Visual Bible Charts

A Step-by-Step Guide to the NEW TESTAMENT

Jonas Dagson

ROSE
PUBLISHING

Visual Bible Charts: A Step-by-Step Guide to the New Testament

Published by Rose Publishing
An imprint of Tyndale House Ministries
Carol Stream, Illinois
rose-publishing.com

ISBN 979-8-4005-0971-1

Illustrations are by Jonas Dagson, except "Imagery in the Book of Revelation," which is by Anders Parsmo.

Printed in China
32 31 30 29 28 27 26
7 6 5 4 3 2 1

Contents

Introduction to the New Testament

Interpreting the New Testament 5
Structure of the New Testament 6
When the New Testament Was Written 7
Two Ways to Read the New Testament 8
Applying the New Testament 9

Gospel Background

Stages in the Life of Jesus 10
Stages in the Life of the Early Church 11
A Chronological Overview of the New Testament 12
Israel in Jesus's Day 14
The Geography of the Gospels 15
Jerusalem in Jesus's Day 16
Cross Sections of Israel's Geography 17
The Jordan River: Headwaters to Dead Sea 18
Israel under Roman Rule 19
How the Gospels Harmonize 20
An Overview of Jesus's Life 26
A Comparison of the Gospels 27
Sixteen Writers in the New Testament 28
What the Bible Teaches about Jesus Christ 29
Forty-Five Prophecies about Jesus 30
Sixty-Four Days in Jesus's Life 31

The Gospels

Matthew 34
Reading a Thematic Gospel 35
Mark 36
Seeing Peter as Mark's Source 37
Luke 38
Doctor Luke's Medical Notes 39
John 40
Signs, Words, and Testimonies 41
Dating Jesus's Birth and Death 42
Jesus and His Earthly Family 43
Elizabeth and Mary: Chosen by God 44
Bethlehem: Where Jesus Was Born 45
We Saw His Star 46
Christmas Story Fact-Checking 47
The Silent Years: Jesus Grows Up 48
An Overview of John the Baptist's Life 49
Different Views of Baptism 50
Jesus Is Tempted by the Devil 51
Jesus's Three Years of Public Ministry 52
A Conversation in the Early Hours 53
Four Truths from "the Gospel in a Nutshell" 54
The Woman at the Well 55
Jesus Relocates to Capernaum 56
The Man Lowered through the Roof 57
Jesus Debates the Sabbath 58
Seasons in the New Testament 59
Fourteen New Testament Apostles 60
Jesus and His Disciples 61
Interpreting the Sermon on the Mount 62
The Sermons on the Mountain and the Plain 63
The Prayer Jesus Taught 64
The Day Jesus Did Not Heal Everyone 65
Jesus Heals a Centurion's Servant 66
When Jesus Calms the Storm 67
Revenge on the Dance Floor 68
When Jesus Was Stopped in His Tracks 69
Herod the Great's Family Tree 70
All the Miracles Jesus Performed 71
When Jesus Fed the Multitudes—Twice 72
Jesus Makes Footprints on the Water 73
All the Parables Jesus Told 74
Parables: How Do We Interpret Them? 75
Men and Women in the Gospel of Luke 76
Jesus's Active Triangle 77
Four Time Jesus Withdrew 78
Peter's Confession of the Messiah 79
Jesus on the Mount of Transfiguration 80
The Woman Caught in Adultery 81
Attacks of Religious Leaders 82
Fourteen Rulers in the New Testament 83
Who Exactly Is My Neighbor? 84
Fourteen Groups in Jesus's Day 85
Thousands of People around Jesus 86
Jesus and the Children 87
What Does it Cost to Be a Disciple? 88
How Did Jesus Teach? 89
What We Can Learn from Jesus's Prayers 90
What We Can Learn from Jesus's Miracles 91
The Feasts of the New Testament 92
Jesus Raises Lazarus 93
Bartimaeus and Zacchaeus in Jericho 94
Holy Week: Day by Day 95
The Triumphal Entry into Jerusalem 96
Jesus and the Great Debate 97
The Disciples' Questions about the Future 98
The Last Night in the Upper Room 99
The Conversation in the Upper Room 100
Different Views of Communion 101
Toward Gethsemane: Through the Night 102
The Betrayal in the Garden of Gethsemane 103
Jesus Is Sentenced to Death 104
Via Dolorosa: The Road to the Cross 105
Where Was the Road to Calvary? 106
The Cross: The Cruelest Death 107
Jesus's Six Hours on the Cross 108
The People around Jesus's Cross 109
Why Did Jesus Have to Die? 110
What Happened When Jesus Died? 111
Golgotha and the Tomb of Jesus 112
The Alternative Burial Site 113
Those Who Saw Jesus Resurrected 114
The Conversation on the Road to Emmaus 115
What Jesus Talked about on the Road to Emmaus 116
The Four Pillars of the Great Commission 118
Why the Resurrection Is So Important 119
Jesus Ascends to Heaven 120

Contents

The Book of Acts

Acts of the Apostles ... 121
Pentecost and the Baptism of the Spirit ... 122
The First Two Years in Jerusalem ... 123
Seven Deacons Are Elected ... 124
On to Judea and Samaria ... 125
The Greatest Sinner Is Saved ... 126
All the Sermons in the Book of Acts ... 127
All of the Miracles in Acts ... 128
Taking the Gospel to Asia Minor ... 129
Taking the Gospel to Athens and Corinth ... 130
Athens in Paul's Day ... 131
Using Ephesus as a Base ... 132
Ephesus in Paul's Day ... 133
Events in Caesarea by the Sea ... 134
Through the Storm to Rome ... 135
Fourteen Disciples Who Followed Paul ... 136
An Overview of Paul's Life ... 137

Paul's Letters

An Overview of Paul's Thirteen Letters ... 138
Four Major Themes of the Letters ... 139
All the Letters in the New Testament ... 140
How to Interpret the Letters ... 142
Romans ... 143
The Path to Faith in Romans ... 144
What It Means to Come to Faith ... 145
The Pillars of the Christian Life ... 146
Balancing the Christian Life ... 147
Views on Israel and the Church ... 148
First Corinthians ... 149
Problems in the Corinthian Church ... 150
Six Questions to Paul in 1 Corinthians ... 151
About the Gifts of the Spirit ... 152
Love: What It Is and What It Is Not ... 153
Second Corinthians ... 154
Paul and All the Corinthian Letters ... 155
Seven Images of the Believer ... 156
Paul's Trials and Tribulations ... 157
Galatians ... 158
Who Exactly Were the Galatians? ... 159
Paul's Words on God's Grace ... 160
Five Different Meanings of "Law" ... 161
Nine Aspects of the Fruit of the Spirit ... 162
Ephesians ... 163
What We Have "in Christ" ... 164
Nine Images of the Church ... 165
The Whole Armor of God ... 166
Philippians ... 167
Philippi in Paul's Day ... 168
Doctrines and Heresies about Jesus ... 169
Colossians ... 170
The Shadows and the Reality ... 171
Heresies in the Early Church ... 172
First Thessalonians ... 173
What Happens when Jesus Returns? ... 174
Three Approaches to the End Times ... 175
Second Thessalonians ... 176
What Misled the Thessalonians? ... 177
First Timothy ... 178
An Overview of Timothy's Life ... 179
Paul's Journeys after the Book of Acts ... 180
Twenty Criteria for Leadership ... 181
Second Timothy ... 182
Paul's Words in the Waiting Room of Death ... 183
The Origin and Purpose of Scripture ... 184
Titus ... 185
Doing Good Deeds ... 186
Crete and Other Mediterranean Islands ... 187
Philemon ... 188
The Story of the Slave Onesimus ... 189

The General Letters and Revelation

Overview of the General Letters ... 190
Hebrews ... 191
Who Wrote Hebrews? ... 192
Jesus Is Bigger, Better, Greater ... 193
Different Stages in the Christian Life ... 194
A Gallery of Heroes of the Faith ... 195
James ... 196
Clothing in Biblical Times ... 197
Theology of the Tongue and Face ... 198
First Peter ... 199
An Overview of Peter's Life ... 200
To Whom Did Jesus Preach? ... 201
Second Peter ... 202
The Signs of False Teachers ... 203
Some Troublemakers in the New Testament ... 204
First John ... 205
An Overview of John's Life ... 206
Do Not Love This World ... 207
Second John ... 208
How Love, Truth, and Obedience Are Connected ... 209
Third John ... 210
Don't Follow Bad Examples ... 211
Jude ... 212
The Way Down and the Way Up ... 213
Revelation ... 214
Five Ways of Interpreting Revelation ... 215
How to Interpret Revelation ... 216
The Seven Churches in Revelation ... 217
Letters to the Seven Churches ... 218
Imagery in the Book of Revelation ... 219
What (Almost) Everyone Agrees On ... 220

Summary

The New Testament: Book by Book ... 221
Three Aspects of Spiritual Maturity ... 222
How to Grow a Christian Character ... 223
Comparing the Beginning and the End ... 224

Interpreting the New Testament

The transition from the old covenant to the new is not found between Malachi and Matthew. It happens at Jesus's death and resurrection. The Gospels and Acts are historical books that describe the transition between the old and new covenants. Here are seven important things to keep in mind when reading the New Testament.

> "Nothing less than the death of Christ was the close of the Old [Covenant]. Nothing less than His resurrection from the dead,... the opening of the New. (Andrew Murray)

1 Whole Bible is inspired
The entire text of the Bible is equally God's Word. Jesus's words do not have a higher status than other parts.

2 Epistles written first
Most of the letters (epistles) were written before the Gospels were. The teaching did not come afterward.

3 Know the type of text
The narrative texts (stories) only describe what happened. This doesn't mean that we must imitate all of the events.

4 The author's intention
Ask: What did the author want his original audience to know, believe, and do? We want to agree with the author's intent.

5 Read in context
The texts were not written in a vacuum. They must be understood in the context in which they were written.

6 Understand then apply
First ask what the text means. Once you have identified the author's intent, then you can ask what it means for you.

7 No secret codes
God's message is what the author wrote. The Bible was not written in secret messages or codes (2 Cor. 1:13).

❶ "The day is coming," says the LORD, "when **I will make a new covenant** with the people of Israel and Judah" (Jer. 31:31).

❷ "Don't misunderstand why I have come. **I did not come to abolish the law** ... No, I came to accomplish their purpose" (Matt. 5:17).

❸ "**The Spirit had not yet been given,** because Jesus had not yet entered into his glory" (John 7:39).

❹ "When the Spirit of truth comes, **he will guide you into all truth**" (John 16:13).

❶ "**This cup is the new covenant** between God and his people" (Luke 22:20).

❸ "**Everyone present was filled with the Holy Spirit** and began speaking in other languages" (Acts 2:4).

❹ "**For it seemed good to the Holy Spirit and to us** to lay no greater burden on you than these few requirements" (Acts 15:28).

❷ "When you are directed by the Spirit, **you are not under obligation to the law of Moses**" (Gal. 5:18).

Examples of the transition from the Old Testament to the New Testament

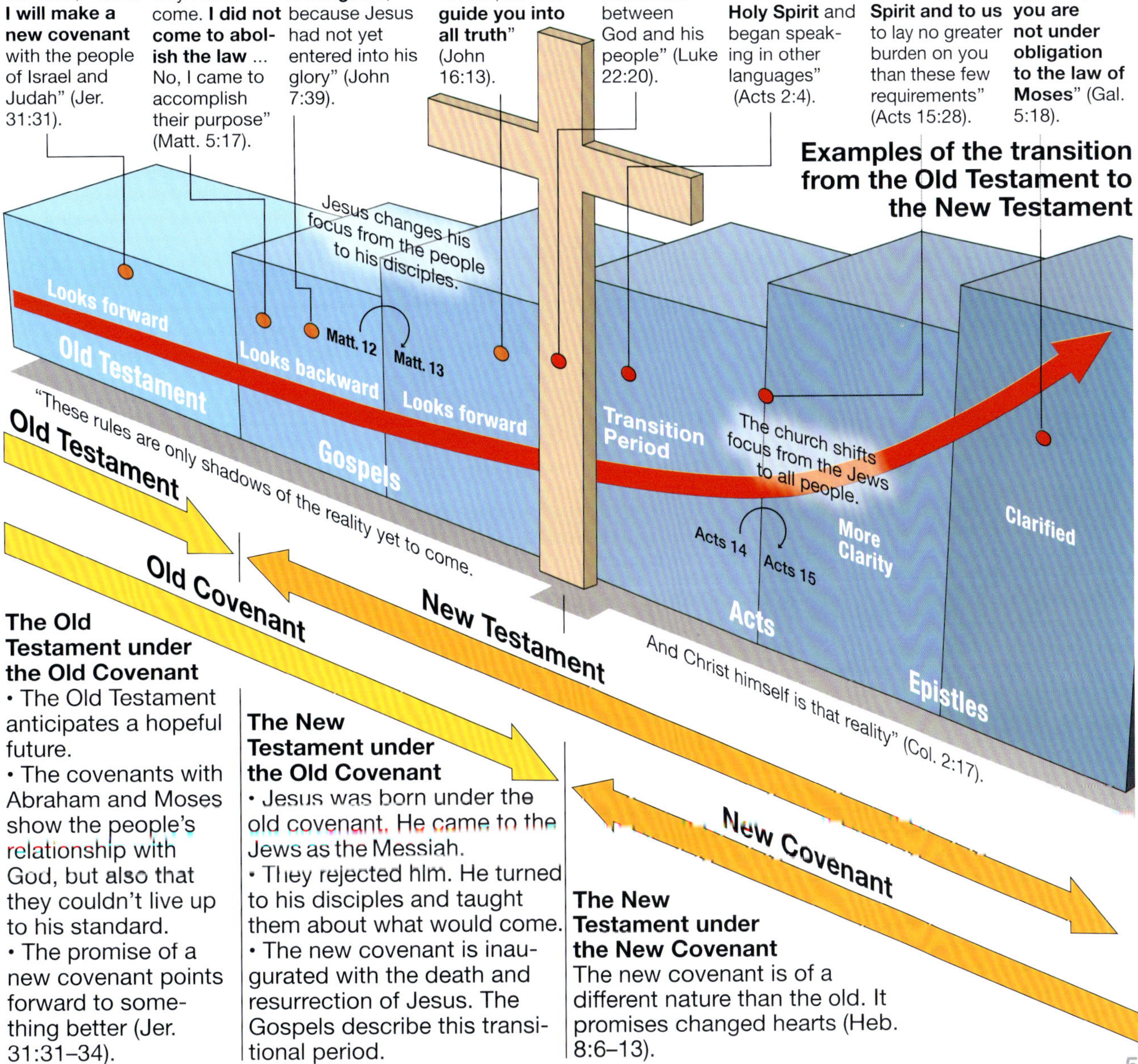

The Old Testament under the Old Covenant
- The Old Testament anticipates a hopeful future.
- The covenants with Abraham and Moses show the people's relationship with God, but also that they couldn't live up to his standard.
- The promise of a new covenant points forward to something better (Jer. 31:31–34).

The New Testament under the Old Covenant
- Jesus was born under the old covenant. He came to the Jews as the Messiah.
- They rejected him. He turned to his disciples and taught them about what would come.
- The new covenant is inaugurated with the death and resurrection of Jesus. The Gospels describe this transitional period.

The New Testament under the New Covenant
The new covenant is of a different nature than the old. It promises changed hearts (Heb. 8:6–13).

Structure of the New Testament

The New Testament has 27 books:
- **Historical Books**—the four Gospels and Acts (5)
- **Letters (Epistles)**—usually split into two groups: Paul's letters (13) and the general letters (8), a total of 21
- **Prophetic Literature**—Revelation (1)

New Testament Records

- **Shortest book:**
3 John (minimum word count 219*—15 verses)
2 John (minimum number of verses 13—245 words)
- **Longest book:**
Luke (19,482 words—1,149 verses)
- **Shortest chapter:**
Revelation 15 (minimum word count 217)
- **Longest chapter:** Luke 1 (80 verses)
- **Shortest verses:** Luke 20:30 (12 letters); 1 Thessalonians 5:16 (14); John 11:35 (16)
- **Longest verse:** Revelation 20:4 (58 words)
- **The book in the middle:** 2 Thessalonians
- **The chapter in the middle:** Romans 13
- **Middle verse:** Acts 17:17
- **Average in the NT:**
On average, a book has 255 verses.

Three ways of categorizing the New Testament Letters

1. By Author
13 letters from Paul
3 letters from John
2 letters from Peter
3 letters from other people

2. By Recipient
16 letters to churches
5 letters to individuals
(2 John was probably written to a church and 3 John was probably written to an individual.)

3. By Theme
4 letters primarily about the Savior
4 letters primarily about salvation
8 letters primarily about the church
5 letters primarily about the future

✪ The author of Hebrews is unknown. Some believe that it was written by Paul or someone close to him such as Barnabas, Apollos, or Luke. The letter does have Pauline features.

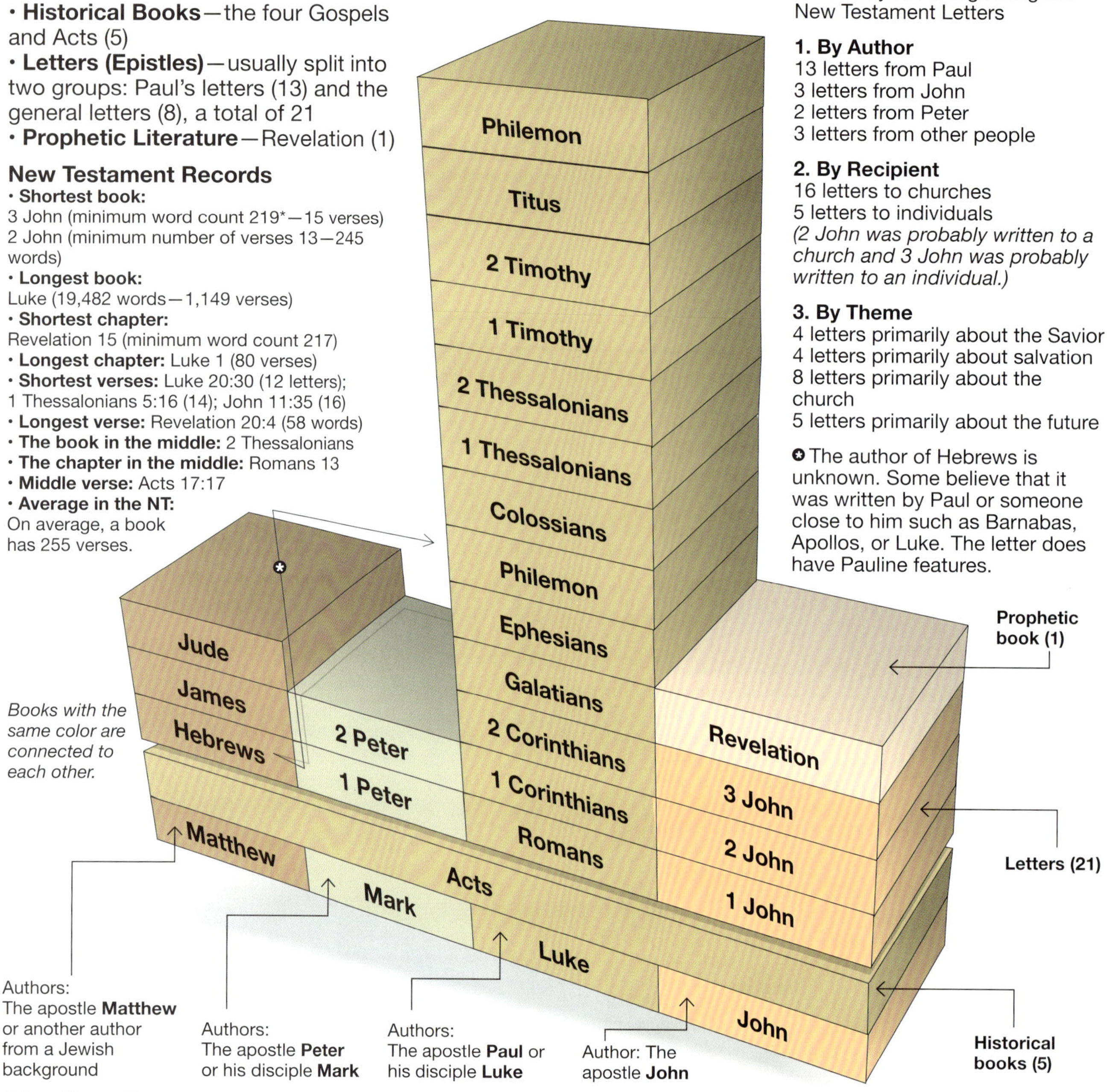

The New Testament Book by Book

	Book	Chapters	Verses		Book	Chapters	Verses		Book	Chapters	Verses
1	Matthew	26	1,068	**10**	Ephesians	6	155	**19**	Hebrews	13	303
2	Mark	16	673	**11**	Philippians	4	104	**20**	James	5	108
3	Luke	24	1,149	**12**	Colossians	4	95	**21**	1 Peter	5	105
4	John	21	878	**13**	1 Thessalonians	5	89	**22**	2 Peter	3	61
5	Acts	28	1,002	**14**	2 Thessalonians	3	47	**23**	1 John	5	105
6	Romans	16	432	**15**	1 Timothy	6	113	**24**	2 John	1	13
7	1 Corinthians	16	437	**16**	2 Timothy	4	83	**25**	3 John	1	15
8	2 Corinthians	13	256	**17**	Titus	3	46	**26**	Jude	1	25
9	Galatians	6	149	**18**	Philemon	1	25	**27**	Revelation	22	404

** All counts (words and letters) are based on the Greek text Nestle-Aland Novum Testamentum Graece version 27.*

When the New Testament Was Written

When to date some of the New Testament books is debated. The dating of the Gospels is particularly uncertain, and there are many theories. This chart shows possible time frames for the writing of each book.

Book	Date written (AD)
Matthew	55–68
Mark	55–65
Luke	58–64
John	80–90
Acts	62–64
Romans	56–57
1 Corinthians	55–56
2 Corinthians	56–57
Galatians	48–49 / 53–56
Ephesians	60–61
Philippians	61–62
Colossians	60–61
1 Thessalonians	51–52
2 Thessalonians	51–52
1 Timothy	62–66
2 Timothy	66–67
Titus	62–66
Philemon	60–61
Hebrews	64–68
James	44–49
1 Peter	62–65
2 Peter	64–67
1 John	85–95
2 John	85–95
3 John	85–95
Jude	60–80
Revelation	94–96

Timeline: AD 10 · AD 30 · AD 50 · AD 70 · AD 90

Jesus's death AD 33

Time period described in the book

Luke written before Acts (see Acts 1:1)

Destruction of the temple AD 70

Nero's persecution AD 64

Two theories on the dating of Galatians

Domitian's persecution AD 93

Paul is executed about AD 67

Paul imprisoned in Rome AD 60–62

Possibly the oldest book in the New Testament

The New Testament was written over a period of about fifty years.

Peter executed about AD 67

Jude cites 2 Peter (or vice versa)

The dates indicate the time span within which the book was probably written. This does not mean that the writing took place throughout the entire period.

Clues for Determining Dates

1. Luke and Acts are linked
They have the same author (Luke 1:1–4; Acts 1:1), so the books date each other.

2. Parallels between Scriptures
Peter mentions Paul's letters and there are parallels between events in Acts and Paul's letters.

3. Persecution under Emperor Nero
Rome burned in AD 64, which led to Nero's persecution of Christians. Possible background to Hebrews.

4. Destruction of the temple
The Romans captured Jerusalem and destroyed the temple in AD 70. Biblical texts that mention its future destruction were written earlier.

5. Persecution under Emperor Domitian
Domitian persecuted Christians who would not worship the Roman gods. Probable reason for John's exile (Rev. 1:9).

6. References by the church fathers
Early church fathers cite and refer to dates of New Testament books and letters. This helps in dating the books.

Two Ways to Read the New Testament

Bible reading can be done from different starting points. Two common approaches are (1) seeing the whole (the synthetic method) and (2) looking at the details (the analytic method).

Read with a telescope … …and a microscope

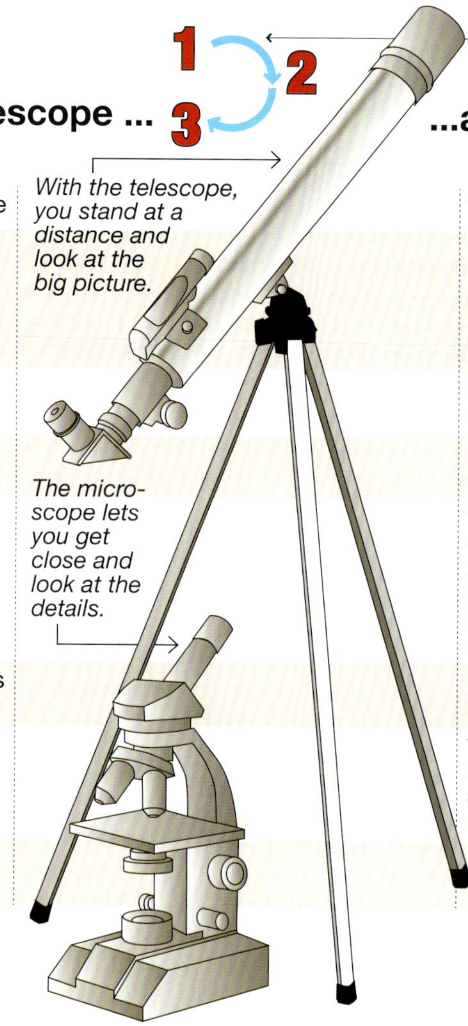

	Telescope	Microscope
Look at	The big picture	The details
Focus	Chapters, whole books, longer passages. Read the book in one sitting.	Words, concepts, and different verses. Read short passages several times. Look for the details in the stories and the reasoning.
Examine the text	Look for the plot, main ideas, and outline.	Look at phrasing, word choice, and grammar.
Look for	Development and trends	Nuances and theological clarifications
Ask questions	1. What is the main idea of the book or section? 2. How does the author develop his main idea? 3. How is the book or section structured?	1. What is the meaning of this word? 2. How do the sentences tie together? 3. How is the argument structured?
Methods	Learn lessons from events and structures.	Draw conclusions from arguments and teachings.
Learn from the other approach	The microscopic view gives the conclusions of the telescopic view a more detailed content.	The telescopic view gives an overall context for the details discovered through the microscopic view.
Perspective	Like an eagle in the sky.	Like an ant on the ground.

How do we go about reading and studying a book of the Bible?

The key to studying a book of the Bible is to see the relationship between the telescopic perspective and the microscopic perspective. Here is one way you can visualize it.

To apply the text is to show the relevance of the text. Application must always grow out of the text and stay in harmony with its intended meaning.

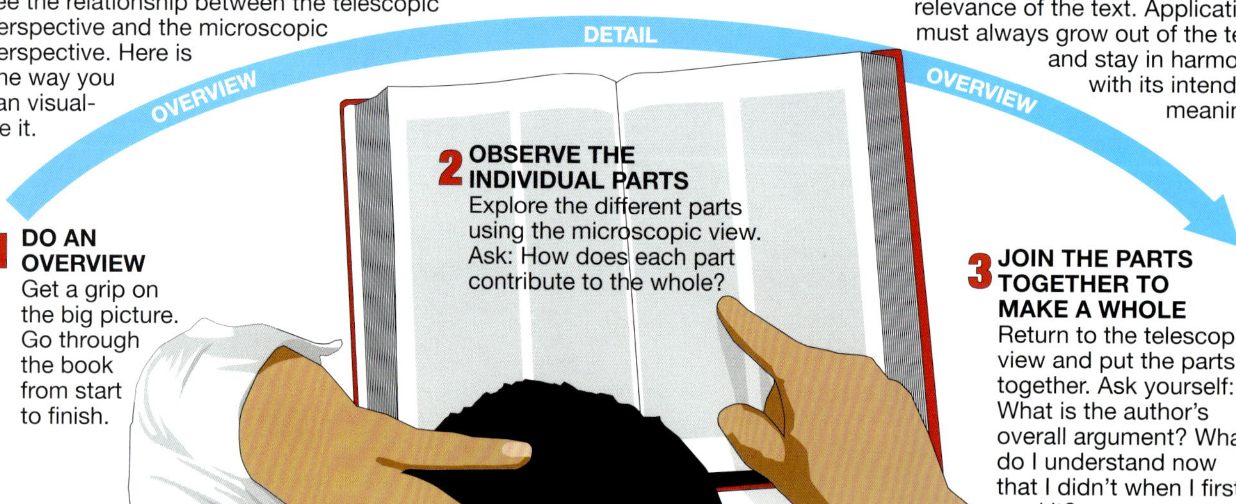

1 DO AN OVERVIEW
Get a grip on the big picture. Go through the book from start to finish.

2 OBSERVE THE INDIVIDUAL PARTS
Explore the different parts using the microscopic view. Ask: How does each part contribute to the whole?

3 JOIN THE PARTS TOGETHER TO MAKE A WHOLE
Return to the telescopic view and put the parts together. Ask yourself: What is the author's overall argument? What do I understand now that I didn't when I first read it?

Applying the New Testament

Moving from interpretation to application always involves a few specific steps. This is how it works—step by step.

Application is always based on a sound interpretation of the text. A text has only one interpretation but it can have several different applications.

TIME BOUND — TIMELESS — APPLIED

1

WHAT DID THE TEXT MEAN TO THE ORIGINAL RECIPIENTS?
Interpretation works to determine what the author intended to say to the people to whom the text was originally addressed. It is, or can be, influenced by its time. We start by searching for what the text meant in its own time.

THEN

2

WHAT IS THE TIMELESS PRINCIPLE BEHIND WHAT THE TEXT SAYS?
What is a principle? From the Latin *principium*—meaning "beginning, foundation, or basic concept." It is what constitutes the ultimate basis or cause of something; a general rule that guides practical actions. Here, we ask the question: What is the underlying cause—the fundamental principle—in the text that points to the actions that it promotes?

NOW

3

HOW DO WE APPLY THE PRINCIPLE IN OUR OWN CONTEXT?
The final step is to ask how we apply the timeless principle to our day and age and in our own lives. While the applications are sometimes the same as in the text, at times they differ, as the application can be tied to its time.

Four steps toward a sound application

1 Start from the text
What does this actually mean? How can I understand its meaning? You must be able to trace the application to the text(s) on which it is based.
• **Danger:** Jumping immediately from your observations to an application.
• **Example:** In the first century, Paul instructs the believers in Thessalonica to stay away from all kinds of evil (1 Thess. 5:22).

2 Application (I)—Find the principle
Next is to look for the timeless underlying principle. Why does the Bible say this? Different difficulties come up when interpreting different types of text.
• **Danger:** Not distinguishing between what is timeless and what is specific to its time period.
• **Example:** All believers at all times should stay away from all evil is the principle behind 1 Thess. 5:22.

3 Application (II)—Make it personal
The third step is to ask: How does the timeless principle apply to me today? It is about looking for the implications of the biblical text.
• **Danger:** Allowing the spirit of the times to influence me, to color my conclusions.
• **Example:** Since all believers at all times should stay away from all evil, as a believer I should also stay away from all evil.

4 Application (III)—Make it practical
The final step is to ask: How can I put this truth into practice in my everyday life? It's about taking practical steps here that help me put the meaning of the Bible text into everyday life.
• **Danger:** Not being concrete enough.
• **Example:** I make concrete decisions such as choosing to avoid certain TV programs and certain websites.

> "Application asks us to take that original interpretation and connect it to our lives. Therefore, each person may have a different application stemming from the same interpretation. Furthermore, one might come back to the same passage some time later and find a completely different application because their life situation has changed.
> (Ken Carson)

Different types of applications to consider

1 Absolute Moral Imperatives
We encounter timeless exhortations that apply in all situations and in all times.
• **Dealing with them:** The timeless principles challenge us and call us to obedience in action.
• **Example:** "Stop telling lies. Let us tell our neighbors the truth" (Eph. 4:25). This also applies to all of us.

2 General Principles
We encounter fundamental truths in the text. These are not direct exhortations, but guiding principles and beliefs.
• **Dealing with them:** We must understand the implications of what they mean in our context.
• **Example:** "Share each other's burdens" (Gal. 6:2).

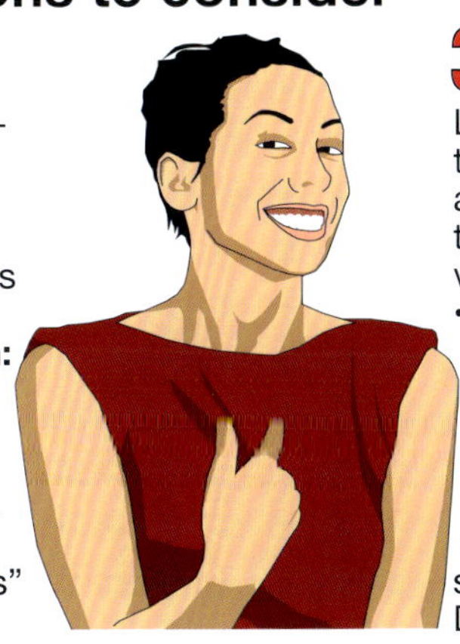

3 Standardizing Patterns
Look for examples in the text of how people act or reason. From them we can draw valid principles.
• **Dealing with them:** We should consider if the principle might apply to us.
• **Example:** After one parable, Jesus tells a man to "go and do the same" (Luke 10:37). Does this apply to us?

4 Time Bound Applications
We will also encounter principles or exhortations addressed to people in specific situations.
• **Dealing with them:** In these cases, it is difficult to find any timeless principles to apply to ourselves.
• **Example:** Paul's specific instructions to Timothy do not apply to us (2 Tim. 4:21).

Stages in the Life of Jesus

1 Birth and Childhood

Time*:** About 35 years, 7–4 BC to AD 29 ***Texts*:** Matt. 1:1–2:23; Luke 1:1–2:52; 3:23b–38; John 1:1–18 ***Share*: 5.7% ***Events:*** Born in Bethlehem, flees to Egypt, settles in Nazareth, visits Jerusalem at age 12, becomes a carpenter

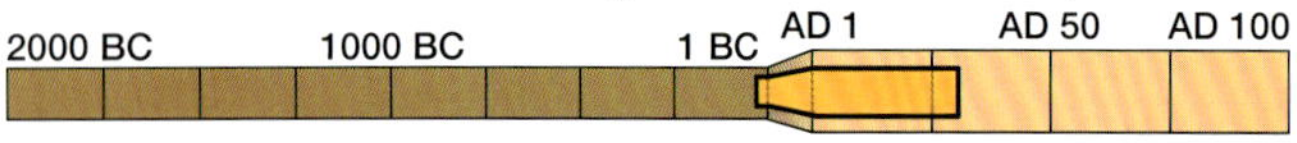

From Jesus with the Father in heaven → To Jesus as a man on earth
From the glory of heaven → To the simplicity of the manger
From equality with God → To human form as a man

2 Initial Ministry

Time*:** 4 months, Jan. to April AD 30 ***Texts*:** Matt. 3:1–4:11; Mark 1:1–13; Luke 3:1–18, 21–23a; 4:1–13; John 1:19–51 ***Share*:** 2.9% ***Events: John the Baptist appears, Jesus baptized by John in the Jordan, Jesus tempted by the devil in the desert

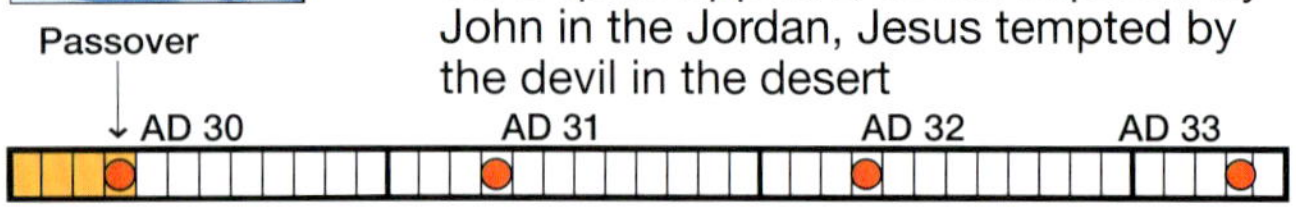

From prophetic silence → To a prophet's voice
From the forerunner in the desert → To the one who comes after
From heavenly confirmation → To confrontation with the devil

3 Early Judean Ministry

Time*:** About 8 months, May to Dec. AD 30 ***Texts*:** Matt. 4:12; Mark 1:14–15; Luke 3:19–20; 4:14a; John 2:1–4:42 ***Share*:** 2.9% ***Events: Jesus performs first miracle, cleanses the temple, has discussion with Nicodemus, preaches in Judea

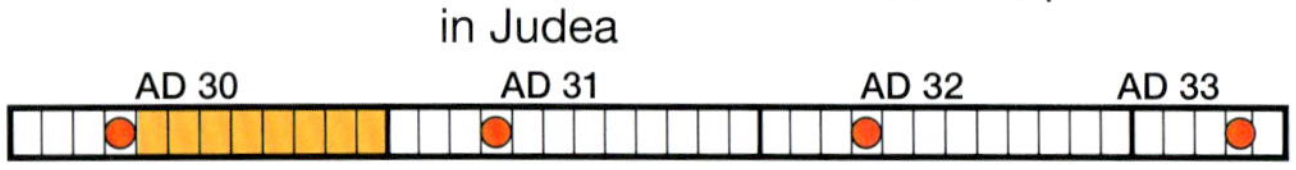

From public confrontation → To nocturnal conversation
From a natural birth → To being born of the Spirit
From visiting Jerusalem → To teaching in Judea

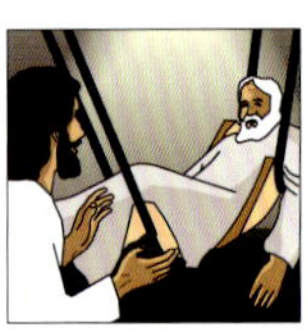

4 Early Galilean Ministry

Time*:** About 4 months, Jan. to April AD 31 ***Texts*:** Matt. 4:13–25; 8:2–4, 14–17; 9:1–17; Mark 1:16–2:22; Luke 4:14b–5:39; John 4:43–54 ***Share*:** 4.5% ***Events: Talks with Samaritan woman at a well, is driven out of Nazareth, to Capernaum, travels around Galilee

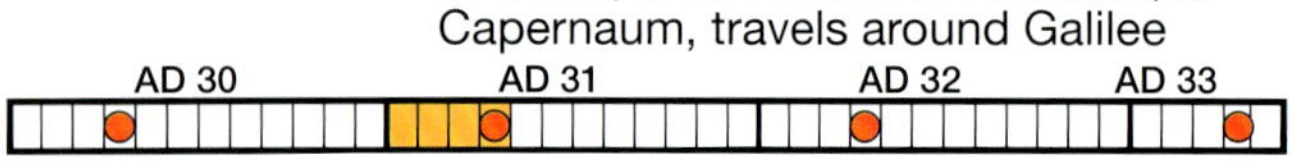

From his hometown of Nazareth → To his new home in Capernaum
From thirst for water → To thirst for eternal life
From proclamation → To discipleship

5 Mid-Galilean Ministry

Time*:** 12 months, May AD 31– April AD 32 ***Texts*:** Matthew 5:1–8:1; 8:5–13, 18, 23–34; 9:18–15:20; Mark 2:23–7:23; Luke 6:1–9:17; John 5:1–7:1 ***Share*:** 23.5% ***Events: Chooses the Twelve, gives the Sermon on the Mount, travels around Galilee, calms the storm

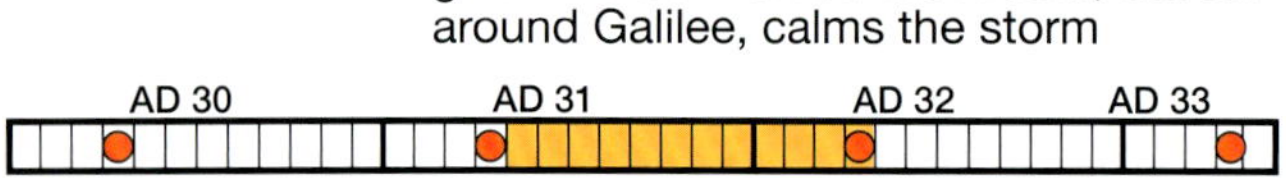

From choosing the Twelve → To teaching the Twelve
From proclaiming the message → To rejection of the message
From disciples following him → To disciples leaving him

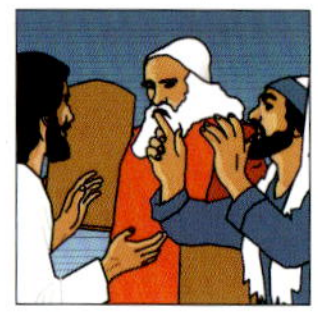

6 Late Galilean Ministry

Time*:** About 6 months, May to Oct. AD 32 ***Texts*:** Matt. 8:19–22; 15:21–18:35; Mark 7:24–9:50; Luke 9:18–62; John 7:2–10 ***Share*:** 7.0% ***Events: Jesus withdraws from Galilee, on the Mount of Transfiguration, predicts his death and resurrection

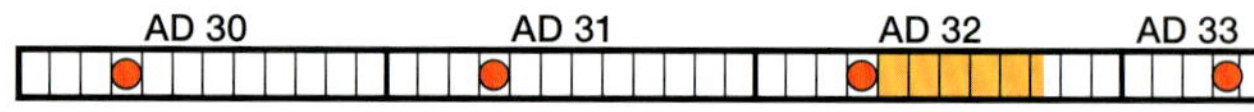

From active public life → To withdrawal from public life
From people's doubts → To Peter's confession
From the clarity on the mountain top → To the reality in the valley

7 Late Judean Ministry

Time*:** About 3 months, Nov. to Jan. AD 32–33 ***Texts*:** Luke 10:1–13:21; John 7:11–10:39 ***Share*:** 9.5% ***Events: Pharisees want to stone Jesus, he sends out the 72, visits Martha and Mary, teaches about true discipleship

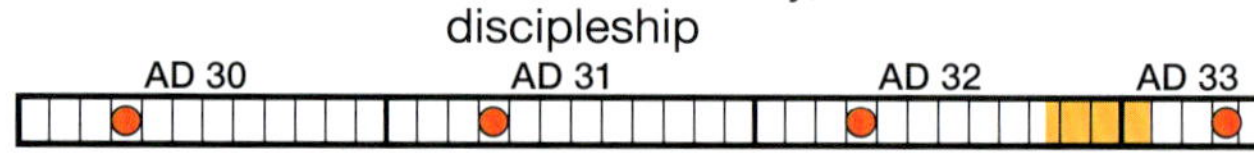

From Galilee in the north → To Jerusalem in the south
From his forgiving words → To religious leaders' hateful words
From fleeing Herod Antipas → To fleeing religious leaders

8 Late Perean Ministry

Time*:** About 3 months, Feb. to April AD 33 ***Texts*:** Matt. 19:1–20:34; Mark 10:1–52; Luke 13:22–19:28; John 10:40–11:54 ***Share*:** 10.4% ***Events: Jesus raises Lazarus from the dead, heals Bartimaeus, visits Zacchaeus in his house

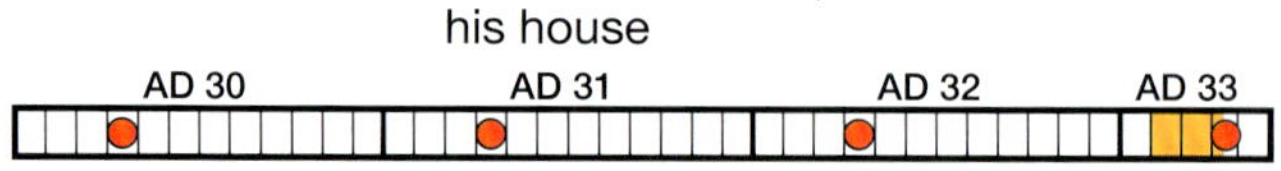

From Judea west of the Jordan → To Perea east of the Jordan
From words of life for Lazarus → To words of death for Jesus
From escaping death threats → To facing death threats

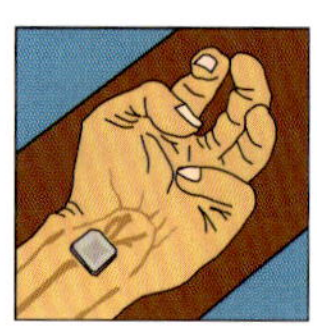

9 The Last Passover

Time*:** One week, April AD 33 ***Texts*:** Matt. 21:1–27:66; Mark 11:1–15:47; Luke 19:29–23:56; John 11:55–19:42 ***Share*:** 29.7% ***Events: Jesus institutes the Lord's Supper, on trial six times, convicted despite his innocence, is crucified, dies, is buried

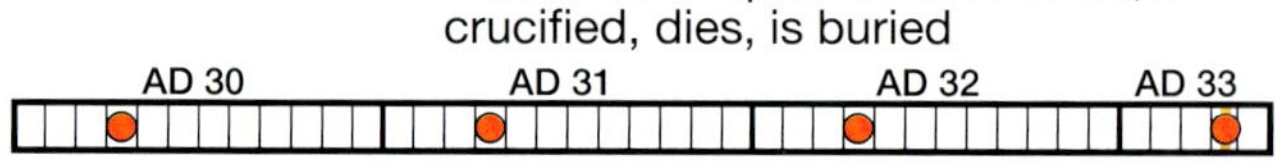

From joyful reception → To cruel death sentence
From praying hands in Gethsemane → To pierced hands on Calvary
From living with people → To dying for people

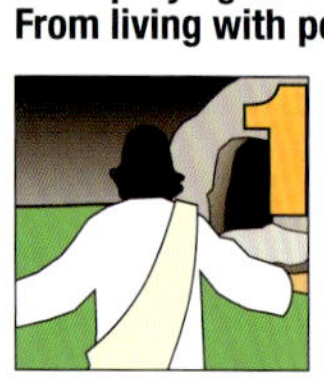

10 Post-Resurrection

Time*:** 40 days, April to May AD 33 ***Texts*:** Matt. 28:1–20; Mark 16:1–20; Luke 24:1–53; John 20:1–21:25 ***Share*:** 4.0% ***Events: Jesus rises from the dead, appears to the disciples, gives the Great Commission, is taken up to heaven

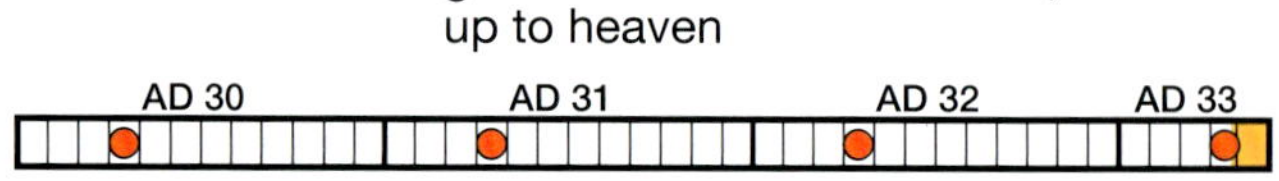

From the realm of the dead → To the kingdom of heaven
From an empty cross → To an empty tomb
From Jesus as man on earth → To Jesus with the Father in heaven

** Percentage of the text in the four Gospels*

Stages in the Life of the Early Church

11 Birth of the Church

Time: About 2 years, AD 33–35
Texts: Acts 1:1–7:60 ****Share***: 25.8%
Events: Jesus ascends, the Spirit is given to believers on Pentecost, church is founded and grows in Jerusalem, Stephen is stoned to death and becomes a martyr

30 40 50 60 70 80 90 AD 100

From Jesus with the disciples on earth → To Jesus with Father in heaven
From the Spirit with the Father → To the Spirit on earth
From the resurrected body of Jesus → To the church body of Jesus

12 Persecution

Time: 13 years, AD 35–48 ***Texts***: Acts 8:1–40; 9:31–11:18; 12:1–23 ***Share***: 12.0% ***Letters***: James ***Events:*** Persecution erupts, Ethiopian eunuch converted, gospel to the Samaritans, Spirit given to gentiles in Cornelius's house, Peter is imprisoned

30 40 50 60 70 80 90 AD 100

From resistance → To persecution
From Jerusalem → To Judea and Samaria
From Philip the deacon → To Philip the evangelist

13 Saul's Conversion

Time: 13 years, AD 35–48 (parallels Stage 12) ***Texts***: Acts 9:1–30; 11:19–30 ***Share***: 4.3% ***Events:*** Saul is converted on the Damascus road, spends time in the desert, Jerusalem, Tarsus, and Antioch, preparing for future missionary journeys

30 40 50 60 70 80 90 AD 100

From Saul the persecutor → To Paul the preacher
From hating Christians → To loving Christ
From Jewish legalism → To Christian freedom

14 First Missionary Journey

Time: 2 years, April AD 48–April AD 50 ***Texts***: Acts 12:24–15:35 ***Share***: 11.8% ***Letters***: Galatians ***Events:*** Paul journeys to Cyprus and Asia Minor (Antioch in Pisidia, Iconium, Lystra, Derbe), council in Jerusalem affirms gentile inclusion in faith

30 40 50 60 70 80 90 AD 100

From Antioch → To Cyprus and Galatia
From the call to mission → To the work of mission
From the gospel on Jewish terms → To the gospel on everyone's terms

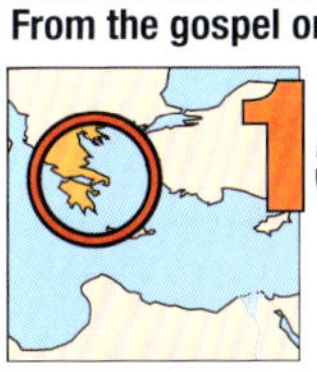

15 Second Missionary Journey

Time: About 3 years, April AD 50–spring AD 53 ***Texts***: Acts 15:36–18:22 ***Share***: 10.4% ***Letters***: 1 and 2 Thessalonians ***Events:*** Paul travels through Asia Minor to Troas, Philippi, Thessalonica, Berea, Athens, Corinth, and Ephesus, returns to Jerusalem

30 40 50 60 70 80 90 AD 100

From Antioch in Asia → To Athens and Corinth in Europe
From a vision in Troas → To Lydia's conversion in Philippi
From ex-Pharisee from Jerusalem → To debate with Greek philosophers

*** Percentage of the text in Acts*

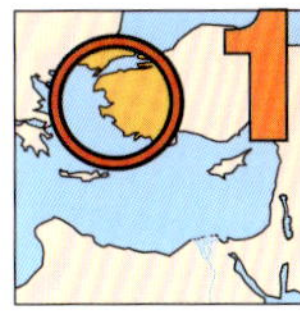

16 Third Missionary Journey

Time: 4 years, spring AD 53–May 57
Texts: Acts 18:23–21:16 ***Share***: 10.2%
Letters: 1 and 2 Corinthians, Romans
Events: Paul travels through Asia Minor to Ephesus, through Macedonia to Corinth, returns to Ephesus and Jerusalem

30 40 50 60 70 80 90 AD 100

From Antioch in Syria → To Ephesus in Asia Minor
From the pillared halls of Solomon → To the lecture halls of Tyrannus
From going from town to town → To staying two years in Ephesus

17 Imprisoned in Caesarea

Time: 2 years, May AD 57–Aug. AD 59 ***Texts***: Acts 21:17–26:32 ***Share***: 17.8 % ***Events:*** Paul is taken to Caesarea, goes through three trials in two years—before Felix, Festus, and King Agrippa—release is possible, but he appeals to the emperor

30 40 50 60 70 80 90 AD 100

From freedom to travel the Roman Empire → To captivity in Caesarea
From preaching to the gentiles → To preaching to Roman rulers
From determined forward movement → To patient enforced waiting

18 Journey to Rome

Time: 3 years, Aug. AD 59–spring AD 62 ***Texts***: Acts 27:1–28:31 ***Share***: 7.7% ***Letters***: Ephesians, Colossians, Philemon, Philippians ***Events:*** Paul sails across the Mediterranean, arrives in Rome via Malta, placed under house arrest, ministers and writes letters

30 40 50 60 70 80 90 AD 100

From a prison cell in Caesarea → To a prison ship to Rome
From the calm of the prison cell → To the storms on the Mediterranean
From the fringes of the empire → To the capital of the empire

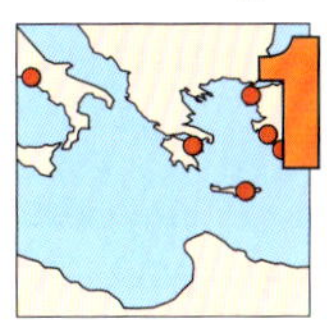

19 Paul's Later Journeys

Time: About 6 years, spring AD 62–68 ***Letters***: 1 and 2 Timothy, Titus, Hebrews, 1 and 2 Peter, Jude ***Events:*** Paul travels to Ephesus, Colossae, Macedonia, Asia Minor, Crete, Nicopolis, Greece, Rome, possibly travels to Spain

30 40 50 60 70 80 90 AD 100

From captivity in Rome → To freedom to travel the empire
From traveling for the gospel → To captivity for the sake of the gospel
From living for his Master → To dying for his Master

20 John's Writings

Time: 5 to 10 years, around AD 85–95 ***Letters***: Gospel of John, 1, 2, and 3 John, Revelation ***Events:*** John's letters were probably written from Ephesus, while Revelation was written during his captivity on the island of Patmos, offering hope to believers.

30 40 50 60 70 80 90 AD 100

From captivity in the body → To freedom in the Spirit
From Patmos on earth → To God's throne in heaven
From insight into what is now → To hope for what is to come

A Chronological Overview of the New

The numbers correspond to those in Stages in the Life of Jesus and the Early Church, pages 10–11.

1

MARY
The virgin who became the mother of the Son of God

2

JOHN THE BAPTIST
The forerunner of the Messiah

3

NICODEMUS
Pharisee who became a disciple of Jesus

4

PETER
Was entrusted with leading the church

ANDREW
One of the first four disciples to be called

- The announcement to Mary (c. 7–6 BC)
- The birth of John the Baptist
- The birth of Jesus in Bethlehem (c. 7–4 BC)
- Jesus to Egypt
- Jesus at the age of 12 in the temple (c. AD 6)
- Jesus grows up in Nazareth

Jesus is baptized by John

Jesus is tested by the devil

Jesus calls his first disciples

Jesus meets the woman at the well

Jesus is driven from Nazareth, moves to Capernaum

Jesus in Galilee, preaches and heals

Jesus chooses twelve disciples

Jesus gives the Sermon on the Mount

PETER

JESUS

JOHN THE BAPTIST

John the Baptist appears

AD 30

Jesus's first miracle, in Cana

Jesus in Jerusalem at Passover (I), talks with Nicodemus

Jesus in Judea

AD 31

Jesus calls four disciples (Peter, Andrew, John, and James), and later Levi (Matthew)

JESUS
God's Son who became a man

Jesus in Jerusalem at Passover (II)

■ AT THE BEGINNING OF THE GOSPELS

... we meet a people under Roman occupation. Many religious leaders have compromised their faith for power. There is hope that the Messiah will appear and restore freedom, but few expect him to arrive as a humble newborn baby.

11

STEPHEN
Became the first martyr

12 & 13

PHILIP
Deacon who became a pioneer missionary

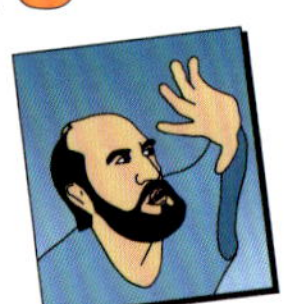

PAUL
The persecutor who became a preacher

14

1 James

2 Galatians

15

3 1 Thessalonians

4 2 Thessalonians

16

5 1 Corinthians

6 2 Corinthians

7 Romans

17

BARNABAS
The link between Peter and Paul

■ AT THE BEGINNING OF ACTS

... we meet a small group of eleven bewildered disciples, all of whom have abandoned or denied Jesus, now huddled with a few other men and women in a secluded upstairs room in Jerusalem.

Jesus's death and resurrection

Pentecost

Stephen is martyred.

Paul's conversion

Paul in Jerusalem (I)

Paul travels to Antioch.

Peter preaches to the gentiles

James is martyred.

Paul to Antioch

Paul to Europe

Paul in Athens and Corinth

Paul in Jerusalem (IV) and Antioch

Paul in Corinth

Paul prisoner in Caesarea

PAUL 2 3, 4 5, 6, 7

PETER

JOHN

1

AD 30 · AD 35 · AD 40 · AD 45 · AD 50 · AD 55 · AD 60

Acts begins.

Paul in Arabia and Damascus

Paul to Tarsus

Paul in Jerusalem (II)

Paul in Cyprus

Paul in Galatia

The Council of Jerusalem (III)

Paul to Ephesus

Paul to Jerusalem (V)

Paul's journey to Rome

Testament

Several chronological options have been proposed, covering the length of Jesus's public ministry and the timing of his death and resurrection (AD 30 or 33). This overview mostly follows Dr. Harold Hoehner's chronology.

5

JAMES
John's brother who was later martyred

MATTHEW
A tax collector, also called Levi

JUDAS
Disciple who betrayed Jesus

6 7 8 9 10

AT THE END OF THE GOSPELS
... we meet a Messiah whose kingdom is not of this world. Having died and risen, he lays its foundation, promises his disciples the Holy Spirit as their Helper, and sends them out to proclaim the gospel throughout the world.

Timeline continues below

Jesus again in Galilee, preaches and heals

Jesus speaks in parables

Jesus calms the storm

Jesus feeds 5,000

Jesus withdraws to Tyre and Sidon

Jesus withdraws to the Decapolis

Jesus predicts his death and resurrection

Jesus on the Mount of Transfiguration

Jesus to Perea, east of Jordan

Jews want to stone Jesus

Jesus visits Martha and Mary

Jesus raises Lazarus in Bethany

Jesus meets Zacchaeus in Jericho

Jesus raised from death

Jesus on the road to Emmaus

Jesus in the upper room, twice

Jesus gives the Great Commission

AD 32

AD 33

Jesus is rejected by the religious leadership

John the Baptist is executed

Jesus walks on water

Jesus sends out the disciples

Jesus in Jerusalem at Passover (III)

Peter's declaration at Caesarea Philippi

Jesus in silence through Samaria to Jerusalem

Jesus sends out the 72 disciples

The ascension of Jesus

Jesus's entry into Jerusalem at Passover (IV)
Jesus cleanses the temple.
Jesus in the upper room................ Thursday evening
Jesus prays in Gethsemane..... Thursday late evening
Jesus before Jewish leaders.............. Thursday night
Jesus before Roman leaders............. Friday morning
Jesus is crucified and dies......... Friday, 9 am to 3 pm
Jesus is buried................................ Friday afternoon

18 19 20

8 Ephesians
9 Colossians
10 Philippians
11 Philemon

12 1 Peter
13 1 Timothy
14 Titus
15 2 Peter

16 2 Timothy
17 Hebrews
18 Jude

TIMOTHY
Became Paul's closest coworker

TITUS
A Greek who had a heart for Corinth

JOHN
Who received a revelation of the end times

19 1 John
20 2 John
21 3 John
22 Revelation

LUKE
A doctor who became God's historian

ONESIMUS
The slave who became a Christian

AT THE END OF ACTS
... we meet a growing church. Bold disciples have spread the gospel to rulers and commoners across Africa, the Middle East, Greece, and Rome, undeterred by opposition.

Acts ends.

Peter executed in Rome

Paul executed in Rome

Jerusalem is destroyed by the Romans.

John to Patmos

8, 9, 10, 11 — 13, 14 — 16

12, 15 — 17, 18

19, 20, 21, 22

Paul a prisoner in Rome

Paul free again, traveling around

AD 65

Paul in prison in Rome again

AD 70

John to Ephesus (?)

AD 75

AD 80

AD 85

AD 90

Israel in Jesus's Day

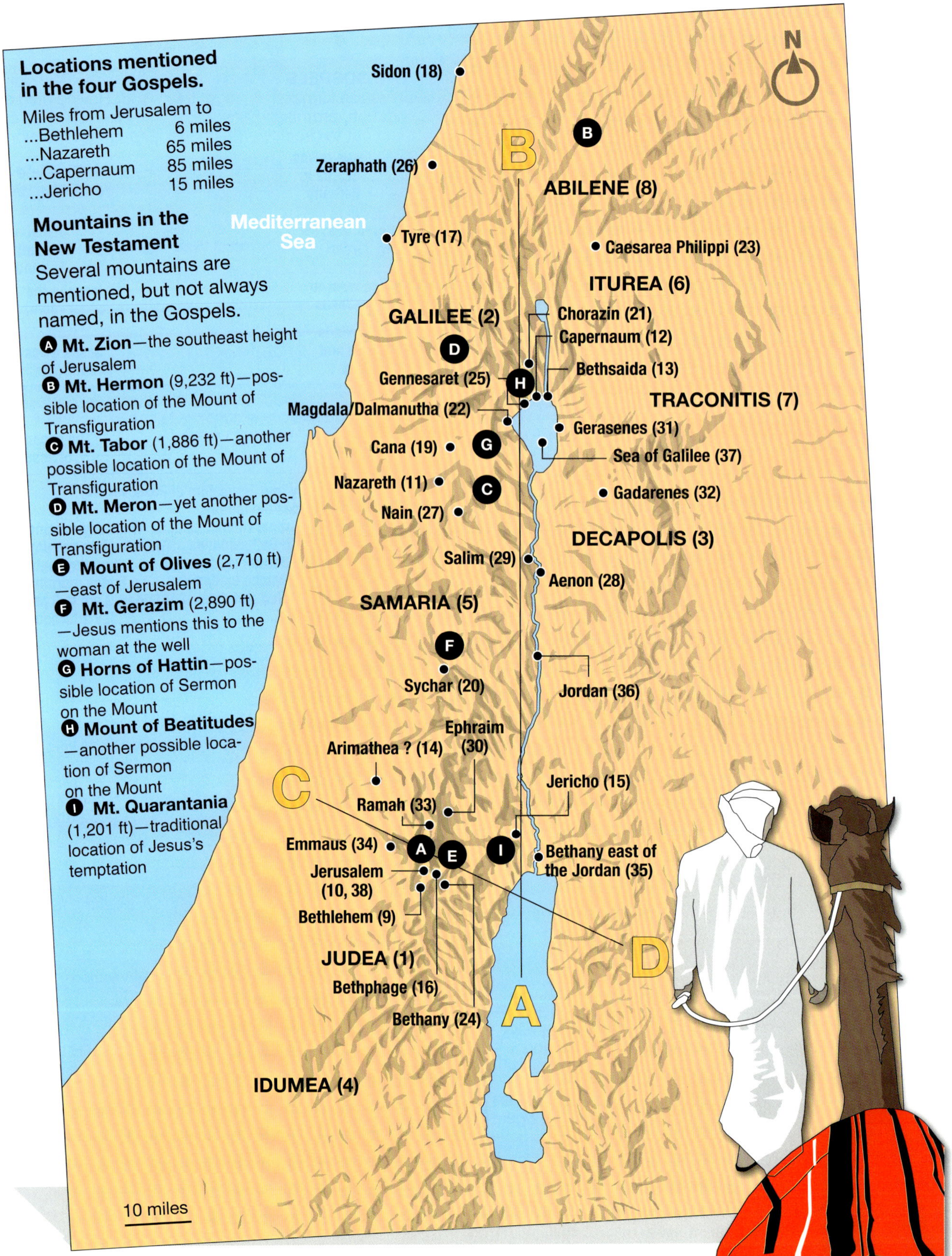

The Geography of the Gospels

The Gospels are set in a number of locations across Israel. This is a compilation of all the places associ-ated with the life and ministry of Jesus. Note which locations each Gospel writer emphasizes.

• REGIONS		MATTHEW	MARK	LUKE	JOHN
Judea	**1**	2:1, 5, 22; 3:1; 4:25; 19:1; 24:16	1:5; 3:8; 10:1; 13:14	1:5, 39, 65; 2:4; 3:1; 4:44; 5:17; 6:17; 7:17; 21:21; 23:5, 51	3:22; 4:3, 47, 54; 7:1, 3; 11:7, 54
Galilee	**2**	2:22; 3:13; 4:12, 15, 23, 25; 11:1; 17:22; 19:1; 21:11; 26:32, 69; 27:55; 28:7, 10, 16	1:9,14, 28, 39; 3:7; 6:21; 9:30; 14:28; 15:41; 16:7	1:26; 2:4, 39; 3:1; 4:14, 31; 5:17; 8:26; 17:11; 23:5, 49, 55; 24:6	1:43; 2:1, 11; 4:3, 43, 45–47, 54; 7:1, 3, 9, 41, 52; 12:21; 21:2
Decapolis	**3**	4:25	5:20; 7:31		
Idumea	**4**		3:8		
Samaria	**5**			17:11	4:4–5
Iturea	**6**			3:1	
Traconitis	**7**			3:1	
Abilene	**8**			3:1	
• CITIES					
Bethlehem	**9**	2:1, 5–6, 8, 16		2:4,15	7:42
Jerusalem *(see details on "Jerusalem in Jesus's Day")*	**10**	2:1, 3; 3:5; 4:25; 5:35; 15:1; 16:21; 20:17–8; 21:1, 10; 23:37	1:5; 3:8, 22; 7:1; 10:32, 33; 11:1, 11, 15, 27; 15:41	2:22, 25, 38, 41, 43, 45; 4:9; 5:17; 6:17; 9:31, 51, 53; 10:30; 13:4, 22, 33–4; 17:11; 18:31; 19:11, 28, 41; 21:20, 24; 23:7, 28; 24:13, 18, 33, 47, 52	1:19; 2:13, 23; 4:20–21, 45; 5:1–2; 7:25; 10:22; 11:18, 55; 12:12
Nazareth	**11**	2:23; 4:13; 21:11; 26:71	1:9, 24; 10:47	1:26; 2:4, 39, 51; 4:14, 16, 34; 18:37; 24:19	1:45–6; 18:5, 7; 19:19
Capernaum	**12**	4:13; 8:5; 11:23; 17:24	1:21; 2:1; 9:33	4:23, 31; 7:1; 10:15	2:12; 4:46; 6:17, 24, 59
Bethsaida	**13**	11:21	6:45; 8:22	9:10; 10:13	1:44; 12:21
Arimathea	**14**	27:57	15:43	23:51	19:38
Jericho	**15**	20:29	10:46	10:30; 18:35; 19:1	
Bethphage	**16**	21:1	11:1	19:29	
Tyre	**17**	11:21–22; 15:21	3:8; 7:24, 31	6:17; 10:13–4	
Sidon	**18**	11:21–2; 15:21	3:8; 7:31	4:26; 6:17; 10:13–14	
Cana	**19**				2:1, 11; 4:46; 21:2
Sychar	**20**				4:5
Chorazin	**21**	11:21		10:13	
Magdala/ Dalmanutha	**22**	15:39; 27:56, 61; 28:1	8:10		
Caesarea Philippi	**23**	16:13	8:27		
Bethany	**24**	21:17; 26:6	11:1, 11–22; 14:3	19:29; 24:50	11:1,18; 12:1
Gennesaret	**25**	14:34	6:53		
Zeraphath	**26**			4:26	
Nain	**27**			7:1	
Aenon	**28**				3:23
Salim	**29**				3:23
Ephraim	**30**				11:54
Gerasenes	**31**		5:1		
Gadarenes	**32**	8:28			
Ramah	**33**	2:18			
Emmaus	**34**			24:13	
Bethany (east)	**35**				1:28
• BODIES OF WATER					
Jordan River	**36**	3:5–6, 13; 4:15, 25; 19:1	1:5, 9; 3:8; 10:1	3:3; 4:1	1:28; 3:26; 10:40
Sea of Galilee, Lake Tiberias, Lake Kinnereth	**37**	4:18; 15:29	1:16; 7:31	5:1	6:1; 21:1
• MOUNTAIN					
Mount of Olives	**38**	21:1; 24:3; 26:30	11:1; 13:3; 14:26	19:29, 37; 21:37; 22:39	8:1

* *Possibly also Magadan*

Jerusalem in Jesus's Day

Some of the details are uncertain.

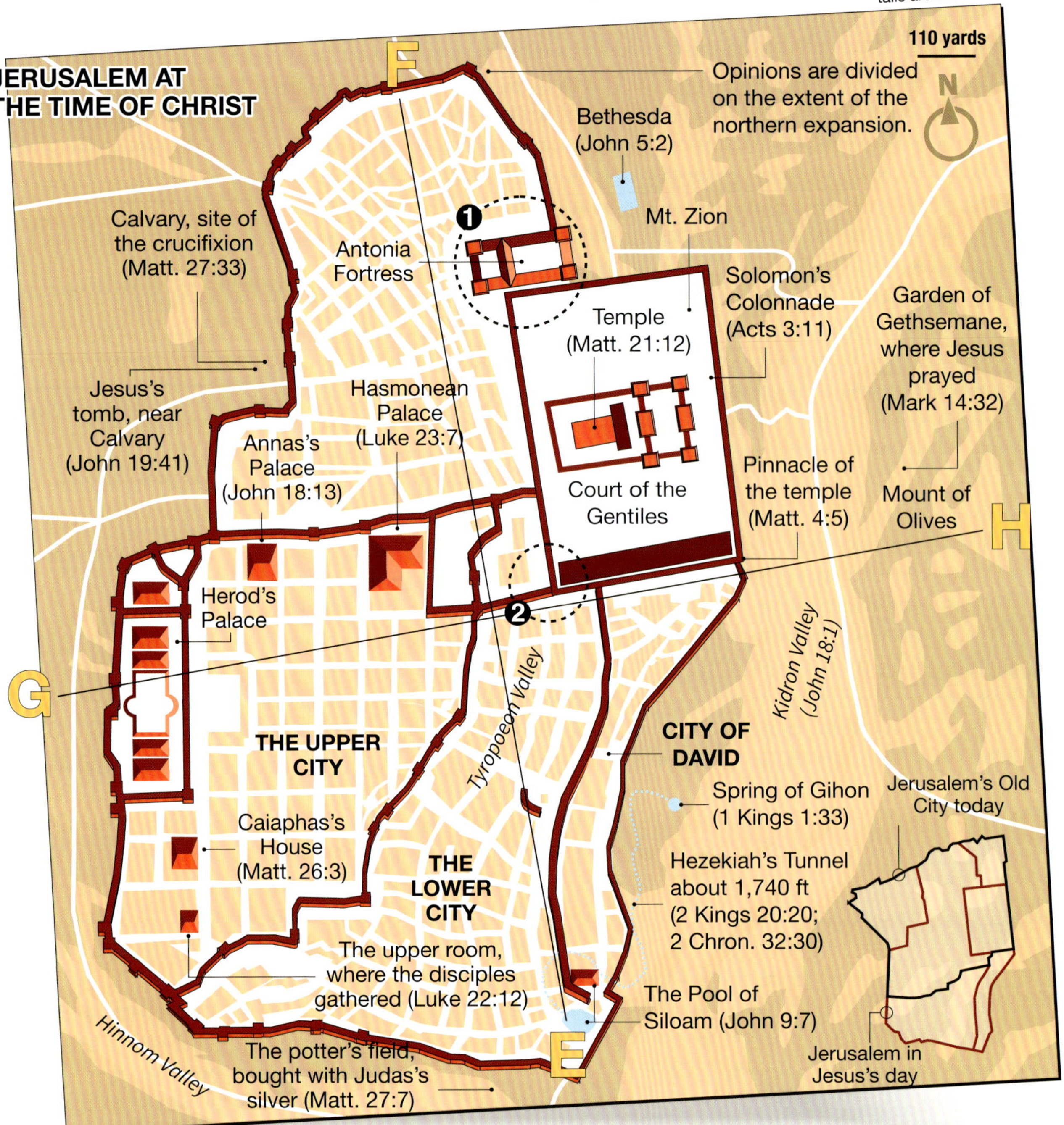

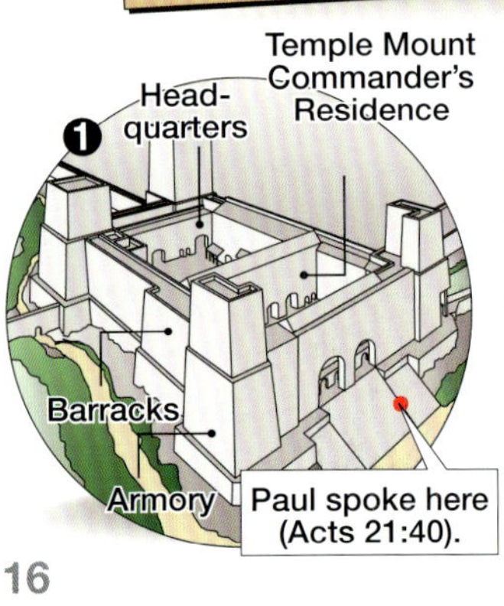

Antonia Fortress

• Fortress built by Herod the Great to protect the Temple Mount. It is named after Marcus Antonius, a friend of Herod. Probably built before 30 BC, destroyed in AD 70.

• Also called "the barracks" (Acts 21:37; 22:24). Paul was standing on its steps when he spoke (21:40).

• The Via Dolorosa starts here, thought by some to be the path of Jesus's suffering.

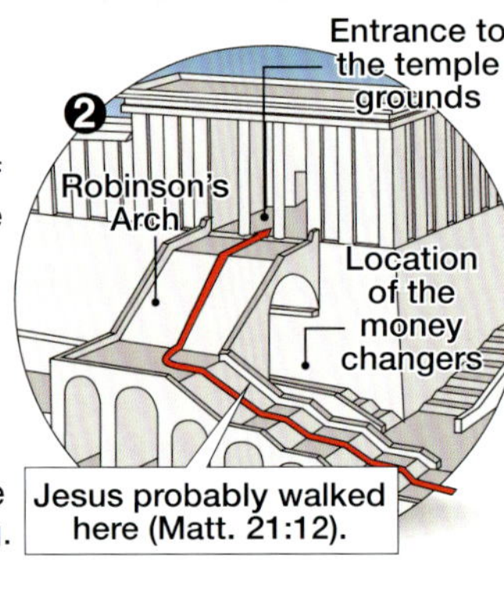

Robinson's Arch

• Robinson's Arch is a staircase at the southwest corner of the Temple Mount.

• The staircase, over 65 feet high, led up to the Temple Mount. It was completed around AD 20 and destroyed in AD 70.

• The staircase is named for archaeologist Edward Robinson, who discovered its remains during excavations in 1838.

Cross Sections of Israel's Geography

Cross section through Israel from south to north, facing west: The Jordan Valley is below sea level, and the surface of the Dead Sea is the lowest point on earth, while Mount Hermon rises high in the north.

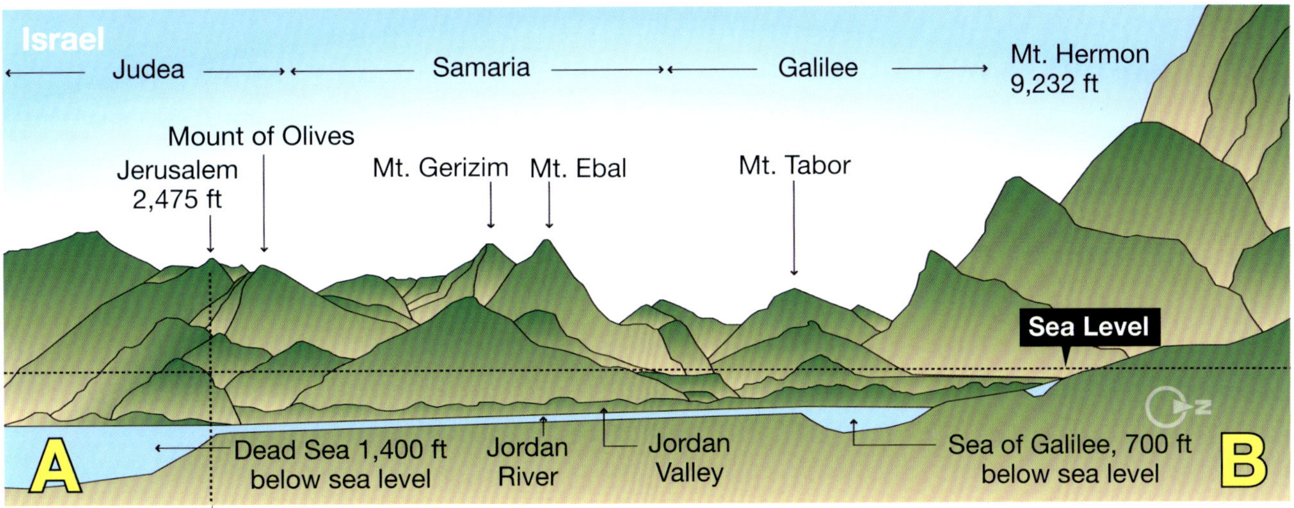

Cross-section through Israel from west to east, facing north: From the Mediterranean in the west to the mountains in the east, Israel has distinct zones: the coastal strip, the central highlands, and the Jordan Valley.

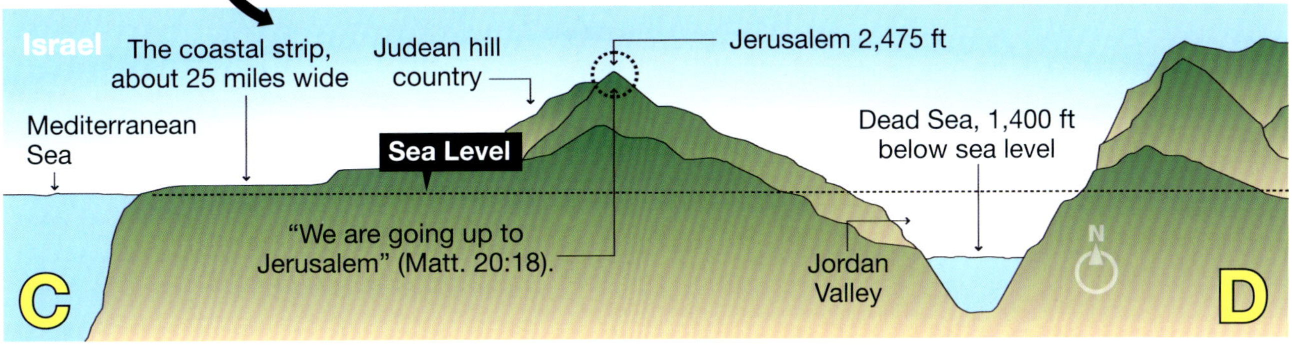

Cross section through Jerusalem from south to north, facing west: Jerusalem is a hilly city. From the Lower City it is a steep climb up to the Temple Mount.

Cross section through Jerusalem from west to east, facing north: In the west-east direction, the city is also hilly. Down to the Temple Mount, and to the Kidron Valley, and then up the Mount of Olives.

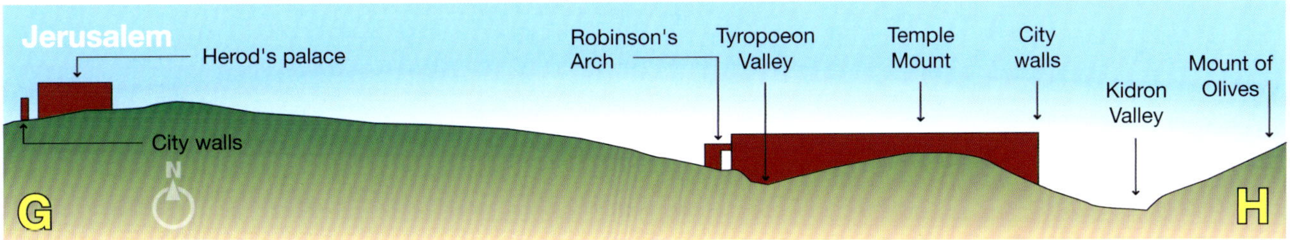

The Jordan River: Headwaters to Dead Sea

Length: 156 miles
Elevation Drop: 1,365 feet

- **The Jordan River** flows through a large fault basin which extends from northern Turkey down to Africa in the south.
- **The ecosystem** around the Jordan deteriorated in the latter part of the twentieth century. In 1964, Israel built a pumping station that feeds water into the national water system. Both Jordan and Syria have diverted water from the Yarmouk tributary.
- **In the past**, 343.5 billion gallons of water flowed annually through the river channel; today it is just under 7.9 billion gallons. But efforts are now being made to improve the ecosystem. For example, Israel's water needs are increasingly being met by desalinated seawater.

Length compared with other rivers

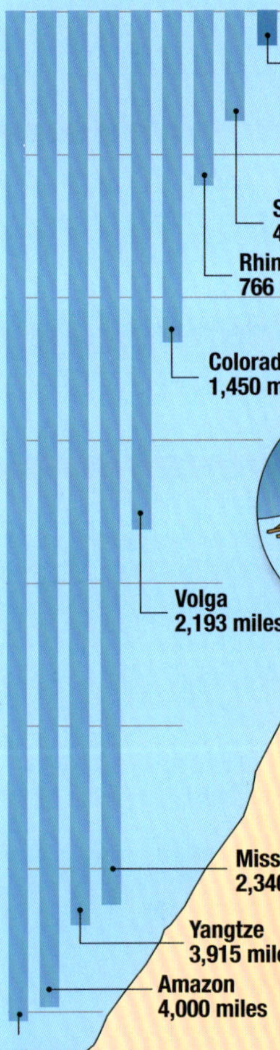

1 Jordan's headwaters

Mt. Hermon's snowmelt flows from springs at the base of the mountain. These form the tributaries of the upper Jordan: Dan, Hasbani, Ayun, and Banias.

2 Lake Hula

Before 1950: Surface: 5.5 sq mi **Length:** 3 miles **Width:** 2.5 miles The water entered the wetland before flowing into the lake. Between 1951 and 1958, authorities drained the lake for irrigation and to prevent the spread of malarial mosquitoes. The lake is now largely dried up. However in 1964, part of the wetland was restored and is now a nature reserve. Around 500 million migratory birds pass through the reserve annually.

3 Upper Jordan

From Lake Hula down to the Sea of Galilee, the river drops 890 feet in about 12 miles, its steepest section.

Notable birds:

4 Sea of Galilee

Surface: 64 sq mi **Depth:** 141 ft **Length:** 18 miles **Width:** 7.5 miles It is the lowest freshwater lake in the world, also called Lake Kinnereth, Lake Gennesaret, or Lake Tiberias. Just south of its outlet is the Degania Dam, which has regulated the lake's water since the 1930s. Nearby is the Yardenit Baptismal Site, built in 1981.

Fishing boat on the Sea of Galilee in Jesus's day

5 Lower Jordan

In Joshua's time, the Jordan was so powerful that it took a miracle to enable the Israelites to cross it (Josh. 3:14–17). Today, it is a quiet and shallow river. It is about 65 miles from the Sea of Galilee to the Dead Sea, but the river's meandering makes the actual length 140 miles. Its tributaries include the Yarmouk and Zarqa (also called Jabbok, Gen. 32:23).

Qumran Caves

6 Dead Sea

Surface: 233 sq mi **Depth:** 977 ft **Length:** 40 miles. This is the lowest point on earth. Surrounded by hills and having no outlet, it forms a salt lake. The salinity is around 34%, more than 8 times saltier than normal seawater.

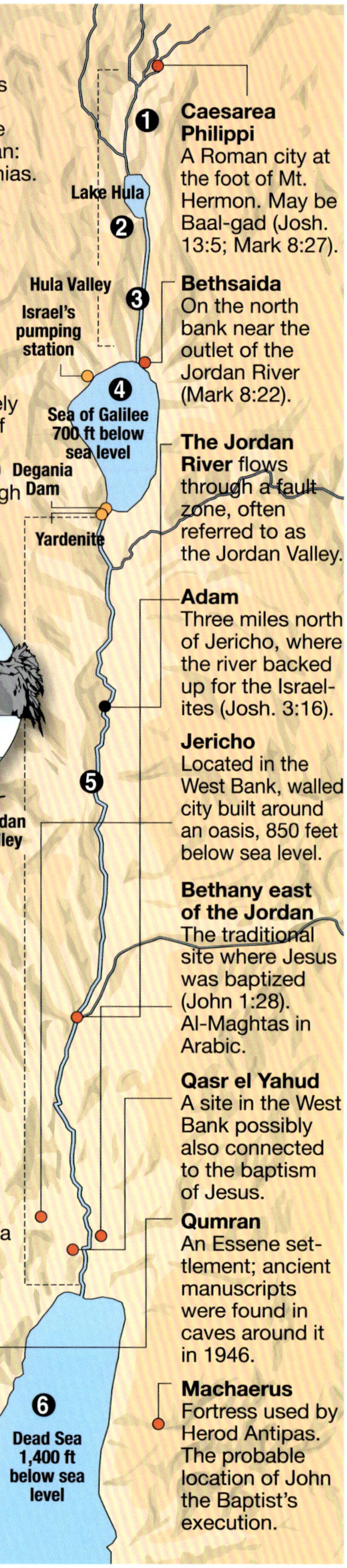

Caesarea Philippi A Roman city at the foot of Mt. Hermon. May be Baal-gad (Josh. 13:5; Mark 8:27).

Bethsaida On the north bank near the outlet of the Jordan River (Mark 8:22).

The Jordan River flows through a fault zone, often referred to as the Jordan Valley.

Adam Three miles north of Jericho, where the river backed up for the Israelites (Josh. 3:16).

Jericho Located in the West Bank, walled city built around an oasis, 850 feet below sea level.

Bethany east of the Jordan The traditional site where Jesus was baptized (John 1:28). Al-Maghtas in Arabic.

Qasr el Yahud A site in the West Bank possibly also connected to the baptism of Jesus.

Qumran An Essene settlement; ancient manuscripts were found in caves around it in 1946.

Machaerus Fortress used by Herod Antipas. The probable location of John the Baptist's execution.

Israel Under Roman Rule

GALILEE AND PEREA
After the death of Herod the Great in 4 BC, these territories passed to his son Herod Antipas. He was deposed in AD 39.

- **GALILEE:** The northernmost of the three regions west of the Jordan. Cities in the area include Nazareth, Capernaum, Sepphoris, and Tiberias.
- **PEREA:** Means "beyond" (Matt. 4:15). Refers to the area east of the Jordan. Jews from Galilee traveling to Jerusalem who wanted to avoid going through Samaria chose the route through Perea.

PHOENICIA
The area, a narrow coastal strip about twelve miles long, was home to a number of trading and maritime cities such as Tyre and Sidon. Captured by the Romans in 64 BC.

ITUREA
Philip the Tetrarch, also a son of Herod, reigned over the northeastern territory east of the Jordan from AD 4 to 34.

- **ITUREA, TRACONITIS, AND ABILENE:** Areas north and east of the Sea of Galilee. Caesarea Philippi was also in the area. Primarily a non-Jewish population.

JUDEA, SAMARIA, AND IDUMEA
After Herod's death in 4 BC, his son Herod Archelaus ruled the area. When Archelaus was exiled in AD 6, Roman prefects based in Caesarea were appointed as rulers, including Pontius Pilate.

- **SAMARIA:** After Assyria conquered Israel in 722 BC, those left in the land mixed with foreign settlers, forming the Samaritans.
- **JUDEA:** Of the three regions west of the Jordan, it was the southernmost, with Jerusalem at its center.
- **IDUMEA:** The Greek name for Edom. In the fifth century, the Edomites were driven from their homeland near Petra and founded a kingdom in southern Judea.

AREA OF THE DECAPOLIS

- Originally ten Hellenistic cities that created a confederation around 65 BC. Other cities joined later.
- The cities were independent of the local tetrarch, ruled instead by the governor in Syria.
- In the Gospels, Decapolis usually refers to the area southeast of the Sea of Galilee. Also called the Ten Towns.
- Cities include Gadara, Gerasa, Capitolias, Hippos, and Damascus (Matt. 8:28; Mark 5:1).

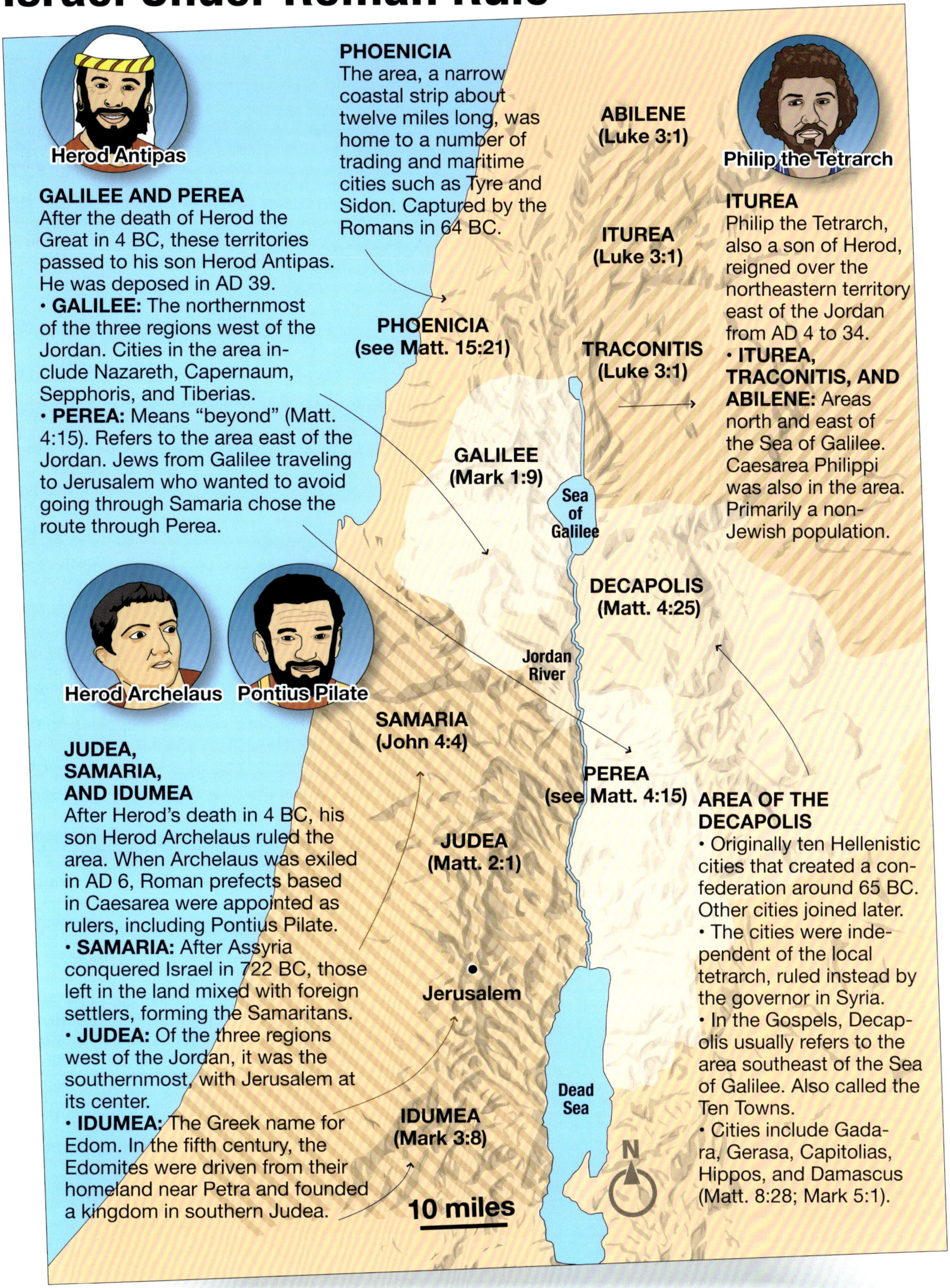

How the Gospels Harmonize (1)

The four Gospels are accounts of the life of Jesus from four different authors. This is an attempt to harmonize the ten stages of Jesus's life and work as described by Matthew, Mark, Luke, and John.

This harmony mostly follows *A Harmony of the Gospels* by A. T. Robertson

MATTHEW	MARK	LUKE	JOHN
Total: *1,068 verses* *28.3%*	**Total:** *673 verses* *17.9%*	**Total:** *1,149 verses* *30.5%*	**Total:** *878 verses* *23.3%*

1 BIRTH AND CHILDHOOD

213 verses, 5.7% of the Gospels

Two major events: the annunciation and the birth of Jesus. **Time:** From 4–7 BC to around AD 29, about 35 years in total

	Number of verses/percentage of the Gospel:	*48/4.5%*	*0/0%*	■ *147/12.8%*	*18/2.1%*	*Number of times found in the Gospels*
1	Luke's investigative method			• 1:1–4		1
2	Jesus is the Word before the incarnation				• 1:1–18	1
3	The genealogy of Jesus	1:1–17		3:23–38		2
4	John the Baptist's birth foretold			• 1:5–25		1
5	Annunciation: Jesus's birth foretold			• 1:26–38		1
6	Elizabeth blesses Mary			• 1:39–45		1
7	Mary's song of praise			• 1:46–56		1
8	Early life of John the Baptist			• 1:57–80		1
9	Jesus's birth foretold to Joseph	• 1:18–25				1
10	The birth of Jesus			• 2:1–7		1
11	Jesus's birth announced to shepherds			• 2:8–20		1
12	Jesus is circumcised			• 2:21		1
13	Simeon and Anna meet baby Jesus			• 2:22–38		1
14	The wise men visit Jesus	• 2:1–12				1
15	Joseph, Mary, and Jesus flee to Egypt	• 2:13–15				1
16	The infanticide in Bethlehem	• 2:16–18				1
17	Jesus's family moves to Nazareth	2:19–23		2:39		2
18	Jesus grows up in Nazareth			• 2:40		1
19	Jesus visits Jerusalem at age twelve			• 2:41–50		1
20	Jesus as an adult in Nazareth			• 2:51–52		1

Squares show the Gospel with most verses in the stage.

Dots indicate events only recorded in one Gospel.

Nothing about the birth of Jesus (Mark)

Nothing about the birth of Jesus (John)

Matthew and Luke tell different parts of the birth narrative.

2 INITIAL MINISTRY

108 verses, 2.9% of the Gospels

TRANSITION: Jesus's life in Nazareth comes to an end. He takes the first steps of his public ministry—his time has come (see Gal. 4:4). John the Baptist has paved the way, and now Jesus appears on the scene. **Time:** From January to April AD 30, about 4 months

	Number of verses/percentage of the Gospel:	*28/2.6%*	*13/1.9%*	■ *34/3.0%*	*33/3.8%*	
21	John the Baptist appears	3:1–6	1:1–6	3:1–6		3
22	John the Baptist preaches	3:7–10		3:7–14		2
23	John the Baptist speaks of the Messiah	3:11–12	1:7–8	3:15–18		3
24	John the Baptist baptizes Jesus*	3:13–17	1:9–11	3:21–23	*Told afterwards*	3
25	Jesus is tempted in the desert	4:1–11	1:12–13	4:1–13		3
26	John the Baptist speaks of Jesus's baptism				• 1:19–28	1
27	John the Baptist reveals Jesus as Messiah				• 1:29–34	1
28	Jesus calls his first disciples				• 1:35–51	1

Synoptics and John offer different views of the event.

3 EARLY JUDEAN MINISTRY

171 verses, 4.5% of the Gospels

TRANSITION: At the Passover, Jesus begins preaching publicly, coming into direct conflict with the Jewish religious leaders. Beyond this first Passover, we know very little about the details of his early ministry. **Time:** From May to December AD 30, about 8 months

	Number of verses/percentage of the Gospel:	*1/0.1%*	*1/0.1%*	*3/0.3%*	■ *103/11.7%*	
29	Jesus's first miracle, in Cana				• 2:1–11	1
30	Jesus's first trip to Capernaum				• 2:12	1
31	Jesus cleanses the temple the first time				• 2:13–22	1
32	Jesus talks to Nicodemus				• 2:23–3:21	1
33	Jesus and John the Baptist active at the same time				• 3:22–36	1
34	Jesus's reasons for leaving Judea**	4:12	1:14–15	3:19–20; 4:14	4:1–4	4
35	Jesus and the woman at the well				• 4:5–42	1

The three are silent about this stage.

The texts are not entirely parallel.

One verse, John 3:22, summarizes 8 months.

** If John's account is taken retrospectively, Jesus's baptism is the first event described in all four Gospels **Although there are accounts in each Gospel, the accounts are not entirely parallel. John gives one aspect of the reasons for Jesus to leave Judea, Luke gives another aspect, and Mark and Matthew a third.*

How the Gospels Harmonize (2)

4 EARLY GALILEAN MINISTRY

171 verses, 4.5% of the Gospels

TRANSITION: John the Baptist is imprisoned by Herod Antipas, so Jesus chooses to retreat to Galilee. He is driven out of Nazareth, moves to Capernaum, and preaches in Galilee.
Time: From January to April AD 31, about 4 months

	MATTHEW	MARK	LUKE	JOHN	Number of times found in the Gospels
Number of verses/percentage of the Gospel:	*37/3.5%*	*53/7.9%*	■ *69/6.0%*	*12/1.4%*	
36 Jesus arrives in Galilee	4:17		4:14–15	4:43–45	2
37 Jesus heals an official's son from a distance				• 4:46–54	1
38 Jesus is driven out of Nazareth			• 4:16–31		1
39 Jesus moves to Capernaum	• 4:13–16				1
40 Jesus calls four disciples	4:18–22	1:16–20	5:1–11*		3
41 Jesus heals a possessed man on the Sabbath		1:21–28	4:31–37		2
42 Jesus heals Peter's mother-in-law	8:14–15	1:29–31	4:38–39		3
43 Jesus heals many possessed people	8:16–17	1:32–34	4:40–41		3
44 Jesus's first ministry tour through Galilee	4:23–25	1:35–39	4:42–44		3
45 Jesus heals a leper	8:2–4	1:40–45	5:12–16		3
46 Jesus heals a man who was lowered through a roof	9:1–8	2:1–12	5:17–26		3
47 Jesus calls Levi (Matthew)	9:9–13	2:13–17	5:27–32		3
48 Jesus teaches about fasting	9:14–17	2:18–22	5:33–39		3

Matthew is not chronological here.

5 MID-GALILEAN MINISTRY

884 verses, 23.5% of the Gospels

TRANSITION: Accused of being demon-possessed, Jesus withdraws from the crowds and devotes himself to the disciples. He chooses the Twelve and delivers the Sermon on the Mount.
Time: From May AD 31 to April AD 32, about 12 months

	MATTHEW	MARK	LUKE	JOHN	Number of times found in the Gospels
Number of verses/percentage of the Gospel:	■ *391/36.6%*	*203/30.2%*	*172/15.0%*	*118/13.4%*	
49 Jesus heals a lame man on the Sabbath				• 5:1–3, 5–47	1
50 Jesus's disciples pick grain on the Sabbath	12:1–8	2:23–28	6:1–5		3
51 Jesus heals a man on the Sabbath	12:9–14	3:1–6	6:6–11		3
52 Jesus teaches and heals at the Sea of Galilee	12:15–21	3:7–12			2
53 Jesus prays and chooses the Twelve		3:13–19	6:12–16		2
54 Sermons on the Mount and Plain	5:1–8:1		6:17–49		2
55 Jesus heals an official's servant	8:5–13		7:1–10		2
56 Jesus raises a widow's son in Nain			• 7:11–17		2
57 John the Baptist asks about Jesus	11:2–19		7:18–35		2
58 Jesus denounces cities, reveals the Father	• 11:20–30				1
59 A sinful woman anoints Jesus's feet			• 7:36–50		1
60 Jesus's second ministry tour through Galilee			• 8:1–3		1
61 Jesus accused of coming from Satan	12:22–37	3:20–30			2
62 Scribes and Pharisees request a sign	12:38–45				1
63 Jesus's family concerned about him	12:46–50	3:31–35	8:19–21		3
64 Jesus explains his parables	13:1–53	4:1–34	8:4–18		3
65 Jesus calms the storm	8:18, 23–27	4:35–41	8:22–25		3
66 Jesus drives out an evil spirit	8:28–34	5:1–20	8:26–39		3
67 Jesus heals a woman and raises a girl	9:18–26	5:21–43	8:40–56		3
68 Jesus heals two blind men, faces accusations	• 9:27–34				1
69 Jesus's last visit to Nazareth	13:54–58	6:1–6			2
70 Jesus's third ministry tour of Galilee	9:35–11:1	6:6–13	9:1–6		3
71 Herod worries about Jesus	14:1–12	6:14–29	9:7–9		3
72 Jesus feeds 5,000	14:13–21	6:30–44	9:10–17	6:1–13	4
73 Jesus rejects being made king	14:22–23	6:45–46		6:14–15	3
74 Jesus walks on the water during a storm	14:24–33	6:47–52		6:16–21	3
75 Jesus received at Gennesaret	14:34–36	6:53–56			2
76 Disciples begin to leave Jesus				• 6:22–71	1
77 Pharisees attack Jesus over hand washing	15:1–20	7:1–15, 17–23		7:1	3

Over one third of Matthew deals with this stage.

Almost nothing about this period in John.

Luke reports the events in chronological order. But this is an exception.

Matthew is not chronological in this section.

The first story found in all four Gospels.

The beginning of what is known as the travel narrative.

* Luke says he will give "an orderly account" (Luke 1:3). We therefore assume that Luke is the most chronological gospel. But there are a few chronological deviations. This is the first. Simon and the others (Mark 1:36) were with Jesus when he traveled, so they had already been called in Luke 5:1–11.

How the Gospels Harmonize (3)

6 LATE GALILEAN MINISTRY

265 verses, 7% of the Gospels

TRANSITION: Jesus's Galilean ministry falls apart, and many disciples abandon him. He withdraws from Herod Antipas's territory. Yet an inner core of disciples confesses him as the Messiah. **Time:** From May to Oct. AD 32, about 6 months

#	Event	MATTHEW	MARK	LUKE	JOHN	Number of times found in the Gospels
	Number of verses/percentage of the Gospel:	■ *111/10.4%*	*100/14.9%*	*45/3.9%*	*9/1.0%*	
78	Jesus withdraws to Tyre and Sidon	15:21–28	7:24–30			2
79	Jesus in Phoenicia, heals a deaf man	15:29–38	7:31–8:9			2
80	Jesus visits Magadan, attacks Pharisees	15:39–16:4	8:10–12			2
81	Jesus in Bethsaida, heals a blind man	16:5–12	8:13–26			2
82	Jesus asks who people say he is	16:13–20	8:27–30	9:18–21		3
83	Jesus predicts his suffering and death	16:21–26	8:31–37	9:22–25		3
84	Jesus talks about his return in glory	16:27–28	8:38–9:1	9:26–27		3
85	Jesus transfigured, Moses and Elijah present	17:1–8	9:2–8	9:28–36		3
86	Conversation descending the mountain	17:9–13	9:9–13	9:36		3
87	Jesus heals a possessed boy	17:14–20	9:14–29	9:37–43		3
88	Jesus speaks of his death and resurrection	17:22–23	9:30–32	9:43–45		3
89	Jesus pays the temple tax	• 17:24–27				1
90	The disciples discuss who will be first	18:1–5	9:33–37	9:46–48		3
91	Jesus rebukes through a parable	18:6–14	9:38–43, 45, 47–50	9:49–50		3
92	Jesus instructs on church discipline	• 18:15–35				1
93	Jesus's challenge to count the cost	• 8:19–22		9:57–62		2
94	Jesus's brothers try to advise him				• 7:2–9	1
95	Jesus secretly travels to Jerusalem			9:51–56	7:10	2

Deviates from the chronology (Matthew 8:19–22)

Almost nothing about this period in John

Another exception in Luke's chronology (Luke 9:51–56)

7 LATE JUDEAN MINISTRY

358 verses, 9.5% of the Gospels

TRANSITION: Jesus begins to speak openly about his death and resurrection. He travels to Jerusalem in secret, sends out his disciples, and is threatened twice with stoning. **Time:** From November AD 32 to January 33, about 3 months

#	Event	MATTHEW	MARK	LUKE	JOHN	Number of times found in the Gospels
	Number of verses/percentage of the Gospel:	*0/0.0%*	*0/0.0%*	*176/15.3%*	■ *182/20.7%*	
96	Jesus at the temple for Feast of Tabernacles				• 7:11–52	1
97	Jesus confronted with the adulteress				• 7:53–8:11	1
98	Jesus says he is the light of the world				• 8:12–20	1
99	Pharisees try to stone Jesus				• 8:21–59	1
100	Jesus heals a man born blind				• 9:1–41	1
101	Jesus teaches on the Good Shepherd				• 10:1–21	1
102	Jesus sends out 72 disciples			• 10:1–24		1
103	Jesus tells the parable of the Good Samaritan			• 10:25–37		1
104	Jesus visits Martha and Mary			• 10:38–42		1
105	Jesus teaches on prayer, Lord's Prayer			• 11:1–13		1
106	Jesus accused again of being from Satan			• 11:14–36		1
107	Jesus harshly criticizes the Pharisees			• 11:37–54		1
108	Jesus admonishes the disciples and tells parables			• 12:1–59		1
109	Jesus calls everyone to repent			• 13:1–9		1
110	Jesus heals a crippled woman on the Sabbath			• 13:10–21		1
111	Jesus's opponents try again to stone him				• 10:22–39	1

Jesus goes to Jerusalem in secret (John 7:10). It is possible that Matthew and Peter were not present when this happened.

Matthew and Mark are silent about this period.

It is doubtful that John 7:53–8:11 was originally included in the Gospel of John.

8 LATE PEREAN MINISTRY

392 verses, 10.4% of the Gospels

TRANSITION: Jesus leaves Jerusalem and goes to Perea, across the Jordan, where he preaches about discipleship. On hearing of Lazarus's death, he returns and calls him out of the tomb. **Time:** From February to April AD 33, about 3 months

#	Event	MATTHEW	MARK	LUKE	JOHN	Number of times found in the Gospels
	Number of verses/percentage of the Gospel:	*64/6.0%*	*52/7.7%*	■ *219/19.1%*	*57/6.5%*	
112	Jesus leaves Jerusalem, crosses the Jordan				• 10:40–42	1
113	Jesus teaches in Perea, warned about Herod			• 13:22–35		1
114	Jesus heals on a Sabbath, tells parables			• 14:1–24		1
115	Jesus talks about the cost of discipleship			• 14:25–35		1
116	Jesus tells three parables against critics			• 15:1–32		1
117	Jesus tells three more parables			• 16:1–17:10		1
118	Jesus goes to Bethany, raises Lazarus				• 11:1–44	1

How the Gospels Harmonize (4)

(Stage 8 continued)

		MATTHEW	MARK	LUKE	JOHN	Number of times found in the Gospels
119	Jesus's opponents plot to kill him				• 11:45–54	1
120	Jesus heads to Jerusalem for last time			• 17:11–35, 37		1
121	Jesus tells two parables about prayer			• 18:1–14		1
122	Jesus in Perea, teaches about divorce	19:1–12	10:1–12			2
123	Jesus blesses the children	19:13–15	10:13–16	18:15–17		3
124	Jesus and the rich young man	19:16–20:16	10:17–31	18:18–30		3
125	Jesus predicts his death and resurrection	20:17–28	10:32–45	18:31–34		3
126	Jesus heals Bartimaeus in Jericho	20:29–34	10:46–52	18:35–43		3
127	Jesus meets Zacchaeus in Jericho			• 19:1–28		1

From this point onward, the Synoptic Gospels are parallel.

There are four Gospels with one Christ, four accounts with one purpose, and four sketches of one person. (Henrietta C. Mears)

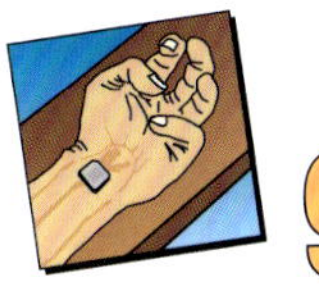

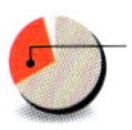

1,120 verses, 29.7% of the Gospels

9 THE LAST PASSOVER

TRANSITION: Jesus returns to Jerusalem, fully aware of what awaits him. He is arrested, offering his life on the cross. His life's work now nears its climax as he is laid in a tomb.
Time: April AD 33, one week

	Number of verses/percentage of the Gospel:	*368/34.4%*	*231/34.3%*	*231/20.1%*	*290/33%*	
	1. Friday (would not have traveled on a Sabbath)					
128a	Jesus arrives in Bethany, near Jerusalem				• 11:55–12:1, 9–11	1
	2. Saturday					
	Saturday probably with his disciples in Bethany					
	3. Sunday (Palm Sunday)					
128b	Jesus enters Jerusalem on a donkey	21:1–11, 14–17	11:1–11	19:29–44	12:12–19	4
	4. Monday					
129	Jesus cleanses the temple, curses the fig tree	21:18–19a,12–13	11:12–18	19:45–48		3
130	Jesus speaks again about his death				• 12:20–50	1
	5. Tuesday					
131	Jesus shows that the fig tree is now withered	21:19b–22	11:19–25	21:37–38		3
132	Sanhedrin questions Jesus's authority	21:23–22:14	11:27–12:12	20:1–19		3
133	The question of paying taxes to Caesar	22:15–22	12:13–17	20:20–26		3
134	The Sadducee's question about resurrection	22:23–33	12:18–27	20:27–40		3
135	Pharisees ask about greatest commandment	22:34–40	12:28–34			2
136	Jesus asks the Pharisees about David's son	22:41–46	12:35–37	20:41–44		3
137	Jesus's last public speech, against the Pharisees	23:1–13, 15–39	12:38–40	20:45–47		3
138	Jesus comments on the widow's offering		12:41–44	21:1–4		2
139	Jesus's speech on the Mt. of Olives (evening)	24:1–25:46	13:1–37	21:5–36		3
140	Jesus predicts his death in two days (evening)	26:1–5	14:1–2	22:1–2		3
141	Jesus with Simon the leper (evening)	26:6–13	14:3–9		12:2–8	3
142	Judas decides to betray Jesus (evening)	26:14–16	14:10–11	22:3–6		3
	6. Wednesday					
	Jesus remains in Bethany					
	7. Thursday					
143	Disciples prepare the Passover meal	26:17–19	14:12–16	22:7–13		3
144	Jesus and the start of the Passover meal (evening)	26:20	14:17	22:14–16, 24–30		3
145	Jesus washes the disciples' feet (evening)				• 13:1–20	1
146	Jesus identifies Judas as the traitor (evening)	26:21–25	14:18–21	22:21–23	13:21–30	4
147	Jesus predicts Peter's denial (evening)	26:31–35	14:27–31	22:31–38	13:31–38	4
148	Jesus institutes the Lord's Supper (evening)	26:26–29	14:22–25	22:17–20	(1 Cor. 11:23–26)	3
149	Jesus's speech in the upper room (evening)				14:1–31	1
150	Jesus on the way to Gethsemane (evening)				15:1–16:33	1
151	Jesus's High Priestly Prayer (evening)				17:1–26	1
152	Jesus's agony in Gethsemane (evening)	26:30, 36–46	14:26, 32–42	22:39–46	18:1	4

These are the last words of Jesus during his public ministry. (Luke 21:1–4)

Some believe that this is the same story as in Luke 7:36–50 (59). But it is unlikely. (John 12:2–8)

One of the few occasions when Luke seems to deviate from the chronology. (Luke 22:21–23, 22:31–38, 22:17–20)

How the Gospels Harmonize (5)

	(Stage 9 continued)	MATTHEW	MARK	LUKE	JOHN	
	8. Friday (Good Friday)					
153	Jesus is betrayed by Judas (night)	26:47–56	14:43–52	22:47–53	18:2–12	4
154	(I) Jesus before the high priest Annas (night)			22:54–62	• 18:12–14, 19–23	1
155	(II) Jesus is questioned by the Sanhedrin (night)	26:57, 59–68	14:53, 55–65	22:54a, 63–65	18:24	4
156	Peter denies Jesus three times (night)	26:58, 69–75	14:54, 66–72	22:54b–62	18:15–18, 25–27	4
157	(III) Jesus is declared guilty (morning)	27:1	15:1a	22:66–71		3
158	Judas commits suicide (morning, Acts 1:18–19)	• 27:3–10				1
159	(IV) Jesus before Pilate the first time (morning)	27:2, 11–14	15:1b–5	23:1–5	18:28–38	4
160	(V) Jesus before Herod Antipas (morning)		15:16–19	• 23:6–12		1
161	(VI) Jesus before Pilate a second time (morning)	27:15–26	15:6–15	23:13–16, 18–25	18:39–19:16	4
162	Roman soldiers mock Jesus (6:00–9:00 am)	27:27–30	15:16–19	23:33–43		2
163	Jesus on the way to Calvary (before 9:00 am)	27:31–34	15:20–23	23:26–33a	19:16–17	4
164	The first three hours on the cross (9:00–12:00)	27:35–44	15:24–27, 29–32	23:33b–43	19:18–27	4
165	Three hours of darkness (12:00–3:00 pm)	27:45–50	15:33–37	23:44–45a, 46	19:28–30	4
166	The death of Jesus and related events (3:00 pm)	27:51–56	15:38–41	23:45b, 47–49		3
167	Jesus is buried	27:57–60	15:42–46	23:50–54	19:31–42	4
168	The women go to the tomb (3:00 pm–Saturday)	27:61–66	15:47	23:55–56		3

10 Post-Resurrection

149 verses,
4% of the Gospels

TRANSITION: After the resurrection, Jesus appears to his disciples in Jerusalem and then in Galilee. Their final meeting together is on the Mount of Olives, where he ascends to heaven.
Time: From April to May AD 33, 40 days in total

	Number of verses/percentage of the Gospel:	*20/1.9%*	*20/3%*	*53/4.6%*	*56/6.4%*	
	9. Sunday					
169	The women go to the tomb (Sunday morning)	28:1	16:1			2
170	Earthquake rolls away the stone (morning)	• 28:2–4				1
171	Women come to the tomb, meet an angel	28:5–8	16:2–8	24:1–8	20:1	4
172	The women tell, Peter and John go to the tomb			24:9–12	20:2–10	2
173	Jesus appears to Mary Magdalene		16:9–11		20:11–18	2
174	Jesus appears to the women	• 28:9–10				1
175	The guards tell the chief priests what happened	• 28:11–15				1
176	Jesus meets two disciples going to Emmaus		16:12–13	24:13–32		2
177	Reports from the two disciples and Peter	*Mark 16:9–20 is disputed and not in the earliest manuscripts.*		• 24:33–35		1
178	Jesus appears to the disciples (except Thomas)		16:14	24:36–43	20:19-25	3
	10. After the Resurrection					
179	Jesus appears to the disciples (with Thomas)				• 20:26–31	1
180	Jesus appears to seven disciples				• 21:1–25	1
181	Jesus appears to 500, the Great Commission	28:16–20	16:15–18			2
182	Jesus appears to the disciples			• 24:44–49		1
183	Jesus ascends into heaven		16:19–20	24:50–53		2

** There are also references to encounters with the resurrected Christ outside the Gospels; see Acts 1:3–11 and 1 Cor. 15:5–7.*

> "A harmony [of the Gospels] cannot give all the aid that one needs, but it is the one essential [thing] for the serious study of the life of Jesus.... One who has never read a harmony will be amazed at the flood of light that flashes from the parallel and progressive record of the life of Jesus Christ.
> (A. T. Robertson)

How the Gospels Harmonize (6)

Statistical consultant: *Josef Dagson*

The Gospel writers chose to emphasize different aspects of Jesus's life in their accounts. Here is how they organized their material.

Reading and comparing the Gospels horizontally

Distribution of the Gospels in each stage.

Percentage of material in stage/ Number of verses

Stage	Verses	MATTHEW	MARK	LUKE	JOHN
1. Birth and Childhood 4–7 BC–AD 29	213 verses	22.5%/48	0.0%/0	69.0%/147	8.5%/18
2. Initial Ministry 4 months, Jan.–April AD 30	108 verses	25.9%/28	12.0%/13	31.5%/34	30.6%/33
3. Early Judean Ministry 8 months, May–Dec. AD 30	108 verses	0.9%/1	0.9%/1	2.8%/3	95.4%/103
4. Early Galilean Ministry 4 months, Jan.–April AD 31	171 verses	21.6%/37	31.0%/53	40.4%/69	7.0%/12
5. Mid-Galilean Ministry 12 months, May AD 31–May 32	884 verses	44.2%/391	23.0%/203	19.5%/172	13.3%/118
6. Late Galilean Ministry 6 months, May–Oct. AD 32	265 verses	41.9%/111	37.7%/100	17.0%/45	3.4%/9
7. Late Judean Ministry 3 months, Nov. AD 32–Jan. 33	358 verses	0.0%/0	0.0%/0	49.2%/176	50.8%/182
8. Late Perean Ministry 3 months, Feb.–April AD 33	392 verses	16.3%/64	13.3%/52	55.9%/219	14.5%/57
9. The Last Passover One week, April AD 33	1,120 verses	32.9%/368	20.6%/231	20.6%/231	22.9%/290
10. Post-Resurrection 40 days, April–May AD 33	149 verses	13.4%/20	13.4%/20	35.6%/53	37.6%/56
		Total: 28.3%	17.9%	30.5%	23.3%

Reading and comparing the Gospels vertically

Distribution of the stages in each Gospel.

Stage	%	MATTHEW 1,088 verses	MARK 673 verses	LUKE 1,149 verses	JOHN 878 verses
1. Birth and Childhood Total: 213 verses	5.6%	4.5%	0%	12.8%	2.1%
2. Initial Ministry Total: 108 verses	2.9%	2.6%	1.9%	2.9%	3.8%
3. Early Judean Ministry Total: 108 verses	2.9%	0.1%	0.1%	0.3%	11.7%
4. Early Galilean Ministry Total: 171 verses	4.5%	3.5%	7.9%	6.0%	1.4%
5. Mid-Galilean Ministry Total: 884 verses	23.5%	36.6%	30.2%	15.0%	13.4%
6. Late Galilean Ministry Total: 265 verses	7.0%	10.4%	14.9%	3.9%	1.0%
7. Late Judean Ministry Total: 358 verses	9.5%	0%	0%	15.3%	20.7%
8. Late Perean Ministry Total: 392 verses	10.4%	6.0%	7.7%	19.1%	6.5%
9. The Last Passover Total: 1,120 verses	29.7%	34.4%	34.3%	20.1%	33.0%
10. Post-Resurrection Total: 149 verses	4.0%	1.9%	3.0%	4.6%	6.4%

The proportion of material in this section in this Gospel

An Overview of Jesus's Life

Seven basic theological truths about Jesus

1 Jesus existed in eternity before he became man

Jesus was with God in the beginning, sharing divine glory with the Father (John 1:1). Jesus also spoke about this (John 8:58; 17:5).

2 Jesus was born of a virgin

He was born of a virgin and perfectly fulfilled God's ancient promises as prophesied (Isa. 7:14; Matt. 1:22–23; Luke 1:26–38).

3 Jesus was aware of his divinity

By calling God his Father, Jesus claimed equality with him (John 5:17–18). He also stated that he existed before Abraham (John 8:58–59).

> "Christus, the originator of this name, was executed in the reign of Tiberius by the procurator Pontius Pilate ... superstition broke out ... even in the City [of Rome]. (Tacitus, Roman historian)

4 Jesus knew he would die on the cross

Jesus knew beforehand that he would suffer and die and revealed it to his disciples (Matt. 16:21; Mark 8:31; Luke 9:22).

5 Jesus rose bodily from the dead

His resurrection was bodily and forms the basis for our hope of a future resurrection (John 20:19–29; 1 Cor. 15:12–28).

6 Jesus sits at the Father's right hand

Jesus ascended into heaven and sits at the right hand of God the Father (John 14:2–3; Acts 1:9–11; 1 Peter 3:21–22).

7 Jesus will return bodily to earth

He will return to earth to judge the living and the dead and to establish his righteous reign (Acts 1:6–7; 2 Tim. 4:1).

	Pre-existence	Incarnation	Revealing	Training	Atonement	Resurrection	Glorification
KEY POINTS	• In eternity with the Father • Created everything • Prophesied in Old Testament	• Became human • Born in Bethlehem • Grew up in Nazareth	• Baptized by John • Preached to the Jews • Rejected as Messiah	• Chose the disciples • Taught the disciples • Sent out the disciples	• Judged by Pilate • Crucified on Calvary • Died an atoning death	• Rose from the dead • Seen by more than 500 • Ascended to heaven	• At the right hand of the Father • Will return to earth • Will judge all people
TOPICS	He is the creator (Col. 1:16–17).	He takes on humanity (Isa. 9:6).	He shows himself as the Messiah (Matt. 16:16–20).	He teaches with authority (Matt. 7:29).	He is our Savior (1 Tim. 4:10).	He wins the victory for us (1 Cor. 15:55–57).	He will judge in righteousness (2 Thess. 1:5–10).
	Jesus, eternal member of the Trinity	Jesus becomes human, born on earth	Jesus emerges as the Messiah	Jesus is rejected, turns to the disciples	Jesus gives his life, dying on the cross	Jesus is raised, shows himself to many	Jesus is coming back to judge
	Planning salvation from eternity	Creating opportunities to be mediator	Offering himself to the Jews as the Messiah	Preparing disciples for the future	Reconciling fallen humanity with God	Triumphing over and defeating death	Establishing at last a new heaven and earth
PEOPLE	God the Father, God the Holy Spirit	Elizabeth, Zechariah, Mary, Joseph, Herod	First disciples he meets, Nicodemus	The Twelve, inner circle of three	Judas, the High Priest Caiaphas, Pontius Pilate	The women at the tomb, Peter, John, James	The disciples, Thomas, Stephen, Paul
LOCATIONS	Heaven	Bethlehem, Egypt, Nazareth	Jerusalem, Judea, Samaria	Galilee, Tyre and Sidon, Decapolis	Jerusalem	Jerusalem, road to Emmaus, Galilee	Heaven and earth
TEXTS	Mic. 5:2; John 1:1; 17:5; Heb. 7:3; 13:8; 1 Peter 1:20	Luke 1:5–38; 2:1–21; Phil. 2:5–11	Matt. 3:13–17; 9:35; Mark 10:1; John 1:11	Matt. 10:1–4; Luke 6:12–16; 24:27	Matt. 16:21; 26:28; Mark 15:1–15; Rom. 3:25; 5:9–11	Luke 24:5–6; John 11:25; 1 Cor. 15:1–11	Acts 1:9–12; Rom. 8:34; 1 Peter 4:5
TIME PERIOD	From eternity to about 4/7 BC	About 35 years 4/7 BC–AD 29	About 1 year AD 30–31	About 1 year AD 31–32	About 1 year AD 32–33	40 days, April to May AD 33	From AD 33 to eternity

A Comparison of the Gospels

While the four Gospels share common themes, each offers a unique perspective. This overview shows each evangelist's contributions to the multifaceted portrait we have of Jesus's life and ministry.

	MATTHEW	MARK	LUKE	JOHN
Author	According to tradition	According to tradition	According to tradition (also authored Acts)	Inner testimony of the book (John 21:7, 24) and tradition
Profession	Tax collector (Matt. 9:9–10)	Missionary (Acts 12:25)	Physician (Col. 4:14)	Fisherman (Mark 1:19)
What we know about him	An apostle, also called Levi (Matt. 10:3; Mark 2:14)	Traveled with Paul and Peter (Acts 15:37; Col. 4:10; 1 Pet 5:13)	Traveled with Paul (Acts 16:10; 2 Tim. 4:11; Philem. 1:24)	An apostle, "whom Jesus loved" (Mark 3:17; John 21:20)
Family	Son of Alphaeus (Mark 2:14), brother of James and Joseph	Son of Mary (Acts 12:12), cousin of Barnabas (Col. 4:10)	Unknown	Son of Zebedee, brother of James (Mark 1:19)
Target audience	Primarily Jews	Primarily Romans	Primarily Greeks	All people/all the world
How we know who the target audience was	Assumes readers know Jewish customs (15:1–2), describes how Jesus fulfills OT prophecies, sees Jesus as Messiah	Explains Jewish traditions (7:2–4), uses Latin words (12:42*), emphasizes Jesus's actions over his teachings	Explains the geography (4:31; 24:13), portrays Jesus as the perfect man, a Greek ideal	"To all" (John 1:12), stated purpose of the book is that "you may believe" (John 20:31)
Jesus portrayed as	The King	The Servant	The Perfect Man	The Son of God
Number of chapters/ verses/words**	28/1,071/18,346	16/678/11,304	24/1,151/19,482	21/879/15,658
Key verse	Matt. 21:5	Mark 10:45	Luke 19:10	John 20:31
Ministry emphasis	Five major sermons	Many miracles	Many parables	Private teaching
Arrangement	By themes	Chronological	Chronological	By subjects
Perspective	Prophetic	Practical	Historical	Spiritual
Jesus's Genealogy	Traced from Abraham forward (1:1–17)	None	Traced back to Adam (Luke 3:23–38)	None
Amount of Gospel that is Jesus's words	60%	42%	50%	50%
Amount of material unique to Gospel	42%	7%	59%	93%
Gospel Type	Synoptic Gospel	Synoptic Gospel	Synoptic Gospel	Complementary Gospel
Symbols of the Gospel writers				
Temporal focus	Looks back	Looks at the present	Looks at the present and future	Looks toward eternity
Sphere of ministry	More about the public sphere	More about the public sphere	More about the personal sphere	More about the personal sphere
Geographical focus	More in Galilee	More in Galilee	The journey to Jerusalem (9–19)	Many visits to Jerusalem
Emphasis	What Jesus does and says	What Jesus does	What Jesus says	What Jesus says
Language	Greek with many Jewish influences	Greek that is somewhat grammatically simple	Greek that is elegant, literary, of high standard	Greek that is simple but with symbolic depth
Literary features	Structured around five long sermons	Rapid shifts between episodes ("then," "now")	Paired stories, many parables, many prayers	Many ironies, paradoxes, and testimonies
Opening of the Gospel	A structured genealogy from Abraham (1:1–17)	"This is the Good News about Jesus the Messiah" (1:1).	"Many people have set out to write accounts" (1:1–4).	A cosmic theological hymn (John 1:1–18)

** The word translated "two small coins" is Latin in the Greek text. Other examples: Mark 5:9; 6:27; 12:14, 15; 15:39, 44, 45.*

*** Numbers are from the Greek New Testament.*

Sixteen Writers of the New Testament

MATTHEW

Book: Gospel of Matthew. The Gospel is anonymous, but there is strong support for the apostle Matthew being the author. In the second and third centuries, Irenaeus, Papias, and Eusebius supported Matthew's authorship.

MARK (JOHN MARK)

Book: Gospel of Mark. The Gospel is anonymous, but there is strong support in extra-biblical sources pointing to John Mark (Acts 12:25) as the author (Polycarp, Papias, and others). Peter is seen as the apostolic source.

LUKE

Books: Gospel of Luke and Acts. Some think he may have been the scribe for 1 & 2 Timothy and Titus ("only" 2 Tim. 4:11). The Gospel is anonymous, but strong extra-biblical support exists for Luke's authorship.

JOHN

Books: Gospel of John, 1, 2, & 3 John, Revelation. The Gospel is anonymous, but there is strong support in extra-biblical sources for John being the author (Irenaeus). "We" in John 21:24 suggests he may have had a scribe.

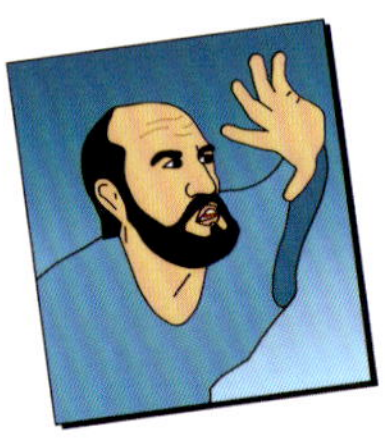

PAUL

Books: Majority of NT letters. Thirteen name Paul as author: Romans, 1 & 2 Corinthians, Galatians, Ephesians, Philippians, Colossians, 1 & 2 Thessalonians, 1 & 2 Timothy, Titus, and Philemon. He used several scribes.

TERTIUS

Book: Romans. "I, Tertius ... the one writing this letter for Paul" (Rom 16:22). All we know from the NT is that he was Paul's scribe. Later tradition says he was among the 70 disciples Jesus sent out (Luke 10:1).

SOSTHENES

Book: 1 Corinthians. The introduction can be seen as a presentation: "From Paul ... and our brother Sosthenes" (1 Cor. 1:1, see Acts 18:17). Paul's personal greeting at the end shows he used a scribe, Sosthenes (16:21).

TIMOTHY

Books: 2 Corinthians, Philippians, Colossians, and Philemon, possibly also 1 & 2 Thessalonians. A disciple of Paul and one of his closest associates (2 Tim. 1:2). Was the scribe for many of his letters.

SILAS (SILVANUS)

Books: 1 & 2 Thessalonians, and 1 Peter. The scribe for the letters to the Thessalonians is not named, but Silas is a strong contender (1 Thess. 1:1–2; 2 Thess. 1:1). Peter mentions Silas helped him (1 Peter 5:12).

JAMES

Book: James. Named in the introduction as the author: "James, a slave ... of Jesus Christ" (James 1:1). Likely Jesus's half-brother (Mark 6:33). Supported by extra-biblical sources, like Origen in third century.

PETER

Books: 1 & 2 Peter. The introduction identifies the author: "From Peter, an apostle of Jesus Christ" (1 Peter 1:1; 2 Peter 1:1). The difference in writing style between the two letters suggests the use of different scribes.

PROCORUS

Books: Gospel of John, possibly Revelation. "We" (John 21:24) suggests a scribe was involved. According to apocryphal tradition, Procorus, one of the first deacons (Acts 6:5), was John's scribe.

JUDE

Book: Jude. The author named in the introduction is "Jude … a brother of James" (Jude 1). He is most likely the half-brother of Jesus ("Judas" Matt. 13:55), which also makes him James's brother.

POSSIBLY THREE OTHERS

Mark 16:8–20 and John 7:53–8:11 might be later additions to the books by two unknown authors. The author of Hebrews is also unknown to us but was known to the letter's recipients (Heb. 13:19, 22–23).

What the Bible Teaches about Jesus Christ

Philippians and Colossians provide some of the key texts that shape our understanding of the person and work of Jesus Christ. Paul talks about Jesus's eternal nature, his role in creation, and his coming in the flesh. What follows are some of the central features of a biblical Christology.

1 Christ is eternally God —his pre-existence
Jesus is the second person of the Trinity. He existed before creation, and there was never a time when he did not exist (Col. 1:15–17; Phil. 2:6; John 1:1–18; 17:5, 24).

2 Christ is the author of everything —his creation
Jesus is not created. He is the eternal author and creator of everything in the universe, including all things great and small, visible and invisible (Col. 1:15–17; John 1:10; Heb. 1:2).

3 Christ appears in a fallen world —his theophanies
A theophany is an appearance of God. Some believe that "the Angel of the Lord" in the Old Testament was an appearance of Christ in physical form (Gen. 18:1–3; 32:24–30; Josh. 5:14).

4 Christ becomes man —his incarnation
Incarnation means "in the flesh." At a certain point in history, Jesus takes human form while remaining God. He is true God and true man, his two natures inseparably united (Phil. 2:6–8; John 1:14).

5 Christ gives his life in our place —his substitutionary atoning death
Jesus dies on the cross in our place. He carries our sin and pays our debt to God. All barriers that stood between God and us have been removed (Isa. 53:3–7; 2 Cor. 5:21; 1 Peter 2:24; 3:18).

6 Christ rises from the dead —his resurrection
Jesus rises from the dead on the third day, leaving the tomb empty. The resurrection confirms that he has triumphed over death and is the Son of God (1 Cor. 15:1–11, 14; Matt. 28:1–10; John 20:1–10).

7 Christ sits at the Father's right hand —his ascension
Jesus is lifted to heaven. He sits at the Father's right hand and intercedes for us. All powers and authorities submit to him (Luke 24:50–53; Acts 1:6–11; 1 Peter 3:22; 1 John 2:1).

8 Christ is coming back —his role as judge
Jesus will come back to earth the same way he left. He will come to judge everyone, and his judgment will always be just (Matt. 25:31-32; John 5:22; 2 Thess. 1:7-9; 2 Tim. 4:1).

9 Christ finally becomes all in all —his final triumph
In the end, eternity will break through. All creation will be set free. Those who have received God's salvation will live eternally in Jesus's presence (Rom. 8:22–23; Rev. 22:4–5).

Forty-Five Prophecies about Jesus

The Old Testament foretells the coming of Jesus (Luke 24:27), confirming God's sovereign control over history, his eternal plan of salvation, and the trustworthiness of Scripture. Here is a selection of some of these messianic prophecies.

Prophecies about Jesus, the promised Messiah

	Old Testament Prophecy	Prophecy—He will ...	New Testament Fulfillment
1	Gen. 12:3; 17:7; 18:18; 22:18	... be descended from Abraham	Matt. 1:1; Acts 3:25; Rom. 9:5
2	Gen. 17:19; 21:12	... be descended from Isaac	Luke 3:34
3	Num. 4:24–17	... be descended from Jacob	Matt. 1:2; Luke 3:34
4	Gen. 49:10	... be of the tribe of Judah	Luke 3:33; Heb. 7:14
5	Ps. 110:4	... be a priest like Melchizedek	Heb. 5:5–6; 7:1–22
6	Deut. 18:15–19	... be a prophet like Moses	Acts 3:22–23; 7:37
7	2 Sam. 7:12–13; Isa. 9:7	... be heir to David's throne	Luke 1:32–33; Rom. 1:3; Acts 13:32–34
8	Mic. 5:2	... be born in Bethlehem	Matt. 2:1; Luke 2:4–7
9	Isa. 7:14	... be born of a virgin	Matt. 1:18, 21–23; Luke 1:26–31
10	Isa. 7:14	... be called Immanuel	Matt. 1:23
11	Jer. 31:15	... be met with opposition from the start	Matt. 2:16–18
12	Hos. 11:1	... flee to Egypt and return	Matt. 2:14–15
13	Mal. 3:1; 4:5–6	... be preceded by a messenger	Matt. 11:13–14; Mark 1:2–3
14	Isa. 40:11	... be seen as a shepherd	John 10:11–16
15	Deut. 5:18	... be seen as a prophet	Acts 3:20–22
16	Ps. 110:4	... be seen as a priest	Heb. 5:5–6
17	Ps. 2:6; Zech 9:9	... be seen as a king	Matt. 27:37; Mark 11:7–11
18	Ps. 2:7	... be called the Son of God	Matt. 3:16–17
19	Isa. 8:14	... be a stumbling block	Rom. 9:32–33
20	Ps. 8:2	... be praised by children	Matt. 21:16
21	Isa. 29:18–19	... make the deaf hear and the blind see	Matt. 11:5; Mark 7:37; John 9:39
22	Ps. 69:8; Isa. 53:3	... be rejected by his own people	John 1:11; 7:5
23	Zech. 9:9	... enter Jerusalem triumphantly	John 12:13–14
24	Ps. 41:9; Zech 11:12–13	... be betrayed	Matt. 26:14–16; Luke 22:47–48
25	Ps. 35:11	... be falsely accused	Mark 14:57–58
26	Ps. 38:13–14; Isa. 53:7	... be silent before his accusers	Matt. 26:62–63; Mark 15:4–5
27	Ps. 69:9	... carry the insults directed at God	Rom. 15:3
28	Ps. 22:7–8; Isa. 50:6	... be spat on and mocked	Matt. 26:67; 27:39–44; Luke 23:35
29	Isa. 53:12	... be executed with criminals	Mt 27:38; Mk 15:27–28; Lk 23:37; Jn 19:18
30	Num. 21:8–9	... be lifted up like the bronze snake	John 3:14–15
31	Pss. 22:15; 69:21	... be given wine with myrrh when thirsty	Matt. 27:34, 48; John 19:28–30
32	Ps. 22:16; Zech 12:10	... have his hands pierced	John 20:25–27
33	Ex. 12:46; Ps. 34:2	... not have his bones broken	John 19:33–36
34	Ps. 22:18	... have clothes divided among soldiers	Matt. 27:35–36; Luke 23:34
35	Ps. 109:4	... pray for his enemies	Luke 23:34
36	Ps. 22:1	... be forsaken by the Father	Matt. 27:46
37	Zech. 12:10	... be pierced in the side	John 19:34–37
38	Isa. 53:9	... be buried among the rich	Matt. 27:57–60
39	Isa. 53:4–6	... be the Messiah, the redeemer	John 1:29
40	Ex. 12:1–11	... be the sacrificial Passover lamb	John 1:29; Rev. 5:12
41	Isa. 53:5–12	... take humanity's sin on himself	Rom. 5:6–8
42	Pss. 16:10; 22:23; 49:15; Hos. 6:2	... rise on the third day	Matt. 16:21; 28:2–7; Rom. 4:25; 1 Cor. 15:4
43	Pss. 24:7–10; 68:18	... be taken up to heaven	Mark 16:19; Luke 24:51
44	Ps. 110:1	... sit at the right hand of the Father	Matt. 22:44; Mark 16:19
45	Ps. 22:27–29; Isa. 49:6–10	... be a light to the gentiles	Acts 13:47

" One of the authenticating proofs for the inspiration of the Bible ... are the many fulfilled prophecies which find their fulfillment in the person and life of Christ. (Hampton Keathley III)

• **More prophetic messages in the Old Testament:** Several other biblical passages can be understood as prophetic—for example, that he would be connected to Galilee (Isa. 9:1–2) and that he would heal people from diseases (Isa. 53:4; Matt. 8:17). • **There are also prophecies about issues other than those directly related to the Messiah:** There will be a forerunner (Mal. 3:1; 4:5–6), and the Spirit will come upon God's people (Joel 2:28–32). Consider also the words of the high priest Caiaphas concerning Jesus (John 11:49–51).

Sixty-Four Days in Jesus's Life (1)

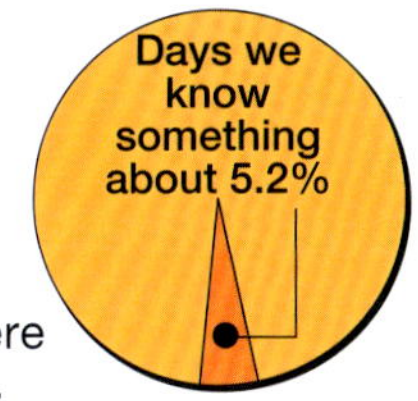

Jesus's public ministry lasted around 1,220 days.

Although Jesus's public ministry lasted over three years (AD 30–33), the Gospels only provide detailed accounts of events that occurred on sixty-four separate days. Days with general descriptions aren't included in this overview.

1 Jesus is baptized by John the Baptist

Jesus goes to the Jordan to be baptized by John the Baptist. "Then Jesus went … to the Jordan … to be baptized by John" (Matt. 3:13–17; Mark 1:9–11; Luke 3:21–22).

2 Jesus is tempted by the devil on the 40th day

The Spirit leads Jesus into the desert, where "for forty days and forty nights he fasted… then the devil came" (Matt. 4:2–3). The tempter approaches on the 40th day. Matt. 4:1 is not noted as a separate day; it may be the same day as Day 1 (see Mark 1:12). (Matt. 4:1–11; Mark 1:12–13; Luke 4:1–13).

3 Jesus goes to John

"The next day" (John 1:29), after his first testimony, John again testifies about Jesus (John 1:29–34).

4 Jesus calls two disciples

"The following day" (John 1:35), Jesus calls his first two disciples—Andrew and his brother Peter (John 1:35–42).

Peter and Andrew

5 Jesus calls two more disciples

"The next day" (John 1:43), Jesus decides to go to Galilee. He calls two more disciples, Philip and Nathanael. He finds them before heading north. The 10-mile journey to Galilee takes multiple days (John 1:43–51).

6 Jesus turns water into wine in Cana

"On the third day" (John 2:1 NIV) or the third day of the week (Tuesday), Jesus is in Cana for a wedding, where he miraculously turns water into wine (John 2:1–12).

7 The first Passover

Jesus is in Jerusalem for the Passover (John 2:13), when he cleanses the temple and then talks to Nicodemus in the evening. "One evening" (John 2:23–25; 3:2) might refer to a different day, but more likely to the same day (John 2:13–3:21).

8 Meeting the woman at the well

Jesus leaves Judea and returns to Galilee, passing through Samaria (John 4:3–4). On the way, he stops at a well outside Sychar, where he talks with a woman. His two days in the village are not counted in the 64 days (John 4:1–38).

9 Heals the son of an official

Jesus is in Cana (John 4:46) when an official from Capernaum goes to see him, begging him to heal his sick son, who is in Capernaum. Jesus tells him his son will live (John 4:46–54). Verses 51–54 are not about Jesus, so they are not counted in the 64 days.

An official

Anger

10 Driven out of the synagogue in Nazareth

Jesus arrives in his hometown, Nazareth. "On the Sabbath" (Luke 4:16), he goes to the synagogue and reads the Scripture, applying it to himself. In anger, the people try to throw him off a cliff, but he walks through the crowd (Luke 4:16–30).

11 Calls four disciples for a second time

"One day" (Luke 5:1), Jesus calls Peter, Andrew, James, and John at the Sea of Galilee. Luke's text is seen as the same event (Matt. 4:18–22; Mark 1:16–20; Luke 5:1–11).

12 Heals the sick on the Sabbath

Jesus heals a possessed man, Peter's mother-in-law, and many other sick people "on the Sabbath" (Luke 4:31). The previous day they had been fishing, so it wasn't a Sabbath (Matt. 8:14–17; Mark 1:21–34; Luke 4:31–41).

13 Withdraws to a lonely place

"Early the next morning", even "before daybreak" (Luke 4:42; Mark 1:35) Jesus withdraws to pray. Peter and others search for him (Mark 1:35–39; Luke 4:42–44).

14 Heals a man with leprosy

"When" (Luke 5:12) a leper begged Jesus to heal him, he did. Possibly a continuation of the previous day, unlikely (Matt. 8:1–4; Mark 1:40–45; Luke 5:12–16).

Down through the roof

15 Heals a lame man, calls Levi, and eats with sinners

"One day" (Luke 5:17) Jesus heals a lame man who is lowered through the roof by his friends. He "later" (Luke 5:27) calls Levi who is sitting at the tax booth and eats at Levi's house, leading to a discussion with the Pharisees and scribes about eating with sinners. This day describes the most events of any day yet (Matt. 9:1–17; Mark 2:1–22; Luke 5:17–39).

16 Heals a lame man at the pool of Bethesda

On "one of the Jewish holy days" and a Sabbath (John 5:1, 9), Jesus heals a lame man at Bethesda in Jerusalem, and later discusses the miracle with the Jews, declaring that he is the Son of God (John 5:1–47).

17 Disciples pick grain on the Sabbath

On a "Sabbath day" (Mark 2:23) the disciples pick grain and eat it, leading to a discussion with the Pharisees; Jesus declares himself Lord of the Sabbath (Matt. 12:1–8; Mark 2:23–28; Luke 6:1–5).

18 Jesus heals a man with a withered hand

"On another Sabbath" (Luke 6:6), Jesus heals a man with a withered hand, outraging the Pharisees. While Matthew allows it to be the same Sabbath, Luke does not (Matt. 12:9–14; Mark 3:1–6; Luke 6:6–11).

A man with a withered hand

19 Chooses the Twelve, Sermon on the Mount

"At daybreak" (Luke 6:13), Jesus chooses the Twelve, gives the Sermon on the Mount, heals an officer's servant, and raises a widow's son (Luke 6:12–7:17; Matt. 5–7; 8:5–13; 11:1; 12:15; Mark 3:7–19).

20 A woman anoints Jesus's feet

Jesus answers John the Baptist and judges the towns in Galilee. A woman anoints Jesus's feet. "At that time" (Matt. 11:25; compare Luke 7:21) can be seen as referring to another day, but it need not do so (Matt. 11:2–30; Luke 7:18–50).

21 One of Jesus's busiest days

The Pharisees accuse Jesus of getting power from Satan; he also speaks of his true family, explains a series of parables, takes a boat across the lake, and calms the storm. He heals two possessed men on the other side, then returns by boat. "Later that same day" (Matt. 12:22–13:53; 8:18, 23–34; Mark 3:20–5:20; Luke 8:4–39).

Sixty-Four Days in Jesus's Life (2)

22 Jesus heals a woman and raises a girl
"Jesus ... went back" across the lake (Mark 5:21), where he heals a woman who had been sick for twelve years, raises Jairus's daughter, and heals two blind men and one mute man. "As" in Matt. 9:18 links it to the preceding passage, but Mark and Luke's chronology disagrees (Matt. 9:18–34; Mark 5:21–43; Luke 8:40–56).

Raises a dead girl

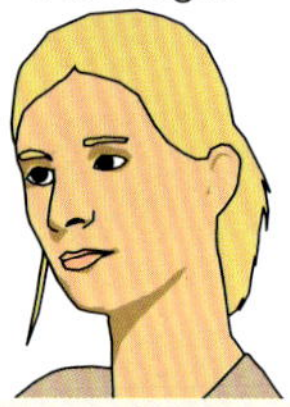

23 Jesus back in Nazareth
On his last visit to Nazareth, Jesus goes to the synagogue on the Sabbath (Mark 6:2). Some link this to Luke 4:14–30, but that is unlikely (Matt. 13:54–58; Mark 6:1–6).

24 Jesus sends out the Twelve
"Jesus called together" his twelve disciples (Luke 9:1), gives them instructions, and sends them in pairs to proclaim the good news (Matt. 9:35–11:1; Mark 6:7–13; Luke 9:1–6).

25 Jesus feeds 5,000 and walks on water
Near the Jewish Passover (John 6:4), Jesus heals the sick. "That evening" (Matt. 14:15) he feeds 5,000 with 5 loaves and 2 fish. The disciples collect twelve baskets of leftovers, and he walks on water to the disciples' boat (Matt. 14:13–36; Mark 6:30–56; Luke 9:10–17; John 6:1–21).

26 Jesus is abandoned by many disciples
"The next day" (John 6:22), Jesus speaks of himself as the bread of life, and his ministry dwindles. It is possible that "at this point" (John 6:66) refers to another day, but not necessarily (Matt. 15:1–20; Mark 7:1–23; John 6:22–71).

27 Jesus to Tyre and Sidon
"Then" (Matt. 15:21) Jesus goes to Tyre and Sidon, meets a faith-filled Canaanite woman, and drives an evil spirit from her daughter (Matt. 15:21–28; Mark 7:24–30).

Canaanite woman

28 Heals sick and feeds 4,000
Jesus "left Tyre and Sidon" (Mark 7:31) for the Decapolis, heals a deaf-mute and other sick people, and provides food for 4,000. The distance from Tyre indicates that it must be another day (Matt. 15:21–39; Mark 7:31–8:10).

29 Discussion with religious leaders
After he "had arrived" (Mark 8:11) near Dalmanutha, Jesus talks with the Pharisees and Sadducees. Possibly the same as Day 28 but the distance makes it unlikely (Matt. 15:29–16:4; Mark 8:10–13).

30 Jesus warns the disciples and heals a blind man
Jesus "crossed to the other side of the lake" (Mark 8:13) and warns against the leaven of the Pharisees and Sadducees. Spitting on the man's eyes, he heals a blind man in two stages, then crosses to Bethsaida. How far Jesus could go in one day is uncertain (Matt. 16:5–12; Mark 8:14–26).

31 Disciples confess their faith
"One day" (Luke 9:18), Peter confesses Jesus as Messiah. Jesus speaks of his coming death and the cost of following him (Matt. 16:13–28; Mark 8:27–9:1; Luke 9:18–27).

32 Jesus on the Mount of Transfiguration
About six or eight days later (Matt. 17:1; Luke 9:28), Jesus takes three disciples up the Mount of Transfiguration, probably staying overnight on the mountain (Matt. 17:1–8; Mark 9:2–13; Luke 9:28–36).

33 Jesus descends the mountain
"The next day, after they had come down the mountain" (Luke 9:37), Jesus heals a boy possessed by a spirit (Matt. 17:9–20; Mark 9:14–29; Luke 9:37–42).

34 Jesus gives a new teaching
"In Capernaum" (Matt. 17:24), Jesus predicts his death again. Disciples discuss who is greatest. He teaches them. Capernaum is 50 miles from Caesarea Philippi, so it must be another day (Matt. 17:22–18:14; Mark 9:30–50; Luke 9:43–50).

35 The cost of discipleship
Jesus teaches about the cost of following him, on "the other side of the lake" (Matt. 8:18) "As they were walking along" (Matt. 8:18–22; Luke 9:57–62).

Teaching: The cost of discipleship

36 Jesus is mocked by his brothers
When "it was time for the Jewish Festival of Shelters" (John 7:2), Jesus's brothers tell him that they do not believe. Luke 9:51–56 and John 7:10 could possibly be another day (Luke 9:51–56; John 7:2–10).

37 Jesus teaches in the temple
"Midway through the festival" (John 7:14), Jesus went to the temple and began to teach, probably on the fourth day. The Festival of Shelters lasted seven days (John 7:14–36; Lev. 23:39).

38 Jesus talks about living water
"On the last day, the climax of the festival" (John 7:37), Jesus promises the Holy Spirit and speaks about living water flowing from the believer. This is three days after Day 36 (John 7:37–8:1).

39 Jesus is the light of the world
"Early the next morning" (John 8:2), Jesus meets the adulteress.* Among other things, he tells the Pharisees that he is the light of the world. John 7:53–8:11 is controversial (John 8:2–59).

40 Another day with many events
At the Festival (John 10:22), Jesus heals a blind man, discusses spiritual blindness with leaders, and presents himself as the gate for the sheep and the good shepherd. The context is unclear, with several solutions proposed, and some think it took more than one day. One possibility is that 9:1–10:21 took place on Day 37 (John 9:1–10:21).

41 Jesus sends out 72 disciples
Jesus "now"(Luke 10:1) chooses seventy–two disciples, sending them out in pairs. He gives detailed instructions for the mission, warning them of what they might encounter. There are chronological questions here (Luke 10:1–16).

42 The 72 return and report
"When" (Luke 10:17) the disciples returned, they reported to Jesus. He tells the parable of the Good Samaritan and visits Martha and Mary. It has to be another day (Luke 10:17–42).

How do Days 40–42 relate?
Context raises questions:
1) Does all of John 9:1–10:39 belong in one day, or should it be split between 10:21 and 10:22?
2) In what order should the different episodes be arranged? Should Luke 10:1–13:21 be placed before John 9:1–10:42? Or after? Or between 10:21 and 10:22? Or where? Conclusion: Several days.

John 7:53–8:11 probably was not in the original text.

Sixty-Four Days in Jesus's Life (3)

43 Jesus teaches about prayer
"Once" (Luke 11:1) when Jesus was praying, the disciples ask him to teach them to pray. He teaches them the Lord's Prayer and explains the meaning of prayer (Luke 11:1–13).

44 An intense day in Jesus's life with constant interruptions
Jesus drives out an evil spirit, warns against unbelief, teaches about the inner light, attacks the religious leadership, gives a series of warnings, calls to repentance, and tells the parable of the fig tree. All on "one day" (Luke 11:14); see "As Jesus was speaking" (Luke 11:37) and "Meanwhile" (Luke 11:14–13:9).

45 Jesus heals a woman and talks about the kingdom of God
"One Sabbath" (Luke 13:10), Jesus speaks in a synagogue, heals a crippled woman, debates the Sabbath, and teaches about the kingdom of God using two parables. Some commentators believe that it is the same as Day 46 (Luke 13:10–21).

46 Attempt to stone Jesus
"At the time of ... the Festival of Dedication" (John 10:22), Jesus debates with Jews, who ask if he is truly the Messiah (see discussion in Days 38–40, John 10:22–39).

47 Jesus and the narrow door
"Pressing on toward Jerusalem" (Luke 13:22), Jesus teaches about the narrow door and, "at that time" (Luke 13:31) grieves over Jerusalem (Luke 13:22–35).

48 Jesus tells the parable of the prodigal son
"One Sabbath" (Luke 14:1), Jesus visits a Pharisee, talks on the cost of discipleship, tells parables—including the great feast, the lost sheep, the prodigal son, the rich man and Lazarus—and discusses faith and forgiveness (Luke 14:1–17:10).

49 Jesus learns that Lazarus is sick
Jesus is in Perea when Lazarus of Bethany becomes sick, and his sisters send a message asking him to come. "When Jesus heard about it" (John 11:1–5), he chooses not to depart immediately.

50 Jesus heads toward Bethany
Jesus "stayed where he was for ... two days" before saying, "'Let's go'" (John 11:6–7). He then begins the journey from Perea to Bethany. It took several days to arrive (John 11:6–16).

51 Jesus raises Lazarus
When Jesus arrives in Bethany, Lazarus had been "in his grave for four days" (John 11:17). He talks to Martha and Mary, then raises Lazarus to life. "From that time on" (John 11:17–54; compare Luke 13:22).

Lazarus

52 Jesus travels from Galilee toward Jerusalem
"As Jesus continued" (Luke 17:11), he heals ten lepers, tells two parables, teaches on marriage and divorce, blesses children, and meets a rich man. Mark 10:32 may indicate several days; 10:46, "to Jericho." (Matt. 19:1–20:34; Mark 10:1–52; Luke 17:11–19:27).

53 Friday or Saturday: Jesus to Bethany
"Six days before the Passover" (John 12:1), Jesus arrives in Bethany and meets Lazarus, whom he had previously raised from the dead. There is debate over which day is referred to (John 11:55–12:1, 9–11).

Jesus's entry

54 Sunday: Jesus rides into Jerusalem
"The next day" (John 12:12), Jesus rides into Jerusalem to cries of "Hosanna!" He visits the temple then returns to Bethany. (John 12:12–19; Matt. 21:1–11, 14–17; Mark 11:1–11; Luke 19:28–44).

55 Monday: Jesus cleanses the temple
"The next morning" (Mark 11:12), Jesus cleanses the temple by expelling merchants, curses a fig tree, and speaks of his approaching death (Mark 11:12–19; Matt. 21:12–13, 18–19; Luke 19:45–48; John 12:20–50).

56 Tuesday: The speech on the Mount of Olives
"The next morning" (Mark 11:20), Jesus speaks against the Pharisees on the Mount of Olives. Nothing recorded for Wednesday (Matt. 21:19b–26:16; Mark 11:20–14:11; Luke 20:1–22:6; John 12:2–8).

57 Thursday: The Last Supper
"The first day of the Festival" (Matt. 26:17), Jesus washes the disciples' feet, institutes the Lord's Supper, is betrayed by Judas and arrested in Gethsemane (Matt. 26:17–56; Mark 14:12–50; Luke 22:7–54; John 13:1–18:12).

58 Good Friday: Jesus is tried, crucified, and buried
On "the day of preparation, the day before the Sabbath" (Mark 15:42), Jesus is taken through six trials—three before the Jews, three before the Romans—then sentenced by Pontius Pilate, crucified, dies, is taken down and laid in a tomb (Matt. 26:57–27:66; Mark 14:53–15:47; Luke 22:55–23:56; John 18:13–19:42).

He is risen!

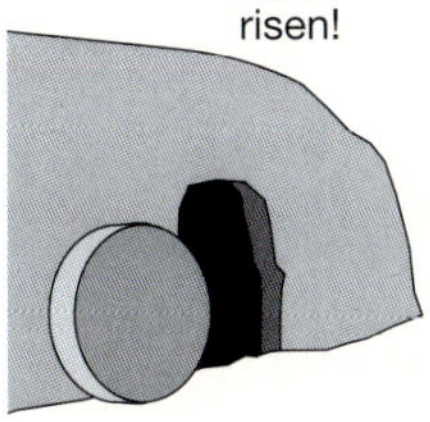

59 Sunday: Jesus rises from the dead
"Early on Sunday morning" (Matt. 28:1), Jesus rises from the dead, appearing to the women, the travelers to Emmaus, and the disciples. (Matt. 28:1–15; Mark 16:1–8;* Luke 24:1–43; John 20:1–25). Note: Nothing from Saturday.

60 On the eighth day after the resurrection
"Eight days later" (John 20:26), Jesus appears to the Eleven disciples. Thomas is now present and can touch Jesus's wounds. Probably the eighth day, the following Sunday (John 20:26–29; compare 1 Cor. 15:5).

61 Jesus meets seven on the shore
"Later, Jesus appeared again" (John 21:1) to seven disciples at the Sea of Galilee. The order and number of Jesus's instructions are uncertain, Days 60–61 (John 21:1–25).

62 Jesus joins disciples in Galilee
Jesus meets the Eleven on a mountain in Galilee. "Jesus came" (Matt. 28:18) and then gave them the Great Commission (Matt. 28:16–20; compare 1 Cor. 15:6).

63 Jesus meets the Eleven while eating
"Still later" (Mark 16:14), Jesus appears while the disciples are at a meal and gives the Great Commission again. The text is disputed. Could possibly be the same as Day 60, 61, or 62 (Mark 16:14–18).**

64 Jesus is taken up into heaven
Jesus speaks to the disciples in Jerusalem, goes with them to the Mount of Olives, and announces the coming Spirit. "When ... Jesus had finished talking" (Mark 16:19) he is lifted up to heaven (Mark 16:19–20;** Luke 24:44–53; see Acts 1:3–8).

Jesus taken up into heaven

** Could possibly be perceived as a summary of events. The total then becomes 63 days. ** Mark 16:9–20 probably does not belong to the original text.*

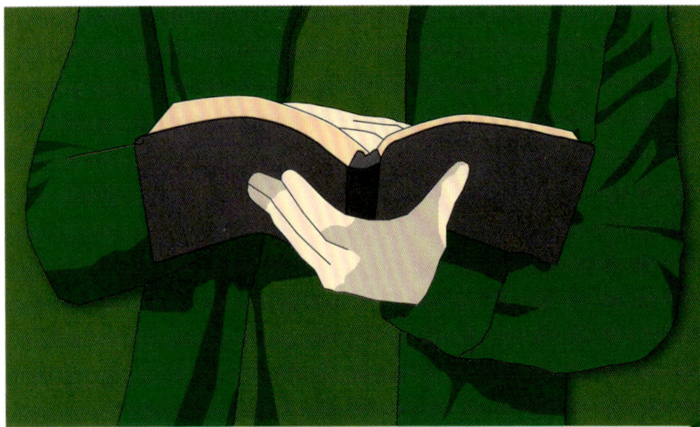

MATTHEW

"A sign was fastened above Jesus' head, announcing the charge against him. It read: "This is Jesus, the King of the Jews" (Matt. 27:37).

A FEW WORDS ABOUT THE AUTHOR

Officially, the book is anonymous, but there is strong support among early church fathers for Matthew as the author (Irenaeus, Papias, Eusebius, and others). No one else has been suggested as a possible author. Matthew, also called Levi, was one of Jesus's disciples (Matt. 10:3; Mark 2:14). Jesus called him at the tax collector's booth in Capernaum; he left everything and followed Jesus (Matt. 9:9; Luke 5:28).

A FEW WORDS ABOUT THE RECIPIENTS

Matthew's audience is generally understood to be Jewish-Christians. He often quotes Old Testament prophecies to show that Jesus is God's promised Messiah. One possible recipient is the church in Antioch, Syria. There were many Greek-speaking Jewish Christians who were involved in missionary work. Several church fathers at the turn of the first century mention the Gospel and quote from it.

A FEW WORDS ABOUT DATES

According to tradition, Matthew was the first to write down Jesus's teachings. The Gospel may have been written in Hebrew, perhaps using only the words of Jesus. Later scholars suggest that Mark may have been written earlier and served as a source for Matthew. The Greek version we have was probably written between AD 55 and 68. It covers the time from the birth of Jesus, around 6 BC, to his death and resurrection in AD 33.

THE WHOLE BOOK IN 25 WORDS

The promised Messiah, Jesus, comes. The Jewish leaders misunderstand. The disciples understand but fail at the crucial moment. The Sermon on the Mount—a classic.

A SIMPLE STRUCTURE

1. Commission – Jesus sends disciples to serve
(Matt. 1:1–12:50)

2. Calling – Jesus calls followers to faith
(Matt. 13:1–20:34)

3. Climax – Jesus fulfills his mission
(Matt. 21:1–28:20)

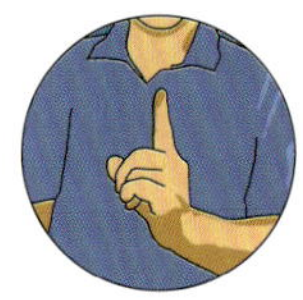

A FEW WORDS ABOUT KEY THEMES

- **Jesus the King—**Jesus is portrayed as the King, the coming Messiah (18:23; 21:5; 22:2; 25:34, 40; 27:11, 29, 37, 42). He is also repeatedly referred to as the "Son of David" (12:23; 15:22; 20:30; 21:15; 22:45).
- **Kingdom of Heaven—**The phrase is only used by Matthew, occurring 31 times. It parallels the kingdom of God in other Gospels, perhaps out of sensitivity for Jewish reluctance to speak God's name (3:2; 4:17; 5:3, 10; 10:7; 25:1).
- **Sermons—**The Gospel contains five sermons around which the book is structured. Note how the narratives lead up to each sermon (5:1–7:27; 10:1–42; 13:1–52; 18:1–35; 24:1–25:46).
- **Passages unique to Matthew—**Some passages are unique, including the one about the wise men (1:20–24; 2:1–18; 27:3–10, 19, 52; 28:19–20). A total of 42% of the Gospel is unique to Matthew.

A FEW TIPS ON WHAT TO LOOK FOR

Theme of the book:
Jesus, the King

- Anything that speaks of Jesus as the Messiah, the King
- Over 100 quotes from and allusions to the Old Testament, note the fulfillment of prophecies
- The use of "heaven" and "heavenly Father"
- "When Jesus had finished" (5 times)
- All the numerical data
- Angels and dreams
- First use of word "church" (16:18; 18:17)
- Care for gentiles

Reading a Thematic Gospel

Matthew is a thematic gospel rather than a chronological one. The events aren't presented in the order they occurred but are arranged to highlight the themes Matthew wishes to emphasize.

Overall Thematic Structure

The Gospel is organized around five longer sermons, creating an interplay between story and teaching.

Story	Teaching	Structure marker
Story (1–4): Jesus's birth and early ministry	**Teaching (5–7):** Sermon on the Mount	"When Jesus had finished saying these things" (7:28)
Story (8–9): Jesus demonstrates that he is Messiah	**Teaching (10):** The Mission Discourse	"When Jesus had given ... these instructions" (11:1)
Story (11–12): Jesus meets resistance and accusations	**Teaching (13):** The Parable Discourse	"When Jesus had finished telling these stories" (13:53)
Story (14–17): Jesus focuses on the disciples	**Teaching (18):** The Church Order Discourse	"When Jesus had finished saying these things" (19:1)
Story (19–23): Jesus heads toward Jerusalem and the cross	**Teaching (24–25):** The Olivet Discourse	"When Jesus had finished saying all these things" (26:1)
Story (26–28:17): Jesus dies and rises from the dead	**Teaching (28:18–20):** The Great Commission	

Structure markers: Each sermon ends with a new start.

Thematic Structure: Matthew 8–10

By looking at one of the sections, we can see how Matthew builds his thematic narrative:

	Three Stories			One Challenge
1 First cycle	Jesus cures a leper (8:1–4)	Jesus heals an officer's servant (8:5–13)	Jesus heals Peter's mother-in-law (8:14–17)	Jesus explains the cost of discipleship (8:18–22)
2 Second cycle	Jesus calms the storm (8:23–27)	Jesus heals two men who are possessed (8:28–34)	Jesus heals a man who is lame (9:1–8)	Jesus calls Matthew to become his disciple (9:9–17)
3 Third cycle	Jesus heals Jairus's daughter and a sick woman (9:18–26)	Jesus heals two men who are blind (9:27–31)	Jesus casts a demon out of a mute man (9:32–34)	Jesus talks about the need for disciples (9:35–38)

The three stories lead to a challenge about discipleship

The three challenges lead to a concrete mission

4 Final Teaching

Sermon: The Mission Discourse	Jesus sends out his twelve disciples (10:1–4)	Jesus gives instructions to them (10:5–15)	Jesus warns of difficulties they will face (10:16–33)	Jesus explains the cost of following him (10:34–42)

Leading into the next section, the opposition to Jesus grows, culminating in accusations that he uses the power of Beelzebub, the devil (11–12). In response, Jesus turns to the disciples and begins telling parables (13).

A Different Way of Dividing Matthew

1 **Addressing the people: "From then on** Jesus began to preach, "Repent of your sins and turn to God, for the Kingdom of Heaven is near'" (4:17).

2 **Addressing the disciples: "At that time** Jesus prayed 'thank you for hiding these things from those who think themselves wise ... revealing them to the childlike'" (11:25).

3 **Turning to the cross: "From then on** Jesus began to tell his disciples [he must] go to Jerusalem … suffer … be killed, but on the third day … be raised" (16:21).

MARK

"For even the Son of Man came not to be served but to serve others and to give his life as a ransom for many" (Mark 10:45).

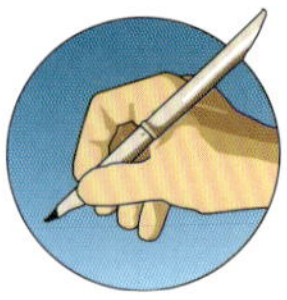

A FEW WORDS ABOUT THE AUTHOR

Officially, the book is anonymous, but early church fathers support the view that John Mark is the author. Around AD 100, Papias writes: "When Mark became Peter's interpreter, he carefully wrote down everything he remembered of Christ's words and deeds." Mark accompanied Paul at first, but later he became Peter's assistant in Rome (1 Peter 5:13). They eyes are Peter's the pen is Mark's.

A FEW WORDS ABOUT THE RECIPIENTS

The recipients are not specified, but the book was likely written for a non-Jewish Christian audience, probably in Rome. Both Irenaeus and Clement of Alexandria (writing in the AD 100s) state that the Gospel was composed in the Roman capital. Mark's explanations of Jewish customs and his use of many Latin expressions—such as *praetorium* and *denarius*—support this view (7:3–4; 12:15; 15:16).

A FEW WORDS ABOUT DATES

The dating of the book is uncertain. Irenaeus says that the Gospel was written after Peter's death (AD 67), while Clement of Alexandria claims it was written earlier. It is usually considered to be the earliest of the gospels, probably written between AD 55 and 65. Mark's story of Jesus covers the time from his baptism by John the Baptist in the Jordan River in early AD 30 to Jesus's death and resurrection in April AD 33.

THE WHOLE BOOK IN 25 WORDS

Things happen quickly, emphasizing action over teaching. Mark shows a Roman audience how Jesus, the servant, lives obediently and ultimately sacrifices his life for others.

A SIMPLE STRUCTURE

1. Proclamation – Jesus announces God's kingdom
(Mark 1:1–7:37)

2. Persecution – Opposition and growing resistance
(Mark 8:11–13:36)

3. Passion – Jesus suffers, dies, and rises
(Mark 14:1–16:20)

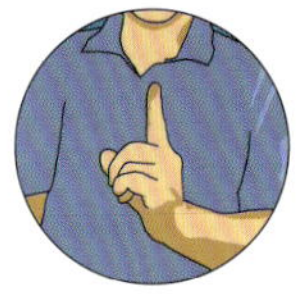

A FEW WORDS ABOUT KEY THEMES

- **Jesus as servant**—Portrays Jesus as the servant who came to serve us and sacrifice his life as payment for our sins (9:35, 10:43–45; 12:1–8).
- **Jesus's suffering**—Talks about human suffering and Jesus's suffering for our sake (5:26; 8:31; 9:12, 30–31).
- **The pace of the book**—The story moves at a fast pace. Jesus "immediately" moves from one event to another. Look for the words "immediately," "quickly," "soon," and "already."
- **Mark stresses Jesus's humanity**—Notes his emotions (1:41; 3:5; 6:34; 8:12), human limitations ("sleep" 4:38, "hungry" 11:12; 13:32), and other observations (9:36; 10:13–16).
- **Unique in Mark**—Most of Mark is in other Gospels; just 7% is unique to Mark (4:26–27; 7:32–37; 8:22–26; 14:51–52).
- **Debate about the ending**—Many believe that 16:9–20 is a later addition.

A FEW TIPS ON WHAT TO LOOK FOR

Theme of the book:
Jesus, the servant

- Note "immediately," "thereafter," "next"
- Interest of the crowds
- People's feelings and reactions
- Explanations of Jewish customs and Aramaic words
- All the references to time
- References to beach, lake, ship, storm
- Notice how Jesus looks at people, and the idea of blindness and sight
- All references to Peter
- References to "the road"
- Talk about discipleship

Seeing Peter as Mark's Source

According to an early tradition, Mark was Peter's scribe (1 Peter 5:13). With careful study, we can see how Peter's observations and experiences permeate the narrative of the Gospel of Mark.

1 Fisherman's interest in boats and the sea

Peter was a fisherman. The Gospel contains many references to boats and fishing.

- **The boat:** "Jesus instructed his disciples to have a boat ready" (3:9, also 1:19, 20; 4:1, 36–37; 5:2, 18, 21; 6:32, 34, 45, 47, 51, 54; 8:10, 13).
- **The sea:** "Better for you to be thrown into the sea" (9:42 also 11:23).
- **The nets:** "Throwing a net into the water" (1:16, also 1:18, 19).
- **The lake:** "Jesus went out to the lake with his disciples" (3:7, also 1:16; 2:13; 3:7; 4:1, 39, 41; 5:1, 13, 21; 6:47, 48, 53; 8:13).
- **The lakeshore:** "Jesus began teaching by the lakeshore" (4:1).
- **The storm/winds:** "A fierce storm came up" (4:37, also 4:39, 41; 6:48, 51).
- **The waves:** "High waves were breaking into the boat" (4:37).

2 Unique Details

Mark gives many details which can only have come from an eyewitness, such as Peter.

- **One who** noticed that the whole city gathered outside Peter's house (1:33)
- **One who** saw men digging a hole in the roof of a house (Peter's house) for their sick friend (2:4)
- **One who** saw the waves breaking and the boat starting to sink (4:37)
- **One who** saw the man screaming and hurting himself, and how he came running (5:5–6)
- **One who** saw how the people were seated in groups and the size of each group (Mark 6:39–40)

3 Details about Peter

Mark gives details about Peter that are not found in the other gospels, which could only come from Peter.

- Peter leads the search for Jesus (1:35–37).
- It is Peter's house in Capernaum (1:29–31; 2:1–5, see Matt. 4:13–16).
- Peter remembers the fig tree (11:20–21, see Matt. 21:18–19).
- A disciple [Peter?] (13:3) asks Jesus about the temple (13:1–4, see Matt. 24:1–3).

4 Compare Peter's speech (Acts 10:34–43) ...	... with the outline of the Gospel of Mark (Mark 1–16).
• "The Good News" (10:36).	• "This is the Good News" (1:1).
• "God anointed Jesus of Nazareth with the Holy Spirit" (10:38).	• "The heavens splitting apart and the Holy Spirit descending on him like a dove" (1:10).
• "Beginning in Galilee" (10:37)	• "Jesus went into Galilee" (1:14).
• "He went around doing good and healing all" (10:38).	• Jesus went around healing the sick and performing miracles (1:16–8:26).
• "We apostles are witnesses of all he did ... in Jerusalem" (10:39).	• "Jesus came to Jerusalem and went into the Temple"(11:1–14:72)
• "They put him to death by hanging him on a cross" (10:39).	• "They crucified him ... then Jesus ... breathed his last" (15:25, 37).
• "God raised him to life on the third day" (10:40).	• "You are looking for Jesus ... who was crucified. He isn't here! He is risen!" (16:6).

5 Peter is mentioned in nine of the sixteen chapters of Mark's Gospel

Chapter	1	2	3	4	5	6	7	8	9	10	11	12	13	14	15	16
Mentions			1x		1x			3x	2x	1x	1x		1x	10x		1x
Verses			3:16		5:37			8:29, 32, 33	9:2, 5	10:28	11:21		13:3	14:29, 31, 33, 37, 54, 66, 67, 70 (2x), 72		16:7

Peter: Twenty-one references in total, he is also called Simon in four verses 1:16, 36; 3:16; 14:37.

THE GOSPEL WHERE EVERYTHING HAPPENS IMMEDIATELY

Here are the 42 times that *euthys* is used in Mark.

1:10*	1:42	4:29	6:50*	11:2
1:12*	1:43*	5:2*	6:54	11:3*
1:18	2:8	5:29	7:25	14:43
1:20	2:12	5:30	7:35	14:45
1:21*	3:6	5:42	8:10	14:72
1:23	4:5	5:42*	9:15*	15:1*
1:28	4:15	6:25*	9:20*	
1:29*	4:16	6:27	9:24	
1:30	4:17	6:45	10:52	

The Greek word *euthys* means *at once, suddenly, quickly, right away, immediately, instantly* or *as soon as*. This word is used 87 times in the New Testament, including 42 times in Mark. *Sometimes *euthys* does not correspond to any word used in the English translation.

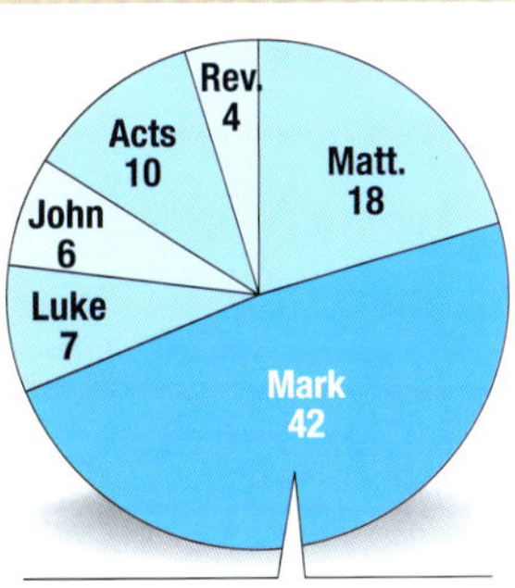

48% Almost half of all references in Mark

Here are the 87 times *euthys* is used in the New Testament.

Matthew	18
Mark	42
Luke	7
John	6
Acts	10
Galatians	1
James	1
3 John	1
Revelation	1

LUKE

"For the Son of Man came to seek and to save the lost" (Luke 19:10).

A FEW WORDS ABOUT THE AUTHOR

Officially, the book is anonymous, but there is strong extra-biblical support for Luke as the author (Irenaeus and Eusebius). In addition to the Gospel, he also wrote Acts (compare Luke 1:1–4 with Acts 1:1–2). He was a medical doctor and disciple of Paul (Col. 4:14; 2 Tim. 4:11), According to tradition, Luke came from Antioch of Syria. He is the only non-Jewish author who wrote a book in the New Testament.

A FEW WORDS ABOUT THE RECIPIENT

Theophilus, meaning "friend of God," is also named in Acts (Luke 1:3; Acts 1:1). The phrase "most honorable" (1:3) may refer to a Roman political dignitary. Some suggest King Agrippa II (Acts 25:13); others a Roman official, possibly Titus Flavius Sabinus. Still others think it refers to Paul's defense lawyer during his imprisonment in Rome. Several theories exist, but the evidence is mostly circumstantial and remains debated.

A FEW WORDS ABOUT DATES

The book was likely written between AD 58 and 64, before Acts—which was composed no earlier than Paul's release from prison around AD 62 (Acts 28:30). It is believed that Luke was written after Mark's Gospel, therefore no earlier than the late AD 50s. Luke's gospel covers events from the birth of Jesus around 6 BC to his death and resurrection at Passover in AD 33, providing a carefully detailed historical context.

THE WHOLE BOOK IN 25 WORDS

In Luke's orderly account, we see how both faith in and resistance to Jesus grow side by side. The key—counting the cost of discipleship.

A SIMPLE STRUCTURE

1. Preparation – God establishes salvation history
(Luke 1:1–9:50)

2. Pilgrimage – Jesus journeys toward Jerusalem
(Luke 9:51–19:27)

3. Passion – Christ triumphs through resurrection
(Luke 19:28–24:53)

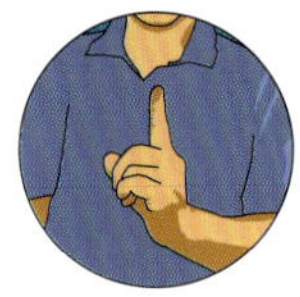

A FEW WORDS ABOUT KEY THEMES

- **Many miracles**—Luke the physician is interested in details that others do not notice (4:38–40; 5:15–25; 6:17–19; 7:11–15; 8:43–47, 49–56; 9:2, 6, 11; 13:11–13; 14:2–4; 17:12–14; 22:50–51).
- **Highlighting women**—Note Jesus's encounters with women, who were marginalized in the culture of the time (7:12–15, 37–50; 8:2–3, 43–48; 10:38–42; 13:11–13).
- **Luke's method**—He is a researcher and historian. Luke "carefully investigated" to "write an accurate account" so Theophilus "can be certain of the truth of everything [he was] taught" (1:3–4).
- **The Travel Narrative**—Jesus's journey toward Jerusalem (9:51–19:27).
- **What's unique about Luke**—About 35% of his material is unique to Luke (Text 4:18–21, 24–27; 7:41–43; 10:18–20, 25–37, 41–42; 11:5–8; 12:16–20, 36–38, 42–46; 16:19–31; 18:1–4).

A FEW TIPS ON WHAT TO LOOK FOR

Theme of the book: Jesus, the true man

- Son of Man (28 times)
- Note Jesus's human traits
- Note all the parables, more than in any other gospel (24)
- All the women Jesus meets
- Money, poverty, and wealth
- Jesus's prayers, other people's prayers, parables about prayer
- Joy and praise (five times just in chapters 1–2).
- All the medical and anatomical terms
- Note verses about the Spirit

Doctor Luke's Medical Notes

Luke was a doctor (Col. 4:14) and the traces of his professional career permeate his writings. He frequently refers to diagnosis and healing. The following examples show how his expertise is reflected in the text.

HIGH FEVER

Simon's mother-in-law had "a high fever" (Luke 4:38). The other gospels (see Matt. 8:14) use a general Greek word for fever (*pyresso*) while Luke uses a specific medical term (*synechomene pyreto megalo*) which means "afflicted with high fever." The difference is clear.

FULL OF LEPROSY

Again, Luke differs from the other Gospels. He writes about a man who came to Jesus with "an advanced case of leprosy" (Luke 5:12), the others write that "a man with leprosy came" (Matt. 8:2; Mark 1:40). The word Luke uses for "full" (Gr. *pleres*) means complete, fully developed.

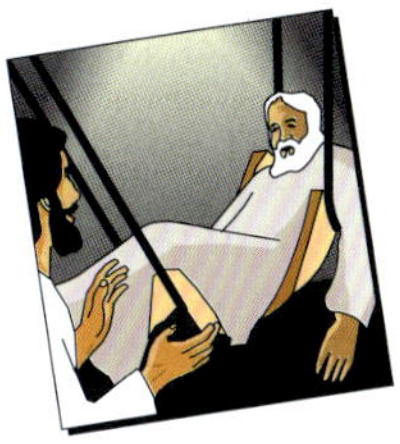

PARALYZED MAN

Luke uses a Greek different word (*paralelymenos*; Luke 5:24; Acts 8:7, 9:33) than the other Gospels (*paralytikos*, Matt. 9:1–7; Mark 2:3–12, see Matt. 4:24; 8:6). Luke's word means "losing a side," "from the side," or "weakened limbs," while the word used in the other Gospels is more general, a paralyzed man. Notice how careful Luke is to note the background of the various paralytics, two were paralyzed from birth, another for eight years (Acts 3:2; 9:33; 14:8).

TWISTED HAND

Luke notes that it was the man's "right hand" (Luke 6:6). The other gospels only mention "one hand" (Matt. 12:10; Mark 3:3).

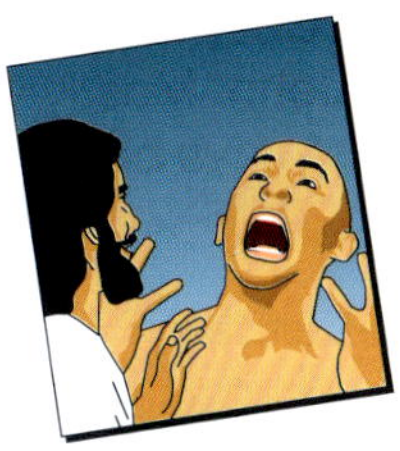

MEETS A POSSESSED MAN

Though no medical terms appear in Luke 8:26–27, Luke the physician is more observant about the man's condition than the other gospel writers. Luke notes that "for a long time he had been homeless and naked" (Luke 8:27)—specific details that are not included by either Matthew or Mark.

BLEEDING FOR TWELVE YEARS

Luke is careful to describe the woman's detailed medical history: "for twelve years" and that she persistently sought help (Luke 8:43–44). Luke even uses the word "stopped" (Greek *este*) a medical term for how different kinds of bodily fluids stop. Neither Matthew (9:20–22) nor Mark (5:30–34) use such precise terminology.

Luke was probably Paul's family doctor (Col. 4:14).

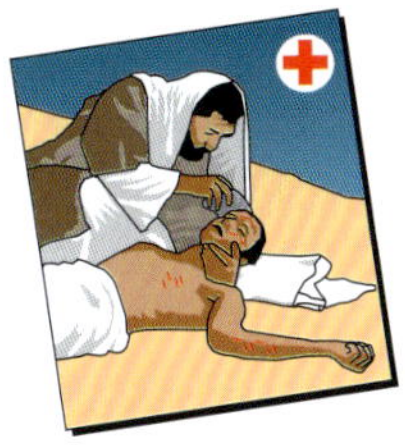

FIRST AID

The Good Samaritan gives the injured man good first aid for the times, "soothed his wounds with olive oil and wine" (Luke 10:33–34). Hippocrates* recommended alcohol because it was antiseptic and was believed to have a soothing effects. Oil was also believed to aid in healing and protect the surface of a wound (Luke 10:34; 1 Tim. 5:23; James 5:14).

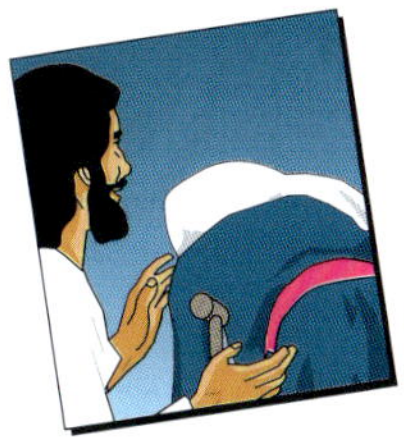

A CRIPPLED WOMAN

The Greek word for "sickness" (Luke 13:11–13) shows lack of strength. Luke carefully describes the history of the woman's illness ("bent double for eighteen years," "unable to stand up straight"). He uses Greek medical terms for "crippled" and "free from," meaning to release tension or to remove bandages.

SWELLING OF THE BODY

Luke speaks of a man "whose arms and legs were swollen" referring to an edema, an abnormal accumulation of fluid. It is the only place the Greek word is used in the New Testament, and it is a medical term. Jesus uses the man's illness to start a discussion about whether it is permissible to do good on the Sabbath (Luke 14:2–3).

VENOMOUS SNAKE BITES

The word "bit" (Acts 28:3) was used by doctors to describe poison entering the body. To "swell up" (Acts 28:6) is the technical term for inflammation. The Greek word for "drop dead" (Acts 28:6) is only used by Luke in the NT (Luke 8:6; Acts 26:14) and describes when someone suddenly collapses due to a wound.

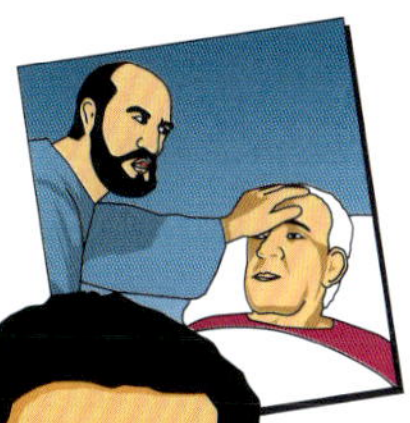

FEVER AND SEVERE DIARRHEA

The Greek words for "fever and dysentery" (Acts 28:8) are medical terms. Also, the word for fever is in the plural, which is medically correct (4:38–39), but Matthew 8:15, Mark 1:31, and John 4:52 use the singular form.

SOME MORE OBSERVATIONS

- "Struck at the high priest's slave, slashing off his right ear" (Luke 22:50). Matthew and Mark just say ear.
- "[Jesus] touched the man's ear and healed him" (Luke 22:51). Luke uses a specific Greek word for ear, *ous*, probably referring to the earlobe.
- Luke says a "mulberry fig tree" (Luke 17:6, 19:4). Dioscorides** notes there is a difference in the medicinal effect compared to an ordinary fig tree (compare Mark 11:13; John 1:48).

** Hippocrates (c. 460–370 BC), often called the "father of medicine," turned medicine into a profession. ** Dioscorides (40–AD 90). Describes in his works various medicinal plants. Source: Medical Terminology in Luke, Reuben Hubbard; Luke the physician, Isak Lindstedt, Läkartidningen Nr 51–52/2008.*

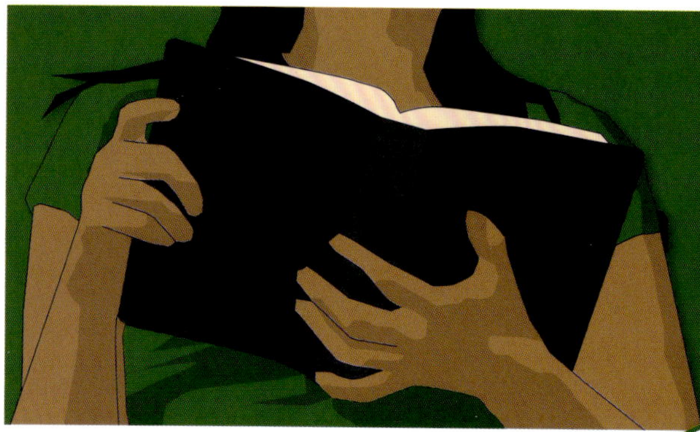

JOHN

"For this is how God loved the world: He gave his one and only Son, so that everyone who believes in him will not perish but have eternal life" (John 3:16).

A FEW WORDS ABOUT THE AUTHOR

Officially, the book is anonymous, but the author was probably an eyewitness to the events. John 21:2, 7 names just six possible candidates, as Peter is improbable. The most likely is John, son of Zebedee and brother of James, often identified as "the disciple Jesus loved" (John 13:23; 21:20). There is also strong support for John the apostle's authorship from early church fathers, such as Irenaeus, Clement of Alexandria, and Eusebius.

A FEW WORDS ABOUT THE RECIPIENTS

If John was in Ephesus, we can assume that he was writing to the church there and others in the region (see Rev. 2–3). It has been debated whether the book is addressed to Greeks (non-believers), Jews, and/or Christians. Since the purpose is "that you may continue to believe that Jesus is the Messiah, the Son of God" (John 20:31). The message is universal, speaking to believers and seekers alike.

A FEW WORDS ABOUT DATES

In the AD 100s, Polycarp writes that John was an elderly man when he wrote the Gospel. According to tradition, he was active in Ephesus in the latter part of the first century. The book was probably written between AD 85 and 95, before John was exiled to the island of Patmos (Rev. 1:9). It tells about the life of Jesus from AD 30 to 33, with a strong focus on the days leading up to his trials, death, burial, and resurrection.

THE WHOLE BOOK IN 25 WORDS

John tells everyone that Jesus is God's Son. Highlights seven words and seven miracles. Offers unique memories of Jesus's last hours. Includes famous Bible verses.

A SIMPLE STRUCTURE

1. Light – The Word became flesh
(John 1:1–12:50)

2. Love – Jesus washes disciples' feet
(John 13:1–17:26)

3. Life – Resurrection conquers death
(John 18:1–21:25)

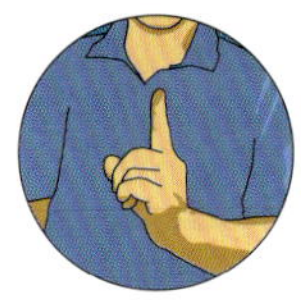

A FEW WORDS ABOUT KEY THEMES

- **Son of God**—Repeats and clarifies the truth that Jesus is the Son of God, who came to earth as a human (5:19–27; 6:40; 8:36; 10:36; 13:31; 17:1; 20:31).
- **Faith**—Not just a belief but a trust in the person and work of Jesus (1:12, 50; 11:25; 12:36; 14:11, 29; 16:27; 20:8, 29, 31).
- **People's responses**—The reactions and responses of those Jesus meets (1:11–12, 29–31; 3:1–21; 6:14–15; 7:10–13; 9:8–12; 11:21–27, etc.).
- **Eternal life**—What fellowship with the Son brings (3:15–16, 36; 4:14; 5:24; 6:47; 10:28)
- **"I Am" statements**—Jesus describes himself using "I am ..." (6:35; 8:58; 10:7, 14; 11:25; 14:6; 15:1, see Exodus 3:14).
- **Material not in the other Gospels**—As much as 93% is unique to John. Mostly material surrounding the last days before Jesus's death (14:1–17:26; 20:26–21:25).

A FEW TIPS ON WHAT TO LOOK FOR

Theme of the book:
Jesus,
Son of God

- "Son of God" (20:31)
- "My Father" (35 times)
- Witnesses, testify (50 times)
- Signs, the miracles of Jesus (7)
- Life, live, eternal life (36 times)
- Stop, stay (32 times)
- Light (21 times), darkness (8), truth (14), love (57), faith (100)
- Jesus's words about the world
- All the people Jesus meets
- Emphasis on the last days of Jesus's life (chapters 13–20)

Signs, Words, and Testimonies

John shows that Jesus is the Son of God by highlighting seven signs, seven "I Am" statements,* and seven testimonies. Together, they give a compelling portrait of his divine identity and mission.

Seven signs to create faith

1

Turns water into wine (2:1–11)*
With this sign, Jesus shows his power over the very nature of things. He turns gallons of water into the finest wine.

2

Heals a sick boy (4:46–53)
With this sign, Jesus shows his power is not limited by distance. Jesus is in Cana and the boy is in Capernaum.

3

Heals a lame man (5:1–29)*
With this sign, Jesus shows his power over time. He immediately heals a man who had been ill thirty-eight years.

4

Feeds 5,000 (6:1–14)
With this sign, Jesus shows his power over quantity. Five loaves and two fish become enough to feed a large crowd.

5

Walks on water (6:16–21)
With this sign, Jesus shows his power over nature. Creation obeys him as he walks to the boat through the strong wind.

6

Heals a man born blind (9:1–12)*
With this sign, Jesus shows his power over circumstances that are out of our control. This man was born blind.

7

Raises Lazarus (11:1–44)*
With this sign, Jesus shows his power over death and the grave. Death cannot hold Lazarus—even after four days.

Seven times Jesus says "I am ..."**

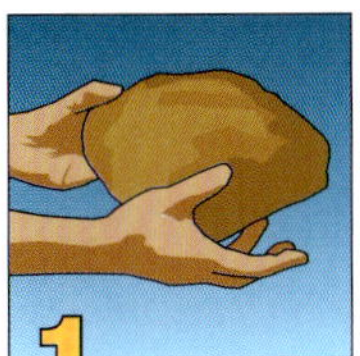

1

"I am the bread of life" (6:35).
With this statement, Jesus shows us he is the true bread. Jesus not only provides, but he himself satisfies our needs.

2

"I am the light of the world" (8:12).
With this statement, Jesus shows us he is the light. He speaks God's holiness and reveals truth in his incarnation.

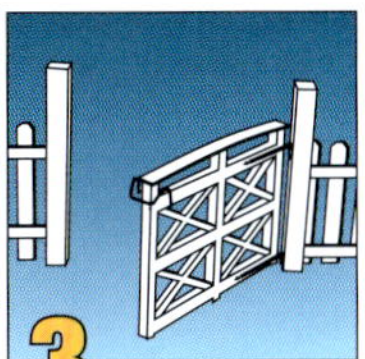

3

"I am the gate for the sheep" (10:7).
With this statement, Jesus shows us he is the gate of the enclosure where the sheep are protected and safe.

4

"I am the good shepherd" (10:11).
With this statement, Jesus shows us he is the good shepherd. He protects us, even giving his life for us.

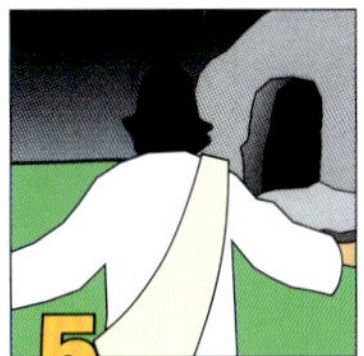

5

"I am the resurrection and the life" (11:25).
With this statement, Jesus shows us he is the resurrection and eternal life, both made possible only through him.

6

"I am the way, the truth, and the life" (14:6).
With this statement, Jesus shows us he is the way, the truth, and life. Through him we have a relationship with God.

7

"I am the true vine" (15:1).
With this statement, Jesus shows us he is the true vine. Believers belong to him and are cared for by the Father.

Seven testimonies to Jesus's identity

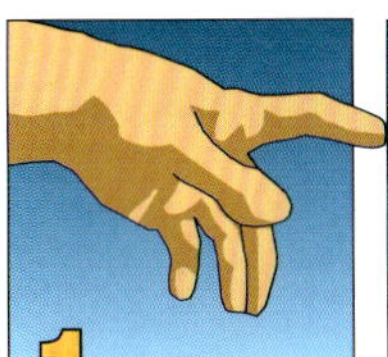

1

The testimony of the Father (5:37)
This testimony says, "The Father who sent me has testified about me himself." He confirms Jesus's identity.

2

The testimony of the Son (8:14)
This testimony says, "These claims are valid even though I make them about myself." Shows the truth of who he is.

3

The testimony of the Spirit (15:26)
This testimony says, "When [the Advocate comes he will] testify about me." The Spirit reveals the truth of who Jesus is.

4

The testimony of God's Word (5:46)
This testimony says, "If you really believed Moses, you would believe me, because he wrote about me."

5

The testimony of Jesus's works (10:25)
This testimony says, "The proof is the work I do in my Father's name." It demonstrates God's plan for humanity.

6

The testimony of John the Baptist (1:6–7)
This testimony says, "God sent a man ... to tell about the light so that everyone might believe because of his testimony."

7

The testimony of the disciples (19:35)
This last testimony says, "This report [John's Gospel] is from an eyewitness giving an accurate account."

** Only in John. ** Jesus uses the phrase "I am ..." over fifty times in the Gospel, but only seven times is it linked to concrete images.*

Dating Jesus's Birth and Death

When was Jesus born?

1 Caesar Augustus (Luke 2:1) He became emperor of the Roman Empire in 44 BC and died in AD 14. His appearance in Luke is consistent with extra-biblical sources but does not pinpoint the time of Jesus's birth.

2 The Census (Luke 2:1) Several sources note that Augustus ordered a census of the Roman Empire around the time of Jesus's birth. But none provide clear details to help determine the exact date.

3 Governor Quirinius He was governor of Syria at the time of Jesus's birth, but his official appointment came in AD 6. Luke 2:2 can be translated "before Quirinius was governor"—one possible explanation among others.

4 King Herod (Matt. 2:1) Became King of Judea in 37 BC and reigned until his death in 4 BC. Josephus links his death to a solar eclipse in April 4 BC. Jesus must have been born before that time.

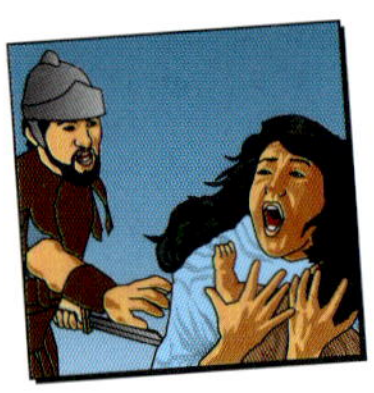

5 Boys under two (Matt. 2:16) The boys who were killed were no older than two. This may indicate the length of time that elapsed between the wise men seeing the star and Herod ordering the killing of the boys.

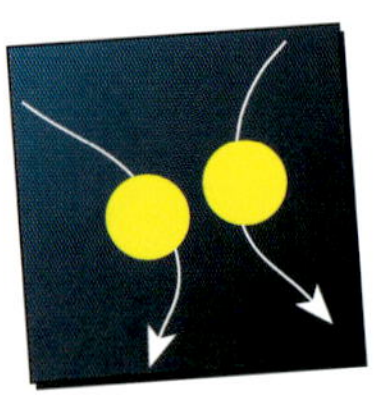

6 The Star of Bethlehem In 7 BC, several planetary conjunctions were visible. Another explanation for the star is a comet. There's no clear evidence for comets or planetary encounters. The theory is of little importance.

When did Jesus appear in public?

John the Baptist appeared in the fifteenth year of Emperor Tiberius's reign (Luke 3:1). Tiberius began ruling in AD 14, making his fifteenth year AD 28 or 29. John may have ministered for one or two years before Jesus came to him at the Jordan (Matt. 3:13). So, Jesus most likely began his public ministry in late AD 29 or early AD 30, probably sometime early in AD 30.

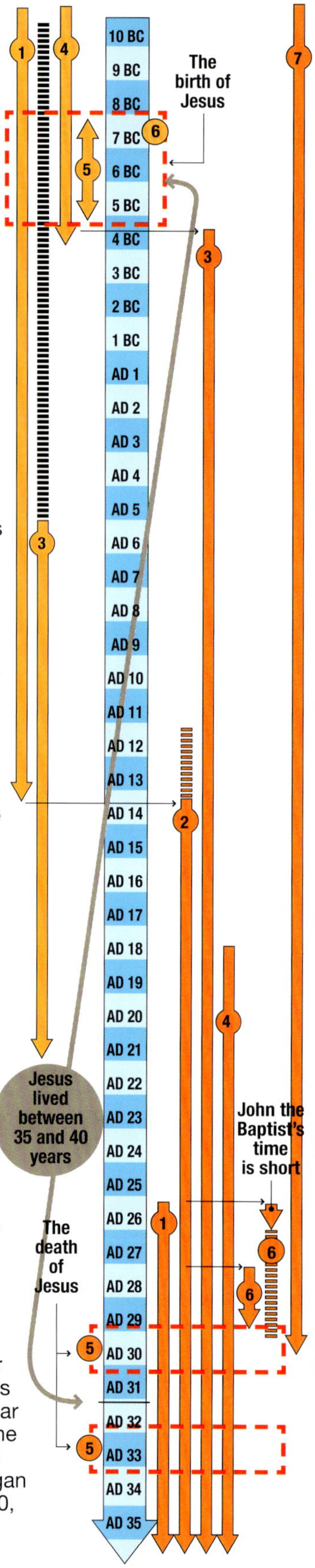

When did Jesus die?

1 Pontius Pilate (Luke 23:1) Became governor in AD 26 and ruled from Caesarea until AD 37 when he was summoned to Rome. He was governor when Jesus died, but this does not clarify the dating.

2 Caesar Tiberias (Luke 3:1) Became emperor in AD 14. His fifteenth year was AD 29. He began to co-rule with Augustus in AD 12, but that is usually not counted as part of his reign.

3 Herod Antipas (Luke 23:6–12) Appointed tetrarch of Galilee and Perea in 4 BC and deposed in AD 39. After their father's death, his brother Philip ruled Iturea from 4 BC to AD 34 (Luke 3:1).

4 High Priest Caiaphas (John 11:49) Installed as high priest in AD 18 and deposed in AD 36. He was high priest at the time of Jesus's death, but this does not help to clarify the date.

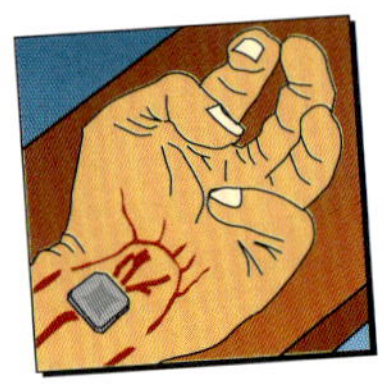

5 Died on a Friday (Mark 15:42) Jesus died just before the Sabbath and Passover, which is celebrated at the full moon (John 18:28). The only Passovers that fit this timing are in AD 30 and 33.

6 John the Baptist (Luke 3:1–3) He began ministering in the fifteenth year of Tiberius's reign, around AD 28 or 29. Jesus started his public ministry after John's and it lasted at least two years.

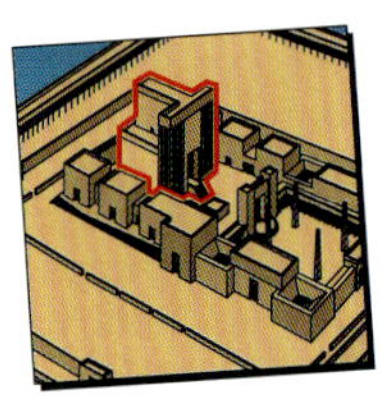

7 The Temple (John 2:20) Herod's expansion of the Temple began in 20 BC, lasting 46 years. This verse refers to the central building, begun around 16 BC, pointing to Jesus's death in AD 33.

Jesus and His Earthly Family

There's no clear genealogy of Jesus's extended family, so we piece the puzzle together from Scripture. The early church fathers offer some information, though their reliability is debatable. Here is one possibility.

1 John 19:25 says, "his mother's sister, Mary (the wife of Clopas)." It is unclear in the Greek if this refers to one or two women. (1) If it is one Mary, the wife of Clopas (see far right) is the Virgin Mary's sister-in-law. (2) But if it is two women, Mary's sister is someone else, either an unnamed woman or James and John's mother Salome (Matt.10:2; 27:56; Mark 15:40).

2 Matthew and Luke list different fathers for Joseph. One explanation is that Luke gives Mary's family line and Heli is her father (Luke 3:23; Matt. 1:16).

3 Another suggestion: Joseph's mother was first married to Heli who died childless (Luke 3:23); his half-brother Jacob then married her (Matt. 1:16). Jacob's son would then be counted as Heli's son (Deut. 25:5–6).

4 About Mary, Clopas's wife, there are at least two suggestions. (1) Based on John 19:25, she is the sister of Mary, Jesus's mother. (2) But if Clopas was Joseph's brother, it would make Mary the sister-in-law of Jesus's mother, Mary.

NOTE: Elizabeth and John the Baptist are also related to Jesus, but we don't know how (Luke 1:36).

5 Tradition has Joseph dying early. He was in Jerusalem when Jesus was twelve but is not seen again (Luke 2:41). However, some believe he was still alive when Jesus appeared in public (John 6:42).

6 If James the Younger is the apostle James, the two theories are: (1) Alphaeus (Matt. 10:3) is identical with Clopas, or (2) Alphaeus died and Clopas married his widow, compare Point 3.

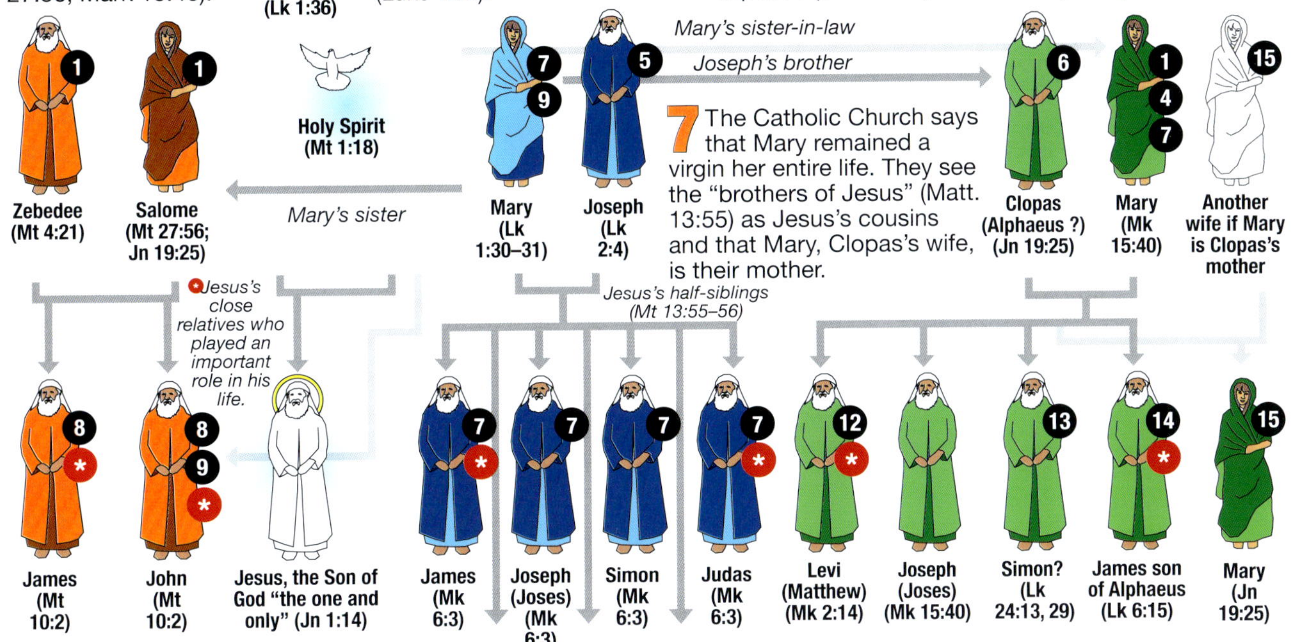

7 The Catholic Church says that Mary remained a virgin her entire life. They see the "brothers of Jesus" (Matt. 13:55) as Jesus's cousins and that Mary, Clopas's wife, is their mother.

8 If Salome is Mary's sister (John 19:25), it means that the apostles James and John were both Jesus's cousins.

9 Jesus speaks to his mother and John from the cross. His words implied that John should care for her after Jesus's death (John 19: 26–27). John takes Mary into his home from that moment. There is no formal kinship in such an arrangement.

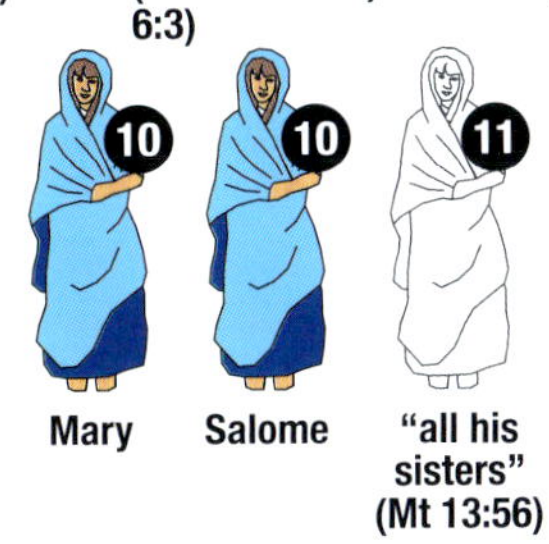

10 Tradition names Jesus's half-sisters Salome and Mary, both common Jewish names. But there is no biblical support.

11 In Greek, the word for "all" implies at least two. So we believe that Jesus had (at least) two half-sisters.

12 If Clopas and Alphaeus are the same person (see 6), then the third brother might be Levi (Matthew), who is referred to as the son of Alphaeus (Mark 2:14).

13 Extra-biblical sources say that one of the travelers on the road to Emmaus was a son of Clopas named Simon.

14 James is called "the younger" (Mark 15:40). This was to distinguish him from others with the same name. He was neither Jesus's half-brother nor James, the son of Zebedee. He is probably the apostle James, son of Alphaeus (Acts 1:13). If Clopas is Joseph's brother, he is also Jesus's cousin.

15 John 19:25 literally says "Mary of Clopas." It is often interpreted as "wife," but could also mean "daughter" or "mother."

• **Three views on Mary's sons: 1) Protestant view:** Believes Jesus had half brothers **2) Orthodox view:** Believes Jesus had stepbrothers **3) Catholic view:** Believes Mary was a virgin all her life, and Jesus's "brothers" were his cousins by her sister.

Elizabeth and Mary: Chosen by God

ELIZABETH

• Married to the priest Zechariah and mother of John the Baptist (Luke 1:5, 57).
• Relative of Mary, Jesus's mother (Luke 1:36).
• Was barren but late in life an angel revealed that she would have a son (Luke 1:7, 13).
• When she met Mary, the child in her womb leapt and she was filled with the Holy Spirit (Luke 1:41).

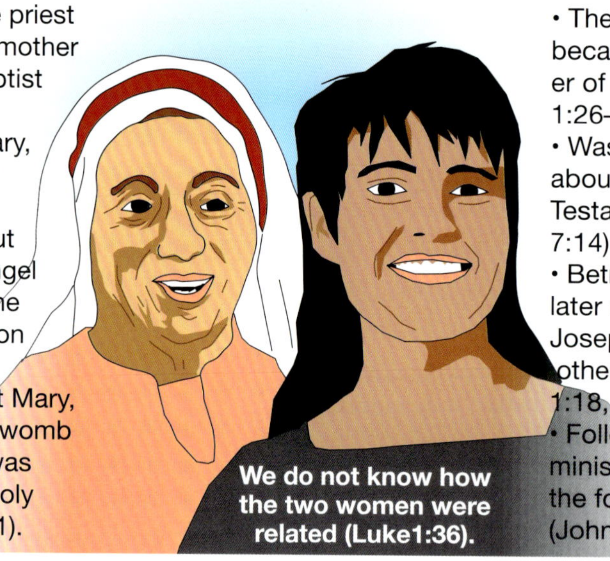

We do not know how the two women were related (Luke1:36).

MARY

• The virgin who became the mother of Jesus (Luke 1:26–38).
• Was prophesied about in the Old Testament (Isa. 7:14).
• Betrothed to and later married to Joseph and had other children (Matt. 1:18, 25; 12:46).
• Followed Jesus's ministry and was at the foot of the cross (John 19:26).

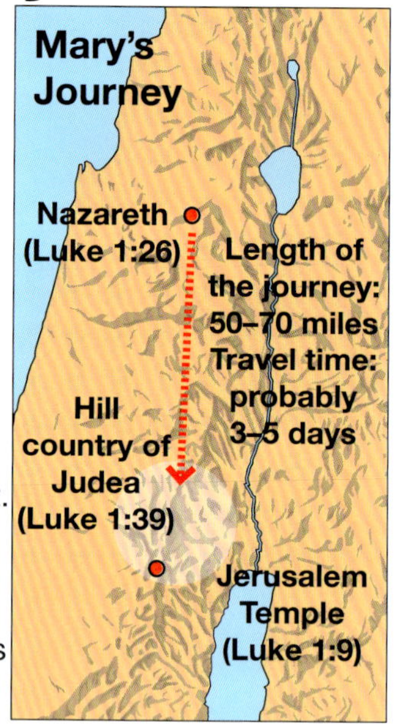

An angel, two women, two men, a meeting, and two children

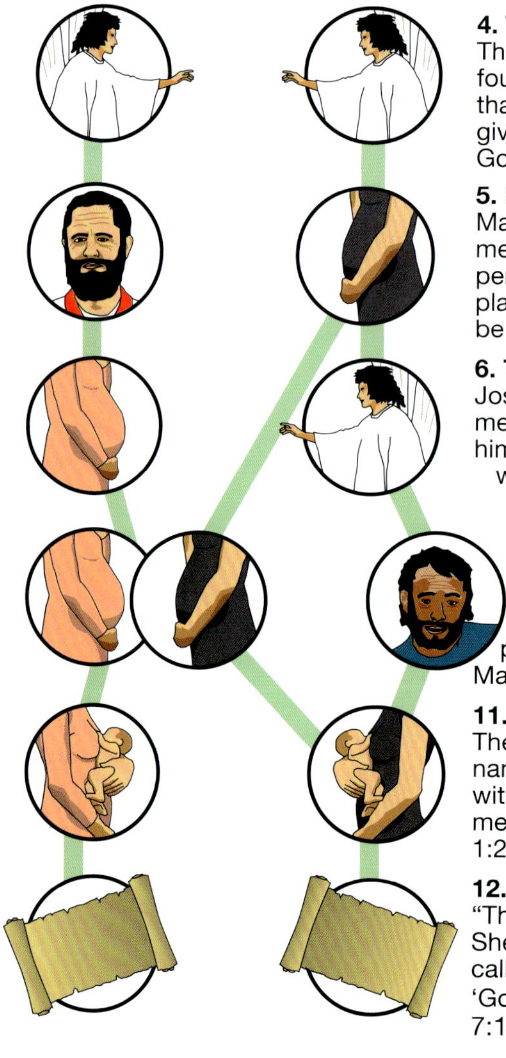

1. The message to Zechariah
God is in control of the timing as the angel speaks to Zechariah (not to Elizabeth). It is a natural pregnancy with a supernatural purpose (Luke 1:5–17).

2. Zechariah's reaction
Despite the supernatural encounter, Zechariah doubts. As a result, he becomes mute. But human weakness is not an obstacle to God's work (Luke 1:18–23).

3. Elizabeth becomes pregnant
After Elizabeth becomes pregnant, she thanks God and sees the child as the removal of her disgrace. The pregnancy is described as a miracle of God (Luke 1:24–25).

8. The expectant mothers meet
Mary learns from the angel that Elizabeth is also expecting a baby and travels to her. Both expectant mothers give praise to God (Luke 1:39–56).

9. The baby is named John
The baby is born and named John, as instructed by the angel. John means "God is gracious." Zechariah receives his voice back (Luke 1:57–80).

10. How the prophecy is fulfilled
John "will be a man with the spirit of Elijah ... [preparing] the people for ... the Lord" and "I am sending you the prophet Elijah ... before the ... day of the Lord" (Luke 1:17; Mal. 4:5).

4. The angel's message to Mary
The angel tells Mary that she has found favor with God. He says that she will become pregnant and give birth to a son. She submits to God's will (Luke 1:26–38).

5. Mary becomes pregnant
Mary does not doubt the angel's message but asks how it will happen. The angel describes God's plan and Mary learns the child will be the Son of God (Luke 1:34–35).

6. The message to Joseph
Joseph plans to break the engagement but in a dream, an angel tells him not to fear, to take Mary as his wife and to name the child Jesus (Matt. 1:19–23).

7. Joseph's reaction
Joseph believes the angel and acts accordingly. He follows the angel's instructions and proceeds with the plan to marry Mary (Matt. 1:24–25).

11. Mary's baby is named Jesus
The child is born and the parents name him Jesus, in accordance with the angel's message. Jesus means "God is salvation" (Matt. 1:25).

12. How the prophecy is fulfilled
"The virgin will conceive a child! She will give birth to a son and will call him Immanuel (which means 'God is with us')" (Matt. 1:23; Isa. 7:14).

Bethlehem: Where Jesus Was Born

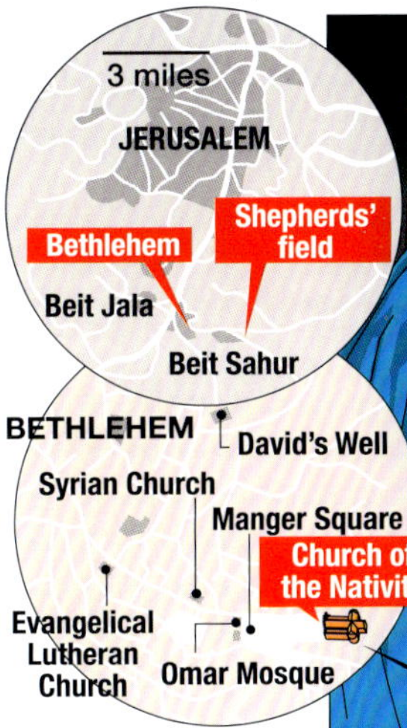

It is about 1 mile from the Shepherds' Field to the Church of the Nativity.

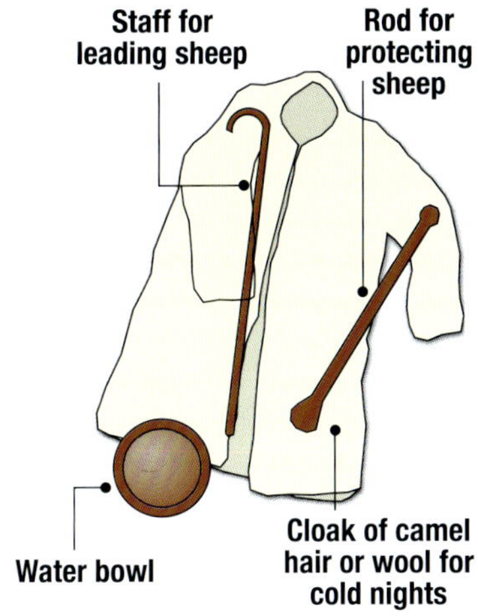

Some other shepherds in the Bible: Abel, Lot, Abraham, Isaac, Jacob, Rachel, Laban, the twelve sons of Jacob, Moses, David, the Shulamite, and Amos.

Church of the Nativity in Bethlehem

Bethlehem in the Bible

- The name means "house of bread."
- Rachel gave birth to Benjamin and died "on the way to Ephrath (that is Bethlehem)" (Gen. 35:19).
- Ruth married Boaz (Ruth 1:2; 4:13).
- David was born and grew up here (1 Sam. 16:4–13; Luke 2:4).
- Micah predicted that a savior would be born in Bethlehem (Mic. 5:2).
- Jesus was born here (Luke 2:7).

Bethlehem today

- According to tradition, the Church of the Nativity was built on the site where Jesus was born.
- The church was built in 326–339 and renovated in the 530s.

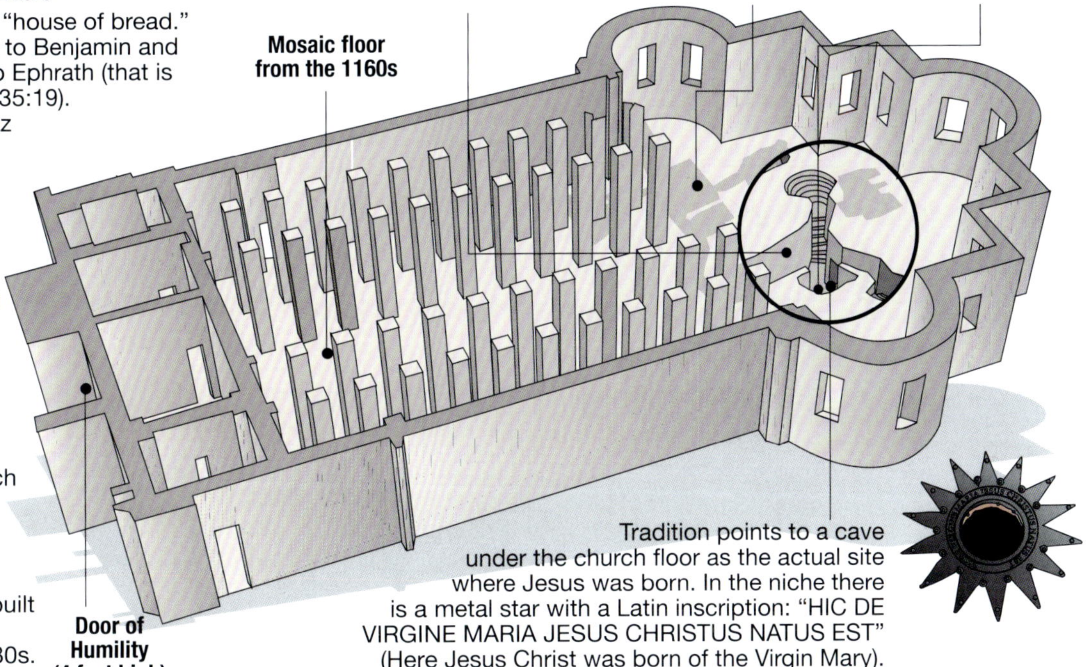

Tradition points to a cave under the church floor as the actual site where Jesus was born. In the niche there is a metal star with a Latin inscription: "HIC DE VIRGINE MARIA JESUS CHRISTUS NATUS EST" (Here Jesus Christ was born of the Virgin Mary).

THE HISTORY OF THE CHURCH OF NATIVITY

- **About AD 155–160:** Justin Martyr identifies a cave in Bethlehem as the place of Jesus's birth.
- **About AD 326–339:** Saint Helena, mother of Roman emperor Constantine, initiates construction of a church over the cave.
- **AD 386–429:** Jerome translates the Bible into Latin while working near the church.

Jerome

- **Around AD 529:** The original church is destroyed or damaged during the Samaritan revolts.
- **AD 535–565:** Justinian I rebuilds the church into the basilica that largely still stands today.
- **AD 1130–1169:** During the Crusader period, the church undergoes further renovations.
- **AD 1852:** The Greek Orthodox, Armenian, and Catholic churches share responsibility for its care under the "Status Quo."
- **AD 2002:** The church is besieged by Israeli forces during clashes with the Palestinians.
- **AD 2012:** Church is designated a UNESCO World Heritage Site.

We Saw His Star

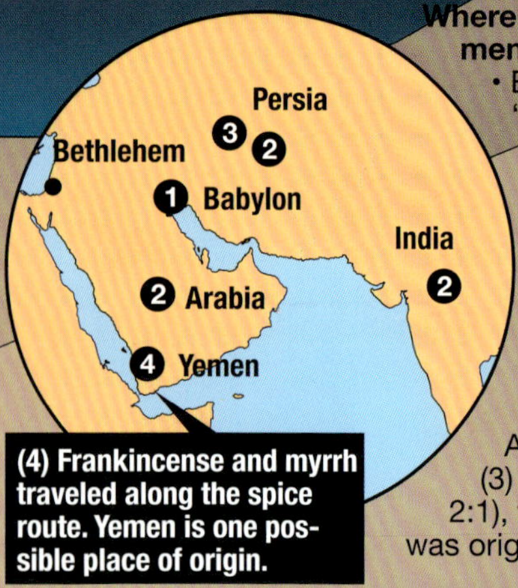

(4) Frankincense and myrrh traveled along the spice route. Yemen is one possible place of origin.

Where did the wise men come from?

- Eastern lands" (Gr. *anatole*, "where the sun rises"), though we don't know exactly (Matt. 2:1).
  (1) Usually assumed to refer to Babylon, often associated with astrologers (Dan. 1:20).
  (2) An Armenian tradition speaks of wise men from three different places: Arabia, Persia, and India.
  (3) The word *magi* (Matt. 2:1), translated "wise men," was originally used in Persia.

In Arabia and Persia, camels were primarily used as pack animals (see "camels loaded" 1 Kings 10:2). The wise men probably arrived on horses.

Possible Explanations for the Star of Bethlehem

A COMET
It was a comet. But in those days, comets were considered bad omens. Also, there is no evidence of any comets visible at the time.

A NOVA OR SUPERNOVA
A supernova or a group of novas (novas are exploding stars). But there are no records of novas or supernovas that fit the biblical text.

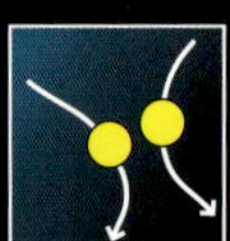

A PLANETARY CONJUNCTION
There were three encounters between Saturn and Jupiter in 7 BC. But the planets never came close enough to be viewed as a single star. *See below.*

AN ESP PHENOMENON
It was something that they became aware of by means other than their ordinary senses. But this is inconsistent with the biblical text.

A PROPHECY
Imagery taken from the Bible, "A star rises" (Num. 24:17). They concluded that the time was right. But why now? And why only these wise men?

A MIRACLE
For those who believe in a sovereign God, the star was a divine intervention, a true miracle, or even an angel sent by God (Rev. 9:1).

The night sky over Baghdad

May 27, 7 BC, 4:55 am (Speculative time of Jesus's birth)

The expression "from eastern" refers to where the sun rises (Matt. 2:1). "Saw his star as it rose" is the same Greek word, used here as an astronomical term referring to a star or conjunction of planets appearing in the sky (Matt. 2:2).

> **"The truth is that no one knows [what the star refers to]. No ordinary star or bright planet seems fit the description. (Peter Nilsson, astronomer)**

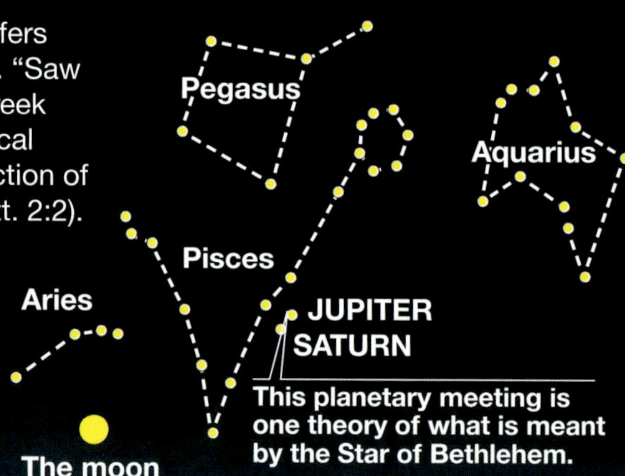

This planetary meeting is one theory of what is meant by the Star of Bethlehem.

The Wise Men's Gifts

GOLD
Precious metal from Arabia or Persia.

FRANKINCENSE
Dried resin from burned balsam trees.

MYRRH
Dried resin from the myrrh bush.

The sale of these valuable gifts may have financed the journey to and stay in Egypt.

Christmas Story Fact-Checking

Was Jesus born in the year 0?
Not possible. There is no year 0, as 1 BC is followed by AD 1. Jesus was not born in AD 1 either, since King Herod (Matt. 2:1) died in 4 BC. The probable date for Jesus's birth is therefore between 7 and 4 BC.

Was Jesus born December 25?
We don't know. December 25 is first given as the day of Jesus's birth in the early 300s. Other proposed dates are January 6, March 21, April 15, May 20, and Nov 17. There is no certainty that it was at the end of December.

Did Mary ride on a donkey?
We don't know. It would have been difficult for a pregnant woman to ride a donkey for any length of time. The journey probably took at least four to six days. Joseph and Mary probably walked, or Mary rode in a cart.

Was Jesus born immediately?
Unlikely. "While they were there, the time came" (Luke 2:6). It is doubtful that they arrived in Bethlehem the same day Jesus was born. They probably arrived some time before the birth, possibly several months.

Was Jesus born in a stable?
Unlikely. The text mentions a manger (Luke 2:7) which is why people assume it was a stable. But in Jesus's day, people's houses had space for the animals on the ground floor and a place upstairs where they slept.

Was the inn full?
Sort of. The Greek word *katalyma*, traditionally translated "inn" (Luke 2:7), means "room for temporary accommodation." It does not necessarily mean an "inn." It may imply that the guest room was too small for the birth.

Did the angels sing?
Unknown. The first angel that appeared to the shepherds *spoke* to them (Luke 2:10). Luke then speaks of the angels "praising God and saying" (Luke 2:13). The word for praise, *aineo*, does not indicate the type of praise.

Did the star shine over the stable?
Probably not. The text says nothing about a star shining when Jesus was born. Matthew says the wise men came after Jesus was born, "the star ... guided them" (Matt. 2:9). The star arrived with the wise men.

Were there three wise men?
We have no idea. The Bible says the wise men brought three gifts (Matt. 2:11), but it doesn't say how many there were. There may have been more, one tradition even claims that there were twelve.

Typical House in Jesus's Day

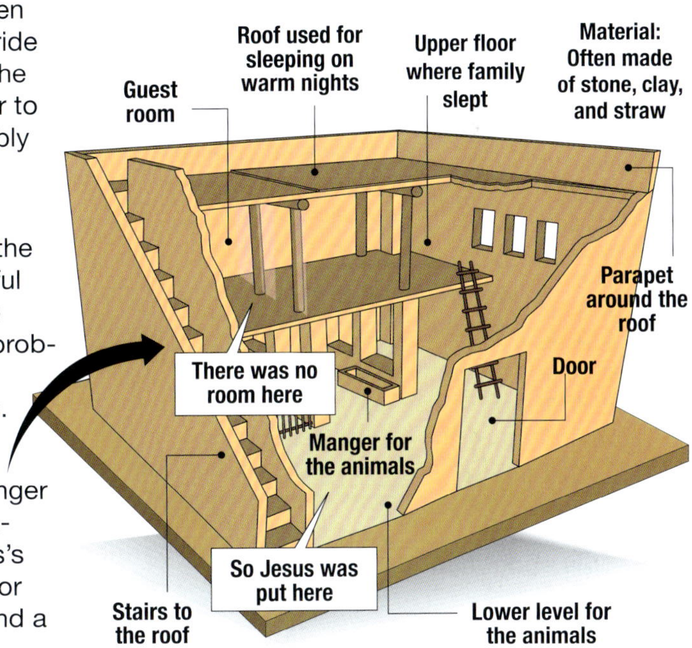

Did the wise men come on camels?
Unlikely. The text does not mention camels. While camels carried goods in Arabia and Persia (see 1 Kings 10:2), it is more likely that the wise men arrived on horses, which were seen as symbols of wealth in Arabia.

Did they arrive thirteen days later?
Unlikely. If the star appeared when Jesus was born, their journey would have taken much longer to complete. Ezra's trip from Babylon took four months (Ezra 7:8–9; see Matt. 2:16).

The Silent Years: Jesus Grows Up

Although Jesus lived about thirty-five years, admittedly we don't know much about the majority of them. Scripture only has a few verses which give us details, or hints, of his life before being baptized by John the Baptist at the Jordan. It is from these hints that we can form a general understanding of Jesus's early years.

1 What do we know about his infancy?

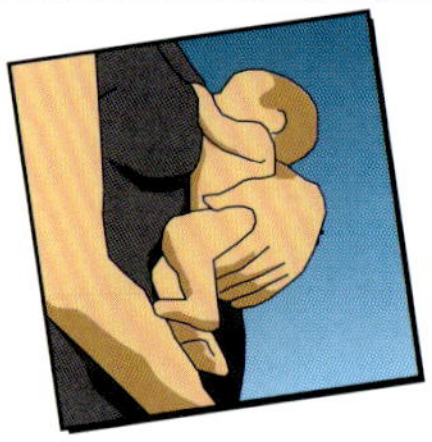

Circumcision: Jesus was circumcised on the eighth day after his birth, probably in Bethlehem (Gen. 17:10–14).
Purification sacrifice: Jesus was presented in the temple thirty-three days after his circumcision (Ex. 13:2; Lev. 12:1–8; Luke 2:22–24).
The flight to Egypt: Some time afterward, the family fled to Egypt to escape Herod's wrath (Matt. 2:13–15).

2 What do we know about his childhood?

Jesus grew: Just like all children, Jesus's body matured, growing healthy and strong (Luke 2:40).
Jesus matured: His maturity, understanding, and insight attracted attention (Luke 2:47).
Jesus knew or came to know, his identity: The distance from his parents was remarkable and revealed his awareness of his identity and mission at age twelve (Luke 2:49–51).

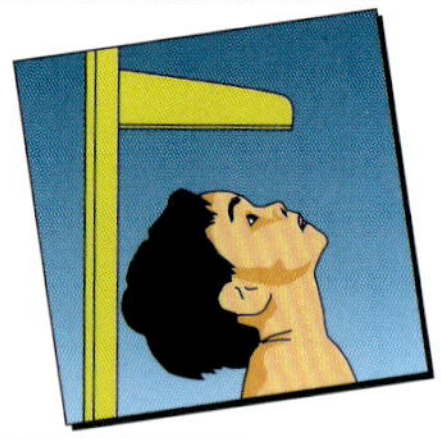

3 What do we know about his adolescence?

Jesus continued to grow: He was noted for his wisdom, the ability to use his knowledge well (Luke 2:52).
Jesus gained the trust of those around him: He had the gift of being accepted and liked by those around him (Luke 2:52).

> "The story of Jesus's entire upbringing, from infancy to religious awareness, is described in one single Bible verse, Luke 2:40.
> (G. Campbell Morgan)

4 What do we know about his home life?

He grew up in Nazareth: Jesus spoke Aramaic, probably with a noticeable accent (Matt. 26:69–75). People from Galilee were held in low regard, as it was distant from Jerusalem, the nation's heart (John 1:46; 7:52).
He was a natural part of the family: Jesus was understood to be Joseph's son (Luke 3:23; 4:22; John 1:45). He had at least four half-brothers and two half-sisters (Mark 6:3).

5 What do we know about his profession?

He was a carpenter: Jesus learned his father's trade, which may have been house construction. Today we might call him a master builder (Mark 6:3).
Or a stonemason: Timber was scarce in Galilee and the Greek word, *tekton*, means "craftsman," not just "carpenter." The provincial capital of Sepphoris, near Nazareth, was being rebuilt in Jesus's day, so he and Joseph may have worked there.

6 What do we know about his appearance?

We know nothing: The only description we have in the Bible is in Revelation and is figurative: "His head and his hair were white like wool, as white as snow. And his eyes were like flames of fire ... and his face was like the sun" (Rev. 1:12–16).
Ordinary appearance: We can assume he looked ordinary. Isaiah says: "There was nothing beautiful or majestic about his appearance, nothing to attract us to him" (Isa. 53:2).

7 What do we know about his education?

Taught by his father: Joseph probably taught him the law of Moses from an early age (Deut. 6:6–7).
Probably went to school: Jesus could read and write Hebrew and also spoke Greek (Luke 4:16–19; 23:3).
No further studies: In contrast, he seems to have lacked formal studies, but reasoned with rabbis as one of them (Luke 2:46–47; John 7:15).

An Overview of John the Baptist's Life

Key events in the life of John the Baptist

1 The angel Gabriel announces his arrival
The angel Gabriel tells Zechariah that he will have a son who will fulfill Malachi's prophecy (Luke 1:11–17; Mal. 3:1; 4:5).

2 Begins his prophetic ministry
Dressed in camel's hair and eating locusts, John calls the people to repent (Matt. 3:4–12).

3 Fulfills Old Testament prophecies
Jesus confirms that John is the Elijah to come, the fulfillment of Malachi's prophecy (Matt. 11:11–15).

"Make a straight highway through the wasteland for our God!" (Isa 40:3).

> "John was bold yet humble—he faithfully pointed followers to Jesus, not himself (Alistair Begg)

4 Baptizes Jesus in the Jordan
Jesus comes to John and is baptized in the Jordan. By baptizing him, John confirms Jesus's identity and mission (Matt. 3:13–17).

5 Disciples leave John for Jesus
Disciples who followed John the Baptist choose to follow Jesus. But John does not object (John 1:35–39).

6 Imprisoned and killed by Herod Antipas
John criticizes Herod Antipas, is imprisoned by him, and is then dramatically executed (Mark 6:17–28).

7 Confirmed as one of the greatest by Jesus
Jesus says, "I tell you the truth, of all who have ever lived, none is greater than John the Baptist" (Matt. 11:11).

	The Prophecies	The Promise	The Preparer	The Baptizer	The Prisoner	The Martyr	The Aftermath
KEY POINTS	• Prepared the way • Came in the spirit of Elijah • Will turn the hearts of fathers	• Promised to Zechariah • Born of Elizabeth • Leaped in the womb	• Called for repentance • Pointed to his successor • Baptized the people	• Baptized Jesus • Proclaimed Jesus as the Lamb of God • Left by some of his followers	• Criticized Herod Antipas • Sent to prison • Asked questions about Jesus	• Executed by Herod • Head given to Herodias • Buried by his disciples	• Believed to have risen • Compared to Jesus • Feared by Herod Antipas
TOPICS	A forerunner promised by the prophets	A child who gives hope to the people	A preacher who calls for repentance	A prophet who meets the one to come	A prisoner who confronts Herod Antipas	A martyr killed for his message	A memory that lives on among the people
	John is foretold in the Old Testament	John is promised to his parents	John appears and preaches	John baptizes Jesus	John speaks truth to power	John is executed on a whim	John is compared to Jesus
	Isaiah and Malachi prophesy	The angel Gabriel speaks to Zechariah	John eats locusts and honey	Jesus is baptized by John	Herod Antipas imprisons John	Herodias has John executed	Some believe that John has returned
PEOPLE	Isaiah and Malachi	Zechariah and Elizabeth (Lk 1:5)	The people, Pharisees, and Sadducees	Jesus, the people, tax collectors, and soldiers	Jesus, John's disciples, Herod Antipas	Herod Antipas, Herodias, Salome	Jesus, John's disciples, Herod, the people
LOCATIONS	Judah	The hill country of Judah	Judea and Jerusalem	Around the Jordan, Ainon near Salim	Galilee, Machaerus	Galilee, Machaerus	Galilee, the whole country (?)
TEXTS	Isa. 40:3; Mal 4:5–6	Luke 1:5–25, 44, 57, 80	Matt 3:1–12; Mark 1:1–8; Luke 3:1–20; John 1:19–28	Matt 3:13–19; Mark 1:9–11; Luke 3:21–22; John 1:29–42	Matt 11:2–19; Mark 6:17–20; Luke 7:18–23; John 3:22–36	Matt 14:3–12; Mark 6:21–29	Matt 14:1–2, 16:13–16; Mark 6:14–16
TIME PERIOD	About 700 BC and 430 BC, respectively	Around 7–5 BC	AD 28–29	Winter AD 30	AD 30	AD 31	AD 31–33

Different Views of Baptism

Baptism is practiced in most churches and congregations. However, views on baptism differ. There are two main ways of baptizing; pouring and immersion. And there are several different interpretations of the meaning of baptism. The baptism that Jesus experienced by John the Baptist was a very different kind of baptism than Christians practice today (Matt. 3:13–17; Acts 19:3–5; 1 Peter 3:20–21).

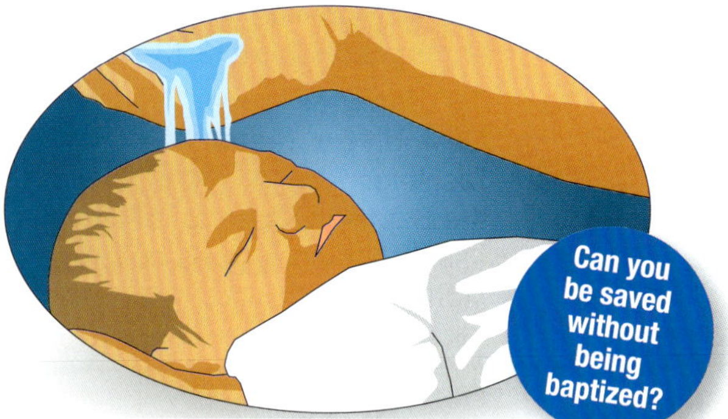

Baptism by pouring		Baptism by immersion
According to the faith of the parents: Entire families, including children, were baptized (Acts 16:15). Jesus said: "Let the children come to me" (Mark 10:14). The parents' faith is sufficient for the child, who is confirmed when older (1 Cor. 7:14).	**Who is baptized?**	**After the person has come to faith:** Only after confessing faith in Jesus can someone be baptized. Points out that faith always comes before baptism and that there are no biblical texts that explicitly mention baptizing children (Acts 2:41; 18:8).
By Pouring/Sprinkling: The Greek word *baptizo* is understood to refer to the ceremony of baptizing. The method used is not crucial, but pouring can be more practical with small children. Adults can be baptized later in life.	**Method of baptism**	**By Immersion:** Emphasizes that the Greek word *baptizo* means "to immerse, dip something in liquid." For example, the word is used to refer to make clean with water, to the process of dyeing fabrics, or about sunken ships.
Usually at a baptismal font: In some traditions, the children are completely immersed. Families often have a special gown that the baby wears, handed down for generations. 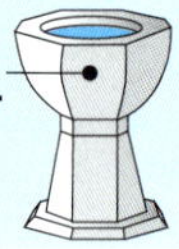	**Location of baptism**	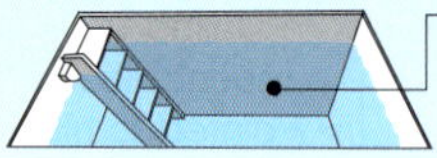 **Often in a baptism pool:** But it isn't uncommon for baptisms to be outdoors at a lake, river, or even in the ocean (Acts 8:36).
Emphasizes that God works in baptism: Baptism is seen as a promise from God to be with the child in a personal way. The child is said to share in the Holy Spirit. Some see it as a saving sacrament (called *ex opere operato*). Baptism is perceived as inclusion into the family of God.	**What is emphasized?**	**Emphasizes that the believer chooses baptism:** Emphasizes that baptism is primarily an act of obedience, publicly proclaiming one's willingness to follow Jesus (Matt. 28:18–20). It is often linked to church membership. Most view it as a symbolic act, some see it as part of salvation (Mark 16:16).

NOTE: Acts 19:4–5 is the only text in the New Testament that mentions rebaptism.

SEVEN DIFFERENT BAPTISMS IN THE NEW TESTAMENT

1 Baptism of John
As a result of conversion under the old covenant. Nothing happens in the baptism itself (Matt. 3:13–17), it is a purely symbolic act that marks repentance.

2 Disciples' baptism
We know little about it. A baptism of conversion under the old covenant. A symbolic mark of repentance, similar to John the Baptist's baptism (John 3:22; 4:1–2).

3 Baptized into Moses
Those who passed through the Red Sea were identified with Moses. It does not refer to a single event but symbolically to the whole journey (1 Cor. 10:2).

4 Baptized with Jesus
Jesus talks about baptism in a figurative way, referring to his suffering and death (Mark 10:39; Luke 12:50). He is not talking about the act of baptism.

5 Christian baptism
Jesus urged his disciples to baptize those who come to faith. This is the baptism that the church practices today (Matt. 28:18–20; Acts 2:41; 19:3–5).

6 Baptized in the Spirit
The Holy Spirit takes up residence in every believer, identifying them as belonging to Christ. Only used as a verb (1 Cor. 12:13; Acts 1:5; Eph. 1:13).

7 Baptism for the dead
Paul writes about the practice of being baptized for the dead. We don't really know what he meant but he does warn against the practice (1 Cor. 15:29).

Jesus Is Tempted by the Devil

Jesus's Three Temptations

1 Temptation: To make bread of stones
Meaning: False independence from the Father **Temptation:** Becoming significant **Affects:** Jesus personally (Matt. 4:1–4; Mark 1:12; Luke 4:1–4).

2 Temptation: To command angels
Meaning: Mistaken dependence on heavenly powers. **Temptation:** To be spectacular **Affects:** The nation (Matt. 4:5–7; Luke 4:9–12). **Note:** Jesus's movement to "the temple" (Matt. 4:5) and to "a high mountain" (Matt. 4:8).

3 Temptation: To worship Satan
Meaning: Unacceptable compromise with God's plan **Temptation:** To become powerful **Affects:** All of humanity (Matt. 4:8–11; Mark 1:13; Luke 4:5–8, 13).

Was Jesus tempted or tested?

1 Jesus was able not to sin
The text should be understood as temptation. As a true man, Jesus was subjected to the same kind of temptations as we are (Heb. 2:18; 4:15).

2 Jesus could not sin
The text should be understood as a test. As true God, Jesus cannot sin. Would it be sinful for God to make bread out of stones? Satan challenges Jesus to abandon his incarnation, offering him a shortcut without the cross.

> "The real question is: Was He unable to sin? Was He not only able to overcome temptation, but also unable to be overcome by it? The answer: of course, has to be "yes". It is not that He is able not to sin, but He is not able to sin. (S. Lewis Johnson Jr.)

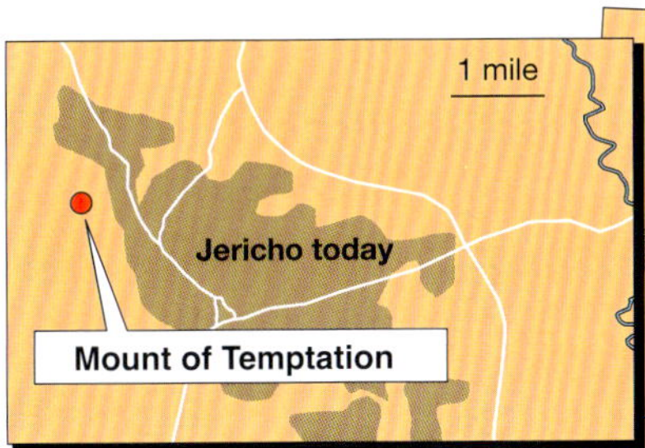

MOUNT OF TEMPTATION
Tradition points to Jabal al-Qarantal, a mountain about one mile north of Jericho, known as the Mount of Temptation (Matt. 4:8). There is now cable car to the top.

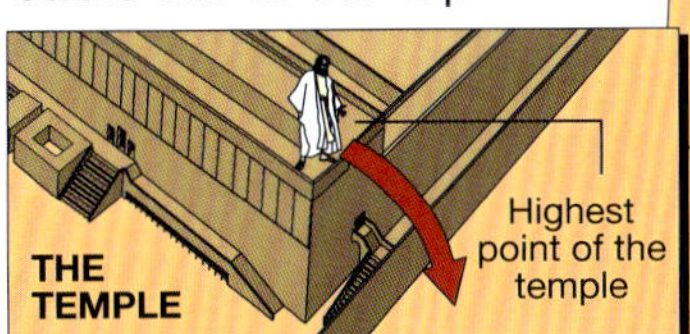

THE TEMPLE
To "the highest point of the temple" (Matt. 4:5), probably the temple roof or the boundary wall. It was about 165 feet high.

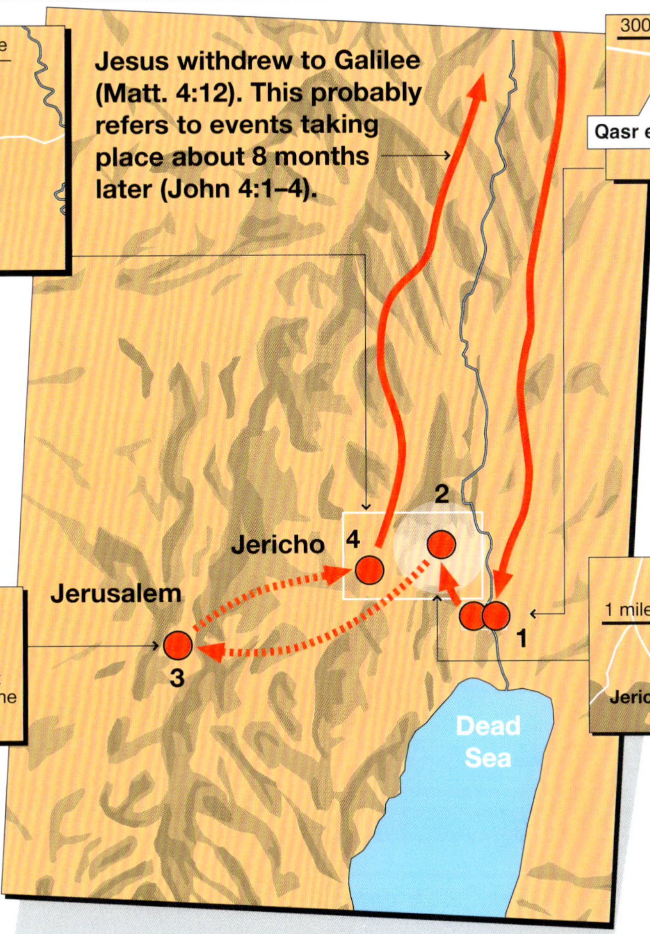

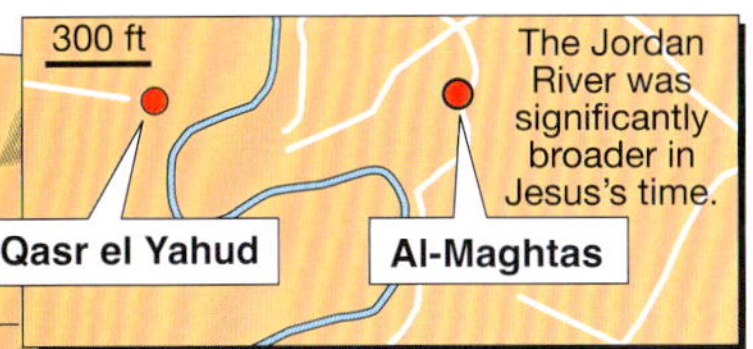

JORDAN
Two sites are traditionally identified as the place where John the Baptist was active.
- Qasr el Yahud, located in the West Bank.
- Al-Maghtas (Bethany, John 1:28). Located on the Jordanian side, it is a more likely site.

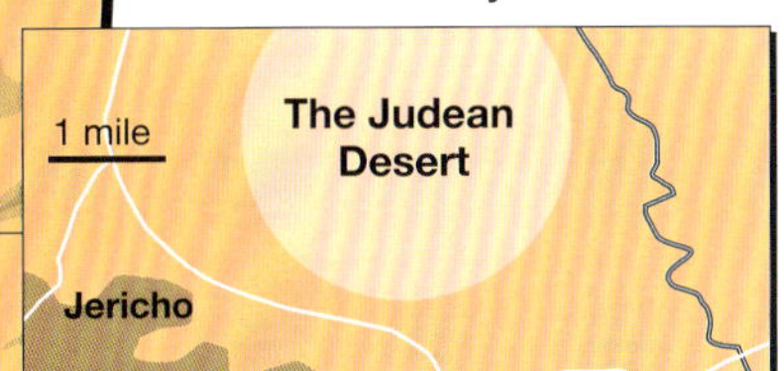

THE DESERT
Unclear. Jesus "was led ... into the wilderness" (Matt. 4:1). Most take this to be between the site of the baptism and Jericho.

Jesus's Three Years of Public Ministry

Jesus's public ministry is the time from his appearance to John the Baptist (Matt. 3:13–17) until his ascension into heaven (Luke 24:50–53). The ministry most likely lasted 3½ years. However, not everyone agrees.

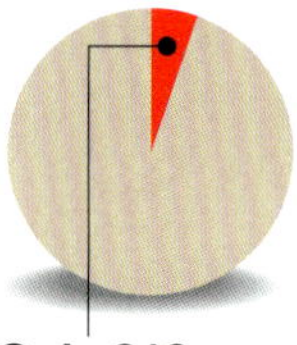

Only 213 verses, 5.7% of the gospel text, talk about Jesus's birth and childhood.

"Jesus was about thirty years old when he began his public ministry" (Luke 3:23).

More than thirty years of preparation

The Gospels contain comparatively little material on the birth and childhood of Jesus. Matthew and Luke tell of Jesus's birth. There is only one account of him as a child, when he visits the temple in Jerusalem at the age of 12. There are a few references in later texts, such as "He's just the carpenter's son" (Matt. 13:55; Luke 4:22; John 2:12; 6:42).

1 The Year of Silence (AD 30)

Average 18 verses/month

2 The Year of Success (AD 31)

Average 74 verses/month

3 The Year of Resistance (AD 32)

Average 65 verses/month

½ The Half Year of Sacrifice (AD 33)

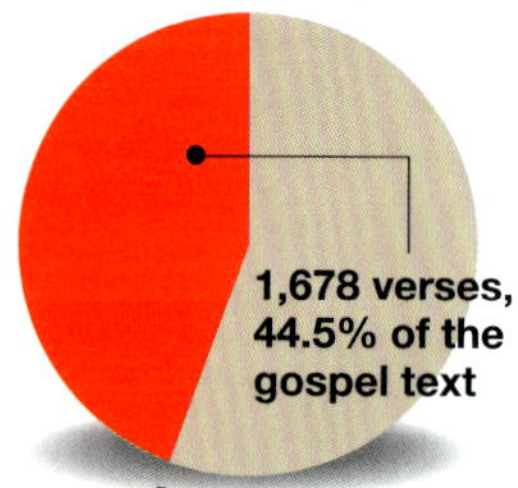

Average 280 verses/month

	The Year of Silence (AD 30)	The Year of Success (AD 31)	The Year of Resistance (AD 32)	The Half Year of Sacrifice (AD 33)
Things to Note	Eight months in Judea are captured in a single verse (John 3:22).	To Galilee. Reactions in Nazareth bring him to Capernaum.	Turns away from the public, withdraws, devotes time to disciples.	Walks purposefully toward Jerusalem, knowing what awaits him.
Year Marked By	Jesus works in silence. We know little about what he did (John 4:1).	Jesus appears in public. Many more people follow him.	Resistance grows, disciples begin to leave, plans are made to kill him.	The resistance culminates. The plan to kill Jesus is put into action.
Locations	Jerusalem, Judea, and through Samaria.	Around Galilee, based in Capernaum.	Galilee, Tyre, Sidon, Phoenicia, Jerusalem, and Judea.	Judea, Perea, and then back to Jerusalem.
Key Events	• Baptized by John the Baptist • Tempted in the desert • Spoke with Nicodemus • Preached in Judea • Met the woman at the well	• Driven out of Nazareth • Chose the Twelve • Gave the Sermon on the Mount • Began to speak in parables • Fed 5,000	• Withdrew from Galilee • Disciples confessed their faith • Transfiguration • Attempted stoning • Visited Martha and Mary	• Taught in Perea • Raised Lazarus • Instituted the Lord's Supper • Crucified and died • Raised from the dead

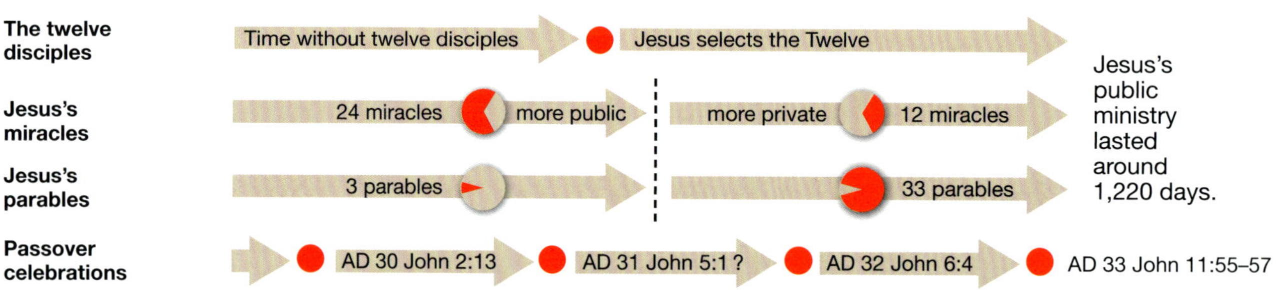

Jesus's public ministry lasted around 1,220 days.

A Conversation in the Early Hours

During the day: Jesus cleanses the temple (John 2:13–25)

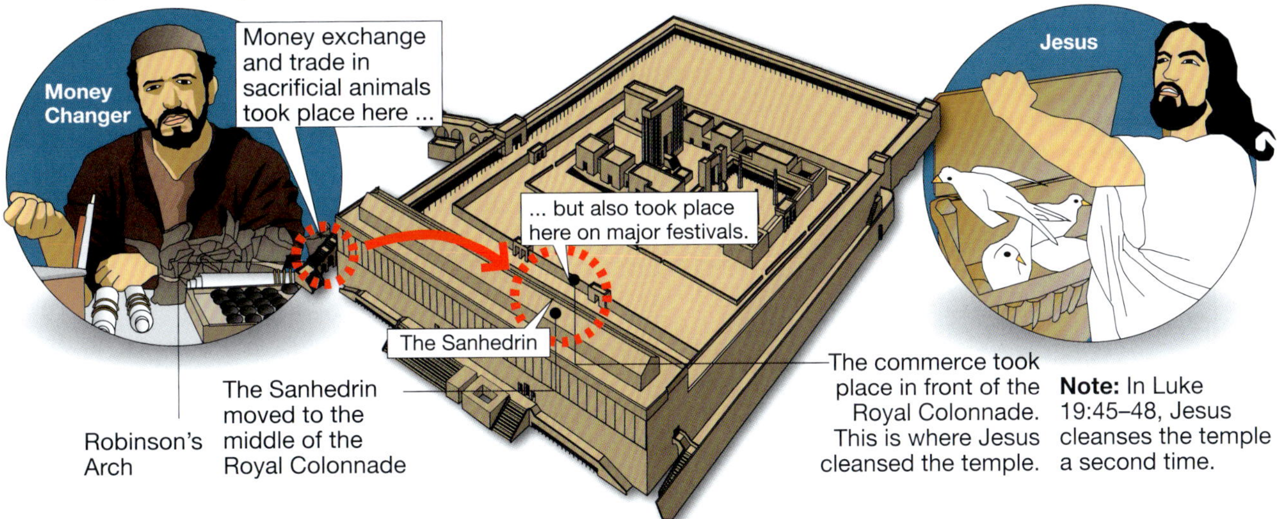

Note: In Luke 19:45–48, Jesus cleanses the temple a second time.

1 The lucrative money exchange

Pilgrims coming to Jerusalem had to purchase sacrificial animals at the temple. The temple used a special temple currency, which the pilgrims had to buy, at a bad rate, at the booths just outside the temple.

2 Caiaphas's sons controlled the trade

At major festivals, the money exchange and animal trade also took place inside the temple courtyard (John 2:14). Both lucrative businesses (money and animals) were controlled by high priest Caiaphas's sons.

3 Caiaphas sat in the Sanhedrin

According to rabbinic writings, the Sanhedrin moved from the priests' courtyard to the "bazaars" around AD 30. The bazaars were located where the trade in sacrificial animals took place during the festivals.

4 Jesus attacked Caiaphas's trade

When Jesus attacked the trade (John 2:15–16), he did it outside the Sanhedrin. The high priest was a Sadducee. Nicodemus, a Pharisee, belonged to the other party. In the evening he came to Jesus.

After dark: Nicodemus comes to Jesus (John 3:1–21)

Nicodemus to Jesus:

We know you are a teacher (3:2)
Jesus's action in the temple is compelling. Nicodemus calls Jesus a teacher. He says "we," he is the spokesman for several people. He understands that God is with Jesus.

How then to be born again? (3:4)
Nicodemus does not understand what Jesus means by being born again. He asks for an explanation. The question "How" is about how he can change.

How is it possible? (3:9)
Nicodemus accepts Jesus's answer, but does not quite understand. He asks: What should I do? Can it become a reality for me?

Jesus to Nicodemus:

1 You must be born again (3:3)
Jesus responds with something completely different. He says that man must be *born again* in order to enter and see the Kingdom of God.

2 Being born in a new way (3:5–8)
Jesus replies: You must repent [be born of water and the Spirit]. It is about an inner change. You don't see the new birth, but you can see its consequences.

3 Teaching is not enough (3:10–21)
Jesus clarifies: The Son of Man will give His life. Whoever believes in Me will have eternal life. Conclusion: I am more than a teacher: I am the Son of God.

Four Truths from "the Gospel in a Nutshell"

Probably the most famous verse in the Bible, John 3:16 is spoken by Jesus to Nicodemus. It is often called "the gospel in a nutshell" for it summarizes the Bible's central message in a single verse.

"(1) For this is how God loved the world:

1 The word "For" refers to the preceding verses.
John 3:13–15 speaks of Jesus's incarnation and death. The Greek *outos*, often translated "how" or "so," means "in this way." Verse 16 speaks of the motive.

2 Talks about God's motivation for orchestrating the plan of salvation.
The verse underlines the intensity of God's love for humanity. "The world" refers to humanity in rebellion against God (1 John 2:15–17).

Four major points in John 3:16

1. God's motive
2. God's action plan
3. God's purpose
4. Intended outcome
   a. rescued from
   b. rescued to

(2) He gave his one and only Son,

3 How God expressed his love for humanity.
He sent Jesus (Phil. 2:6–8), who took on bodily form, entered into our condition and became our mediator, our go-between (1 Tim. 2:5).

4 What Jesus's incarnation meant—in all its aspects.
It encompasses the whole of Jesus's ministry on earth—incarnation, ministry, death, and resurrection. He took our guilt, reconciling us to God.

What does "one and only" mean?
At times translated "only begotten," it means to be the only child, the only one of its kind.

(3) so that everyone who believes in him

5 Describes who can benefit from salvation.
Jesus came for the whole world but salvation is not automatic. It is not given to everyone, but only to those who meet God's criteria—faith.

6 Describes what is necessary to receive salvation.
Salvation is given to all who believe in him. To believe is to rely on, to trust in the finished work of Jesus on the cross.

(4a) will not perish

7 Describes the implications for people.
"Not" and "but" show the contrast between what we receive from him and what we suffer without him.

8 Describes the scope of what the verse is talking about.
There is clearly a risk of being lost. The Greek word *apoletai* means to perish (Matt. 8:25), to be lost (Luke 15:8).

(4b) but have eternal life (John 3:16).

9 Describes what God gives to all who believe.
Finally, the text describes what the believer receives instead—eternal life. Christ's work on the cross enables people, through faith and trust, to spend eternity with God.

Other noteworthy verses about salvation:
Rom. 4:4–5
Eph. 2:4–5
1 Pet. 2:24–25

The Woman at the Well

• Jesus begins a conversation with a woman at Jacob's well outside Sychar (John 4:5–10).
• The woman was a Samaritan, a people of mixed ancestry who came out of the Assyrian migration in the eighth century BC.
• The Samaritans were considered ceremonially unclean and not permitted to participate in Jewish society.
• A Jew who drank from a Samaritan woman's cup would be considered ritually unclean (John 4:9, 21–22).

TO TALK ABOUT YOUR FAITH

Jesus's conversation with the woman at the well can serve as a model for conversations about your Christian faith.

1 Grab their attention
A question on a mundane topic starts the conversation. Jesus asks the woman for a drink (John 4:7).

2 Spark an interest
Jesus says there is a different kind of water, living water. The woman's curiosity is piqued (John 4:10).

3 Create a desire
Jesus talks about what this other water can do, give eternal life. The woman says she wants some (John 4:14–15).

4 Lead to action
Jesus reveals who he is and what he knows about her. She publicly confesses her faith in Jesus (John 4:17–18).

Jesus returns to Galilee

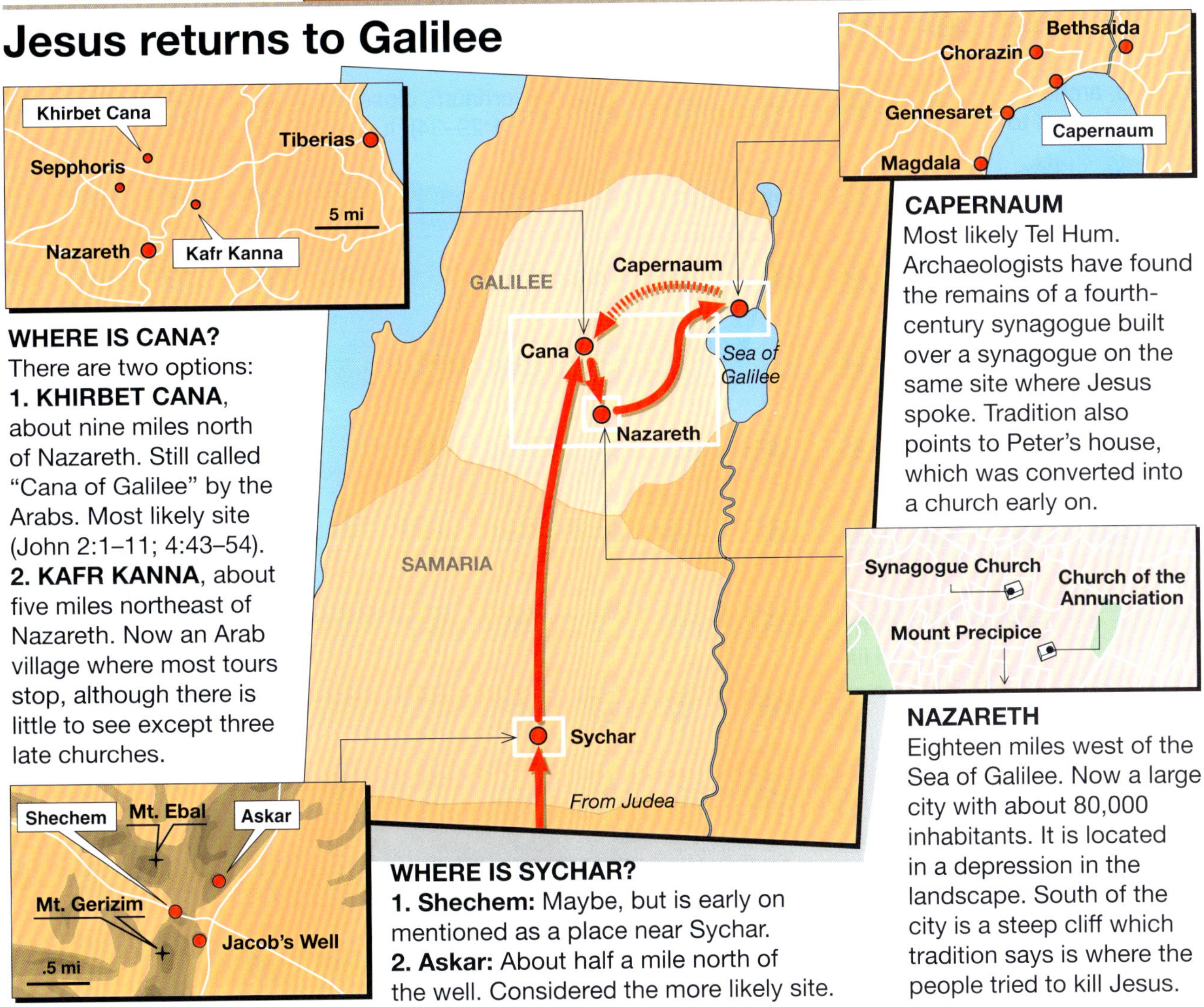

WHERE IS CANA?

There are two options:
1. KHIRBET CANA, about nine miles north of Nazareth. Still called "Cana of Galilee" by the Arabs. Most likely site (John 2:1–11; 4:43–54).
2. KAFR KANNA, about five miles northeast of Nazareth. Now an Arab village where most tours stop, although there is little to see except three late churches.

CAPERNAUM

Most likely Tel Hum. Archaeologists have found the remains of a fourth-century synagogue built over a synagogue on the same site where Jesus spoke. Tradition also points to Peter's house, which was converted into a church early on.

NAZARETH

Eighteen miles west of the Sea of Galilee. Now a large city with about 80,000 inhabitants. It is located in a depression in the landscape. South of the city is a steep cliff which tradition says is where the people tried to kill Jesus.

WHERE IS SYCHAR?

1. Shechem: Maybe, but is early on mentioned as a place near Sychar.
2. Askar: About half a mile north of the well. Considered the more likely site.

Jesus Relocates to Capernaum

Jesus relocates from Nazareth to Capernaum (Matt. 4:13) and calls it his "own town" (Matt. 9:1). Here are six reasons for the move.

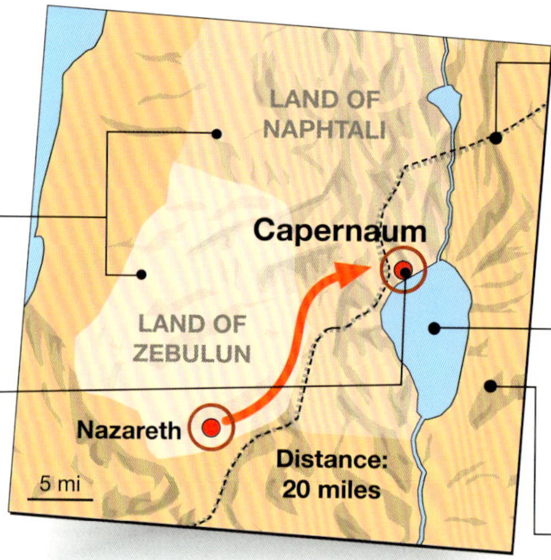

1 Fulfilled prophecy
Isaiah talks about "the land of Zebulun and Naphtali" (Isa. 9:1; Matt. 4:15). Nazareth is in Zebulun and Capernaum in Naphtali.

2 Access to housing
Peter lived in Capernaum and Jesus probably lived in his house. This is the town he called his home (Mark 2:1).

3 A larger population
Capernaum was a bigger town. Jesus came into contact with more people.

4 Close to a trade route
Capernaum was on the Via Maris (Isa. 9:1) trade route that connected modern-day Syria and Iraq with Egypt. Both information and goods traveled along the road.

5 Close to the Sea of Galilee
Proximity to the Sea of Galilee made it possible to travel quickly around the region—a strategic hub.

6 Close to gentiles
Capernaum was a cosmopolitan town with a Roman garrison. It was also close to cities where many non-Jews lived.

Peter's house in Capernaum

In 1968, archaeologists discovered the ruins of a house in Capernaum, close to the synagogue, that may have belonged to Peter and where Jesus may have lived (Mark 1:29–34). It could have looked like this.

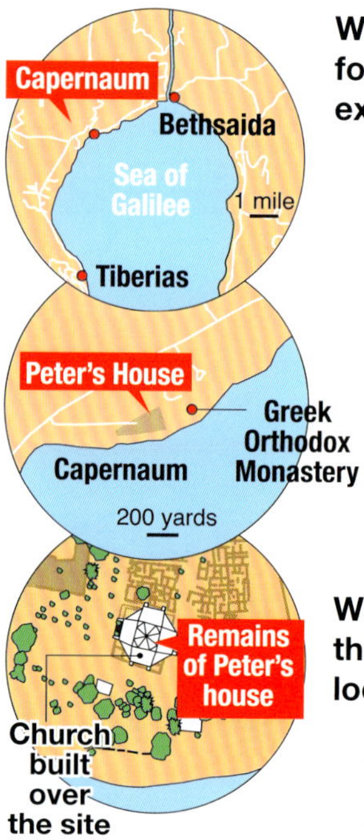

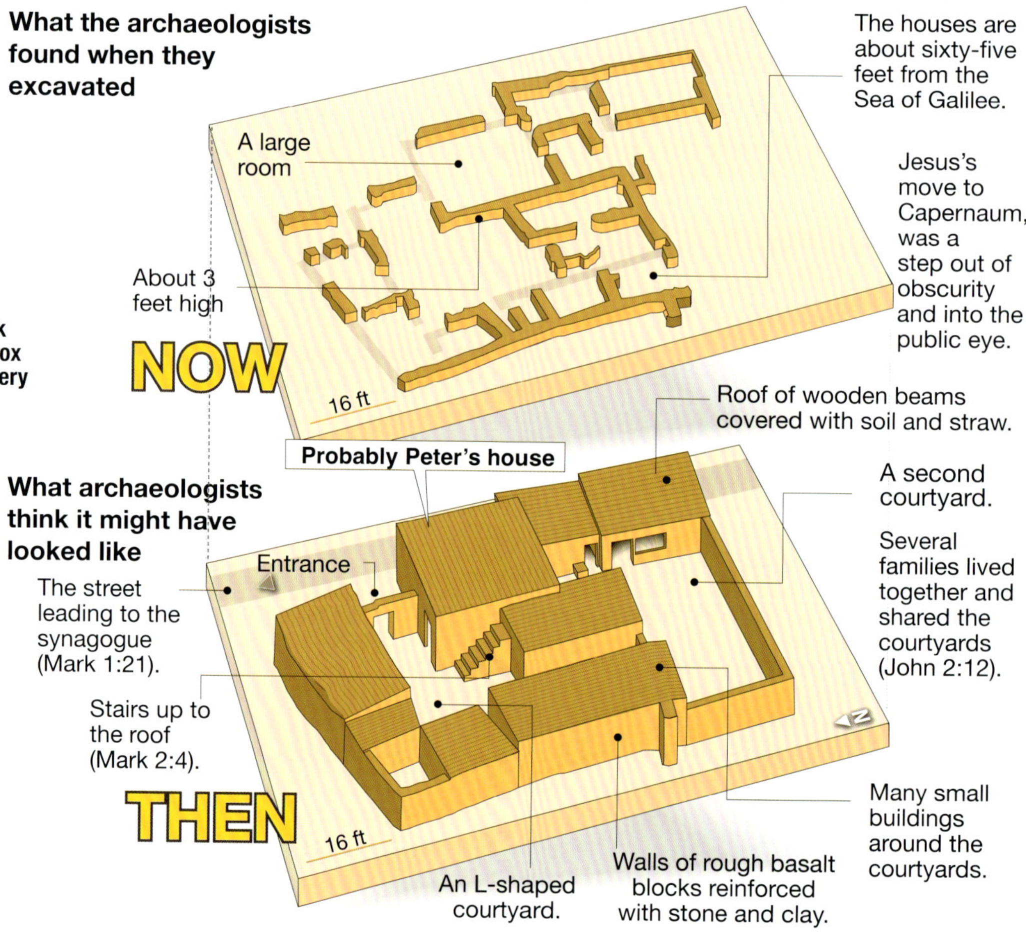

FACTS ABOUT CAPERNAUM
Name: Capernaum, means the city of Nahum.
Called today: Tell Hum
Population in Jesus's day: around 1,500
Location: About two miles from the mouth of the Jordan River

The Man Lowered Through the Roof

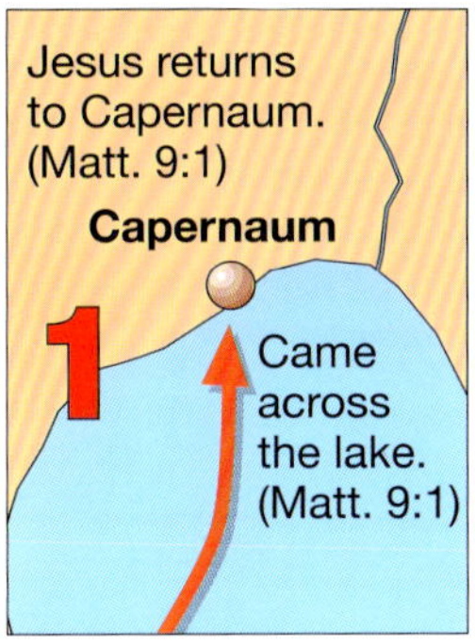

		Matt.	Mark	Luke
1	Jesus arrives in Capernaum	9:1	2:1–2	5:17
2	The paralyzed man is lowered through the roof	9:2	2:3–4	5:18–19
3	Jesus forgives the man's sins	9:2	2:5	5:20
4	The Pharisees react to Jesus's statement	9:3	2:6–7	5:21
5	Jesus responds to the Pharisees' thoughts	9:4–5	2:8–9	5:22–23
6	Jesus heals the paralyzed man	9:6–7	2:10–12	5:24–25
7	The people comment on what they have seen	9:8	2:12	5:26

2 Through the roof
Four friends lower a paralytic through the roof (Mk 2:4; Lk 5:18–19).

3 Expression of faith
Lowering the man down expresses the faith of the friends. Jesus forgives the man his sins (Mk 2:5; Lk 5:20).

4 Silent protest from the Pharisees
The Pharisees are silent, but think to themselves that Jesus cannot forgive sins, because only God can (Lk 5:21).

5 Jesus's penetrating question
Jesus knows their thoughts and asks which is easier, "to say 'Your sins are forgiven,' or 'Stand up and walk'?" (Lk 5:23).

6 The paralytic gets up and walks
Jesus heals the man. He immediately gets up, takes his mat, and goes home praising God (Lk 5:24–25).

7 The reaction of the crowd
The people praise God, at the same time they are amazed at what has happened and are filled with awe (Lk 5:26).

1 Four miracles in the text
The text mentions four miracles. Jesus 1) sees the faith of the man's friends, 2) forgives sins, 3) knows people's thoughts, and 4) heals a paralytic.

2 What is not said
The text never makes a connection between the man's sins and his illness. The sickness is never seen as a punishment from God (Jn 9:3).

3 What we need to know
The phrase "I will prove to you" (Lk 5:24) highlights the text's purpose: Jesus is the Son of Man—human and Son of God, inseparably united.

4 What is clearly stated
Jesus demonstrates that he has the authority to forgive sins and the power to heal the sick. The latter confirms the former (Lk 5:20–24).

5 The challenge of the text
Everything takes place in the tension between the faith of the friends and the doubts of the religious leadership. Which side do you choose?

Jesus's Preaching and Teaching Tours

The Gospels describe several preaching tours: first by Jesus, then with the disciples, and finally the disciples on their own (Luke 10:1).

1 The First Tour
Texts: Matt. 4:23–25; Mark 1:35–39; Luke 4:42–44
Where: In Galilee and Judea.
Events: Taught, proclaimed, healed, and cast out demons.
Result: Word spread, large crowds followed him.

2 The Second Tour
Text: Luke 8:1–3
Where: In towns and villages.
Participants: Jesus, the Twelve, and some women, Mary Magdalene, Joanna, Susanna, and many others.
Events: Preached the gospel.

3 The Third Tour
Texts: Matt. 9:35–11:1; Mark 6:6–13; Luke 9:1–6
Participants: Jesus sends out the disciples and goes himself (Matt. 11:1).
Where: Only to the lost sheep of Israel.

4 The Fourth Tour
Text: Luke 10:1–24
Where: Every town and place where Jesus would go.
Participants: Jesus sends out the seventy-two.
Events: "Even the demons obey us when we use your name!"

Jesus Debates the Sabbath

Should we keep the Sabbath? Jesus declares that he is "Lord, even over the Sabbath!" (Matt. 12:8). But what does that mean? How should a Christian relate to the commandment to keep the Sabbath (Ex 20:8)? There are four different ways believers have interpreted the command in the light of the New Testament.

	SATURDAY	SUNDAY	ANY DAY	EVERY DAY
When should the Sabbath be observed?	**Observed from Friday evening to Saturday evening**	**Observed on Sunday, preferably with a church service.**	**Observed with rest on any day during the week.**	**Through Christ, every day is a day of rest.**
What is the argument for the view?	Believes the requirement to keep the Sabbath is rooted in creation, so it applies to everyone, regardless of when they are living.	Believes the requirement to keep the Sabbath has been replaced with Sunday, the first day of the week, to remind us of Jesus's resurrection.	Believes the requirement to keep the Sabbath is no longer in effect, but that the idea of resting after work should still be applied.	Believes the requirement to keep the Sabbath was a shadow, the reality is salvation in Christ. He gives us true rest, so every day is a day of rest.
Key Bible passages	"And God blessed the **seventh day** and declared it holy, because it was the day when he rested from all his work of creation" (Gen. 2:3). "Remember to observe the **Sabbath day** by keeping it holy" (Ex. 20:8).	"Very early on **Sunday morning**, just at sunrise, they went to the tomb. ... You are looking for Jesus ... He is risen from the dead!" (Mark 16:2, 6). "On **the first day of the week,** we gathered ... to share in the Lord's Supper" (Acts 20:7).	"You would not have condemned my innocent disciples if you knew the meaning of this Scripture: 'I want you to show mercy, not offer sacrifices.' **For the Son of Man is Lord, even over the Sabbath!**" (Matt. 12:7–8).	"So don't let anyone condemn you for what you eat or drink, or for not celebrating ... Sabbaths. For these rules are only shadows of the reality yet to come. **And Christ himself is that reality**" (Col. 2:16–17).

" Many may be surprised to learn that connecting Sunday with the fourth commandment finds very little warrant in the early church, and that calling Sunday 'the Sabbath' is a relatively new phenomenon ... there are very few passages that might seem to claim that the Christian Lord's Day has taken the place of the Sabbath. (Justo Gonzalez)

Jesus in seven controversies over the understanding of the Sabbath

Jesus is confronted seven times about breaking the Sabbath.

1 The disciples pick grain
Texts: Mt 12:1–8; Mk 2:23–28; Lk 6:1–5
The disciples pick grain in the field and eat it. Jesus responds to the criticism with "The Son of Man is Lord, even over the Sabbath."

2 Jesus heals a man
Text: Jn 5:1–18
Jesus heals a man who cannot walk. The man is criticized for carrying his mat on the Sabbath and replies that the one who healed him said, "Pick up your mat and walk."

3 Jesus heals a man's hand
Texts: Mt 12:9–14; Mk 3:1–6; Lk 6:6–11
In the synagogue, Jesus heals a man's shriveled hand. He then says to his critics, "The law permits a person to do good on the Sabbath."

4 Compares to circumcision
Text: Jn 7:22–23
Jesus challenges the Jews by asking, "If the correct time for circumcising ... falls on the Sabbath, you ... do it. So why ... be angry with me for healing a man on the Sabbath?"

5 Jesus heals a blind man
Text: Jn 9:1–34
Jesus heals a man who was born blind. The religious leaders believe it is a violation of the Sabbath, so they call the man a sinner and drive him out of the synagogue.

6 Jesus heals a woman
Text: Lk 13:10–17
Jesus heals a woman crippled by a spirit, angering the leaders. He calls them hypocrites. If they care for animals on the Sabbath, why can't he free her on the Sabbath?

7 Jesus heals a sick man
Text: Lk 14:1–6
Jesus asks the religious leaders if healing is allowed on the Sabbath and they don't answer. So he heals a sick man, saying that in emergencies, people intervene on the Sabbath.

Seasons in the New Testament

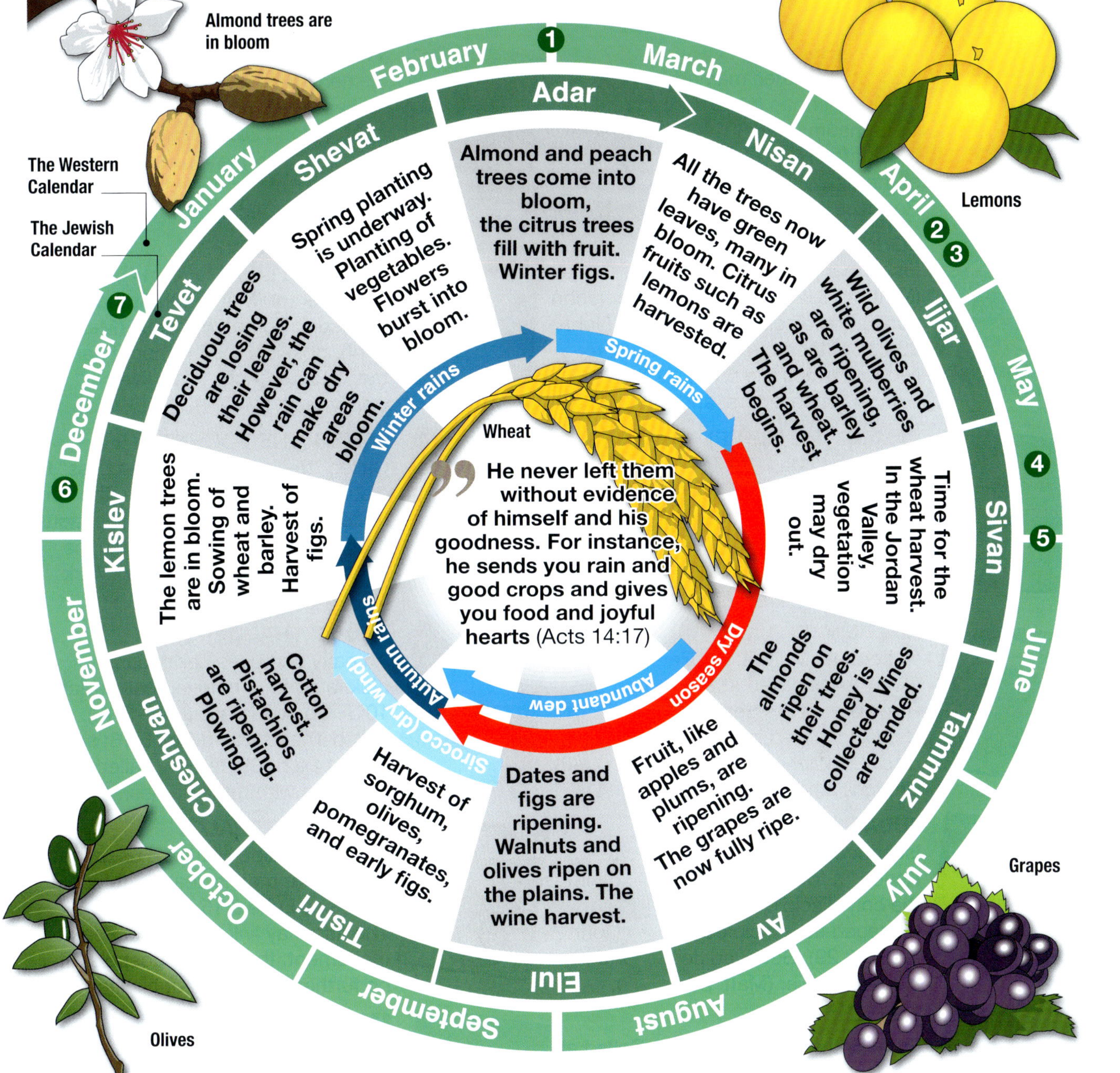

Texts that can be dated by the season

1. Text: "Have the people sit down in groups on the green grass" (Mark 6:39). **Date:** In spring (February—March) when the grass is green from the spring rains.

2. Text: "When the [fig tree] leaves come out, you know without being told that summer is near" (Luke 21:30). **Date:** In April when the trees leaf out and bud.

3. Text: "He cuts off every branch of mine that doesn't produce fruit, and he prunes the branches that do bear fruit so they will produce even more" (John 15:2). **Date:** At Passover when the grapes begin to appear.

4. Text: "His disciples were hungry, so they began breaking off some heads of grain and eating them" (Matt. 12:1). **Date:** Probably May when the wheat ripens for harvest.

5. Text: "So pray to the Lord who is in charge of the harvest; ask him to send more workers into his fields" (Luke 10:2; Matt. 9:37–38). **Date:** In May and June when the wheat is harvested.

6. Text: "It was now winter, and Jesus was in Jerusalem at the time of Hanukkah, the Festival of Dedication" (John 10:22). **Date:** In December, the 25th day of the month Kislev.

7. Text: "Four months between planting and harvest" (John 4:35). **Date:** In December and January when the harvest is four months away.

Fourteen New Testament Apostles

SIMON PETER

Andrew's brother, married (Matt. 8:14), fisherman (Mark 1:16), lived in Capernaum (Mark 1:21, 29). Called at the Jordan River (John 1:40), and again at the Sea of Galilee (Matt. 4:18–19). Received new mission (John 21:17–19).

JOHN

Fisherman, called at the Sea of Galilee (Matt. 4:18–22), James's brother (John 19:25), the disciple Jesus loved (John 13:23). Later moved to Ephesus, exiled to Patmos (Rev. 1:9). Author of a Gospel, three letters, and Revelation.

JAMES (THE ELDER)

Fisherman (Mark 3:17), called at the Sea of Galilee (Matt. 4:18–22), John's brother (Matt. 4:21), son of Zebedee (Mark 3:17) and Salome (Matt. 27:56; Mark 15:40). With his brother, called a Son of Thunder by Jesus (Mark 3:17).

ANDREW

Fisherman (Matt. 4:18), Peter's brother (John 1:41), called at the Jordan River, later at the Sea of Galilee. From Bethsaida, lived in Capernaum, disciple of John the Baptist (John 1:40). Brought others to Jesus (John 1:41).

JUDAS ISCARIOT

Iscariot could mean "a man from Keriot," a town in Judea, making him the only disciple not from Galilee. Managed the disciples' money (John 12:6; 13:29). Betrayed Jesus for thirty pieces of silver (Matt. 26:14–16).

PHILIP

From Bethsaida (John 1:44). Called at Bethany when Jesus left for Galilee (John 1:28, 43). Brought Nathanael to Jesus (John 1:45–46). Present at the feeding of the 5,000 (John 6:5–7). All the details about him are in John.

NATHANAEL (BARTHOLOMEW)

Also called Bartholomew (Matt. 10:3; John 1:45). Brought to Jesus by Philip and always listed with him (Luke 6:14; John 1:43). From Cana in Galilee (John 21:2). Saw Jesus at the Sea of Galilee after the resurrection (John 21:2).

THOMAS

Remembered as "Doubting Thomas" as he doubted Jesus's resurrection at first (John 20:25). Nicknamed "the Twin," was willing to die with Jesus (John 11:16). Among those who went fishing after resurrection (John 21:2).

MATTHEW (LEVI)

Also called Levi (Mark 2:14), was a tax collector (Matt. 9:9). Author of a Gospel. Son of Alphaeus (Mark 2:14), possibly the brother of James the Younger (Acts 1:13), lived in Capernaum (Matt. 9:1, 9).

JAMES (THE YOUNGER)

Called "the Younger" or "the Less" to distinguish him from James, the son of Zebedee (Mark 15:40). If Alphaeus and Clopas are the same man, he could be Matthew's brother (Mark 2:14; John 19:25).

JUDAS (THADDEUS)

An early text uses Lebbaeus, a nickname for a beloved child (Matt. 10:3). Son of James (Luke 6:16). Also called Thaddaeus (Mark 3:18; see John 14:22). St. Jerome called him "the man with three names."

SIMON THE ZEALOT

Called a Zealot, Matthew uses the a form that means zealous (Matt. 10:4; see Luke 6:15; Acts 1:13). The title may link him to the Zealot movement, though the gospels offer no further details about his life.

MATTHIAS

Chosen to replace Judas Iscariot (Acts 1:26). Described as one who had been with the disciples the entire time they traveled with Jesus (Acts 1:21) and witnessed Jesus's resurrection (Acts 1:22).

PAUL (SAUL)

Born in Tarsus (Acts 9:11), he was a Pharisee and tentmaker (Acts 18:3; 23:6). Met Jesus on the road to Damascus (Acts 9:4–7; 22:6). Roman citizen and eager missionary. Wrote thirteen letters in the New Testament.

Jesus and His Disciples

Early in the gospels, Jesus had many followers and disciples. But toward the end, most of them seem to have disappeared.

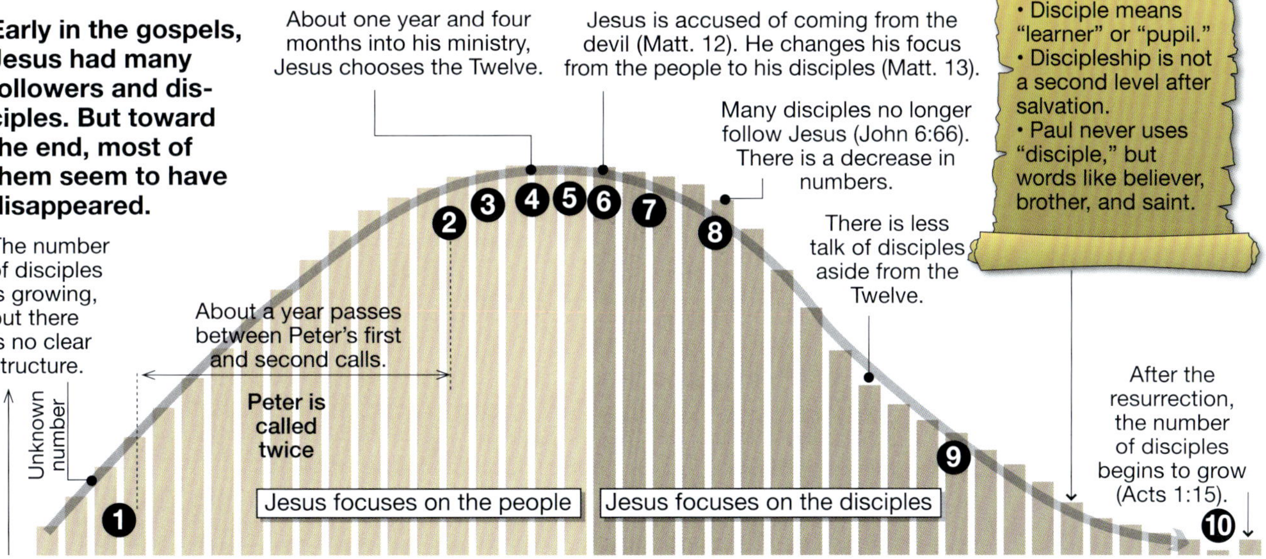

What is a disciple?

- Disciple means "learner" or "pupil."
- Discipleship is not a second level after salvation.
- Paul never uses "disciple," but words like believer, brother, and saint.

Chronological Overview of Jesus's Ministry

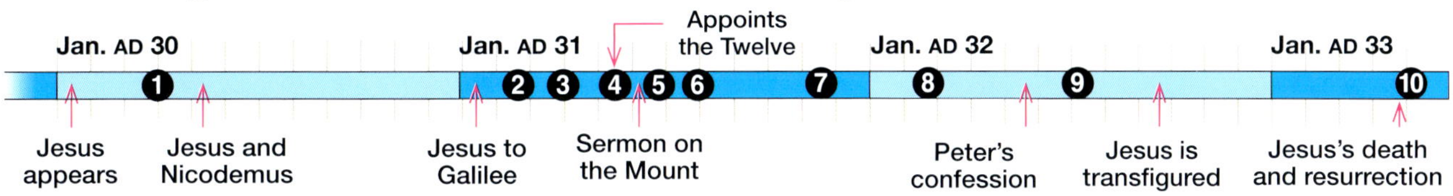

Peter, the Three, the Twelve, the Seventy, and Followers

Although we often speak of the Twelve, there was a larger group of somewhat loosely organized disciples around Jesus. Here is one way of representing this larger group.

Large crowds came out to listen to Jesus out of curiosity, but not all became his followers (Luke 5:1).

Followers
Those who believed and followed Jesus.

Seventy*
Jesus appoints 70 "others" whom he sends out two by two (Luke 10:1–20).
• Possibly **Joseph Barsabbas**, **Matthias** (Acts 1:23), **Nicanor** and **Nicholas** (Acts 6:5).

Twelve—Jesus chooses twelve who are given a special status. He calls them apostles (Mark 3:14). Among them are:
• **Judas**, managed the money (John 12:6) and **Andrew**, link between the disciples (John 12:21–22).

Three—There was also an inner group of three disciples, **Peter, James,** and **John**. They were with Jesus at the transfiguration and other events (Matt. 17:1–13; 26:37; Mark 5:37).

Peter He has a leading role and often acts on behalf of all the disciples (Matt. 16:16). He clearly states the disciples' confession and perseveres the longest before failing (Matt. 26:74). After the resurrection, Jesus commissions him to "take care of my sheep" (John 21:16) and he emerges on the day of Pentecost as the church's leader (Acts 2:14).

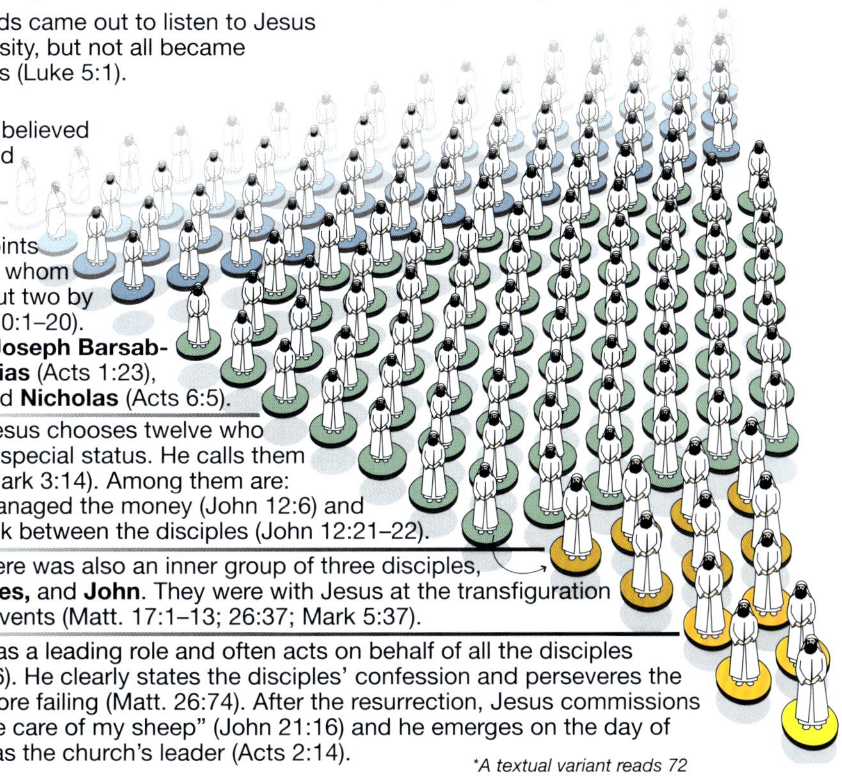

*A textual variant reads 72

The growth and decline of Jesus's followers

❶Jesus calls some to follow him, including Peter (Jn 1:35–51). Some followers have no recorded calling.
❷Jesus specifically calls four to follow him. Calls Peter a second time (Mt 4:18–22).
❸Jesus calls more disciples, including Levi (Mt 9:9–13), and the crowds also follow him (Lk 6:1).
❹Jesus chooses twelve men from among all the disciples (Lk 6:13).
❺Jesus sends out the Twelve (Mt 10:1–11:1).
❻Jesus shifts focus from the crowds to the disciples (Mt 13:10–13).
❼Jesus chooses from the Twelve an inner circle of three disciples (Mt 17:1; Mk 5:37; Lk 8:51).
❽Many disciples begin to leave him (Jn 6:60–71).
❾Jesus chooses a wider circle of 70 (72) disciples and sends them out (Lk 10:1, 17).
❿Judas betrays Jesus (Mt 26:49), nine disciples fail him (Mt 26:56), eventually including Peter (Mt 26:73).

Interpreting the Sermon on the Mount

There is a lively debate about how to interpret and understand the Sermon on the Mount (Matt. 5–7). Several issues need to be considered when coming to a conclusion.

1 Who was Jesus's audience? The disciples (believers, 5:1) or the people (who did not yet believe, 8:1)?

2 What is the purpose of the sermon? Evangelization, disciple-making, a goal to strive for, a goal we can reach?

3 Does Jesus reinterpret the law? Does Jesus fulfill the law (5:17) or abolish it (5:21–22; Rom. 7:4)?

4 What about historical distance? Jesus speaks of being brought before the altar (5:22–23). Does it apply to us?

5 Why nothing about the Spirit? Can it be about the Christian life, since nothing is said about the Holy Spirit?

6 Why nothing about salvation? Can it be aimed at Christians, since nothing is said about salvation?

7 Why nothing about the church? Why doesn't Jesus mention the church? Isn't it central to the Christian life?

An Interpretive Guide to the Sermon on the Mount

This guide can help you determine your own understanding of the Sermon on the Mount. (Chart inspired by James Leake.)

START HERE: What do you think about the Sermon on the Mount?

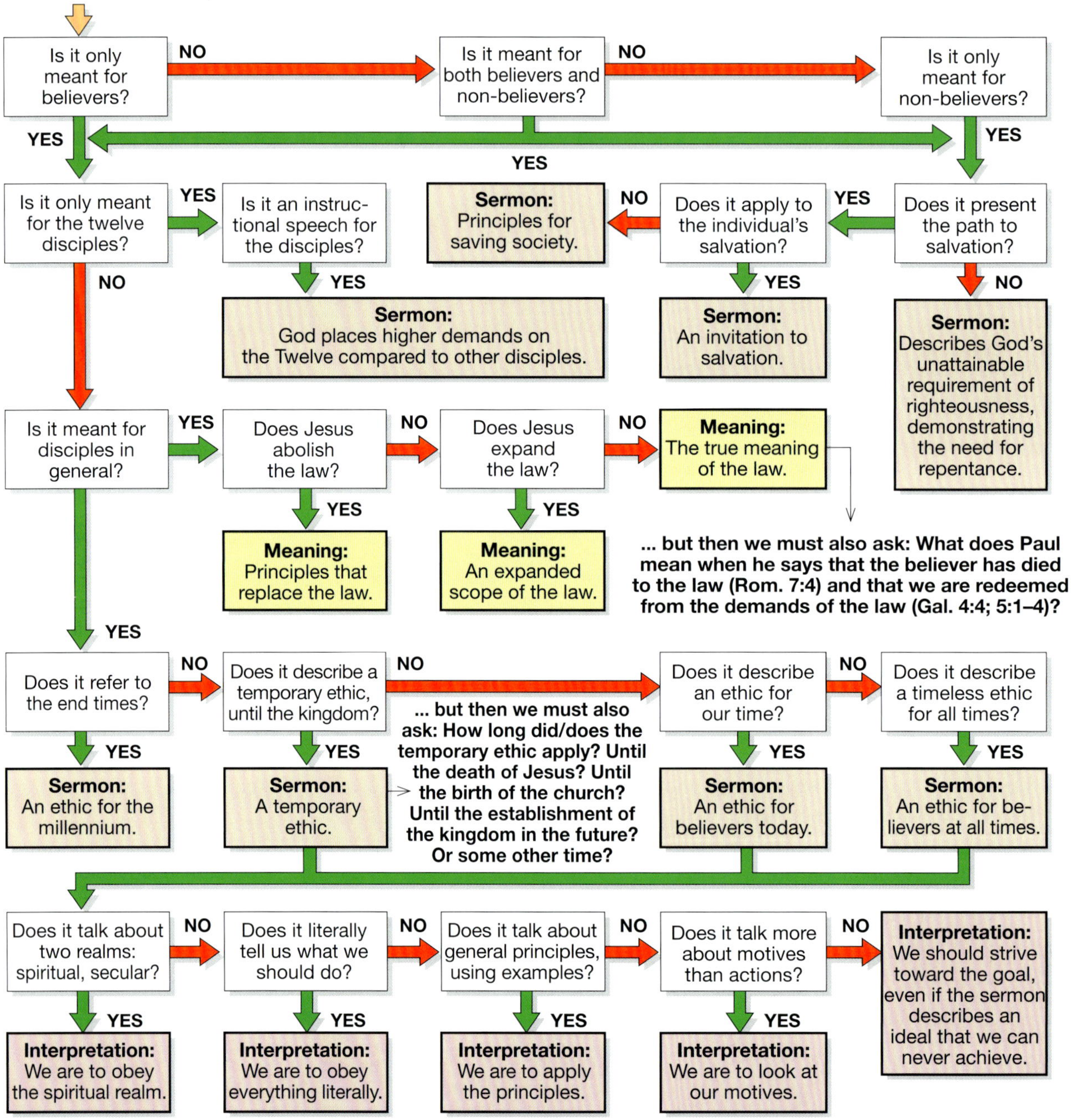

The Sermons on the Mountain and the Plain

Matthew's Sermon on the Mount and Luke's Sermon on the Plain are similar, but also different. Are they the same sermon or did Jesus use his material more than once?

TO CONSIDER WHEN COMPARING THE SERMONS

1 Is it one sermon or two different sermons?
Some believe that it is the same sermon with Luke summarizing Matthew. Others believe they were two different sermons and Jesus uses the same material twice. The question of how to interpret "mountainside" (Matt. 5:1) and "level area" (Luke 6:17) becomes crucial.

2 Note differences in the arrangement.
This applies to both selections and order. Notice what is unique in each sermon and how the placement of the material differs between them. Some of the material in one sermon appears in a different context in the other sermon.

3 Who is the intended audience of the gospel?
Matthew primarily writes for a Jewish audience while Luke's audience is mainly Roman. The parts that Luke includes have a more general, timeless message.

> "Most people are willing to take the Sermon on the Mount as a flag to sail under, but few will use it as a rudder by which to steer. (Oliver Wendell Holmes Jr.)

*Wording varies and verses aren't identical.

Sermon on the Mount (Matt. 5:3–7:27) / Sermon on the Plain (Luke 6:20–49)

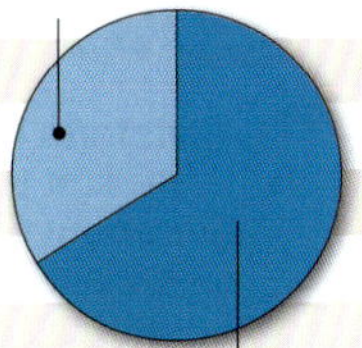

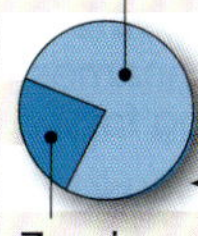

Sermon on the Mount	Elsewhere in Matthew		Sermon on the Plain	Elsewhere in Luke
(4:23–25)		Audience	(6:17–19)	
(5:1–2)		Introduction	(6:20a)	
5:3–4, 6, 10-11		Beatitudes (1)	6:20b–22	
5:5, 7–9		Beatitudes (2)		
5:12		Reward in heaven	6:23	
5:13		Salt of the earth		14:34–35
5:14		Light of the world		11:33
5:15–17		Fulfillment of the law		
5:18		The smallest detail		16:17
5:19–24		Do not get angry		
5:25–26		Settle your differences		12:57–59
5:27–30		About adultery		
5:31–32		About divorce		16:18
5:33–37		About making vows		
		Four sorrows	6:24–26	
5:43–44		Love your enemies	6:27–28	
5:38–42		Turn the other cheek	6:29–30	
7:12		Golden Rule	6:31	
5:46–47		Go above and beyond	6:32–34	
5:48		To be perfect		
5:45		Children of Most High	6:35	
		Be compassionate	6:36	
6:1–2		Not like the hypocrites		
7:1		Do not judge	6:37a	
6:14–15		Forgive each other	6:37b	
6:3–4		About giving	6:38a	
7:2		Judged by own standard	6:38b	
6:5–8		Don't pray as hypocrites		
	15:14	Blind leading the blind	6:39	
	10:24–25	Teacher and disciple	6:40	
6:9–13		The Lord's Prayer		11:2–4
6:16–18		Right fasting		
6:19–21		Treasures in heaven		12:33–34
6:22–23		The lamp of the body		11:34–36
6:24		Can't serve two masters		16:13
6:25–34		Seek first the kingdom		12:22–34
7:3–5		Speck in the eye	6:41–42	
7:6		Pearls before pigs		
7:7–11		Ask and will receive		11:9–13
7:13–14		The narrow gate		13:23–24
7:15		About false prophets		
7:16–20		Recognized by fruit	6:44–44	
	12:35	Good comes from heart	6:45	
7:21		"Lord! Lord!"	6:46	
7:22–23		Never known you		13:23–24
7:24–27		Foundation on the rock	6:47–49	
(7:28–29)		Closing	(7:1)	

Verses in red are unique to Matthew

Verses in blue can be found elsewhere in Matthew

Verses in red are unique to Luke

Verses in blue can be found elsewhere in Luke

The Prayer Jesus Taught

The Lord's Prayer is the prayer that Jesus taught his disciples. Many believe that it is not a prayer to be recited word for word, but a model prayer that provides a pattern, helping us form our own prayers to God.

"Our Father in heaven, may your name be kept holy.

1 Who the prayer is addressed to
In the Old Testament, people rarely call God "Father."

2 Reminds us who God is
God is Spirit and has all power.

3 Both praise and a call to give to God the honor he is due
To sanctify God's name is to revere and respect God for who he really is.

May your Kingdom come soon.

4 Asking for the messianic kingdom to come soon
Emphasizes the nearness of God's kingdom and that believers long for it and prepare for its coming.

Divisions in the prayer:
- The first three phrases are about God [your].
- The last three phrases are about us [we, us].

May your will be done on earth, as it is in heaven.

5 What we long to have happen as we anticipate the coming kingdom
God's will expresses his righteousness and justice, and his wise plan.

6 Asking that what happens in heaven will happen on earth
God's will reigns in heaven, and we ask that it will also reign on earth.

Give us today the food we need,

7 The focus shifts from God to our needs
"Today" refers to what we need now.

8 We ask for daily food so that we can survive
God cares even about our most basic physical needs.

Note:
- **1382:** First version in English (Wycliffe)
- **1611:** "Trespasses" becomes "debts" (KJV), later "sins" (NLT)
- **1978:** "from evil" becomes "from the evil one" (NIV)
- **1989** "Temptation" becomes "trial" (NRSV)
- **1996:** "You" and "your" used for God (NLT)

and forgive us our sins,

Note: "And" links the last three phrases.

9 Talks about our need to have God forgive our sins
Forgiveness involves two elements: confession and repentance. God forgives (1 John 1:9).

as we have forgiven those who sin against us.

10 "As" is a comparison
It connects the two phrases.

11 Describes the scope of what the verse is talking about
Some translations use "debt." When we see the extent to which God forgives us, the sins of others become insignificant (Matt. 6:15; 18:35).

And don't let us yield to temptation,

12 A request for God to direct our daily lives
Talks about God's guidance and protection in our lives.

13 Protect us from life's trials
Temptation does not only mean temptation to sin, but also trial, testing.

but rescue us from the evil one. (Matt. 6:9–13)

14 Gives a contrast
Instead of temptation.

15 Describes the scope of the verse
Here, rescue means save, protect, lead us away from.

16 Suggests that temptations may come from the evil one
Probably refers to "the evil one" but can also be translated "evil."

"For yours is the kingdom and the power and the glory, forever. Amen." is not in modern translations. The addition is based on 1 Chronicles 29:11 and is only found in later manuscripts.

The Day Jesus Did Not Heal Everyone

1 Jesus asks one man
There were many sick, blind, and crippled people at the pool of Bethesda. Jesus asks **one** man if he wants to get well (John 5:1–6).

2 The man answers
The man says he has no one to help him (John 5:7). The belief was that the first one in the water after it moved was healed.

3 Jesus heals the man
Jesus says "Stand up!" The man starts walking (John 5:8). And Jesus leaves all the other sick people at the pool.

4 The man is questioned
Jewish leaders confront him on the Sabbath. He refers to "the man who healed me," but doesn't know who it was (John 5:9–13).

5 Who is this Jesus?
Jesus meets the man and tells him to "stop sinning" (John 5:14–15). He then tells the leaders that it was Jesus who healed him.

6 They plot to kill Jesus
Jewish leaders plan to kill Jesus because of his claim to be God: "My Father is always working, and so am I" (John 5:17).

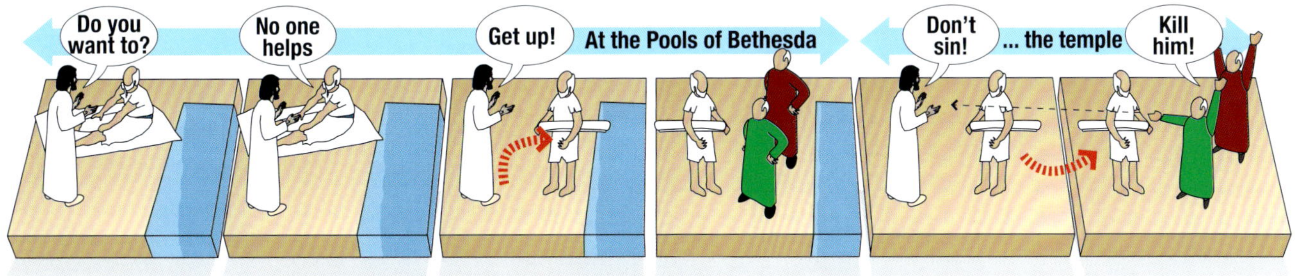

1 Jesus did not heal everyone
There were "crowds of sick people ... blind, lame, or paralyzed" present (John 5:3). Jesus heals only one man and leaves the rest. Jesus did not heal all the sick he met.

2 Text that does not belong here
Verses 5:3b–4 are missing in the oldest manuscripts. These verses mention an angel who would make the waters move. It is not considered part of the original text.

3 Which feast is referred to?
Jesus comes to Jerusalem for a feast (John 5:1). Which one? Probably one of the three pilgrim feasts, possibly Passover. Or maybe the Feast of Purim. We don't know.

4 Man healed without faith
Notice that the lame man does not know who Jesus is, seek him out, or express any kind of faith in him. One could say that the lame man was healed involuntarily.

5 Intended to provoke
Jesus healed the lame man in order to provoke the religious leaders into a discussion about his divinity, using a discussion about healing on the Sabbath.

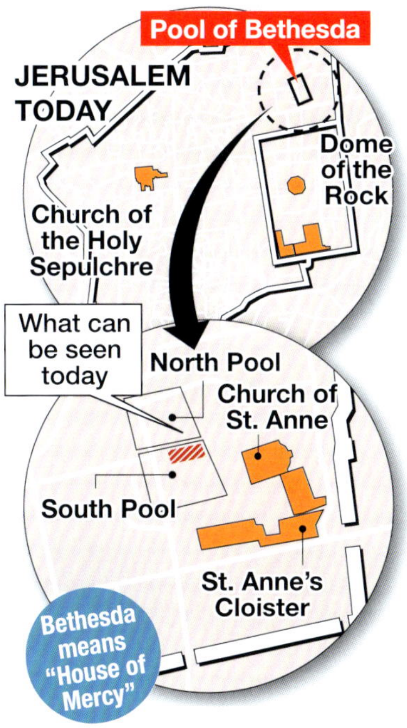

How the Pool of Bethesda might have looked

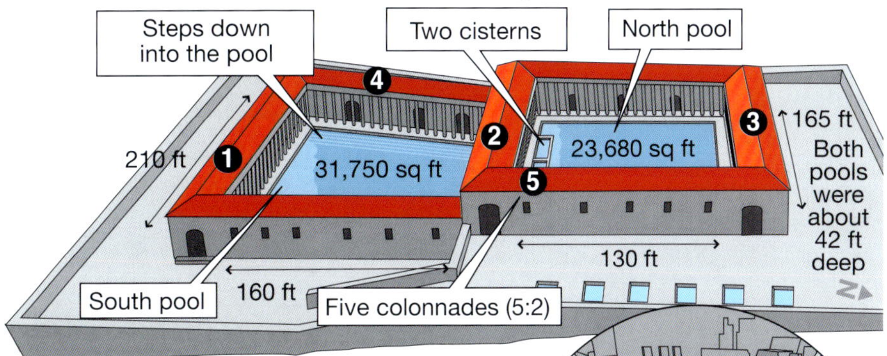

1 Is it a sheep gate or a sheep pool?
It is uncertain whether it should be translated "sheep gate" (John 5:2) or "sheep pool." Both are possibilities but "gate" is preferable (see Neh. 3:1, 32).

2 How did the water move?
It is possible that there was an underground spring that moved the water. The idea that an angel stirred the water was probably a superstition.

Jesus Heals a Centurion's Servant

1 Jesus comes to Capernaum
When Jesus arrives in Capernaum, a centurion who has a servant near death hears about it (Luke 7:1–2).

2 The centurion sends elders
First, the centurion sends some Jewish elders who plead on his behalf for the servant (Luke 7:3–6).

3 The centurion sends friends
Then the centurion sends his friends to ask Jesus to heal the servant from a distance (Luke 7:6–8).

4 The centurion goes himself
Then the centurion speaks directly to Jesus, and he declares his faith. Jesus heals from afar (Matt. 8:5–13).

5 The servant is healed
When the friends return, they find the servant fully healed (Matt. 8:13; Luke 7:9–10).

1 Understanding the faith
The centurion's words indicate that he put his faith in the authority that Jesus had. It was this belief in Jesus that showed him the possibility of healing.

2 A healing without faith
The story makes it clear that healing is not dependent on the faith of the sick person. The faith of the servant is never mentioned.

3 A healing without touch
The story also shows that the laying on of hands, special rituals, or even physical presence are not required for God's healing to take place.

Did the centurion talk to Jesus?
1) No, he did not talk to Jesus
Since what was said to Jesus came from the centurion, it is presented as if he said it. One possibility.
2) Yes, he did talk to Jesus
The centurion himself went to meet Jesus and plead for his servant—a second possibility.

The woman who anointed Jesus's feet

1 The needy were allowed at parties
Those in need were allowed to be present at meals like this, as well as when rabbis visited town (Luke 7:36–37).

2 She began to wet his feet with her tears ...
Jesus is at the table and the woman kneels behind him. As she weeps, her tears fall on his feet (Luke 7:38).

3 ... and dried them with her hair ...
Letting one's hair down could be seen as provocative. But here it is a sign of her humility (Luke 7:38).

4 ... and she kissed his feet ...
Kissing someone's feet was a sign of affection, respect, and submission (Luke 7:38).

5 ... and anointed them with perfume.
She poured expensive perfume from an alabaster bottle over Jesus's feet (Luke 7:38). The fragrance spread throughout the room (John 12:3), a sign of great financial and personal sacrifice. In this single gesture, she declared that Jesus's worth was above all earthly treasures.

• **Other texts where women anoint Jesus.** All happen in Bethany (Matt. 26:6–13; Mark 14:3–9; John 12:1–8).

CONCLUSION: The woman did what the host, Simon the Pharisee, ought to have done. His attitude should have been the same as hers. That is the point of the story (Luke 7:44–48).

1 The very expensive perfume (Mark 14:3; John 12:3). Pure nard is a fragrant oil with an earthy and spicy scent. It was imported from the slopes of the Himalayas. The perfume cost an entire year's wages.

2 The tear bottle (Luke 7:38). Can you cry enough to make someone's feet wet? The idea of tear bottles is a fairly recent and popular phenomenon. There is no historical evidence for them.

When Jesus Calms the Storm

(Matt. 8:18, 23–27; Mark 4:35–41; Luke 8:22–25)

The discovery of a unique fishing boat

- In 1986, northern Israel was hit by a severe drought.
- When the Sea of Galilee water level dropped, a fishing boat was revealed in the mud on the shore.
- The boat has been dated to the first century, around the time of Jesus.
- It is estimated that the boat could have carried a maximum of fifteen people.
- The boat had a mast for sails and space for oars and a steering oar.

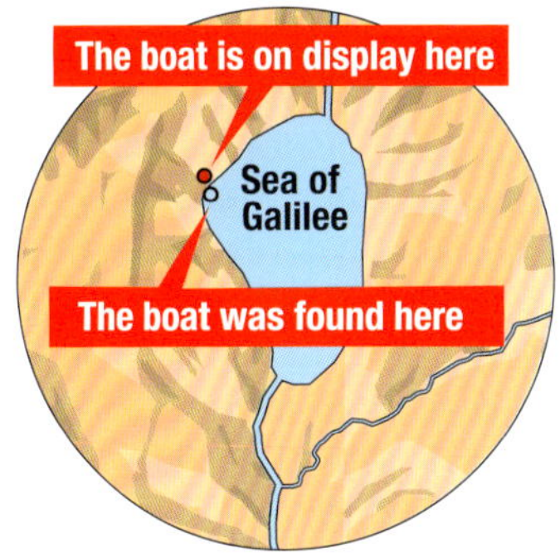

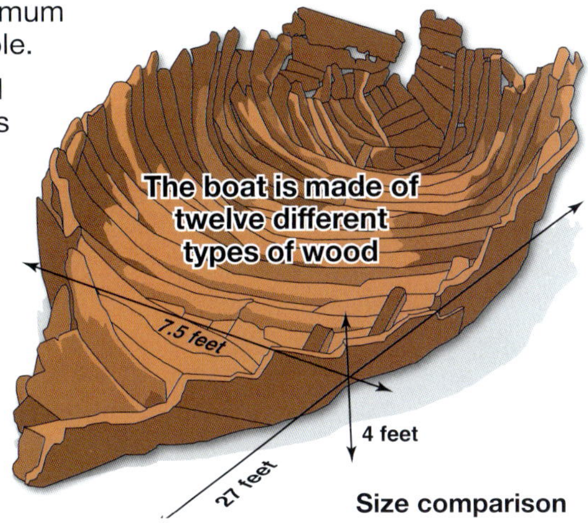

1 Power over creation

That Jesus, as true God, can command the storm to subside points to his divinity. He is the Lord of creation (Ps. 107:25; 135:7; Col. 1:15–17).

2 That time Jesus slept

This is the only text that describes Jesus sleeping. It points to his humanity (Ps. 121:4). In his humanity, he needed to sleep.

3 Disciples are challenged

The disciples were afraid that they would drown. But Jesus says: "Do you still have no faith?" They had not yet fully understood who he was.

Size comparison

The Jesus Boat: 27 ft

Ford F-150: 18 ft

How storms form on the Sea of Galilee

The Sea of Galilee is the lowest freshwater lake in the world, lying in a natural basin that is about 700 feet below sea level.

1 The sun warms the air

The sun heats the air over the lake, which causes the warm air to rise. This rising air creates a low pressure system that sits over the lake.

2 The wind from south

This low pressure attracts air masses from different directions, depending on where the wind is coming from. When the wind comes from the south, the storms are usually less intense, but coming over the desert, they bring drier air and fine dust with them.

Three characteristics of the storms:

- They arise suddenly
- They are unpredictable
- They are violent

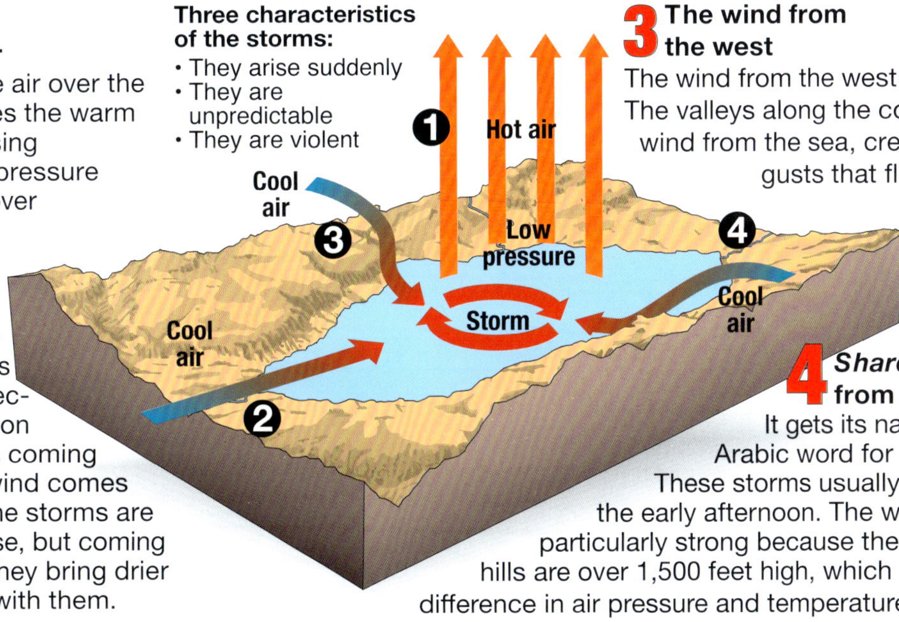

3 The wind from the west

The wind from the west rises suddenly. The valleys along the coast collect the wind from the sea, creating powerful gusts that flow down and turn the lake into a foaming cauldron.

4 *Sharqia*—the wind from the east

It gets its name from the Arabic word for east, *sharq*. These storms usually begin in the early afternoon. The wind can be particularly strong because the surrounding hills are over 1,500 feet high, which creates a big difference in air pressure and temperature conditions.

Revenge on the Dance Floor

Machaerus, a Roman fortress on the eastern shore of the Dead Sea, is not mentioned in the Bible. However, extrabiblical sources claim that it was the site of John the Baptist's execution by Herod Antipas.

1 Herod condemned
John the Baptist condemned Herod Antipas for marrying Herodias, his brother's wife. Herodias hated John and looked for opportunities to have him killed (Matt. 14:3–5; Mark 6:17–20).

2 Salome's dance
During Herod's banquet, Salome, Herodias's daughter, pleased him with her dance. He publicly swore to give her anything she asked for, up to half his kingdom (Matt. 14:6–7; Mark 6:21–23).

3 Herodias's revenge
Salome sought her mother's advice about what she should request. Herodias urged her to demand the head of John the Baptist on a platter, which she did (Matt. 14:8; Mark 6:24–25).

4 John's execution
Because of his public vow, Herod reluctantly agreed. John was beheaded in prison and his head was brought to Salome on a platter, who gave it to Herodias (Matt. 14:9–11; Mark 6:26–28).

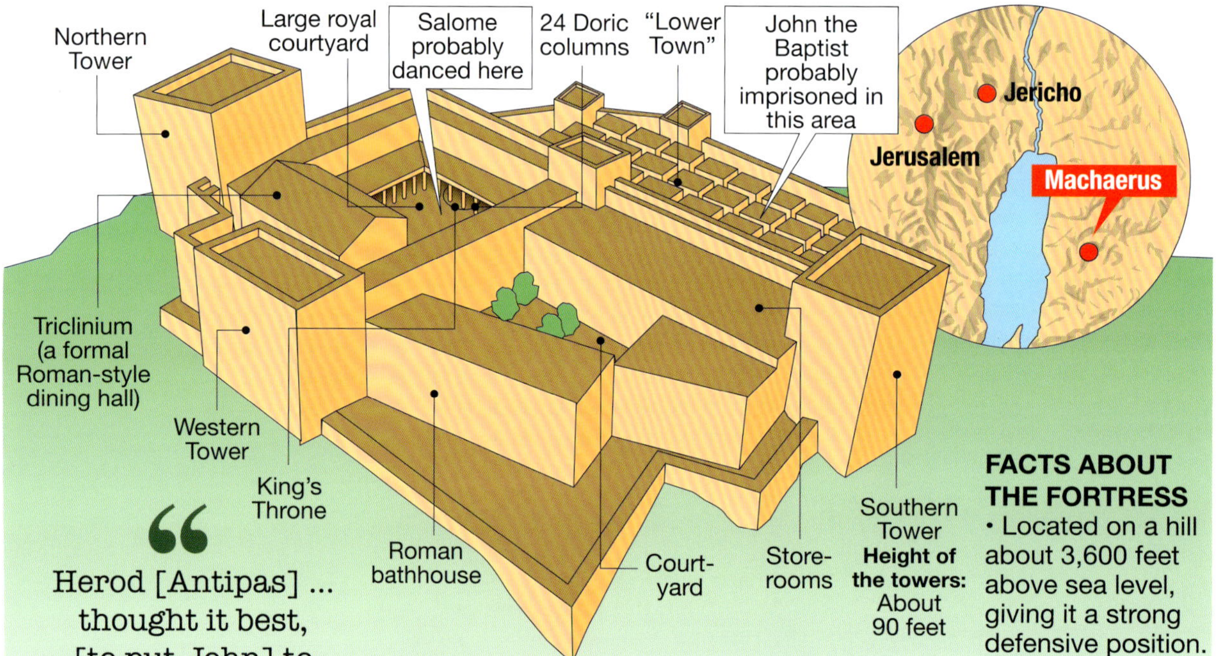

"Herod [Antipas] ... thought it best, [to put John] to death... Accordingly he was sent a prisoner, out of Herod's suspicious temper, to Macherus,... and was there put to death." (Josephus)

Facts about beheading

- A common method of execution for Roman citizens sentenced to death for crimes such as treason, rebellion, or military offenses.
- It was seen as a quick and relatively dignified form of execution as compared to crucifixion or burning, which were reserved for slaves and non-citizens (which did not apply to John).

FACTS ABOUT THE FORTRESS

- Located on a hill about 3,600 feet above sea level, giving it a strong defensive position.
- The steep cliffs and elevated position made it strategic, allowing rulers to monitor both external and internal threats.
- **Perimeter wall:** 330 ft long by 200 ft wide

THE HISTORY OF MACHAERUS

- **About 90 BC:** Built by the Hasmonean king Alexander Janneaus
- **57 BC:** Destroyed by Roman general Gabinius
- **30 BC:** Rebuilt by Herod the Great as a military base
- **4 BC:** The fortress passed to Herod Antipas.
- **About AD 31–32:** John the Baptist was imprisoned and beheaded in the fortress.
- **AD 72:** Conquered by Romans during the first Jewish-Roman War, leading to its destruction

Jerry Vardaman

- **1807:** The German explorer Ulrich Seetzen rediscovered the fortress of Machaerus
- **1968–1969:** Archaeologist Jerry Vardaman led the first modern excavation at the site. Further excavations were carried out by others and the work is ongoing.

When Jesus Was Stopped in His Tracks

1 Jesus goes to raise a girl
Jairus asks Jesus to raise his daughter who just died. Jesus follows (Mt 9:18–19; Mk 5:21–43; Lk 8:40–56).

2 A woman touches him
In the crowd, a woman touches Jesus's robe and is healed. Jesus, aware he was touched, stops (Matt. 9:20–21).

3 Jesus talks about faith
Jesus speaks to the woman about her faith, and confirms that her faith is what healed her (Matt. 9:22).

4 "The girl isn't dead"
Jesus arrives at the house and tells the mourners to go, saying that the girl is "asleep" (Matt. 9:23–24).

5 Jesus raises the girl
Jesus takes the girl by her hand, bringing her back to life (Matt. 9:25).

6 People are amazed
"News of this spread through all that region" (Matt. 9:26).

1 The issue of God's time
Jairus must have seen the incident with the sick woman as a frustrating delay. But for Jesus, time was not a problem. God is never in a hurry.

2 The issue of the power of God
Touching Jesus's cloak produced no magical effect. In the end, it was not the woman who touched Jesus, it was Jesus who touched her.

3 The issue of the woman's faith
The woman's faith was in the healer. Jesus calls her daughter and tells her to "Go in peace" (Mark 5:34). Peace is more than freedom from illness.

4 The issue of power over death
Jesus was not troubled that the girl was dead (Mark 5:35–36). For Jesus there is no difference, to resurrect is no more difficult than healing.

Other people who were raised

All of these people were raised to the same life they had before their death.

ELIJAH RAISES A WIDOW'S SON
Text: 1 Kings 17:17–24
While staying at a widow's house, her son gets sick and dies. Elijah prays to the Lord, who restores the boy to life.

ELISHA RAISES A SHUNNAMITE'S SON
Text: 2 Kings 4:18–37
The woman's boy dies and she goes to find Elisha. He comes and lays on the boy, who then opens his eyes.

AFTER TOUCHING BONES A DEAD MAN IS RAISED
Text: 2 Kings 13:20–21
A dead man is thrown into Elisha's tomb. When his body touches Elisha's bones, he comes back to life.

JESUS RAISES A WIDOW'S SON
Text: Luke 7:11–17
Jesus sees a widow in Nain burying her only son. He touches his body and raises him back to life.

JESUS RAISES LAZARUS TO LIFE
Text: John 11:1–44
Event: Lazarus had been dead four days. At the tomb, Jesus calls his name and he comes out alive.

THE DEAD ARE RAISED AT JESUS'S RESURRECTION
Text: Matt. 27:51–53
When Jesus dies on the cross, many graves are opened and those in them are resurrected.

PETER RAISES TABITHA FROM THE DEAD
Text: Acts 9:36–42
A believer in Joppa dies. Peter comes and prays for her, saying, "Get up, Tabitha." Her life is restored.

PAUL RAISES A MAN WHO FELL OUT A WINDOW
Text: Acts 20:7–12
Eutychus sits in the window on the third floor, falls out, and dies. Paul prays and he comes back to life.

Herod the Great's Family Tree

This family tree shows the relationships between Herod's descendants mentioned in the New Testament.

Herod the Great married ten women: (1) Doris, (2) Mariamne I, (3) Mariamne II, (4) Malthace, (5) Cleopatra of Jerusalem, (6–10) Pallas, Phaidra, and Elpis and two whose names we don't know.

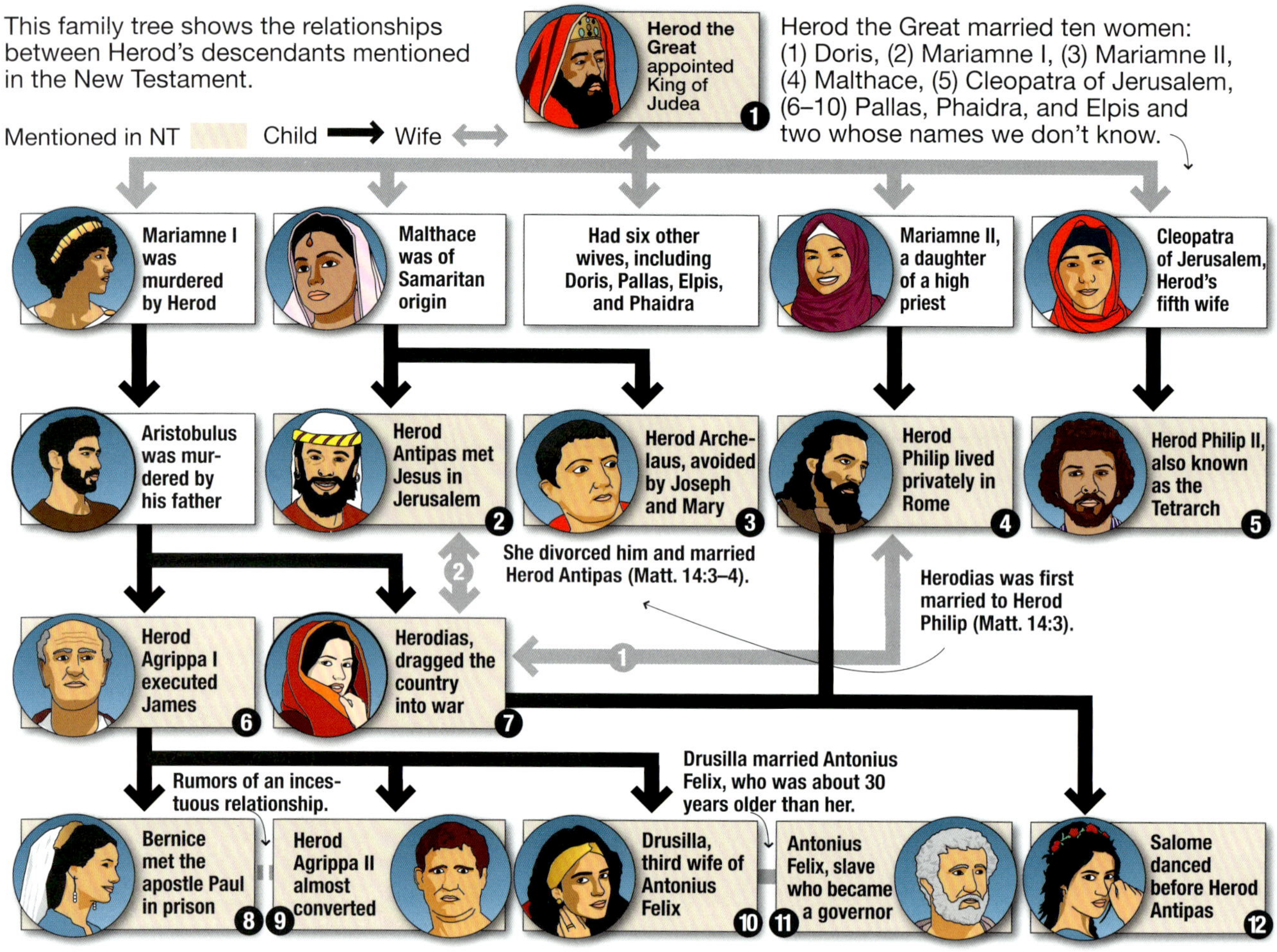

All the Bible References to Herod and His Family

1 **Herod the Great:** From Idumea (Edom), king of Judea 37–4 BC. Built the temple in Jerusalem, met the wise men, ordered the killing of baby boys in Bethlehem (Matt. 2:1–19, 22; Luke 1:5).

2 **Herod Antipas:** Prince of Galilee, ruled in Perea 4 BC–AD 39. Killed John the Baptist, met Jesus in Jerusalem (Matt. 14:1–12; Mark 6:14–29; 8:15; Luke 3:1, 19–20; 8:3; 9:6–9; 13:31; 23:7–15; Acts 4:27; 13:1).

3 **Herod Archelaus:** Herod the Great's successor and a cruel ruler. Jesus may be alluding to him in the parable of the ten talents (Matt. 2:22; Luke 19:11–27). Deposed in AD 6.

4 **Herod Philip:** Disinherited by Herod the Great. Lived privately in Rome. Married Herodias, who left him for Herod Antipas. Was the father of Salome (Matt. 14:3; Mark 6:17; Luke 3:19).

5 **Herod Philip II:** Ruled from 4 BC to AD 34. Married a woman named Salome, either Herodias's daughter or possibly a half-sister with same name, the daughter of Herod's wife Elpis (Luke 3:1).

6 **Herod Agrippa I:** Deposed Herod Antipas and ruled Galilee from AD 39 and Judea from AD 41. Was a devout Jew. Executed James and imprisoned Peter. Died in AD 44 (Acts 12:1–22).

7 **Herodias:** Married to Herod Philip and was the mother of Salome. Left Philip to live with Herod Antipas and was behind the death of John the Baptist (Matt. 14:1–12; Mark 6:17–29; Luke 3:19).

8 **Bernice:** Had multiple marriages, possible incestuous relationship with her brother Agrippa II. Met Paul in prison in Caesarea. Later was the mistress of Emperor Titus (Acts 25:13, 23; 26: 30).

9 **Herod Agrippa II:** Visited Festus in Caesarea. Conversed with Paul and came close to being convinced of Christ. Was nearly converted to Christ (Acts 25:13–26:32).

10 **Drusilla:** Daughter of Herod Agrippa I. According to historian Josephus, she was known for her beauty. Her second marriage was to Antonius Felix, who also met Paul in Caesarea (Acts 24:24–25:14).

11 **Antonius Felix:** A former slave who became governor. Married Drusilla, daughter of Agrippa I. Considered greedy and cruel, interrogated Paul in Caesarea, hoping for a bribe (Acts 23:23–24:27).

12 **Salome:** Daughter of Herodias who danced before the guests at Herod Antipas's birthday. At her mother's request, she asked for John the Baptist's head on a platter (Matt. 14:6–12; Mark 6:21–29).

All the Miracles Jesus Performed

Jesus worked many miracles. To interpret the miracles, we need to answer the question: In what capacity did Jesus perform his miracles? Here are two different views.

1) AS THE SON OF GOD AND OUR SAVIOR

• Emphasizes that Jesus, unlike us, is the Son of God. Sees the miracles in the gospels as a way in which Jesus shows and confirms that he is the Messiah.

• The miracles should mainly be seen historically. Rejects any idea that healing is found in the atonement. Only sins need to be atoned for, and diseases are not sins that separate us from God (John 9:1–3; Matt. 9:5–8).

2) AS OUR EXAMPLE AND ROLE MODEL

• Emphasizes that Jesus became human just like us (Phil. 2:5–8). Sees Jesus's miracles as a pattern. Points out that Jesus says we will do even greater miracles than he did (John 14:12)

• Sees the miracles as a way of confirming the message. Often sees a promise of healing in the atoning death of Jesus and that healing is received in the same way as salvation (Isa. 53:4–5).

Jesus's Miracles in the Gospels

	Miracle	Location	Matthew	Mark	Luke	John	Healing	Raising dead	Deliverance	Nature miracle	Number of versions
1	Turns water into wine	Cana	-	-	-	2:1–11	□	□	□	■	1
2	Heals a royal official's son	Cana	-	-	-	4:46–54	■	□	□	□	1
3	Frees possessed man in synagogue	Capernaum	-	1:21–28	4:33–37	-	□	□	■	□	2
4	Heals Peter's mother-in-law	Capernaum	8:14–15	1:29–31	4:38–39	-	■	□	□	□	3
5	First miraculous catch of fish	Sea of Galilee	-	-	5:1–11	-	□	□	□	■	1
6	Heals a leper	Galilee	8:2–4	1:40–45	5:12–15	-	■	□	□	□	3
7	Heals man lowered through the roof	Capernaum	9:1–8	2:1–12	5:17–26	-	■	□	□	□	3
8	Heals a sick man at Bethesda	Jerusalem	-	-	-	5:1–15	■	□	□	□	1
9	Heals a man with a withered hand	Galilee	12:9–13	3:1–5	6:6–11	-	■	□	□	□	3
10	Heals a centurion's servant	Capernaum	8:5–13	-	7:1–10	-	■	□	□	□	2
11	Raises a widow's son	Nain	-	-	7:11–17	-	□	■	□	□	1
12	Casts an evil spirit out of a deaf-mute	Galilee	12:22–32	-	-	-	□	□	■	□	1
13	Calms a storm	Sea of Galilee	8:23–27	4:35–41	8:22–25	-	□	□	□	■	3
14	Frees a possessed man in Gadara	Gadara	8:28–34	5:1–20	8:26–39	-	□	□	■	□	3
15	Heals a woman with bleeding	Capernaum	9:20–22	5:25–34	8:43–48	-	■	□	□	□	3
16	Raises Jairus's daughter	Capernaum	9:18–26	5:22–43	8:41–56	-	□	■	□	□	3
17	Heals two blind men	Capernaum	9:27–31	-	-	-	■	□	□	□	1
18	Casts an evil spirit out of a mute	Capernaum	9:32–34	-	-	-	□	□	■	□	1
19	Feeds 5,000 people	Near Bethsaida	14:13–21	6:30–44	9:10–17	6:1–14	□	□	□	■	4
20	Walks on water	Sea of Galilee	14:22–33	6:45–52	-	6:16–21	□	□	□	■	3
21	Casts out an evil spirit in Phoenicia	Phoenicia	15:21–28	7:24–30	-	-	□	□	■	□	2
22	Heals a deaf-mute man	Decapolis	-	7:31–37	-	-	■	□	□	□	1
23	Feeds 4,000 people	Decapolis	15:32–38	8:1–9	-	-	□	□	□	■	2
24	Heals a blind man outside Bethsaida	Bethsaida	-	8:22–26	-	-	■	□	□	□	1
25	Casts an evil spirit out of a young boy	Mount Hermon	17:14–21	9:14–29	9:37–42	-	□	□	■	□	3
26	Finds money in a fish's mouth	Capernaum	17:24–27	-	-	-	□	□	□	■	1
27	Heals a man born blind	Jerusalem	-	-	-	9:1–7	■	□	□	□	1
28	Casts an evil spirit out of a deaf-mute	Uncertain (?)	-	-	11:14–23	-	□	□	■	□	1
29	Heals a crippled woman	Perea (?)	-	-	13:10–17	-	■	□	□	□	1
30	Heals a man with abnormal swelling	Perea	-	-	14:1–6	-	■	□	□	□	1
31	Raises Lazarus	Bethany	-	-	-	11:1–44	□	■	□	□	1
32	Heals ten lepers	Samaria	-	-	17:11–19	-	■	□	□	□	1
33	Heals the blind Bartimaeus	Jericho	20:29–34	10:46–52	18:35–43	-	■	□	□	□	3
34	Curses a fig tree	Jerusalem	21:18–19	11:12–14	-	-	□	□	□	■	2
35	Heals Malchus's severed ear	Jerusalem	-	-	22:49–51	-	■	□	□	□	1
36	Second miraculous catch of fish	Sea of Galilee	-	-	-	21:1–13	□	□	□	■	1
		Number of miracles:	20	18	20	8	17	3	7	9	

When Jesus Fed the Multitudes—Twice

The Gospels tell about two miracles with bread. Jesus first feeds 5,000 and later another 4,000. After the second miracle, Jesus says, "Don't you understand yet?" (Mark 8:21). The miracles have a clear purpose.

Food for 5,000	Food for 4,000

BEFORE THE MIRACLES

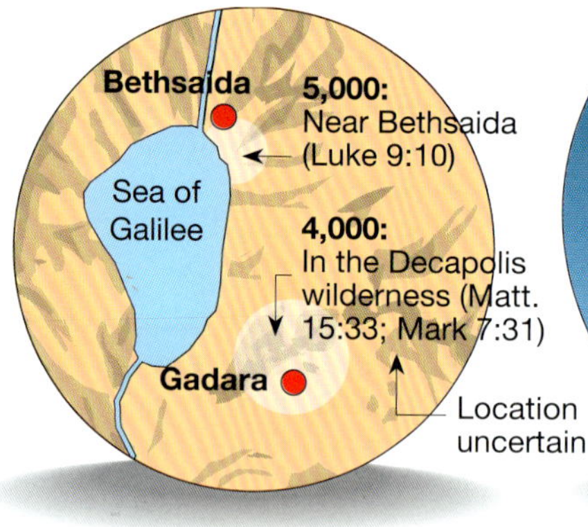

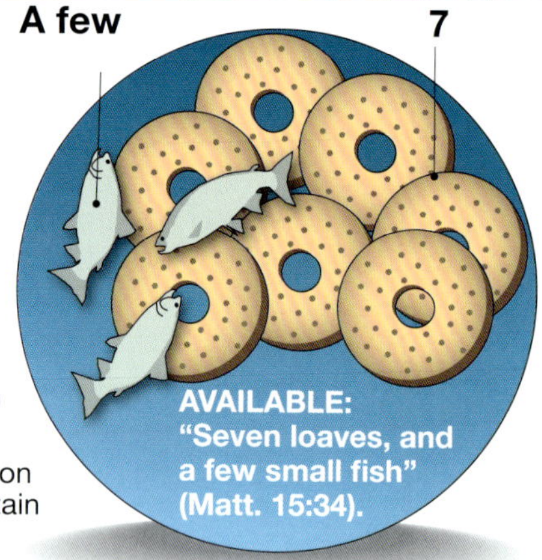

THE MIRACLES

• **TEXTS:** Matt. 14:13–21; Mark 6:31–44; Luke 9:10–17; John 6:1–14 (4 versions).
• **NUMBER:** About 5,000 men, plus women and children (Mt 14:21).
• **GROUP:** Probably with a Jewish background (Mt 14:13; Lk 9:10).
• **AREA:** A deserted place near Bethsaida (Mk 6:32; Lk 9:10).
• **TIME OF YEAR:** Late spring (Jn 6:4), maybe March or April AD 32 (Mk 6:39).
• **RESPONSE:** "When Jesus saw that they were ready to force him to be their king, he slipped away" (Jn 6:15).

• **TEXTS:** Matt. 15:32–38; Mark 8:1–9 (2 versions).
• **NUMBER:** About 4,000 men plus women and children (Mt 15:38).
• **GROUP:** Probably people with a gentile background (Mk 7:31).
• **AREA:** In the wilderness in the region of the Decapolis (Mk 7:31).
• **TIME OF YEAR:** Summer AD 32, a few month later, maybe May or June.
• **RESPONSE:** No response from those who were fed. Jesus criticizes the disciples for not understanding (Mk 8:21).

AFTER THE MIRACLES

1 The only miracle in all four Gospels

Food for 5,000 is the only miracle recorded in all four Gospels (Mt 14:13–21; Mk 6:30–44; Lk 9:10–17; Jn 6:1–14).

2 Jesus used bread as a metaphor

The Gospels mention the word "bread" often. It is a central image culminating with Jesus's words: "I am the bread of life" (Jn 6:35, 48).

Baskets (Greek *kophinous*). This is a small, portable basket often used by Jewish travelers to carry provisions. It is the size of a small backpack (holding 7–10 quarts) and can carry food for a few days for one or two people.
12 baskets equal 100–125 quarts.

The two stories use different Greek words to refer to the baskets which the disciples filled with the leftover bread and fish.

Baskets (Greek *spyris*). This is a larger basket, sometimes large enough to hold a person (see Acts 9:25). It ranges from the size of a bucket to a barrel (holding between 27 and 80 quarts) and is used to transport and store grain.
7 baskets equal 200–550 quarts.

Jesus Makes Footprints on the Water

1 Jesus sends his disciples away

Several reasons: (a) The people wanted to make Jesus king (John 6:15), (b) Jesus wanted time for prayer (Matt. 14:23), (c) Jesus needed rest (Mark 6:31–32), and (d) Jesus wanted the disciples to learn to believe.

2 Jesus is both God and man

Note Jesus's human and divine sides. He wanted to be alone (Mark 6:46), and he walks on water and uses God's name: "I AM" (John 6:20; Ex. 3:14).

3 Jesus's prayers show dependence

On three occasions Jesus withdraws to pray (Mark 1:35; 6:45–46; 14:32–36). His prayers point to his dependence on the Father (John 10:30).

4 Jesus appears coming toward them

When the disciples saw Jesus, they thought he was a ghost (Matt. 14:26). The Greek word means "an optical illusion." Did the darkness, rain, or fog make them think Jesus was a ghost?

5 Focus of the story: Who is Jesus

The central question of the story is: Who is Jesus? The disciples have not yet fully understood who he is (Mark 6:52). Jesus demonstrates his power over nature (walking on water). The disciples' reaction was finally "[they] worshiped him. 'You really are the Son of God!'" (Matt. 14:33).

Peter Tries to Walk on Water

1 The first of several similar events

This is the first occasion when Jesus singles out Peter. Others are the confession (Matt. 16:13–20), the transfiguration (Matt. 17:1–8), the temple tax (Matt. 17:24–27), the denial (Matt. 26:34), and the restoration (John 21:15–16).

2 Only Matthew talks about Peter walking on water

Only Matthew tells us how Peter wants to go to Jesus. The phrase "If it's really you" (Matt. 14:28) can also be understood as Peter saying "Because it is you."

3 Jesus asks why Peter doubts

When Peter gets out of the boat and starts to sink, Jesus reproaches him. Afterward, Jesus asks: "Why did you doubt me?" He asks Peter for an explanation, not for his faith but for his doubts. What are the reasons for your doubts?

Where were they going?

• **TIME:** "Night fell" (Matt. 14:23) includes the time from late afternoon to sunset.
• "About three o'clock in the morning" (Matt. 14:25), literally: "In the fourth watch of the night." The Romans divided the night into four parts, the same as three to six a.m.
• **DISTANCE:** "Three or four miles" literally "25 or 30 stadia" (John 6:19). About 4 mi; 1 stadia is about 600 ft.

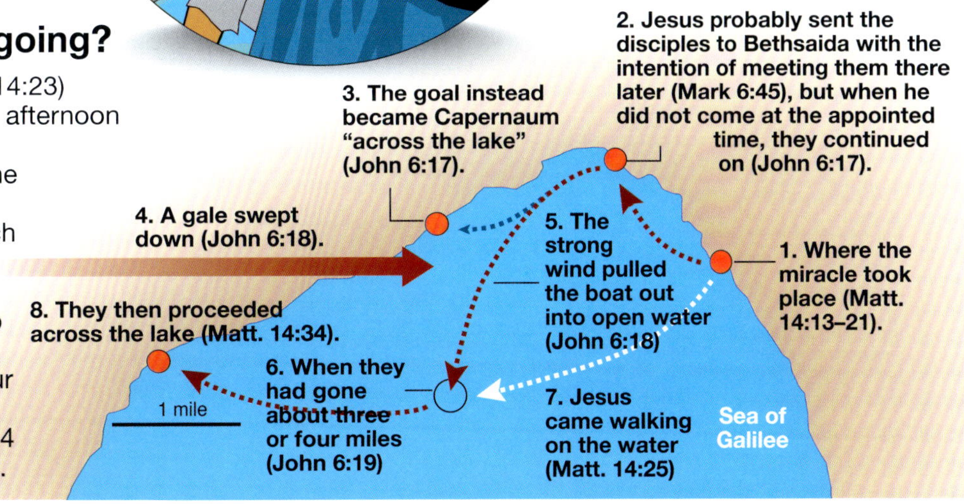

All the Parables Jesus Told

A parable is a story in which a spiritual truth is explained by comparing it to an image. The purpose of the parable is to make the message clear to some and hide it from others.

• The parable of the sower (Matt. 13:3–9, 18–23) explains why Jesus changed strategies and what he expects of those who hear the message.

The only thing that differs is the soil, the way in which they receive Jesus's words.

Through Matthew 12: Preaching to the people
From January AD 30 to fall 31, around 20 months

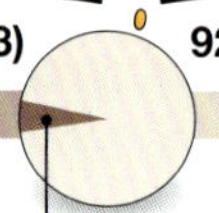

From Matthew 13: Teaching to the disciples
From fall AD 31 to April 33, around 20 months

The breaking point: Matthew 13:1–23

All Jesus's Parables

	The Parable of ...	Matthew	Mark	Luke	John	Kingdom of God	The Gospel	Discipleship	The future		Number of versions
1	the Old Garment	9:16	2:21	5:36					■	About a new time	3
2	the New Wineskins	9:17	2:22	5:37–39					■	About a new time	3
3	the Wise and Foolish Builders	7:24–27		6:47–49				■		About application	2
4	the Sower	13:3–8	4:3–8	8:5–8		■				About obedience	3
5	the Growing Seed		4:26–29			■				About God's power	1
6	the Weeds in the Wheat	13:24–30				■				About timing	1
7	the Mustard Seed	13:31–32	4:30–32	13:8:5–8		■				About growth	3
8	the Yeast in the Bread	13:33		13:20–21		■				About extent	2
9	the Treasure in the Field	13:44				■				About price	1
10	the Pearl of Great Price	13:45–46				■				About cost	1
11	the Net	13:47–48				■				About judgment	1
12	the Unmerciful Servant	18:23–35						■		About forgiveness	1
13	the Good Samaritan			10:25–37				■		About neighbors	1
14	the Friend at Midnight			11:5–8				■		About prayer	1
15	the Rich Fool			12:16–21				■		About money	1
16	the Watchful Servants			12:35–48					■	About faithfulness	1
17	the Barren Fig Tree			13:6–9				■		About sanctification	1
18	the Great Banquet			14:16–24					■	About attendance	1
19	the Cost of Being a Disciple			14:28–32				■		About the prize	1
20	the Lost Sheep	18:10–14		15:3–7			■			About salvation	2
21	the Lost Coin			15:8–10			■			About salvation	1
22	the Prodigal Son			15:11–32			■			About forgiveness	1
23	the Shrewd Manager			16:1–13				■		About wisdom	1
24	the Rich Man and Lazarus			16:19–31				■		About stewardship	1
25	the Obedient Servant			17:7–10				■		About service	1
26	the Persistent Widow			18:1–8				■		About prayer	1
27	the Pharisee and the Tax Collector			18:9–14				■		About inner life	1
28	the Workers in the Vineyard	20:1–16						■		About reward	1
29	the Ten Talents			19:11–27				■		About service	1
30	the Two Sons	21:28–32						■		About obedience	1
31	the Tenants	21:33–46	12:1–12	20:9–19					■	About responsibility	3
32	the Wedding Banquet	22:1–14							■	About willingness	1
33	the Lesson of the Fig Tree	24:32–35	13:28–31	21:29–33					■	About timing	3
34	the Faithful Servant	24:45–51							■	About faithfulness	1
35	the Ten Bridesmaids	25:1–13							■	About preparedness	1
36	the Talents	25:14–30						■		About faithfulness	1
	Number of parables:	20	7	24	0	8	3	16	9		

No parables in the Gospel of John

At times the parables come in groups. These three parables belong together. See Luke 15:3

3 (parables 6–8) · 3 (parables 9–11) · 3 (parables 20–22)

Parables: How Do We Interpret Them?

DEFINITION

What is a parable?

- The dictionary defines a parable as a "short fictitious story that illustrates a moral attitude or a religious principle." Parables are not built on real events and people.*
- The word parable comes from the Greek "*paraballo*" which means "to place things side by side."
- A parable is a story in which a spiritual truth is explained or illustrated by comparison with an image, often an everyday situation (such as sowing/harvesting, a wedding, fishing, or money).
- Parables must be interpreted with care and caution.

PURPOSE

1 Pointing to the truth

One of the purposes of parables is to illustrate and clarify truth to those who already believe. Jesus uses parables to teach, explain, and answer questions that people ask him (Mark 4:30; Luke 10:29).

2 Hiding the truth

At the same time, Jesus uses parables to hide the truth, so that those who criticize him do not understand and thus are not given new grounds to criticize him (Mark 4:11; Matt. 13:13).

3 Key to the parables

A central parable is the story of the sower, where three soils illustrate those who will not listen, while the good soil refers to those who will listen and allow the message to take root (Matt. 13:3–9).

4 Later part of Jesus's ministry

Of Jesus's thirty-six surviving parables, thirty-three were told during the latter part of his public ministry. The parable fits his purpose when he turns away from the masses to focus more on his disciples.

5 Interpretation by itself

The parable is often characterized by separating the narrative and interpretation (Matt. 13:3–9 and 13:18–23), in contrast to illustrations where the story and the interpretation are closely interwoven (John 15:1–17).

> "No doctrine should be grounded on a parable as its primary or only source.
> (Henry Virkler)

6 A call for caution

As parables, by their very nature, have a tendency to hide the truth, interpreters are advised to be cautious. A parable should therefore be understood primarily as an illustration of a truth or a text pointing to an application.

INTERPRETATION

1 Interpret as usual

The text of a parable should be interpreted in the same way we interpret other narrative texts. Parables are not allegories and there is no secret code. The story is the message.

2 Note the context

Context is important. Clues to the interpretation can often be found in the circumstances leading up to the story. Note when the parable was told, to whom, and its conclusion.

3 See parables in sequence

On several occasions, parables seem to be ordered sequentially so that several parables belong together but Jesus only interprets one of them (Matt. 13:24–30, 31–32, 36–43).

4 Seek the central idea

Seek to understand the central message, often at the end, the answer to the question that gave rise to the parable (Luke 16:19–31). A parable has only **one truth** that it wants to convey.

5 The importance of details

When details are significant, they only have meaning in relation to the central truth. You should not read other conclusions into the text. There is danger in pushing the text too far.

6 Examples to illustrate

The parable of the shrewd manager (Luke 16:1–15) is an example. Jesus commended the shrewd manager, not for his dishonesty but for his wisdom (16:8). Wisdom is the "only truth."

7 Search application

The focus of Jesus's parables often is to point out the practical application. For example, when Jesus tells the parable of the Good Samaritan, he instructs the man to "go and do the same" (Luke 10:37).

*There may be exceptions. For example, some think that the parable of the Ten Talents (Lk 19:11–27) may allude to Herod Archelaus.

Men and Women in the Gospel of Luke

The evangelist Luke highlights women alongside men. There is a balance where a story of a man is often followed by a corresponding story of a woman. This pattern can be followed throughout the gospel.

Men		Women
The message to Zechariah An angel appears to Zechariah. Announces the birth of John the Baptist (1:5–25).	1	**The message to Mary** An angel appears to Mary. Announces the birth of Jesus (1:26–38).
Zechariah's song of praise When John the Baptist is born, Zechariah sings a song of praise to the Lord (1:67–79).	2	**Mary's song of praise** Mary is filled with joy and sings a song of praise to the Lord (1:46–56).
Simeon prophesies about Jesus When the child Jesus is brought to the temple, Simeon prophesies over him (2:25–35).	3	**Anna talks about Jesus** When Jesus is in the temple, Anna sees him and praises God for the child (2:36–38).
Elijah healed a leper from Syria Of all the lepers in Elijah's time, Naaman the Syrian was the only one healed (4:27).	4	**Elijah was sent to a widow** Of all the widows in Elijah's time, he was sent to the widow of Zarephath (4:25–26).
Possessed man delivered A possessed man in Capernaum is delivered by Jesus (4:31–37).	5	**Woman with a fever healed** Peter's mother-in-law is healed by Jesus in Capernaum (4:38–39).
Man makes his way to Jesus A lame man is lowered through the roof and receives forgiveness from Jesus (5:19–26).	6	**Woman makes her way to Jesus** An outcast woman goes to Jesus and receives forgiveness of her sins (7:36–50).
List of men who follow A list of the twelve disciples Jesus chooses for his inner circle (6:12–16).	7	**List of women who follow** A list of three women who also accompany Jesus on his travels (8:1–3).
A servant saved from death The officer pleads for his servant and Jesus heals him from a distance (7:1–10).	8	**A son saved from death** The widow in Nain has her son raised to life when Jesus comes to town (7:11–17).
Men of Nineveh will stand up The men of Nineveh listened to Jonah's sermon. It was credited to them (11:32).	9	**Queen of Sheba will stand up** The queen of Sheba came to listen to Solomon's wisdom (11:31)
A man sows a mustard seed Jesus likens the kingdom of God to a mustard seed a man sows (13:18–19).	10	**A woman bakes with yeast** Jesus likens the kingdom of God to a woman baking with yeast (13:20–21).
Heals a man on the Sabbath Despite the Sabbath, Jesus heals a man with abnormal swelling (14:1–4).	11	**Heals a woman on the Sabbath** Despite the Sabbath, Jesus heals a woman crippled by a spirit (13:10–17).
A shepherd loses a sheep A shepherd with 100 sheep searches for and finds a lost one (15:4–7).	12	**A woman loses a coin** A woman with 10 coins searches for and finds a lost one (15:8–10).
Two men in the same bed When Jesus comes, one will be taken and the other left behind (17:34).	13	**Two women grinding grain** When Jesus comes, one will be taken and the other left behind (17:35).
A man going to Emmaus A man named Cleopas walking from Jerusalem is joined by Jesus (24:13,18).	14	**A woman (?) going to Emmaus** One possibility is that the other disciple is Cleopas's wife, Mary (24:13, 29 "with us").

Jesus's Active Triangle

"Then Jesus began to denounce the towns where he had done so many of his miracles, because they hadn't repented of their sins.... "What sorrow awaits you, Korazin and Bethsaida! ... And you people of Capernaum, will you be honored in heaven? No, you will go down to the place of the dead" (Matt. 11:20–21, 23).

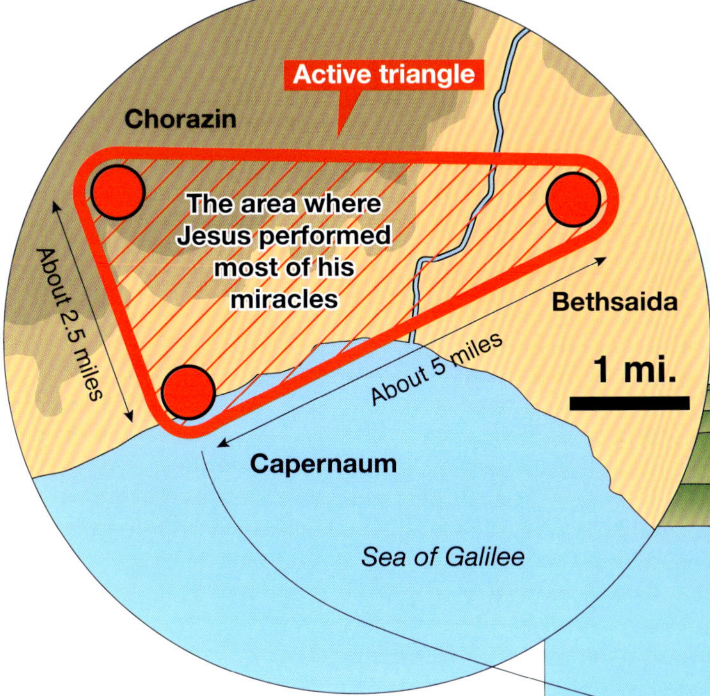

Jesus's miracles in the three cities

Chorazin: Nothing specific is described (Mt 11:21; Lk 10:13).
Bethsaida: Jesus heals a blind man outside the town (Mk 8:22–26).• Nothing specific is described (Mt 11:21; Lk 10:13).
Capernaum: Jesus frees a man from an evil spirit (Mk 1:21–28; Lk 4:31–41).
• Jesus heals Peter's mother-in-law (Mt 8:14–15; Mk 1:29–31; Lk 4:38–39). • Jesus heals a centurion's servant (Mt 8:5–13; Lk 7:1–10). • Jesus heals a paralyzed man lowered through the roof (Mt 9:1–8; Mk 2:1–12; Lk 5:17–26). • Jesus heals a woman with constant bleeding (Mt 9:20–22; Mk 5:25–34; Lk 8:43–48). • Jesus raises Jairus's daughter (Mt 9:18–26; Mk 5:22–43; Lk 8:40–56).
• Jesus heals an official's son (Jn 4:46–54).
• Jesus heals two blind men and a demon-possessed mute (Mt 9:27–33; 12:22–45; Lk 11:14).

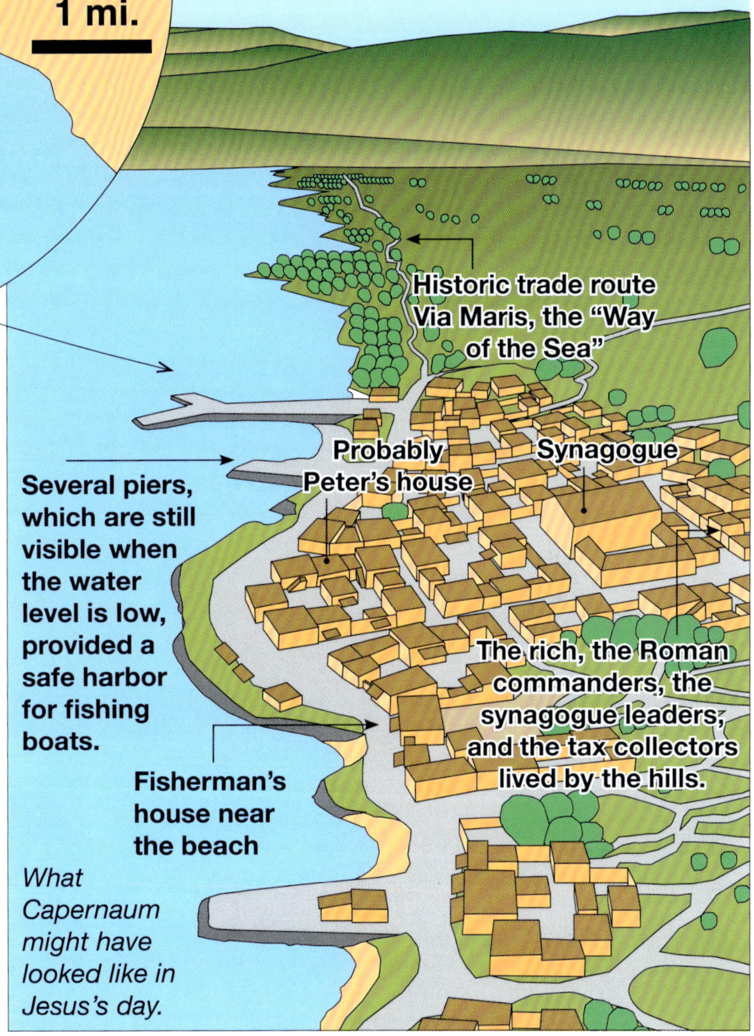

What Capernaum might have looked like in Jesus's day.

WHAT HAPPENED IN THE ACTIVE TRIANGLE?
This is where Jesus spent most of his time and did most of his miracles.

1 Spent the most time here
The area on the north shore of the Sea of Galilee is where Jesus was most active during his public ministry.

2 We don't know all Jesus did
Although we know about a few of them, most of the miracles Jesus performed in the three cities are unknown to us.

3 It eventually came to an end
The towns did not repent. So Jesus chose to lead the blind man out of the town to heal him (Mark 8:23).

4 Miracles met with rejection
Even after witnessing Jesus perform amazing miracles, these towns chose to reject Jesus.

Four Times Jesus Withdrew

Starting in Mark 6:31, Jesus increasingly withdraws from the crowd. We see at least four occasions.

1 **First time:** "Let's go off by ourselves to a quiet place" (Mark 6:31), "toward the town of Bethsaida" (Luke 9:10; Matt. 14:13).

2 **Second time:** "To the region of Tyre and Sidon" (Matt. 15:21). The area was dominated by Phoenicians (Mark 7:26).

3 **Third time:** "To Sidon before going back to the Sea of Galilee and the region of the [Decapolis]" (Mark 7:31).

4 **Fourth time:** "They arrived at Bethsaida" (Mark 8:22). "Went up to the villages near Caesarea Philippi" (Mark 8:27).

Why Jesus withdrew

1. To keep away from Herod Antipas who thought he was John the Baptist (Mark 6:14).
2. To retreat from fanatics who wanted to make him king (John 6:15).
3. To withdraw from the Jewish leaders who sought to provoke him (Mark 8:11).
4. To have more time with his disciples (Mark 9:30–31).
5. To find rest and peace (Mark 6:31; Mark 8:31).
6. To have more time to pray for himself (Luke 9:18).

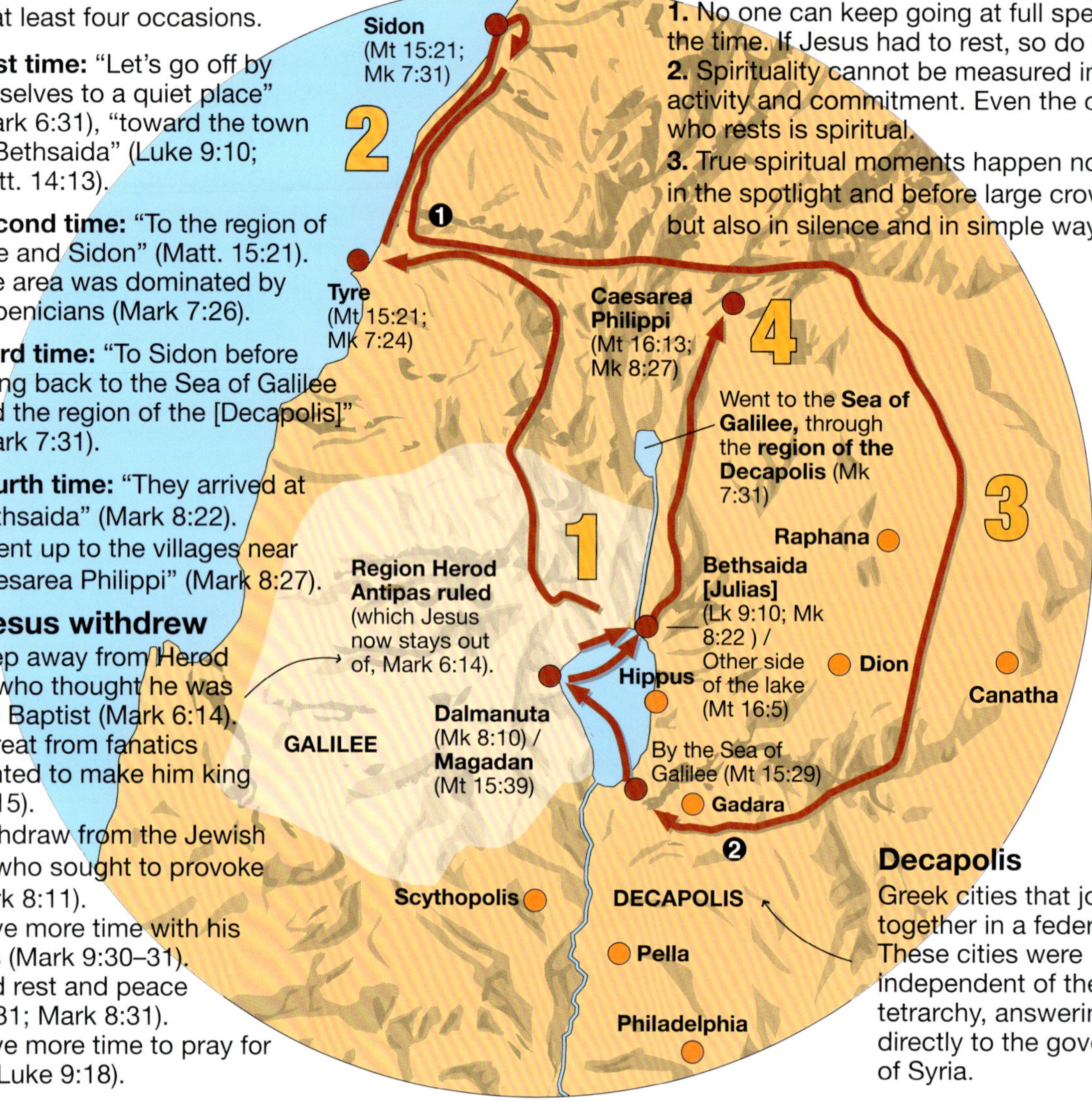

Lessons from Jesus's example

1. No one can keep going at full speed all the time. If Jesus had to rest, so do we.
2. Spirituality cannot be measured in activity and commitment. Even the one who rests is spiritual.
3. True spiritual moments happen not only in the spotlight and before large crowds, but also in silence and in simple ways.

Decapolis

Greek cities that joined together in a federation. These cities were independent of the local tetrarchy, answering directly to the governor of Syria.

(1) The Canaanite woman of Tyre
Jesus meets a woman of Syrian-Phoenician descent with strong faith. From a distance, he heals her daughter from an evil spirit (Matt. 15:21–28; Mark 7:24–30).

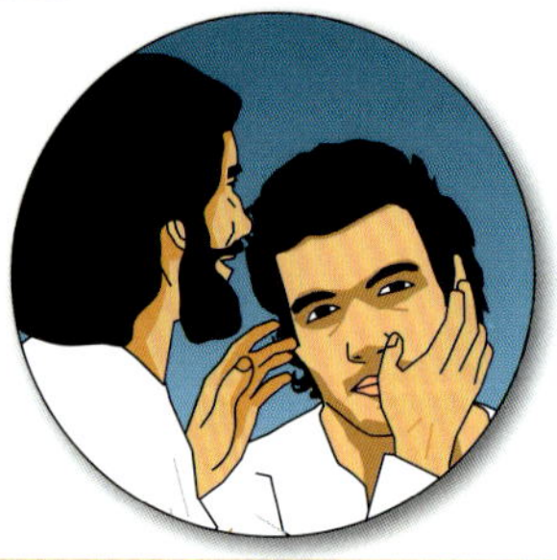

(2) The deaf-mute man in the Decapolis
Jesus encounters a deaf-mute man whom he takes aside from the people and heals by saying the word *Ephphatha*, meaning "Be opened" (Matt. 15:29–31; Mark 7:31–37).

WHY JESUS STAYED AWAY FROM HEROD ANTIPAS

- Herod Antipas was the tetrarch of Judea and Perea from 4 BC to AD 39.
- John the Baptist accuses him over his marriage (Mark 6:17).
- Antipas has John the Baptist killed in revenge (Matt. 14:6–11).
- Herod believes that Jesus is John the Baptist (Matt. 14:1; Mark 6:14–16).
- Jesus calls Antipas "that fox" (Luke 13:32).
- Jesus is warned about Antipas (Luke 13:31).
- **That is why he withdraws from Antipas's region.**
- But, in the end, the two would meet (Luke 23:7, 9).

Peter's Confession of the Messiah ...

Jesus asks the disciples two questions. The purpose of both questions is to make them reflect: who do they think he is? The first question leads to the second.

1 Who do people say the Son of Man is?
The first question (Matt. 16:13). The disciples answer:
1. Some say John the Baptist (Matt. 14:2)
2. Or Elijah (Mal. 4:5–6)
3. Others say Jeremiah
4. Or one of the other prophets (Matt. 16:14).

2 Who do you say I am?
The second question is addressed directly to the disciples (Matt. 16:15). Simon Peter speaks as the leader of the group.

1 Jesus asks the whole group
Jesus uses a plural form of "you" and asks: "Who do you say I am?" He turns to the group of disciples. Peter's answer must therefore be seen as coming from the whole group of disciples.

2 The confession was something God gave
Peter's insight into who Jesus is was something that had been given to him (Matt. 11:27; John 6:44). He did not learn it from a human being. The insight had been revealed by God.

3 Jesus's response to Peter
When he says, "Upon this rock I will build my church" (Matt. 16:18), Jesus alludes to Peter's name, which means rock. The question is, what does "this rock" mean?

4 The first time the church is mentioned
It is the first time (Matt. 16:18) that the Bible speaks of the church (Matt. 18:17). The church is founded on the day of Pentecost and then becomes a central theme in Acts and the Epistles.

UNDERSTANDING PETER'S CONFESSION
In response to Peter's confession, Jesus says: "Upon this rock I will build my church" (Matt. 16:18). There are four views:

1 Peter as a disciple
The words refer to Peter personally. It is he, and no one else, who becomes the foundation on which the church is built (Acts 2:14).

2 Successor of Peter
The words refer to Peter and others after him. Through apostolic succession there is one who acts in Peter's place (the pope).

3 Peter's confession
The words do not refer to Peter, but to his confession. It is on this confession, that Jesus is the Messiah, that the church is built.

4 Jesus himself
The words refer to Jesus himself. It is he, and he alone, who is the rock on which the church is built (Rom. 9:33; 1 Cor. 3:11; 10:4).

Chronological overview

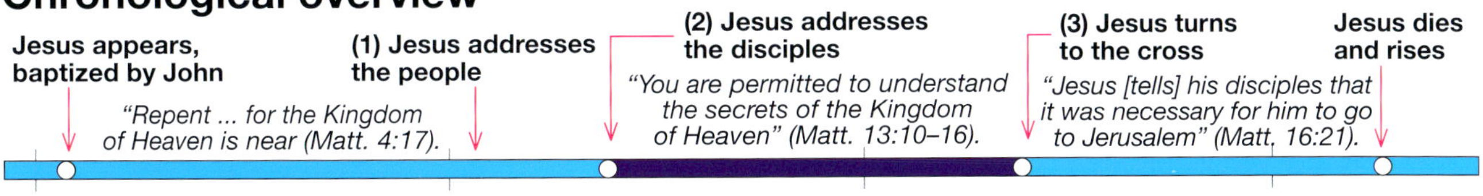

... and Jesus's announcement

1 Jesus changes direction
The confession meant that Jesus changed the focus of his ministry (Matt. 16:21). He now turns his focus to his task as reconciler.

2 First mention of his death
This is the *first time* Jesus tells them that he must die and rise from the dead (Matt. 17:22–23; 20:18–19; Mark 8:31; Luke 9:22).

3 A compelling necessity
The word "necessary" (Matt. 16:21) tell us that there is a compelling necessity behind Jesus's atoning death—it was necessary for God.

4 Resurrection and sacrifice
Jesus must not only die but also rise from the dead (Matt. 16:21). His death and resurrection defeats death once and for all (1 Cor. 15:14).

Jesus on the Mount of Transfiguration

The transfiguration is a central event in Jesus's life. God's voice from heaven confirms that Jesus is the Messiah (Luke 9:35), as it did at the beginning of his public ministry (Matt. 3:17).

1 They walk up the mountain

Jesus chooses three disciples—Peter, James, and John—and takes them up a high mountain, where they are alone, to pray.
• Matt. 17:1; Mark 9:2a; Luke 9:28

2 Jesus is transfigured

Jesus is transfigured before their eyes. His face is transformed and his clothes become white.
• Matt. 17:2; Mark 9:2b–3; Luke 9:29

3 Moses and Elijah visit

They see Moses and Elijah talking to him. Peter suggests they build three shelters so they can stay on the mountain.
• Matt. 17:3–4; Mark 9:4–6; Luke 9:30–33

4 God speaks directly

A cloud descends and a voice is heard from heaven saying: "This is my dearly loved Son ... Listen to him!"
• Matt. 17:5–8; Mark 9:7–8; Luke 9:34–36a

5 They walk down the mountain

They come down from the mountain. Jesus tells them not to tell anyone about what they have seen until after his resurrection.
• Matt. 17:9–13; Mark 9:9–13; Luke 9:36b

1 A glimpse of the Kingdom of God

What the disciples see is not eternity breaking through, but a glimpse of the coming messianic kingdom that will be established on earth. They will see it before they die.

2 A guarantee of things to come

The presence of Moses and Elijah is a reminder (proof) that there is a conscious life after death and it also gives strength to the hope of our coming resurrection.

3 Live in the valley, not on the mountaintop

Peter wants to stay but Jesus takes them down to the valley. The Christian life is not primarily about "spiritual experiences" (mountaintops), but about everyday life (the valley).

4 God's mercy toward Moses

Moses was not allowed to enter the land after he hit the rock (Num. 20:12). But 1,400 years later, God displays his mercy and allows him to enter the land after all.

Where was the Mount of Transfiguration?

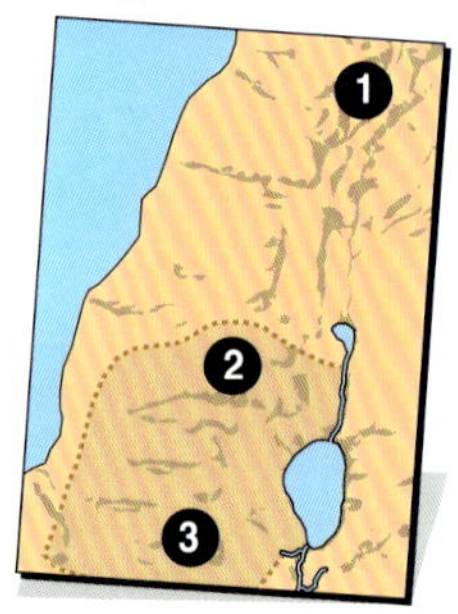

Here are three possibilities:

1. Mount Hermon (9,232 ft)
The mountain is high and located near Caesarea Philippi (Mark 8:27). Most of the population was gentile, with few Jewish teachers of the law (see Mark 9:14).

2. Mount Meron (3,960 ft)
The highest in the region, seems to match the text although it's is centrally located in the region Herod Antipas ruled.

3. Mount Tabor (1,886 ft)
Supported by tradition. The Basilica of the Transfiguration is at the top now. But in Jesus's day there was a fortification here, and the text says they went there "to be alone" (Mark 9:2).

Some observations from the events on the mountain

Some observations that can be made from the texts about Jesus, Moses, and Elijah on the mountain.

1 The event was an answer to prayer

Jesus goes up the mountain to pray. The transfiguration before their eyes must be understood as a direct answer to Jesus's prayer. (Luke 9:27–29).

2 Confirms that Jesus is the Son of God

The events on the Mount of Transfiguration confirm that Jesus is indeed Messiah, the Son of God. With the words "This is my dearly loved Son," there is no doubt (Matt. 17:5).

3 The individual's resurrection

The transfiguration of Jesus (Mark 9:2)—that his face shines like the sun—shows the transformation that those who believe in him will experience (Phil. 3:21; Col. 3:4).

4 The event confirms prophecies

Peter says, "We also have the prophetic message as something completely reliable." What was previously accepted in faith, had been confirmed (2 Pet. 1:19–21).

The Woman Caught in Adultery

1 An adulteress is caught
The Pharisees and scribes come to Jesus with a woman they have caught in adultery (John 7:53–8:4).

2 They put Jesus to the test
They want to test Jesus by demanding that she be stoned to death according to the law (John 8:5–6a; Ex. 20:10).

3 Jesus writes in the dust
To their surprise, Jesus just stoops down to the ground and writes in the dust with his finger (John 8:6b).

4 The religious leaders leave
Jesus says: "Let the one who has never sinned throw the first stone!" The religious leaders leave (John 8:7–9).

5 Jesus does not judge
Jesus then speaks to the woman. "Neither do I [condemn you]. Go and sin no more" (John 8:10–11).

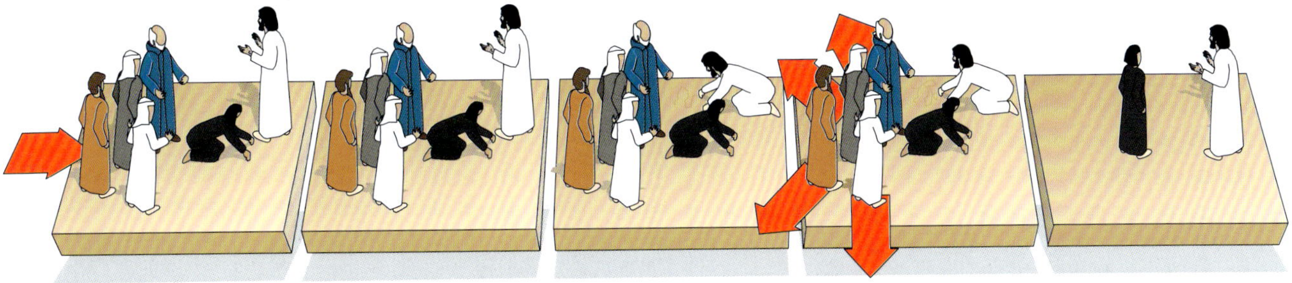

1 The whole set-up was a trap
There is no doubt that they were once again trying to frame Jesus: (a) if he wanted to stone the woman he would lose the support of his followers, (b) if he did not allow her to be stoned, he would openly disregard the law.

2 The sin was not their concern
It was a trap so the woman herself was unimportant and the man was not brought to Jesus. (The law stipulates the same punishment for both.) This shows the Pharisees' disregard for the law.

3 The writing in the dust?
There are several suggestions: (a) He keeps his distance. (b) He lists the sins of the accusers themselves. (c) He writes Exodus 23:1. (d) He refers to Isaiah 10:22 about Israel's sin "as the sand of the seashore" We do not know.

4 A matter of perspective
(a) Jesus saw the woman with love, the Pharisees with contempt.
(b) Jesus looked at her with mercy, they wanted to punish her.
(c) Jesus looked toward her future, they only looked at her past.

5 The origin of the text
The text is missing from the oldest manuscripts and few Church Fathers cite it. It was probably not originally part of the gospel but is still considered to describe an authentic event (John 21:25).

> "The entire section, John 7:53–8:11, traditionally known as the *pericope adulterae*, is not contained in the earliest and best [manuscripts] and was almost certainly not an original part of the Gospel of John.... but represents a later addition to the text.... The evidence for the non-Johannine origin of the pericope... is overwhelming. (The NET Bible)

Verses that do not belong to the biblical text

About 36 verses in total

Textual research has shown that as well as the story of the woman caught in adultery, some other verses do not belong to the original text. They are most likely redundant duplicates copied from other gospels.

1 Texts in Matthew
17:21 (see Mark 9:29); 18:11 (see Luke 19:10); 23:14 (see Mark 12:40; Luke 20:47).

2 Texts in Mark
Mark 7:16 ("Anyone with ears to hear should listen and understand."); 9:44, 46 (see Luke 9:48); 11:26 (see Matt. 6:15); 15:28 (see Luke 22:37).
Mark 16:9–20 is missing in the oldest manuscripts. Some documents have a shorter, alternative ending.

3 Texts in Luke
17:36 (see Matt. 24:40); 23:17 (see Matt. 27:15; Mark 15:6; John 18:39).

4 Texts in John
5:3b–4 "waiting for a certain movement of the water, for an angel of the Lord came from time to time and stirred up the water. And the first person to step in after the water was stirred was healed of whatever disease he had."
John 7:53–8:11 is missing in the oldest manuscripts, but included as it is considered credible.

Attacks of the Religious Leaders

The religious leadership took an interest in Jesus, debated with him and finally conspired to have him executed. Here is a summary of the confrontations and the different groups mentioned on each occasion.

Jewish Leaders' Conflicts with Jesus

In the confrontations with Jesus, two main issues came up: (1) His relationship with God the Father and claim to be God, and (2) His relationship with people that he socialized with, especially the lowest in society.

	Event		Matthew	Mark	Luke	John	Pharisees	Sadducees	Scribes	High Priest	Elders	Lawyers	Councilors		Number of versions
1	Heals a lame man lowered down through the roof		9:1–8	2:1–12	5:17–26		■	□	■	□	□	■	□		3
2	Asks Jesus about eating with sinners		9:9–13	2:13–17	5:27–31		■	□	■	□	□	□	□		3
3	Pharisees ask about the Sabbath		12:1–8	2:23–28	6:1–5		■	□	□	□	□	□	□		3
4	Jesus heals man with withered hand		12:9–15	3:1–6	6:6–11		■	□	■	□	□	□	□	1)	3
5	Jesus heals a centurion's son				7:1–10		□	□	□	□	■	□	□		1
6	Eats with a Pharisee and anointed by a sinner				7:36–50		■	□	□	□	□	□	□		1
7	Jesus accused of having power from Satan		12:22–32	3:20–30			■	□	■	□	□	□	□		2
8	Critics ask for a sign		12:38–45				■	□	■	□	□	□	□		1
9	Accused of being helped by the prince of demons		9:27–34				■	□	□	□	□	□	□		1
10	Accused of violating the tradition of elders		15:1–9	7:1–13		(7:1)	■	□	■	□	□	□	□	2)	3
11	Critics ask for a sign		16:1–4	8:10–12			■	■	□	□	□	□	□		2
12	Leaders try to seize Jesus					7:31–52	■	□	□	■	□	□	■		1
13	Woman caught in adultery					8:2–11	■	□	■	□	□	□	□		1
14	Jesus is not allowed to testify about himself					8:12–20	■	□	□	□	□	□	□		1
15	A blind man receives his sight					9:13–41	■	□	□	□	□	□	□		1
16	An expert in the law asks about eternal life				10:25–37		□	□	□	□	□	■	□		1
17	Jews surround Jesus in the temple					10:22–39	□	□	□	□	□	□	□	2)	1
18	Pharisees warn Jesus				13:31–35		■	□	□	□	□	□	□		1
19	Eats with a Pharisee, heals a sick man				14:1–6		■	□	□	□	□	■	□		1
20	Leaders constantly criticize Jesus				15:1–2		■	□	■	□	□	□	□		1
21	Jesus and the Pharisees on money				16:1–15		■	□	□	□	□	□	□		1
22	The question of when the Kingdom of God will come				17:20–21		■	□	□	□	□	□	□		1
23	The question of marriage		19:3–9	10:2–9			■	□	□	□	□	□	□		2
24	Jesus rides into Jerusalem				19:29–44		■	□	□	□	□	□	□		1
25	Jesus and the children in the temple square		21:12–17				□	□	■	■	□	□	□		1
26	Jesus cleanses the temple			11:15–19	19:45–48		□	□	■	■	□	□	□	3)	2
27	Leaders demand answers about Jesus's authority		21:23–46	11:27–12:12	20:1–19		■	□	■	■	■	□	□		3
28	Jesus on paying taxes to Caesar		22:15–22	12:13–17	20:20–26		■	□	□	□	□	□	□	1)	3
29	Jesus on the question of the resurrection		22:23–33	12:18–27	20:27–40		□	■	■	□	□	□	□		3
30	Jesus on the greatest commandment		22:34–40	12:28–34			■	■	■	□	□	■	□		2
31	Jesus asks whose son the Messiah is	Passion Week	22:41–46	12:35–37	20:41–44		■	□	□	□	□	□	□		3
32	Jesus is arrested and detained		26:47–56	14:43–52	22:47–53	18:1–14	■	□	■	■	■	□	□	2,4)	4
33	Jesus before the high priest Annas					18:19–24	□	□	□	■	□	□	□		1
34	Jesus before the high priest Caiaphas		26:57–68	14:53–65	22:54–65		□	□	■	■	■	□	□	5)	3
35	Jesus before the Sanhedrin		27:1	15:1	22:66–71		□	□	■	■	■	□	□		3
36	Jesus is accused before Pilate		27:2, 11–14	15:1–5	23:1–5	18:28–38	□	□	□	■	■	□	□	2,5)	4
37	Jesus before Herod Antipas				23:6–12		□	□	■	■	□	□	□		1
38	The leaders incite the people		27:15–26	15:6–15	23:13–25	18:39–19:16	□	□	□	■	■	□	■	2)	4
39	Jesus is mocked on the cross		27:41–43	15:27–32	23:33–38		□	□	■	■	■	□	■		3

• A few more expressions and groups are mentioned: **1) Herodians:** Matt. 22:16; Mark 3:6; 12:13 **2) Jews** (as a critical group): John 2:18; 7:1; 10:22–42; 18:1–14; 18:28–38, 39–19:16. See also John 5:10, 15–16, 18; 6:41, 52; 7:1, 13, 15, 35; 8:22,48, 52, 57; 9:18, 22; 10:19; 11:8, 54 **3) The leaders of the people:** Luke 19:45–48 **4) The temple guard:** Luke 22:47–53; see also John 7:32, 45; 18:3 **5) The Sanhedrin:** Matt. 26:57–68; Mark 14:55; Mark 15:1.

Fourteen Rulers in the New Testament

EMPEROR AUGUSTUS
Born 63 BC, he founded the Second Triumvirate in 44 BC. The others were ousted and he became Rome's first emperor in 27 BC. Died Aug. 19, AD 14. Issued a decree for an empire-wide census (Luke 2:1).

EMPEROR TIBERIUS
Born 42 BC. Stepson of Augustus. Became the second emperor on Sept. 18, AD 14. Enlarged the Roman Empire. Died March 16, AD 37. Helps date John the Baptist (Luke 3:1–2; Matt. 22:17; John 19:12).

EMPEROR CLAUDIUS
Born Aug. 1, 10 BC. Was lame and hard of hearing. Elected emperor Jan. 24, AD 41. Died on Oct. 13, AD 54, probably killed by his wife. In AD 49 he ordered all Jews to leave Rome (Acts 18:2; 11:28; 17:7).

HEROD THE GREAT
Born 74/73 BC. Became king of Judea in 40 BC. Undertook major construction projects including the temple in Jerusalem. Died in 4 BC. Ordered massacre of the children in Bethlehem (Matt. 2:1–22; Luke 1:5).

HEROD ARCHELAUS
Herod the Great's son, born in 23 BC. Appointed prince of Judea, Samaria, and Idumea in 4 BC, exiled in AD 6. Died in AD 18. Joseph didn't return to Bethlehem after Archelaus took over (Matt. 2:22).

(HEROD) PHILIP II
Herod the Great's son, he ruled over the northeastern part of his father's kingdom from 4 BC until his own death in AD 34. This helps to date the ministry of John the Baptist (Luke 3:1).

HEROD ANTIPAS
Herod the Great's son, born before 20 BC. Tetrarch of Judea and Perea from 4 BC to AD 39. Executed John the Baptist (John 14:10), rebuked by Jesus (Luke 13:31–32), mocked Jesus (Luke 23:7, 11).

HEROD AGRIPPA I
Also called Julius Agrippa. Born in 10 BC, son of Aristobulus. Began ruling in AD 37 and died suddenly in AD 44 (Acts 12:23). Persecuted Christians, killed James, and imprisoned Peter (Acts 12:1–23).

HEROD AGRIPPA II
Born in AD 27 the son of Agrippa I. Rumors of an incestuous relationship with his sister Bernice (Acts 25:13). Died AD 92/93 or 100. He interrogated Paul in prison. Close to becoming Christian (Acts 26:28).

KANDAKE
Probably the title of a female ruler of Kush in the Nile Valley, Sudan (at the time called Ethiopia). May refer to Queen Amanitore. Mentioned as the one under whom the Ethiopian eunuch served (Acts 8:27).

ANTONIUS FELIX
Governor of Judea from AD 52 to 59/60. Paul was imprisoned in Caesarea. Felix interrogated him there, hoping for a bribe. He kept Paul in custody for two years (Acts 23:24–24:27).

PORCIUS FESTUS
Governor of Judea, probably AD 59 to 62. Succeeded Felix (Acts 24:27). Festus interrogated Paul while he was imprisoned in Caesarea (Acts 25:6–12). During the hearing, Paul appealed to Rome (Acts 25:12).

PONTIUS PILATE
Governor of Judea from AD 26 to 36. Ruthless toward the Jews and Samaritans. Although Jesus was innocent, he sentenced him to death (John 19:12, 16). Mentioned in both the Apostles' and Nicene Creeds.

SULPICIUS QUIRINIUS
Born in 50 BC. He was a special representative in the eastern Roman Empire between 12 BC and AD 16. Appointed governor of Syria in AD 6 and died in AD 21. Carried out the census mentioned in Luke 2:2–5.

Who Exactly Is My Neighbor?

The only parable addressed to a critic

1 A man attacked by robbers

An expert in religious law wants to test Jesus (Luke 10:25–29). The question is: "Who is my neighbor?" In response, Jesus tells a parable about a man who was attacked by robbers on the road to Jericho (Luke 10:30). After the attack, the man is left lying on the road.

2 A priest came along the way

A priest came down the road but he passed by the man (Luke 10:31). If the man had been dead and the priest touched him, he would have become unclean (Lev. 21:1–4).

3 A Levite came down the road

A Levite, a temple servant from the tribe of Levi, also came by. Like the priest, he made a detour around the man and left him lying beaten in the road (Luke 10:32).

4 A Samaritan stopped

Then a Samaritan arrived on the scene (Luke 10:33–34a). He was despised by the Jews. But filled with compassion, he stayed and bound up the man's wounds.

5 Who is my neighbor?

He took the beaten man to an inn, paid for his ongoing care, and promised that he would return (Luke 10:34b–35). Jesus asked the expert: "Which of these three … was a neighbor?" His answer: "The one who showed him mercy." Jesus's response: "Go and do the same" (Luke 10:36–37).

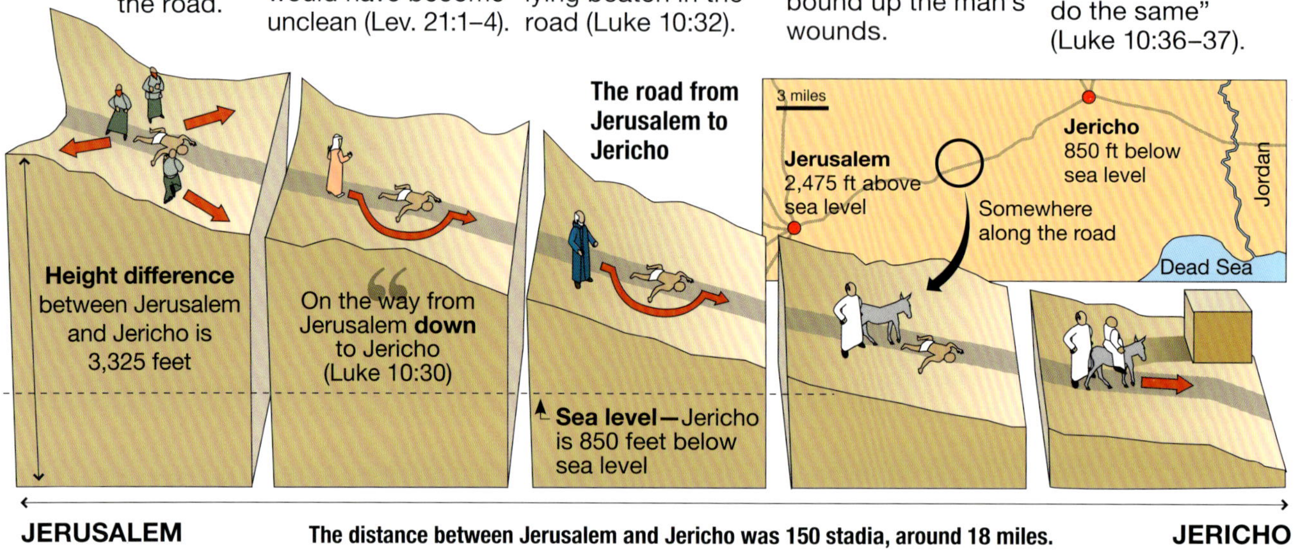

1 The road to Jericho was very dangerous

The road from Jerusalem to Jericho was about 18 miles long, mostly downhill. The mountains and steep slopes were a haunt for robbers and the road was considered dangerous to travelers in both directions.

2 Never a neighbor to a Jew

The word "neighbor" means "someone who is close." The Jews interpreted it as referring only to other Jews. They excluded Samaritans and foreigners from that group. This is the background to the story.

3 Not what you say but what you do

Jesus illustrates the difference between saying you believe something and showing compassion. Those who are expected to help the man don't. Your compassion is the essential element, not your words.

4 Jesus turns the question around

The expert in religious law asks: "Who is my neighbor?" But Jesus turns the question around and says: "To whom are you a neighbor?" And the answer is: You are a neighbor to the one you show mercy to.

Some other Samaritans

A MAN WITH LEPROSY
Text: Luke 17:11–19
Jesus heals ten men with leprosy, one of them is a Samaritan.

WOMAN AT THE WELL
Text: John 4:1–42
Jesus meets a Samaritan woman in Sychar.

SIMON THE SORCERER
Text: Acts 8:18–24
Philip meets Simon the sorcerer in the city of Samaria.

OTHER SAMARITANS
Texts: John 4:39–42; Luke 9:51–56; Acts 8:4–17.

Fourteen Groups in Jesus's Day

HIGH PRIESTS
The high priest was both a religious and a political leader. When the High Priest Annas was deposed by Rome, his son-in-law Caiaphas assumed the role (Matt. 2:4; 20:18; Mark 15:11; John 11:49; 18:13).

PRIESTS
Men who could prove descent from Aaron were allowed to become priests (Neh. 7:64). They participated in making religious sacrifices and other ritual duties (Mark 1:44; Luke 10:31; Acts 6:7).

LEVITES
Men from the tribe of Levi who could not prove descent from Aaron were called Levites. They could not serve as priests but performed other temple duties, like serving as temple guards (John 1:19; Luke 22:4).

SCRIBES/LAWYERS
Men who had many years of training were considered capable of interpreting the law. May be seen as bureaucrats who formulated the rules of life (Acts 23:9). Ezra is often seen as the first scribe (Ezra 7:10).

THE SANHEDRIN
The Sanhedrin was the highest Jewish judicial and political body. It had 71 members, composed of the chief priest and representatives from the Pharisees and Sadducees (Luke 23:13; John 7:26; 12:42).

PHARISEES
An influential group that was concerned with personal piety. They wanted to break the power of the priests. They were legalistic and some considered them hypocrites (Matt. 5:20; 12:2; Mark 2:18).

SADDUCEES
More of a political party than a religious one. Included members of aristocratic families and many priests. Had great political influence and cooperated with the Romans (Matt. 22:23, 34; Acts 5:17; 23:7).

TAX COLLECTORS
Rome leased the right to collect taxes at city gates and similar places. Tax collectors were despised and considered traitors. The disciple Matthew and Zacchaeus were both tax collectors (Matt. 10:3; Luke 19:2).

HERODIANS
A political party that sympathized with the rule of the Herodian dynasty. Many members came from the aristocracy and they embraced the traditions of Rome (Matt. 22:16; Mark 3:6; 8:15; 12:13).

ESSENES
An ascetic religious group that was critical of the clergy. Mainly in Judea, they had a stronghold in Qumran by the Dead Sea. They hid the Dead Sea Scrolls. John the Baptist may have had contact with them.

SAMARITANS
Samaritans emerged in the seventh century BC when peoples displaced by the Assyrians mixed with the remaining Jews in Samaria (2 Kings 17). Their religious beliefs were mixed, too (Luke 10:33; John 4:20).

JEWS OF THE DIASPORA
Diaspora means "scattered" and refers to Jews who lived outside the land of Israel (Acts 8:1; 15:21). This group also included non-Jews who converted to the Jewish faith, called proselytes (John 7:35; 1 Peter 1:1).

ZEALOTS
Their goal was the overthrow of Roman rule. They may have started as a tax rebellion but later became religiously motivated. Simon the Zealot might have come from this group (Luke 6:15; Acts 1:13; 5:37).

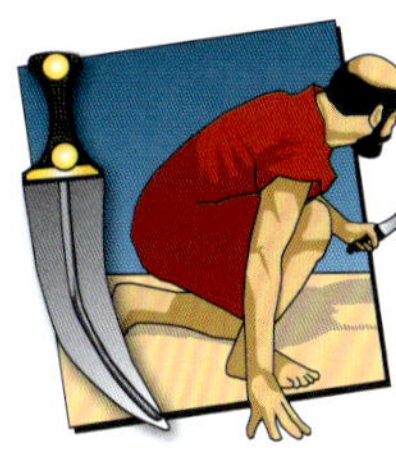

ASSASSINS (*SIKARIOS*)
Cutthroats who hid daggers (Latin *sicarii*) in their cloaks and stabbed political opponents in crowds, slipping away unnoticed. A violent group that splintered off from the Zealots (Acts 21:38).

Thousands of People around Jesus

Luke 11:14–13:9 describes an intense and busy day in the life of Jesus. He moves quickly from miracles to teaching and from discussion to proclamation. Follow him step by step as he moves from confrontation to spiritual care and concern.

1

Jesus drives out a demon

A miracle begins the hectic day. Jesus drives out an evil spirit. The people are amazed but also question his power. Jesus warns them of the danger of spiritual blindness (11:14–26).

3

Jesus addresses the people

More people flock in, seeking signs. Jesus rebukes their unbelief and condemns their generation. He speaks of the eye as the lamp of the body (11:29–36).

5

Jesus confronted by critics

On his way out, he is suddenly confronted by religious teachers who aggressively try to trap and frame him (11:53–54).

7

Jesus speaks to the disciples (I)

Jesus first addresses his disciples. He warns them about the leaven of the Pharisees, saying that they should not be afraid (12:2–12).

9

Jesus speaks to his disciples (II)

Jesus urges them not to worry but to seek the Kingdom of God above all else, trusting fully in God's provision and timing (12:22–40).

11

Jesus speaks to the people

Jesus says that people can read the weather but sadly cannot discern or understand the true spiritual signs of the times (12:54–59).

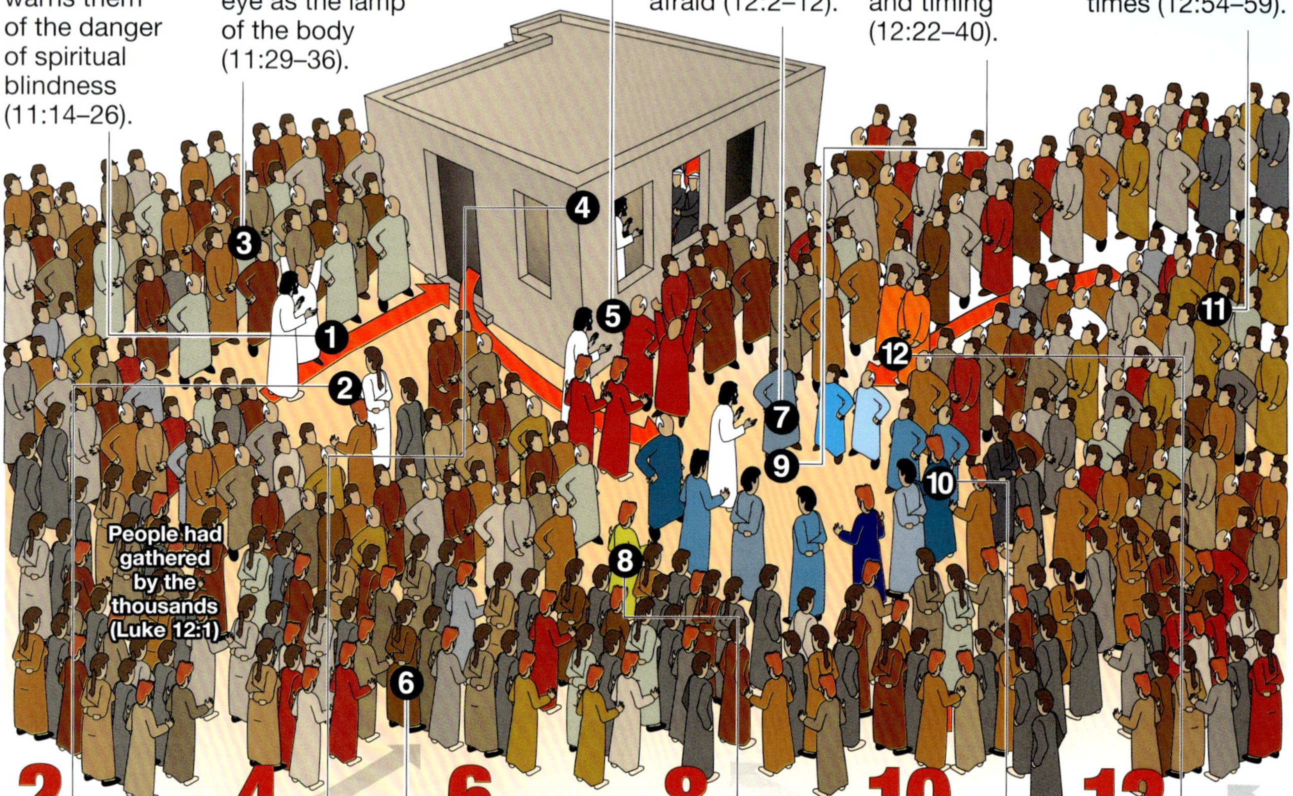

2

Jesus speaks with a woman

As Jesus is speaking, a woman cries out from the crowd. He answers her that blessing comes from obeying God's word (11:27–28).

4

Jesus is a Pharisee's guest

Jesus eats with the Pharisees, rebuking those who care more about the outside than the inside, exposing their hypocrisy (11:37–52).

6

The crowd grows larger

New people keep arriving. Thousands now wait to hear him. They are drawn by his authority, urgency, and radical message (12:1).

8

Jesus replies to someone in the crowd

Jesus responds to a person who asks for help in distributing an inheritance by warning him against greed (12:13–21).

10

Jesus replies to Peter

Jesus talks about stewardship, pointing out that motivation must come from within, emphasizing inner conviction (12:41–53).

12

People come with bad news

New people arrive and tell of misfortunes and violence. Jesus says it is not God's punishment but a warning for all (13:1–9).

Jesus and the Children

Jesus's view of children seems to have contradictions. Perhaps they also apply to every Christian's view of their own life. We are, after all, children of God.

1 • **Children are God's gift** to parents and family, to the church, and to society. They are a sign of his blessing (Ps. 127:3–5; 128:3–6; Luke 1:14; John 16:21).
• At the same time, **children are morally responsible** for their actions, born into and carrying sin, and they are at risk of being lost (Gen. 8:21; Ps. 51:5–6; Prov. 20:11; Matt. 18:14; Rom. 3:9–10).

2 • **Children are fully human,** created in the image of God. They are able to have their own independent relationship with God through faith. God both calls and uses children for good (1 Sam 3:3–14; Isa. 49:5; Matt. 18:5, 10).
• At the same time, **children are developing humans**, in need of guidance and instruction, who need to make a personal commitment to the gospel (Gen. 18:19; Deut. 31:12–13; Prov. 22:6; Eph. 6:4).

3 • **Children are role models of faith**, sources of revelation, examples of worship, and representatives of Christ. Adults are to learn from their uncomplicated faith and trust (Matt. 18:1–5, 10; 19:14; 21:16; Mark 10:15).
• At the same time, **children are vulnerable**, poor, and sometimes orphaned. Parents and other adults are expected to protect them, care for them, and take responsibility for them (Ex. 22:22; Deut. 10:18; Matt. 18:6).

Some children Jesus met

(We do not always know the children's ages.)

A WIDOW'S SON IS RAISED FROM THE DEAD BY JESUS
Jesus comes to Nain where a widow's son has died. As the boy is carried out Jesus touches the "young man," raises him, and gives him back to his mother.
Lesson: Children are a gift to their parents (Luke 7:11–17).

JAIRUS'S DAUGHTER IS RAISED FROM THE DEAD BY JESUS
Jairus's daughter has died. Despite Jairus's doubts, Jesus accompanies him home. The girl receives her life back (Matt. 9:18–26; Mark 5:21–43; Luke 8:40–56).
Lesson: Even if we think all hope is lost, it is never too late for Jesus.

THE BOY WITH FIVE LOAVES AND TWO FISH
Jesus teaches a hungry crowd but there is not much food. A boy shares his meal and Jesus feeds all (Matt. 14:13–21; Mark 6:30–44; Luke 9:10–17; John 6:1–13).
Lesson: Everyone's contribution matters. Jesus can multiply it.

A BOY WITH SEIZURES IS HEALED BY JESUS
A boy is possessed by an evil spirit. His father asks Jesus for help, but doubts. Jesus rebukes the spirit, delivering the boy (Matt. 17:14–18; Mark 9:14–27; Luke 9:37–42).
Lesson: A parent's faith does not have to be perfect to be effective.

THE CHILD THAT JESUS PLACES IN THE CENTER
Jesus puts a child among his disciples saying: "Anyone who becomes as humble as this little child is the greatest" (Matt. 18:1–5; Mark 9:36–37; Luke 9:47–48).
Lesson: Comparing ourselves to a child calls us to humility.

THE CHILDREN THAT JESUS TAKES IN HIS ARMS
Small children are brought to Jesus. He takes them in his arms and blesses them (Matt. 19:13–14; Mark 10:13–16; Luke 18:15–17).
Lesson: Even small children are valuable, they are fully human in the eyes of God.

SOME BIBLE TEXTS ABOUT JESUS AND CHILDREN
Jesus came into the world as a child (Luke 2:16–17) • Jesus reveals truth to the childlike (Matt. 11:25; Luke 10:21) • Jesus affirms children (Matt. 18:2; 9:47) • Jesus accepts help from children (Matt. 18:1–5; Mark 9:36–37; John 6:9) • Jesus lays hands on and blesses children (Mark 10:13, 16; Luke 18:15) • Jesus prays for children (Matt. 19:13) • Jesus heals children (Luke 8:42, 54; John 4:49).

What Does It Cost to Be a Disciple?

Jesus emphasizes that while salvation is free, following him as a disciple comes at great cost. Salvation assures us of heaven, but it also demands wholehearted devotion to him—not in order to earn heaven, but as the response of a grateful heart for the gift received!

> “The theme of the cost of accompanying Jesus runs like a refrain throughout Luke. (Howard Marshall)

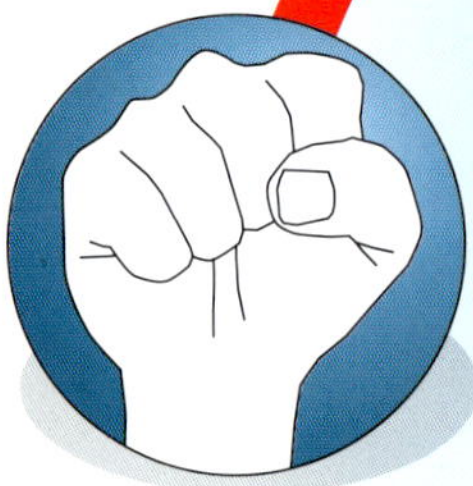

1 “Hating” father and mother
Love for Jesus should be so great that all other relationships—with parents, spouses and children, siblings, even self—seem like hatred by comparison (Luke 14:25–26).

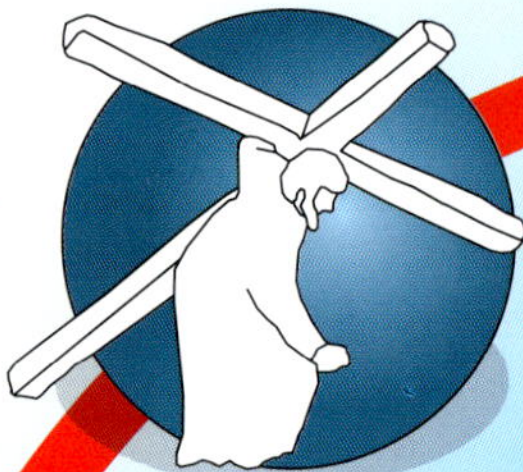

2 Taking up your cross
Taking up your cross meant that you were headed to your own execution. Those who are condemned have lost their right to life. Being a disciple includes giving up the right to your life (Luke 14:27).

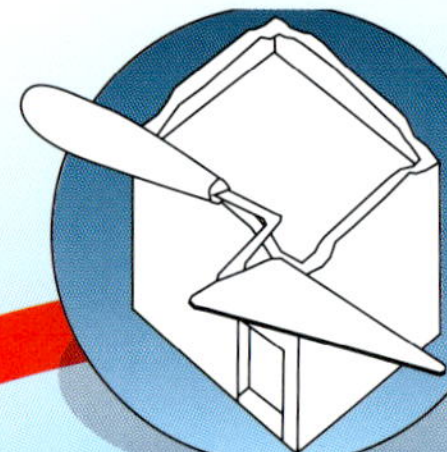

3 The cost of building a tower
The builder, like the disciple, is asked to count the cost—otherwise he risks becoming a public laughingstock for his failure to complete his plans (Luke 14:28–30).

4 Cost of going to war
The king going to war, like a disciple, is asked to calculate the cost—otherwise his actions could lead to disaster not only for himself, but also for what he claims represent (Luke 14:31–33).

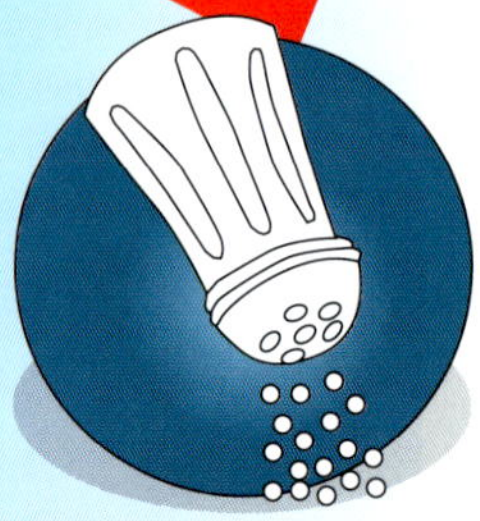

5 Salt without saltiness
Salt from the Dead Sea came in blocks. When rain dissolved the salt, the blocks became useless. Submission is the salt of the Christian (Luke 14:34–35).

Three parables with the same theme

- In Luke 15, Jesus tells three parables in a row, each having the same theme: something that was lost is found.
- This suggests that the parables are not independent of each other, but build on each other.
- **Note:** “This story” (15:3), implies that the three parables are one story.

1 The parable of the lost sheep
The emphasis of the first parable is the condition of the lost. It focuses on the shepherd’s effort (Luke 15:3–7).

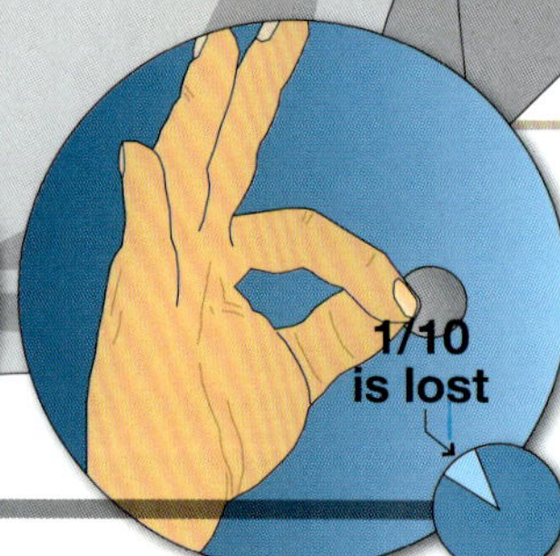

2 The parable of the lost coin
The emphasis of the second parable is the search itself. The focus is on a woman’s dogged pursuit (Luke 15:8–10).

3 The parable of the lost son
The third parable emphasizes the redemption of the lost. It points to the father’s willingness to forgive (Luke 15:11–32).

NOTE: An ever-increasing percentage of what had been lost is recovered.

How Did Jesus Teach?

We often discuss what Jesus preached, but pay less attention to *how* he preached. These were his methods.

EDUCATION

1. SPEECHES/SERMONS—Jesus's sermons include word pairs (Matt. 5:21–48), words of wisdom (Matt. 5:13–14), and repetitions (Matt. 5:3–11). **Examples:** Matt. 5–7; 24–25; John 13–17.

2. (WRITTEN) REFERENCES—Jesus refers to and draws on Old Testament texts to support his views. **Examples:** Matt. 5:21–48; 22:41–46; Mark 7:5–13.

3. PARABLES—Stories based on everyday life with a theological or moral point that the listener is expected to interpret. **Example:** Matt. 13:1–52.

4. ILLUSTRATIONS—Illustrative stories to clarify and make it easy to remember. **Examples:** Luke 14:28 (the tower), 14:31 (the war), 14:34 (the salt).

5. SILENCE—Jesus sometimes chooses not to answer questions. Silence should lead to reflection on the part of those who expected an answer. **Examples:** Matt. 15:21–23; John 8:6–9.

INTERACTIONS

6. DIALOGUE—Jesus talks to people and through their exchange, he helps lead them to insight and understanding. **Examples:** Matt. 6:1–18; 8:5–13; 9:14–17; 17:19–21; Mark 2:18–22.

7. DISCUSSION—The discussion weaves back and forth, exchanging positions and arguments, before reaching understanding. **Examples:** Matt. 12:1–8, 9–14, 38–42; 15:1–20; 21:23–27; Mark 2:23–28; 7:1–13.

8.QUESTION AND COUNTER-QUESTION—Jesus answers questions. But his answer is often a counter-question. This leaves the original questioner to think for himself and answer his own question. **Examples:** Matt. 21:24–27; 22:16–17, 28–33.

ACTIVITY

9. ILLUSTRATIVE EXAMPLES—Jesus uses people, animals, and things to illustrate what he wants to convey. The images reinforce the message. **Examples:** Matt. 6:26 (birds), Matt. 18:1–4 (a child).

10. DRAMATIZATION—Jesus shows his message in action. **Example:** His cleansing of the temple becomes an educational drama. Matt. 21:12–17; Mark 11:15–19; Luke 5:24.

11. DEMONSTRATION—By his actions, Jesus shows what the message he proclaims means and that it is credible and true. **Example:** Matt. 11:4–6.

12. PROJECT/INTERNSHIP—Jesus sends his disciples out discover for themselves how to put into practice what they have learned. **Example:** Matt. 10:1–42.

OTHER METHODS

13. REPETITION—Jesus repeats themes, making them easier to remember. **Examples:** Matt. 5:3–11; 16:21–23; 17:22–23; 20:17–19.

14. WORDS OF WISDOM—Short sentences (proverbs and adages), pithy and easy to remember. **Examples:** Matt. 5:13–14; 7:16; 13:57; 15:14; 24:28; Mark 4:21; Luke 4:23; 6:40; 10:7.

All Jesus's Sermons

	Sermon	Matthew	Mark	Luke	John	Audience	Number of versions
1	In the synagogue in Nazareth			4:17–27		All the people (4:28)	1
2	On the authority of the Son				5:19–47	Jewish leaders (5:16)	1
3	Sermons on the Mount and the Plain	5:1–7:29		6:17–49		Disciples & crowds (5:1)	2
4	Defense against the Pharisees (1)	12:22–45	3:20–30			Pharisees (12:24)	2
5	Parables of the kingdom of God	13:1–52	4:1–34	8:4–18		Crowds & disciples (13:2, 10)	3
6	First sending out of the disciples	10:1–4	6:7–11	9:1–5		The Twelve (10:1)	3
7	About defilement	15:1–20	7:1–23			Pharisees & scribes (15:1)	2
8	On the greatest in the kingdom	18:1–35	9:33–50	9:46–50		The disciples (18:1)	3
9	At the Feast of Tabernacles				7:37–39	Crowds (7:40)	1
10	The Good Shepherd				10:1–18	Pharisees (9:40)	1
11	Second sending out of the disciples			10:1–24		Seventy-two disciples (10:1)	1
12	Defense against the Pharisees (2)			11:14–54		Crowds (11:14)	1
13	On the cost of discipleship			14:25–35		Crowds (14:25)	1
14	Parables of the lost			15:1–16:31		Pharisees & scribes (15:1)	1
15	Defense against the Pharisees' attack	23:1–39	12:38–40	20:45–47		People & disciples (23:1)	3
16	The Olivet Discourse on the end times	24–25	13:1–37	21:5–36		The disciples (24:1)	3
17	In the Upper Room and on way to Gethsemane				13:31–16:33	The Eleven (13:31)	1

Source: Tomas Kroksmark, Didaskalos: Teaching Methodology at the Beginning of Our Era

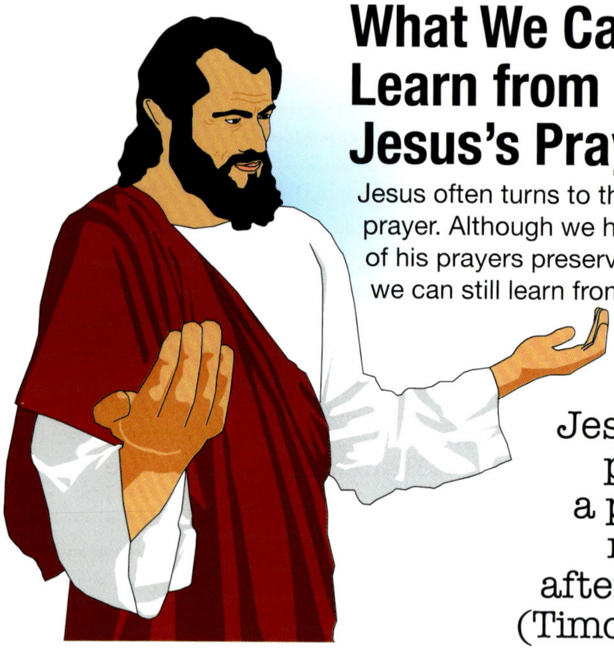

What We Can Learn from Jesus's Prayers

Jesus often turns to the Father in prayer. Although we have relatively few of his prayers preserved in the Bible, we can still learn from his example.

> "Jesus made prayer a priority, not an afterthought. (Timothy Keller)

Four Types of Prayer

1 Prayers of Worship
Prayers that focus on thanking God and exalting his name. These prayers remind us of who God is (Ps. 145:1–21).

2 Prayers of Confession
Prayers that confess sins and express a willingness to repent. This does not apply to Jesus (Ps. 51:1–21).

3 Prayers of Thanksgiving
Prayers of gratitude for what God has done through history as well as what he has done for us (Ps. 100:1–5).

4 Prayers of Intercession
Prayers where we turn to God, asking him to intervene, both for our own sake and for the sake of others (Ps. 67:1–8).

All of Jesus's Prayers

	Prayer	Location	Matthew	Mark	Luke	John	Has no words*	Has words	Number of words**	Number of versions
1	At his baptism in the Jordan	Jordan			3:21–22		■	□	0	1
2	In morning before leaving for Galilee	A lonely place		1:35–36			■	□	0	1
3	After healing people	The wilderness			5:16		■	□	0	1
4	Before choosing the Twelve	On a mountain			6:12–13		■	□	0	1
5	Speaking to Jewish leaders	Unclear	11:25–26				□	■	← 38	1
6	Before feeding 5,000	A lonely place	14:19	6:41	9:16	6:11	■	□	0	4
7	Before walking on water	On a mountain	14:23	6:46		6:15	■	□	0	3
8	When he heals a deaf-mute man	Sea of Galilee		7:31–37			□	■	← 1	1
9	Before feeding 4,000	The wilderness	15:36	8:6–7			■	□	0	2
10	Before Peter calls him Christ	Unclear			9:18		■	□	0	1
11	On the Mount of Transfiguration	A mountain			9:28–29		■	□	0	1
12	When the seventy return	Unclear			10:21		□	■	← 38	1
13	Before teaching the Lord's Prayer	"A certain place"			11:1		■	□	0	1
14	Teaching the Lord's Prayer	On a mountain	6:9–13		11:2–4		□	■	← 66	2
15	When he raises Lazarus	Bethany				11:41–42	□	■	← 33	1
16	When he blesses the children	Judea	19:13–15	10:13–16			■	□	0	2
17	After his Triumphal Entry	Jerusalem				12:27–28	□	■	← 20	1
18	At the Last Supper	The upper room	26:26	14:22–23	22:19		■	□	0	3
19	When praying for Peter	Jerusalem			22:31–32		■	□	0	1
20	The High Priestly Prayer	To Gethsemane				17:1–26	□	■	← 600	1
21	First prayer in Gethsemane	Gethsemane	26:36–39	14:32–36	22:39–46		□	■	← 27	3
22	Second prayer in Gethsemane	Gethsemane	26:40–42	14:37–40			□	■	← 17	2
23	Third prayer in Gethsemane	Gethsemane	26:43–46	14:41–42			■	□	0	2
24	When he was nailed to the cross	Golgotha			23:34		□	■	← 11	1
25	Prayer on the cross	Golgotha	27:46	15:34			□	■	← 4	2
26	At the moment of his death	Golgotha			23:46		□	■	← 8	1
27	Praying over the bread	Emmaus			24:30		■	□	0	1
28	For the disciples at the ascension	Bethany			24:50–53		■	□	0	1
	Number of prayers:		11	10	18	5	16	12	863	

• **In addition:** Some verses can be interpreted that Jesus is still praying for us: Romans 8:34; Hebrews 7:25; 9:24; 1 John 2:1.

**The text talks about Jesus praying without reproducing his words. **Version with the most words, based on the New Living Translation.*

What We Can Learn from Jesus's Miracles

We know that Jesus performed many miracles, but how often do we think to look beyond the events themselves and see something more? Miracles are also teaching tools used by Jesus that convey truth in specific situations. Here are some of the lessons that he communicated with his miracles.

1 THEY AFFIRM THAT JESUS IS TRUE GOD
The scribes state, "Only God can forgive sins!" Jesus answers: "[I have] the authority ... to forgive sins" (Mark 2:7–11), confirmed by the miracle.

2 THEY CONFIRM THAT JESUS IS THE MESSIAH
Jesus frees many who were possessed. "Because the demons knew who he was, [Jesus] did not allow them to speak" (Mark 1:34; 3:11–12).

3 THEY DEMONSTRATE GOD'S POWER OVER NATURE
Jesus's power over creation is displayed when he turns water into wine (John 2:7–10), calms the sea (Mark 4:39), and walks on water (Matt. 14:25).

4 THEY SHOW GOD'S POWER OVER DISEASE
Seventeen of Jesus's miracles recorded in the Gospels involve healing people who suffer from various physical ailments. Jesus is the great healer.

5 THEY SHOW GOD'S GRACE TO US
Grace is receiving something without having earned it. Many people are healed without their active participation (John 5:1–9; Mark 7:24–30).

6 THEY SHOW GOD'S MERCY ON US
A leper comes to Jesus and asks to be healed (Mark 1:40) "Moved with *compassion* ... Jesus reached out and touched him. 'Be healed!'" (Mark 1:41).

7 THEY SHOW GOD'S POWER OVER DEATH
Jesus raises several people from the dead, including Jairus's daughter (Mark 5:42) and Lazarus (John 11:44). And then he is raised from the dead.

8 THEY CONFIRM JESUS'S TEACHING
Jesus asks which is easier, to forgive someone's sin or heal their body? (Matt. 9:3–5). He then says "I will *prove* to you" (Matt. 9:6; Mark 3:1–5).

> "We modern people think of miracles as the suspension of the natural order, but Jesus meant them to be the restoration of the natural order.... His miracles are not just proofs that he has power but also wonderful foretastes of what he is going to do with that power. Jesus' miracles are not just a challenge to our minds, but a promise to our hearts, that the world we all want is coming.
> (Timothy Keller)

9 THEY DEMONSTRATE THAT GOD FORGIVES SINS
The healing in Mark 2 is linked with forgiveness of sins. "Jesus saw their faith and said to the lame man, 'My child, your sins are forgiven'" (Mark 2:5).

10 THEY FULFILL OLD TESTAMENT PROPHECIES
The miracles fulfill prophecies that people would be healed. "This fulfilled the word of the Lord through the prophet Isaiah" (Matt. 8:16–17).

11 THEY CHALLENGE US TO BELIEVE AND WORSHIP
Jesus meets a woman with constant bleeding and says "'Your faith has made you well.' And the woman was healed" (Matt. 9:22; 15:22–28; Mark 10:52).

12 THEY SHOW GOD'S POWER OVER EVIL
Time and again, Jesus shows that he has power over evil and the evil one "Even evil spirits obey his orders!" (Mark 1:27; Luke 4:33–36).

13 THEY GIVE HOPE FOR THE WORLD TO COME
The miracles give us a glimpse of what is to come. Everything on earth will be restored to perfection as the miracles restored people in Jesus's day.

14 THEY ARE THE EXCEPTION, NOT THE RULE
Jesus heals many, but not all. "Inside these porches [at the Pool of Bethesda] lay many sick people." But Jesus only heals one of them (John 5:3–5).

15 THEY DID NOT ALWAYS LEAD TO REPENTANCE
The miracles were not always met with a response of faith. Jesus rebukes three cities because they *did not* repent (Matt. 11:20–24; Luke 10:13–16).

16 THEIR PURPOSE IS ALWAYS TO GLORIFY GOD
Jesus heals ten sick people. One returns and thanks God (Luke 17:15). Jesus asks him why the others did not give God the glory (Luke 17:18).

The Feasts of the New Testament

START HERE

There are seven major Jewish holidays, and most are listed in Leviticus 23. Two of them, Purim and Hanukkah, were added after the account in Leviticus 23.

1 Passover*, Feast of Unleavened Bread, and Firstfruits

Texts: Lev. 23:4–14; John 2:13; 6:4; 11:55; 18:28. **Dates:** Observed for eight days: Passover on 14 Nisan, Unleavened Bread on 15–21, and Firstfruits on the Sunday of that week. Commemorates the liberation from slavery in Egypt. The Passover meal is eaten the first day and Psalms 113–118 are sung (Matt. 26:30).

2 Shavuot*—Feast of Harvest

Text: Lev. 23:15–22
Date: 6(–7) Sivan.
Commemorates the receiving of the Law on Mount Sinai. Also a harvest festival when offerings of the first harvest were brought to the temple. Today, the Torah is celebrated during the weekend in memory of the receiving of the Law. Flowers and leaves are often picked and the home is decorated with them.

3 Rosh Hashanah—(also New Year)

Texts: Lev. 23:23–25; Matt. 24:31; 1 Thess. 4:16–17
Date: 1 Tishri, celebrated for two days. It is the day the shofar is blown. People look back on their lives and reflect on whether they have followed God's laws.

4 Yom Kippur

Texts: Lev. 16:1–34; Acts 27:9 **Date:** 10 Tishri. The holiest day for Jews. The Day of Atonement. On this day, people ask God for forgiveness.

5 Sukkot*—Feast of Tabernacles

Texts: Lev. 23:33–43; John 7:2, 10 **Date:** 15–22 Tishri. To remember the wandering in the desert. A sukkah (simple hut) is built.

Festival added after Leviticus 3:23.
↓

6 Hanukkah—Festival of Lights

Texts: 1 Macc. 4:36; 2 Macc. 1:18; John 10:22
Date: 25 Kislev to 3 or 4 Tevet. Commemorates the Jewish recapture and rededication of the temple in 165/164 BC. The soldiers only found enough oil for one day, but the lampstand burned for eight days.

7 Purim—honors the rescue by Esther

Text: Est. 9:18–32
Date: 14 or 15 Adar.
Celebration to commemorate how Esther saved her people from Haman's wrath. The book of Esther is read in the synagogue. When Haman's name is mentioned, there is much booing and stamping of feet.

• There are two Jewish calendars. (1) Exodus 12:1–2 establishes one in which the month of Nisan begins the year. (2) In Jesus's day (and today) another is used in which the month of Tishri begins the year.

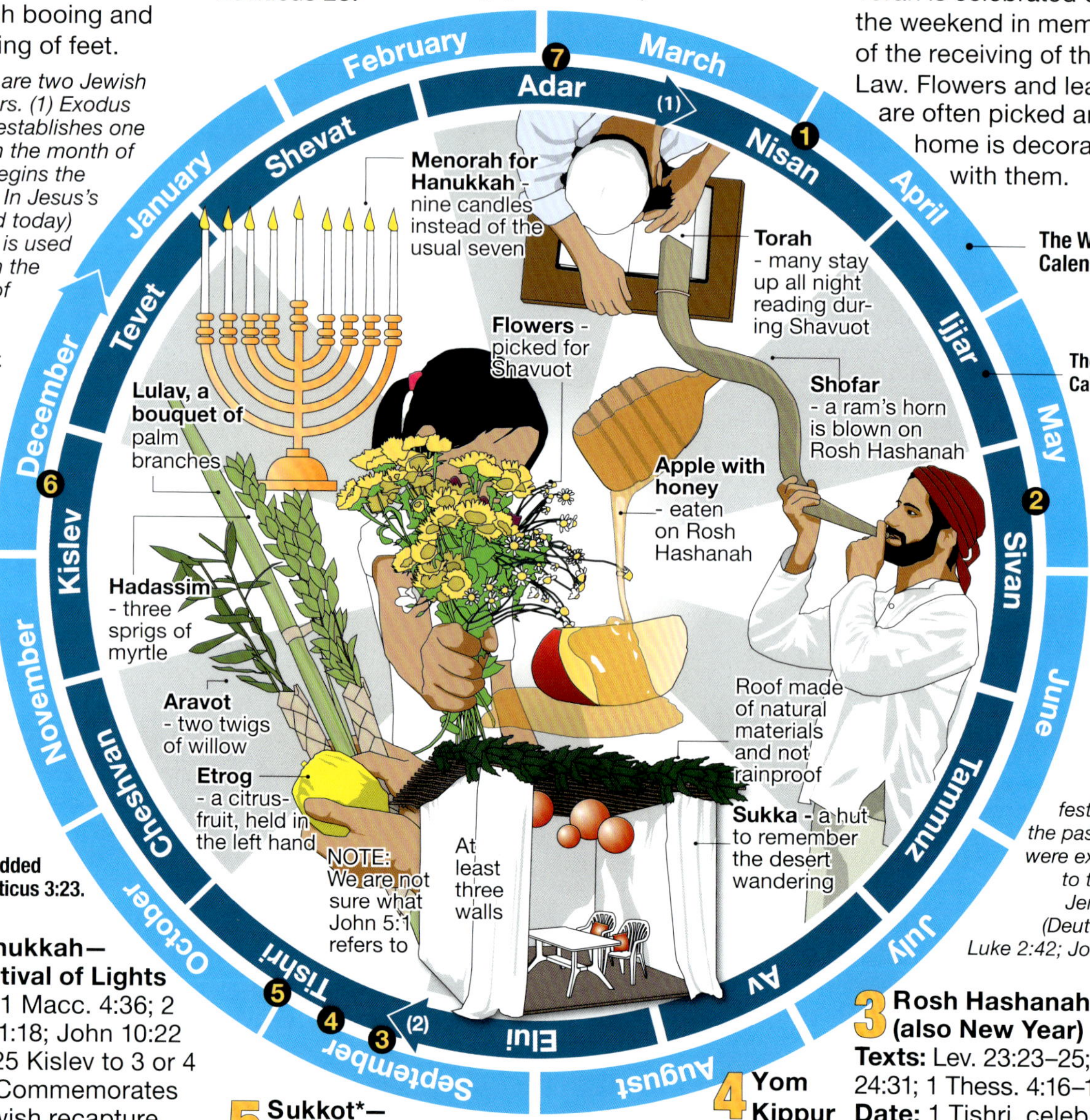

**Called pilgrim festivals. In the past, Jews were expected to travel to Jerusalem (Deut. 16:16; Luke 2:42; John 5:1).*

Jesus Raises Lazarus

Martha and Mary's brother Lazarus was sick. They had faith that Jesus could make him well, but possibly not that Jesus could raise him from the dead.

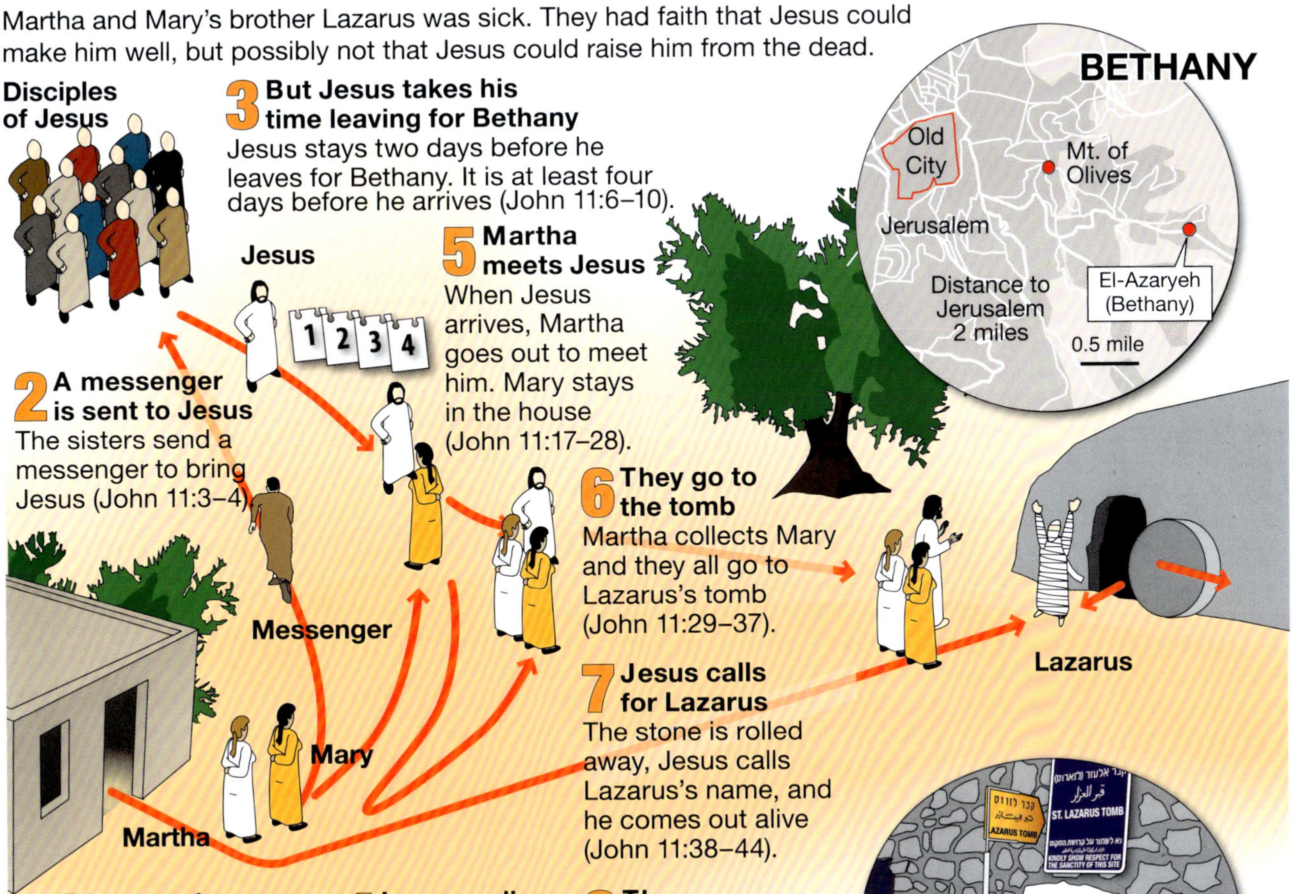

1 Lazarus becomes very sick
Lazarus, who is in Bethany, is quite ill. His sisters, Mary and Martha, send for Jesus in Perea (John 11:1–2, 5).

2 A messenger is sent to Jesus
The sisters send a messenger to bring Jesus (John 11:3–4).

3 But Jesus takes his time leaving for Bethany
Jesus stays two days before he leaves for Bethany. It is at least four days before he arrives (John 11:6–10).

4 Lazarus dies and is buried
As Jesus heads toward Bethany, Lazarus dies and his body is laid in a tomb (John 11:11–16).

5 Martha meets Jesus
When Jesus arrives, Martha goes out to meet him. Mary stays in the house (John 11:17–28).

6 They go to the tomb
Martha collects Mary and they all go to Lazarus's tomb (John 11:29–37).

7 Jesus calls for Lazarus
The stone is rolled away, Jesus calls Lazarus's name, and he comes out alive (John 11:38–44).

8 The consequences
Many come to faith. But when the Pharisees hear, they want to kill both Jesus and Lazarus (John 11:45–57).

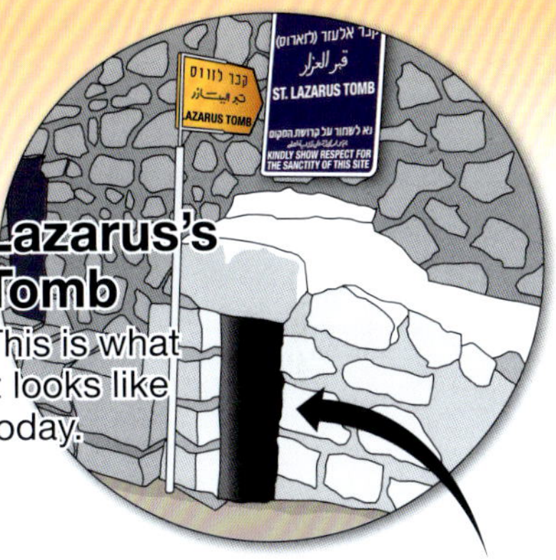

Lazarus's Tomb
This is what it looks like today.

1 Lazarus dead for four days
According to Jewish tradition, the soul stayed close to the body for three days in the hope of returning. "Four days" may mean that all hope was gone (John 11:17).

2 No immediate answers
God's answer is not always immediate. Even for those who pray and wait for an answer, the situation may get worse before it gets better. God answers prayer in his own time.

3 Not always explained
Both Martha and Mary state: "If you had been here" (John 11:21, 32). But they received no explanation, God is never obliged to tell us the reason for his actions.

4 The miracle's consequence
In a way, Jesus gave his life for Lazarus. It was as a result of the raising of Lazarus from the tomb that the religious leaders decided to kill Jesus (John 11:18, 45–53).

5 The grave in Bethany
There is a place in El-Azaryeh in the West Bank called Lazarus's Tomb. It is possible, but not certain, that this is where Jesus performed the miracle.

> "The Jewish system of preparing a body for burial provided for swathing it in bandage-like wrappings ... leaving the shoulders bare ... Such enswathement would effectively prevent any ordinary means of locomotion on the part of Lazarus. The only explanation of his appearance at the door of the tomb is that the power that galvanized him into life brought him forth to the door. (Merrill Tenny)

Bartimaeus and Zacchaeus in Jericho

On his way to Jerusalem, Jesus arrives in Jericho where two dramatic events occur—the healing of two blind men and the encounter with the tax collector Zacchaeus (Matt. 20:29–33; Mark 10:46–52; Luke 18:35–19:10).

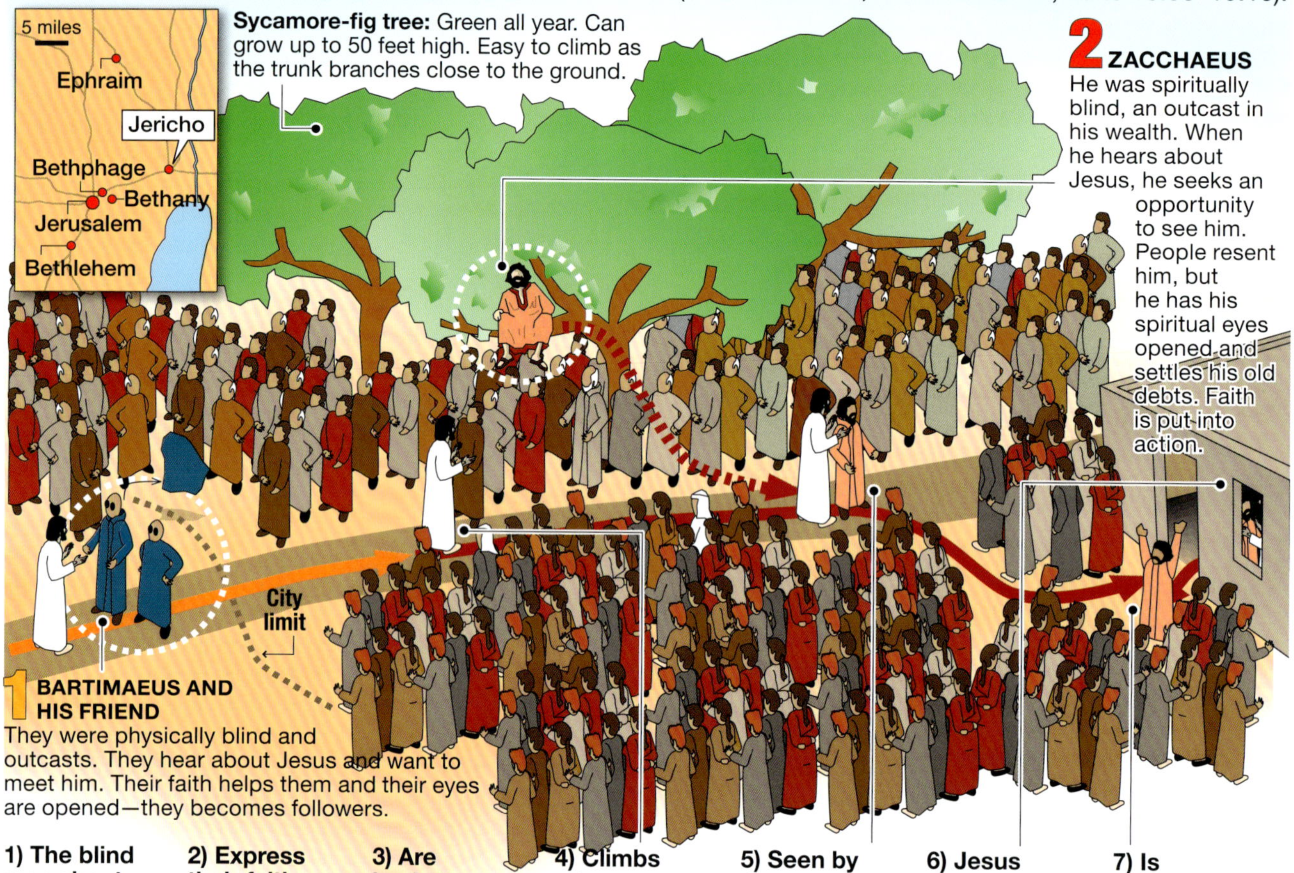

1) The blind men shout
Two blind men sitting by the road cry out to Jesus for help (Mt 20:29–31; Lk 18:35–39).

2) Express their faith
One of them throws aside his coat as an expression of faith (Mk 10:49–52a; Lk 18:40–43a).

3) Are healed
Jesus touches their eyes, and restores their sight (Mt 20:32b–34; Lk 18:43b).

4) Climbs a tree
The tax collector Zacchaeus climbs a tree so he can see Jesus better (Lk 19:1–4).

5) Seen by Jesus
Jesus sees him and stops, saying, "I must be a guest in your home today" (Lk 19:5).

6) Jesus invited
The tax collector climbs down, invites Jesus home in great joy (Lk 19:6–7).

7) Is changed
As a result, Zacchaeus promise to make up for all his wrongdoing (Lk 19:8–10).

Meals Attended by Jesus

		Matthew	Mark	Luke	John	Present at the meal	Location	Number of versions
1	The wedding in Cana				2:1–11	Wedding guests	Cana	1
2	Guest in Matthew's house	9:10–17	2:15–22	5:29–39		Tax collectors and sinners	Capernaum	3
3	Meal with a Pharisee			7:36–50		The Pharisee and a sinner	Unknown	1
4	Feeding 5,000 people	14:15–21	6:35–44	9:12–17	6:10–13	The people	Bethsaida	4
5	Feeding 4,000 people	15:32–38	8:1–9a			The people	Deserted area	2
6	Home of Martha and Mary			10:38–40		Martha and Mary	Bethany	1
7	Home of a Pharisee			11:37–54		Scribes and Pharisees	Unknown	1
8	Home of a leading Pharisee			14:1–24		A leading Pharisee	Unknown	1
9	Eating with sinners			15:1–2		Tax collectors and sinners	Unknown	1
► 10	Guest of Zacchaeus			19:1–10		The tax collector Zacchaeus	Jericho	1
11	Guest of Simon the Leper	26:6–13	14:3–9		12:1–11	Simon & a woman with perfume	Bethany	3
12	Evening meal with the Twelve	26:26–29	14:22–25	22:17–20	13:1–17	The twelve disciples	Upper room	4
13	Guest of the disciples in Emmaus		16:12–13	24:13–32		Cleopas and someone else	Emmaus	2
14	Eating fish with the disciples		16:14	24:36–43	20:19–25	Ten disciples	Upper room	3
15	Eating fish at the Sea of Galilee				21:11–14	Seven disciples	Galilee	1

Holy Week: Day by Day

"[They] took palm branches and went down the road to meet him" (John 12:13).

Palm Sunday (March 29, AD 33)*

1 Jesus rides into Jerusalem

Texts: Matt. 21:1–11,14–17; Mark 11:1–11; Luke 19:29–44; John 12:12–19; Zech. 9:9 • Jesus arrives via Bethany and Bethphage • Sends two disciples to bring a donkey and foal • Rides into Jerusalem on the donkey • Weeps over Jerusalem

Monday (March 30)

2 Jesus in Jerusalem

Texts: Matt. 21:18–19,12–13; Mark 11:12–18; Luke 19:45–48; John 12:20-50
• Jesus curses the fig tree
• Clears the temple • Speaks of his impending death

Tuesday (March 31)

3 Jesus appears in Jerusalem

Texts: Matt. 21:18–26:16; Mark 11:19–14:11; Luke 21:37–22:6; John 12:2–8
• The great debate • Comments on the widow's offering • The Olivet Discourse • Predicts his death • Jesus at Simon the leper's house**
• Judas makes a deal to betray Jesus**

Wednesday (April 1)

4 Jesus remains in Bethany

Text: No text
• Perhaps at the home of Martha, Mary, and Lazarus (Luke 21:37). • Bethany is located on Mt. of Olives 2.5 miles from Jerusalem

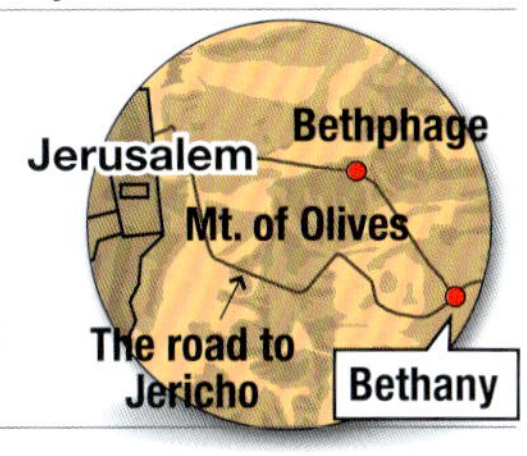

Thursday (April 2)

5 Jesus's last evening

Texts: Matt. 26:17–46; Mark 14:12–42; Luke 22:7–46; John 13:1–18:1
• Jesus washes the disciples' feet • Identifies Judas as the traitor • Predicts Peter's denial
• Institutes the Lord's Supper • Talks on the way to Gethsemane • Anguish in Gethsemane

Good Friday (April 3)

6 Jesus is convicted, crucified, and dies

Text: Matt. 26:47–27:66; Mark 14:43–15:47; Luke 22:47–23:56; John 18:2–19:42
• Jesus is betrayed by Judas • Interrogated by Jewish leaders • Peter denies Jesus • Jesus before Herod Antipas • Condemned by Pilate
• Crucified • Dies on the cross and is buried

Saturday (Easter eve, April 4)

7 Jesus is in the grave

Text: No text
• Jesus is in the tomb.
• There is debate about whether 1 Peter 3:19–20 refers to this time, but that is unlikely

"On the third day he will rise again (Luke 18:33).

Sunday (Easter day, April 5)

8 The tomb is empty, Jesus appears

Texts: Matt. 28:1–15; Mark 16:1–14; Luke 24:1–43; John 20:1–25
• The women come to the tomb • Peter and John run to the tomb • Jesus appears to Mary Magdalene • Jesus meets the travelers to Emmaus
• Appears to all the disciples except Thomas

1 2 3 On third day

"When Jesus had tasted it, he said, 'It is finished!' Then he bowed his head and gave up his spirit (John 19:30).

Church of the Holy Sepulchre

• Constantine built a church on the site in AD 335. Since then, it has been destroyed and rebuilt, expanded and renovated several times.

• Under the rotunda is the place which is identified as the tomb of Jesus.

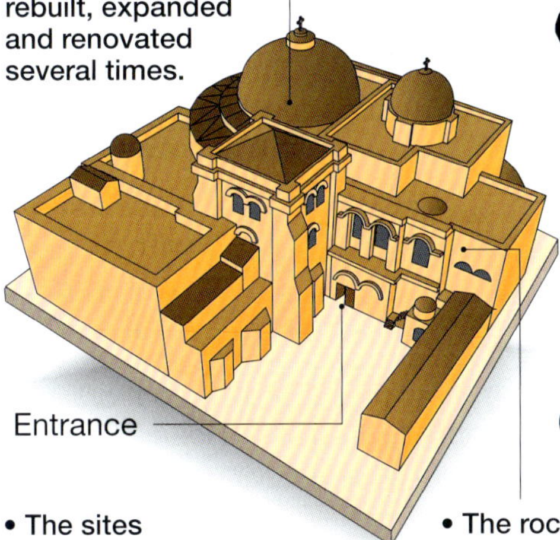

• The sites identified by tradition as Calvary and the burial ground are located inside the Church of the Holy Sepulchre. The superstructure was built in 1810 in the so-called Turkish Rococo style.

• The rock of Calvary is up the stairs.

* *Probable dates of Jesus's death and resurrection*
** *Possibly on Wednesday*

The Triumphal Entry into Jerusalem

Jesus's entry into Jerusalem is a public proclamation that he is the Messiah. ("Now the time has come," John 12:23).

1 The Donkey
Brought by the disciples (Matt. 21:6–8). Jesus may be riding both donkeys ("them," 21:2).

2 The Colt
Jesus rides on a donkey's colt (Mark 11:2). The donkey is often seen as a symbol of peace. (see Zech. 9:9).

3 The Shouts
The people shout "Hosanna!" (Ps. 118:25–26; Isa. 62:11). This links Jesus to the hope of the Messiah.

4 The Palm Branches
Palm branches symbolize righteousness (Ps. 92:13). Only John mentions them (John 12:13).

5 The Cloaks
To spread cloaks was to exalt, showed respect (2 Kings 9:13); also tied to righteousness (Job 29:14).

1 The disciples
They bring Jesus's donkeys, join the procession, cut branches, and shout. But only later do they realize the significance of the event (John 12:16).

2 People outside the walls
The crowd is made up of people on their way to Jerusalem, pilgrims who know the deeds of Jesus (John 12:17). The cry comes from the pilgrim psalms.

3 People inside the walls
When Jesus enters the city, they ask, "Who is this?" (Matt. 21:10). Here it is people from Jerusalem who do not know Jesus. The pilgrims respond.

4 The Pharisees
The Pharisees ask Jesus to rebuke his followers, he replies: "If they kept quiet, the stones along the road would burst into cheers!" (Luke 19:40).

5 The children
Finally, the children in the temple join in. They shout "Praise God" (Matt. 21:15; see Ps. 118:25). The Pharisees want Jesus to stop them but he refuses.

ABOUT THE CRY HOSANNA
This was a prayer call in Hebrew. Used five times in the Greek (Mt 21:9; 21:15; Mk 11:9, 10; Jn 12:13).

1 Two words put together
One means "save," the other indicates a petition. It is a prayerful cry to God: "O, save, O, save us."

2 Prayer for the Messiah
Psalm 118:25 uses the word translated "Lord, please save us." It is a cry of hope that the Messiah will come soon.

3 Greeting the Messiah
They were voicing their desire to see him as the promised Messiah of the Old Testament.

4 Associated with hope
At the Feast of Tabernacles it was customary to shout or sing "Hosanna" as a cry of hope and thanksgiving.

The Old Testament Prophecy of the Entry into Jerusalem

The meaning of Zechariah 9:9 (This is how the Messiah comes)

- **"People of Zion, people of Jerusalem"**—personification, refers to the whole people.
- **"Your king is coming to you"**—refers to the awaited Messiah.
- **"Righteous"**—speaks of his character.
- **"Victorious"**—tells us that he is coming to establish his kingdom.
- **"Riding on a donkey"**—symbol, says "he is coming with peace."

Note also
As in many other prophecies, two perspectives are interwoven: the first coming of Jesus (Zech. 9:9) and the second coming of Jesus (Zech. 9:10–11).

Jesus and the Great Debate

Jesus has ridden into Jerusalem and been hailed by the people (Matt. 21:1–11). This is followed by an exchange with the religious leadership in the temple (Matt. 21:23). This is known as the Great Debate.

THE BACKGROUND
• **Text:** Matt. 21:1–22:14
• **Time:** March/April AD 33
EVENTS: Jesus rides into Jerusalem (21:1–11) and cleanses the temple a second time (21:12–17). This is the beginning of an open confrontation with the religious leadership.

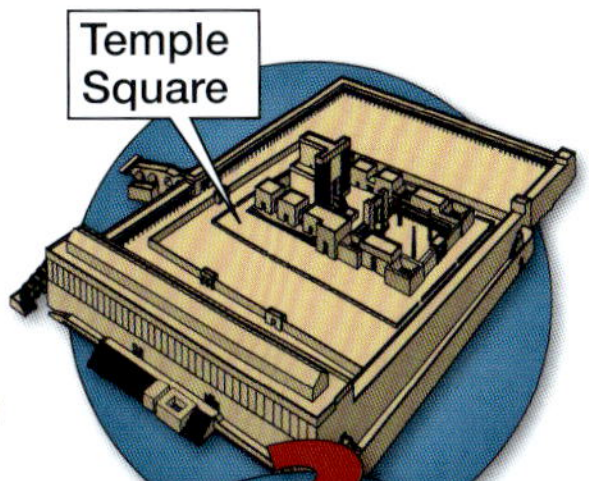

Jesus is confronted by the high priests and elders (21:23–27). He curses the fig tree (21:18–22) and tells three parables (21:28–22:14). In the temple square the following day, the religious leaders begin their attack (21:18, 23). This is referred to as the Great Debate.

1 JESUS AND POLITICS
• **Text:** Matt. 22:15–22
• **Attackers:** Pharisees, Herodians
THE DEBATE: The Pharisees opposed Rome; the Herodians collaborated. Question to Jesus: "Is it right to pay taxes to Caesar?"

Should a person pay taxes to the emperor or not?

No matter how he answered, one group would be angry. Jesus asks for a coin: "Whose image is on it?" Answer: the emperor's. "Give to Caesar what belongs to Caesar, and to God what belongs to God." **Reaction:** Amazement, and they leave.

2 JESUS AND DEATH
• **Text:** Matt. 22:23–33
• **Attackers:** Sadducees
THE DEBATE: The Sadducees didn't believe in the resurrection. They present a scenario that makes it seem illogical and slightly absurd.

In the resurrection, whose wife will she be?

Jesus exposes their false assumptions. Resurrection is not a return to the former life—it is a transformed life. Doesn't the Old Testament speak of Abraham, Isaac, and Jacob as if alive? **Reaction:** The people are astounded, but the Sadducees are unresponsive.

3 THE GREATEST COMMANDMENT
• **Text:** Matt. 22:34–40
• **Attackers:** Pharisees, one in particular, an expert in religious law.
THE DEBATE: The question: "Which is the most important commandment?" Jesus replies from the Old Testament.

Which is the greatest commandment?

"Love God and your neighbor. All the law and prophets are based on these." The foundation of the law is love. It is also the motivation for following the law and cannot be used as a motive for breaking the commandments. **Reaction:** There is no comment.

4 JESUS AND THE MESSIAH
• **Text:** Matt. 22:41–45
• **Attacker:** Jesus, who now asks the Pharisees a counter-question
THE DEBATE: "Whose son is [the Messiah]?" This is the important question. Their response: "The son

Whose son is the Messiah?

of David." Jesus counters: "Why does David call the Messiah 'my Lord'?" The idea: Whoever is son of David must also be Messiah, the Lord. Jesus shows the Messiah was both God and man. **Reaction:** No one could answer, and no one dared to ask more.

The Disciples' Questions about the Future

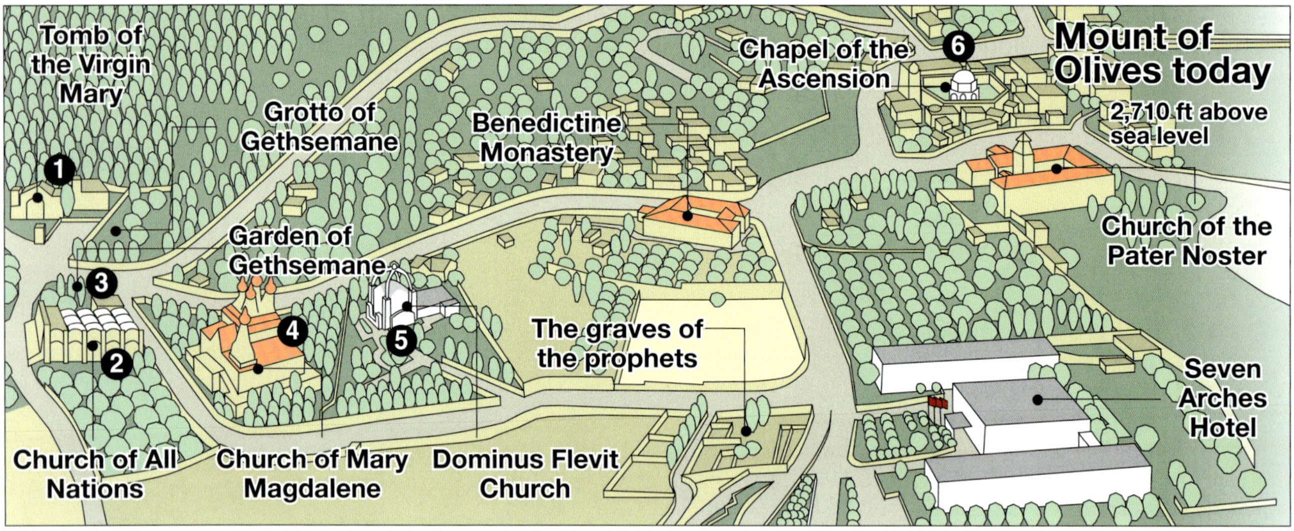

1 Tomb of the Virgin Mary
Traditionally believed to be the burial site of Mary, the mother of Jesus. But it is doubtful. The church is built underground.

2 Church of All Nations
There are three patches of bare rock inside the church. These are said to be where Jesus prayed before his arrest.

3 Garden of Gethsemane
This is where it is believed that Jesus prayed in anguish. Some of the olive trees are said to date from the first century.

4 Mary Magdalene Church
Russian Orthodox church built in 1885–86. It has seven gilded onion domes, each topped with a Russian Orthodox cross.

5 Dominus Flevit Church
Means "the Lord wept." Said to be where Jesus wept over the city when he arrived in Jerusalem. Built in 1955.

6 Chapel of the Ascension
An octagonal chapel where, according to tradition, Jesus ascended to heaven. Today it is used as a mosque.

Jesus's Mount of Olives Sermon on the Future

• The disciples ask two questions: **1. "Tell us, when will all this happen?"** (Matt. 24:3) and **2. "What sign will signal your return and the end of the world?"** (Matt. 24:3).
• Jesus answers (1) "when" (Matt. 24:4–28) and (2) "the sign of the second coming" (Matt. 24:29–31).
• The rest deals with the consequences for believers (Matt. 24:32–25:46).

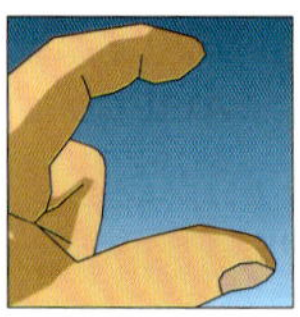

1 First comes this, then the end is coming

• "The end won't follow immediately" refers to events occurring before Jesus's return (Matt. 24:6).
• Before the end, there will be persecution and the gospel will be preached everywhere (Matt. 24:1–14).

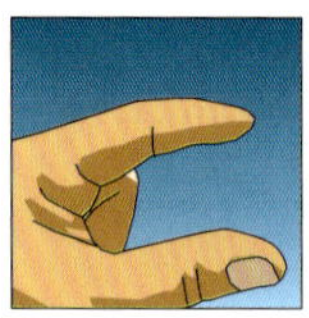

2 When this happens, then it is near

• "When you see" describes what will happen (Matt. 24:15).
• "Then" talks about how to respond to the events that will occur before the return of the Messiah (Matt. 24:15–28).

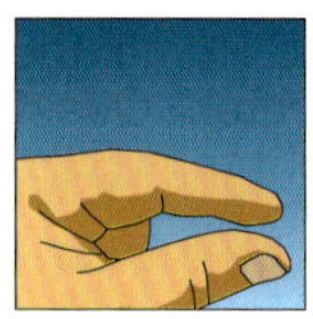

3 And this is the sign of his coming

• When the time comes, the Son of Man will appear. The sign is the Messiah coming in glory (Matt. 24:30a).
• All the chosen ones are gathered from around the world (Matt. 24:29–31).

4 You do not know when, so be prepared

• Only the Father knows when Jesus will return (Matt. 24:36).
• Therefore, we should always be ready for Jesus's return. It can happen when we least expect it (Matt. 24:32–51).

5 You do not know when, so stay awake

• Only the bridesmaids who prepared were allowed to participate in the wedding feast.
• The wise prepared and were ready. When Jesus returns, it will be too late to prepare (Matt. 25:1–13).

6 You do not know when, so serve faithfully

• "After a long time" tells us that the return of Jesus may be delayed (Matt. 25:5, 19).
• Faithful service is rewarded. Is Jesus only talking about believers (Matt. 25:14–30)?

7 But when he comes, he will judge

• Different interpretations.
• Some say it describes the final judgment in Revelation 20:11–15.
• Others that it is the non-Jewish peoples who are judged at Jesus's return (Matt. 25:31–32).

The Last Night in the Upper Room

JERUSALEM TODAY

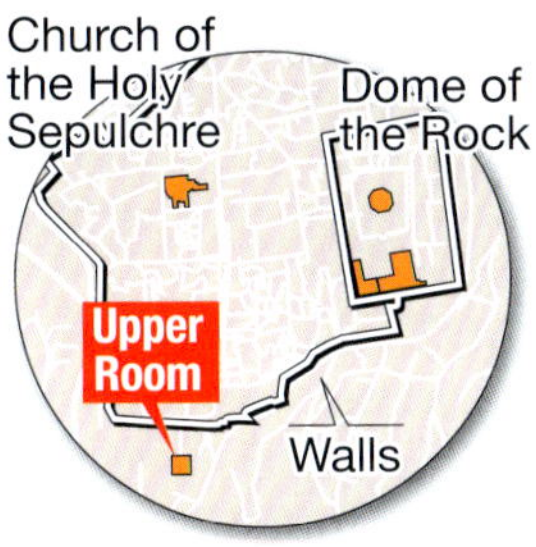

WHAT DO WE KNOW ABOUT THE UPPER ROOM IN JERUSALEM?

- It was common for wealthy people to have a second floor, used for banquets.
- The room was often larger, more airy, and better furnished than the rooms on the ground floor.
- The disciples asked for a guest room and were offered something nicer, the upper room.
- The location of the site is uncertain.
- There is a tradition that places the upper room in the house of John Mark's mother (Acts 12:25).
- However, some questions remain: Was there one upper room or two? Acts 1:13 uses a different expression than the one used in Mark 14:15 and Luke 22:12.
- The site identified as the upper room is in a building above what is known as David's Tomb. Several archaeologists argue this is probably where the upper room was.

THE MAN WHO CARRIED A JAR OF WATER

- When Jesus instructs John and Peter on how to find the upper room, he says: "As you enter the city, a man carrying a jar of water will meet you. Follow him" (Lk 22:10–11).
- It was usually the women who fetched water, so seeing a man carrying a jar of water was unusual (Jn 4:7).
- The man is an example of someone who is used by God without even knowing it.
- Yet, Jesus knew the man would be there and where he would be headed.

Does Jesus instruct us to wash each other's feet?

Jesus takes on the role of a servant. He pours water into a basin and starts washing the disciples' feet, drying them with a towel he had wrapped around his waist. How should we understand Jesus washing his disciples' feet? There are three main interpretations.

1. JESUS IS SPEAKING LITERALLY

- Jesus is teaching us that we should wash each other's feet.
- Jesus's own words are emphasized, "you ought to wash each other's feet" (John 13:14).
- Some consider washing one another's feet a sacrament (see 1 Tim. 5:10 NIV).
- In practice, we are expected to wash each other's feet.

2. JESUS IS SPEAKING SYMBOLICALLY

- Jesus is teaching us about our continual inner cleansing.
- Jesus says: "A person who has bathed all over does not need to wash, except for the feet, to be entirely clean" (John 13:10).
- "Bathed" is thought to refer to baptism, so in practice, the saved (clean) man should take sanctification seriously (washing feet).

3. JESUS IS GIVING AN EXAMPLE

- Jesus is modeling a servant attitude for us.
- He himself calls his actions an example (John 13:15).
- This means we should follow Jesus's example. Instead of protecting our status, we should have a servant attitude, which is expressed in actions appropriate to our day (such as giving practical help to those in need).

The Conversation in the Upper Room

In New Testament times, people ate reclining at a table (Matt. 26:20). Although we do not know what it looked like in the upper room, we can imagine that the disciples followed this custom. It is likely that they ate lying on their sides on padded couches next to a low table. This is what it might have looked like.

THEY LAY AROUND THE TABLE

The custom of reclining at the table like this came from the Greeks and was later adopted by the Romans and the Jews.

1 U-shaped table
The Jews had adopted the tradition and now gathered around a U-shaped table. The arrangement is called a *triclinium*.

2 Lying on couches
The table was surrounded by large, low couches with padding. It was open in the middle for the purpose of serving and entertaining.

3 Lying on left side
The guests lay on their left side and could therefore eat with their right hand. The legs were stretched out (Luke 7:38).

4 The host
There were rules for how people sat. The host reclined on his left side, second from the left. To his right was a loyal friend.

5 Guest of honor
The guest of honor for the day was placed on the host's left. The other guests were then seated in order of importance.

6 Chance to talk
The guests were seated so close to each other that one could lean against the neighbor on the left and speak confidentially.

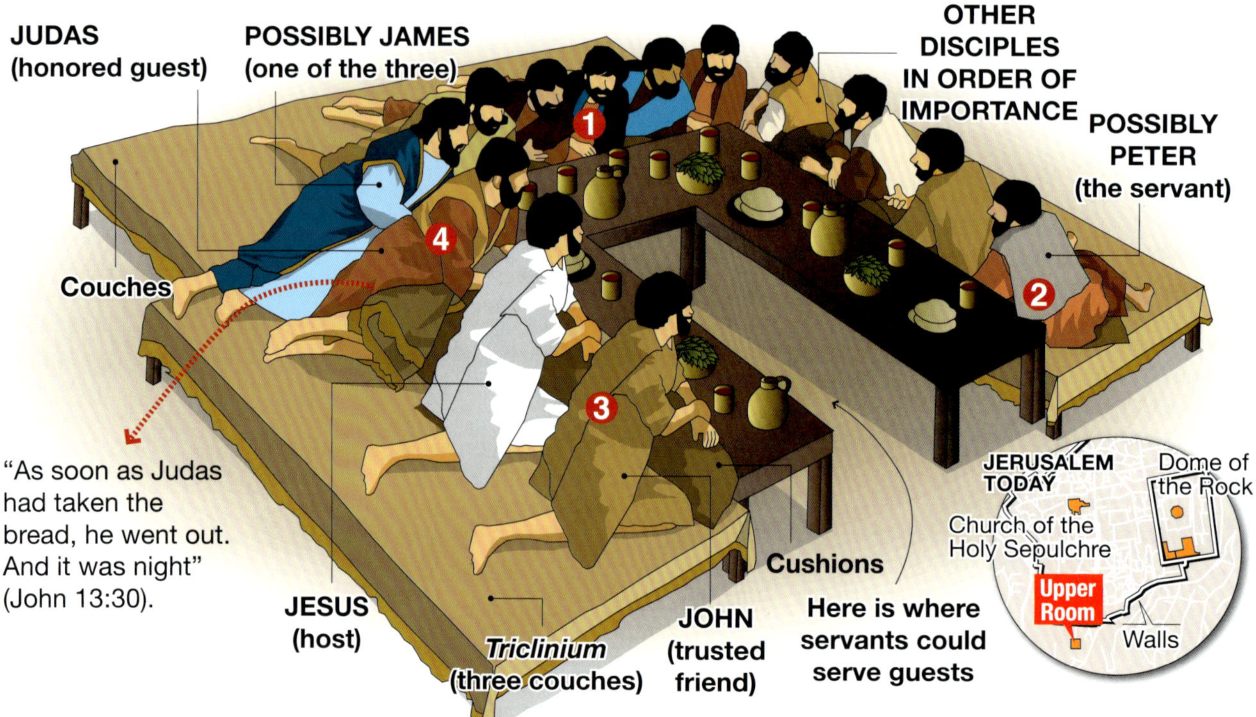

What happened around the table on the last evening?

1 Disciples' questions
• "Jesus sat down at the table with the Twelve" (Matt. 26:20).
• During the meal, Jesus said, "I tell you the truth, one of you will betray me" (Matt. 26:21).
• The disciples asked, "Am I the one, Lord?"
• John, the disciple Jesus loved, was seated at his right hand (John 12:23).

2 Peter's question
• Peter is probably seated at the bottom right of the table, the servant's seat (Matt. 23:11; Luke 22:27; John 13:16).
• Since Peter isn't close enough to ask quietly, he signals to John, seated across from him, to ask Jesus who he means (John 13:24).

3 John's question
• John leaned on Jesus's chest and whispered to him, "Lord, who is it?" (John 13:25).
• Jesus replied, "One of you who has just eaten from this bowl with me" (Matt. 26:23; Mark 14:20).
• Probably only John understood. It's unclear if he told Peter immediately.

4 Judas's question
• Judas sat next to Jesus on his left, eating from the bowl (Matt. 26:23).
• He also asked Jesus, "Rabbi, am I the one?" Jesus said, "You have said it" (Matt. 26:25; John 13:27).
• No one except John understood why Jesus said that (John 13:28).

Different Views of Communion

What does it mean to share the bread and wine with other believers?

How Communion Was First Celebrated

- Communion was not originally celebrated in a church service. Instead, it was part of a communal meal (1 Cor. 11:17–22).
- Communion began to be separated from the meal in the 100s, and by the 300s they were completely separate.
- Communion seems to have been an informal meal, usually celebrated in the home (Acts 2:42).
- Therefore, many of our customs surrounding Communion are different from those of the early Christians.
- Scripture suggests that Communion was instituted in two parts, the bread first, during the meal, and the wine later, after the meal (Luke 22:19–20; 1 Cor. 11:25).

Who should participate? In the Bible, Communion is never used as a tool for evangelization. It is a meal for the church, for believers in Christ (1 Cor. 11:22, 24). Paul warns against celebrating Communion without reflection (1 Cor. 11:29).

What should be done with any left-overs?

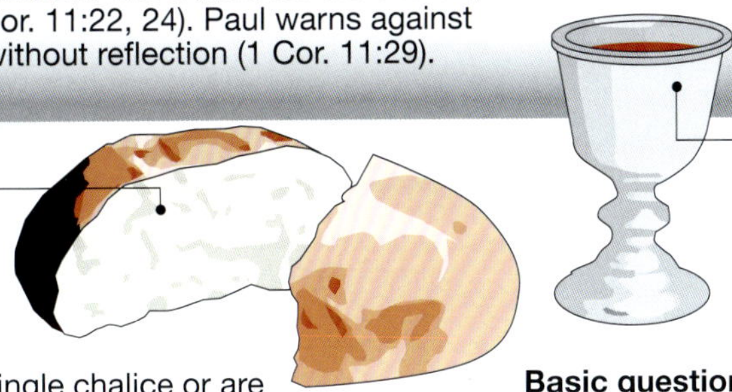

Bread Discussion: Should it be unleavened as during the Passover meal, or is using bread with yeast acceptable?

The wine Discussion: Is it okay to use wine? Is it okay to use grape juice?

Other questions: Is it a single chalice or are individual cups okay? Does the bread have to be broken (Luke 22:19)?

Basic question: Do the form and distribution of the elements, bread and wine, even matter?

An interpretive guide to Communion

START HERE: What about Communion?

Here is a guide to help you find your own understanding of Communion.

*The elements are the bread and wine.

- Is Jesus present in the elements* in a particular way?
  - NO → Is Jesus present in the same way he always is? So how does that presence differ from God's omnipresence and Christ's being with us always? (Ps. 139:1–10; Isa. 66:1; Jer. 23:23–24; Matt. 28:18–20; Acts 17:24–28)
    - YES → Communion: A memorial of Jesus's work
  - YES → Is Jesus physically present in the elements?
    - YES → Communion: An encounter with the physical Jesus
    - NO → Is Jesus invisibly present in the elements?
      - YES → Communion: An encounter with the spiritual Jesus
      - NO → Is Jesus spiritually present in the elements?
        - YES → Communion: A spiritual encounter with Jesus

Other terms:
- The Lord's Supper
- Eucharist (*thanksgiving*)
- Mass (*to go forth*)
- Breaking of the bread
- Memorial

Commonly referred to as	Transubstantiation	Consubstantiation	Real Spiritual Presence	Memorial of Christ's Sacrifice
How the elements* are viewed	The bread becomes the body of Christ, the wine becomes the blood of Christ.	The bread contains the body of Christ, the wine contains the blood of Christ.	The bread and wine are not affected, but Christ is spiritually present in them.	The bread is just bread, the wine is just wine. Communion is only a symbol.
Traditionally held by	Catholics	Lutherans	Reformed, Anglicans, and Presbyterians	Baptists and Pentecostals
Bible text often cited as central But does this text have anything to do with Communion?	[Jesus said]: "I tell you the truth, unless you eat the flesh of the Son of Man and drink his blood, you cannot have eternal life within you" (John 6:53).	"He took some bread ... Then he broke it in pieces and gave it to the disciples, saying, "This is my body, which is given for you" (Luke 22:19a).	[Jesus said]: "This cup is the new covenant between God and his people—an agreement confirmed with my blood" (1 Cor. 11:25a).	[Jesus said:] "Do this in remembrance of me as often as you drink it" (1 Cor. 11:25b; Luke 22:19b).
The position summarized	Jesus is really (not just in a symbolic way), truly (not just subjectively or as an image) and in substance (not just in his power) present in the bread and wine.	Jesus is not the bread and not the wine, but Christ is "in, with, and under" the bread and wine. "Out of two kinds of objects a union has taken place, which I shall call a 'sacramental union'" (Luther).	The body and blood of Jesus are not physically present in the elements, but "the Spirit truly unites things separated by space" (Calvin). Therefore, Christ is spiritually present in the elements.	Because Jesus is in heaven, his body is not present in the elements. Therefore his presence at Communion is spiritual, but in exactly the same way that he is always spiritually present with us (Matt. 28:20).

Toward Gethsemane: Through the Night

The Road to Gethsemane

1. Jesus is in the upper room with his disciples (Matt. 26:30; Luke 22:12; John 13:2). After the meal, he says: "Come, let's be going" (John 14:31).

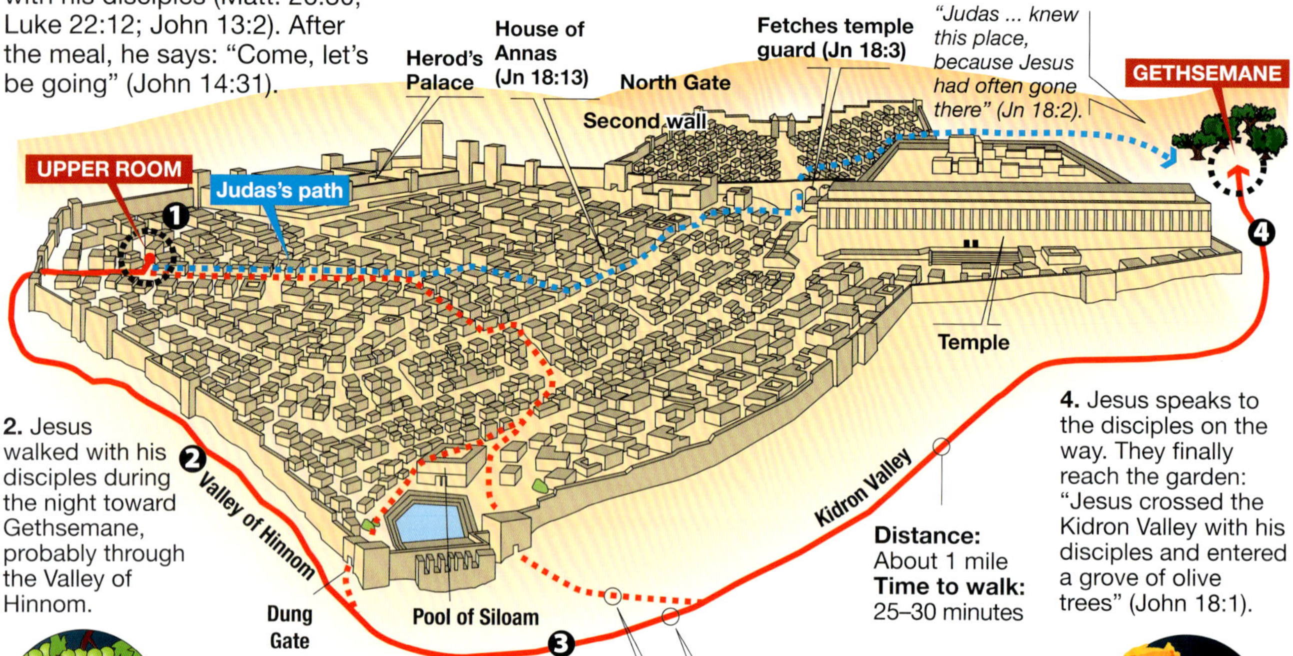

2. Jesus walked with his disciples during the night toward Gethsemane, probably through the Valley of Hinnom.

4. Jesus speaks to the disciples on the way. They finally reach the garden: "Jesus crossed the Kidron Valley with his disciples and entered a grove of olive trees" (John 18:1).

Distance: About 1 mile
Time to walk: 25–30 minutes

The vine
There may have been a vineyard along the road (John 15:1).

3. Jesus heads up the Kidron Valley, knowing his destination (Luke 22:39; John 18:1).

The road
We do not know which way Jesus chose. He may have walked through the city.

Torches
These were sticks with rags dipped in tar, carried at night (John 18:3).

Jesus's words to his disciples on the road

1 Jesus is going to the Father · **2 Jesus speaks of the future** · **3 Jesus promises another helper** — Jesus addresses the disciples

4 Jesus prays to the Father — and the Father

1 Jesus is going to the Father

Key messages:
- Explains the way to the Father (Jn 14:1–14).
- The promise of another helper (Jn 14:15–31).

Jesus answers three questions from the disciples:
1. Thomas asks: "How can we know the way?" (Jn 14:5).
2. Philip pleads: "Lord, show us the Father" (Jn 14:8).
3. Judas asks: "Why are you going to reveal yourself only to us?" (Jn 14:22).

2 Jesus speaks of the future

Key messages:
- The true vine (Jn 15:1–17).
- Being hated by the world (Jn 15:18–16:4).

Jesus gives five admonitions—remember my warning (16:4).
1. "Remain in me" (Jn 15:4–5).
2. "Remain in my love" (Jn 15:9).
3. "Love each other" (Jn 15:12, 17).
4. "Testify about me" (Jn 15:27).
5. "[Don't] abandon your faith" (Jn 16:1).

3 Jesus promises another helper

Key messages:
- "I am going away" (Jn 16:5–7a).
- You will have the Spirit (Jn 16:7b–15).
- "You will see me again" (Jn 16:16–31).
- "You will be scattered" (Jn 16:32–33).

Four new admonitions
1. Let the Spirit guide you (Jn 16:13).
2. Sorrow will turn to joy (Jn 16:20).
3. Pray in my name (Jn 16:23–24).
4. "Take heart" (Jn 16:33).

4 Jesus prays to the Father

Key message:
- The High Priestly Prayer (Jn 17:1–26)

Jesus's prayer to the Father:
- *For himself:* "Glorify your Son" (Jn 17:1–5).
- *For the disciples:* "Protect them" (Jn 17:6–12). Keep them from the evil one (Jn 17:13–19).
- *For future disciples:* His care for future generations (Jn 17:20). May they all be one (Jn 17:21–26).

The Betrayal in the Garden of Gethsemane

Gethsemane was a garden on the Mount of Olives that Jesus had visited on many occasions (John 18:2). In the garden, Judas betrays him, marking the beginning of the Passion drama. Just twelve hours later, he is condemned, tortured, and crucified.

5 The temple guards arrive with soldiers and a crowd of armed men

Jesus goes to meet them as they make their way through the garden. He asks who they want. They reply: "Jesus the Nazarene." Jesus answers: "I AM he" (John 18:2–9).

6 Judas betrays Jesus with a kiss

Judas identifies Jesus by kissing him on the cheek. They immediately arrest Jesus (Matt. 26:48–50).

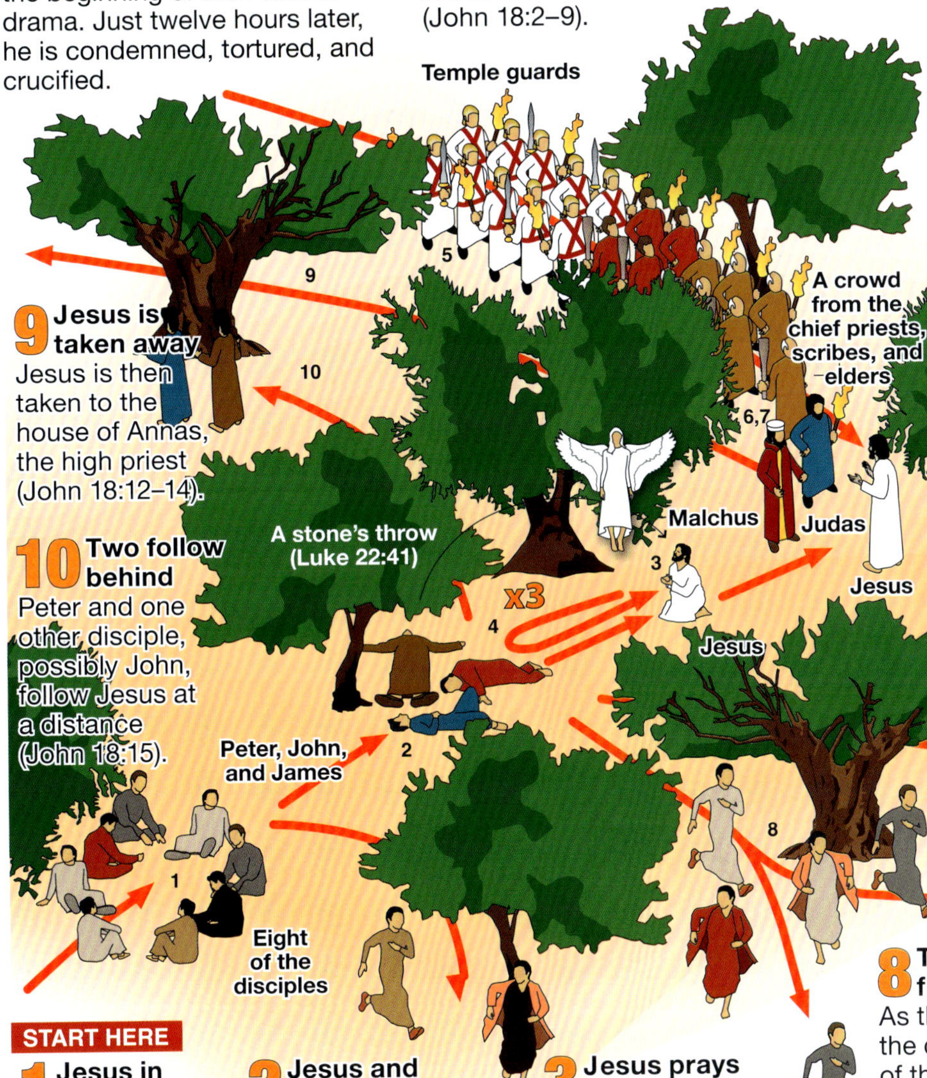

9 Jesus is taken away

Jesus is then taken to the house of Annas, the high priest (John 18:12–14).

10 Two follow behind

Peter and one other disciple, possibly John, follow Jesus at a distance (John 18:15).

7 Peter tries to protect Jesus

Peter cuts off the right ear of the slave Malchus. But Jesus heals him immediately (Luke 22:50–51).

4 Back to the three

Jesus returns to the three, finding them asleep. He admonishes them and returns to his prayer. This cycle happens three times (Matt. 26:40–46).

8 The disciples flee

As the disciples flee, the crowd grabs one of them. He slips out of his shirt and flees naked (Matt. 26:56; Mark 14:50–52).

START HERE

1 Jesus in Gethsemane

The group arrives. Jesus tells eight of the disciples to sit and wait while he prays farther away (Mark 14:32).

2 Jesus and the three

Taking Peter, John, and James with him, Jesus goes farther into the garden. He is deeply grieved and troubled (Matt. 26:37–38).

3 Jesus prays to the Father

Jesus goes on alone, kneels, and prays: "Take this cup of suffering away from me." An angel strengthens him (Luke 22:41–43).

Gethsemane Today

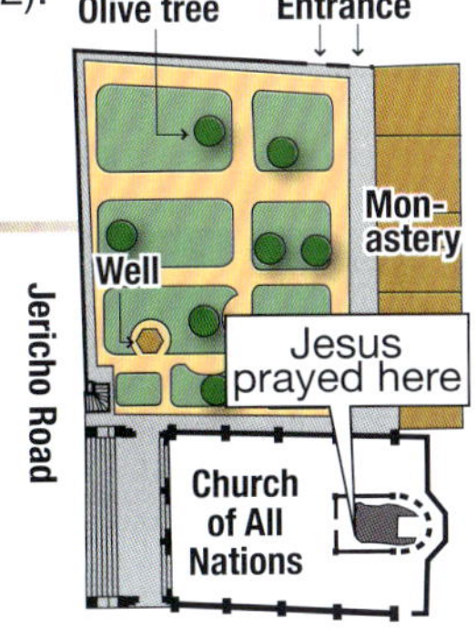

1 Jesus says "I AM"

When they ask for his name, Jesus's confession is clear. "I AM" is the name of God and he confesses it without hesitation (John 18:5; Ex. 3:14).

2 Jesus knew the future

Jesus already knew what would happen in Gethsemane and the next day (Matt. 26:45–46). His was a prayer born of anguish, not a plea for an escape.

3 Peter and his weapon

It is highly likely that the disciples carried weapons; knife-like swords were common (Luke 22:38, "we" 22:49). But it was wrong to use one in that situation.

4 Malchus's ear is healed

Malchus's ear was cut off, but also healed (Luke 22:51). For the rest of his life, his healed ear would remind him of Jesus. Did he ever ask: Who can do such a thing?

Jesus Is Sentenced to Death

After his arrest, Jesus is taken by the temple guard to the house of the high priest Annas. This is the first in a series of interrogations and trials in which Jesus is falsely accused and eventually convicted.

One of the greatest miscarriages of justice in history.

The Six Trials of Jesus	1 Before Annas	2 Before Caiaphas	3 Before the Sanhedrin	4 Before Pilate (I)	5 Before Herod	6 Before Pilate (II)
Matthew		26:57–58	26:59–27:1	27:2, 11–14		27:15–26
Mark		14:53–65	15:1	15:1–5		15:6–15
Luke		22:54, 63–65	22:66–71	23:1–5	23:6–12	23:13–25
John	18:19–24			18:28–38		18:39–19:16
Time of day	After midnight 2:00–2:30 a.m.	After midnight 2:30–5:00 a.m.	Friday at daybreak 6:00 a.m. (Lk 22:66)	Friday morning 6:30 a.m. (Jn 18:28)	Friday morning around 7:00 a.m.	Friday morning 7:30–8:00 a.m.
Approximate location	High Priest Annas's house	High Priest Caiaphas's house	Sanhedrin Council Room	The Praetorium (John 18:28)	Herod Antipas's Palace	The Praetorium (John 18:28)
In front of	← Religious trials		→	← Political trials		→
	 High Priest Annas	 High Priest Caiaphas	 Sanhedrin	 Pontius Pilate (I)	 Herod Antipas	 Pontius Pilate (II)
Accusations against Jesus	A pre-trial hearing with false accusations. Public hearing to obtain information.	An informal trial. Direct question: Do you claim to be the Messiah, the Son of God?	A formal, mock trial. Direct question: Do you claim to be the Messiah, the Son of God?	Jews accuse Jesus of treason (Luke 23:2), a crime that could lead to death by the Romans.	Jesus is not accused of anything. The trial is mostly a show.	Pilate bargains with the crowd, washes his hands, frees Barabbas, and condemns Jesus.
How the process worked	An interrogation at night, without legal grounds. Jesus is slapped across the face.	It was without legal basis, with false witnesses and violence against Jesus.	A formal trial to confirm the death sentence they had already passed (John 11:53).	Outside the Praetorium, then inside. It is more like a conversation than a trial.	Jesus is shouted at, mocked, ridiculed, and dressed in a royal robe.	Pilate finds no evidence of guilt but he allows the mob to decide Jesus's fate.
How Jesus responded	"Everyone knows what I teach.... If I said anything wrong, you must prove it" (John 18:20–23).	"I AM. And you will see the Son of Man seated in the place of power at God's right hand" (Mark 14:62).	"If I tell you, you won't believe me ... You say that I am" (Luke 22:67, 70).	"My Kingdom is not an earthly kingdom... You say I am a king" followed by silence (John 18:36–37).	Jesus did not give an answer (Luke 23:9).	Jesus is not spoken to.
Judgment passed	Accused of disrespecting Annas.	Considered guilty of blasphemy.	Convicted of blasphemy.	Pilate puzzled, sees no crime.	Contempt from Herod.	**Innocent—but sentenced to death.**

Via Dolorosa: The Road to the Cross

In a travelogue from AD 380, a pilgrim described the Via Dolorosa—the route Jesus might have taken from Pilate to the site of his crucifixion and burial. Today, the route blends biblical accounts with church tradition.

Red numbers: station not in Bible

1 **STATION I:** Pilate sentences Jesus to death at the Antonia Fortress. **Site:** 100 ft. from the Lion Gate **Text:** Mt 27:26

2 **STATION II:** Jesus takes up his cross and begins the long walk to Golgotha. **Site:** Chapel of the Flagellation **Text:** Jn 19:17

3 **STATION III:** Tradition says that Jesus falls for the first time here. **Site:** Just inside El-Wad Street **Text:** No biblical evidence

4 **STATION IV:** Tradition says that Jesus meets his mother here. **Site:** Armenian Catholic Church **Text:** No biblical evidence

5 **STATION V:** Simon from Cyrene is forced to carry the cross of Jesus. **Site:** At a Franciscan chapel **Text:** Mk 15:21

6 **STATION VI:** Veronica wipes Jesus's face with a cloth. **Site:** The Chapel of the Holy Face **Text:** No biblical evidence

7 **STATION VII:** Tradition says that Jesus falls for the second time here. **Site:** At Khan ez-Zeit Market **Text:** No biblical evidence

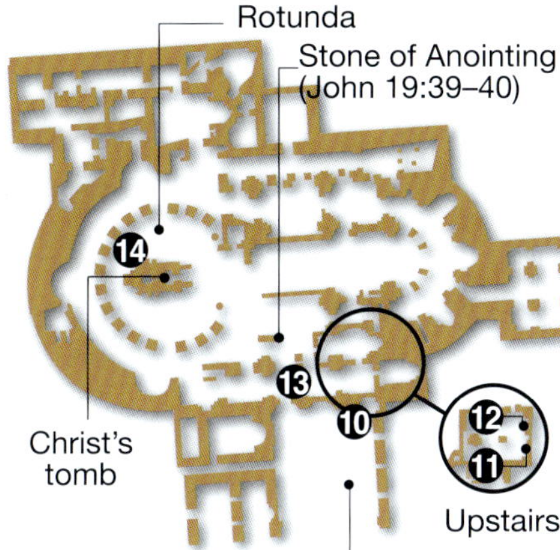

CHURCH OF THE HOLY SEPULCHRE
The site where the church is was already considered sacred in the first century.

"Carrying the cross by himself (John 19:17).

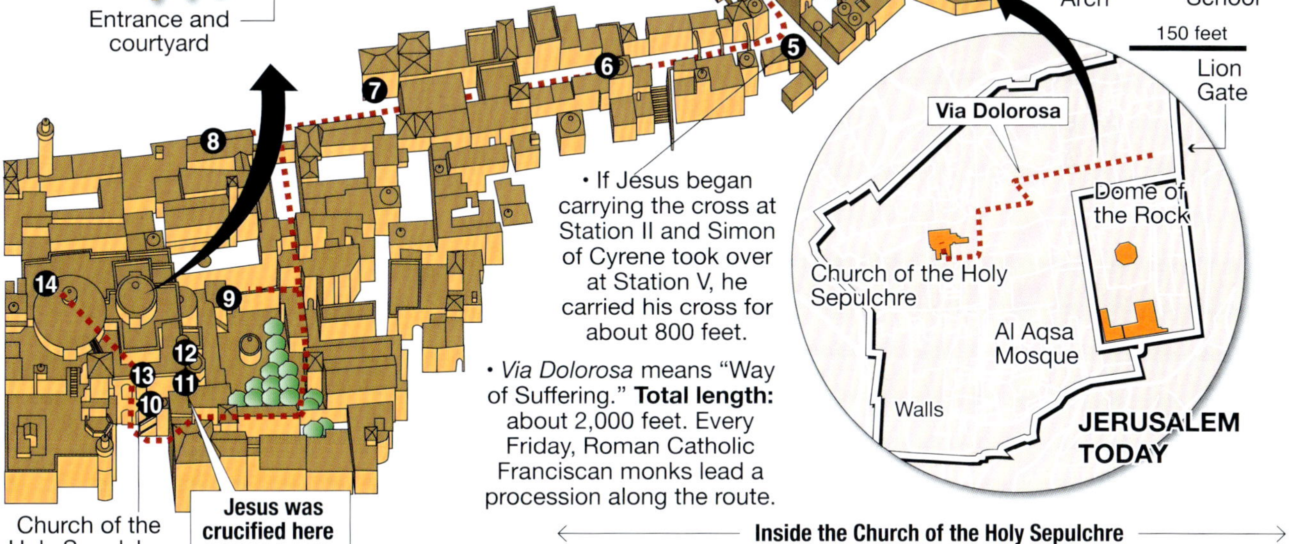

- If Jesus began carrying the cross at Station II and Simon of Cyrene took over at Station V, he carried his cross for about 800 feet.
- *Via Dolorosa* means "Way of Suffering." **Total length:** about 2,000 feet. Every Friday, Roman Catholic Franciscan monks lead a procession along the route.

Inside the Church of the Holy Sepulchre

8 **STATION VIII:** Jesus speaks to the weeping women of Jerusalem. **Site:** At the Monastery of Charalampus **Text:** Lk 23:28

9 **STATION IX:** Where tradition says Jesus falls the third time. **Site:** By the Coptic Queen Helena church **Text:** No biblical evidence

10 **STATION X:** The soldiers divide up Jesus's clothes. **Site:** Just outside the Church of the Holy Sepulchre **Text:** Mk 15:24

11 **STATION XI:** Jesus is nailed to the cross. **Site:** In the church and up the stairs, the Franciscan altar on the right **Text:** Lk 23:33

12 **STATION XII:** Jesus dies on the cross. **Site:** Adjacent to Station XI, the Greek Orthodox altar on the left **Text:** Mt 27:50

13 **STATION XIII:** Jesus's body is taken down. **Site:** In the church, at the Stone of Anointing **Texts:** Lk 23:53; Jn 19:38

14 **STATION XIV:** The body of Jesus is laid in the grave. **Site:** The Holy Sepulchre, located inside the Rotunda **Text:** Mt 27:59–60

Where Was the Road to Calvary?

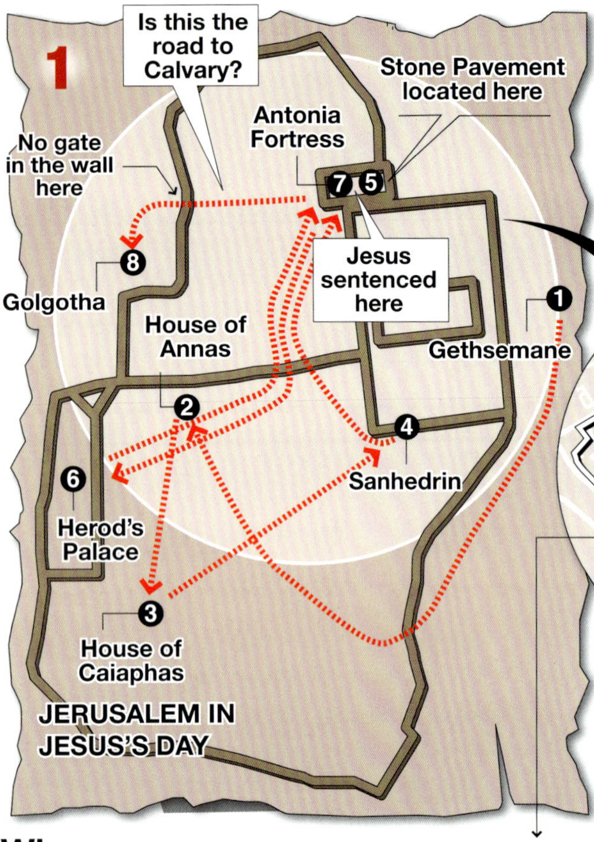

There is ongoing debate about the route that Jesus took to the cross on the morning of the crucifixion. The heart of the issue is the location of the Stone Pavement, where Jesus was condemned by Pilate (John 19:13).

1. The Traditional Route

The Via Dolorosa's route is based on the theory that Pilate judged Jesus in the Antonia Fortress. Given this, the Stone Pavement was thought to be located at the arch that is now called Ecce Homo (John 19:5).

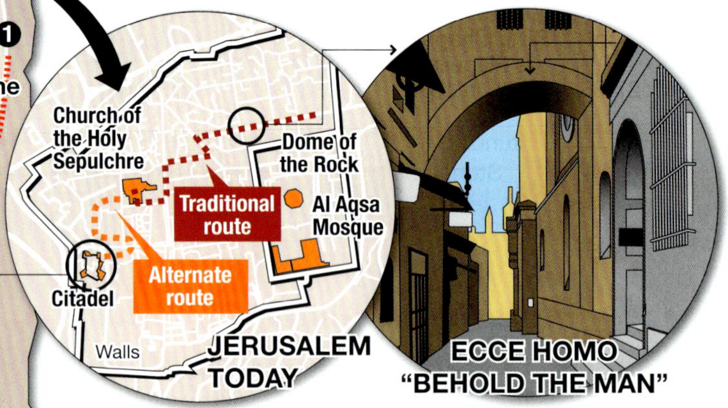

2. An Alternate Route

Research, including new archaeological finds, suggests it is more likely Pilate stayed in Herod's former palace. This places the Stone Pavement in what is now the Citadel. If so, the route of the Via Dolorosa is incorrect.

Where was *Gabbatha*?

- John 19:13 mentions the Stone Pavement, *gabbatha* in Hebrew.
- Archaeologist Pierre Benoit showed that the pavement at the Antonia Fortress was first laid in the second century.
- Mark used the word "courtyard" (15:16) which can be associated with a palace.
- Herod the Great's palace, the Citadel, became Roman property when he died in 4 BC. Pilate used it as his residence when visiting Jerusalem.
- It is unclear exactly which feature in the Citadel complex is meant by the term "Stone Pavement."

CITADEL

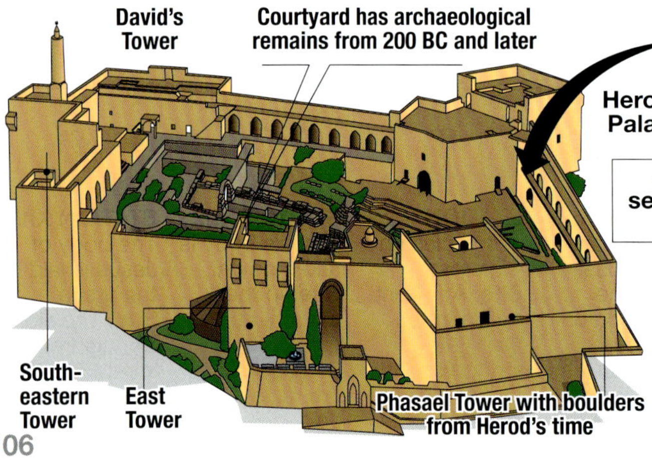

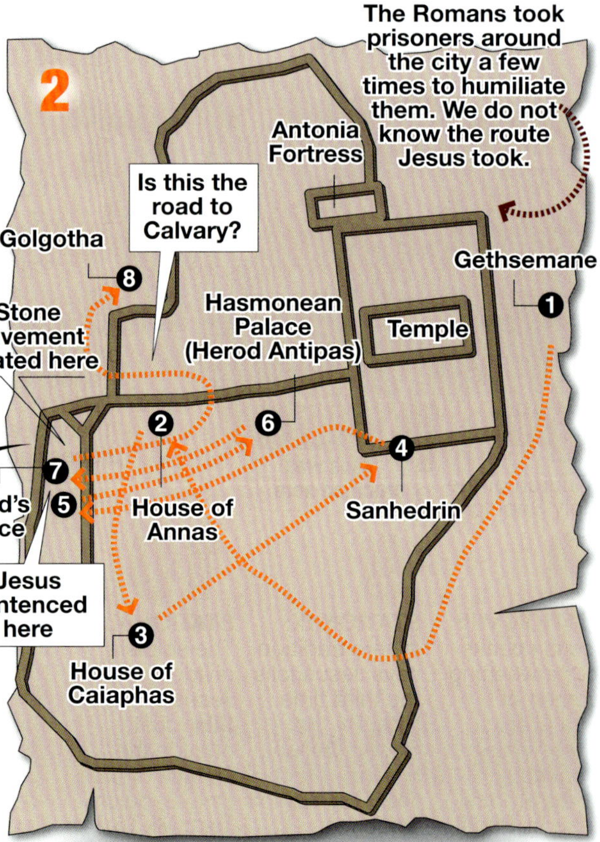

The Cross: The Cruelest Death

1 The flogging
A whip, set with stones and pieces of bone, tears up the back. These wounds rub painfully against the wooden cross.

2 An upright pole
A pole is set securely in the ground. It wasn't very high—the prisoner's feet were only about eighteen inches off the ground.

3 The crossbeam
The prisoner is put on his back with his arms outstretched on the crossbeam. To prevent tearing, the nails go through the wrists.

4 Raised up
The crossbeam, with the prisoner on it, is hoisted onto the pole and then secured in place.

5 A seat is attached
A seat nailed to the pole allows the prisoner to sit, relieving the strain on the arms. This only serves to prolong the agony.

6 Nail in the feet
With knees bent, one or two nails are driven through the feet into the pole, allowing the prisoner to brace against the nail.

7 Dulling the pain
If the pain was too great, the prisoner was offered sour wine for relief, often on a sponge placed on a long stick (Prov. 31:6).

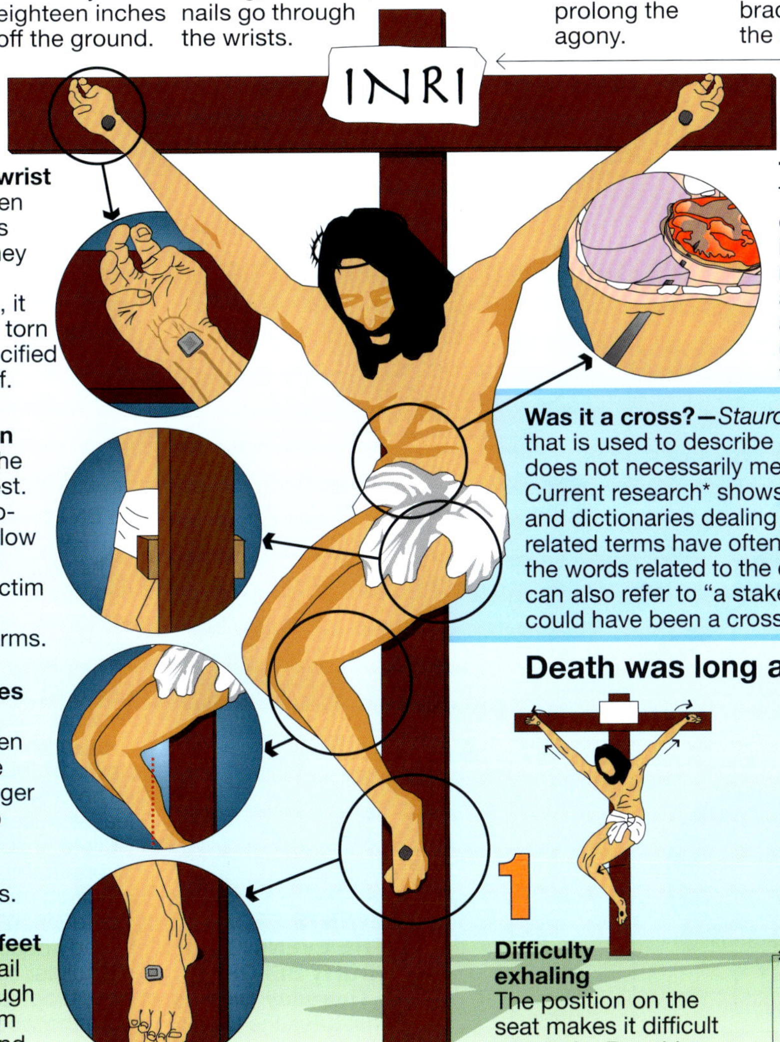

• INRI—an abbreviation of the Latin *Iesus Nazarenus, Rex Iudaeorum* [Jesus Nazareth King Jews] (John 19:19)

The nails in the wrist
The nails are driven through the wrists (John 20:25). If they had been driven through the hand, it would have been torn apart and the crucified man would fall off.

The spear in the side
To ensure that the prisoner was dead, soldiers thrust a spear into the side (John 19:34), most likely through the lungs and into the heart. Pericardial and pleural fluids (water) came out with the blood.

The seat to sit on
The seat allows the crucified some rest. But the body's position does not allow deep breaths. To bring in air, the victim must pull himself upright with his arms.

Was it a cross?—*Stauros*, the Greek word that is used to describe Jesus's execution, does not necessarily mean "a cross." Current research* shows that wordbooks and dictionaries dealing with crucifixion-related terms have often overinterpreted the words related to the crucifixion. *Stauros* can also refer to "a stake or a pole." But it could have been a cross.

On a pole

The broken bones
To hasten death, the legs are broken (John 19:32). The victim can no longer pull himself up to breathe. Death usually occurs shortly afterwards.

The nails in the feet
In order for the nail to be driven through the feet, the victim was forced to bend his knees. The weight of the body now came to rest on the nail.

Death was long and painful

1 Difficulty exhaling
The position on the seat makes it difficult to exhale. Breathing becomes shallow and carbon dioxide builds up, causing cramps.

2 In order to breathe
Straightening the legs and pulling up with the arms allows breathing for a short time. But cramps and pain take over and the body sinks back onto the seat.

CAUSE OF DEATH BY CRUCIFIXION: Crucifixion becomes a prolonged agony. The victim could hang on a cross for days if no measures were taken to his shorten life. The cause of death was often hemorrhagic shock (too little blood volume) or acute oxygen deprivation. Other possible causes were dehydration, cardiac arrhythmia caused by stress, or acute heart failure, resulting in rapid accumulation of fluid in the lungs. Death always came as a relief.

Sources: On the physical death of Jesus Christ, JAMA, March 21, 1986 and Crucifixion in Antiquity, Gunnar Samuelsson, 2010.

Jesus's Six Hours on the Cross

Jesus most likely died on Friday, April 3, AD 33

The priests mock Jesus
Similarly, the leading priests and religious leaders mock him. "He saved others,... but he can't save himself!" (Mark 15:31).

The soldiers mock Jesus
Even the soldiers join in and mock Jesus saying, "If you are the King of the Jews, save yourself!" (Luke 23:36–37).

The two thieves on the cross
One of the thieves mocks him, but the other one says: "Jesus, remember me" (Luke 23:39–42).

2 Jesus's second words
"I assure you, today you will be with me in paradise" (Luke 23:43).

3 Jesus's third words
Jesus sees his mother and the disciple he loves and says: "'Dear woman, here is your son.' And he said to this disciple, 'Here is your mother'" (John 19:26–27).

Darkness over the earth
About noon, darkness falls across the whole land, and it lasts until three o'clock (Matt. 27:45).

4 Jesus's fourth words
At three o'clock, Jesus cries with a loud voice: "My God, my God, why have you abandoned me?" (Matt. 27:46; Ps. 22:2).

Passersby mock Jesus
Those who walk by mock him (Matt. 27:39).

5 Jesus's fifth words
"I am thirsty." He receives sour wine on a hyssop branch to drink (John 19:28–29).

The soldiers divide his clothes
The soldiers divide Jesus's clothing between them (Mark 15:24; Ps. 22:18).

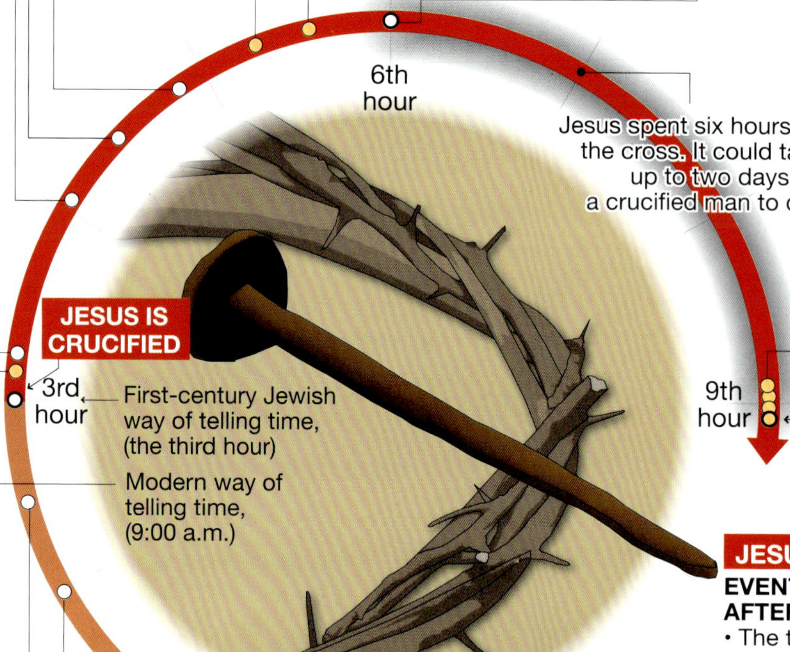

6 Jesus's sixth words
"It is finished!" (John 19:30).

1 Jesus's first words
"Father, forgive them, for they don't know what they are doing" (Luke 23:34).

7 Jesus's seventh words
Jesus cries out with a loud voice: "'Father, I entrust my spirit into your hands!' And with those words he breathed his last" (Luke 23:46).

Jesus is crucified
"It was nine o'clock in the morning when they crucified him" (Mark 15:25).

Jesus is led to Golgotha
Jesus is flogged and then taken away to the place of crucifixion, called The Skull (Luke 23:26, 33).

Jesus is sentenced to death
The mob pressures Pilate, demanding the crucifixion of Jesus and the release of Barabbas. Pilate decides to give them what they demand, and releases Barabbas (Luke 23:23–25).

JESUS DIES

EVENTS IMMEDIATELY AFTER JESUS'S DEATH

- The temple curtain is torn in two, the earth shakes, rocks split apart, and tombs are opened (Matt. 27:51–52).
- The officer and those guarding Jesus were terrified by what happened, saying, "This man truly was the Son of God!" (Matt. 27:54).
- The crowd of onlookers leaves in sorrow (Luke 23:48).
- Pilate orders the soldiers to break the legs of the crucified men. But Jesus is not touched because he is already dead (John 19:31–33).
- A soldier spears Jesus in the side, blood and water flow from the wound (John 19:34).
- Joseph of Arimathea takes down the body (John 19:38).
- Nicodemus joins him with the burial spices (John 19:39).
- Jesus is buried in a rich man's tomb (John 19:41; Isa. 53:9).
- The tomb is sealed and guards are posted to secure it (Matt. 27:66).

START HERE

EVENTS FROM THE EVENING AND NIGHT BEFORE

- **Thursday evening:** Institutes the Lord's Supper (Luke 22:14).
- **After midnight:** Prays in Gethsemane (Matt. 26:36) and is arrested (John 18:12).
- **Friday morning:** Tried before Annas, Caiaphas, and the Sanhedrin (Luke 22:54–71).

Jesus is brought to Pilate (I)
Early in the morning, the entire Sanhedrin makes its decision. They bind Jesus, take him away, and hand him over to Pontius Pilate (Mark 15:1).

Jesus is sent to Herod Antipas
Pilate asks if he was from Galilee. When he learns that Jesus came from the territory of Herod Antipas, he sends him to Herod (Luke 23:6–7).

Jesus sent back to Pilate (II)
Herod Antipas and his soldiers mock Jesus cruelly before they send him back to Pilate (Luke 23:11).

The People around Jesus's Cross

SIMON FROM CYRENE

The man forced to carry Jesus's cross to Calvary. He was from Cyrene, located in present-day Libya. Father of two sons, Alexander and Rufus (Matt. 27:32; Mark 15:21; Luke 23:26; Rom. 16:13).

THE SOLDIERS

At least four soldiers are active at the cross. They give Jesus wine, crucify him, and divide up his clothes between them. One of them pierces his side with a spear (Matt. 27:34–35; Luke 23:34, 36–37; John 19:34).

THE MOCKING THIEF

One of the thieves crucified alongside Jesus joins in with the mocking. He does not hold back when he says "So you're the Messiah, are you? Prove it!" (Matt. 27:38, 44; Mark 15:27; Luke 23:32–33, 39; John 19:18).

THE REPENTANT THIEF

The second thief turns directly to Jesus: "Jesus, remember me when you come into your Kingdom." Jesus immediately replies: "Today you will be with me in paradise" (Luke 23:32–33, 40–43).

THE SOLDIER WHO GIVES WINE

Jesus says, "I am thirsty." Near the cross is a jar of sour wine. A soldier takes a sponge and dips it in the wine. He puts it on a hyssop branch and holds it up to Jesus (Matt. 27:48; Mark 15:36; John 19:28–29).

THE OFFICER WHO BELIEVED

An officer standing near the cross sees how Jesus gives up his spirit and feels the earthquake. He is deeply impressed, worships God, and states: "This man truly was the Son of God!" (Matt. 27:54; Luke 23:47).

MARY MAGDALENE

Many women watch the crucifixion from a distance. Among them is Mary Magdalene, who had followed Jesus for some time. She will be the first to see the risen Christ (Matt. 27:56; Mark 15:40; Luke 23:49; John 19:25).

MARY AND SALOME

Two others are Mary (the wife of Clopas) and Salome. According to tradition, Salome was the wife of Zebedee and the mother of James and John (Matt. 20:20–21; 27:56; Mark 15:40; John 19:25).

MARY, THE MOTHER OF JESUS

Jesus's mother is also at the cross, where Jesus urges her to take John as her son. The last time Scripture mentions Mary, she is with the disciples on Pentecost (John 19:25–27; Acts 1:14).

JOHN, THE BELOVED

"The disciple [Jesus] loved" (understood to be the apostle John) seems to be the only disciple at the cross. Jesus asks him to take up the role of Mary's son (John 19:26–27).

THE OTHER WOMEN

A large group of women watch the crucifixion from a distance. Among them are Joanna and possibly Susanna (Luke 24:10; 8:3, Matt. 27:55; Mark 15:40–41; Luke 23:49).

THE CHIEF PRIESTS

The leading priests ridicule Jesus. "He saved others ... but he can't save himself!" They also complain about Pilate's sign that reads: "The King of the Jews" (Matt. 27:41–43; Mark 15:31–32; John 19:21).

THE TEACHERS OF THE LAW

The teachers of the law take the opportunity to mock Jesus. The elders and counselors also join in. These men are all part of the Jewish religious leadership (Matt. 27:41–43; Mark 15:31).

THE PEOPLE WHO WALKED BY

The people of the city come out to watch. Some walk by and mock him. There were probably hundreds of people who stood around the cross (Matt. 27:39–49; Mark 15:29–36; Luke 23:35, 48).

Why Did Jesus Have to Die?

Matthew writes: "From then on Jesus began to tell his disciples plainly that it was *necessary* for him to ... suffer many terrible things [and] be killed, but on the third day he would be raised from the dead" (Matt. 16:21). The key word is "necessary." Why did Jesus have to die? He didn't just choose to die, he knew that there was a compelling reason for it.

Cornerstones of the Atonement

1 Our condition: the legacy of sin
Our sinful nature separates us from God, preventing us from seeking after him (Rom. 3:10–11, 23).

2 God's character: infinite holiness
God is holy, and sinful people cannot enter into his presence (1 Peter 1:16; Ex. 33:20; Isa. 59:2).

3 Our need: a representative
Sinful people are therefore in need of someone who can take their place and solve the problem of sin (1 Tim. 2:5).

4 God's offer: a savior
God did what we were unable to. He sent his Son to be our Savior and Mediator (Rom. 8:3; John 3:16; 1 Tim. 2:5).

> "With his own blood ... [Jesus] entered the Most Holy Place once for all time and secured our redemption forever (Hebrews 9:12).

THREE VIEWS ON THE ATONEMENT:	1 JESUS HAD TO DIE FOR THE DEVIL'S SAKE	2 JESUS HAD TO DIE FOR HUMANITY'S SAKE	3 JESUS HAD TO DIE FOR GOD'S SAKE
Why Jesus Dies	Jesus dies to redeem us from the power of the devil.	Jesus dies to demonstrate the extent of God's love for us.	Jesus dies to satisfy God's holiness and righteousness.
Called	Ransom view of the atonement	Moral Example view of the atonement	Satisfaction view of the atonement
The Focus	The focus is the battle between God and the devil. The devil holds sinful people captive. God offers Jesus as a ransom for humanity and the exchange takes place on the cross. But Jesus defeats the devil and is resurrected. In Jesus, God has thus freed humanity from the grip of the devil.	The focus is on humanity's need to see and understand God's love. Emphasizes that God is love and that he wants fellowship with people. Jesus is the ultimate example of God's love, and by looking at his voluntary sacrifice, we can understand God's love and will desire to turn to him.	The focus is on human guilt before God. Because of sin, humans owe a debt to God they cannot repay. And a holy God cannot accept sinful people. Jesus becomes our substitute. He takes our guilt upon himself and dies in our place. In a legal sense, the debt is thus paid and the sin atoned for.
Key Biblical Texts	"The Son of Man came not to be served but to serve others and to give his life as a ransom for many" (Mark 10:45; Rev. 5:9).	"There is no greater love than to lay down one's life for one's friends" (John 15:13; 2 Cor. 5:19).	"Since we have been made right in God's sight by the blood of Christ, he will certainly save us from God's condemnation" (Rom. 5:9; 3:25).
Weakness of the View	The devil has no power over God. Humans owe a debt to God, not to the devil (Job 1–2).	Does not present any atonement for sin. Jesus's death is only an invitation to come to God.	Describes a mechanical view of atonement. Humans are declared righteous without actually being so.

Sources: The doctrine of the atonement in Swedish Theology, Roland Hellsten, DTS thesis 1973

What Happened When Jesus Died?

Jesus died on Good Friday at three in the afternoon. The Bible describes four dramatic phenomena that occurred in connection with his death. We can assume that all of them were the result of divine intervention.

1 “At noon, darkness fell across the whole land until three o’clock (Matt. 27:45).

DARKNESS GIVES WAY TO LIGHT
The darkness was supernatural. Darkness often represents judgment (Ex. 10:21–23; Amos 8:8–9). After three hours, Jesus cried out in despair as the judgment on human sin fell (Matt. 27:46; 2 Cor. 5:21). When sin is atoned for, light breaks forth (Acts 26:18; Eph. 5:8; 1 John 1:5–7; 2:8).

2 “The earth shook, the rocks split apart (Matt. 27:51).

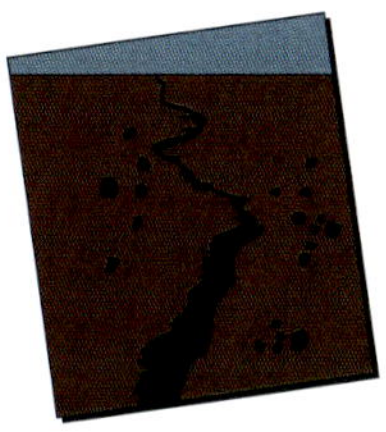

EARTHQUAKE SHAKES JERUSALEM
Several fault lines run through Israel, posing a risk of earthquakes. Jerusalem has been hit several times. Sometimes quakes coincide with God’s intervention (Isa. 29:6; Jer. 10:10). This is an indication of God’s direct action (see Rom. 8:21–22).

3 “Tombs opened. The bodies of many godly men and women who had died were raised from the dead (Matthew 27:52).

DEAD CAME OUT OF THE GRAVES
There is debate over how to understand Matthew’s statement about the bodies (Matt. 27:52–53), both what is meant and when it happened. Regardless of the meaning, one thing is agreed on: The liberation of the dead from their tombs is a prophetic (anticipatory) picture of the saving significance of the death of Jesus.

4

CURTAIN IN THE TEMPLE TORN
• The curtain tore at three o’clock in the afternoon, at the time of the incense offering (Luke 1:8–10). The tearing of the curtain “from top to bottom” (Matt. 27:51) indicates that it was God who caused it to tear.
• The tearing of the curtain indicates that the way into the Most Holy Place is now open through Jesus Christ (Heb. 10:19–20).

HOW DID THE DEAD RISE?
Matthew 27:52–53 does not say clearly whether the dead were raised to their old physical life or resurrected into a new, transformed existence. This leaves room for interpretation.

1 Awakened to their old life
Some believe that the text should be understood as they were raised to their old life (like Lazarus, John 11:43–44). They lived for awhile and then died again, returning to the grave until the final resurrection.

2 Resurrected after Jesus
Some believe that they rose to the new life, like Jesus. But this happened after his resurrection. Jesus is the first born from the dead, the guarantee of eternal life for all who follow him (1 Cor. 15:23).

3 Waited in their graves
Still others say they were resurrected when Jesus died. They stayed in their tombs and only entered the city “after Jesus’s resurrection” (Matt. 27:53), serving as visible proof of God’s power and the coming resurrection.

4 May need to be left open
Whether their resurrection was to the old or the new life may need to be left open. Either way, it was a sign of the impact of the atoning death of Jesus and demonstrated God’s power over death, giving us hope.

Golgotha and the Tomb of Jesus

The Church of the Holy Sepulchre is the probable site of Jesus's death, burial, and resurrection, for lack of a better alternative. Pilgrims have visited the site since at least AD 326, when construction of a basilica began.

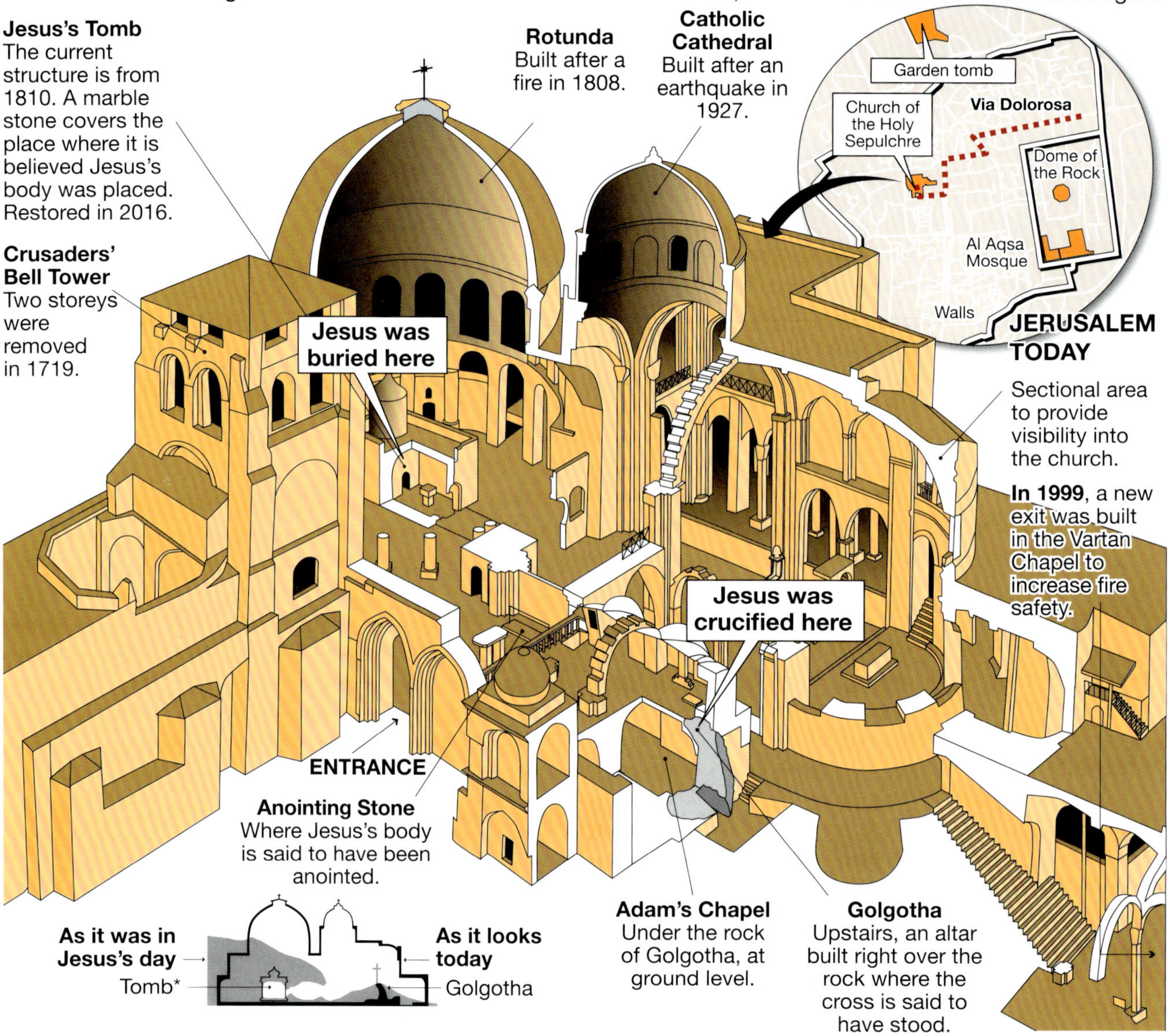

This is what it might have looked like

Archaeologists have found evidence of an abandoned quarry that is believed to have been used as a cemetery.

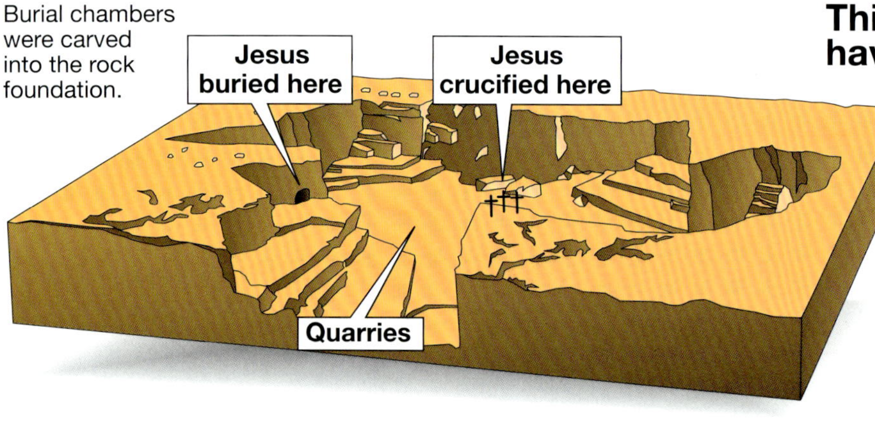

> "We may not be absolutely certain that [it] is the site of Jesus' burial, but we ... have no reason to reject the authenticity.
> (Dan Bahat)

* Guilhem D. "Golgotha cross-section.svg." in Wikimedia 21 April 2007.

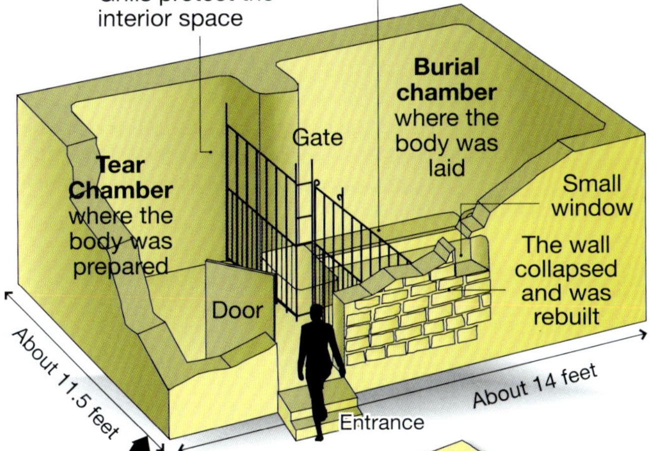

The Alternative Burial Site

The Garden Tomb, located north of the Damascus Gate, is an alternative to the Church of the Holy Sepulchre. The tomb and its garden are close to a rocky escarpment, known as Skull Hill. Jesus was crucified "near a garden, where there was a new tomb" (John 19:41).

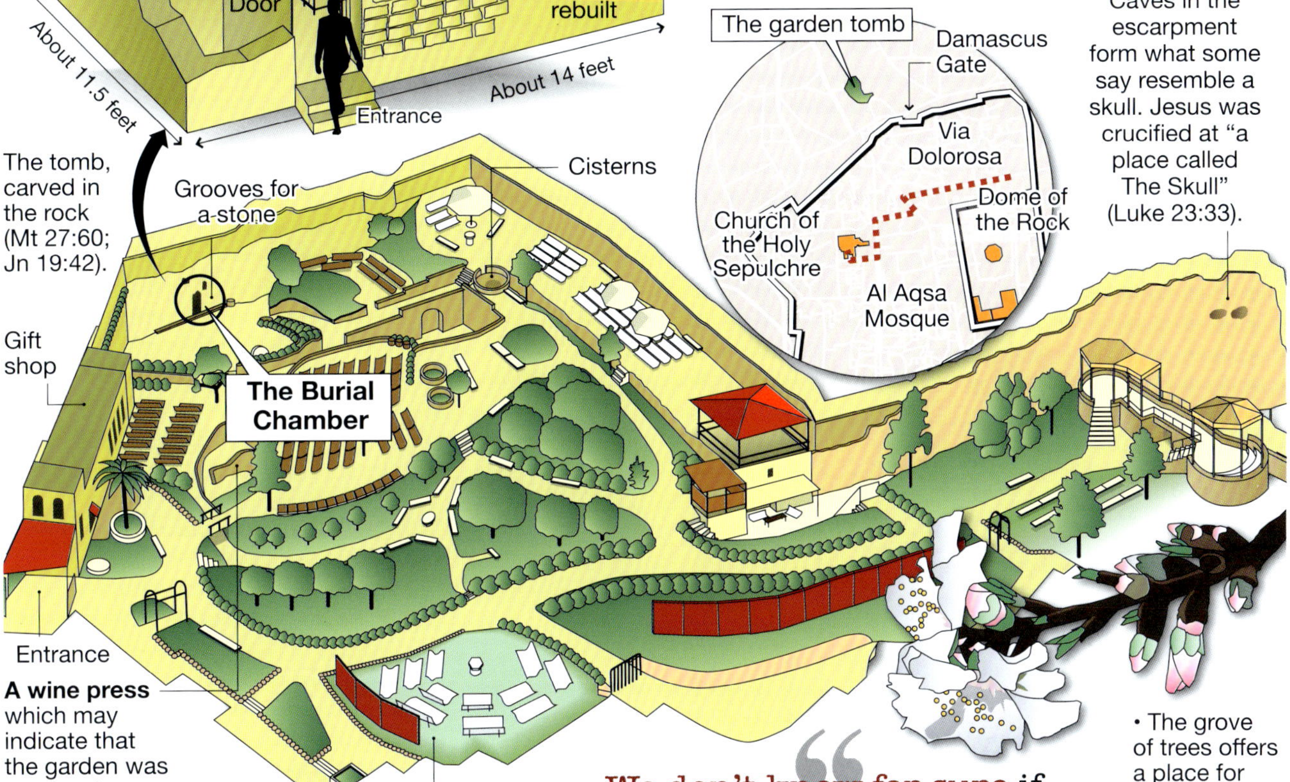

"We don't know for sure if this is the place where Jesus was ... buried. (Garden Tomb Foundation)

• The grove of trees offers a place for silence and reflection.
• This contrasts with the ornate and crowded Church of the Holy Sepulchre, which can be overwhelming for visitors.

THOSE WHO BURIED JESUS

JOSEPH OF ARIMATHEA
He was a member of the Sanhedrin (Mark 15:43), a secret disciple of Jesus who offered his new tomb (Matt. 27:57–60).

NICODEMUS
He came with a mixture of myrrh and aloe to anoint and wrap Jesus's body (John 19:39).

THE WOMEN
Mary Magdalene (Matt. 27:61), Mary (Mark 15:47), and others (Matt. 27:56, 61; Luke 23:55).

THE HISTORY OF THE GARDEN TOMB

• **1842:** Otto Thenius sees a rock that resembles a skull outside the Damascus Gate (Luke 23:33). He identifies the site as an alternative location for the biblical Golgotha.
• **1867:** The site is excavated and a tomb is found in a nearby garden (John 19:41; 20:15).
• **1870:** A large cistern is found.
• **1883:** After visiting the site, the British General Charles Gordon increases awareness of it, leading to it being referred to as Gordon's Calvary.
• **1894:** The site is bought by a British foundation, which now owns and manages it. It has been open to the public ever since then.

Charles Gordon

• **1924:** A wine press is discovered inside in the garden.
• **2015:** Part of the limestone rock that formed the skull comes loose. The rock is very porous and has crumbled over the years.
NOTE: The Garden Tomb has never undergone proper archaeological excavation.

Those Who Saw Jesus Resurrected

SOLDIERS (?)
Sunday morning, at the tomb. Roman guards were there to make sure no one stole the body. But it is unlikely that they saw the risen Jesus (Matt. 27:62–66; 28:1–4, 11–15).

MARY MAGDALENE
Sunday morning, at the tomb. She came with four other women (Luke 24:10; Mark 16:1), saw that the stone had been rolled away from the tomb, and later met Jesus alone (John 20:11–18).

MARY, MOTHER OF JAMES
Sunday morning, at the tomb. She came with four other women (Luke 24:10), saw the stone was rolled away from the tomb, and met Jesus on the way to the disciples (Matt. 27:56; 28:1, 9–10; Mark 16:1).

THE OTHER WOMEN
Sunday morning, at the tomb. Salome, Joanna, and at least one other woman came to the tomb (Mark 16:1; Luke 24:10). Probably met Jesus ("them" Matt. 28:9; Mark 16:1; Luke 23:55–24:11).

THE TRAVELERS TO EMMAUS
Sunday during the day, on the road to Emmaus. Only Cleopas is named (Luke 24:13–35; Mark 16:12–13). His companion may have been his wife, Mary (John 19:25), but it is unknown.

SIMON PETER
Sunday, possibly at the tomb. That evening, the disciples shared that Jesus had also appeared to Peter (Luke 24:34), but exactly when this had happened is not stated (Luke 24:12, 34; 1 Cor. 15:5).

TEN DISCIPLES
Sunday evening, in the upper room. At least ten disciples were present (Mark 16:14). Judas was dead and Thomas wasn't there (John 20:24). It is possible that others were there (Luke 24:36–43; John 20:19–23).

ELEVEN DISCIPLES
Eight days later, in the upper room. The Eleven, including Thomas, were gathered together (Mark 16:14). Jesus appeared and told Thomas to place his finger in Jesus's wounds (Mark 16:14–18; John 20:26–28).

SEVEN DISCIPLES
Within 40 days, by the Sea of Galilee. Jesus met with Peter, Thomas, Nathanael, James, John, and two other disciples not named. Jesus offered them grilled fish and bread, then reinstates Peter (John 21:1–23).

ELEVEN AND MATTHIAS (?)
Within 40 days, on a mountain in Galilee (Matt. 28:16). "The Twelve" (1 Cor. 15:5) may include Matthias. Peter said that Judas's replacement "will join us as a witness of Jesus' resurrection" (Acts 1:22, 26).

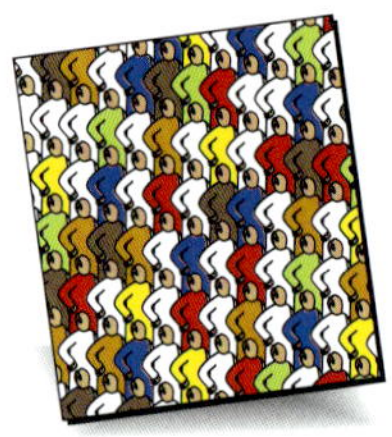

MORE THAN 500 BELIEVERS
Within 40 days, unknown location, probably in Galilee. Jesus appeared to over 500 people at one time. Matthias and Joseph Barsabbas may have been present (Acts 1:22–23; 1 Cor. 15:6).

JAMES, BROTHER OF JESUS
Within 40 days, unknown location. Jesus also appeared to his half-brother, James, who only comes to faith after the resurrection. He later becomes a leader in the church (John 7:5; Ac 21:18; 1 Cor. 15:7).

THE TWELVE (?) DISCIPLES
After 40 days, on the Mount of Olives. The disciples gathered again. Jesus took them to the Mount of Olives and ascended to heaven (Mark 16:19; Luke 24:50–52; Acts 1:4–12; 1 Cor. 15:7).

SAUL/PAUL
About two years later, on the road to Damascus. But did Paul meet the risen Christ or was it only a vision of him? Paul himself clearly believed that had met Jesus in person (Acts 9:1–6; 1 Cor 9;1; 15:8).

See also: Stephen (Acts 7:55), Paul (Acts 22:17–22; 23:11), and John (Rev. 1:10–19).

The Conversation on the Road to Emmaus

WHERE WAS EMMAUS?

• The location of Emmaus is unclear, even though we know how far it was from Jerusalem "about seven miles" (Luke 24:13, literally "60 *stadia*").

• Some manuscripts say 160 *stadia* (15.6 miles) instead.

• The travelers walked to Emmaus and were back in Jerusalem before nightfall (Luke 24:33–36). Walking 320 *stadia* seems too far; 120 is more realistic.

• Four main sites for Emmaus have been proposed, all east of Jerusalem.

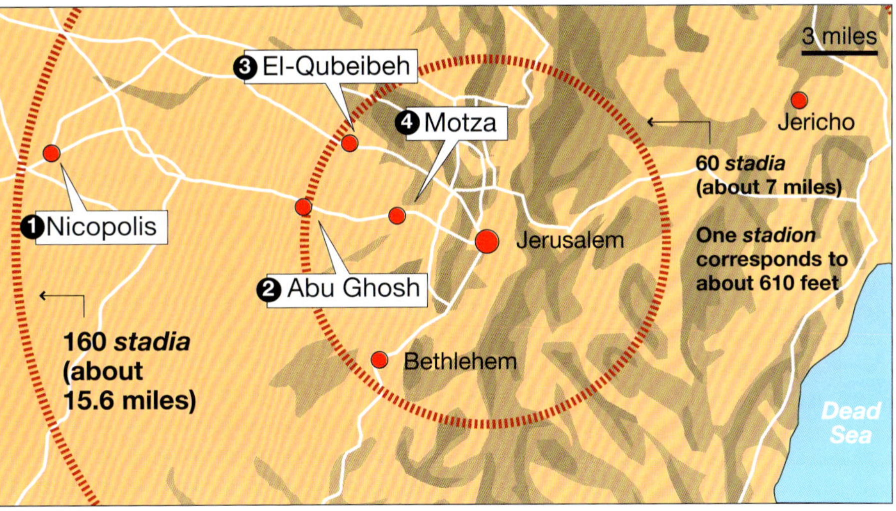

1. NICOPOLIS
Also called: Imwas. Identified as Emmaus in the third century. In the fourth century, Jerome suggested that a church was built on the site of Cleopas's house. Was laid waste by Israel in the 1967 Six-Day War.
Problem: Located too far away from Jerusalem (Luke 24:33).

2. ABU GHOSH
Location: Near Kiriath-jearim, where the ark of the covenant was kept for thirty years before being taken to Jerusalem (1 Sam. 6:21). A church was built there by the Crusaders in 1140.
Problem: The village was not identified with Emmaus until the twelfth century.

3. EL-QUBEIBEH
Also called: Al-Qubeiba. When the Crusaders were driven out, Christians were not allowed to use the road that led to Jaffa. In 1280, this site on the alternative route to Jaffa was designated as Emmaus instead.
Problem: The site was not identified as Emmaus until the thirteenth century.

4. MOTZA
Also called: Colonia, Qalunya, Ammaous, or Amassa. Possible location according to many modern scholars. Josephus mentions the village. Was destroyed by war in 1948.
Problem: It is too close to Jerusalem. No early Christian tradition identifies it as Emmaus.

Who were the three travelers?

CLEOPAS (CLOPAS)
One of the travelers was Cleopas (Luke 24:18), usually identified as Clopas (John 19:25). According to tradition, he was Jesus's uncle, the brother of his stepfather, Joseph.

THE OTHER DISCIPLE
Uncertain. One possibility is Mary, the wife of Clopas (John 19:25). This Mary, who was present at the crucifixion, may be the sister-in-law of Mary, the mother of Jesus. Another suggestion is that Clopas's companion was his son, Simon. According to tradition, he became a leader in the church. Several other candidates have been suggested, including the author Luke himself.

JESUS
Jesus joined the travelers (Luke 24:15). The event takes place after the resurrection and they do not recognize him at first.

What did the travelers learn?

• **THE WALK:** Jesus walked with the disciples to Emmaus. They knew about the empty tomb but were unsure of what it meant.

• **THE CONVERSATION:** Jesus wanted them to understand. So he explained "from all the Scriptures [the Old Testament] the things concerning himself" (Luke 24:27).

• **THE MEAL:** They invited him in and it was when he broke the bread (did they see his wounds?) that they realized who he was. This was probably a regular evening meal, not communion.

• **THE RESPONSE:** When they realized who he was, they said: "Didn't our hearts burn within us as he talked with us ... and explained the Scriptures to us?" (Luke 24:32). Jesus's explanation of the Scriptures, not seeing him resurrected, seems to have made the strongest impression on them.

What Jesus Talked about

• We don't know what Jesus said to his companions on the road to Emmaus (Luke 24:13–35), but he probably explained to them how the Old Testament portrays him...

GENESIS
• As the offspring of the woman who strikes the serpent's head (Ge 3:15) • As the promised offspring through whom all the families of the earth are blessed (Ge 13:15; Gal 3:16)

EXODUS
• As the Passover lamb whose blood saves (Ex 12:5–6; Jn 1:29, 36; 1Co 5:7; 1Pe 1:19) • As the tabernacle where God displays his glory (Ex 25:9; Jn 1:14; Heb 8:5; 9:11)

LEVITICUS
• As the sacrificial goats on the Day of Atonement which are a picture of His atoning sacrifice (Lev 16:1–34; Heb 9:13) • As our eternal high priest (Lev 21:10; Heb 5:1–6)

NUMBERS
• As the bronze serpent that is lifted up in the desert and gives life (Nu 21:4–9; Jn 3:14)
• As the rock in the desert that gives water (Ex 17:6; Nu 20:8; 1Co 10:4)

DEUTERONOMY
• As a prophet like Moses whom God raises up (Dt 18:15; Ac 3:22–25; 7:37)
• As a refuge we can flee to for safety and live (Dt 4:41; Nu 35:9–34; Mt 11:28)

JOSHUA
• As a savior, whose name means "the LORD saves" (Jos 1:1; Ac 4:12), • As "the commander of the LORD's army", a vision of the Lord (Jos 5:13–15; Ex 3:5)

JUDGES
• As a judge, the judges illustrate the work of Jesus. Their role as savior and leader points forward to the righteous leader who will bring justice to the people (Jdg 2:16; 2Ti 4:8)

RUTH
• As our redeemer (Ru 3:9), one who is not only able to redeem those in need, but is also willing to do so (Ru 2:1; 3:11–13; Mt 20:28). Jesus is our redeemer (Tit 2:14)

FIRST SAMUEL
• As a king like David, a man after God's own heart (Ac 13:22)
• As the "anointed one," the Messiah. To be anointed for a special task (1Sa 2:10; Lk 2:26; Jn 1:41)

SECOND SAMUEL
• As the fulfillment of the promises to David of an eternal throne, an eternal kingdom, and an exalted offspring. Jesus is the Son of David (2Sa 7:12–16; Lk 1:32–33; Mt 22:45)

FIRST KINGS
• As a king who is greater than Solomon in all of his splendor (1Ki 10:4–9; Mt 12:42)
• As a prophet who is of greater importance than Elijah (1Ki 18:15–40; Mt 16:13–16)

SECOND KINGS
• As a descendant of the tribe of Judah, the line that is preserved by God (2Ki 8:19; 11:3; Lk 2:4; 3:33) • As a prophet like Elijah and Elisha (2Ki 2:8, 19–22; Lk 24:19)

FIRST CHRONICLES
• As the offspring of King David whom God promises to exalt to kingship and to establish his throne forever: "I will be his father, and he will be my son" (1Ch 17:12–13).

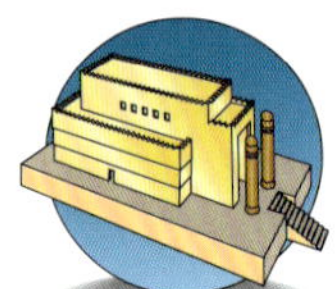

SECOND CHRONICLES
• As one who is greater than the magnificent temple Solomon built in Jerusalem, and greater than the sacrifices the priests offered in the temple (2Ch 2:1–5:14, Mt 12:6)

EZRA
• As the one who brings freedom to the captives, as illustrated by Zerubbabel and Ezra in their roles as leaders of those allowed to return from Babylon (Ezr 3:1–2; 7:1–8; Lk 4:18)

NEHEMIAH
• As one who restores, illustrated by Nehemiah as he rebuilds the wall around Jerusalem (Ne 6:16) • As one who renews the covenant (Ne 10:28–29; Mt 18:3; Lk 22:20)

ESTHER
• As a savior who gives his life for his people, illustrated by Esther (Est 4:16; Jn 18:9) • As an example of events happening according to the plan of God (Est 4:13, 16; Gal 4:4)

JOB
• As the living redeemer in whom Job places his hope (Job 19:25–27; Isa 44:6; 47:4) • As the one to whom Job cries out in all of his distress (Job 9:33; 16:20; 33:23; 1Ti 2:8)

"And beginning with Moses and all the Prophets, he explained to them what was said in all the Scriptures concerning himself (Luke 24:27).

PSALMS
• As the Son of God (Ps 2:7; Heb 1:5) • As the Creator of all things (Ps 19:1–7) • As the One whose hands will be pierced (Ps 22:16) • As the One who rules over all (Ps 8:6–7; Eph 1:22)

on the Road to Emmaus

PROVERBS
• As the wisdom of God who is from the beginning, in whom are hidden all the treasures of wisdom, God's eternal wisdom personified (Pr 8:22; 1Co 1:24; Col 2:3)

ECCLESIASTES
• As the one who fills the desire that God has placed in every human heart (Ecc 3:11; Lk 24:32) • As the one whose laws we should keep (Ecc 12:11–14; Jn 14:21)

SONG OF SONGS
• As our loving bridegroom, the One of whom the song is an illustration (SS 2:9–10, Isa 54:5–6; 2Co 11:2, Rev 19:7–9) • As an illustration of true love (SS 2:4; Eph. 5:32)

ISAIAH
• As the suffering servant who takes on the sin of the world (Isa 53:5–7) • As the child who is called Mighty God and Prince of Peace (Isa 9:6, Mt 1:23, Lk 1:32–33)

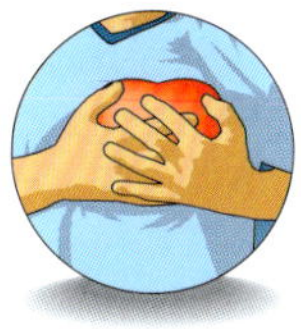

JEREMIAH
• As the giver of the new covenant, one that offers a new heart (Jer 31:31–33, Lk 22:20; Ro 6:17) • As the descendant of David (Jer 33:15; Zec 6:12; Luke1:32)

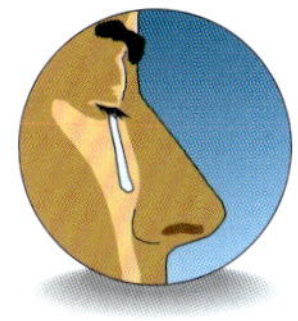

LAMENTATIONS
• As "a man of sorrows," illustrated by the pain and grief felt by the prophet (La 1:12; 3:19–20; Isa 53:3)
• As the One who weeps over Jerusalem (La 1:16; Mt 23:37–38)

EZEKIEL
• As the branch from the top of the tall cedar that will become a majestic cedar (Eze 17:22–24; Da 2:44–45) • As the rightful king who is to come (Eze 21:26–27; Mt 21:1–11)

DANIEL
• As the son of God in the furnace (Da 3:25)
• As the Son of Man, Jesus is also the true man (Dn 7:13; Mt 9:6).
• As the rock that crushes kingdoms (Dn 2:34–35, 44; Ac 4:11)

HOSEA
• As the son called out of Egypt, an image linked to Joseph and Mary leaving Egypt (Hos 11:1; Mt 2:15).
• As an illustration of God's boundless love (Hos 3:1–2; Gal 3:13)

JOEL
• As the one by whose name everyone who calls on him will be saved (Joel 2:32; Jn 14:6; Ac 2:21) • As the judge who will judge all people (Joel 3:2, 12; 1Pe 4:5)

AMOS
• As the one for whom the sun went down at noon and darkened the land (Am 8:9; Mt 27:45)
• As the one who opens for Gentiles a way to come to faith (Am 9:11–15; Ac 15:13–19)

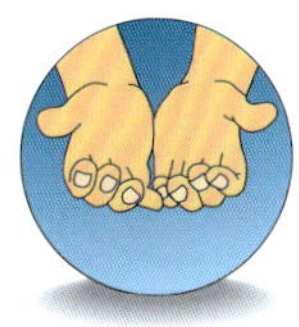

OBADIAH
• As a model of God's protection of his people Israel (Ob 1:17–20) while judging the nations that rise against them (Ob 1:15–16) "The Lord himself will be king!" (Ob 1:21).

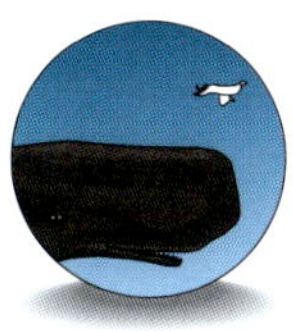

JONAH
• As the one who, like Jonah, remained three days and nights in the "belly of the great fish," Jonah is an image of Jesus's death and resurrection (Jnh 2:1; Mt 12:39–41).

MICAH
• As the child who will be born in Bethlehem, whose origin is from eternity and who will rule over Israel (Mic 5:2; Mt 2:5–6) • As the one who will judge many peoples (Mic 4:1–8)

NAHUM
• As the one that the messenger says will proclaim peace (Na 1:15) • As one who is both a strong refuge in the day of trouble and a zealous avenger (Na 1:2–7)

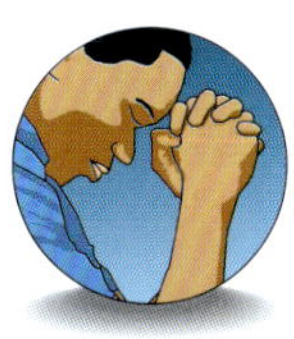

HABAKKUK
• As the one through whom the righteous live by faith (Hab 2:4; Ro 1:17; Gal 3:11)
• As the one who will fill the earth with the knowledge of the glory of the Lord (Hab 2:14)

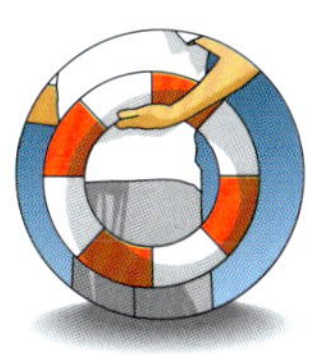

ZEPHANIAH
• As the one who lives in you, a mighty savior who saves, rejoicing over you (Zep 3:17) • As the one who will remove the judgments from us and disperse our enemies (Zep 3:15)

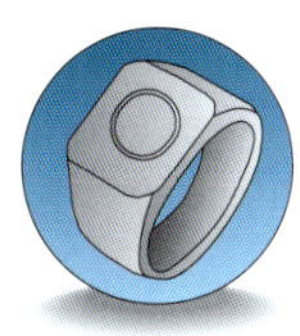

HAGGAI
• As a signet ring like Zerubbabel's (Hag 2:23; Jer 22:24; Eph 1:13)
• As the one who will shake the heavens and the earth and fill the temple with glory (Hag 2:6–9; Heb 12:25–27)

ZECHARIAH
• As the pierced one on whom they will look (Zec 12:10, Jn 19:34, 37)
• As the one who comes riding on a donkey (Zec 9:9; Mt 21:7) • As the one sold for thirty pieces of silver (Zec 11:12–13; Mt 27:3)

MALACHI
• As the one through whom the sun of righteousness will rise (Mal 4:2; 1:11) • As the promised one who is preceded by one coming in the power of Elijah (Mal 4:5; Mt 11:13–14; Mk 9:11)

HOW LONG DID THE WALK TAKE?
• It is seven miles from Jerusalem to Emmaus (Lk 24:13). A normal walking pace is about three mph, so the journey was probably between two and two and one-half hours.

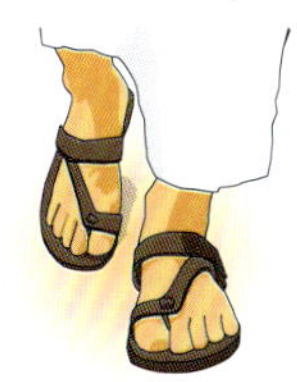

The Four Pillars of the Great Commission

Before his ascension, Jesus gave the Great Commission to his disciples. In it are four all-encompassing statements. These lay the foundation for the mission to spread the word of God to the whole world.

1 ALL authority (Matt. 28:18)
Jesus has been given all authority in heaven and on earth by the Father. This authority is the basis for the rest of the Great Commission. Without it, his disciples would not be able to do what Jesus asks of them.

2 ALL the nations (Matt. 28:19a)
Therefore, "for this reason," Jesus sends the disciples out to make disciples of all nations. This command is clearly about every single nation, not just the Jewish nation.

3 ALL the commands (Matt. 28:19–20a)
Those who come to faith are to be taught all that Jesus commanded. He gives two instructions: 1) **to baptize** them and 2) **to teach** them to keep what Jesus has commanded.

4 ALWAYS (Matt. 28:20b)
A promise that they will not carry out the mission in their own strength. Jesus promises that he is with them all the way to the end of time. Although he is not physically present today, he is with us spiritually.

All Authority | All Nations | All Commands | Always

DID THE DISCIPLES MISUNDERSTAND THE GREAT COMMISSION?

1 THE WHOLE WORLD
Jesus said: "Make disciples of all nations" (see Acts 1:8)—yet they stayed in Jerusalem for two years. Only when persecution broke out did they spread further (Acts 8:1).

2 ALL PEOPLE
Jesus said: "Make disciples of all nations" (Matt. 28:19)—yet at first they only preached to Jews (Acts 2:22). Peter was even attacked by the other believers for entering a gentile's house (Acts 11:1–3).

3 ALL THE COMMANDS
Jesus said: "Obey all the commands I have given you" (Matt. 28:20)—yet for years, some continued to live and teach as if receiving Christ was not enough, insisting on obedience to the Jewish religious laws (Gal. 2:9–13).

OTHER VERSIONS OF THE GREAT COMMISSION

Mark 16:15–16 was probably not in the original text.

1 LUKE 24:47–49
"It was also written that this message **would be proclaimed in the authority of his name to all the nations**, beginning in Jerusalem: 'There is forgiveness of sins for all who repent.' You are witnesses of all these things."

2 JOHN 20:21–23
"'As the Father has sent me, so I am sending you.' Then he breathed on them and said, 'Receive the Holy Spirit. If you forgive anyone's sins, they are forgiven. If you do not forgive them, they are not forgiven."

> "We must be global Christians with a global vision because our God is a global God. (John Stott)

THE GLOBAL IMPACT OF THE GOSPEL

The spread of the gospel has had periods of advance and periods of setback. Here is a quick overview of the history of the church.

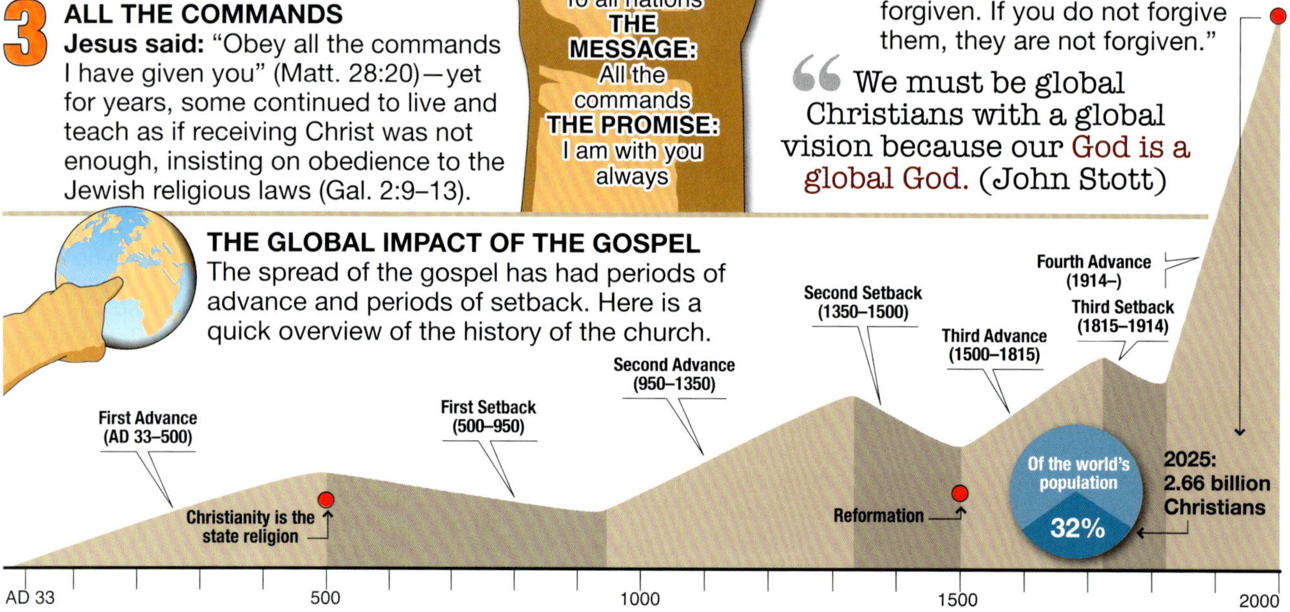

Source: chart from Bible Atlas by H. H. Rowley, statistics from Operation World

Why the Resurrection Is So Important

Jesus explained to his disciples that "it was necessary for him ... [to] be killed, but on the third day he would be raised from the dead" (Matt. 16:21). What would the gospel be without the resurrection of Jesus?

DEFINITION

What does the resurrection mean?

- The resurrection is the belief that Jesus came back from the dead on the third day.
- There is a difference between the resurrection of Jesus to a new life and the examples of restoration back to the old life that we encounter in other texts in the Bible, such as with Lazarus (John 11:43–44).
- In 1 Corinthians 15:12–19, Paul uses a particular method of reasoning. For the sake of argument, he assumes that Jesus did not rise from the dead. He then shows all of the contradictions that arise if one believes this.

> Since we have been united with him in his death, we will also be raised to life as he was (Rom. 6:5).

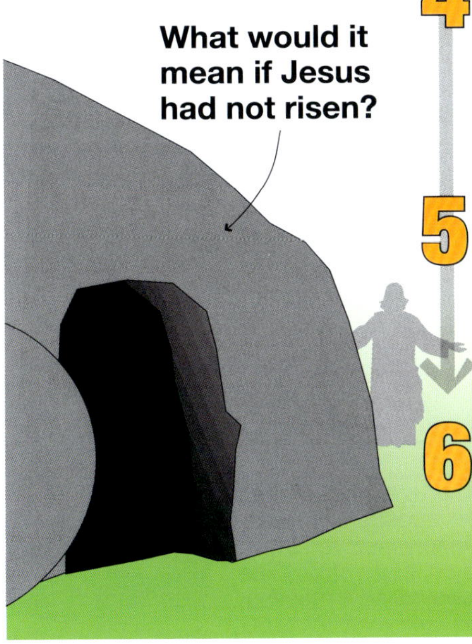

IT CONFIRMS ...

1 ... that Christ is the Messiah. The resurrection from the dead is God's confirmation of the Messiah, the crucified one. It confirms both his divinity and his role as the final judge (Acts 2:36; 5:30–31; 10:40–42).

2 ... that his death is sufficient. Confirms that Jesus's death is sufficient to bring reconciliation. God can offer forgiveness of sins and salvation to everyone who believes (Acts 13:32–33, 38–39; Rom. 4:23–25; 1 John 5:11–13).

3 ... that our faith is true. It is the ultimate proof that our faith is true, this is the basis for our assurance of salvation. "We will certainly be saved through the life of his Son" (Rom. 5:10; 8:15–17; 1 Peter 1:21).

> For the apostles, "to preach Christianity meant primarily to preach the Resurrection." (C. S. Lewis)

4 ... our own resurrection. It is a promise to all who are in Christ that their bodies will be resurrected. It changes our view of death and gives us hope (Acts 4:2; Rom. 8:10–11; 1 Cor. 15:12–58; 2 Cor. 4:14).

5 ... the call to be sanctified. Death, resurrection, and ascension are the pattern. Having died and risen with him, we should see ourselves as new creations (Rom. 6:3–11; 2 Cor. 4:10–11; Eph. 2:4–6).

6 ... the whole revelation. It becomes the ultimate proof that God's revelation is true. It moves Christian faith from a philosophical speculation to an affirmation of God's existence and activity in history.

BUT IF NOT ...

1 ... then our preaching is useless. If Jesus did not rise bodily from the dead, then the teaching about him and the claim that he is alive are based on a lie (1 Cor. 15:14a).

2 ... then your faith is useless. Then faith is also empty, having no true content. Denying the resurrection takes the very heart out of the gospel (1 Cor. 15:2, 14b).

3 ... then the apostles are all lying. Those who testified that they met the risen Christ are to be regarded as false witnesses. They claim things that never happened (1 Cor. 15:15).

4 ... then your faith is futile. Faith is then futile, serving no good purpose. It only exists in the mind and has no connection to any real-world event (1 Cor. 15:17a).

5 ... then you are still guilty of your sins. Without the resurrection, the promise of salvation is a lie, and there would be no atonement and no forgiveness for sin (1 Cor. 15:17b).

6 ... then those who died in Christ are lost. If Christ has not risen, we can have no expectation of rising from the dead one day. We are eternally lost, regardless of what we believe (1 Cor. 15:18).

7 ... then we are more to be pitied than anyone. This summarizes the passage. Paul shows the consequences of denying the truth that Jesus has indeed risen from the dead (1 Cor. 15:19).

Jesus Ascends to Heaven ...

Forty days after his resurrection, Jesus gathers with his disciples at Bethany on the Mount of Olives (Luke 24:50; Acts 1:12). He gives a final speech and is then lifted up. A cloud takes him out of their sight. But what is the significance of the ascension?

1 Jesus is confirmed as the final sin offering (Heb. 10:11–14)

The Father confirms the significance of Jesus's life, death, and resurrection by seating Jesus at his right hand. Jesus "offered himself to God as a single sacrifice for sins, good for all time" (Heb. 10:12).

2 Jesus speaks for us before the Father (1 John 2:1; Rom. 8:34)

Jesus is now seated at the right hand of the Father, and he takes upon himself the task of pleading for us before the Father. This gives us the assurance that we always have access to the Father through Christ (John 14:6).

3 Jesus takes his place as head of the church (Eph. 1:22–23; 4:15–16)

"God has ... made [Christ] head over all things for the benefit of the church" (Eph. 1:22). As his body, the church works together and grows.

4 Jesus reigns over all enemies (1 Peter 3:22; 1 Cor. 15:25)

As Jesus is lifted up, he will reign over all his enemies. "[Christ] is seated in the place of honor next to God, and all the angels and authorities and powers accept his authority" (1 Peter 3:22).

5 Now is the opportunity for the Spirit to come (John 7:39)

Jesus explained that the Spirit could not come "because [he] had not yet entered into his glory" (John 7:39). But now that he was lifted up, the Spirit could come.

Versions of the Ascension: Mark 16:19–20; Luke 24:50–53; Acts 1:6–12
• **Other texts about Jesus's ascension:** Luke 9:51; John 6:62; 7:33; 14:2, 12, 28; 16:5, 10, 16–17, 28; Eph 4:8–10.

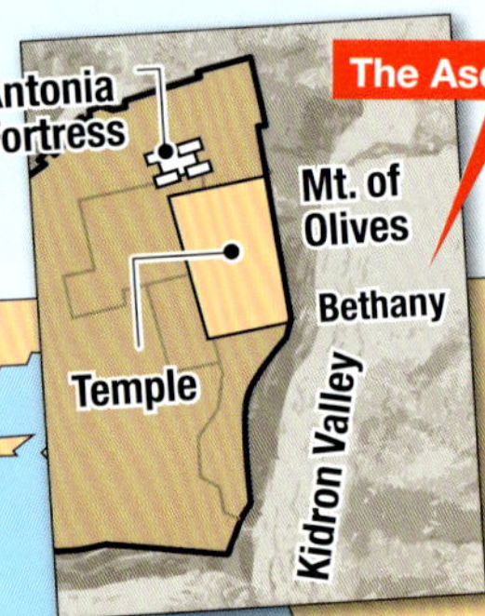

Chapel of the Ascension on the Mt. of Olives

... and then the message of Pentecost spreads

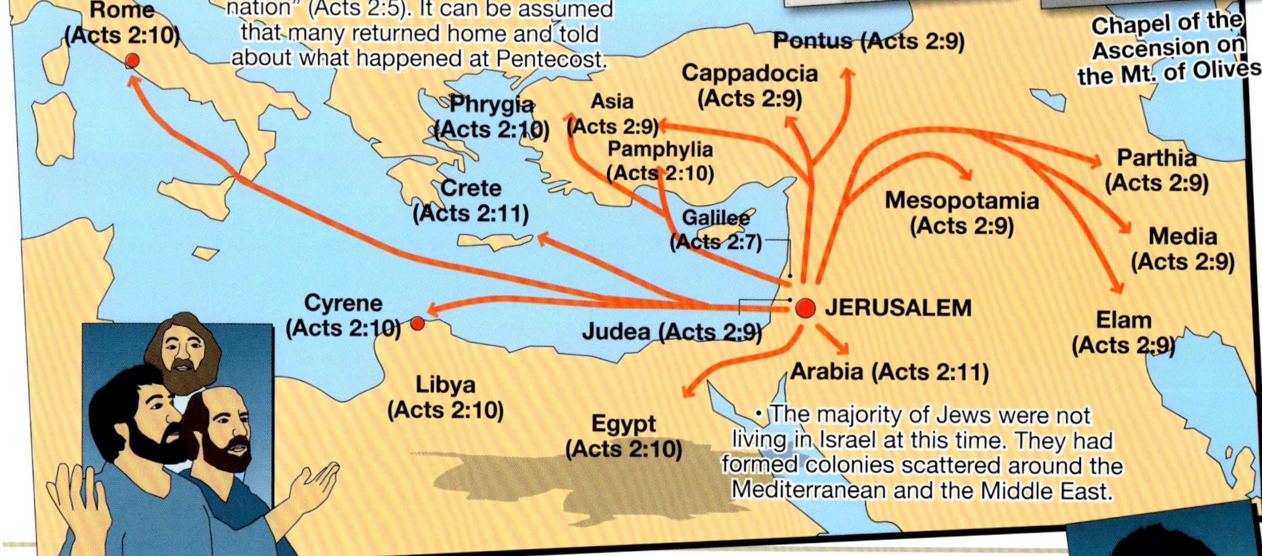

THE CHOICE OF MATTHIAS
After Judas's death, someone else was needed to take his place (Acts 1:20).

• The new apostle needed to be someone who had followed Jesus and witnessed Jesus's death and resurrection (Acts 1:21–22).

• They prayed and drew lots between two men, with the lot falling on Matthias (Acts 1:23–26).
• Matthias is never mentioned again, but neither are most of the other apostles. He was definitely involved in church leadership: "The Twelve called a meeting of all believers" (Acts 6:2).

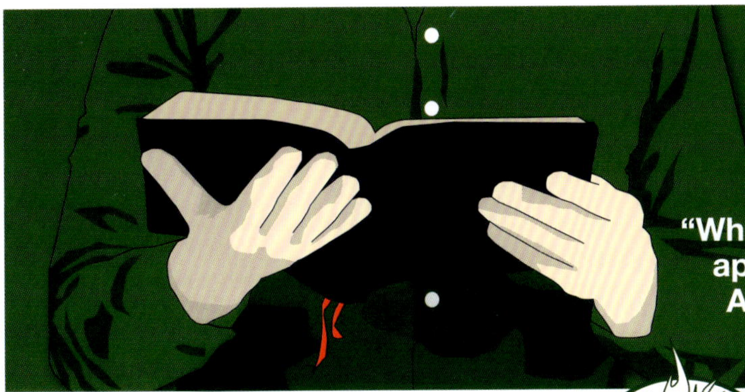

ACTS OF THE APOSTLES

"What looked like flames or tongues of fire appeared and settled on each of them. And everyone present was filled with the Holy Spirit" (Acts 2:3–4).

A FEW WORDS ABOUT THE AUTHOR

From the introduction, we can conclude that Acts has the same author as the Gospel of Luke (Luke 1:1–4; Acts 1:1–2). From the "we" passages in the book, we can conclude that the author traveled with Paul for great stretches (16:10–17; 20:5–21:18; 27:1–28:16). He also seems to have had access to written sources (15:23–29; 23:26–30). And early church fathers (Clement of Alexandria, Tertullian, and Jerome) confirm Luke as the author.

A FEW WORDS ABOUT RECIPIENT

Called Theophilus, "friend of God," the same as in Luke (1:1). "Most honorable" (Luke 1:3) seems to refer to a Roman political leader. Some say it was King Agrippa II (Acts 25:13). Others speak of a Roman official, possibly Titus Flavius Sabinus, still others that it was Paul's defense lawyer when imprisoned in Rome. Some say it is a symbolic name for all believers, which is less likely. Other ideas exist, but we just don't know.

A FEW WORDS ABOUT DATES

Acts ends abruptly. In one of the last verses, we are told that Paul was under house arrest for two years in Rome (28:30). His release is usually dated to AD 62. Some say that the book was written before Paul was released from prison; others that it was written shortly after, perhaps before AD 64. It was certainly written before his execution in AD 67.There are those who want to date the book later, but this seems less likely.

THE WHOLE BOOK IN 25 WORDS

Pentecost marks the church's birth and Spirit's arrival. Jesus works through Peter, Philip, Paul, and others to carry the gospel all the way to Rome.

A SIMPLE STRUCTURE

1. Proclamation – Christ's message spreads boldly
(Acts 1:1–7:60)

2. Progress – Church growth despite persecution
(Acts 8:1–12:25)

3. Preaching – Paul's travels spread the gospel
(Acts 13:1–28:31)

A FEW WORDS ABOUT KEY THEMES

- **The Holy Spirit**—Given in four steps through the book: on the day of Pentecost (2:1–13); in Samaria (8:14–25); in the house of Cornelius (10:44–47); and in Ephesus (19:1–7).
- **The Way**—A term describing those who receive the gospel and follow Jesus (9:2; 19:9, 23; 22:4; 24:14, 22).
- **The Church**—Refers to a chosen group. Born on the day of Pentecost and became the bearer of the message and instrument of mission (5:11; 7:38; 8:1, 3; 9:31; 11:22, 26; 12:1, 5; 13:1, 43; 14:27; 15:3–4, 22, 30, etc.).
- **The New Covenant**—Describes the transition from the Old to the New Covenant (Luke 22:20). Not all the pieces fell into place at once. Note for example 1:4–5; 3:25; 8:14–17; 10:9–20; 11:1–18; 15:1–29; 19:1–7; John 7:37–39; Gal. 2:11–14; Heb. 9:15).
- **The Opposition**—Note how resistance to the gospel grows (2:13; 4:1–22; 5:17–42; 6:9–8:4; 12:1–5; 13:6–50, etc.).

A FEW TIPS ON WHAT TO LOOK FOR

Theme of the book:
The gospel's journey from Jerusalem to Rome

- "The name of Jesus" or just "the name" (about 30 times)
- The Holy Spirit (about 40 times)
- The Church—its birth and growth
- Sermons and speeches (20 instances)
- Miracles that God does for and through the apostles (31 different)
- Prayers (about 20 times)
- To testify/testimony
- The relationship between the church and Israel (2:22, see Gal 6:16).
- The background to some of Paul's letters

Pentecost and the Baptism of the Spirit

The story of Pentecost tells of how Holy Spirit appeared on the disciples like tongues of fire and they started speaking in other languages. The phrase "baptism of the Spirit" is not found in the New Testament. There are only seven texts (1–7) where the verb "baptize" is directly linked to the Holy Spirit.

The texts about being baptized in the Holy Spirit

John the Baptist: "He will baptize you with the Holy Spirit" (Matt. 3:11). ①

John the Baptist: "He will baptize you with the Holy Spirit" (Mark 1:8). ②

John the Baptist: "He will baptize you with the Holy Spirit" (Luke 3:16). ③

John the Baptist: "The one who will baptize with the Holy Spirit" (John 1:33). ④

Jesus says: "In just a few days you will be baptized with the Holy Spirit" (Acts 1:5). ⑤

Pentecost ... to the Jews (2:14) "Everyone present was filled with the Holy Spirit and began speaking in other languages" (Acts 2:4).

... to the Samaritans (Acts 8:14) "Peter and John laid their hands upon these believers, and they received the Holy Spirit" (Acts 8:16–17).

... to the gentiles (Acts 10:28) "The Holy Spirit fell upon all who were listening to the message. The Jewish believers ... were amazed" (Acts 10:44–45).

"[Jesus said:] John baptized with water, but you will be baptized with the Holy Spirit" (Acts 11:16). ⑥

... to the disciples of John the Baptist who hadn't heard of the Spirit's baptism: "When Paul laid his hands on them, the Holy Spirit came on them" Acts 19:6).

"You are all children of God ... And all who have been united with Christ in baptism have put on Christ, like putting on new clothes" (Gal. 3:26–27).

According to Paul, "We have all been baptized into one body by one Spirit" (1 Cor. 12:13). ⑦

Paul writes, "Have you forgotten that when we were joined with Christ Jesus in baptism, we joined him in his death?" (Rom. 6:3).

The Spirit seems to have been given in historical steps:
1) to Jews (Acts 2:5, 14; 8:15–16)
2) to Samaritans (Acts 8:17)
3) to gentiles (Acts 10:44–46)
4) on another occasion (Acts 19:1–7)

Why were they amazed?

All three teaching texts contain the concept of "all"
1) "You are **all** children of God" (Gal. 3:26).
2) "We have **all** been baptized" (1 Cor. 12:13).
3) "**All** who are baptized" (Rom. 6:3 NIV).

1 Jesus speaks about the Spirit "who would be given to everyone believing in him. But the Spirit had not yet been given" since Jesus had not yet been glorified (John 7:39).

2 Six of the seven texts using the term "baptized" in reference to the Spirit are in historical texts and all of them are about the giving of the Spirit on the day of Pentecost (Acts 2:1–41).

3 Only one of the seven texts with the term "baptized" in reference to the Spirit is found in a theological text, using "all" to refer to those who have received the Spirit (1 Cor. 12:13).

4 Not everyone received the Spirit at Pentecost, note "fellow Jews" in Acts 2:5, 14. Samaritans and gentiles only received the Spirit later (Acts 8:14–19; 10:45; 19:2).

5 The manifestations of the Spirit seen on Pentecost may have diminished in the early church. "The Holy Spirit fell on them, just as he fell on us at the beginning" (Acts 11:15).

6 Other texts that only contain the word "baptized" probably still refer to being baptized in the Spirit: "All who have been united with Christ in baptism" (Gal. 3:27; Rom 6:3).

7 Speaking in tongues is mentioned three times in Acts: 2:3, 10:46, and 19:6. The only other times it appears is in Mark 16 (an uncertain text) and 1 Corinthians 14.

Narrative text w/"baptism" | Narrative text w/o"baptism" | Theological text

The First Two Years in Jerusalem

In the two years after Pentecost, the activity of the disciples and the church took place primarily in and around Jerusalem. Acts gives us the details and locations of some of the key events from that time.

1 The Ascension of Jesus

After appearing for forty days, Jesus repeats his promise to send the Spirit. While on the Mount of Olives, he is lifted up to heaven before the eyes of the disciples (May 13, AD 33, Acts 1:1–11).

2 Waiting on the Holy Spirit

The disciples gather in the upper room with Mary and others to pray and wait for the Spirit as promised. Matthias is chosen to replace Judas Iscariot (11 days in May AD 33, Acts 1:5, 12–2:4).

3 The Day of Pentecost

The Spirit fills the disciples. Peter speaks, probably in the Court of the Gentiles in the temple. The believers gather in the temple every day (May 24, AD 33, Acts 2:5–47).

4 The healing of a lame man

A crippled beggar at the Beautiful Gate in the temple asks Peter and John for money. They heal him instead. Peter sees an opportunity and preaches inside the temple (summer AD 33, Acts 3:1–26).

5 Brought before the Sanhedrin

John and Peter are brought to the religious leaders, probably in the temple ("arrived" 5:21). They are told not to preach the gospel, but boldly continue (summer AD 33, Acts 4:1–31).

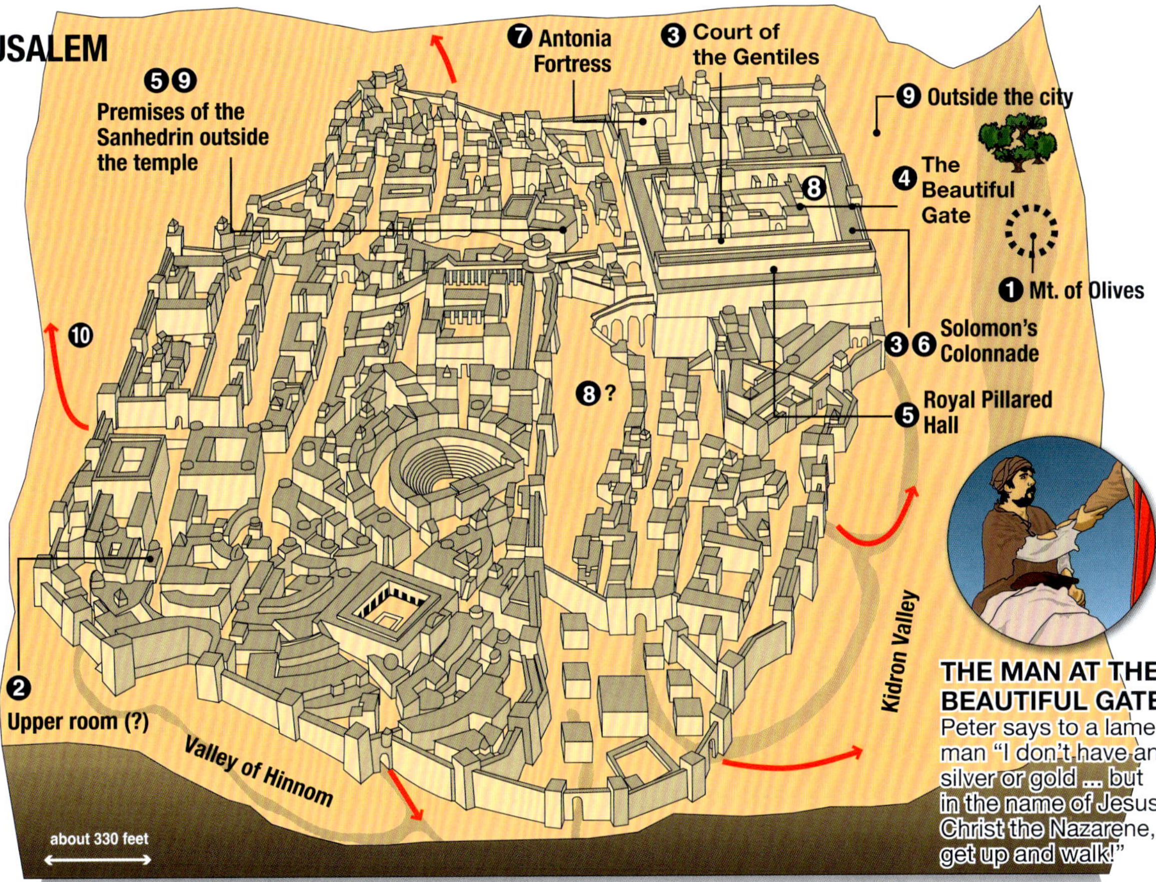

THE MAN AT THE BEAUTIFUL GATE
Peter says to a lame man "I don't have any silver or gold ... but in the name of Jesus Christ the Nazarene, get up and walk!"

6 Lies and Consequences

Ananias and Sapphira die dramatically due to their greed. Regular meetings are held in Solomon's Colonnade in the temple, and many miracles take place (AD 33–34, Acts 3:11; 4:32–5:16).

7 The apostles are rearrested

John and Peter are rearrested. Put in general custody of the Sadducees or possibly in the Antonia Fortress. An angel frees them and they make a speech before the Sanhedrin (AD 34–35, Acts 5:17–42).

8 First deacons are selected

After concerns are raised about the treatment of the Greek-speaking widows in the church, seven deacons are appointed to take charge of practical matters (late AD 34–early 35, Acts 6:1–7).

9 The first martyr is killed

Stephen is arrested and brought before the Sanhedrin. He gives a speech in defense of the faith, but is stoned to death outside the city (Acts 7:58). Saul, looking on, approves (April AD 35, Acts 6:7–7:60).

10 The first persecution

Persecution breaks out. All of the believers, except the apostles, are scattered through Judea and Samaria. This happened about two years after Jesus's death (April AD 35, "began that day" Acts 8:1).

Seven Deacons Are Elected

Acts chapter 6 is the passage in the New Testament that gives us the most insight into how leaders were chosen in the early church. Is it a pattern for us?

3 THEREFORE THE PROBLEM AROSE

A conflict came up between the Greek-speaking and Aramaic-speaking believers. The Greek-speaking believers complained that their widows were not receiving a fair share of the daily food distribution. This complaint came to the apostles' attention.

1 AT LEAST TWO GROUPS

Both groups had Jewish origin (6:1). There were those who lived in Israel and spoke Aramaic (often also Greek) and those who had lived outside Israel but often returned in their old age. They only spoke Greek.

2 TAKES SOCIAL RESPONSIBILITY

The church shared possessions and helped those in need (Acts 2:44–45; 4:32–5:11). Caring for widows, orphans, the poor, and strangers has always been a responsibility of God's people (Ex. 22:22; Deut. 10:18; 1 Tim. 3:4–16).

4 THE CHURCH'S SOLUTION

• **Delegation to others (seven).** In a growing congregation, the leaders' workload can become too heavy.
• **Clear division of responsibilities (Acts 6:2, 4).** No one had control over everything. Some were "in prayer and teaching" and others were "running a food program."

The Seven Deacons

STEPHEN
Tradition says that he was the oldest of the seven. Sometimes called an archdeacon. Preaches boldly, is accused of blasphemy, and stoned to death, the first Christian martyr (Acts 6:5; 6:8–8:2; 11:19; 22:20).

PHILIP
Leaves Jerusalem and preaches in Samaria. Ends up in Caesarea, has four daughters. Paul visits him (Acts 21:8). Early church fathers said that he became a bishop in Tralles in Anatolia (Acts. 6:5; 8:4–40; 21:8).

PROCORUS
Said to have been a cousin of Stephen. May have been the scribe for the apostle John ("we" John 21:24). Either became a bishop of Nicomedia in Bithynia or bishop and martyr in Antioch (Acts. 6:5).

NICANOR
May have been one of the seventy sent out by Jesus on a preaching mission (Luke 10:1). Allegedly martyred in AD 76, possibly in Cyprus according to medieval writings. But very uncertain (Acts 6:5).

TIMON
Some say he had a gift for healing the sick. Said to have become bishop of Bosra in Syria. Others claim that he traveled to Corinth via Cyprus. He is said to have been martyred (Acts. 6:5).

PARMENAS
Preached the gospel in Asia Minor. Said to have been martyred at Philippi in AD 98 under Emperor Trajan. Another tradition says that he became bishop of Soli, uncertain which Soli (Acts. 6:5).

NICOLAS
Called a proselyte from Antioch. That is, one who converted to the Jewish faith and then became a Christian. Possibly one of the seventy sent out by Jesus (Luke 10:1; Acts 6:5).

> Significantly, all seven men had Greek names, implying they were [of Greek origin] ... The early church evidently felt the problem of the unintentional neglect of Grecian Jewish widows would be best solved by the [Greek] Jews, certainly they would not neglect the Aramaic-speaking widows. (Stanley Toussaint)

On to Judea and Samaria

Persecution breaks out after Stephen's death, scattering the believers across Judea and Samaria, but they take the gospel with them (Acts 8:1). Philip and Peter minister in these regions.

PHILIP'S TRAVELS

PHILIP
Appointed one of the church's first seven deacons (6:5). When persecution broke out, he left Jerusalem and preached in Samaria (8:5). He met the Ethiopian eunuch and baptized him (8:26). He eventually landed in Caesarea by the Sea, where he settled. Paul came and lived with him (21:8). He had four daughters, all of whom had the gift of prophecy (21:9).

1 **Location:** Jerusalem
Event: Philip is appointed as a deacon in the church (Acts 6:1–7).

2 **Location:** Samaria
Event: Philip preaches and many come to faith (Acts 8:5–13).

5 **Location:** Jerusalem (?)
Event: Receives a message from an angel of the Lord (Acts 8:26).

6 **Location:** Road to Gaza
Event: Explains the Scripture and baptizes the Ethiopian (Acts 8:27–39).

7 **Location:** Azotus
Event: Spirit snatches Philip away, preaches the gospel (Acts 8:40).

8 **Location:** Arrives in Caesarea and stays there
Event: Paul visits Philip (Acts 8:40; 21:8–10).

PETER'S TRAVELS

PETER
The leader of the church in Jerusalem. Sent with John to investigate what was happening in Samaria (8:14). Using visions, God confirms that the conversion of gentiles is according to his will (10:11). Peter explains his actions to the church in Jerusalem (11:1–4).

3 **Location:** Samaria
Event: Conveys the Spirit through the laying on of hands (Acts 8:14–24).

4 **Location:** Through Samaria to Jerusalem
Event: Preaches in the villages (Acts 8:25).

9 **Location:** Lydda and the region of Sharon
Event: Peter heals Aeneas (Acts 9:32–35).

10 **Location:** Joppa
Event: Peter raises Tabitha and receives a vision from God (Acts 9:36–10:23).

11 **Location:** Caesarea
Event: Peter at Cornelius's house; Holy Spirit falls on gentiles (Acts 10:23–48).

12 **Location:** Jerusalem
Event: Peter explains and defends what happened in Caesarea (Acts 11:1–18).

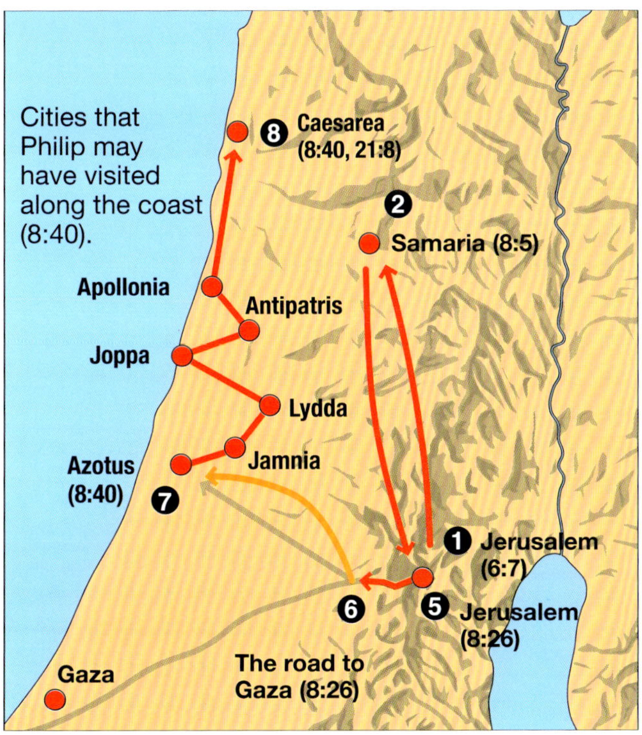

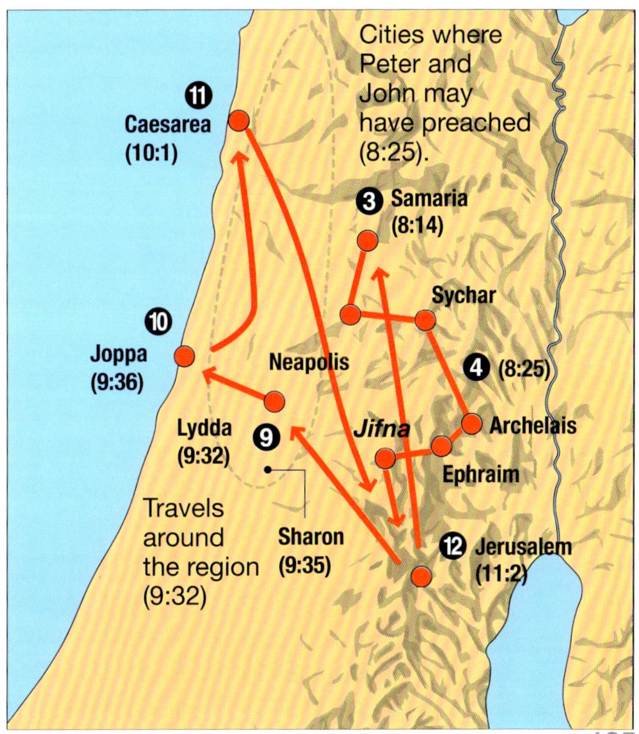

The Greatest Sinner Is Saved

1 Jerusalem (summer AD 35). Saul watches Stephen's martyrdom, then persecutes Christians (Acts 7:58–8:1).

2 Road to Damascus (summer AD 35). Saul is traveling to Damascus when Jesus appears to him. He repents (Acts 9:1–8).

3 Damascus (from summer AD 35). God sends Ananias to Paul. Paul meets opposition for preaching (Acts 9:8–25; 2 Cor. 11:32 ?).

4 Arabia, probably the Nabatean kingdom (for a while, possibly till early summer AD 37). Saul flees, stays away for a time (Gal. 1:17).

5 Damascus (early summer AD 37). Saul returns to Damascus and stays for three years (Acts 9:23–25; 2 Cor. 11:32; Gal. 1:17–18).

6 Jerusalem (first visit since conversion, summer AD 37). Saul meets with Peter and James (Acts 9:26–29; Gal. 1:18–20).

7 Caesarea (summer AD 37). Due to persecution he is sent out of Jerusalem and on to Caesarea (Acts 9:30).

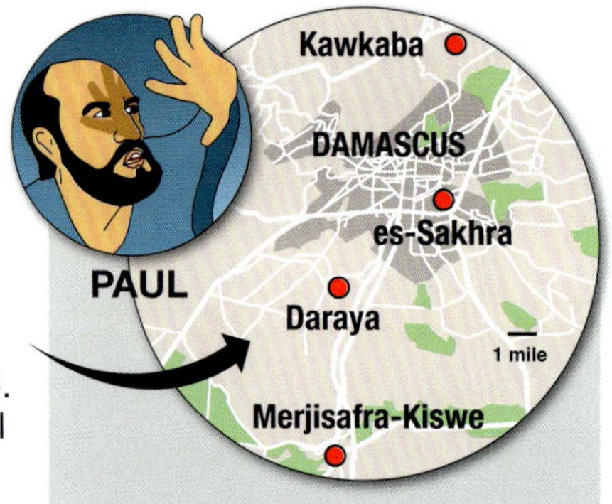

LOCATION OF PAUL'S CONVERSION
The exact place is uncertain. Several options are identified:
- **Daraya,** a suburb of Damascus, southwest of the city center
- **es-Sakhra** in Tabbaleh district, also near the city center. A memorial chapel was built there in 1925, followed by a church in 1971, and a larger one in 2008,
- Other suggested sites are **Merjisafra-Kiswe** south of the city center and **Kawkaba** north of the center.

8 Tarsus (autumn AD 37 to spring 43). Saul returns to Tarsus (Acts 9:27–30).

9 Syria and Cilicia (autumn AD 37 to spring 43). Saul preaches around Tarsus. Some of the events described in 2 Cor. 11:23–27 may have occurred then. Barnabas visits him (Acts 11:22; Gal. 1:21–24).

10 Antioch (spring AD 43 to fall 47). Barnabas takes Saul to Antioch. They teach in the church, believers first called Christians (Acts 11:25–28).

11 Jerusalem (second visit, autumn AD 47). Barnabas, Saul, and Titus in Jerusalem to deliver aid from the church in Antioch (Acts 11:29–30; Gal. 2:1–10).

12 Antioch (autumn AD 47 to spring 48). Barnabas, Saul, and John Mark return. Sent out on their first missionary journey (Acts 12:25–13:3).

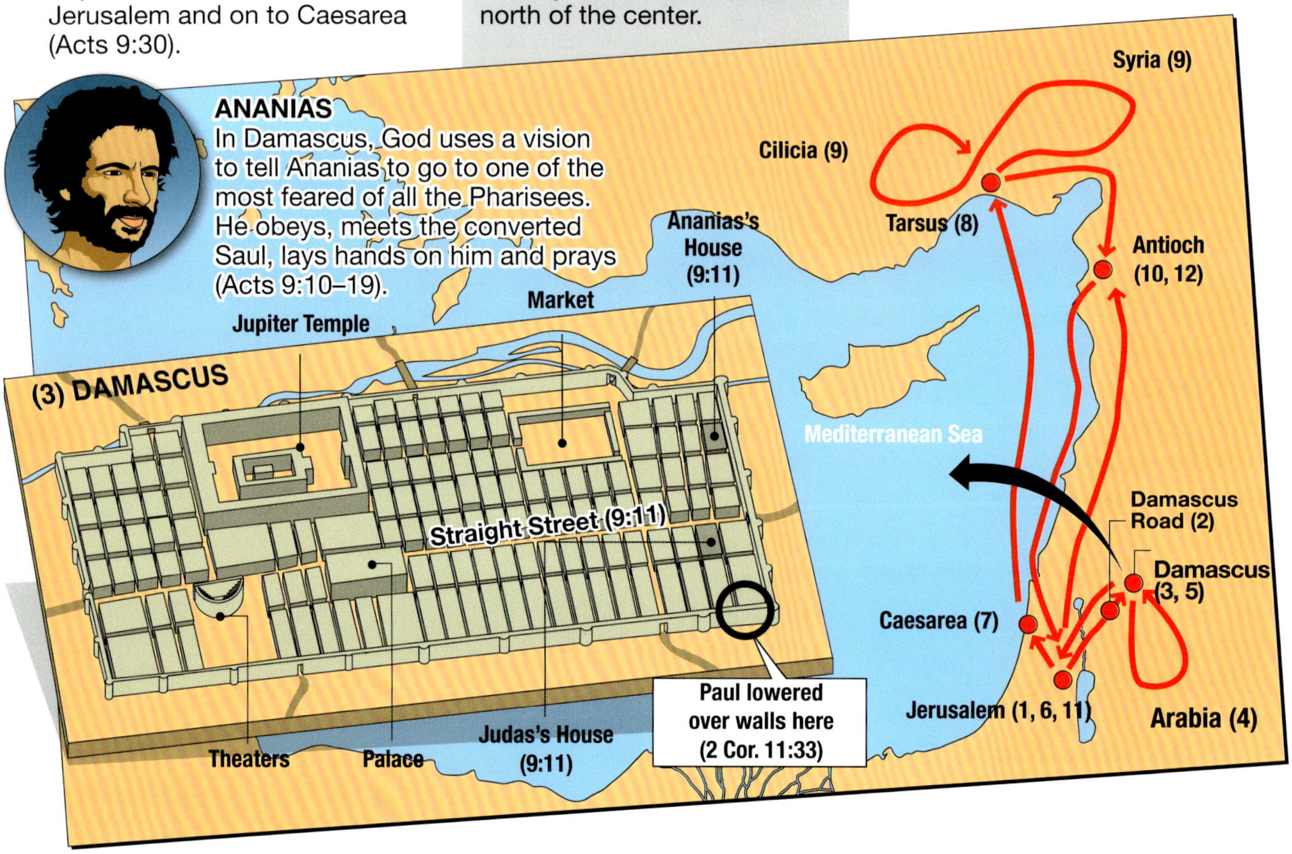

All the Sermons in the Book of Acts

The book of Acts records many of the apostles' sermons and speeches. Here are summaries of three of the most well-known, all of which are examples of great preaching.

Three Major Sermons in Acts

12 *The sermon on the Areopagus*

Speaker: Paul, Text: Acts 17:22–34

1. Introduction: You can know the Unknown God (17:22–23)
2. God is the creator of all things (17:24)
3. God is the sustainer of all things (17:25)
4. God rules over all lands (17:26–27)
5. God is the Father of all (17:28–29)
6. God is the judge of all (17:30–31)
7. His listeners' reaction (17:32–34)

2 *The sermon on Pentecost*

Speaker: Peter, Text: Acts 2:14–40

1. Introduction: What is taking place? What do you see? (2:14–21)
2. Jesus's crucifixion was in accordance with God's plan (2:22–23)
3. Jesus's resurrection from the dead was in accordance with God's plan (2:24–32)
4. Jesus's ascension confirms his exaltation to the right hand of the Father (2:33–35)
5. Conclusion: If he is the Messiah—what will you do? (2:36–40)

5 *Stephen's defense speech*

Speaker: Stephen, Text: Acts 7:2–53

1. God spoke to Abraham (7:2–8)
2. God spoke to Joseph (7:9–19)
3. God spoke to Moses (7:20–43)
4. God spoke through the tabernacle (7:44–47)
5. But God does not dwell in anything man-made (7:48–50)
6. Why don't you listen when God speaks now? (7:51–53)

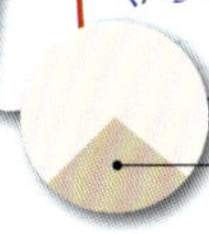

27% of the book of Acts is preaching/teaching.

All the sermons and speeches

	Preacher	Sermon/Speech	Acts	Number of verses	Audience	Location
1	Peter	The speech to choose Judas's replacement	1:16–22	7	The apostles	Jerusalem
2	Peter	The sermon on the day of Pentecost	2:14–36	23	The crowd	Jerusalem
3	Peter	The sermon after the healing of a lame man	3:12–26	15	The crowd	Jerusalem
4	Peter	The speech to the Sanhedrin (I)	4:8–12	5	The Sanhedrin	Jerusalem
5	Stephen	The speech to the Sanhedrin (II)	7:2–53	52	The Sanhedrin	Jerusalem
6	Peter	The sermon in Cornelius's house	10:34–43	10	Cornelius's household	Caesarea
7	Peter	The speech to the church in Jerusalem	11:4–17	14	The church	Jerusalem
8	Paul	The sermon in synagogue in Pisidian Antioch	13:16–41	26	The synagogue	Antioch
9	Paul	The speech in Lystra	14:15–17	3	The crowd	Lystra
10	Peter	The speech to the Council in Jerusalem (I)	15:7–11	5	The church	Jerusalem
11	James	The speech to the Council in Jerusalem (II)	15:13–21	8	The church	Jerusalem
12	Paul	The sermon on the Areopagus	17:22–31	10	The Athenians	Athens
13	Paul	The speech in Miletus	20:18–35	18	The elders	Miletus
14	Paul	The speech to the mob in Jerusalem	22:1–21	21	The mob	Jerusalem
15	Paul	The speech to the Sanhedrin (III)	23:1–6	6	The Sanhedrin	Jerusalem
16	Paul	The speech before Felix in Caesarea	24:10–21	11	Felix	Caesarea
17	Paul	The speech before Festus in Caesarea	25:8, 10–11	3	Festus	Caesarea
18	Paul	The speech before Agrippa in Caesarea	26:1–23	23	Agrippa, Festus	Caesarea
19	Paul	The speech to people on ship in the storm	27:21–26	6	His shipmates	Med. Sea
20	Paul	The speech to the Jewish leaders in Rome	28:17–20, 25–28	8	Leading Jews	Rome

All of the Miracles in Acts

• Paul and Silas, imprisoned in Philippi, are praying and singing to God when an earthquake strikes.
• Believing all of the prisoners had escaped, the jailer plans to kill himself. Paul stops him, saying that they were all there. He asks Paul how he can be saved and comes to faith in Christ (16:25–31).

All the miracles

	Miracle	Acts	No mediator	Peter	Paul	Other	Location	Spiritual	Prophecy	Healing	From death	Deliverance	Punishment
1	The Holy Spirit comes on Pentecost	2:1–4	■				Jerusalem	■					
2	The apostles speak in other languages	2:4	■				Jerusalem	■					
3	A lame man is healed at the Beautiful Gate	3:7		■			Jerusalem			■			
4	Ananias and Sapphira fall down dead	5:1–11	■				Jerusalem						■
5	The apostles are freed from prison	5:19–20	■				Jerusalem	■					
6	Stephen sees Jesus in a vision	7:55–56	■				Jerusalem		■				
7	The Holy Spirit is given to the Samaritans	8:14–17		■		■	Samaria	■					
8	An angel speaks to Philip	8:26	■				Samaria (8:5)		■				
9	Philip is snatched away by the Holy Spirit	8:39	■				Gaza Road (8:26)	■					
10	Paul meets Jesus and is blinded	9:1–7	■				Damascus Road		■				■
11	Ananias has a vision	9:10–16	■				Damascus		■				
12	God restores Saul's sight via Ananias	9:17–19				■	Damascus	■		■			
13	Aeneas who is paralyzed is healed	9:33–35		■			Lydda			■			
14	Tabitha is raised from the dead	9:36–41		■			Joppa				■		
15	Cornelius receives a vision from the Lord	10:1–8, 30–32	■				Caesarea		■				
16	Peter has a vision with many animals	10:9–16	■				Joppa		■				
17	The Holy Spirit is given to the gentiles	10:44–46		■			Caesarea	■					
18	Agabus prophesies about the coming famine	11:28				■	Antioch (11:20)		■				
19	An angel frees Peter from prison	12:5–11		■			Jerusalem	■					
20	Elymas is blinded	13:11			■		Paphos (13:6)	■					■
21	A paralyzed man is healed	14:8–10			■		Lystra			■			
22	Paul miraculously survives being stoned	14:19–20	■				Lystra	■					
23	Paul receives vision of traveling to Macedonia	16:6–9	■				Troas		■				
24	A fortunetelling spirit driven out of a slave girl	16:16–18			■		Philippi					■	
25	An earthquake shakes the prison	16:25–31	■				Philippi	■					
26	Eutychus is raised from the dead	20:10–12			■		Troas				■		
27	Agabus prophesies about Paul	21:10–11				■	Caesarea		■				
28	An angel gives Paul a message on the ship	27:23–26	■				Mediterranean Sea		■				
29	Paul survives a snake bite	28:3–5	■				Malta			■			
30	Publius is healed from fever and diarrhea	28:8–9			■		Malta			■			

There are also summary descriptions of miracles: 2:43; 4:20–30; 5:12–16; 6:8; 8:6, 13; 14:3; 15:12; 19:11–12; 28:9

Taking the Gospel to Asia Minor

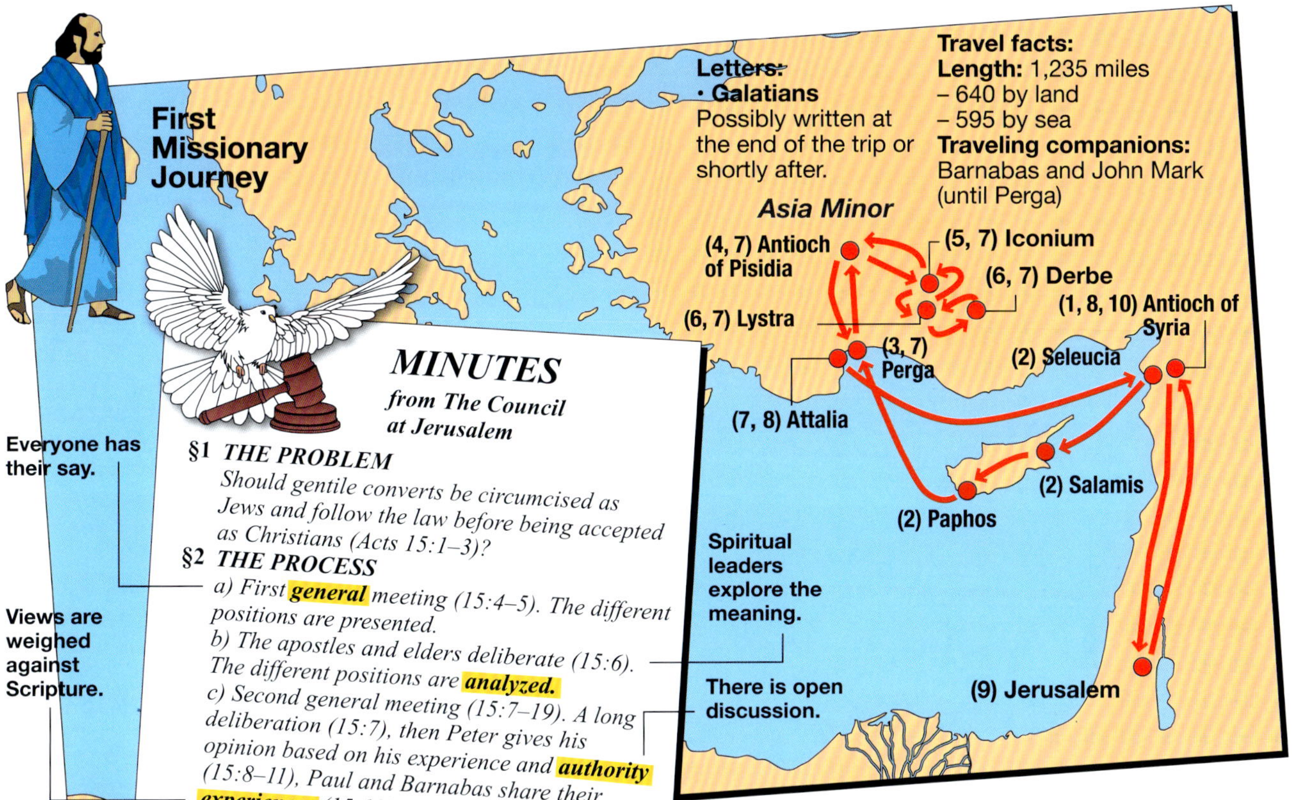

MINUTES

from The Council at Jerusalem

§1 *THE PROBLEM*

Should gentile converts be circumcised as Jews and follow the law before being accepted as Christians (Acts 15:1–3)?

§2 *THE PROCESS*

*a) First **general** meeting (15:4–5). The different positions are presented.*

*b) The apostles and elders deliberate (15:6). The different positions are **analyzed.***

*c) Second general meeting (15:7–19). A long deliberation (15:7), then Peter gives his opinion based on his experience and **authority** (15:8–11), Paul and Barnabas share their **experiences** (15:12), James looks to **Scripture** and makes **suggestions** (15:13–21).*

§3 *THE DECISION*

*The decision is made by **the whole assembly** with the apostles and elders. **"The Holy Spirit and we have decided"** (15:28).*

§4 *THE PROCLAMATION*

*The **practical implications** of the decision are explained to all concerned (15:22–31).*

Everyone has their say.

Views are weighed against Scripture.

The analysis becomes arguments and proposals.

They interpret the decision for everyday life.

Spiritual leaders explore the meaning.

There is open discussion.

The assembly takes a stand.

The Holy Spirit is present in the process as seen in their unity.

1 Antioch of Syria (fall AD 47 to April 48). Saul and Barnabas are set apart for service, John Mark assists them (Acts 12:25–13:5).

2 Via Seleucia to Salamis and Paphos on Cyprus (April to June AD 48). Preaches in synagogues and before the Roman governor. First reference to Saul being called Paul (Acts 13:4–12).

3 Perga in Pamphylia (July AD 48). John Mark leaves Paul and Barnabas, returning to Jerusalem. Later, this leads to strife (Acts 13:13; 15:36–39).

4 Antioch of Pisidia, about a six-day journey from the coast (July to September AD 48). Paul and Barnabas preach to "almost the entire city," are slandered, and run out of town (Acts 13:14–52).

5 Iconium (October AD 48 to February 49). Paul and Barnabas stay "a long time, preaching," meet resistance, and flee (Acts 13:51–14:6).

6 Lystra and Derbe in Lycaonia (March to June AD 49). In Lystra, Paul and Barnabas heal a lame man and are thought to be gods. Jews from Iconium and Antioch incite the crowds who stone Paul, but he survives. Possibly meets Timothy for the first time (Acts 14:6–21; see 2 Tim. 3:11).

7 Back to Lystra, Iconium, Antioch of Pisidia, and Perga to Attalia (June to August AD 49). As Paul and Barnabas revisit these places, they strengthen the disciples (Acts 14:21–25).

8 Back to Antioch of Syria via Attalia (Aug. to Sept. AD 49). Paul and Barnabas sail home, give report. Peter visits Antioch, Paul probably writes Galatians (Acts 14:26–28; Gal. 2:11–14).

9 Through Phoenicia and Samaria to Jerusalem (third visit, fall AD 49). The controversy over Jewish rules deepens. Meeting of the apostles in Jerusalem (Acts 15:1–21).

10 Back to Antioch of Syria (fall AD 49 to March 50). Paul and Barnabas return to Antioch with Silas and Judas Barsabbas. They bring a letter from the apostolic council (Acts 15:22–35).

Taking the Gospel to Athens and Corinth

1 Antioch (March to April AD 50). After a controversy with Barnabas over John Mark, Paul embarks on a new journey, now with Silas (Acts 15:36–40).

2 Through Syria and Cilicia to Derbe, Lystra, and Iconium (April to June AD 50). Paul revisits the churches. Timothy joins him (Acts 15:41–16:5).

3 Through Phrygia, Galatia, and Mysia to Troas (June to July AD 50). Paul receives a vision asking for help in Macedonia. Luke joins the group (Acts 16:6–10, compare "they" in 16:8 with "we" in 16:11).

4 To Philippi via Samothrace and Neapolis (August to October AD 50). Lydia saved, a possessed girl freed, Paul and Silas imprisoned (Acts 16:11–40).

5 To Thessalonica via Amphipolis and Apollonia (Nov. AD 50 to Jan. 51). Preaches to Jews and Greeks, leading to a riot, Paul sent away (Acts 17:1–9; 1 Thess. 1:4–2:14).

6 To Berea (February AD 51). Many Jews receive the gospel, but critics from Thessalonica arrive. Paul is forced to flee to Athens while Silas and Timothy remain behind (Acts 17:10–15).

7 On to Athens (February to March AD 51). Paul speaks in the synagogue and at the Agora, he is asked to give a speech before the Areopagus, a kind of court that could also review teaching. Originally the court met on the Areopagus hill (hence the name) but it had probably moved to a building in the Agora by this time. Paul draws on the images of the gods of Athens and demonstrates his mastery of oratory as well as Greek philosophy (Acts 17:16–34).

8 Then to Corinth in Achaia (March AD 51 to August 52, about one-and-a-half years). Meets Priscilla and Aquila, reconnects with Silas and Timothy. The synagogue leader Crispus is saved and a church is founded. Concerns arise among the Jews, but the Roman governor Gallio does not want to deal with the their criticism of Paul. Paul writes 1 and 2 Thessalonians (Acts 18:1–18; 1 Cor. 2:1–5).

9 To Ephesus via Cenchreae (September AD 52). Speaks in the synagogue and asked to stay longer, he promises to return later. Priscilla and Aquila journey with him from Corinth and remain in Ephesus (Acts 18:18–21).

10 To Jerusalem via Caesarea (fourth visit, September to October AD 52). To Caesarea by ship, then to Jerusalem to visit the church (Acts 18:22).

11 Antioch (November AD 52 to spring 53). Paul returns to Antioch where he stays for a while (Acts 18:22–23).

Travel facts:
Length: 2,705 miles
–1,415 by land
–1,290 by sea
Traveling companions:
Silas (16:40–18:19)
Luke (16:11–18)
Timothy (16:1–17:14; 18:5–18:19)
Priscilla and Aquila (18:18–19)

Letters:
• **1 Thessalonians** From Corinth
• **2 Thessalonians** From Corinth

GALLIO

Proconsul in the province of Achaia when Paul came to Corinth. His rule in AD 51–52 provides a point of reference for the chronology of Paul's life (Acts 18:12–17).

**Note: The boundaries of various Roman provinces are uncertain. Those with asterisks are territories, not provinces.*

Athens in Paul's Day

Data on buildings vary; this is one possible version.

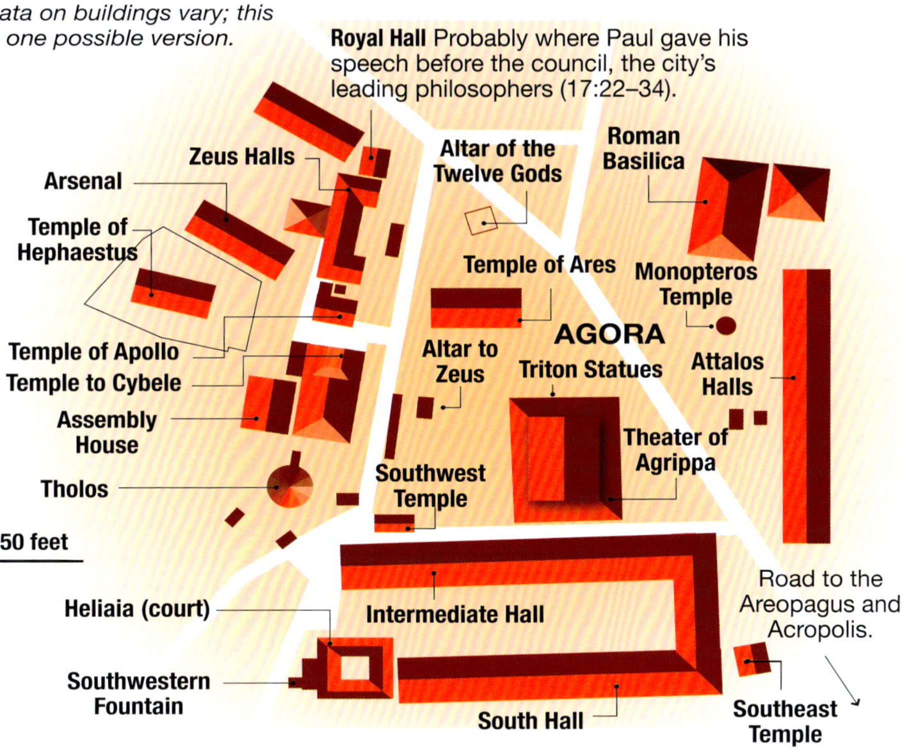

THE AGORA IN ATHENS

A limestone rock northwest of the Acropolis and north of the Areopagus. The Council of Areopagus, a religious court, met on the rock early on. The proceedings were later moved to a building on the Agora.

PAUL IN ATHENS

Paul only visited the city once, during his second missionary journey. He delivered his speech before the Areopagus court. No church seems to have been established in the city during Paul's visit.

Corinth in Paul's Day

CORINTH

The city was strategically located between the Ionian and Aegean Seas. It was also at the meeting point between the Greek mainland and the Peloponnese peninsula.

PAUL IN CORINTH

Paul established the church in Corinth on his second missionary journey. He visited it once or twice on the third journey and once after his release from prison in Rome.

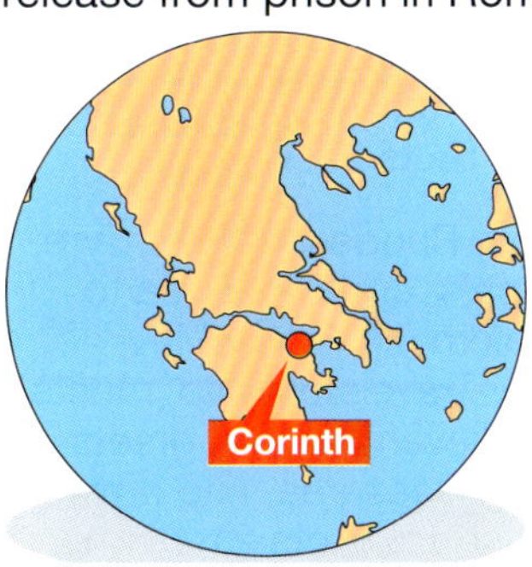

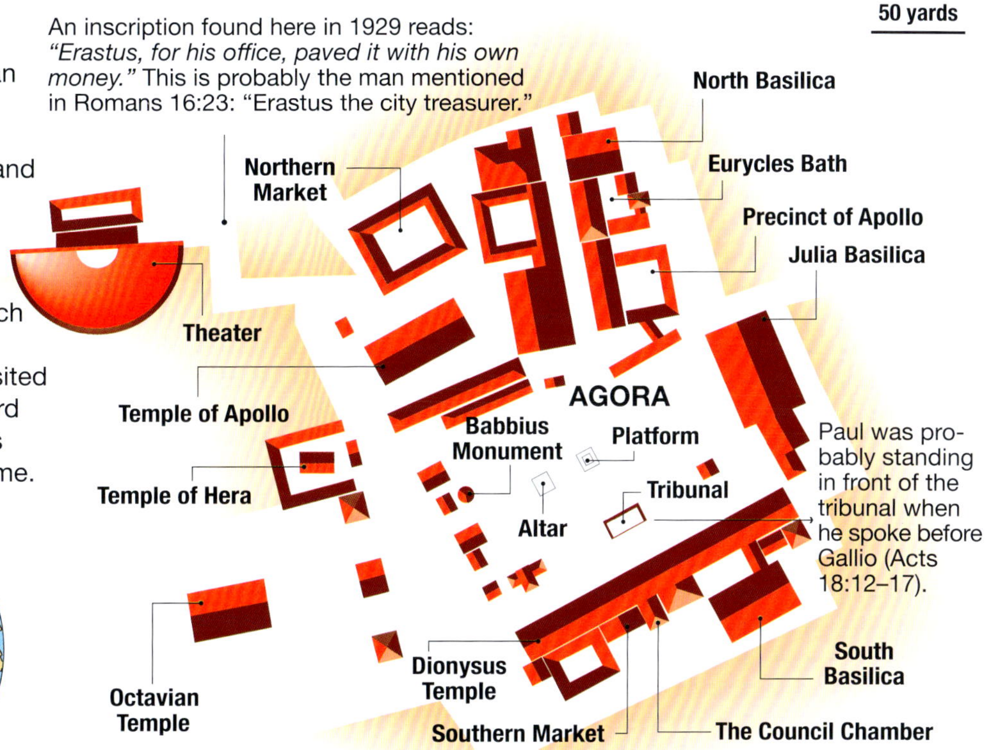

Using Ephesus as a Base

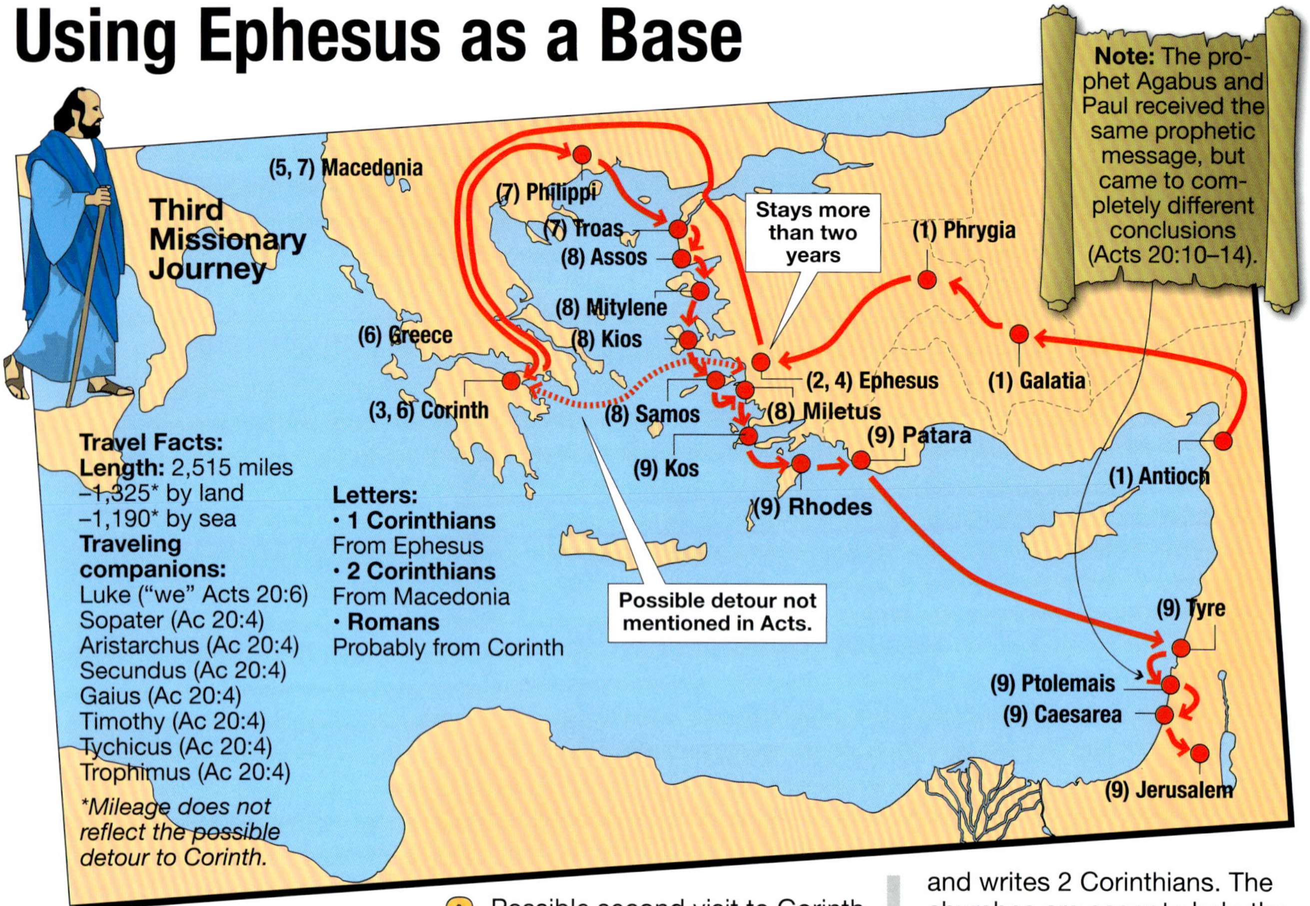

1 Antioch, Galatia, and Phrygia (spring and summer AD 53). Paul visits the disciples (Acts 18:23).

2 Ephesus (from September AD 53, for just over two years). Paul preaches to the Jews and then the gentiles and performs miracles. Silversmiths (idol makers) riot against Paul and his disciples. Paul writes the so-called lost letter, probably from Ephesus (1 Cor. 5:9), and a second letter, the one that we call 1 Corinthians (Acts 19:1–20:1).

3 Possible second visit to Corinth (toward the end of his time in Ephesus?). The visit is not mentioned in Acts but may have taken place during this time (2 Cor. 12:14; 13:1). See below for a more detailed explanation.

4 Back to Ephesus (until May AD 56). After his return, Paul probably writes the "sorrowful letter," which has been lost (2 Cor. 1:4; 2 Cor. 7:8–12).

5 Through Macedonia (June to November AD 56). Paul leaves Ephesus after the riot, encourages the believers, and writes 2 Corinthians. The churches are eager to help the poor among the believers in the Jerusalem church (Acts 20:1–2; Rom. 15:25–26).

6 To Greece, including third visit to Corinth (November AD 56 to February 57). Paul and several disciples visit believers. Writes Romans, a plot against him is discovered (Acts 20:2–4).

7 Through Macedonia, via Philippi to Troas (February to April AD 57). Paul stays a week in Troas, raises Eutychus from the dead (Acts 20:3–12).

8 By land to Assos, by ship to Mitylene, Samos, and Miletus (April AD 57). The elders from Ephesus meet Paul in Miletus, where he gives his farewell speech (Acts 20:13–38).

9 Via Kos, Rhodes, Patara, Tyre, Ptolemais, and Caesarea to Jerusalem (fifth visit, May AD 57). Travels by ship, meets with believers in Tyre, greets Philip in Caesarea, and arrives in Jerusalem (Acts 21:1–17).

Did Paul Visit Corinth a Third Time?

- When Paul writes 2 Corinthians, he mentions that he is "coming to you for the third time" (2 Cor. 12:14; 13:1).
- Second Corinthians is believed to have been written from Macedonia (see 3 above) in the fall of AD 56, before Paul reached Corinth ("traveled down to Greece" Acts 20:2–4).
- Paul's first visit to Corinth was in AD 51–52, during his second journey (Acts18:1–18).
- Therefore the second visit must have taken place sometime between fall AD 52 and winter 56.
- Either Paul made a detour from Ephesus (AD 53–56) or his plans changed and the intended trip never took place.

Ephesus in Paul's Day

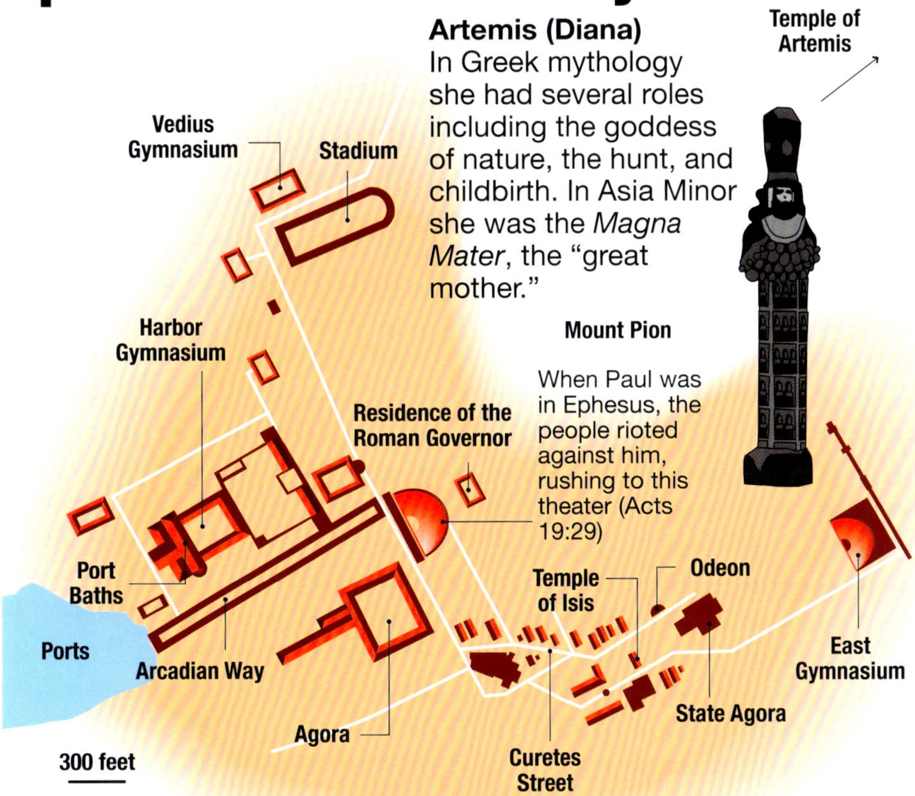

EPHESUS
Became part of the Roman Empire around 130 BC and was one of the largest cities in the empire. Its strategic location made it the gateway to Asia Minor. The Temple of Artemis, built in the third century BC, was there.

PAUL IN EPHESUS
Paul stayed in the city for over two years on his third missionary journey, returning there after his release from prison in Rome. The city became important in the early church. According to tradition, John lived there (Rev. 2:1–7).

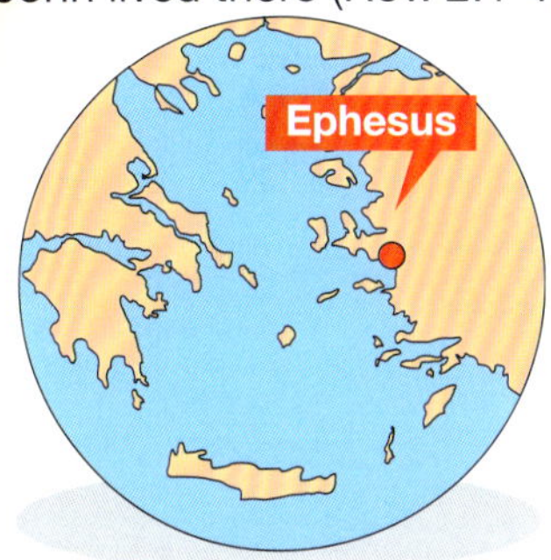

Rome in Paul's Day

ROME
The largest city in the world in Paul's day, with more than a million inhabitants. The historian Tacitus refers to the Christians persecuted under Nero in AD 64 as "a vast multitude."

PAUL IN ROME
Paul visited Rome twice. The first time was when he was brought to Rome after he appealed to the emperor (Acts 27:1–28:31). The second time was at the end of his life when he was imprisoned again and then executed (2 Tim. 1:8; 4:6).

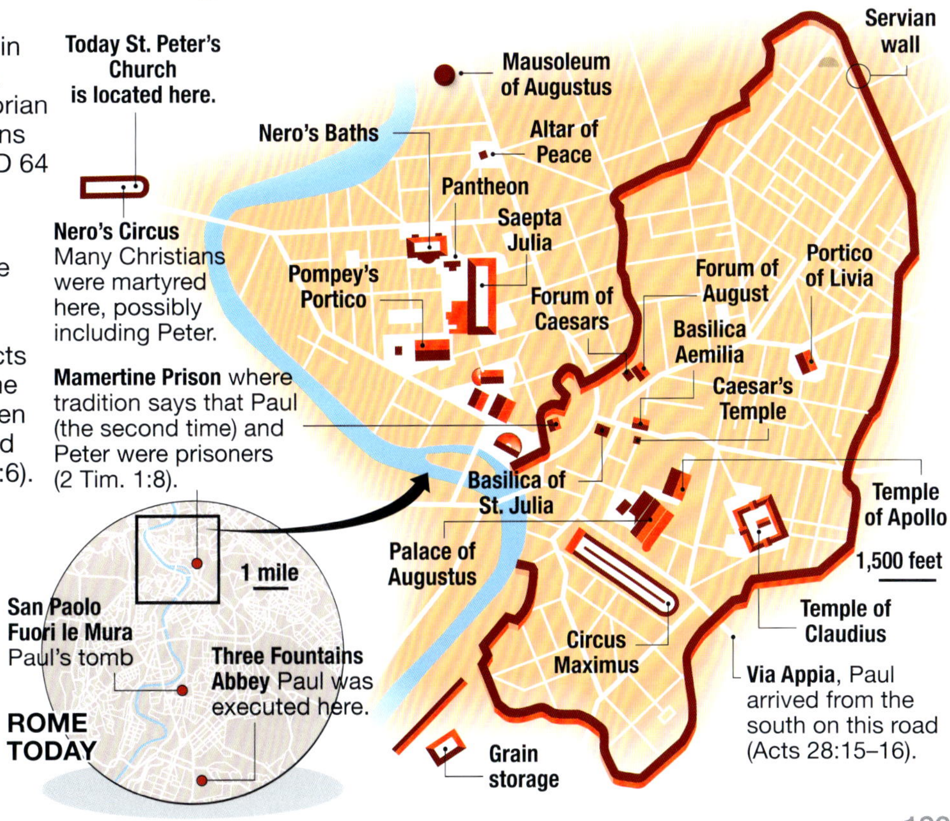

Events in Caesarea by the Sea

1 Philip moves to the city
Philip the evangelist left Jerusalem when persecution broke out. He preached in various places in Samaria, met the Ethiopian eunuch, and finally reached Caesarea by the Sea where he settled (Acts 8:1–40).

2 Peter visits Cornelius
Cornelius, a Roman officer who lived in Caesarea, had a vision telling him to send for Peter, who was in Joppa. When Peter arrived in Caesarea, he preached to Cornelius's household. As he did, the Holy Spirit was given to the gentiles (Acts 10:1–47).

3 Paul passes through the city
On his return from the second missionary journey, Paul's ship docked in Caesarea. He went from there to Jerusalem where he met with the church before returning to Antioch (Acts 18:22).

4 Paul visits Philip
On his way to Jerusalem after the third journey, Paul arrived in Caesarea by boat. He greeted Philip, whose four unmarried daughters had all been given the gift of prophecy (Acts 21:8).

5 Paul imprisoned in the city
While in Jerusalem, the city was stirred up against Paul. The Roman commander took him to Caesarea to protect him from a plot. He remained there for two years under strict Roman guard awaiting trial (Acts 21:15–27:1).

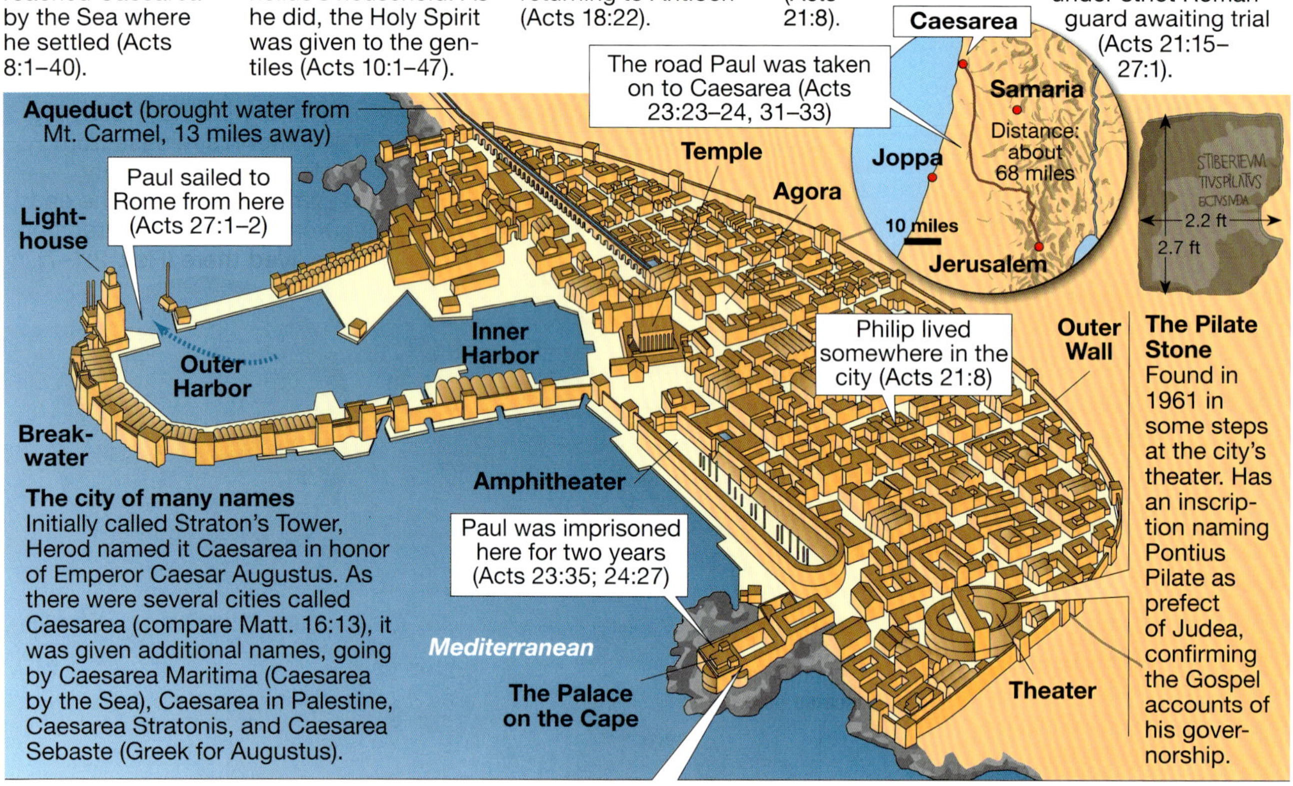

The city of many names
Initially called Straton's Tower, Herod named it Caesarea in honor of Emperor Caesar Augustus. As there were several cities called Caesarea (compare Matt. 16:13), it was given additional names, going by Caesarea Maritima (Caesarea by the Sea), Caesarea in Palestine, Caesarea Stratonis, and Caesarea Sebaste (Greek for Augustus).

The Pilate Stone
Found in 1961 in some steps at the city's theater. Has an inscription naming Pontius Pilate as prefect of Judea, confirming the Gospel accounts of his governorship.

PAUL IS HEARD ON THREE OCCASIONS

During his two years in Caesarea, Paul was interrogated on three occasions. The interrogations finally led Paul to appeal to the emperor in Rome.

1 Before Antonius Felix
Roman governor of Judea AD 52–59. Hard and cruel, he ruled harshly. **Hearing 1:** June AD 57 **Complaint of the Jews:** Paul causes unrest (24:1–9). **Paul's defense:** I did not incite anyone, but I belong to the Way, the Christian movement (24:10–21). **Verdict:** Postponed for a time because Felix hoped to receive a bribe (24:22–26).

2 Before Porcius Festus
Governor of Judea after Felix, AD 59–62. Wise and just. **Hearing 2:** July AD 59 **The Jews' plan:** An ambush (24:27–25:7). **Paul's defense:** I have not committed any crime (25:8). **Festus's ruse:** Threatened to take Paul to Jerusalem (25:9). **Paul's answer:** Opposed the plan and appealed to the emperor (25:10–11). **Verdict:** Postponement (25:12)

3 Before Herod Agrippa II
Tetrarch of Galilee AD 53–66. Diplomatic and tolerant. **Hearing 3:** August AD 59 **Agrippa informed:** (25:13–22). **Festus introduces:** (25:23–27). **Paul defends:** (26:1–29). **Agrippa's reply:** He was almost persuaded to become a Christian. Paul could have been released if he had not appealed to the emperor (26:28, 30–32).

HISTORY OF CAESAREA MARITIMA

- **Around 400 BC:** Straton I, ruler of Sidon, founded the city.
- **30 BC:** After Cleopatra's death, Herod the Great received the city as a reward, making it an important port city and administrative center.
- **AD 41:** King Agrippa I carried out a significant expansion of the city.
- **AD 58–60:** Paul was held captive in the palace for two years (Acts 23:23–27:1).
- **AD 66–70:** At the Jews' revolt against Rome, the city was besieged and captured by the Romans.
- **1265:** The Mamluks conquered the town, which became a small fishing village.
- **1884/1940:** Archaeologists explored the ancient ruins of the town.
- **1952:** Caesarea became part of the modern state of Israel, undergoing extensive restoration.

Through the Storm to Rome

1 Jerusalem (fifth time) (May to June AD 57). Paul meets James, purifies himself in the temple, is saved from death by the Roman commander, speaks to the crowd, and addresses the Sanhedrin. A plot to kill Paul is planned but uncovered. Paul is taken from Jerusalem to safety in Caesarea (Acts 21:15–23:30).

2 Caesarea by the Sea (also called Caesarea Maritima) (June AD 57 to August 59). Paul is taken to Caesarea where he is held captive for two years. He is brought before three Roman representatives, to whom he is allowed to explain himself. He is never convicted and could have been released if he had not appealed to the emperor (Acts 23:30–27:1).

3 Via Sidon to Myra (August to September AD 59). The journey to Rome begins. The ship sails north of Cyprus, following the coast of Cilicia and Pamphylia (Acts 27:2–5).

Storms on the Mediterranean

• **STORM SEASON:** The most dangerous time for sailing on the Mediterranean was between mid-September and early March. Since Paul mentions “the Fast” (the Day of Atonement, Acts 27:9), we know the storm occurred in late September or early October.

• **EURAQUILO:** The sea can produce rapidly developing, intense storms—especially northeasters, also called *Euraquilo* (Acts 27:14). The word combines *euros*, “east wind” and *aquilo*, “north wind.” It is similar to what is called a Mediterranean cyclone today.

• **OFF GUARD:** Because of the surrounding mountain ranges and valleys, winds can be funneled into powerful gales that can catch ships off guard.

4 Along the south coast of Crete to Fair Havens (October AD 59). Continues on new ship via Cnidos, around Salmone to Fair Havens near Lasea. Paul warns against further travel before winter (Acts 27:5–13).

5 Drifting ashore on Malta (November AD 59 to February 60). They sail anyway, toward Phoenix, a storm sets them adrift for fourteen days, they finally land on Malta (Acts 27:13–28:10).

6 The road to Rome (February AD 60). Finishes the journey to Rome on a third ship, meeting believers along the way (Acts 28:10–15).

7 House arrest in Rome (February AD 60 to March 62). Under house arrest while awaiting trial. Writes Ephesians, Colossians, Philemon, and Philippians. Acts ends, he is released after two years. (Acts 28:15–31).

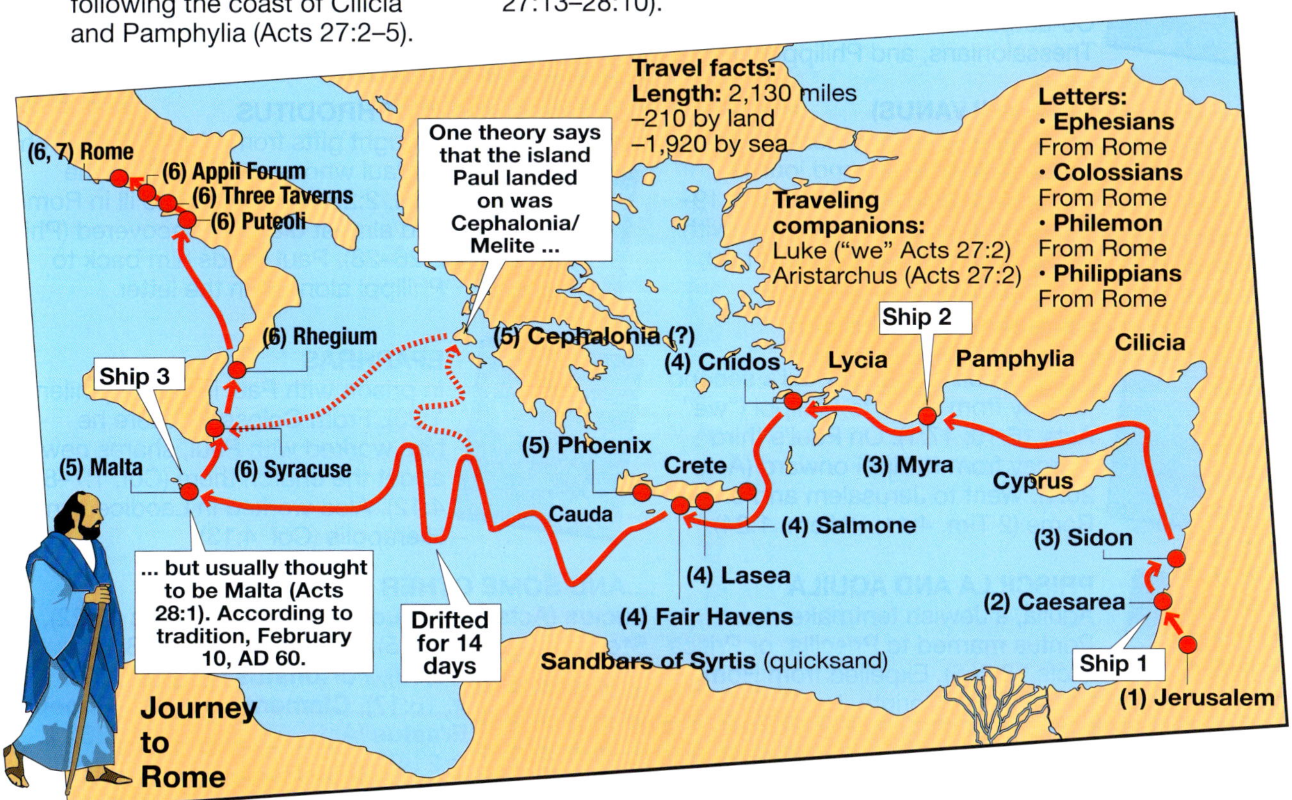

Fourteen Disciples Who Followed Paul

BARNABAS
A Levite from Cyprus (Acts 4:36). Introduces Paul to the apostles (9:27). Travels with Paul on the first journey, leaves after a quarrel over his cousin John Mark (15:39). Later reconciles with Paul (1 Cor. 9:6).

TITUS
Of Greek origin (Gal. 2:3). Paul calls him "my true son in the faith" (Tit. 1:4). Associated with the church in Corinth (2 Cor. 7:6; 8:6, 16, 23; 12:18), visits the churches in Dalmatia and Crete (2 Tim. 4:10; Titus 1:5).

JOHN MARK
Barnabas's cousin (Col. 4:10). Met Paul in Jerusalem (Acts 12:25; Gal. 2:1–3). With Paul on first journey, but deserts him (Acts 13:13). Later with Peter, who calls him his son (1 Peter 5:13). Authored the gospel of Mark.

TIMOTHY
Raised by his Jewish mother and grandmother, who prepared him to receive the faith (2 Tim. 1:5). Called a spiritual son by Paul (Phil. 2:20, 22). Co-author of 2 Corinthians, 1 and 2 Thessalonians, and Philippians.

SILAS (SILVANUS)
Jew from Jerusalem, Roman citizen. With Paul on his second journey, jailed in Philippi (Acts 15:40; 16:19–26). Respected leader, worked with Peter (Acts 15:22, 32; 2 Cor. 1:19; 1 Thess. 1:1; 1 Peter 5:12).

LUKE
Doctor (Col. 4:14). On Paul's second journey from Troas to Philippi ("we" Acts 16:10; 17:1). On Paul's third journey from Philippi onward (Acts 20:1). Went to Jerusalem and on to Rome (2 Tim. 4:11; Philem. 1:24).

PRISCILLA AND AQUILA
Aquila, a Jewish tentmaker from Pontus married to Priscilla, or Prisca (Acts 18:2–3). Expelled from Rome they went to Corinth. Paul took them with him to Ephesus (Acts 18:19; 1 Cor. 16:19; Rom. 16:3; 2 Tim. 4:19).

GAIUS
From Derbe, follows Paul for part of the third journey (Acts 20:4). Travels ahead to both Troas and Assos (20:5, 13). Probably leaves Paul's company in Jerusalem. Doubtful that he is the Gaius in 3 John.

ARISTARCHUS
A Jew (Col. 4:10–11) from Thessalonica who accompanies Paul on his third journey, on to Jerusalem and then Rome (Acts 19:29; 20:4; 27:2). In prison with Paul (Col. 4:10; Philem. 1:24).

TYCHICUS
From Asia Minor. On the third journey and also in Rome (Acts 20:4). Sent by Paul to Ephesus and probably Crete (2 Tim. 4:12; Tit. 3:12). Delivers three letters: Ephesians, Colossians, and Philemon.

ONESIMUS
An escaped slave from Philemon's house in Colossae (Philem. 1:1, 16). Meets Paul in Rome and is converted. Returned to Philemon, along with Tychicus and a letter from Paul (Col. 4: 7, 9; Philem. 1:10).

EPAPHRODITUS
Brought gifts from Philippian church to Paul who is in prison in Rome (Phil. 2:25; 4:18). Became ill in Rome and almost died, but recovered (Phil. 2:26–28). Paul sends him back to Philippi along with the letter.

EPAPHRAS
In prison with Paul in Rome (Philem. 1:23). From Colossae where he had worked with Paul, shares news about the church there (Col. 1:7–8; 4:12). Also worked in Laodicea and Hierapolis (Col. 4:13).

...AND SOME OTHER COWORKERS
Lucius (Acts 13:1), **Judas Barsabbas** (Acts 15:22), **Stephen** (1 Cor. 16:15), **Sosthenes** (Acts 18:17), **Apollos** (1 Cor. 16:12), **Fortunatus** (1 Cor. 16:17), **Achaicus** (1 Cor. 16:17), **Clement** (Phil. 4:3), **Phoebe** (Rom. 16:1–2), **Erastus** (Acts 19:22; Rom. 16:23), **Trophimus** (Acts 21:29), **Jason** (Acts 17:6)

An Overview of Paul's Life

What Saul did, and what Paul suffered.

1 Stoned believers, and was stoned himself
Saul was involved in the stoning of Stephen (Acts 7:58–8:1). Paul himself was stoned several times (Acts 14:19; 2 Cor. 11:25).

2 Whipped believers, and was whipped himself
Saul had those who believed in Jesus flogged (Acts 22:19). Paul himself was flogged three times (2 Cor. 11:23–25).

3 Persecuted believers, and was persecuted himself
Saul persecuted the church and tried to exterminate it (Gal. 1:13). Paul himself was persecuted (2 Cor. 11:32–33).

> "You will always harvest what you plant (Gal. 6:7).

> "The most important event in human history apart from the life, death and resurrection of Jesus ... is the conversion ... of Saul of Tarsus. (William Larkin)

4 Bound believers, and was bound himself
Saul had believers bound and brought to the leading priests (Acts 9:21). Paul himself was bound in Jerusalem (21:11, 13).

5 Imprisoned believers, was imprisoned himself
Saul sought out believers and threw them into prison (Acts 8:3). Paul himself was imprisoned, more than most (2 Cor. 11:23).

6 Chased believers almost to death, was chased himself
Saul persecuted believers "to death" (Acts 22:4). Paul himself was persecuted to the point of death (Acts 14:19).

7 Was won by Christ, and sought to win others
Saul met Christ on the road to Damascus (Acts 9:4). Paul then tried to win others for his master (1 Cor. 9:22).

	Opposition	Conversion	Evangelization	Apologetics	Service	Captivity	Martyrdom
KEY POINTS	• Born in Tarsus • Trained as a Pharisee • Fanatic in Jerusalem	• Met Jesus on the road • Received teaching • Lived in Tarsus	• Preached in Galatia • Founded churches • Spoke at council in Jerusalem	• Went to Greece • Debated in Athens • Founded church in Corinth	• Taught in Ephesus • Said goodbye to Ephesus • Traveled to Jerusalem	• Prisoner in Caesarea • Traveled to Rome • House arrest in Rome	• Traveled in the Mediterranean • Back in prison in Rome • Died a martyr's death
TOPICS	Pharisee (Phil. 3:5)	Disciple (Acts 9:27)	Pioneer (Acts 13:2)	Apologist (Acts 17:22–34)	Teacher (Acts 19:9–10)	Prisoner (Eph. 6:20)	Martyr (2 Tim. 4:6–7)
	The Jewish law (Gal. 1:14)	The revelation from God (Gal. 1:11–12)	The gospel of grace (Gal. 2:21)	The return of Jesus (1 Thess. 4:13–18)	The history of salvation (Rom. 6:23)	The greatness of Christ (Col. 1:15–20)	Leadership and discipleship (Tit. 1; 1 Tim. 3)
	The stoning of Stephen (Acts 7:1–8:1)	The Damascus Road encounter (Acts 9:1–9)	The council in Jerusalem (Acts 15:1–29)	The debate on the Areopagus (Acts 17:22–34)	The riot in Ephesus (Acts 19:1–40)	The meeting with Agrippa (Acts 25:13–26:32)	His spiritual last will (2 Tim. 4)
PEOPLE	Taught by Gamaliel	Ananias, Barnabas	Barnabas, John Mark, Titus	Silas, Luke, Timothy, Aquila and Priscilla	Titus, Apollos, Timothy, Gaius, Aristarchus	Aristarchus, Luke, Tychicus, Epaphras	Luke, Demas, Timothy, Titus, John Mark
TEXTS	Acts 7:58–8:40	Acts 9:1–12:25; Gal. 1:1–20; 2 Cor. 11:32–35	Acts 13:1–15:35 Galatians	Acts 15:36–18:22, 1 & 2 Thessalonians	Acts 18:23–21:16, Romans 1 & 2 Corinthians	Acts 21:17–28:31, Eph., Phil., Col., Philem.	1 & 2 Timothy, Titus
TIME PERIOD	About 25/30 years AD 1/10*-35	12 years AD 35–47	2 years AD 48–49	3 years AD 50–52	4 years AD 53–57	5 years AD 58–62	6 years AD 62–67

**We don't know when Paul was born.*

An Overview of Paul's Thirteen Letters

4. Pastoral Letters: These were written to Timothy and Titus and deal with spiritual leadership. They give advice on various pastoral issues they faced.

1. Early Letters: These were written during Paul's first and second missionary journeys. Galatians is probably the oldest of Paul's letters that has been preserved.

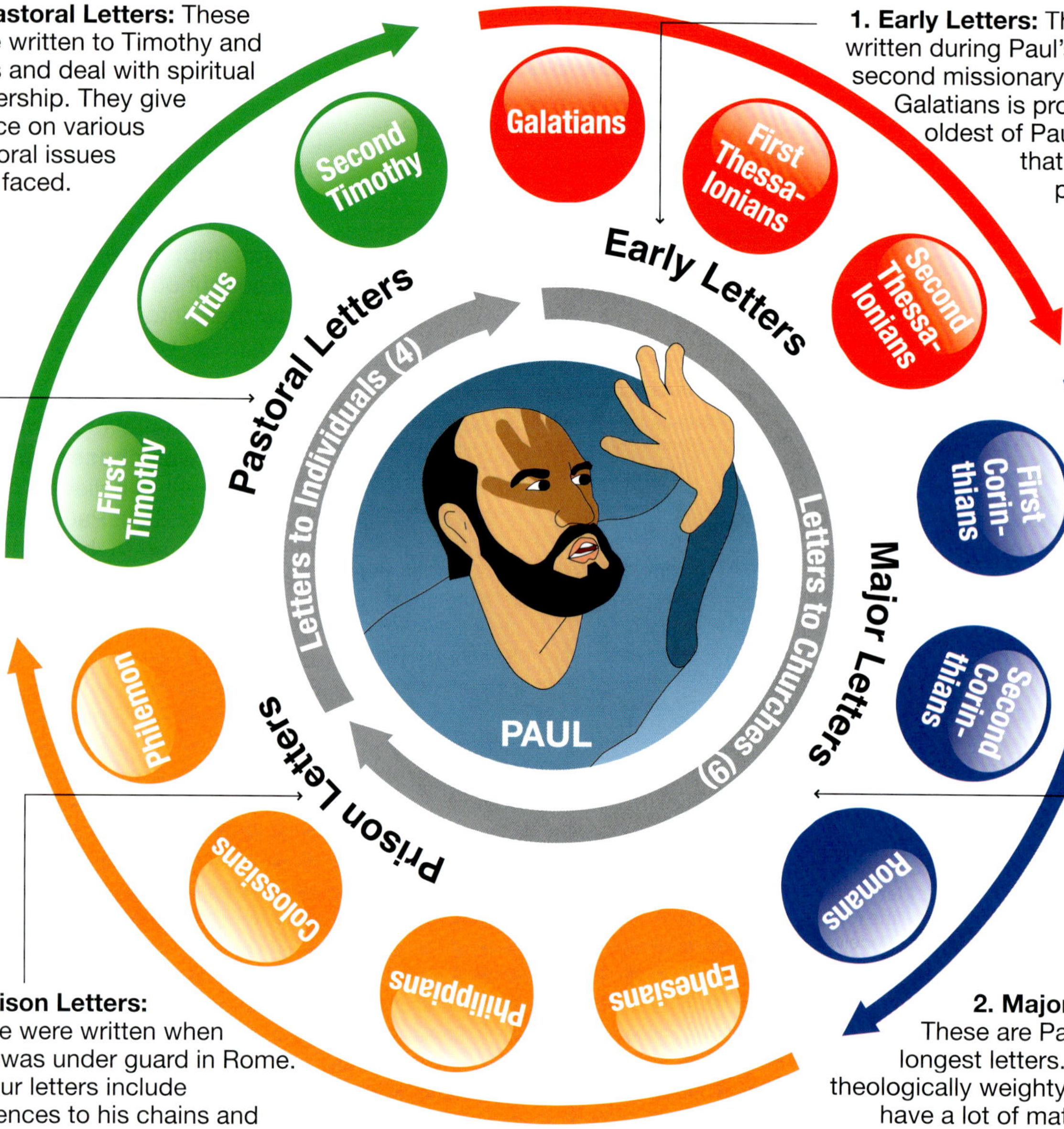

3. Prison Letters: These were written when Paul was under guard in Rome. All four letters include references to his chains and imprisonment.

2. Major Letters: These are Paul's three longest letters. They are theologically weighty and also have a lot of material with practical applications.

Number of chapters in Paul's letters

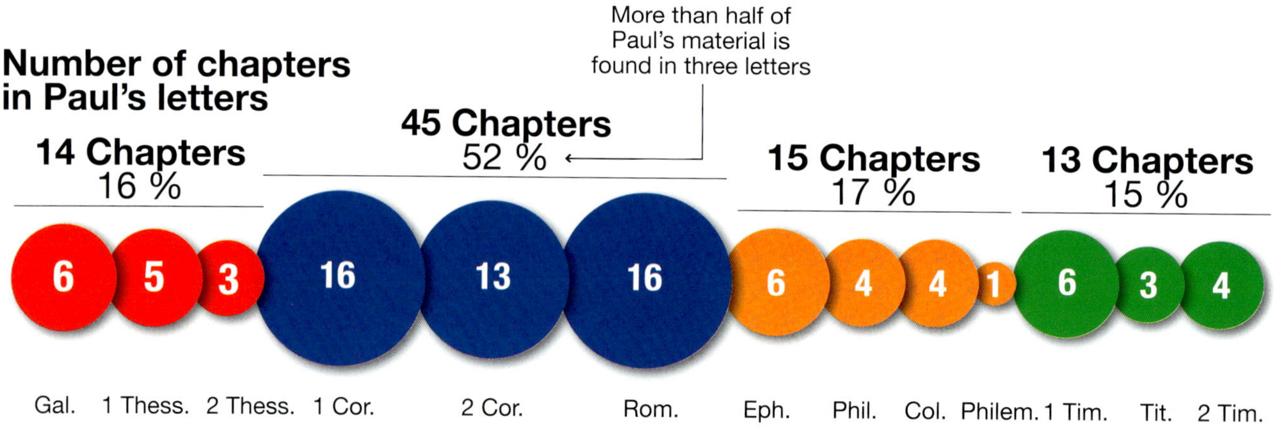

Four Major Themes of the Letters

	The Savior	Salvation	The Church	The Future
Paul's Letters (One author)	**Ephesians:** Christ and the church	**Galatians:** The freedom of salvation	**1 Corinthians:** Problems in the church	**1 Thessalonians** The comfort of Jesus's return
	Colossians: Christ and the cosmos	**Romans:** The way of salvation	**2 Corinthians:** Everyday life in the church	**2 Thessalonians** Waiting for Jesus's return
	Philemon: Christ and forgiveness		**1 Timothy:** Leadership in the church	
	Philippians: Christ and joy		**Titus:** A life worthy of the church	
			2 Timothy: Serving in the church	
The General Letters (Five authors)		**James:** The works of salvation	**1 John:** Community in the church	**1 Peter:** Suffering before Jesus's return
		Hebrews: Saving faith	**2 John:** False teachers in the church	**2 Peter:** The fall and Jesus's return
			3 John: Hospitality in the church	**Jude:** End times and Jesus's return
	4 letters **15 chapters**	**4 letters** **40 chapters**	**8 letters** **49 chapters**	**5 letters** **17 chapters**

Paul's Letters

(One author)

- Named for the recipients of the letters
- **Number of chapters:** 87

- **Ephesians** can also be placed in the category on the church.

- **Soteriology** is the study of salvation. It addresses issues such as the need for salvation, how to be saved, sanctification, final salvation, and whether you can lose your salvation.

- **Eschatology** is the study of the end times. It addresses issues such as the return of Jesus and what happens at the final judgment. But also what happens to the individual when life on earth ends.

- **Ecclesiology** is the study of the church. It addresses questions such as what the church is, who belongs to it, how it should be organized, and how to view baptism and Communion.

> *Faith* with Paul; *hope* with Peter; *love* with John; *works* with James; *zeal* with Jude; and *steadfastness* with 'Hebrews'.
> (Graham Scroggie)

The General Letters

(Five authors)

- Named for the author of the letter (except Hebrews)
- **Number of chapters:** 34

- **Christology** is the study of the person and work of Jesus Christ. It addresses issues such as his eternal existence, the incarnation, the meaning of his life, death and resurrection, and his present and future ministry.

Percentage of all chapters

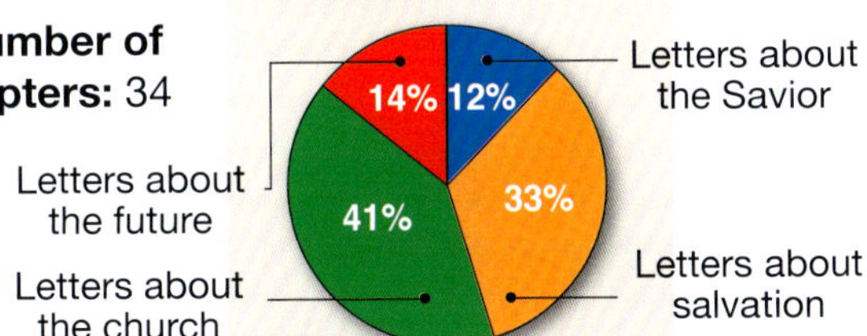

All the Letters in the New Testament (1)

• Marks letters preserved in the New Testament.

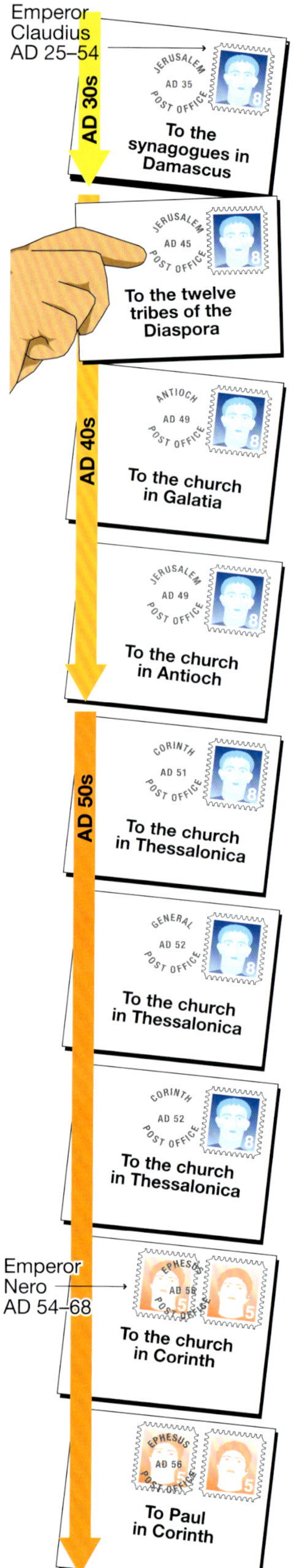

DAMASCUS LETTER
Author: Sanhedrin and High Priests (Acts 9:2; 22:5) **Recipients:** the synagogues in Damascus **Written from:** Jerusalem **Date:** Around AD 35 **Note:** Saul's letter of authorization.

• JAMES
Author: James, half brother of Jesus (1:1) **Recipients:** The twelve tribes of the Diaspora (1:1), probably Christians with Jewish backgrounds **Written from:** Probably Jerusalem **Date:** AD 44–49

• GALATIANS
Author: Paul (1:1) **Recipients:** The churches in Galatia (1:2) **Written from:** Unsure, Antioch or Jerusalem? **Date:** AD 48–49 or 53–56 **Note:** Identification of Galatia determines dating.

• COUNCIL OF JERUSALEM
Author: The apostles and elders (Acts 15:22–23) **Recipients:** The churches in Antioch, Syria, and Cilicia (Acts 15:23–30) **Written from:** Jerusalem (Acts 15:4) **Date:** AD 49

• 1 THESSALONIANS
Author: Paul (1:1) **Recipient:** The church in Thessalonica (1:1) **Written from:** Corinth (3:6; Acts 18:5) **Date:** AD 51–52 **Note:** Dating determined by Paul's travels.

FAKE PAULINE LETTER
Author: Unknown (2 Thess. 2:2) **Recipient:** The church in Thessalonica (2 Thess. 2:2) **Written from:** Unknown **Date:** Sometime before 2 Thessalonians **Note:** False letter sent in Paul's name.

• 2 THESSALONIANS
Author: Paul (1:1) **Recipient:** The church in Thessalonica (1:1) **Written from:** Corinth (1:1; Acts 18:5) **Date:** AD 51–52, shortly after 1 Thessalonians **Note:** Two letters sent in one year.

LOST LETTER
Author: Paul (1 Cor. 5:9) **Recipient:** The church in Corinth **Written from:** Probably Ephesus **Date:** Probably AD 53–56 **Note:** 1 Corinthians 5:9 assumes the existence of an earlier letter that is lost.

LETTER TO PAUL
Author: The church in Corinth (1 Cor. 7:1) **Recipient:** Paul (1 Cor. 7:1) **Written from:** Corinth **Date:** Before 1 Corinthians, AD 55–56? **Note:** Probably delivered by members of Chloe's household (1 Cor. 1:11).

• 1 CORINTHIANS
Author: Paul (1:1) **Recipient:** The church in Corinth (1:1) **Written from:** Ephesus (16:8) **Date:** AD 55–56 **Note:** Actually the second letter to Corinth but the first that is preserved.

FUNDRAISING LETTER
Author: Paul (1 Cor. 16:3) **Recipient:** The church in Jerusalem **Written from:** Corinth (1 Cor. 16:3) **Date:** After 1 Corinthians **Note:** Paul said he would write it.

SORROWFUL LETTER
Author: Paul (2 Cor. 1:1) **Recipient:** The church in Corinth (1:1) **Written from:** Ephesus or Macedonia **Date:** About AD 56, between 1 and 2 Corinthians **Note:** A lost letter (2 Cor. 2:3).

• 2 CORINTHIANS
Author: Paul (1:1) **Recipient:** The church in Corinth (1:1) **Written from:** Macedonia, maybe Philippi, Thessalonica, or Berea **Date:** AD 56–57 **Note:** Four letters to Corinth.

• ROMANS
Author: Paul (1:1) **Recipient:** The church in Rome (1:1) **Written from:** Corinth (Rom. 16:1, 23) **Date:** AD 56–57 **Note:** Phoebe from Cenchreae delivered the letter (16:1–2).

• EPHESIANS
Author: Paul (1:1) **Recipient:** The church in Ephesus (1:1) **Written from:** The prison in Rome (6:20) **Date:** AD 60–61 **Note:** May have been a circular letter.

LETTER TO LAODICEA
Author: Paul (Col. 4:16) **Recipient:** The church in Laodicea **Written from:** The prison in Rome **Date:** AD 60–61 **Note:** Possibly Ephesians, note "Laodicea" (Col. 4:16).

• COLOSSIANS
Author: Paul (1:1) **Recipient:** The church in Colossae (1:2) **Written from:** The prison in Rome (4:18) **Date:** AD 60–61 **Note:** Probably about same time as Ephesians.

• PHILEMON
Author: Paul (1:1) **Recipient:** Philemon of Colossae (1:2) **Written from:** The prison in Rome (Col. 4:18) **Date:** AD 60–61 **Note:** Onesimus was linked to Colossae (Col. 4:7–9).

**Note also Claudius Lysias's letter to Antonius Felix (Acts 23:26–30).*

All the Letters in the New Testament (2)

• **PHILIPPIANS**
Author: Paul (1:1) **Recipient:** The church in Philippi (1:1) **Written from:** The prison in Rome (1:7) **Date:** AD 61–62 **Note:** Paul may have written to them earlier, "telling you these things" (3:1).

• **1 PETER**
Author: Peter (1:1) **Recipients:** The chosen ones living scattered in Pontus, Galatia, Cappadocia, Asia, and Bithynia (1:1) **Written from:** Babylon (Rome) (5:13) **Date:** AD 62–65

• **1 TIMOTHY**
Author: Paul (1:1) **Recipient:** Timothy (1:2) **Written from:** Possibly Macedonia (1:3) **Date:** AD 63–66 **Note:** Uncertain where the letter was written, no clear information.

• **TITUS**
Author: Paul (1:1) **Recipient:** Titus (1:4) **Written from:** Nicopolis (3:12) **Date:** AD 63–66 **Note:** May have been written before 1 Timothy, we do not know for sure.

• **2 PETER**
Author: Peter (1:1) **Recipients:** Same recipients as for 1 Peter (3:1) **Written from:** Rome (See 1 Peter) **Date:** AD 64–67 (1:13–15) **Note:** Some debate over the author.

• **2 TIMOTHY**
Author: Paul (1:1) **Recipient:** Timothy (1:2) **Written from:** The prison in Rome (2:9) **Date:** AD 66–67 **Note:** Letter has feel of a last will, written to a spiritual son.

• **HEBREWS**
Author: Unknown **Recipients:** Persecuted Jewish Christians **Written from:** Unknown **Date:** AD 64–68 **Note:** Several authors have been suggested, including Paul, Barnabas, and Apollos.

• **JUDE**
Author: Jude, half brother of Jesus (1:1) **Recipient:** Unknown church (1:1) **Written from:** Unknown, probably not Israel **Date:** AD 60–80 **Note:** 2 Peter 2:2–3 quotes Jude 1:18, or vice versa.

• **1 JOHN**
Author: John **Recipients:** The churches around Ephesus **Written from:** Ephesus, according to tradition **Date:** AD 85–95 **Note:** Information about the letter comes from the church fathers.

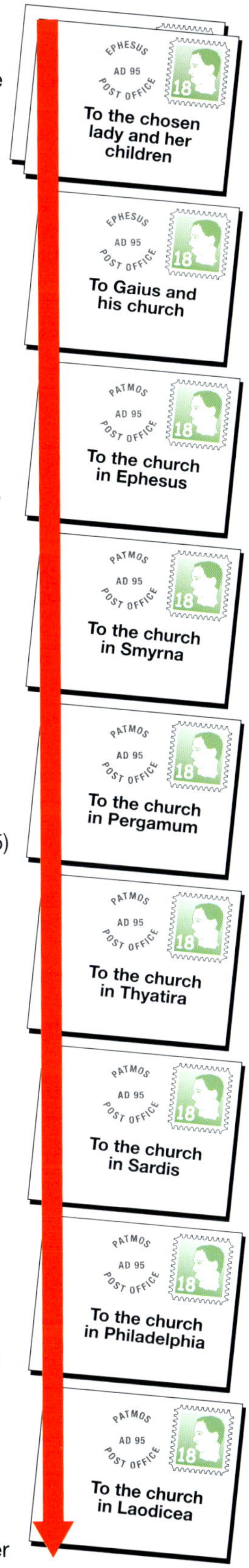

• **2 JOHN**
Author: John, the elder (1:1) **Recipient:** The chosen lady and her children (1:1) **Written from:** Ephesus, according to tradition **Date:** AD 85–95 **Note:** 3 John 1:9 could imply another letter.

• **3 JOHN**
Author: John, the elder (1:1) **Recipient:** Gaius, in a church probably somewhere near Ephesus (1:1) **Written from:** According to tradition, Ephesus **Date:** AD 85–95

• **LETTER TO EPHESUS**
Author: John (Rev. 1:4) **Recipient:** The church in Ephesus (Rev. 2:1) **Written from:** Patmos (Rev. 1:9) **Date:** AD 94–96 **Note:** One of the letters in Revelation to the seven churches.

• **LETTER TO SMYRNA**
Author: John (Rev. 1:4) **Recipient:** The church in Smyrna (Rev. 2:8) **Written from:** Patmos (Rev. 1:9) **Date:** AD 94–96 **Note:** One of the letters in Revelation to the seven churches.

• **LETTER TO PERGAMUM**
Author: John (Rev. 1:4) **Recipient:** The church in Pergamum (Rev. 2:12) **Written from:** Patmos (Rev. 1:9) **Date:** AD 94–96 **Note:** One of the letters in Revelation to the seven churches.

• **LETTER TO THYATIRA**
Author: John (Rev. 1:4) **Recipient:** The church in Thyatira (Rev. 2:18) **Written from:** Patmos (Rev. 1:9) **Date:** AD 94–96 **Note:** One of the letters in Revelation to the seven churches.

• **THE LETTER TO SARDIS**
Author: John (Rev. 1:4) **Recipient:** The church in Sardis (Rev. 3:1) **Written from:** Patmos (Rev. 1:9) **Date:** AD 94–96 **Note:** One of the letters in Revelation to the seven churches.

• **LETTER TO PHILADELPHIA**
Author: John (1:4) **Recipient:** The church in Philadelphia (3:7) **Written from:** Patmos (1:9) **Date:** AD 94–96 **Note:** One of the letters in Revelation to the seven churches.

• **LETTER TO LAODICEA**
Author: John (Rev. 1:4) **Recipient:** The church in Laodicea (Rev. 3:14) **Written from:** Patmos (Rev. 1:9) **Date:** AD 94–96 **Note:** One of the letters in Revelation to the seven churches.

How to Interpret the Letters

The teaching in the letters is more direct than that in the narrative books, like the Gospels and Acts, and is often in response to specific historical situations. One challenge for readers today is determining which teachings are timeless (and apply to us) and which apply mainly to the situation when the letter was written.

1

THE GENRE OF EPISTLE
Be aware of the genre. The letters are epistles, so their teaching is often more straightforward than that found in historical books.

2

THE AUTHOR'S INTENTION
What did the author have in mind? A text cannot mean just anything. It means what the author intended it to mean.

3

THE HISTORICAL AND CULTURAL CONTEXT
• **History:** When did the events take place? • **Culture:** Is there a contemporary cultural expression? • **Theology:** What doctrine is taught? Does it appear in other texts? • **Location:** Where was the letter written? Where did the recipients live?

4

THE CONTEXT OF THE TEACHING
Ask: • What comes before and after it? • Why was it written? What was the author's purpose? • What is the tone? Is it a rebuke or an encouragement? • Who were the recipients? What was their background?

5

HISTORICAL DISTANCE
Some texts are specific to their time and place, like "Do your best to get here before winter" (2 Tim. 4:21), and don't apply to us today.

HOW DO WE INTERPRET?
How can we decide which texts apply to us today and which are tied to their time, and need no modern application?
Example: "Judge for yourselves. Is it right for a woman to pray to God in public without covering her head?" (1 Cor. 11:13).

1 What the text says applies today in the same way as it did in biblical times.

2 What the text says applies today but with a modern expression.

3 What the text says applies now but in a different way than it did then.

4 What the text says applied then, but does not apply today.

THE PRINCIPLE—is it still valid today?

1. **YES** The principle says that a woman should cover her head when she prays to God.
2. **YES** The principle says that a woman should cover her head when she prays to God.
3. **YES** The principle says that a woman should cover her head when she prays to God.
4. **NO** The principle itself is tied to its specific time period, so it does not apply to us today.

APPLICATION—should we do the same today as they did then?

1. **YES** Since the principle is still valid, we should apply it: Women should wear a veil.
2. **KINDA** The principle is valid, but a more modern expression is acceptable.
3. **NO** The text is talking about reverence, which is expressed in the posture of our heart.
4. **NO** Since the principle is tied to its time and place, we do not need to apply it today.

HOW DO WE DECIDE WHAT APPLIES?
How can we determine which of the possible interpretations is valid in each case? Here are some questions to ask.

1 Timeless arguments
Are the reasons for the action tied to a specific time period, or can they be understood as being timeless? (1 Tim. 2:13–14)

2 General application
Is the teaching only applied in one context? Or is it applied in the same way in other passages? (1 Cor. 4:17; 7:17; 14:33)

3 Check the context
Does the interpretation of the text match the context in which it appears? What comes before it and after it in the letter?

4 Look at other texts
Is it consistent with other biblical passages on the same topic? Remember, it is the sum of God's Word that constitutes the truth.

5 Scriptural authority
Are we allowing our cultural attitudes to sway our thinking about the text, or are we letting God's Word speak for itself? (Rom. 12:2)

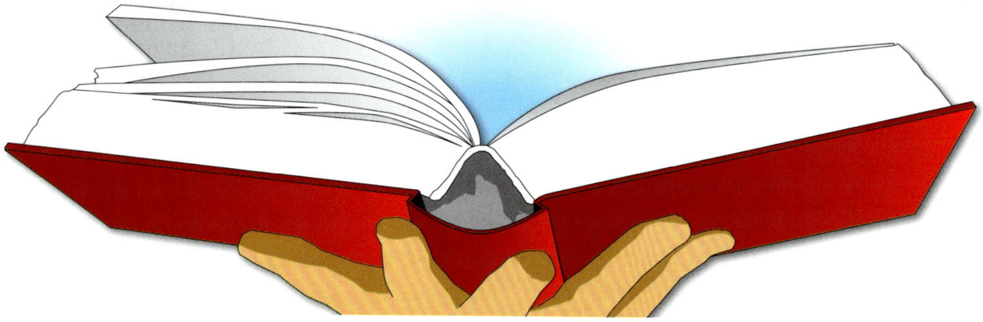

ROMANS

"Now there is no condemnation for those who belong to Christ Jesus. And because you belong to him, the power of the life-giving Spirit has freed you from the power of sin" (Rom. 8:1–2).

A FEW WORDS ABOUT THE AUTHOR

The letter to the Romans names Paul as the author (1:1). It was written during a three-month stay in Corinth during his third missionary journey (Acts 20:2–3). Paul used Tertius as his scribe, who also sent his greetings (16:22). The letter was probably delivered to the Christians in Rome by Phoebe (16:1). Paul sent this letter to prepare the church for his upcoming visit and the journey to Spain that he wanted to make (15:24, 28).

A FEW WORDS ABOUT THE RECIPIENTS

The letter is written to the church in Rome (1:7), which seems to have been founded early (Acts 2:10) and had both Jewish and non-Jewish believers. Early on it consisted of several house churches (16:1–16). Emperor Claudius expelled the Jews from Rome around AD 49 (Acts 18:2) but they were allowed to return in AD 54. Paul had not yet visited the church when he wrote the letter (1:13).

A FEW WORDS ABOUT DATES

The letter was probably written in the fall of AD 56 or spring 57, while Paul was in Corinth. Cenchreae was the port city of Corinth, and Gaius and the city treasurer Erastus were both closely connected to Corinth (16:1, 23; 1 Cor. 1:14). The letter was written toward the end of Paul's third missionary journey, when he was preparing to return to Jerusalem with the money he and others had collected for the poor (15:25).

THE WHOLE BOOK IN 25 WORDS

Paul's journey through the central themes of salvation: sin, justification, and sanctification. He challenges us to practice our faith in all situations of daily life.

A SIMPLE STRUCTURE

1. Sin
– The Need for Righteousness
(Rom. 1:1–3:31)

2. Salvation
– The Provision of Righteousness
(Rom. 4:1–11:36)

3. Service
– The Practice of Righteousness
(Rom. 12:1–16:27)

A FEW WORDS ABOUT KEY THEMES

- **General revelation**—God reveals himself to all humanity through nature and human conscience (1:20; 2:15). This allows no excuse for not knowing God.
- **Human sin**—All people have sinned (3:23). Because of sin, we are unable to turn to God on our own (3:10–11).
- **Righteousness**—It is revealed to us in the gospel and imputed to us by faith (1:17; 4:23–25). We are declared righteous by the blood of Jesus (5:1, 9, 17–18).
- **Death on the cross**—Christ died for us and we are crucified with him (6:6, 8, 11).
- **The Spirit**—Demonstrates that Jesus is the Son of God (1:4); circumcises the heart (2:29); fills the heart with his love (5:5); service to God is now through him (7:6); his law has freed us from the power of sin (8:2); leads the children of God (8:14). (See also 8:1–39; 9:1; 14:17; 15:13, 16, 19, 30).

A FEW TIPS ON WHAT TO LOOK FOR

Theme of the book: The way of salvation

- The steps on the road to salvation
- Saving faith, grace, sanctification
- Meaning of being crucified with Christ
- The terms righteous and righteousness
- Sin, different aspects of sin
- Various meanings of the law
- The Holy Spirit's activities
- The expression "in Christ"
- Paul's rhetorical questions
- The relationship between Israel and the church (9–11)
- Practical challenges (12–15)

The Path to Faith in Romans

Romans describes the way to salvation (1:16) in more detail than any other letter in the New Testament. Step by step, Paul presents the foundations of the Christian gospel: "Everyone who calls on the name of the LORD will be saved" (10:13).

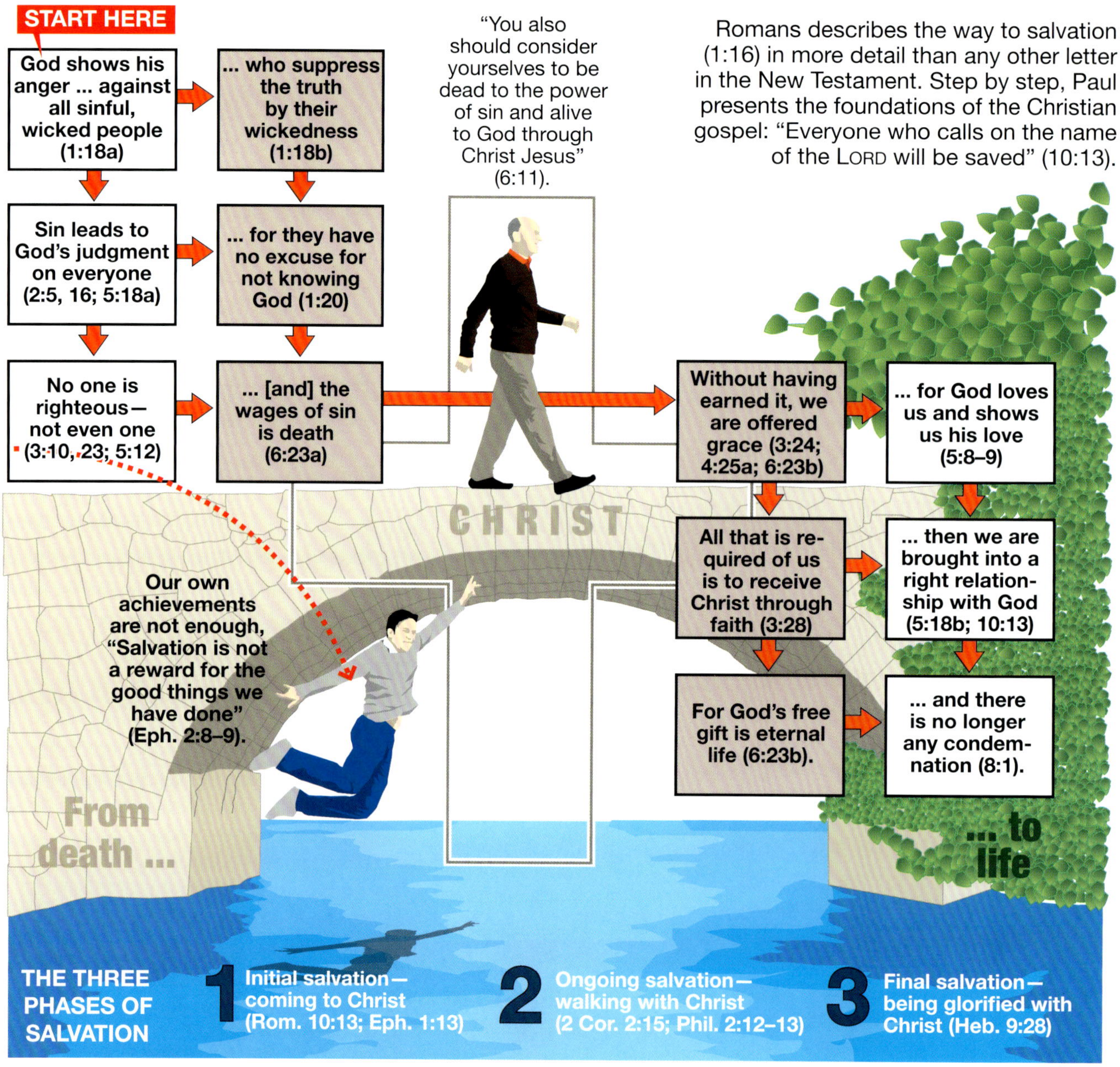

Comparing Adam and Jesus Christ

Adam		Jesus Christ
"The first Adam" (1 Cor. 15:45)—is the representative of all humanity. "The first man" (1 Cor. 15:45)—is the ancestor of the humanity that God created (Gen. 1:27).	**Title**	"The last Adam" (1 Cor. 15:45)—becomes the representative of all humanity. "The second man" (1 Cor. 15:47)—is the first of the new humanity that God will create.
Sinned by eating the forbidden fruit (Gen. 3:1–6).	**Handling**	Gave his life on the cross as payment for humanity's sin (1 John 2:2).
Adam's sin is ascribed to us. We were present with him in the garden. We sinned in him and with him (Rom. 5:12).	**Methodology**	Our sin is ascribed to Christ. We were present with him on the cross. His righteousness is ascribed to us (1 Peter 2:24).
Sin led to all people becoming sinners (Rom. 5:12).	**Consequences**	The atonement led to an offer of justification for all (Rom. 1:16).
Adam came from the earth, we received the old, physical life through him (1 Cor. 15:45–47).	**The nature of life**	Christ came from heaven, we receive the new spiritual life through him (1 Cor. 15:45–47).

What It Means to Come to Faith

Coming to faith in Christ involves more than just accepting facts—it is a personal decision to trust Christ, to receive him, and to begin following him. It is a relationship, not a religion, and it is about allowing God's grace to transform your life from the inside out. **Here are some basic steps.**

WHAT DOES IT MEAN TO BE SAVED?

1. To be forgiven and justified (Rom. 5:1; Col. 2:13–14; 1 John 1:9)

2. To be reconciled to God (Rom. 5:10; 2 Cor. 5:18–19)

3. To become a new creation (2 Cor. 5:17; Eph. 2:4–5)

4. To be a child of God (John 1:12; Rom. 8:15–16; Gal. 4:6–7)

5. To receive the Holy Spirit (Acts 2:38; Rom. 8:9)

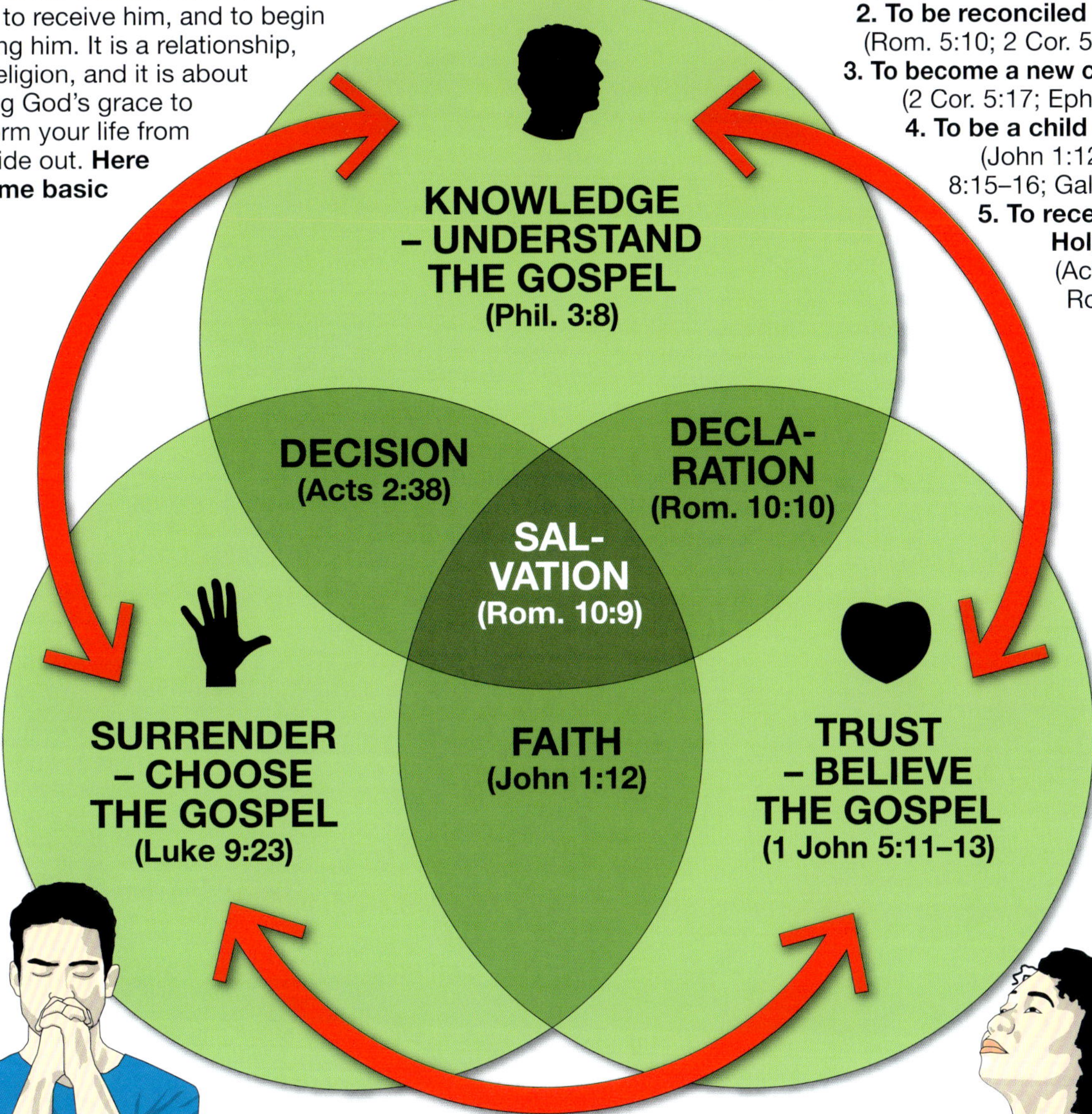

“God saved you by his grace when you believed. And you can't take credit for this; it is a gift from God. Salvation is not a reward for the good things we have done, so none of us can boast about it (Eph. 2:8–9).

Some Who Came to Faith

- **Three thousand**—when Peter preached on the day of Pentecost (Acts 2:41).
- **Five thousand**—when they heard the teaching of Peter and John near the temple (Acts 4:4).
- **Samaritans**—through Philip's preaching (Acts 8:6, 12)
- **Ethiopian eunuch**—on the road to Gaza (Acts 8:36–38).
- **Saul (Paul)**—on the road to Damascus (Acts 9:17–18).
- **Cornelius**—and all his household (Acts 10:44–48).
- **Sergius Paul**—Governor of Cyprus in Paphos (Acts 13:12).
- **Lydia and her family**—by the river outside Philippi (Acts 16:14–15)
- **Philippian jailer**—and all his household (Acts 16:30–34).
- **Many God-fearing Greek men and prominent women**—in Thessalonica (Acts 17:4).
- **Many in Berea**—who willingly accepted the message (Acts 17:11–12).
- **Dionysius, Damaris, and others**—after Paul's speech on the Areopagus (Acts 17:34).
- **The synagogue leader Crispus**—with his household and many others in Corinth (Acts 18:8).
- **Many in Ephesus**—openly confessed their faith (Acts 19:18–20)
- **Onesimus**—a slave Paul met in prison and brought to faith (Philem. 1:10).

The Pillars of the Christian Life

In Romans 4–5, Paul talks about justification, how a Christian comes into a right relationship with God. In chapters 6–8, he goes on to talk about sanctification, how a Christian should live when he or she has come into a right position before God. Romans 6–8 is one of the most central passages on the life of a Christian.

1 Freedom from sin

• WHAT HAS HAPPENED?
We are united with Christ.
1. We have died on the cross with him (6:3–8).
2. We have been buried with him (6:4).
3. We have risen from the dead with him (6:4–10).

• CONSEQUENCES
Jesus died not only as our substitute (he took our sin upon himself) but also as our representative (we died with him, 2 Cor. 5:14). The key to the Christian life is therefore to **look at ourselves** in light of the cross (6:11).

WHAT IS MY RESPONSIBILITY?
1. To know (6:3, 6, 9) Be aware of what took place on the cross.
2. To look at myself (6:11) Trust that it is true.
3. To offer myself for service (6:13, 16, 19) Take practical steps.
4. To obey (6:16–17) Three words summarize the reasons why we should be obedient:
• Grace (6:14–15)
• Freedom (6:16–20)
• Fruit (6:21–23)

2 Freedom from the law

• WHAT HAS HAPPENED?
We have died to the law.
1. We have died with Christ on the cross (6:10–11; 7:1–4).
2. When we died with Christ, we died to the law (7:5–6).
3. We serve God in "the new way of living in the Spirit" (7:6). We are released from the law's rule.

• CONSEQUENCES
God frees us from the law and its demands through our identification with Christ on the cross (6:1–11; 7:3, 6, 24–25). We are not only freed from the guilt of the past, but are also given new conditions for the life that is to come.

WHAT IS MY RESPONSIBILITY?
1. To understand sin and the law. The law could not save me from sin (7:7–13).
2. To understand sin and self. Despite freedom, an inner struggle rages (7:14–20).
3. To understand my inner struggle. Between my desire to obey God and the law of sin at work in me (7:21–23).
4. To understand how I can serve God's law. I do this by throwing myself on Jesus (7:24–25; 8:4).

3 Driven by the Spirit

• WHAT HAS HAPPENED?
We have received the Spirit who leads us to freedom.
1. We are free from judgment. When we died with Christ, we were freed from the law's demands, and the law of the Spirit now reigns (8:1–4).
2. We live in tension, but the Spirit helps us make right choices (8:5–8).
3. Because the Spirit lives in us, he helps and guides us (8:9–11).

• CONSEQUENCES
For those who belong to Christ there is no longer any condemnation (8:1). Life is no longer about performing to please God, but about responding by the Spirit to what God has done.

WHAT IS MY RESPONSIBILITY?
1. To be led by the Spirit The Spirit bears witness with my spirit (8:9–27).
2. To put to death the deeds of the sinful nature. The Spirit helps me to quench my own sinful desires (8:12–13).
3. To wait patiently for the final redemption It will happen one day (8:19–25).
4. To pray with the help of the Spirit The Spirit pleads for me with wordless groans (8:26–39).

Balancing the Christian Life

Being a Christian is balancing the path between lawlessness and legalism. Grace accepts freedom from the law while at the same time inspiring the desire to follow it.

"To call Jesus Lord while rejecting His law is the essence of lawlessness. (R. C. Sproul)

"Legalism may be defined as a fleshly attitude which conforms to a code for the purpose of exalting self. (Charles C. Ryrie)

Lawlessness

• Lawlessness is the sinful condition of rejecting God's will and authority, expressed through disobedience to his Word.
• It is not merely breaking rules, but living in active rebellion against God.
• While legalism distorts God's law by adding to it, lawlessness distorts it by taking away from it (John 3:4; Matt. 7:23; 2 Thess. 2:3–8).

The lawless person must repent, trust in Christ for forgiveness, and submit to the Holy Spirit, who empowers a new life of joyful obedience flowing from the heart in gratitude under God's grace.

Grace

• Grace is God's empowering favor that frees us from the law as a means of earning righteousness, and also transforms us to live out the righteousness the law reveals.
• It leads believers into deeper holiness and more sincere devotion that reflect God's character in everyday attitudes and choices.
• Grace does not abolish the moral law but enables the fulfillment of it through the Spirit. (Eph. 2:8–9; Rom. 6:14; Rom 8:3–4; Titus 2:11)

The legalist must stop relying on personal performance, trust fully in Christ's finished work, and allow the Holy Spirit to produce genuine obedience that flows from grace rather than personal effort.

Legalism

• Legalism is the attempt to earn God's acceptance through rule-keeping rather than through faith in Christ's finished work.
• It replaces inward faith and transformation with external obedience.
• While lawlessness distorts God's law by taking away from it, legalism distorts it by adding to it (Gal. 2:16; 3:3; Matt. 23:23–28; Rom. 10:3).

"There is nothing more devastating to the practice of spiritual living than an imbalance. (Charles C. Ryrie)

Views on Israel and the Church

Romans 9–11 develops the idea of how God's plan of salvation will be accomplished. There are several different views on how the passage should be understood, as well as how we should understand the relationship between Israel in the Old Testament and the church in the New. Here is a simple summary of four of the most common views.

How does the **OLD COVENANT** that God made with his people through Abraham (Gen. 12) and Moses (Ex. 34) ...

... relate to the **NEW COVENANT** that Jesus established with his blood on the cross (Luke 22:20)?

1 God has only one people—the church

• There is only one people of God, those who by faith belong to God through Jesus Christ. This applies to the whole history of salvation.
• Often referred to as covenant theology.

2 God has two peoples

• God has two peoples, Israel and the church, each having its own covenant. Both are still ways to come to God.
• Not commonly held. Sometimes called dual-covenant theology.

3 The church replaces Israel

• Israel is God's people in the Old Testament, but now both its role and promises are fulfilled by the church.
• Often referred to as fulfillment theology or replacement theology.

4 Israel always has a special role

• The church and Israel are two separate groups. The promises made to Israel are not promises to the church and vice versa.
• Often called dispensational theology.

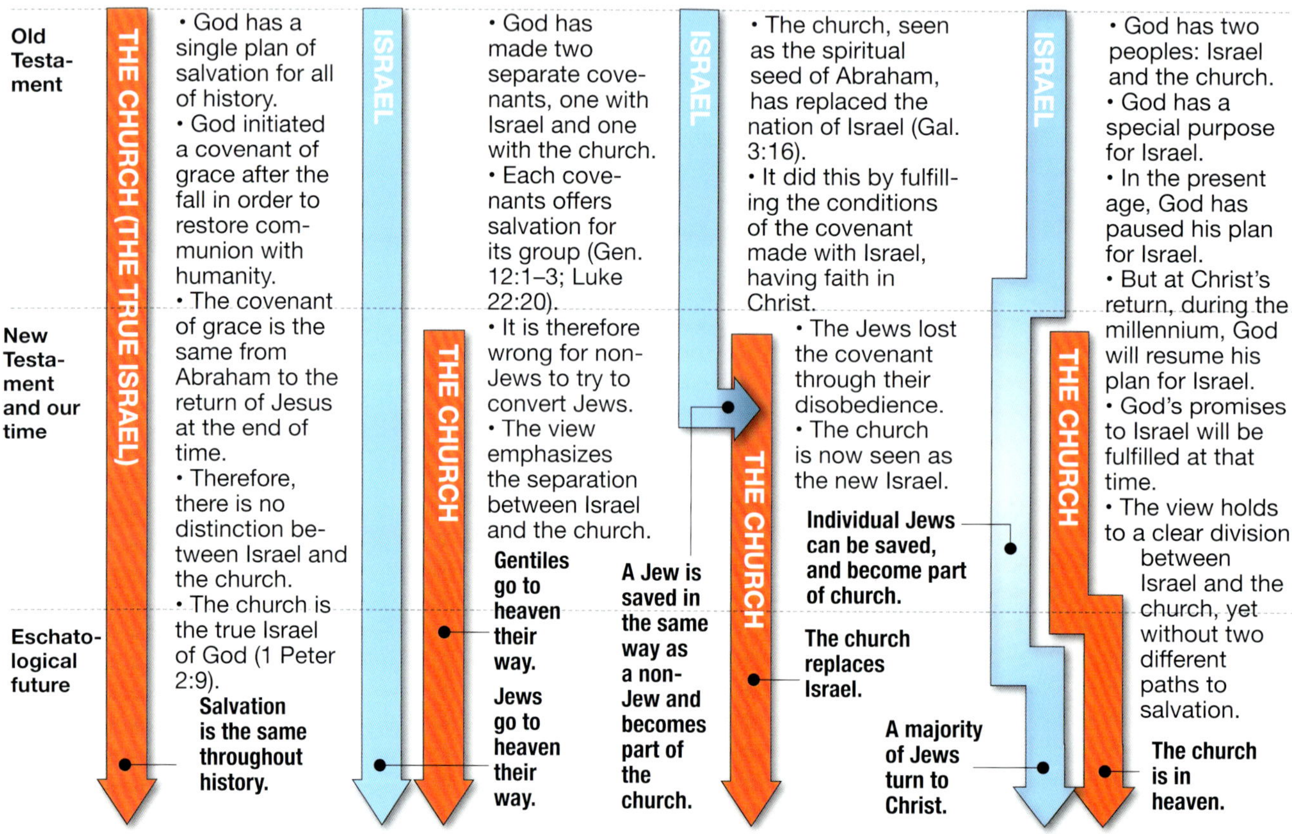

Some questions we need to think about

1 How literal should we be?

Jeremiah 31:31 speaks about God's new covenant with Israel and Judah—is this meant literally, or could it refer to the church?

2 Israel and the church?

Understanding the relationship between Israel and the church is essential. Do they have the same role, or are they distinct from each other?

3 What is the promised land?

The Old testament promises a land to Abraham, Isaac, and Jacob (Gen. 17:8). If the church inherits the promises, what does this mean?

4 Who are Abraham's heirs?

Those who descend from him physically, or must they believe in the atonement? Or is it anyone who receives Christ as their savior (Gal. 3:7)?

5 When was the church born?

Did the church begin at Pentecost? If it did, we must explain what happens to those who belonged to God before the church. Or has it always existed?

FIRST CORINTHIANS

"Three things will last forever —faith, hope, and love —and the greatest of these is love" (1 Cor. 13:13).

A FEW WORDS ABOUT THE AUTHOR

First Corinthians was written by Paul (1:1, 13; 3:4–6; 4:15; 16:21) during his time in Ephesus on the third missionary journey. The authorship has been widely accepted since the first century (see Clement of Rome, Polycarp, Tertullian, and Ignatius), with no serious early opposition. He was assisted by a scribe, most likely Sosthenes (1:1; 16:21; Acts 18:17), who may have helped to deliver the letter.

A FEW WORDS ABOUT THE RECIPIENTS

The recipient is the church in Corinth (1:2). Paul came to Corinth during his second missionary journey and founded the church there (Acts 18:1). He may have made another quick visit later on in that same missionary journey, though the details are not entirely clear (2 Cor. 12:14; 13:1). First Corinthians deals with moral and doctrinal problems within the church. In the letter, he discusses ten problems they were wrestling with.

A FEW WORDS ABOUT DATES

The letter was probably written in AD 55 or 56 in Ephesus, during Paul's third missionary journey (16:8–9,19; Acts 19:1–20:3). He had sent an earlier letter to the church (5:9) and in return received a visit from them (1:11). These visitors probably carried a letter of reply with several questions (7:1). First Corinthians answers their questions and is also meant to prepare them for a possible future visit (4:19; 11:34; 16:7).

THE WHOLE BOOK IN 25 WORDS

Through teaching, admonition, and reproof, Paul guides the church to submit to Jesus as Lord, theologically and practically. The hymn of love—a classic chapter.

A SIMPLE STRUCTURE

1. Correction – Confronting Church Problems
(1 Cor. 1:1–4:21)

2. Cleansing – Calling for Moral Purity
(1 Cor. 5:1–6:20)

3. Counsel – Answering Pastoral Questions
(1 Cor. 7:1–16:24)

A FEW WORDS ABOUT KEY THEMES

- **The Love Chapter**—An epic chapter that ends with the phrase "the greatest of these is love" (13:1–13).
- **Gifts of the Spirit**—Addresses the use of the gifts of the Spirit in the church. As it turns out, the use of the gifts is anything but simple (12:1–30).
- **Trouble in the church**—By no means was Corinth a peaceful church. Paul addresses a variety of problems that arose in their midst.
- **Questions and answers**—Note how the latter part of the letter is like an advice column, with Paul answering a list of questions sent to him (7:1–16:12).
- **The Lord's Supper**—Only chapter in the New Testament that both recounts the Lord's Supper and teaches about it (11:17–33).
- **The resurrection**—The central chapter on the resurrection of Jesus (15:1–58). Faith is meaningless without it (15:14).

A FEW TIPS ON WHAT TO LOOK FOR

Theme of the book:
Problems in the church

- The many different conflicts in the church
- Paul's answers to their many questions (7:1, 25; 8:1; 12:1; 16:1, 12)
- Instructions on living a holy life
- The Lord Jesus Christ
- Jesus's death on the cross (at least 14 times)
- Terms like blood, cross, crucifixion, sacrifice, death
- Passages about preaching (1:23; 2:1–5; 14:9, 19; 15:1)
- Things learned about the church

Problems in the Corinthian Church

Many people talk about wanting to build a New Testament church. Corinth was a New Testament church with all that that meant. In 1 Corinthians, Paul addresses all the craziness, at least ten trouble spots.

1 Contradictions and divisions

The problem: The church was divided into factions with some following Paul and others following Apollos, Cephas, or Christ. **Paul's answer:** Stand united instead (1:10–17).

2 Sexual immorality

The problem: Sexual immorality, including a man in a relationship with his father's wife. **Paul's answer:** Intervene and apply church discipline (5:1–13; 6:15–20).

3 Believers taken to court

The problem: Believers settling their disputes with each other in the secular courts instead of the church. **Paul's answer:** Shame on you! Solve it or leave it (6:1–11).

4 Uncertainty about marriage

The problem: In their pursuit of godliness, they began to question marriage itself. **Paul's answer:** Ideally, stay in the situation they were in when God called them (7:1–40).

5 Meat sacrificed to idols

The Problem: Can Christians buy and eat meat sacrificed to idols, in spite of its origin? **Paul's answer:** Yes, if it doesn't hurt brothers and sisters in the faith (8:1–13; 10:18–11:1).

6 Temptation to idol worship

The problem: Many in the church were tempted to indulge in idol worship with its rituals. **Paul's answer:** Do not go there; protect yourselves from falling away (10:1–22).

7 The role of women

The problem: Arguments and discussions over the role and behavior of women at church gatherings. **Paul's answer:** Women should show propriety and behave in an honorable way (11:1–16; 14:33–35).

8 Behavior at Communion

The problem: The rich gorged themselves before Communion while the poor had nothing. Communion was no longer a meal of unity. **Paul's answer:** Demonstrate your care for each other (11:17–34).

9 Misjudging spiritual gifts

The problem: Some believed their spiritual walk was more important and significant than others'. **Paul's answer:** Be loving instead and strive for order (12:1–14:40).

10 Misunderstanding the resurrection

The problem: Some in the church seemed to believe that there was no resurrection from the dead, therefore Jesus had not risen from the dead. **Paul's answer:** Jesus has risen, therefore we have hope (15:12–34).

Planting, watering, and growing

Paul describes the Corinthian believers as immature (3:1). • They allow their sinful natures to be in control, as shown by the different parties in the church. • So Paul must continue teaching them the basics of the faith (3:2).

Reflections: When someone comes to faith, all the glory belongs to God. Many people are involved in the growth. Who is helping you? Who are you helping? God is always the cause, people are his tools.

1 Different parties

Immaturity made them focus on people instead of looking to God, but true spiritual growth only comes from God (3:3–5).

2 Paul planted

Planting refers to bringing someone to faith. Paul helped in the initial stage of bringing people to Christ (3:6a).

3 Apollo watered

Watering refers to helping someone grow and mature in faith. Apollos helped these new believers to mature in Christ (3:6b).

4 God gave the growth

But neither of them are significant, because God is the one who makes the growth happen, not his instruments (3:6c–7).

Six Questions to Paul in 1 Corinthians

One of the reasons that Paul wrote this letter to the Corinthians was to answer the questions that the Corinthians had asked him. Chloe's people probably brought the written questions to Paul (1:11). He began this section (1 Cor. 7–16) with "now regarding the questions you asked" followed by six answers (7:1).

1 ABOUT BEING MARRIED

"Regarding the questions you asked in your letter" (7:1–24). **Answer:** It is good to be unmarried, but there is nothing wrong with being married. Remain in the position you were in when God called you (7:17, 20, 24). Paul also gives advice on divorce.

NOTES:

- 7:1–7 deals with marriage in general.
- 7:8–24 deals with specific issues.
- Paul's recurring theme in the passage is consistency, "each ... should remain as you were when God first called you" (7:24). Compare verses 7:2, 8, 10, 11, 12–16, 26–27, 37, 40 for deeper insight.

2 ABOUT BEING UNMARRIED

"Regarding your question about the young women" (7:25–40). **Answer:** It is preferable, if possible, to remain unmarried. But if you marry, you are not doing anything wrong (7:38). If you have married, do not focus only on your marriage (7:29).

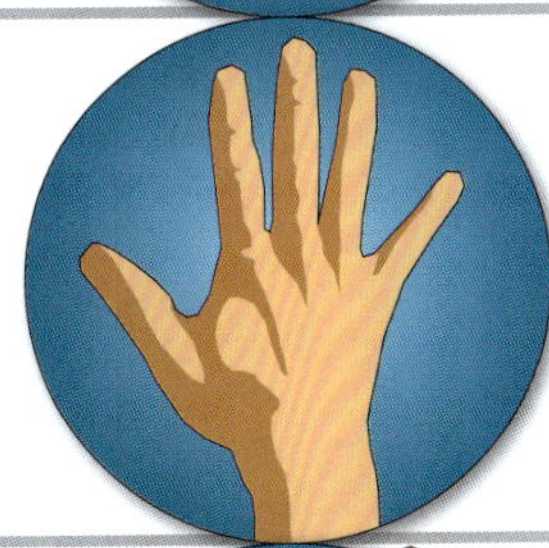

NOTES:

- Three reasons for not marrying: 1) the difficult situation (7:26–28), 2) time is short (7:29–31) and 3) to have time to think about what belongs to the Lord (7:32–35).
- Jesus did not speak on the issue, but Paul, under the inspiration of the Spirit, spoke with wisdom from the Lord (7:25).

3 ABOUT CHRISTIAN FREEDOM

"Regarding your question about food" (8:1–11:34). **Answer:** You are free (8:9; 9:1) but you should not take advantage of your freedom (9:15; 10:23). Your desire should be to live for God's glory, in worship and the celebration of Communion (10:31).

NOTES:

- Don't cause the weak to stumble, but the weak can't demand respect (8:9–11). This principle only applies to practical matters, not to theology.
- 1) All things are lawful (10:23). 2) Don't trip up the weak (8:9) 3) Seek the good of others (10:33). 4) Do everything for God's glory (10:31).

4 ABOUT SPIRITUAL GIFTS

"Regarding your question about the special abilities" (12:1–15:58) **Answer:** Strive for love (13:1–13) but also spiritual gifts (14:1). Make sure everything is done in an orderly way (14:40). Never forget: Jesus's death and resurrection are central (15:14).

NOTES:

- 1) The purpose of the gifts of the Spirit (12:1–30). 2) Love as a better way forward (12:31–13:13). 3) Rules for the proper use of the gifts of the Spirit (14:1–40). "Be sure that everything is done properly and in order" (14:40).

5 ABOUT THE COLLECTION

"Your question about the money being collected" (16:1–11). **Answer:** Collect money regularly, and send it with a trusted group to Jerusalem (16:2–3; Acts 24:17; Rom. 15:25–27; 2 Cor. 8:1–4). I will come to visit you soon, if I can go with them (16:5).

NOTES:

- 1) Let it be done regularly (16:2). 2) In private (16:2; Matt. 6:3). 3) Don't wait until the last minute to collect it (16:2). 4) Choose messengers to deliver it to Jerusalem (16:3–4).

6 ABOUT APOLLOS'S ARRIVAL

"Now about our brother Apollos" (16:12). **Answer:** Paul urged him to go to the Corinthians with Timothy and Erastus (Acts 19:22). But he did not want to go at that time and planned to travel to them later when he had the opportunity (16:12).

NOTES:

- Note Paul's tone. He gives advice and suggestions, but sees Apollos as a fellow worker and allows him to make his own decisions (3:9).

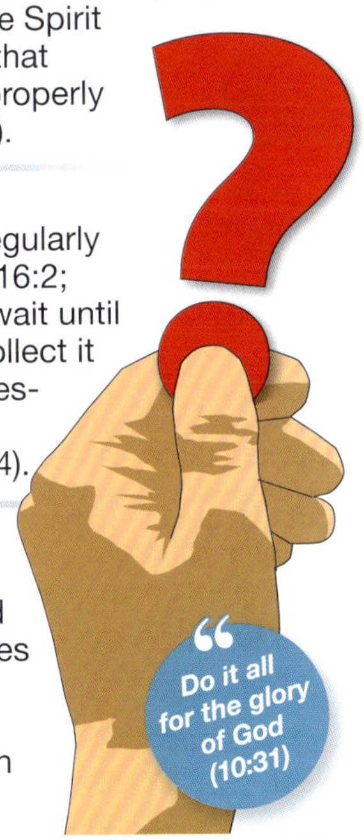

> "Do it all for the glory of God (10:31)

About the Gifts of the Spirit

In 1 Cor. 12, we find two lists of gifts and ministries that the Spirit gives to the church (12:8–10, 28–30). The lists give us examples; they probably are not exhaustive.

1

Gift of wise advice (12:8) The ability to make decisions and give advice based on the truth and in accordance with God's will.

2

Gift of special knowledge (12:8) The ability to comprehend spiritual realities, to grasp spiritual matters.

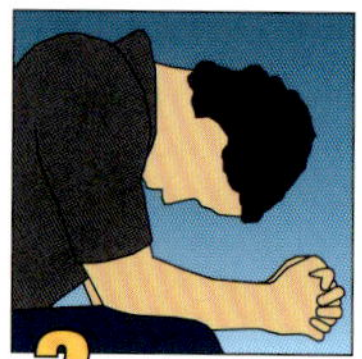

3

Gift of great faith (12:9) It is an unshakeable confidence in God, and helping others to trust him in the same way.

4

Gift of healing (12:9, 28) An ability to impart healing to others: physical, mental, and spiritual healing.

5

Gift of performing miracles (12:10, 28) An ability to convey signs and wonders that confirm the gospel.

6

Gift of prophesying (12:10, 28) To speak the word of God. Not to add to the revelation but to expound and proclaim.

7

Gift of discernment (12:10) The ability to determine whether a message, a person, or an event comes from God.

8

Gift of speaking in unknown languages (12:10, 29) The ability to speak a language not learned in the usual way.

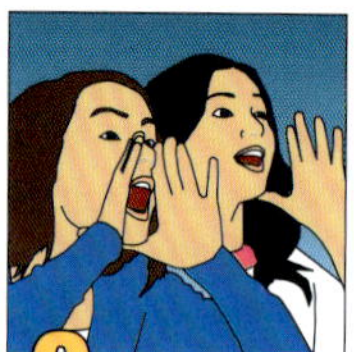

9

Gift interpreting (12:10) The ability to translate what others say back into a language that people can understand.

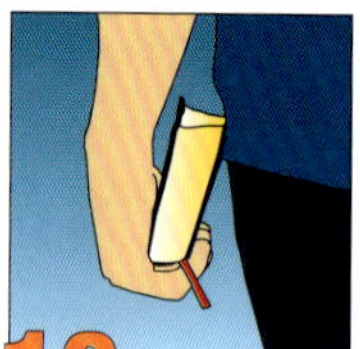

10

Appointed apostle (12:29) A missionary, who plants new churches, who takes the gospel to groups who have not yet heard it.

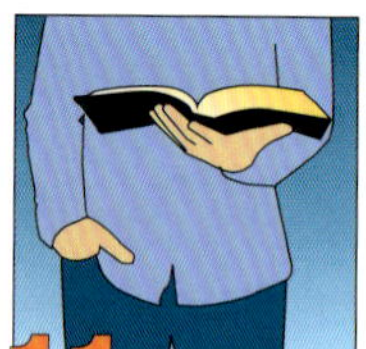

11

Appointed to teach (12:29) One who expounds the Scriptures. Has responsibility to preserve and explain the biblical text.

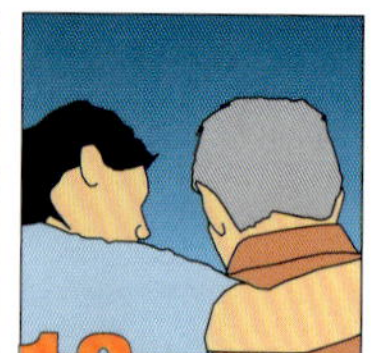

12

Appointed to help others (12:28) An ability to identify the needs of others and being willing to effectively meet the needs.

13

Appointed to lead (12:28) An ability to organize and administer in accordance with God's morals and principles.

Seven Lessons on Spiritual Gifts

Spiritual gifts need to be seen in the right perspective and managed responsibly.

1 The gifts are given by grace and not by merit

Spiritual gifts are not rewards for having a stronger faith than others or for living a more spiritual life. Instead, they are gifts of grace, **given without merit**, in order to enable you to better serve and honor God.

2 Gifts are not a sign of spiritual maturity

Spiritual gifts are not given only to the spiritually mature or those who have been Christian for a long time. Neither are they a reward from God. Spiritual gifts are for all believers, at any stage of their spiritual journey.

3 Everyone gets some, no one gets all gifts

It is God who gives spiritual gifts. Everyone receives at least one gift, no one receives all gifts, and no gift is given to all. The question is not what gifts you have been given, but how you use the gift(s) God has given you.

4 Spiritual gifts can be abused

Spiritual gifts of grace can be abused. The gifts do not have a life of their own, but the recipient has the opportunity and responsibility to steward them well. If this is not done, the use of the gift can get out of hand and become harmful.

5 Spiritual gifts do not give us rights

Having a spiritual gift does not grant you any special rights. Spiritual maturity and character, not a gift, form the basis for responsibility. In order to use their gifts properly, believers have the responsibility of maturing in the faith.

6 The use of gifts should always be tested

The use of spiritual gifts must be tested. Paul writes "Hold on to what is good" (1 Thess. 5:20–21). Not everything that is said or done in the name of God is good. This also means that not all uses of the gifts are necessarily good.

7 Different spiritual gifts never conflict

If the spiritual gifts come from God, we can expect the gifts to work in harmony with each other. If the use of the gifts leads to conflict or hurt, something is wrong.

> "Let all things be done with dignity and order (14:40).

> "It is so easy to become more attached to the gifts of God than to the Giver, and even, I should add, to the work of God than to God Himself. (Watchman Nee)

OTHER GIFTS OF THE SPIRIT: Servanthood (Rom. 12:7) • Encouragement (Rom. 12:8) • Giving (Rom. 12:8) • Leadership (Rom. 12:8) • Kindness (Rom. 12:8) • Evangelism (Eph. 4:11) • Shepherd/Pastor (Eph. 4:11) • Hospitality (1 Peter 4:9) • Speech (1 Peter 4:11) • Celibacy (1 Cor. 7:7–8) • Missionary (Eph. 3:6–8) • Martyr (1 Cor. 13:2–3) • Living in poverty (1 Cor. 13:2–3). No list is complete (Bezalel's gift not found in the NT, Ex. 35:30–33).

Love: What It Is and What It Is Not

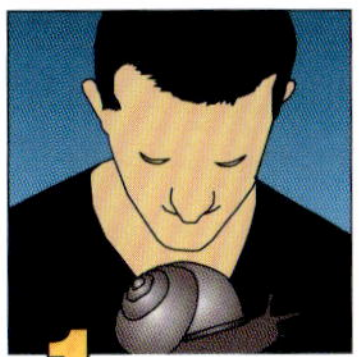

1

Love is patient and kind (13:4) Patient believers wait on God, are self-controlled, their kindness reflects a gentle nature.

2

Love is not jealous (13:4) Jealousy distorts love. True love rejoices in others' good, trusting God's gifts, timing, and grace.

3

Love is not boastful or proud (13:4) Pride elevates, boastfulness draws attention to self. True love lays both aside.

4

Love is not rude (13:5) Rudeness disregards others. True love shows respect and gentleness, reflecting Christ's grace.

5

Love does not demand its own way (13:5) True love is humble and patient, always putting others' needs before self.

6

Love is not irritable (13:5) Love is not quick to anger. Irritability reflects selfishness. True love is patient, calm, and forgiving.

7

Love keeps no record of being wronged (13:5) True love does not hold grudges. It forgives freely, patiently, and continually.

8

Love does not rejoice about injustice (13:5) Love doesn't cheer for what's wrong. It grieves over evil and seeks what is right and just.

9

Love rejoices whenever the truth wins (13:6) Celebrates honesty and righteousness. It is glad when what is right prevails.

10

Love never gives up (13:7) Love holds on through difficulty. It doesn't quit, even when it is costly or hard to hope.

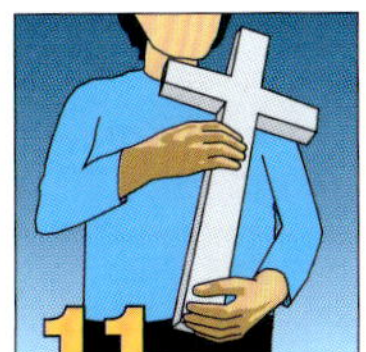

11

Love never loses faith (13:7) Love trusts through every trial and challenge. It never gives up, always hoping and believing.

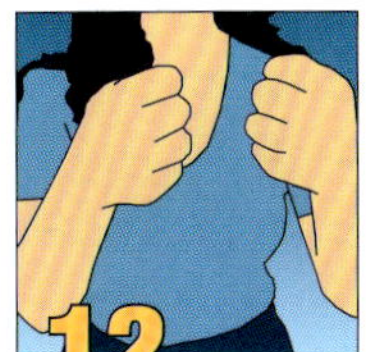

12

Love is always hopeful (13:7) Love holds onto hope, even when the future seems uncertain, and it trusts in God's good plan.

13

Love endures through every circumstance (13:7) Stands firm even in unpleasant circumstances. It does not lose composure.

14

Love will last forever (13:8,13) Can be seen as a summary. The gifts will fail, knowledge is scarce. But love endures.

Love: a road that surpasses all others

"Three things will last forever—

1 These three things are in contrast to the spiritual gifts (13:2, 8, 9).

2 Unlike the gifts that will come to an end (13:8), these continue, endure, abide, and persist.

3 The three things are character qualities, not limited to this life.

faith, hope, and love—

4 Should not be seen as the gift of faith (12:9), but as trust in God.

5 Hope is a confident expectation based on God's character, promises, and faithfulness (Rom. 15:13).

6 Both faith and hope are ultimately expressions and manifestations of true love.

and the greatest of these is love (1 Cor. 13:13).

7 Love is the greatest because when we meet the Lord, love for him will grow. Love is a reflection of God's essence, a sign of Christlikeness. Faith and hope depend on and expect something from God, whereas love is how we reflect God's own character (1 John 4:8, 16).

Four that last forever

- **God's children—**"Everyone who believes in him will not perish but have eternal life" (John 3:16; 1 John 5:11).
- **God's Word—**"The word of the Lord remains forever" (1 Peter 1:25).
- **God's love—**"I have loved you ... with an everlasting love. With unfailing love I have drawn you to myself" (Jer. 31:3).
- **God's mercy—**"Give thanks to the God of gods; his faithful love endures forever" (Ps. 136:2).

SECOND CORINTHIANS

"You are a letter from Christ ... [it] is written not with pen and ink, but with the Spirit of the living God. It is carved not on tablets of stone, but on human hearts" (2 Cor. 3:3).

A FEW WORDS ABOUT THE AUTHOR

Paul is the author (1:1; 10:1; 13:10). His authorship of the letter is rarely questioned. Those who raise doubts argue that the letter is a product of several different letters written by Paul to the church in Corinth. This is based on the fact that there are at least two natural sections in the letter (chapters 1–9 and 10–13). But there is no manuscript evidence to support this idea. So it must be considered speculative.

A FEW WORDS ABOUT THE RECIPIENTS

The letter is written to the church in Corinth. The church's relationship with the apostle had seriously deteriorated, and in the letter he warns against false apostles trying to separate the church from its founder. He is very personal, perhaps more so than in any other of his letters. He speaks frankly of his own internal and external struggles, revealing his weakness, dependence, and God's strength (1:8–9; 12:7–9).

A FEW WORDS ABOUT DATES

The letter was written some years after 1 Corinthians. It seems that before writing this letter, Paul wrote another letter, this lost letter is called the Sorrowful Letter (7:5–8). This gives us a date for 2 Corinthians of AD 56–57, probably the fall of 56. It was likely written from Macedonia, perhaps Philippi (2:12–13; 9:2), and sent to Corinth with Titus and a brother who was well known among the churches (8:16–18).

THE WHOLE BOOK IN 25 WORDS

Paul defends his apostleship in an autobiographical tone. Using irony and sarcasm as weapons, he confronts the false apostles. He calls for giving with joy.

A SIMPLE STRUCTURE

1. Explanation – Defending Paul's Ministry
(2 Cor. 1:1–7:16)

2. Encouragement – Giving Generously
(2 Cor. 8:1–9:15)

3. Exhortation – Confronting Opposition
(2 Cor. 10:1–13:14)

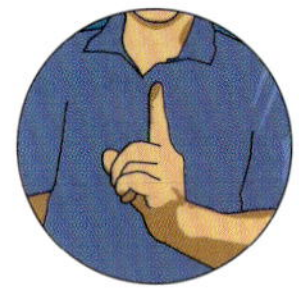

A FEW WORDS ABOUT KEY THEMES

- **Reasons for writing the letter**—Paul explains why he writes, at least seven reasons (1) 1:15–24; 2:1–3, (2) 2:5–9, (3) 7:4, 15, (4) 8:10–11, (5) 11:3–4, 13–14, (6) 11:1–12:21, (7) 12:21–13:2.
- **Truths about salvation in Christ**—Several truths, including the atonement (5:17–21), Jesus's vicarious death (5:21), and assurance of salvation (1:22; 5:5).
- **Description of the Christian life**—Describes the believer as being a letter from Christ (3:3), a new person (5:17), and a Christ-like fragrance (2:15).
- **Paul's feelings, moods, and inner motives**—For example, his physical weakness (1:8–9; 12:7), his anxiety (2:13; 7:5), and the hardships he suffered (4:8–9; 5:4–10).
- **Unique historical data**—the flight from Damascus (11:32–33), visions from God (12:1–4), the overview of his dramatic life (11:23–27).

A FEW TIPS ON WHAT TO LOOK FOR

Theme of the book: Everyday life in the church

- Paul's teaching on generous giving
- Paul's words of comfort (1:4–7; 2:7; 7:4, 6–7, 13), to give and receive comfort
- Paul's change of tone between 1–9 and 10–13
- Serving (18 times)
- Unique biographical information on the life of Paul
- Reasons Paul wrote the letter (7)
- The blessing (13:14)
- Why we face difficulties in life, the meaning of suffering

Paul and All the Corinthian Letters

Paul's relationship with the Corinthians not only includes the visits in Acts and the letters we have in the New Testament, but there must also have been at least three other letters and possibly another visit.

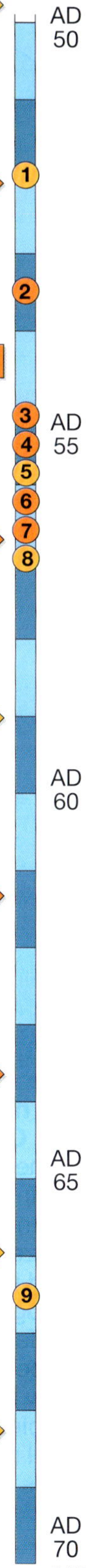

1

Paul visits Corinth for the first time

Text: Acts 18:1, 18 **Time:** AD 51–52 **Context:** During his second missionary journey, Paul stays in Corinth for eighteen months. Timothy and Silas are with him (Acts 18:5). He meets Priscilla and Aquila, who accompany him when he leaves the city (Acts 18:18).

2

Paul writes the lost letter (first letter)

Text: 1 Cor. 5:9 **Time:** AD 53–56 **Context:** Paul writes a letter from Ephesus while he is on his third journey, this letter is not preserved. Apollos is in Corinth, but travels to Paul (Acts 19:1; 1 Cor. 16:12).

3

The Corinthians write a letter to Paul

Texts: 1 Cor. 1:11; 5:1; 7:1, 25; 12:1; 16:12, 17 **Time:** AD 55–56 **Context:** A delegation from Corinth, including members of Chloe´s household and others, comes to Paul with a letter (1 Cor. 1:11; 16:17). They report on the situation in the church and raise several questions.

4

Paul writes 1 Corinthians (second letter)

Text: 1 Cor. 1:1 **Time:** AD 55–56 **Context:** Paul writes a letter from Ephesus in response. Sosthenes is probably his scribe (1 Cor. 1:1). Timothy delivers the letter (1 Cor. 4:17; 16:10–11).

5

Paul visits Corinth for the second time

Texts: 2 Cor. 12:14; 13:1 **Time:** AD 55–56 **Context:** Paul plans a quick visit to Corinth. Acts does not mention this trip, but it fits in sometime during the period Acts 19:1–40. Another possibility is that the texts describe plans that either were revised or never materialized.

6

Paul writes the Sorrowful Letter (third letter)

Text: 2 Cor. 2:1–4 **Time:** AD 56 **Context:** Paul writes another letter that is not preserved, called the Sorrowful Letter. Some believe it is 1 Corinthians, others that the letter is 2 Corinthians 10–13, which was later combined with chapters 1–9.

7

Paul writes 2 Corinthians (fourth letter)

Text: 2 Cor. 1:1 **Time:** AD 56–57 **Context:** From Macedonia, Paul writes a fourth letter to the church. Timothy is probably the scribe (2 Cor. 1:1, 19). Titus and a brother deliver it (2 Cor. 7:6, 8:6, 18; 12:18).

8

Paul visits Corinth for the third time

Text: 2 Cor. 1:16 **Time:** AD 56–57 **Context:** Paul leaves Ephesus and travels overland to Corinth (Acts 20:2). He stays in the city for three months (Acts 20:3), during which time he writes his letter to the Romans (Rom. 16:1). Then he returns to Jerusalem over land and sea.

9

Paul visits Corinth for the fourth time

Text: 2 Tim. 4:20. **Time:** possibly AD 65–67. **Context:** Paul may have visited Corinth a fourth time after his release from Rome. Erastus stayed behind in Corinth, presumably when Paul left the city (2 Tim. 4:20). Erastus was the treasurer of Corinth, confirmed by archaeological finds (Rom. 16:23).

Seven Images of the Believer

In 2 Corinthians, Paul presents at least seven images that describe different aspects of the Christian life. They emphasize the Christian's mission to demonstrate the Christian faith to people we meet.

1 The fragrance of Christ

Your life is a "Christ-like fragrance" that can be perceived (2:14–16).

• Roman military triumphal processions ended with the burning of incense and fragrant spices (2:14).

• Paul compared that aroma to the testimony of Christians who spread the sweet perfume of the one who triumphed on the cross.

2 A letter from Christ

Our lives are like a letter from Christ (3:1–3).

• The false teachers had fake letters of recommendation that were intended to lend them legitimacy (3:1).

• Paul did not believe that he needed any such letter. His legitimacy came from the Christians in Corinth. Their lives were his letter of recommendation (3:2).

3 A minister of the new covenant

The life we live, we live as ministers of the new covenant of the Spirit (3:4–6).

• We are not able to do this on our own, but God qualifies us for this work. This covenant of the Spirit looks at our inner motives, not our fulfillment of written laws.

• Paul lists seven differences between the old and new covenants (3:6–11).

4 A new life in Christ

The new life means that your inner self is made new through faith (5:16–19; Ezek. 36:26).

• God is the creator. Through his initiative and your faith, your old self has been replaced with a new heart, you are a completely new creation.

• Paul says this new life brings us into a deeper knowledge of Jesus as his love leads us further.

5 An ambassador for Christ

Your life is characterized by being an ambassador for Jesus Christ (5:20–21).

• We are representatives of the finished work of Christ (Acts 26:16–18).

• Paul believed that it is Jesus who, through us as his ambassadors, appeals to people to be reconciled with God. A Christian carries the Christian message to others.

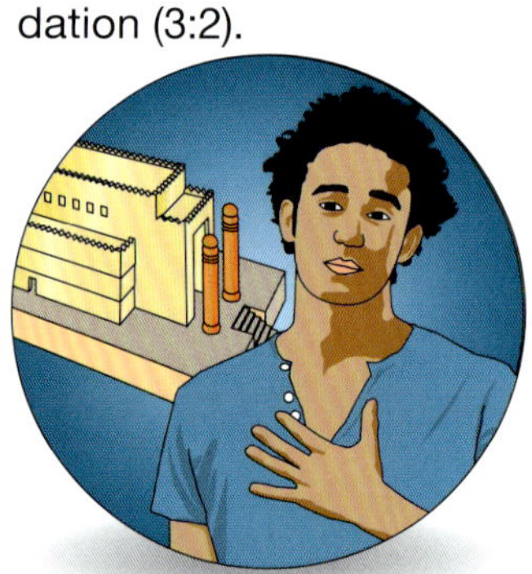

6 A temple of the living God

God lives in us and he is present in our lives (6:16–17).

• In the Old Testament, God revealed his presence among his people in the tabernacle and later in the temple.

• Paul believed that through salvation, believers carry God within them and demonstrate God's presence through their manner of life.

7 A cheerful giver

Your life should be characterized by generous giving to others (9:6–10).

• Three things happen when you give cheerfully and generously: the giver is blessed (9:6–10), the recipient's needs are met (9:11–12), and God, the ultimate giver of all gifts, is glorified (9:13–15). Paul says that a cheerful giver directs the gratitude of others toward God.

Paul's Trials and Tribulations

In 2 Corinthians 11, Paul writes a summary of his life and ministry up to that point. We know about some of the events he describes but have no detailed description for others.

"I can do everything through Christ (Phil. 4:13).

Suffered shipwreck

2 Cor. 11:25 "three times." We have no details. Some suggest it happened when in Tarsus (Acts 9:30). The incident in Acts 27:22–44 happened after this letter was written.

... cities, deserts, oceans

2 Cor. 11:26. Paul was in danger in cities like Damascus and Lystra, and from shipwrecks. We have no examples of danger in deserts (Acts 9:22, 29–39; 2 Cor. 11:32).

Spent time in prison

2 Cor. 11:23 "more often." Imprisonment in Philippi is the only reference (Acts 16:23–39). Possibly in Ephesus, or other times not recorded before this letter was written.

Drifted at sea

2 Cor. 11:25 "a whole night and a day." We know nothing about this event. But later, while traveling to Rome, the ship drifted for fourteen days (Acts 27:27, 33).

... among false brothers

2 Cor. 11:26. Paul speaks of "so-called believers" in Galatia (Gal. 2:4). But it is possible that Paul was betrayed on other occasions that are unrecorded.

Was whipped and beaten

2 Cor. 11:23 "without number." The word used can be understood as a beating (2 Cor. 6:5). It is plural, so refers to many blows, cuts, or stabs (Acts 16:23).

Many long journeys

2 Cor. 11:26. We have descriptions of three long journeys. The letter is written on his third trip. Reference to the journeys introduces the experiences in the verses that follow.

All under toil and hardship

2 Cor. 11:27 "enduring many sleepless nights …. been hungry and thirsty…. shivered in the cold, without enough clothing." (see 1 Cor. 4:9–13; 2 Cor. 4:7–12; 6:4–10).

Often in mortal danger

2 Cor. 11:23. Escaped from Damascus (Acts 9:23) and driven out of Antioch of Pisidia and Iconium (Acts 13:50; 14:5). See also Acts 14:19; 1 Cor. 15:32; 2 Cor. 1:8–10.

Dangers from rivers

2 Cor. 11:26. We do not know what he is referring to. One possibility is the rapids that came down from Mount Lebanon on the road from Jerusalem to Antioch.

The thorn in the flesh

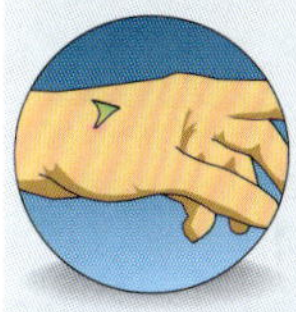

"I was given a thorn in my flesh" (2 Cor. 12:7).

FOUR COMMON EXPLANATIONS

1) A disease: Probable explanation. Possibly an eye disease (Gal. 4:13–15), a recurring fever, or epilepsy.

2) A temptation: The sinful nature that caused constant temptations (Rom. 7:15–16).

3) Persecution: Used figuratively and refers to the fact that Paul constantly faced opposition (2 Cor. 11:23–27).

4) A demon: A fallen angel that tormented Paul (2 Cor. 12:7b). Less likely.

SOME CONCLUSIONS

1) God allowed suffering so that Paul would not boast (2 Cor. 12:7).
2) The suffering had an evil origin (2 Cor. 12:7, see Job 1–2).
3) Prayer did not remove suffering (2 Cor. 12:8).
4) Suffering did show that God's grace is sufficient (2 Cor. 12:9–10).

Received thirty-nine lashes

2 Cor. 11:24 "five different times" (Deut. 25:3; Matt. 10:17). Not described in any text. The Law of Moses forbade more than forty, so thirty-nine were usually given.

Dangers from robbers

2 Cor. 11:26. Again we have no clear reference. But the road across the Taurus Mountains between Perga and Antioch of Pisidia was notorious for robbers.

Beaten with rods

2 Cor. 11:25 "three times." Once in Philippi, the others are unknown (Acts 16:22). A Roman punishment, probably happened in a colony or city under Roman rule (see 2 Tim. 3:11).

Dangers from Jews

2 Cor. 11:26. There are several examples: Damascus (Acts 9:23), Jerusalem (Acts 9:29), Iconium (Acts 14:5–6), Lystra (Acts 14:19), and Corinth (Acts 18:12).

Was stoned

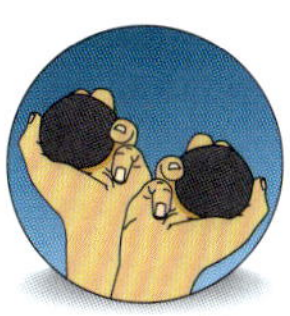

2 Cor. 11:25. Stoned in Lystra to the point that it was thought that he was dead (Acts 14:19). He was threatened with stoning in Iconium but managed to escape (Acts 14:5–6).

Dangers from gentiles

2 Cor. 11:26. There are several examples. In Philippi when Paul was imprisoned (Acts 16:19–40) and in Ephesus when the city rioted after Paul's preaching (Acts 19:23–40).

I have learned ...

"I have learned how to be content with whatever I have." Everything that happened was used to shape his attitude and his trust in God (Phil. 4:11–13).

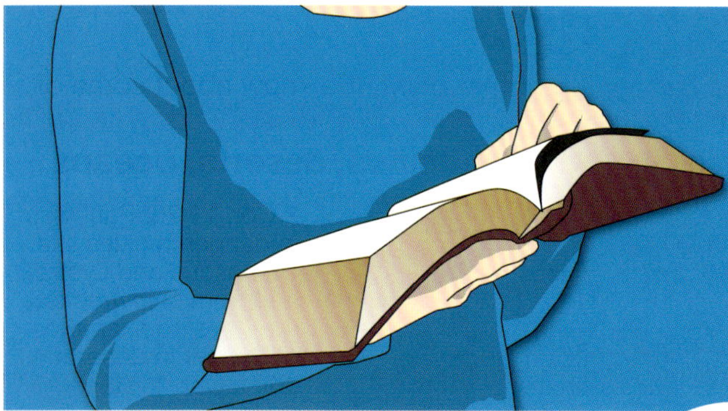

GALATIANS

"The Holy Spirit produces this kind of fruit in our lives: love, joy, peace, patience, kindness, goodness, faithfulness, gentleness, and self-control" (Gal. 5:22–23).

A FEW WORDS ABOUT THE AUTHOR

There is no reason to question the letter's claim that Paul is the author (1:1; 5:2). Galatians is often regarded as one of the most genuine Pauline letters we have. The letter is written to argue against Judaizer teachers who demanded that the new gentile Christians be circumcised and live as Jews. Paul attacks the heresies of the Judaizers with a vengeance, strongly defending the true gospel message.

A FEW WORDS ABOUT THE RECIPIENTS

The letter is written to the churches in Galatia (1:2). Galatia probably refers to the Roman province of Galatia in central present-day Turkey, the southern part of which Paul visited during his first missionary journey (Acts 13:3–14:28). It could also refer to the ancient region of Galatia, farther north, which Paul may have visited on his later journeys (Acts 16:6; 18:23). This uncertainty plays a role in the discussion about the letter's date.

A FEW WORDS ABOUT DATES

The dating is uncertain. If the meeting in 2:1–10 refers to the apostolic council (Acts 15), the letter must be dated late, perhaps AD 53–56. If the text does not, the letter may have been written earlier. The letter is then probably Paul's earliest letter, written in AD 48 or early 49. It also matters how we identify the Galatians because Paul explains that he visited them at least twice when the letter was written ("first brought" 4:13).

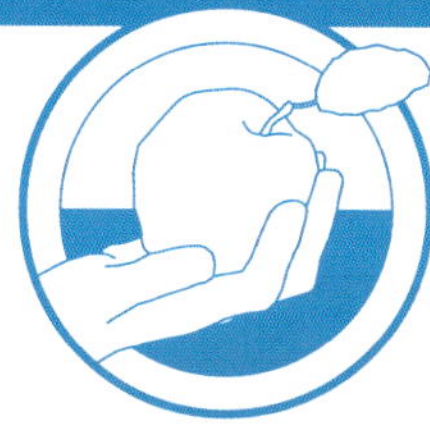

THE WHOLE BOOK IN 25 WORDS

Paul attacks the Judaizers' heresy. He defends his apostleship, rebukes the Galatians for abandoning the gospel of grace, and calls them to freedom in Christ.

A SIMPLE STRUCTURE

1. Defense—Paul's Apostolic Authority
(Gal. 1:1–2:21)

2. Doctrine—Justification by Faith, Not Law
(Gal. 3:1–4:31)

3. Duty—Living by the Spirit, Not the Flesh
(Gal. 5:1–6:18)

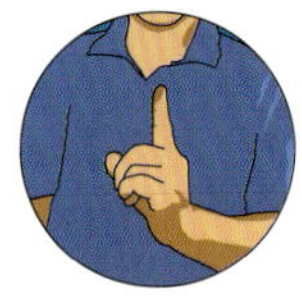

A FEW WORDS ABOUT KEY THEMES

- **Grace**—The main theme of the book is that you are saved by grace (2:16–17, 20–21; 3:2–3, 14, 25–26, 27; 4:6–7; 5:1, 16–18, 22–23; 6:12–14).
- **Justification by faith**—Paul answers the question: How does one become righteous? By your own works or by faith in God? The answer is obvious (2:14–21; 3:6, 11; 5:4–5).
- **The purpose of the law**—Paul explains that the law has never been a path to salvation but a help that leads us to Christ (2:20–21; 3:10–25; 5:1).
- **Contrasts in the letter**—Paul contrasts different positions, such as law versus grace (see 1:6–9, 10; 2:15–20; 3:10–16; 4:1–7; 5:17–18; 6:14).
- **Fruit of the Spirit**—Contrasted with works of the flesh. Speaks of character; love, joy, peace, patience, kindness, goodness, faithfulness, gentleness, self-control (5:22–23).

A FEW TIPS ON WHAT TO LOOK FOR

Theme of the book:
The freedom of salvation

- Grace (7 times), law (27 times), law and grace relationship, believe (26 times)
- The flesh (6 times), slave (16 times)
- The cross (6 times)
- Free, freedom (14 times)
- Titles and names of Jesus (8 different)
- Quotes from and allusions to the Old Testament
- Similarities to Romans
- The contrast between the fruit of the Spirit and the deeds of the flesh
- How many questions can you find?

Who Exactly Were the Galatians?

What does Paul mean when he says Galatians (Gal. 1:1; 3:1)? Is it the Galatian people as a group? Or the people farther south in the Roman province of Galatia? The answer affects the dating of the book.

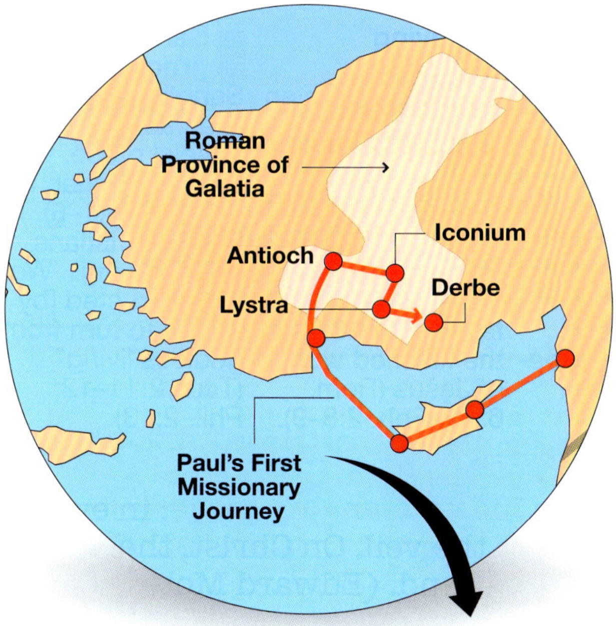

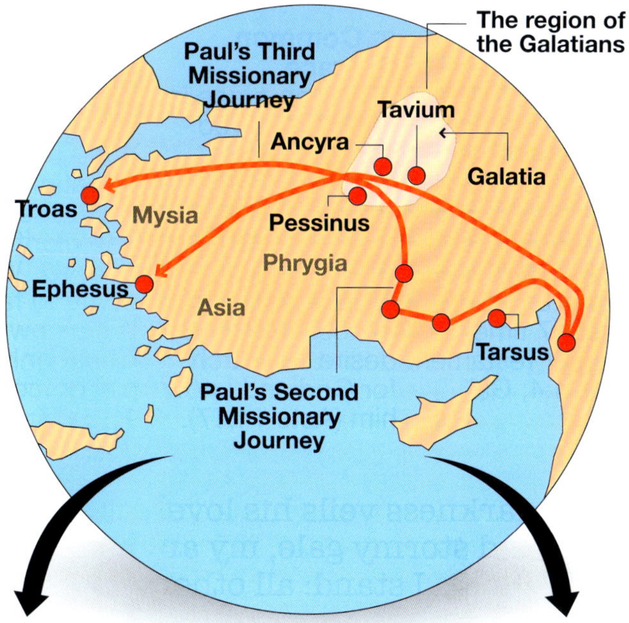

Three different theories about the dating	**1 South Galatian theory—early date**	**2 North Galatian theory–early date**	**3 North Galatian theory– late date**
	Paul is referring to the Roman province of Galatia.	Paul is referring to the region where the Galatian people lived.	
Paul visited them at least twice ("when I first brought" Gal. 4:13). When did these visits take place?	The first visit to Galatia takes place on the outward journey of the first missionary journey (Acts 13:4–14:21) and the second visit on the return journey (Acts 14:21–28). The earliest time the letter could have been written was on the return leg of the first missionary journey.	The other views are based on an assumption: that we know everything about Paul's travels in the region. But suppose that during his time in Tarsus, Paul traveled to the Galatians (Acts 9:30). His two visits may have taken place before the first missionary journey (Gal. 1:21, see Rom. 15:20).	Paul's first visit to the Galatians is on his second missionary journey (Acts 16:6), the second visit on his third journey (Acts 18:23). The earliest the letter could have been written was after Paul had visited the Galatians on his third missionary journey.
Is Paul talking about Roman provinces or territories?	In his letters, Paul talks about geographical locations rather than ethnic groups.	Phrygia, which is not a Roman province, is mentioned alongside Galatia, so why does Galatia have to be the province (Acts 16:6; 18:23)? Paul goes to Galatia after being in Derbe and Lystra, which are in the Roman province (Acts 16:1, 6).	
What about Barnabas?	Barnabas, whom Paul mentions in the letter (2:1), was not with him on the second and third journeys and would therefore be unknown to the Galatians.	Barnabas may have accompanied Paul on a visit to the Galatians before they left for Antioch (Acts 11:25), or the letter was written after the first journey.	Barnabas may have been known to the Galatians for other reasons. Either because of a personal visit or through correspondence (1 Cor. 9:6).
The decision of the apostolic council in Jerusalem	The account in Galatians 2 refers to a different visit to Jerusalem than the apostolic council. Titus is mentioned (2:2) but not in Acts 15. The meeting seems to have taken place in private (2:2) and not in public (Acts 15:6). It would be strange if Paul did not refer to the council's decision, since the Galatians' problems were addressed at the council.		Galatians 2 refers to the apostolic council in Jerusalem (Acts 15). Therefore the text shows that the letter was written after Acts 15.
Conclusion	Galatia refers to the Roman province. The letter was written before the apostolic council (Acts 15:1), but after the visit to Galatia, probably in AD 48–49, possibly in Antioch or Jerusalem.	Galatia is the area where the Galatian people lived. The letter was written before the apostolic council (Acts 15:1), it may have been written before, during, or immediately after the first journey.	Galatia is the area where the Galatian people lived. The letter was written during the third missionary journey, in Ephesus or Macedonia, probably between AD 53–56.

Paul's Words on God's Grace

The Galatians had been exposed to the Judaizers' heresy. The Judaizers said that relying on the finished work of Jesus was not enough and proving one's worth before God was necessary. This letter focuses on grace.

1 Definition of by grace
The word means undeserved goodness, kindness, favor. Grace is receiving something that is not deserved. The word is used at least 157 times in the New Testament (Rom. 4:4; Gal. 2:21).

2 Common grace
Common grace is the undeserved kindness that God shows to all people. It cannot bring someone to saving faith, but it can awaken curiosity and the desire to search for God and know him (Acts 14:17).

3 Special grace
Special grace is what God uses to bring people to salvation. Grace saves, sanctifies, and glorifies the believer. We can come to faith and live a new life in Christ only by special grace (John 1:16–17; 6:44).

4 Saving grace
Saving grace is an aspect of special grace. Salvation is a gift from God that we receive freely, at no cost. Our works do not save us, rather our faith and trust in the finished work of Jesus (Rom. 6:23; Eph. 2:8–9).

5 Sanctifying grace
Sanctifying grace is an aspect of special grace, vital to the Christian life (see Gal. 3:1–6). It spurs Christians to holy living: "We are instructed [by grace] to turn from godless living" (Titus 2:11–12; Phil. 2:13).

> When darkness veils his lovely face, I rest on his unchanging grace; in every high and stormy gale, my anchor holds within the veil. On Christ, the solid Rock, I stand: all other ground is sinking sand. (Edward Mote)

GRACE IN GALATIANS
Throughout this letter, Paul gives reasons why grace is of such importance. Here are four of his points.

1 Active before Paul was born
Paul says, "Even before I was born, God chose me and called me by his marvelous grace." God's grace was already at work before Paul was born, without his having done anything to deserve it (Gal. 1:15).

2 Faith in Christ is the key
"I live in this earthly body by trusting in the Son of God, who loved me and gave himself for me." The only thing that we need to do is trust in the finished work of Jesus; it is all by grace (Gal. 2:16–20).

3 Grace excludes our efforts
"I do not treat the grace of God as meaningless. For if keeping the law could make us right with God, then there was no need for Christ to die." Law refers to our efforts to earn God's favor (Gal. 2:21).

4 Grace leads to order
"God ... give you grace and peace." The word "and" can also be understood to mean "leading to." Grace then leads to peace, meaning the positive presence of God-given harmony and order (Gal 1:3).

> I do not treat the grace of God as meaningless. For if keeping the law could make us right with God, then there was no need for Christ to die (Gal. 2:21).

All the references to grace in Galatians: 1:3, 6, 15; 2:9, 21; 5:4; 6:18

> He is not righteous who does much, but he who, without work, believes much in Christ. The law says, "Do this," and it is never done. Grace says, "believe in this," and everything is already done. (Martin Luther)

Five Different Meanings of "the Law"

The term "law" has several different meanings in the Bible. To correctly understand each passage, we must know which meaning is being used. Here are the five different meanings of "the law."

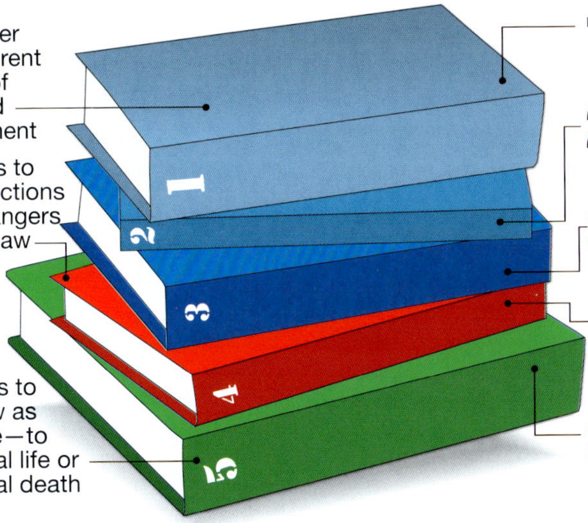

1 Ten Commandments of God
The law refers to the two tablets of stone that Moses received on Mount Sinai (Ex. 24:12).

2 All the laws that Moses received
The law refers to all the commandments and regulations God gave to the Israelite people (Josh. 1:8, 8:34).

3 Part of the Old Testament
The Law refers to the first five books of the Hebrew Scriptures: Genesis through Deuteronomy (Luke 24:44).

4 Deeds to show ourselves righteous
The law refers to deeds we do in order to prove ourselves righteous before God (Gal. 2:16).

5 A prevailing principle
The law refers to a prevailing principle, such as the law of gravity, a power (Rom. 8:2).

The Purpose of Law—to Be Our Educator

If the gospel is given to us by grace, why did God give the law? Paul tries to explain it by telling us about the role played in society by a particular type of slave—the guardian of children (Greek *paidagogos*, Gal. 3:24).

1 The law cannot give us life
Paul says that the law was never intended to be the path to God. "Is there a conflict, then, between God's law and God's promises? Absolutely not! If the law could give us new life, we could be made right with God by obeying it" (Gal. 3:21).

2 The law was our guardian
Instead, it should make us aware of our need for God's grace. "The law was our guardian until Christ came" (Gal. 3:24).

3 The law leads us to Christ
In Christ, we are declared righteous by faith, not by works. "Until we could be made right with God through faith" (Gal. 3:24).

4 The law has played out its role
The law has played out its role in the Christian's life. "Now that the way of faith has come, we no longer need the law as our guardian" (Gal. 3:25).

What is a guardian?
- Greek *paidagogos*, from which we get the word pedagogue. The word literally means "child leader."
- Refers to a slave who went with the children to school. Someone who took the children to the place of knowledge.
- The guardian is not the knowledge but the one who leads to knowledge. Nor is the law the knowledge of salvation, but it leads us to understand our need for true righteousness through Christ.

Grace, not law
Paul says: "I do not treat the grace of God as meaningless. For if keeping the law could make us right with God, then there was no need for Christ to die" (Gal. 2:21; 5:4).

Note: The law still reveals who God is, especially his holiness, and his standard for a holy life (Rom. 8:4).

Nine Aspects of the Fruit of the Spirit

Galatians contrasts the fruit of the Spirit with the sinful nature (Gal. 5:19–21). It refers to one fruit, not many different fruits. We are expected to show all nine aspects, not just the ones we choose.

1 Love (5:22; 1 John 2:10)
A self-giving love that looks out for the good of others. The foundation for the other aspects.

2 Joy (5:22; John 15:11)
A deep-rooted joy regardless of the circumstances. Jesus promises this joy to his followers.

3 Peace (5:22; John 14:27)
We are at peace with ourselves and with others. Another promise from Jesus.

4 Patience (5:22; Col. 1:11; 3:12)
Show generosity even if provoked by others. Not in a hurry but able to wait graciously.

5 Kindness (5:22; see Titus 3:4–5)
An ability to respond and to behave gently and with consideration toward others.

6 Goodness (5:22; Rom. 15:14)
An ability to act in ways that open the path to reaching others.

7 Faithfulness (5:22; 1 Cor. 4:17)
A desire to be considered trustworthy. Also trusting in God, despite difficulties.

8 Gentleness (5:23; Titus 3:2)
A willingness to show consideration for other people, as well as a willingness to humbly receive the Word.

9 Self-control (5:23; Acts 24:25)
Able to practice self-control, to not follow impulses or succumb to temptation.

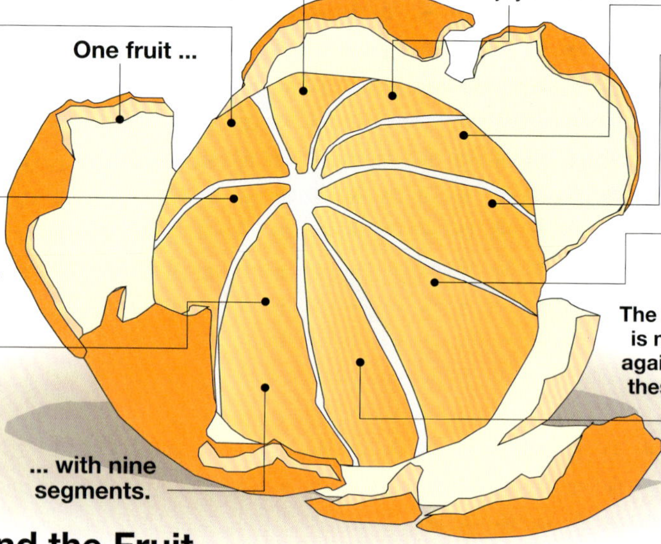

How to Understand the Fruit

1 It's about one fruit—not many
Fruit is in the singular, so there is one fruit, not many. It is a result of the work of the Spirit in the life of the believer.

2 Cannot select the qualities
The Spirit is one and his fruit is one. It is not a buffet where you can choose whatever you like.

3 Comes naturally
Fruit grows quite naturally on trees. It is a reflection of the tree's essential nature and its productive power.

4 Character, not behavior
It's about character more than actions. The fruit of the Spirit describes what our inner motivation should be.

5 Fruit ripens over time
Just as fruit ripens slowly, it takes time for the fruit of the Spirit to transform us. It does not occur overnight.

6 Fruit brings new life
As a fruit is meant for reproducing, the fruit of the Spirit should foster a life that cultivates growth in others.

IN CONTRAST TO THE FRUIT OF THE SPIRIT: The sinful nature is clear: **(1) Sexual sins:** sexual immorality, impurity, lustful pleasures; **(2) Religious sins:** idolatry, sorcery; **(3) Social sins:** hostility, quarreling, jealousy, outbursts of anger, selfish ambition, dissension, division, envy; **(4) Lack of self-control:** envy, drunkenness, wild parties, and other such sins. "Let me tell you again, as I have before, that anyone living that sort of life will not inherit the Kingdom of God" (Gal. 5:21).

To Bear or Not to Bear Burdens

"Share each other's burdens" (Gal. 6:2)

In Galatians 6:2, Paul says we should bear one another's burdens, but a few verses later he says we each should carry our own load (6:5). What's the deal?

1 Share each other's heavy burdens
"Share each other's burdens, and in this way obey the law of Christ" (6:2). Burden here literally means "weight." It refers to the heavy burdens that we are not able to carry on our own.

2 Carry your lighter burdens yourself
"Each one should carry their own load" (Gal. 6:5 NIV). The Greek word for "load," or "burden," is *phortion*. It is a pack, a military term referring to the battle pack every soldier normally wore. We should be able to carry these ourselves.

"Each one should carry their own load" (Gal. 6:5 NIV).

EPHESIANS

"Put on all of God's armor so that you will be able to stand firm against all strategies of the devil" (Eph. 6:11).

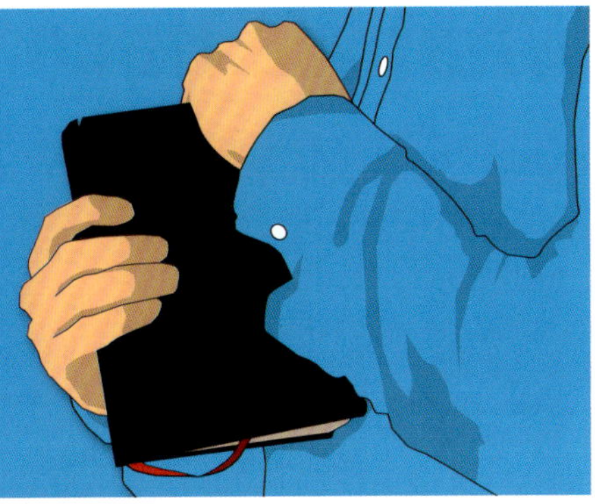

A FEW WORDS ABOUT THE AUTHOR

The letter states that Paul is the author (1:1; 3:1). Ephesians was written by him during his first imprisonment in Rome (Acts 28:16–31). It was probably written at the same time as the letter to the Colossians since the two letters have great similarities (compare Eph. 5:21–32 with Col. 3:18–25). The letter was probably delivered by Tychicus, a trusted companion, who is also mentioned in the letter (Col. 4:7; Eph. 6:21).

A FEW WORDS ABOUT THE RECIPIENTS

The letter may have been a circular letter to several churches in the area of Ephesus. The words "in Ephesus" are missing in some manuscripts (1:1). It also lacks personal greetings to anyone in Ephesus. Ephesians could possibly be the letter to Laodicea (Col. 4:16), or that the Ephesians also read the circular letter meant for a broader church audience. At the very least, this is a letter *also* written to the church in Ephesus.

A FEW WORDS ABOUT DATES

The letter was probably written during Paul's house arrest in Rome, sometime between AD 60 and 61 (Acts 28:30). The letter is one of four letters, along with Philippians, Colossians, and Philemon, collectively referred to as the prison letters. Many think that Ephesians was written in the middle of Paul's time under house arrest, as he does not indicate an imminent release or any foreseeable change in his circumstances.

THE WHOLE BOOK IN 25 WORDS

Paul writes about the church, what we possess in Christ, our walk with him, and our struggle against the devil, wearing the armor of God.

A SIMPLE STRUCTURE

1. Position – our standing in Christ
(Eph. 1:1–3:21)

2. Practice – our walk in the world
(Eph. 4:1–5:33)

3. Power – our struggle against evil
(Eph. 6:1–24)

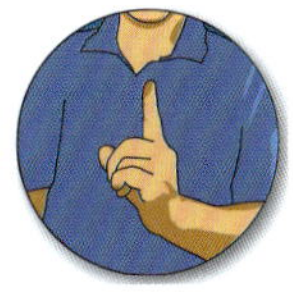

A FEW WORDS ABOUT KEY THEMES

- **What we have "in Christ"** —The letter is permeated with words about all we have in him (1:3–5, 7, 9, 11–13; 2:6, 7, 10, 13, 21; 3:6, 12; 4:32).
- **God's armor**—Paul tells us to "put on the whole armor of God." He talks about the belt, body armor, shoes, shield, helmet, and sword and what they represent (6:13–18).
- **The term "one another"**—The fellowship of the church is expressed in mutual love, service, and caring for one another (4:2, 25, 32; 5:19, 21).
- **Images of the church**—Nine images that help us understand the purpose and function of the church.
- **Paul's speech to the Ephesian elders**—Compare Ephesians with Paul's speech in Miletus (Acts 20:17–35). For example, Acts 20:19 with Eph. 4:2; Acts 20:27 with Eph. 1:11; Acts 20:32 with 3:20; and Acts 2:20 with Eph. 1:14, 18.

A FEW TIPS ON WHAT TO LOOK FOR

Theme of the book: Christ and the church

- The phrase "in Christ," what you have in Christ
- "In the heavenly realms/places" (5 times)
- What is taught about the Holy Spirit
- "Each other/one another" (6 times)
- Images of the church (9)
- The absence (!) of admonitions against heresy
- "Therefore" (at least 8 times)
- "Walk, walking" (7 times)
- The differences and similarities with Colossians

What We Have "in Christ"

The whole of Ephesians 1:3–14 is a single sentence in Greek.

Through Jesus's atonement we are seated "with Christ" in heaven (2:6). Paul uses the Greek expression, and similar ones, 27 times in Ephesians and we can find the expression up to 130 times in the New Testament.

WE ARE BLESSED

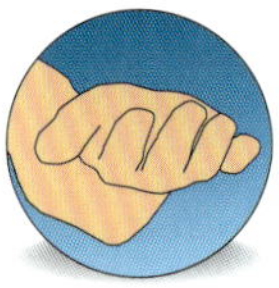

"God ... has blessed us with every spiritual blessing in the heavenly realms because we are united **with Christ"** (1:3). **Comments:** Introduces the section. Shows that we are blessed from before creation, so the blessing is spiritual.

WE ARE CHOSEN

"Even before he made the world, God loved us and chose us **in Christ** to be holy and without fault in his eyes" (1:4). **Comments:** The first blessing is our election. We were chosen from before the creation of the world and for a purpose.

WE ARE IN HIS FAMILY

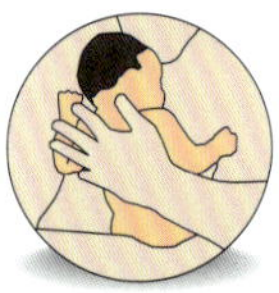

"God decided in advance to adopt us into his own family by bringing us to himself **through Jesus Christ**" (1:5). **Comments:** We are adopted into the family of God so we can praise God for his glorious grace (Rom. 8:15).

WE HAVE FREEDOM

"[God] purchased our freedom with the blood **of his Son**" (1:7a). **Comments:** We are freed from slavery to sin by the death of Jesus on the cross, which fully secured our eternal redemption and restored our relationship with God (see Rom. 8:21).

WE ARE FORGIVEN

"**[In Christ]** he forgave our sins. He has showered his kindness on us" (1:7b–10). **Comments:** The immediate result of our redemption is that God has forgiven our sins (see Rom. 8:1, 38). The believer is accepted eternally into the family of the redeemed.

WE HAVE AN INHERITANCE

"**[In Christ]** we have received an inheritance" (1:11–12). **Comments:** We were predestined, chosen in advance for this, by his will and eternal purpose, rooted in grace and love.

WE HAVE THE SPIRIT

"**[In Christ** he gave] the Holy Spirit ... God's guarantee" (1:13–14). **Comments:** The Spirit is a down payment guaranteeing our future inheritance. The Spirit is God's abiding presence, confirming our salvation and sealing us as his forever.

WE HAVE BEEN GIVEN LIFE

"**[In Christ]** he gave us life when he raised Christ from the dead" (2:4–5). **Comments:** Through his great love and undeserved kindness, we share in Christ's resurrection, being made alive in him. He is the source of our new life.

WE ARE RAISED FROM DEATH

"He raised us from the dead along **with Christ**" (2:6a). **Comments:** We have been raised to a new, different life with him (Rom. 6:4–5), empowered by his Spirit to walk in righteousness, transformed to reflect his holiness and purpose.

WE ARE SEATED IN HEAVEN

"[God has] seated us **with [Christ]** in the heavenly realms" (2:6b). **Comments:** Spiritually, we are seated in heaven (Phil. 3:20). The same power that raised Jesus is at work in us, granting us authority, identity, hope, and access to God's presence.

WE ARE HIS MASTERPIECE

"We are God's masterpiece. He has created us anew **in Christ Jesus**" (2:10). **Comments:** Not only is our salvation through grace, so is our ongoing spiritual growth. We are sustained and guided entirely by his divine grace.

WE ARE CITIZENS

"**Because of what Christ has done ...** [we] are citizens along with all of God's holy people" (2:18–19). **Comments:** We are counted among the saints. Through the Holy Spirit, we are no longer foreigners and strangers, but members of the family of God.

WE ARE SECURE IN GOD

"**Because of Christ** and our faith in him, we can now come boldly and confidently into God's presence" (3:12). **Comments:** Confidence allows us to come before God boldly, without hesitation, trusting in his love, mercy, and faithful acceptance.

WE HAVE INNER STRENGTH

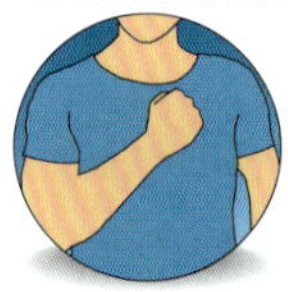

"I pray that from his glorious, unlimited resources **[Christ] will** empower you with inner strength through his Spirit" (3:16). **Comments:** Through Christ and the Spirit we receive inner spiritual power and strength.

WE HAVE RECEIVED LOVE

"Live a life filled with love, following the **example of Christ** ... [who] offered himself as a sacrifice for us" (5:1–2). **Comments:** We are challenged to imitate Christ. His love is the foundation for our love (compare Phil. 2:5).

WE HAVE LIGHT

"For once you were full of darkness, but now you have light **from the Lord**. So live as people of light!" (5:8). **Comments:** In Christ we have received light, righteousness, and insight. We are to be like Christ.

Nine Images of the Church

In Ephesians, Paul uses a number of images to describe the church. Each image reveals something of God's purpose for the church. Together, they provide a multifaceted picture of what God intends for his church.

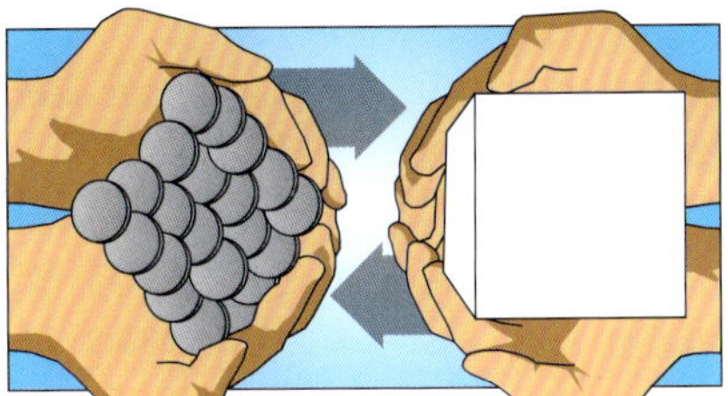

1 A purchased possession (1:14)

The Holy Spirit is a pledge, a down payment, something given in advance as a guarantee that full payment is coming. **Comments:** This inheritance is eternal life in heaven with God. Deliverance is about freedom from the presence of sin (as opposed to in 1:7, where it is about freedom from the guilt of sin). **Parallels:** Rom. 3:24; 8:23; Col. 1:14

2 A chosen group (1:22)

The church is a group of believers called together for a specific purpose (Acts 19:39). **Comments:** This emphasizes that the church is not merely an organization, building, or isolated individuals. It is a living community of people called by God, joined together in fellowship, seeking to discern and carry out God's will. **Parallels:** Eph. 5:23; Matt. 16:18

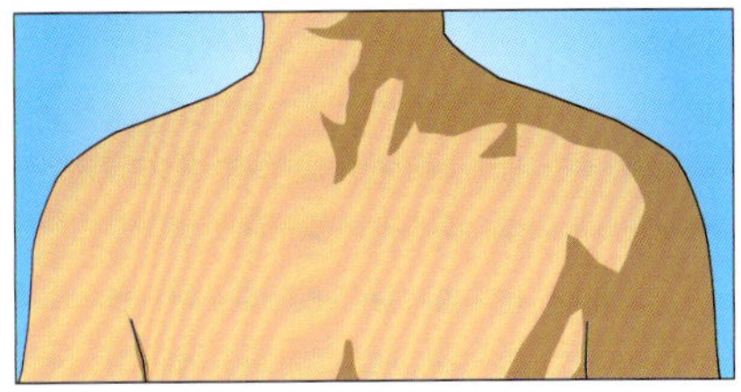

3 A perfect body (1:22–23)

The image of the body emphasizes our unity and togetherness. We are not individual believers, we all belong together. **Comments:** The image of the body speaks of each believer as a unique contribution to the whole, with Christ being the head and leader of the church. (5:23; 1 Cor. 12:14). **Parallels:** Eph. 4:4; 1 Cor. 12:12–27; Col. 1:18

4 A piece of workmanship (2:10)

A masterpiece demonstrates excellence and skill. This presents the church as a work of art shaped and perfected by God through Christ. **Comments:** We are the stuff, the raw material with which Christ works. As a carpenter works with a piece of wood, so Christ works with us, forming us into his masterpiece. **Parallels:** Rom. 1:20; Phil. 2:12–13

5 A new person, a new people (2:15)

The new person, a new people is about a new, changed nature, a better character in Jesus Christ. **Comments:** Emphasizes that salvation is not only the forgiveness of sins but also an inner change, a transformation of heart and mind that is the prerequisite for new life, renewed desires, and a restored relationship with God. **Parallel:** 2 Cor. 5:17

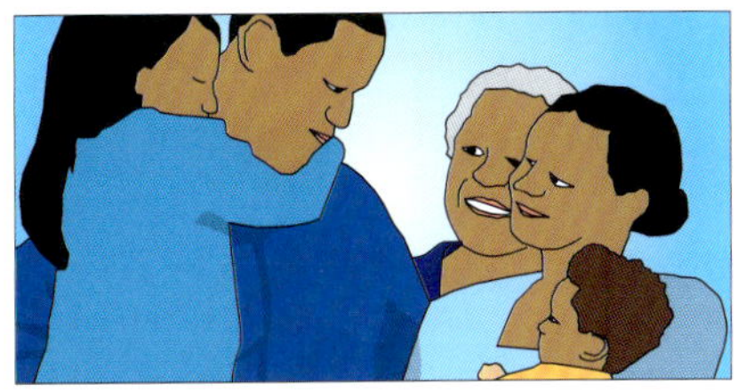

6 A family of God (2:19)

Family describes the close, personal relationship with God that salvation provides, like a child with its loving father. **Comments:** The clear teaching of the New Testament is that we are both born again and adopted into the family of God, also called the family of faith (Gal. 4:1–5; 1 Peter 1:23). **Parallels:** 1 John 3:1–2; Gal. 3:26; 6:10

7 His house, God's holy temple (2:20–22)

The apostles and prophets are the foundation of the church and Christ is its cornerstone. All believers are joined together to form a temple, a dwelling place of the Spirit (1 Peter 2:5). **Comments:** The temple is where God revealed his presence. Believers have now become his dwelling place. **Parallels:** 1 Cor. 3:16; 6:19; 2 Cor. 6:16

8 A bride (5:23–30)

Marriage as a symbol is used for Christ and the church. He is joined to his bride as a husband to his wife. **Comments:** The image beautifully emphasizes the ultimate identity and final destination of the church. The church is eternally united with Christ, belonging to him forever in perfect fellowship. **Parallels:** 2 Cor. 11:2; Rev. 19:7; 21:9

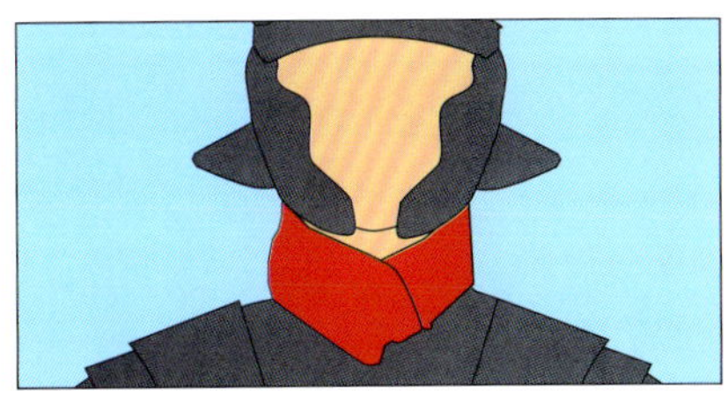

9 A solider with God´s armor (6:10–18)

The church is described as a soldier who stands against evil and defends truth and righteousness. **Comments:** Emphasizes the spiritual resources found in Christ. It is Christ who, through faith and the Spirit, equips the church with strength, spiritual armor, and unwavering courage to actively resist darkness (6:16–17). **Parallel:** 1 Thess. 5:8

The Whole Armor of God

Paul was under house arrest when he wrote this letter, guarded by soldiers (Eph. 6:20; Acts 28:23). Inspired by the their equipment, he urged the Ephesians to "put on all of God's armor" (Eph. 6:11). Paul describes six pieces of the armor, in the order in which the soldier would have put them on.

1 BELT OF TRUTH (6:14)
• The belt holds both the tunic and the scabbard in place.
• Here, truth refers not only to God's Word, his revealed truth, but also to living a life of truth and honesty.

2 BODY ARMOR OF GOD'S RIGHTEOUSNESS (6:14)
• The soldier's armor covered both his front and back.
• For protection against the enemy's attacks, it refers to both the individual's and Christ's righteousness (Isa. 59:17; 1 Thess. 5:8).

3 SHOES OF PREPAREDNESS (6:15)
• The soldiers wore sandals, usually with iron studs in the soles. • Can represent both standing firm in our faith and also our willingness to go out with the message.

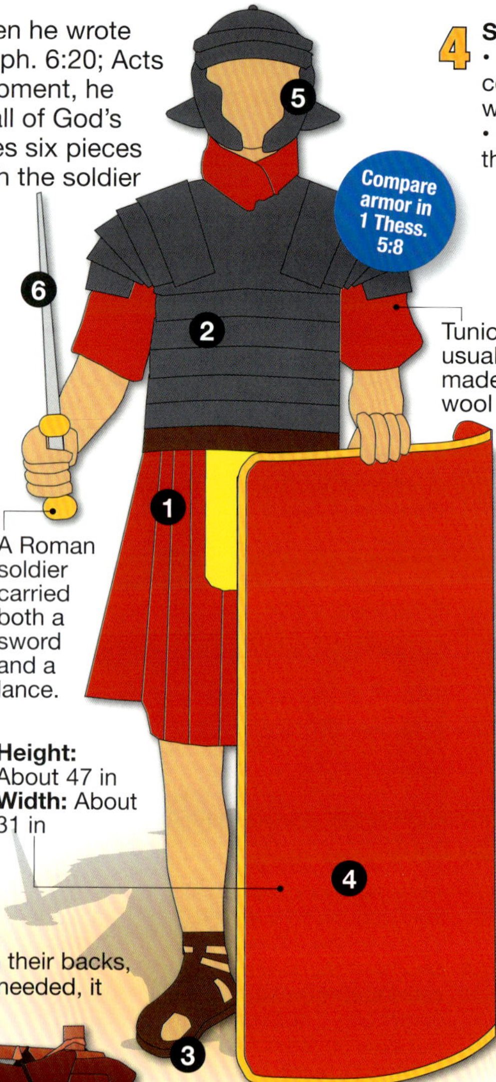

4 SHIELD OF FAITH (6:16)
• The shield was usually made of wood, covered with leather and soaked in water to extinguish burning arrows.
• Represents faith and trust in God and the application of God's Word in life.

5 HELMET OF SALVATION (6:17)
• The helmet protects the head (compare 1 Thess. 5:8). There were two types of helmets, one made of leather, the other of metal. The helmet had protection for the cheeks and for the neck. The main purpose of the helmet was to protect in close combat (Isa. 59:17).
• It is a matter of choice, of accepting and following Christ.

6 SWORD OF THE SPIRIT (6:17)
• The sword was about 1.5 feet long and double-edged (Heb. 4:12). • The sword is the only offensive weapon. It represents the Word of God and is to be understood as the application of God's principles in our lives.

The Soldier's Pack

Roman soldiers carried their pack on their backs, mounted on a T-shaped pole. When needed, it could be quickly dropped.

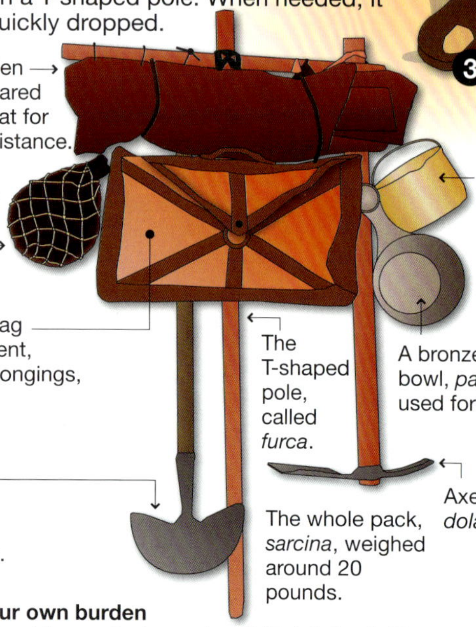

Carrying your own burden
"Each one should carry their own load" (Gal. 6:5 NIV). The text refers to the battle pack, the *sarcina*, that every soldier normally carried. Jesus said that his burden is light (Matt. 11:30). We are expected to take responsibility for the smaller, everyday burdens we have to carry.

Roman Military Terms

• **A legion (garrison)**—3,000–6,000 soldiers (Acts 21:31; Matt. 26:53; Mark 5:9 should be understood as "large numbers").
• **A cohort (guard unit)**—1/10 of a legion, about 600 soldiers (Acts 10:1).
• **A *centuria***—about 50–100 soldiers. Commander is called centurion, often translated "officer" (Mark 15:39; Luke 7:2).
• **The praetorium**—the headquarters of the governor and the place for his soldiers (Matt. 27:27; Mark 15:16; John 18:28, 33; 19:9; Phil. 1:13).

Nine Officers in the New Testament

1. **The officer whose servant was healed** (Matt. 8:5–13; Luke 7:2).
2. **The officer at the cross** (Matt. 27:54).
3. **Cornelius** (Acts 10:1–48).
4. **The commander who arrested Paul** (Acts 22:22–30).

5–7. Lysias and his two officers (Acts 23:16–18, 23–24).

8. The officer with Felix (Acts 24:22–27).

9. Julius on Paul's trip to Rome (Acts 27:1–44).

PHILIPPIANS

"Always be full of joy in the Lord. I say it again—rejoice! Let everyone see that you are considerate in all you do. Remember, the Lord is coming soon" (Phil. 4:4–5).

A FEW WORDS ABOUT THE AUTHOR

The letter was written by Paul toward the end of his first imprisonment in Rome (1:1, 13; 4:22). It is possible that Timothy was his scribe (1:1). Polycarp, a disciple of John, tells us that Paul wrote several letters to the church (see 3:1). Therefore, some think that Philippians is two or three of Paul's separate letters rolled into one. (For example, the break at 3:2 is abrupt.) More likely, it was written by Paul as a single letter.

A FEW WORDS ABOUT THE RECIPIENTS

The church in Philippi had been founded by Paul during his first visit to Macedonia (Acts 16:12–40). Philippi was a military colony in Macedonia, about a mile inland from the Aegean Sea. The letter is filled with the apostle's joy, both at the hope of imminent freedom and at the Philippians' concern for him, as shared by their messenger Epaphroditus, who probably delivered Paul's letter to Philippi (2:25–30).

A FEW WORDS ABOUT DATES

One of Paul's four prison letters (1:7, 17). Unlike the other three prison letters, there are several references to the hope of an imminent release from house arrest in Rome (1:25–26; 2:23–24). This makes it likely that the letter was written toward the end of his imprisonment, perhaps in late AD 61 or 62. Those who claim that the letter is compiled from different letters date the letter much later, but that is improbable.

THE WHOLE BOOK IN 25 WORDS

Paul's great challenge about the Christian life: Have the same mind as Jesus and rejoice in the Lord always. A key text about Jesus's incarnation.

A SIMPLE STRUCTURE

1. Encouragement – Our Confidence in Christ
(Phil. 1:1–26)

2. Example – Our Imitation of Christ
(Phil. 1:27–2:30)

3. Expectation – Our Hope in Christ
(Phil. 3:1–4:23)

A FEW WORDS ABOUT KEY THEMES

- **Joy in Christ**—Paul speaks of being glad and rejoicing in faith in Christ (1:4, 25–26; 2:2, 17–18, 28–29; 4:1, 18).
- **Jesus's incarnation**—What does it mean that he "gave himself up," Greek *kenosis*, literally "emptied himself" (2:5–11; John 1:1–3, 14)?
- **The Spirit**—supports the believer (1:19, 2:1, 3:3).
- **The use of the word "all"**—Paul is all-inclusive in his statements (1:1, 4, 7–8, 13, 18, 25; 2:9–11, 17, 21, 26; 4:5–6, 12, 21–22).
- **What to fix our thoughts on**—Paul's instruction for what to think about: anything that is true, worthy, right, pure, worth loving, appreciating, called virtue, and deserving of praise (4:8).
- **Military terms**—Philippi was a military city so the letter has a lot of military references (1:23, 27, 28; 2:25; 3:14, 21; 4:7).

A FEW TIPS ON WHAT TO LOOK FOR

Theme of the book:
Christ and joy

- "Joy, rejoicing" (at least 15 times)
- Thought, mind, spirit (10 times)
- Allusions to the military due to large military presence in the city
- The word "all" (18 times)
- "In Christ, in him, in the Lord" (18 times)
- The word "gospel" (9 times)
- Paul's personal tone
- Timothy, Epaphroditus, and Christ as examples
- What should we "think about"
- What we learn about Christ

Philippi in Paul's Day

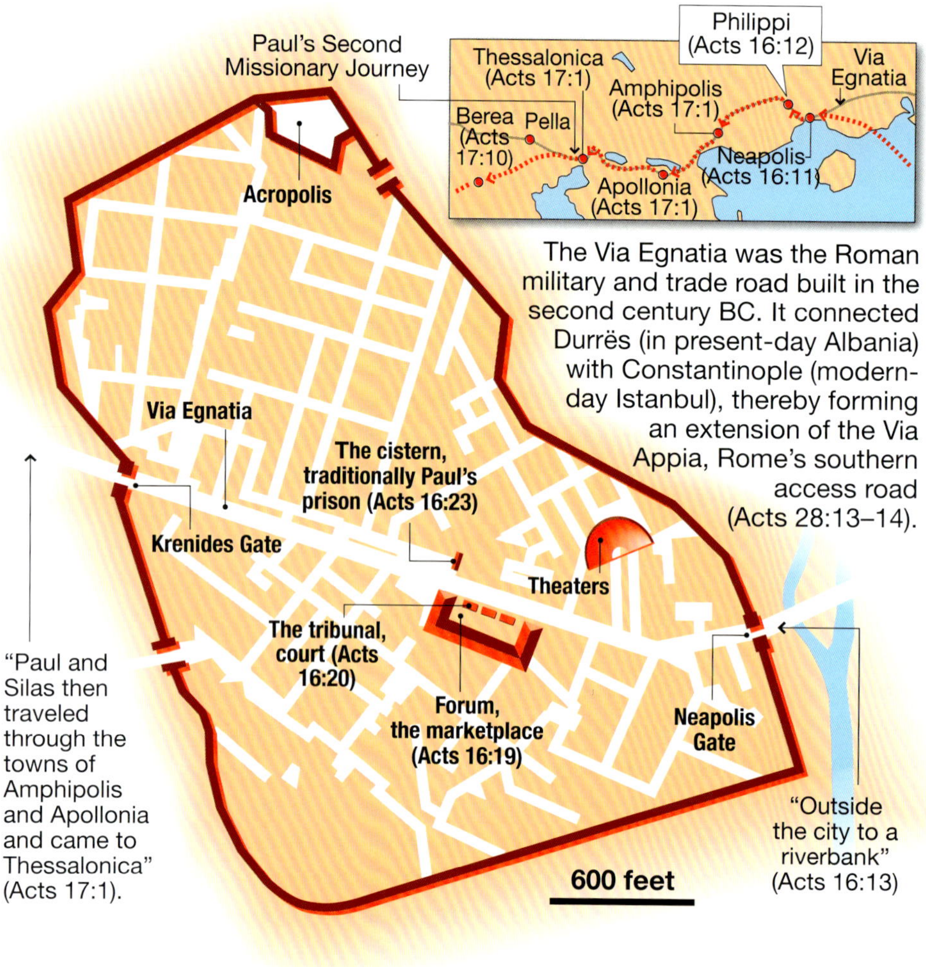

The Via Egnatia was the Roman military and trade road built in the second century BC. It connected Durrës (in present-day Albania) with Constantinople (modern-day Istanbul), thereby forming an extension of the Via Appia, Rome's southern access road (Acts 28:13–14).

PHILIPPI
A Roman colony, having special privileges for Romans (Acts 16:12). It was a military colony where many Roman soldiers settled after completing their service, shaping its culture and language. Sometimes called "little Rome," it mirrored the culture of the Roman Empire.

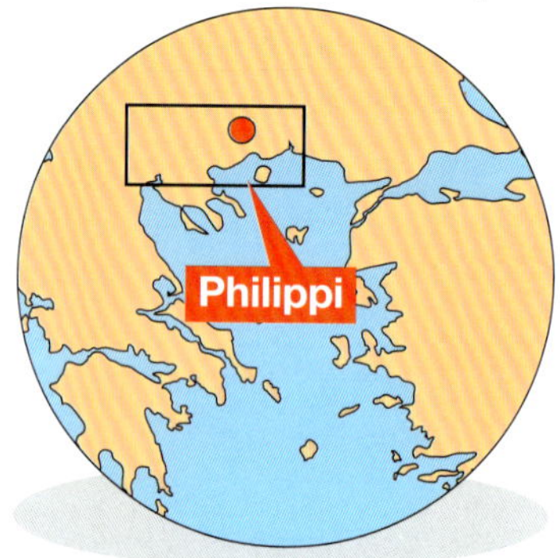

PAUL AT PHILIPPI
Paul came to the city on his second missionary journey and founded a church in the city (Acts 16:11–40). He returned twice on his third trip (Acts 20:1–6). Later, Paul wrote a letter to the church.

Some Military References

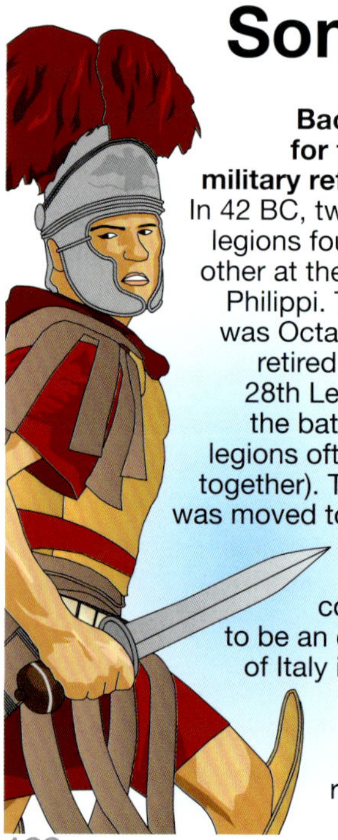

Background for the many military references: In 42 BC, two Roman legions fought each other at the Battle of Philippi. The victor was Octavian, who retired his entire 28th Legion after the battle (whole legions often retired together). The legion was moved to Philippi, a Roman colony, considered to be an extension of Italy itself. The soldiers received generous retirement benefits.

1 Departing the camp (Phil. 1:23)
Describes a military temporary camp where the troops are waiting to head out. Paul was ready to head out like a soldier.

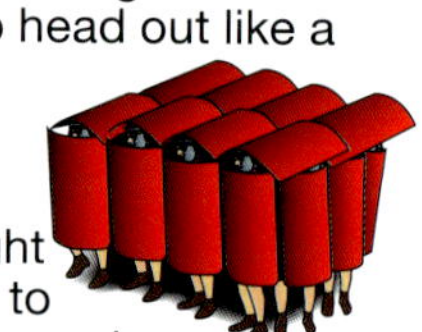

2 Standing firm (Phil. 1:27; 4:1)
The Roman army fought in formation, shoulder to shoulder. Standing firm and remaining in position is important.

3 Resisting intimidation (Phil. 1:28)
Used to describe a surprise attack. We are to resist the surprise attacks of the evil one, which can come like a military attack.

4 Sharing in fight (Phil. 2:25)
Fellow soldiers, two people serving in the same army. Epaphroditus joined Paul in the spiritual fight (compare Philem. 2).

5 Pressing on to the end (Phil. 3:14)
The words describe chariots in the arena—fighting hard to reach the finish line first and claim victory. A role model for us.

6 Subduing all through Jesus's power (Phil. 3:21)
The Roman army's goal was to subdue everything by military force. Jesus has the power to subdue everything and reign forever.

7 Guarding your hearts and minds (Phil. 4:7)
The Greek word *phroureo* ("guard") is a military term describing an armed soldier on sentry duty.

See also: Rom. 13:12; 1 Cor. 9:7; 2 Cor. 10:3–4; Eph. 6:10–18; 2 Tim. 2:3–4.

Doctrines and Heresies about Jesus

Over the centuries, many have tried to define what the Bible teaches about Jesus. In particular, they have wrestled with the question of the relationship between Jesus's divinity and his humanity.

An Interpretive Guide to the Person of Jesus

START HERE

Is Jesus both God and human?

- NO, HE IS ONLY GOD → NO → **Docetism** Jesus is God. He only appears to be human. (Embraced by Gnostics and Marcionites.)
- NO, HE IS ONLY HUMAN → **Is Jesus a human who became divine?**
  - NO → **Atheism** Jesus is not the Messiah. He is only human.
  - NO → **Ebionism** Jesus is the Messiah, but he is only human.
  - YES → **Adoptionism** Jesus is a human who was adopted as God's Son through baptism.
- YES, BOTH GOD AND HUMAN → KIND OF → **Sabellianism** Father, Son, and Spirit are the same person with different roles.
- YES → **Is Jesus of the same essence as the Father?**
  - NO → **Is Jesus like the Father in his essence?**
    - YES → **Homoiousia*** Jesus is like the Father but not fully divine.
    - NO → **Is Jesus unlike the Father in his essence?**
      - YES → **Heteroousia**** Jesus is unlike the Father and not fully divine.
  - YES (ESSENCE) → **1 Homoousia***** Jesus is of the same essence as the Father, fully divine.

In opposition to each other

Arianism
Teaches that Jesus is created, therefore not fully divine.

- YES → **Are Jesus's humanity and divinity united?**
  - NO → **Nestorianism** Jesus's divinity is separate from his humanity.
    - **Teaches that Jesus's humanity can act independently of his divinity.**
  - YES → **Does Jesus have both a human and a divine nature?**
    - NO → **Does Jesus have only a divine nature?**
      - YES → **Apollinarism** Jesus had a divine nature (soul) in a human body.
      - NO → **Does Jesus have a different kind of divine nature?**
        - YES → **Miaphysitism** Jesus is God and human. But his two natures are united in a single nature. They are united without confusion, separation or alteration.
        - NO → **Then what kind of divine nature does Jesus have?**
    - YES (NATURE) → **2 Dyophysitism** Jesus has two natures, human and divine.
      - YES → **Does Jesus have two distinct wills?**
        - NO → **Monothelitism** Jesus only has one will, which is divine.
        - YES (WILL) → **3 Dyothelitism** Jesus has two wills, one human and one divine (see Luke 22:42).

In opposition to each other

Monophysitism
Jesus only had one nature

Jesus's two natures are inseparably and indivisibly united without change or confusion.

Anti-Chalcedonianism

Chalcedonianism

Three Christological Creeds:
1. The Apostolic Creed (dating back to the first century AD).
2. The Nicene Creed (from AD 325/38).
3. The Athanasian Creed: *"there is one Person of the Father, another of the Son ... Such as the Father is, such is the Son"* (sixth century AD).

OUR KNOWLEDGE OF JESUS
Jesus is true God and true human, (1) of the same essence as the Father, (2) with a human nature and a divine nature, inseparably united, and (3) has two wills: one human and one divine. The human will is always subordinate to the divine will.

THE HYPOSTATIC UNION
Jesus's human and divine natures are united and cannot be separated. Jesus is true God and true human in all that he does.

*__Homoiousia__—God's Son is of a similar, but not identical essence as the Father. From *homoios* (similar) and *ousia* (substance).
**__Heteroousia__—God's Son is of a different, distinct essence from the Father. From *heteros* (different).
***__Homoousia__—God's Son is of the same essence as the Father. From *homos* (same).

COLOSSIANS

"God made you alive with Christ, for he forgave all our sins. He canceled the record of the charges against us and took it away by nailing it to the cross" (Col. 2:13–14).

A FEW WORDS ABOUT THE AUTHOR

In the introduction, Paul states that he is the author (1:1, 23). Colossians was written with the help of a scribe, probably Timothy (1:1; 4:18). The letter is closely connected with Paul's letter to Philemon, and the two were probably sent to Colossae at the same time (4:7–9). The letter also has similarities with Ephesians, as they share several themes and sections. They were probably written close together in time.

A FEW WORDS ABOUT THE RECIPIENTS

The letter was addressed to the church in Colossae, in present-day southwest Turkey (1:2). To our knowledge, Paul had not visited the city prior to writing the letter. The church was probably founded by Paul's faithful coworker, Epaphras. He visited Paul during his imprisonment in Rome, bringing news of the church (1:7–8). The letter seeks to encourage the believers in their faith in Christ and to protect them from false teachers.

A FEW WORDS ABOUT DATES

Paul wrote the letter during his imprisonment in Rome, likely sometime between AD 60 and 61 (4:3, 10, 18). It is frequently dated to the middle of Paul's imprisonment, since he does not mention that he has any hope of an imminent release. Because the letter seems to address Gnosticism, which spread at a later date, some believe that it was written near the end of the first century, but that is less likely.

THE WHOLE BOOK IN 25 WORDS

Heresies have ensnared the church. Paul opposes the heresies and offers a healthy alternative, exhorting the Colossians to be rooted in the faith, through teaching.

A SIMPLE STRUCTURE

1. Confession – Our Faith in Christ
(Col. 1:1–2:5)

2. Completeness – Our Fullness in Christ
(Col. 2:6–2:23)

3. Conduct – Our Life in Christ
(Col. 3:1–4:18)

A FEW WORDS ABOUT KEY THEMES

• **The deity of Christ**—He is the image of God (1:15), the creator of all things (1:15–17), he holds all things together (1:17), he is the head of the church (1:18), he bears all the fullness of God (1:19; 2:9), he is the reconciler (1:20), he gives the hope of glory (1:27; 2:2–10; 3:4).

• **Warning against heresies**—Paul warns against empty and treacherous philosophy based on human traditions and worldly powers (2:8, 16–18).

• **Secret/Mystery**—Refers to truths that were previously hidden but are now revealed by God (1:27; 2:2; 4:3).

• **The Christian life**—Paul gave a picture of life in Christ. Set your heart on what is above, your life is hidden with Christ in God (3:1–2, 3), therefore put away ungodliness (3:5–9). Whatever you do or say, do it through your new nature and in the name of Jesus (3:10–17).

A FEW TIPS ON WHAT TO LOOK FOR

Theme of the book: Christ and cosmos

- What is taught about Christ and his greatness
- Take note of all the exhortations (especially in chapter 3).
- Secret/mystery (4 times)
- Knowledge/wisdom
- The many similarities with Ephesians
- Its connection to the letter to Philemon
- Everyone/everywhere/every
- Being filled/fulfilling/fullness
- Similarity with other letters Paul wrote (Rom. 10:12; Gal. 3:28; Eph. 6:8)

The Shadows and the Reality

Legalism is linking God's blessings with our performance. Paul warns against clinging to Old Testament ceremonies and rituals in the false belief that these will bring about closeness with God, calling them shadows.

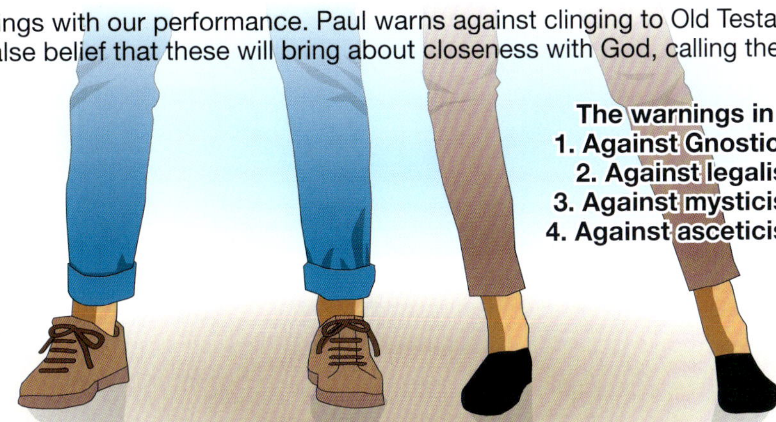

The warnings in Colossians:
1. Against Gnosticism (2:8–10)
2. Against legalism (2:11–17)
3. Against mysticism (2:18–19)
4. Against asceticism (2:20–23)

" So don't let anyone condemn you for what you eat or drink, or for not celebrating certain holy days or new moon ceremonies or Sabbaths. For these rules are only shadows of the reality yet to come. And Christ himself is that reality (Col. 2:16–17).

1 The shadow is just a picture
A "shadow" (Greek *skia*) is just the image that an object casts when illuminated. When you look at the object, the importance of looking at the shadow is gone.

2 The "reality" is Christ's body
The Greek word translated as "reality" means "body" (*soma*) (2:17). As a shadow is only an image of a body, so the ceremonies are only images of Christ.

3 Christ is the opposite of the shadow
The word "reality" indicates that Christ is the opposite of the shadow images. It emphasizes the clear contrast between Christ and the shadow.

4 The risk of legalism
The belief that observing ceremonies is necessary shows a failure to understand what Christ's work on the cross means. This can lead to legalism (Gal. 4:9–11; 5:1).

5 The law is a shadow image
The idea that the reality replaces the shadow is also the main theme of Hebrews: "The law of Moses was only a shadow" (Heb. 8:5–6; 10:1).

6 Don't be attached to the symbols
The warning not to be attached to symbols, shadow images, also applies to practices in the New Testament. No ritual can replace our relationship with Christ.

Similarities Between the "Twin Epistles"

There are clear parallels between Ephesians and Colossians. Several passages or verses are identical, while others deal with similar themes. Here is a summary of parallels between the two letters.

Similarities and...

- Both were written when Paul was in prison (Eph. 6:20; Col. 4:18).
- Tychicus delivered both of them to the churches (Eph. 6:21; Col. 4:7).
- Both emphasize wisdom, knowledge, and mystery.
- In both, the first section deals with doctrine and the second with application (Eph. 4:1; Col. 3:1).
- The letters share many identical or similar verses and passages.

... differences between the letters

- **Ephesians** emphasizes the church as the body of Christ, while **Colossians** emphasizes Christ as the head of the church.
- **Ephesians** is general and less personal, while **Colossians** is more local and more personal.
- **Ephesians** is calm and reasoning in tone, while **Colossians** is more argumentative in tone.
- **Ephesians** is reflective, attacking heresies indirectly. **Colossians** is confrontational, openly attacking heresies.
- **Ephesians** emphasizes Christ and the church, while **Colossians** emphasizes Christ and the cosmos.

WHY ARE THE LETTERS SIMILAR?
There are several explanations for the letters' similarities and differences.

1 Colossians was written first
Colossians was written first and served as the model for Ephesians. The two letters may have had different authors.

2 Ephesians was written first
Ephesians was written first and was the model for Colossians. Again, the two letters may have had different authors.

3 Both have a common model
Both letters were based on a common model, a letter from Paul that is now lost. The origin of both letters is questioned.

4 Paul wrote both close in time
Paul wrote both letters, probably around the same time. One was a circular letter, the other was to a specific audience. Most likely.

Heresies in the Early Church

The New Testament letters shed light on some of the heresies confronting the early church. Other heresies developed in later centuries, but we can see early traces of them in the New Testament.

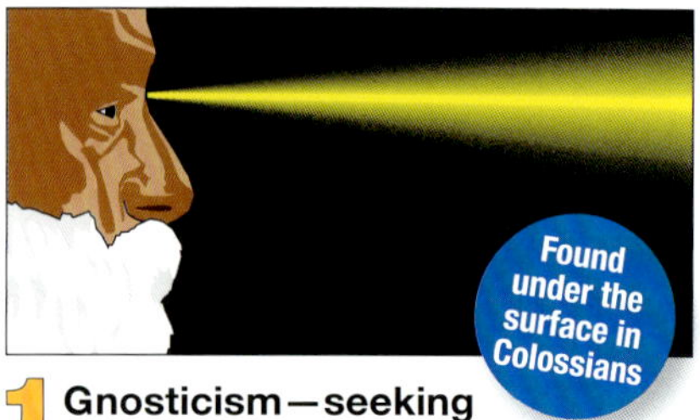

1 Gnosticism—seeking the secret knowledge

From the Greek *gnosis* meaning "knowledge," a hidden knowledge only available to a few. **Description:** A system of thought that despises the physical and exalts the spiritual. The goal is to achieve salvation through higher knowledge of cosmic forces. **Response:** "In [Christ] lie hidden all the treasures of wisdom and knowledge" (Col. 2:2–4).

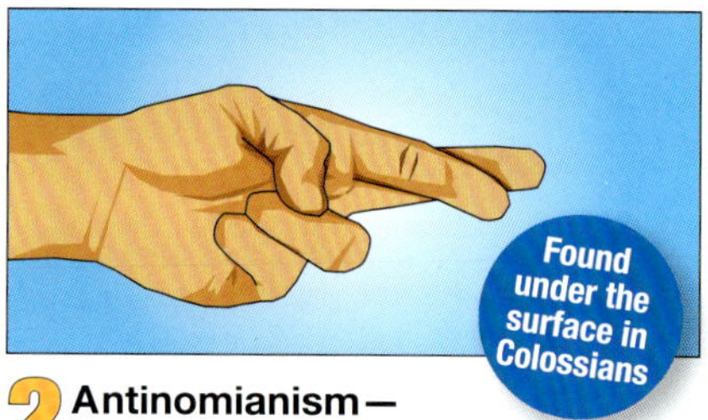

2 Antinomianism—ignoring God's law

Claims that there are no absolute moral values. **Description:** We all decide for ourselves what we think is right, this stems from gnostic thought. When the spiritual is seen as separate from the earthly, the earthly plays a lesser role. **Response:** "You have stripped off your old sinful nature and all its wicked deeds. Put on your new nature" (Col. 3:9–10; 1 Thess. 4:7–8).

3 Judaizing—become Jewish first, Christian second

Claims that all Christians must also become Jews. **Description:** One must become a Jew and follow all the Jewish rules in order to be saved by Jesus. Requires circumcision and observance of the Jewish dietary laws (Gal. 2:11–14). **Response:** "Don't let anyone condemn you for what you eat or drink ... Christ himself is that reality" (Col. 2:16–17; Acts 15:22–29).

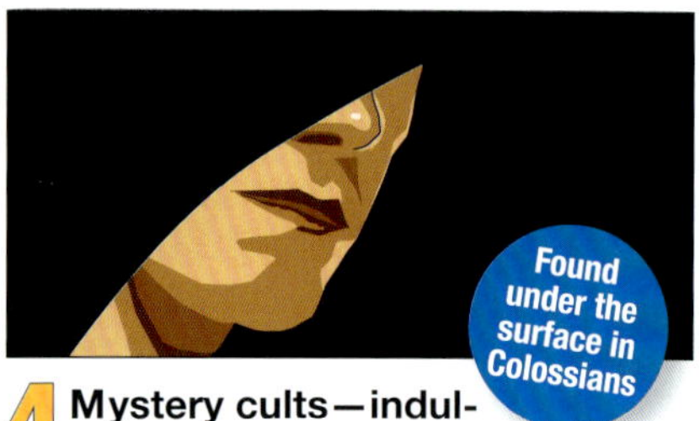

4 Mystery cults—indulging in mystical rituals

A form of religion with secret cultic elements only open to the initiated. **Description:** Gods and spiritual beings are worshiped through rites, sacrifices, and ecstatic elements. Usually borrows elements from other religions. The goal is to be united with the heavenly forces. **Response:** "Christ is the visible image of the invisible God" (Col. 1:15–16; 2:18–19).

5 Arianism—Jesus was created by the Father

Claims that the Son was created by the Father; denying the Trinity. **Description:** The Father is the only true God. The Son is not eternal. The Father gave birth to/created the Son after time began. The Son is not God in the same way as the Father, but the highest of all created beings. **Response:** "Christ ... existed before anything was created" (Col. 1:15–16).

6 Adoptionism—Jesus is not fully divine

Claims that Jesus was born human and later adopted by God as "Son" when Christ/the Spirit descended on him in the form of a dove at his baptism. **Description:** Denies that Jesus always existed. Jesus is not divine in the same way as the Father. **Response:** "Though he was God, he did not think of equality with God as something to cling to" (Phil. 2:6–7).

7 Pelagianism—we are born good, without sin

Claims that we are born without original sin and can achieve salvation by our own efforts. **Description:** Emphasizes free will. Our salvation ultimately depends on our own will. *Semipelagianism*: God's grace helps our free will. **Response:** "God saved you by his grace when you believed... it is a gift from God. Salvation is not a reward" (Eph. 2:8–9).

8 Docetism—Jesus's death was an illusion

Claims that both Jesus's physical body and the crucifixion were illusions. Jesus was a spirit so he could not die. **Description:** Grew out of Gnosticism. Jesus's body was not real. The goal is to be united with God on a spiritual level. **Response:** "If a person claiming ... that Jesus Christ came in a real body, that person has the Spirit of God" (1 John 4:2; 2:22–23; 2 John 1:7).

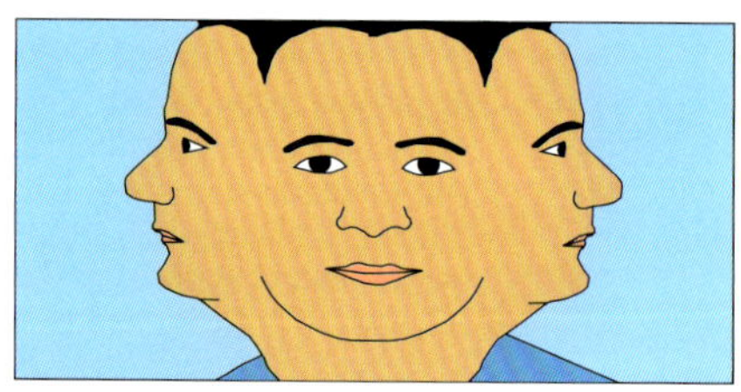

9 Modalism—God is one, and only one person

Claims that God is one person, denying the co-existence of the three persons of the Trinity. **Description:** Claims that God reveals himself in three different ways, or modes: Father, Son, and Spirit—the way ice, water, and steam are different modes of the same thing. **Response:** "I [Jesus] will do what the Father requires of me" (John 14:31; Luke 22:42; Titus 2:13).

FIRST THESSALONIANS

"You know quite well that the day of the Lord's return will come unexpectedly, like a thief in the night ... And there will be no escape" (1 Thess. 5:2–3).

A FEW WORDS ABOUT THE AUTHOR

The introduction states that Paul is the author of the letter (1:1; 2:18). Silas may have been his scribe (1:1). (The "we" in 1:1 cannot refer to Timothy, see 3:1–2). Few question Paul's authorship of the letter but some argue that several short passages have been inserted into the original text (such as 2:13–16). But there is no textual support for the theory and the suggestion has not gained general acceptance.

A FEW WORDS ABOUT THE RECIPIENTS

The letter was written to the church in Thessalonica. Paul founded the church during his second missionary journey but was forced to flee the city after a riot (Acts 17:1–14). Timothy came to Paul in Corinth with good news about the church's faith and love (1:3). Paul wrote the letter to encourage the church (1:3–10), to resolve confusion concerning Jesus's return (4:13–18), and to defend himself against slander (2:9–10).

A FEW WORDS ABOUT DATES

Paul arrived in Corinth after fleeing Thessalonica. Timothy joined him later him, bringing news of the situation in Thessalonica (3:6; Acts 18:5). Paul wrote the letter from Corinth. His time in Corinth can be dated by archaeological finds confirming that Gallio was governor there in AD 51–52 (Acts 18:12–17). The letter must therefore have been written in AD 51 or early 52, making it Paul's second oldest preserved letter, after Galatians.

THE WHOLE BOOK IN 25 WORDS

To a young church under persecution. Paul seeks to clarify misunderstandings and show that Jesus's return is the basis for hope and comfort in suffering.

A SIMPLE STRUCTURE

1. Thanks – Gratitude for Faith
(1 Thess. 1:1–10)

2. Teaching – Growth in Holiness
(1 Thess. 2:1–3:13)

3. Truth – Hope in Christ's Return
(1 Thess. 4:1–5:28)

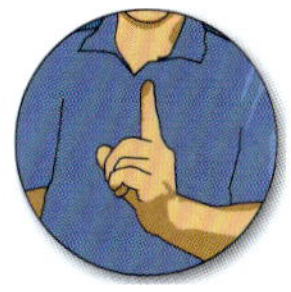

A FEW WORDS ABOUT KEY THEMES

- **The return of Christ**—Each chapter ends with a reference to the hope of Jesus's imminent return (1:10; 2:19; 3:13; 4:15–18; 5:23). The comfort of the thought of his coming is particularly emphasized (4:18).
- **Living as a Christian**—The Thessalonians were examples. They had become followers of Christ (1:6), received the Word (1:6), found joy in the Holy Spirit (1:6), became examples to others (1:7), turned away from idols (1:9), served the true God (1:9), and waited for the return of Jesus (1:10).
- **Testing of prophecy**—Prophetic speech is to be tested and we should only hold on to what is good (5:20–21).
- **Spirit, soul, and body**—The only verse that uses these three together (5:23). The verse is found in a greeting and should not be seen as the basis for a biblical view of humans.

A FEW TIPS ON WHAT TO LOOK FOR

Theme of the book:
The comfort of Jesus's return

- The return of Jesus, in all five chapters
- What is said about the Spirit
- Their love for one another (4:9–10)
- What is said about Paul's character and methods
- Accusations against Paul
- Faith, hope, and love
- Compare "like a mother" and "like a father" (2:7b–8, 11–12)
- Good things Paul commends them for (13 different)
- His appeals to practical action (5:1–28)

What Happens When Jesus Returns?

Paul consistently ends each chapter in 1 Thessalonians by pointing to the return of the Lord and the coming end times.

1 Role models
They were an example to all believers in the area, awaiting the Son of God from heaven (1 Thess. 1:7, 10).

2 Before the Lord
Paul considers them his hope, joy, and reward when he will stand before the Lord Jesus at his coming (1 Thess. 2:19

3 Spotless in holiness
The Lord will strengthen their hearts, so that they will be blameless before him at Jesus's return (1 Thess. 3:13).

4 Comforting the worried
Paul tells them to comfort one another with the firm hope of meeting the Lord and being with Him forever (1 Thess. 4:17).

5 Kept blameless
Paul prays that God's peace will make them holy, preserving them in spirit, soul, and body until Jesus's return (1 Thess. 5:23).

Seven things that will happen at Jesus's return

1 Initial signs
The first signs of the Lord's return: "With a commanding shout, with the voice of the archangel, and with the trumpet call" (1 Thess. 4:16).

2 Down from heaven
At the beginning of the second coming, Jesus will descend from heaven: "The Lord himself will come down from heaven" (1 Thess. 4:16).

3 The dead will rise
The first thing to happen when Jesus returns is the raising of the dead: "First, the believers who have died will rise from their graves" (1 Thess. 4:16).

4 Caught in the clouds
After the dead are raised, those still alive will be caught up with them: "We who are still alive ... will be caught up in the clouds" (1 Thess. 4:17).

5 Meet the Lord
Those who have risen and those still alive will meet the Lord in the clouds: "Together with them ... to meet the Lord in the air" (1 Thess. 4:17).

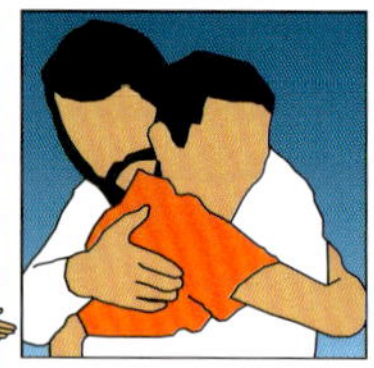

6 How to be together
We have the assurance that after we meet the Lord in the clouds, we will always be with him: "Then we will be with the Lord forever" (1 Thess. 4:17).

7 Words of comfort
The idea that we will all meet the Lord together is a word of comfort: "So encourage each other with these words" (1 Thess. 4:18).

Three themes that Paul highlights

1 Acts of faith
The root word means faith, trust, confidence, or fidelity. **EXAMPLE:** 1) The word of the Lord rang out everywhere their **faith** in God had become known (1:8). 2) They received the word of God and the word was effective in those who **believed** (2:13). 3) They were invited to put on the armor of **faith** (5:8; Eph. 6:16). **OTHER TEXTS:** 1:3, 8; 2:13; 3:2, 57, 10; 5:8

2 Perseverance in hope
The root word means hope, expectation, even confidence rooted in God's future promises. **EXAMPLE:** 1) The believers in the church gave Paul **hope** for the return of Jesus (2:19). 2) The believer has **hope** in light of Jesus's return (4:13). 3) They were invited to put on the **hope** of salvation as a helmet (5:8; Eph. 6:17). **OTHER TEXTS:** 1:3; 2:19; 4:13; 5:8

3 Working in love (1 Thess. 1:3)
The root word means love, benevolence, good will, esteem. **EXAMPLE:** 1) They were to grow and abound in **love** for one another and for all (3:12). 2) Told to show even more **love** for the believers than they had been (4:9–10). 3) They were told to put on **love** as armor (5:8, not mentioned in Eph. 6). **OTHER TEXTS:** 1:3; 2:7; 3:6,12; 4:9 (sibling love),10; 5:8, 13

Three Approaches to the End Times

First Thessalonians 4 says that when Jesus returns, he will come down from heaven and believers will meet him in the clouds. But when does that happen? And how does it fit into God's overall plan? There are three primary views.

THE ORDER OF COMING EVENTS

The Resurrection of Jesus
Luke 24

The Church Age
Acts 2 onward

We are currently here

The Return of Jesus
1 Thess. 4:16–17

The Final Judgment
Rev. 20:11–15

Eternity
Rev. 21–22

Premillennialism

Pre means "before," *millennium* means thousand and refers to the millennium. Jesus will return before the millennium.

The Church

Views on the rapture*
(1 Thess. 4:15–17)
Seen as a separate event during a seven-year period before the millennium. Jesus gathers the believers.
Four views on when the rapture occurs:
1) In the beginning of ...
2) In the middle of ...
3) At the end of ...
4) In several steps during ...
... the seven years.

Return of Jesus (before the millennium)

The Millennial Kingdom

Judgment

New heaven and new earth

Postmillennialism

Post means "after," millennium means *thousand* and refers to the millennium. Jesus will return after the millennium.

The Church

The Millennial Kingdom

Return of Jesus (after the millennium)

Judgment

New heaven and new earth

Amillennialism**

A means "not," *millennium* means thousand and refers to the millennium. Sees the millennium as a symbol of the church age.

The Church—the millennium is now

What is "the millennium"?
The term refers to "a thousand years" in Rev. 20:4. The views differ in how they interpret it, and not all understand it to be a literal one thousand years.

Return of Jesus (after the millennium)

The view of the rapture (1 Thess. 4:15–17)
Seen as the prelude to Jesus's return to earth at the end of time. Believers will meet the Lord in the clouds and immediately return to earth to join him in judging the nations and to be with him forever.

Judgment

New heaven and new earth

** Historical premillennialism does not speak of a period of seven years associated with the return of Jesus. The righteous arise before the millennium, the unrighteous arise and are judged after.*

*** Proponents point out that the term is not accurate, because amillennialists do believe in the millennium; they don't, however, believe it is a literal thousand years. Other terms suggested are nuncmillennialism (where nunc means "now") or inaugurated millennialism (where "inaugurated" means "started").*

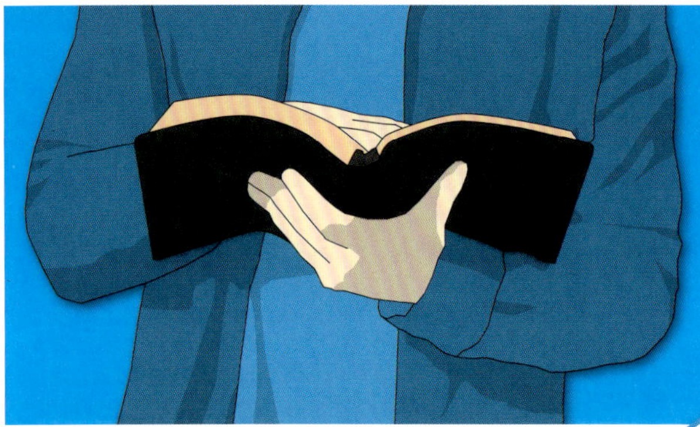

SECOND THESSALONIANS

"Don't be so easily shaken or alarmed by those who say that the day of the Lord has already begun" (2 Thess. 2:2).

A FEW WORDS ABOUT THE AUTHOR

Written by the apostle Paul who was assisted by a scribe, probably Silas (1:1; 3:17). The book deals with the same theme as found in 1 Thessalonians, the return of Jesus. Some argue that there are differences in theology and vocabulary between the two letters. Because of this, they believe that the second letter must have been written later by someone who was using Paul's name. That suggestion is not likely.

A FEW WORDS ABOUT THE RECIPIENTS

The letter was written to the church in Thessalonica. Paul had received information that they misunderstood the doctrine of Jesus's return. This had alarmed them to the extent that some had quit working because they believed Jesus would return momentarily (2:2; 3:6, 11). Paul admonished the believers, telling the idle to get back to work. He also tried to correct their misconceptions about the return of Jesus.

A FEW WORDS ABOUT DATES

Paul most likely wrote 2 Thessalonians within a few months of writing his first letter to the church, during the time when he was still in Corinth. Archaeologists have found an inscription in Delphi that gives a firm date for Gallio's time as governor of Corinth of AD 51–52 (Acts 18:12–17). This allows us to accurately date the writing of 2 Thessalonians to late AD 51 or 52. Proposals for a later dating are based on speculation.

THE WHOLE BOOK IN 25 WORDS

Paul learns that the teachings about Jesus's return are now out of control among the Thessalonians. He warns them against false teaching and irresponsible living.

A SIMPLE STRUCTURE

1. Strength – Suffering shows steadfastness
(2 Thess. 1:1–12)

2. Steadfastness – Stand against deception
(2 Thess. 2:1–17)

3. Separation – Shun the disobedient
(2 Thess. 3:1–18)

A FEW WORDS ABOUT KEY THEMES

- **Healthy view of Jesus's return**—Don't lose heart and don't be intimidated. The day of the Lord is not yet here (2:2). First the apostasy will come, the man of lawlessness will appear (2:3). But Jesus will triumph in the end (2:8).
- **Paul's four prayers**—This short letter contains four prayers (1:11–12; 2:16; 3:3–5; 3:16). Paul asks for prayer for himself (3:1). Also includes examples of thanksgiving (1:3; 2:13–14).
- **Perseverance**—Endure and persevere despite difficulties. Do not tire of doing good (1:4; 3:5, 13).
- **Work ethic**—Work hard and with diligence (3:6–12).
- **Compare the two letters to the Thessalonians**—The first letter emphasizes the comfort of Jesus's return for believers (1 Thess. 4:18). The second emphasizes the judgment of unbelievers at Jesus's return (1:6–7).

A FEW TIPS ON WHAT TO LOOK FOR

Theme of the book: Waiting for the return of Jesus

- What Paul says about the day of the Lord and the lawless one
- What Paul teaches about the return of Jesus, and what must happen first
- What Paul teaches about Jesus
- Four prayers (1:11–12; 2:16; 3:3–5, 16)
- The importance of doctrine (2:15) and which doctrines are mentioned
- What do the Thessalonians do well? What can you learn?
- Paul's exhortations to the believers in Thessalonica

What Misled the Thessalonians?

ANTICHRIST

A godless person, who spreads heresies and misuses God's name, a deceiver who is expected to come in the future (1 John 2:18; 2:22; 4:3; 2 John 1:7).

Other texts: 1 Cor. 15:22–58; 1 Thess. 4:13–5:11

• What was it that led the Thessalonians to believe "that the day of the Lord has already begun" (2 Thess. 2:2)?
• What is Paul's argument that this simply can't be true?

1 The persecution was birth pains
One possibility, they believed that the persecution they suffered were "a pregnant woman's labor pains" (1 Thess. 5:3).

2 Jesus had already returned
They were told that Jesus had already come back and that his kingdom was being establishing somewhere on earth (2 Thess. 2:2).

3 The rapture had occurred
They may have thought that some kind of rapture had already taken place and they had been left behind (1 Thess. 4:15–17).

4 Jesus's mystical return
They had been led to believe Jesus had already returned, but in a mystical way. Perhaps he was embodied in the visible church?

5 Day of the Lord was happening
They had come to believe that the day of the Lord did not require the return of Jesus. It could be realized by living out their faith (1 Cor. 4:8).

What needs to happen first? (2 Thess. 2:3–7)

1 The rebellion must come (2:3a)
• Apostasy, rebellion, revolt (Acts 21:21); an anti-Christian rebellion • The Greek word *apostasis* (apostasy) can also be interpreted as "being moved away."

2 The man of lawlessness (2:3b)
• Refers to the Antichrist (1 John 2:18; Dan. 7:23–26; Rev. 13:11–15). He must first appear. The Antichrist becomes a central character in world history.

3 One who holds back (2:7)
Someone or something that prevents the Antichrist from coming forward. There are many suggestions about what this is; law and order, the church.

Paul or not Paul?

Did Paul write 2 Thessalonians?

Second Thessalonians is one of the letters in the New Testament whose authorship is questioned. Critics argue that although the letter states that Paul is the author, there is reason to believe that the book is a pseudepigrapha, that is, a book written later but put into the mouth of a previously known person—in this case Paul. The arguments for and against the various positions can be summarized as follows.

	Paul wrote the letter	Paul did not write the letter
The claim	The introduction explicitly states that Paul is the author of the letter (1:1).	The writer of the letter has invoked Paul's name to gain authority and trust in the letter.
The view of church history	There was widespread agreement until the nineteenth century that Paul was the author. The letter was included in early Christian writings: the Muratorian Canon, writings by Marcion, and some early church fathers considered it genuine.	Textual research has developed over the centuries and we now have a better understanding of how to analyze the text. With the development of the "New Perspective on Paul," the discussion on authorship has gained new momentum.
Identical material	About one-third of the letter is very similar to 1 Thessalonians. The similarities between the letters suggest that it has the same author.	The fact that so much of the letter is similar to 1 Thessalonians may indicate that the writer of the letter has copied from Paul's earlier letter.
Different tone in the letters	The difference in tone between the letters is due to the situation in Thessalonica. The church had "lost its way" between the writing of the two letters (2:2).	The difference in tone between the letters indicates different authors. Paul is warm and gracious, while the author of the second letter is more demanding.
Different linguistic style in the letters	The distinct writing styles is not problematic and may be due to the different reasons for the letters. It could also be that Paul used different scribes. As both letters are short, there is not a lot of material with which to make far-reaching conclusions.	Although the letters are said to have been written close together in time, they have significantly different writing styles. This indicates that the two letters were written by two different authors, and probably farther apart in time.
Changed theological emphasis	The difference in emphasis points to the issues Paul addressed. In the first letter, he addressed the question of what happens to those who die. In the second letter, he addressed the problem of believers who were ignoring their responsibilities.	The theological differences point to two different authors. The first letter speaks of the day of the Lord being near (1 Thess. 5:2); the second speaks of the day of the Lord being delayed (2 Thess. 2:3). The difference points to different ways of thinking.

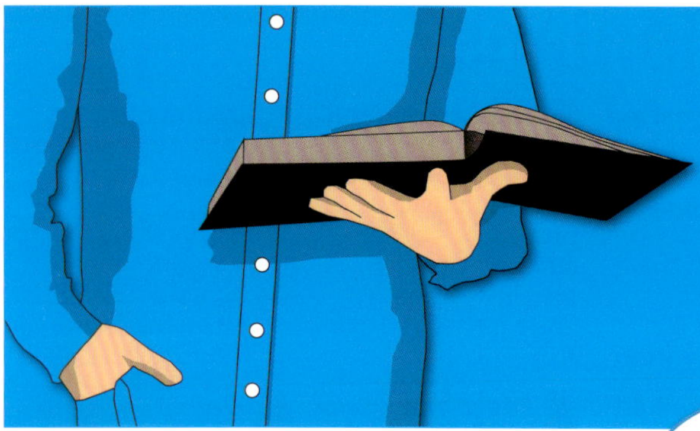

FIRST TIMOTHY

"Physical training is good, but training for godliness is much better, promising benefits in this life and in the life to come" (1 Tim. 4:8).

A FEW WORDS ABOUT THE AUTHOR

The letter was written by Paul, probably from Macedonia (1:1, 3). Early church fathers, such as Irenaeus and Polycarp, quoted from it. Some claim that the letter was written later under a false name. They argue that, among other things, the description of the church is too developed and that the vocabulary differs from Paul's other letters. However, these arguments are not convincing and can be explained by reasons for the letter.

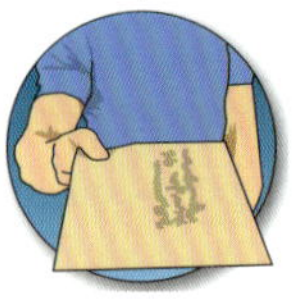

A FEW WORDS ABOUT THE RECIPIENT

The letter was written to Timothy, "my true son in the faith" (1:2). He was close to Paul and a leader in the church at Ephesus, which had previously served as Paul's base of ministry (1:3; Acts 16:1; 19:10; Phil. 2:19–20). Paul gives the young church leader encouragement and detailed instructions on preaching and church organization (4:12). This letter is one of what are known as the Pastoral Letters.

A FEW WORDS ABOUT DATES

The letter (see 1:3) cannot be harmonized with Paul's travels as described in Acts. This suggests that the letter was written after Paul was released from house arrest in Rome (Acts 28:30). As a result, we can date it to between AD 62 and Paul's imprisonment around AD 66. It is widely believed that Paul wrote this letter to Timothy during the first half of that time period, perhaps between AD 62 and 64.

THE WHOLE BOOK IN 25 WORDS

A manual that gives instructions on doctrine and life in the church, especially the requirement for leaders. Challenging texts about contentment and a quiet life.

A SIMPLE STRUCTURE

1. Foundation – Our Faith in Christ
(1 Tim. 1:1–1:20)

2. Formation – Our Function in Christ
(1 Tim. 2:1–3:16)

3. Faithfulness – Our Focus in Christ
(1 Tim. 4:1–6:21)

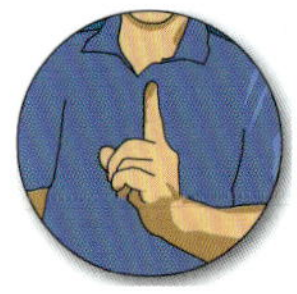

A FEW WORDS ABOUT KEY THEMES

- **Church leadership**—Paul lists fifteen criteria for evaluating leaders in the church (3:2–7). His letter to Titus includes a similar list with five additional criteria (Titus 1:6–9).
- **Sound teaching**—An emphasis on sound doctrine (1:10; 4:1, 6, 13, 16; 5:17; 6:1, 3). The subject is explored further in 2 Timothy and Titus.
- **Faith**—Uses concepts such as genuine faith, drawing nourishment from faith, striving for faith, and fighting the good fight of faith (1:5, 18–19; 3:9; 4:6, 12; 6:11–12).
- **Contentment**—Godliness combined with contentment is indeed a great gain (6:6–10). The love of money is the root of all kinds of evil. We should be content if we have food and clothing.
- **Godliness**—Gives a glimpse into the secret of godliness (2:2, 10; 3:16; 4:7–8; 6:3, 5–6, 11).

A FEW TIPS ON WHAT TO LOOK FOR

Theme of the book: Leadership in the church

- The word "godliness" (8 times)
- Teaching (8 times), sound doctrine, the importance of doctrine
- Criteria for elders and deacons
- What is good (20 times)
- Five exhortations to Timothy (1:18–19; 3:15; 4:11–16; 5:21–23; 6:20)
- A trustworthy saying (3 times)
- What the letter teaches about the Father and Christ
- The misconceptions Timothy was instructed to avoid

An Overview of Timothy's Life

> I have no one else like Timothy, who genuinely cares about your welfare. All the others care only for themselves and not for what matters to Jesus Christ... Like a son with his father, he has served with me in preaching the Good News (Phil. 2:20–22).

Seven challenges for Timothy's ministry

1 Preach the Word
"Preach the word of God. Be prepared, whether the time is favorable or not ... encourage with good teaching" (2 Tim. 4:2).

2 Don't be ashamed of the gospel
"Never be ashamed to tell others about our Lord" (2 Tim. 1:8).

3 Hold fast to the doctrine
"You must remain faithful to the things you have been taught. You know they are true" (2 Tim. 3:14).

4 Preach the resurrection
"Always remember that Jesus Christ ... was raised from the dead. This is the Good News" (2 Tim. 2:8).

5 Follow Paul's example
"Hold on to the pattern of wholesome teaching you learned from me—a pattern shaped by the faith and love that you have in Christ Jesus" (2 Tim. 1:13). "You, Timothy, certainly know what I teach, and how I live" (2 Tim. 3:10).

6 Don't limit the gospel
"The word of God cannot be chained" (2 Tim. 2:9).

7 Work hard, be faithful
"Be a good worker ... who correctly explains the word of truth" (2 Tim. 2:15).

	Preparation	Meeting	Disciple	Maturity	Responsibility	Service	Successor
KEY POINTS	• Born to Eunice • Had a Greek father • Taught by grandmother Lois	• Paul visited Lystra • Maybe met Paul on first visit • Maybe saw Paul being stoned	• Joined Paul • Traveled with Paul • Carried out missions for Paul	• More travels with Paul • Sent to Corinth • Then sent to Ephesus	• Perils during sea voyage • With Paul in Rome • Wrote letters with Paul	• Moved to Ephesus • First letter from Paul • Second letter from Paul	• Imprisoned for his faith • Faithful servant in Ephesus • Died for the faith
TOPICS	Raised by mother and grandmother (2 Tim. 1:5)	Timothy met Paul in Lystra (?) (Acts. 14:8–20)	Timothy was chosen by Paul (Acts. 16:3)	Timothy was sent on a mission (1 Thess. 3:1–2)	Timothy with Paul in prison (Phil. 1:1,7)	Timothy traveled to a final meeting (2 Tim. 4:13, 21)	Timothy imprisoned for his faith (Heb. 13:23)
	God took care of young Timothy (2 Tim. 3:15)	God prepared him for future service (Acts. 16:1–2)	God appointed a companion for Paul (Acts. 16:3)	God used Timothy in his service (Acts. 17:14–15)	God used Timothy for comfort (Phil. 2:19–20)	God prepared a new leader (Phil 2:21–22).	God used Timothy as a leader*
	From a mixed background (Acts. 16:1)	May have seen Paul from afar (Acts. 14:8–20)	Part of Paul's circle of associates (see Rom. 16:21)	Given greater assignments by Paul (1 Cor. 4:17)	Became Paul's scribe for his letters (Col. 1:1)	Given challenges in Paul's "last will" (2 Tim. 2:2)	Died in a riot in Ephesus*
PEOPLE	Eunice, Lois	Paul, Barnabas	Paul, Silas, Luke, Priscilla, and Aquila	Paul, Luke, Titus, Gaius, Apollos	Paul, Titus, Luke, Aristarchus, Onesimus	Paul, Luke, Mark, Erastus	John
TEXTS	2 Tim. 1:5; Acts 16:1	Acts 14:8–20 (see 2 Tim. 3:11)	Acts 16:1–18:22; 1 Thess. 3:1–2; 2 Thess. 1:1	Acts 18:23–21:17; Rom 16:21; 2 Cor. 1:1,19	Phil. 1:1; Col. 1:1; Philem. 1:1	1 Tim. 1:3; 3:14; 2 Tim. 4:13, 21	Heb. 13:23
TIME PERIOD	AD 30/33–48 about 15–20 years	1 year AD 49	2–3 years AD 50–52/53	4–5 years AD 52/53–57	5 years AD 57–62	5 years AD 62–67	30 years AD 67–about 97*

Details after Paul's death (AD 67) are based on comments from church fathers and less reliable texts in apocryphal books.

Paul's Journeys after the Book of Acts

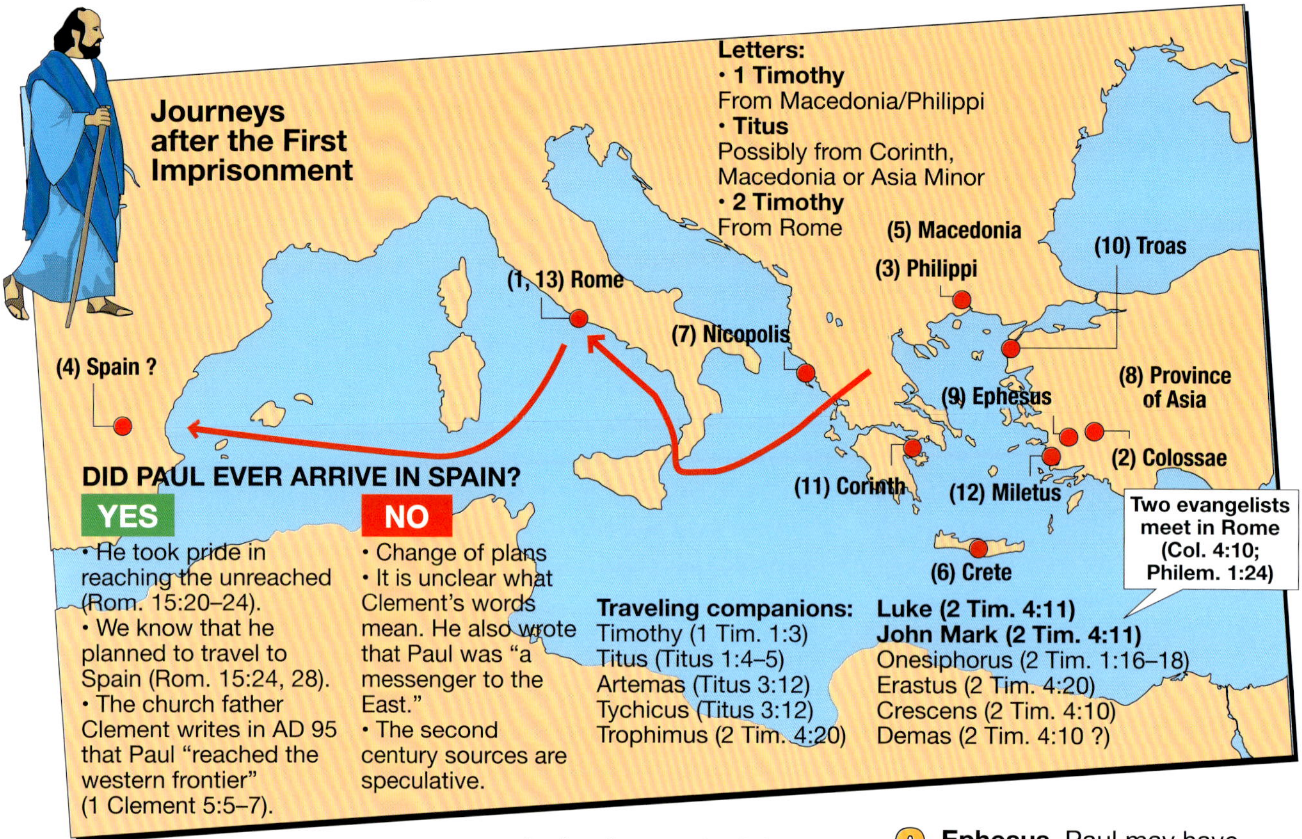

Paul is released from prison after two years (Acts 28:30). We know very little about his travels after that. Here are the places Paul may have visited, in no particular order.

1 **Rome (I).** At the end of Acts Paul is under house arrest in Rome. We do not know if he is brought before the emperor and acquitted (Acts 27:24) or if the case against him is simply dropped. But after two years, Paul is released (Acts 28:30).

2 Possibly **Colossae.** In the letter to Philemon, Paul writes that he plans to go to Colossae when he is released from prison. We do not know if the visit took place (Philem. 1:22).

3 Possibly **Philippi.** Similarly, in his letter to the Philippians, Paul writes that he plans to visit them on his release (Phil. 2:23–24). It is unclear if he did.

4 Possibly **Spain**. In Romans, Paul writes about his plans to travel to Spain. It is uncertain whether he ever had the opportunity to travel there (Rom. 15:20–28).

5 **Macedonia.** Paul travels to the province of Macedonia (1 Tim. 1:3). The cities he could have visited include Philippi (see 3), Thessalonica, Neapolis, Amphipolis, Apollonia, and Berea.

6 **Crete.** Paul visits Crete with Titus, who remains while Paul travels on (Titus 1:5).

7 **Nicopolis.** Paul arrives in Nicopolis, where he spends the winter. He invites Titus to come and visit him there (Titus 3:12).

8 **Asia.** Paul travels in the province, probably on multiple occasions. There are cities like Ephesus (see 9), Colossae (see 2), Troas (see 10), Miletus (see 12), and Laodicea (2 Tim. 1:15). He may have written the letter to Titus there.

9 **Ephesus**. Paul may have accompanied Timothy to Ephesus (1 Tim. 1:3); we know he wanted to visit him there (1 Tim. 3:14). Paul was helped by Onesiphorus while in Ephesus (2 Tim. 1:16–18; 4:19). He sends Tychicus to the city (2 Tim. 4:12).

10 **Troas.** Paul suggests that Timothy travel to Troas where Paul had left a cloak and some books with Carpus (2 Tim. 4:13).

11 **Corinth.** Erastus stays in Corinth when Paul moves on (2 Tim. 4:20).

12 When Paul left **Miletus,** Trophimus remained in the city due to an illness (2 Tim. 4:20).

13 **Rome (II).** At some point, Paul was rearrested and taken back to Rome (2 Tim. 2:9). Writes 2 Timothy and is executed in the fall of AD 66 or possibly 67 (2 Tim. 1:16–17; 4:6–8).

Twenty Criteria for Leadership

In 1 Timothy and Titus, Paul lists twenty characteristics and criteria for leadership. Leaders must be spiritually mature, so these characteristics are also a description of spiritual maturity (1 Tim. 3:6).

What does "be faithful to his wife" mean?

• Literally "husband of one wife," which has been understood in many ways.

Some interpretations:

1. You must be married to be a leader in the church.
2. You cannot be divorced, but compare Matt. 19:8.
3. You can only be married once, remarriage is not allowed.
4. You cannot have multiple wives at the same time (polygamy prohibited).
5. You must not have unhealthy relationships with the opposite sex (it's about your attitude).
6. You must be a man to be an elder (1 Tim. 2:12).

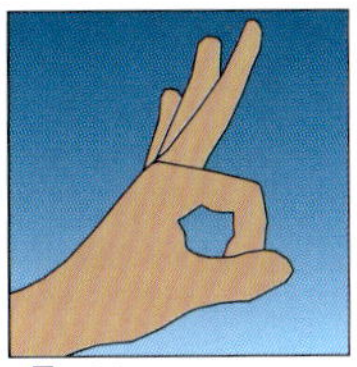

1 Above reproach
Nothing in the person's behavior should invite justified criticism (1 Tim. 3:2; 5:7; 6:14; Tit. 1:6).

2 Faithful to his wife
The focus here is on faithfulness in marriage and respect for others (1 Tim. 3:2; Tit. 1:6).

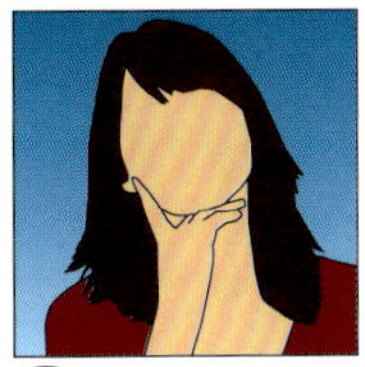

3 Self-controlled
Means sensible, thoughtful, well-balanced, clearheaded, even restrained (1 Tim. 3:2, 11; Tit. 2:3).

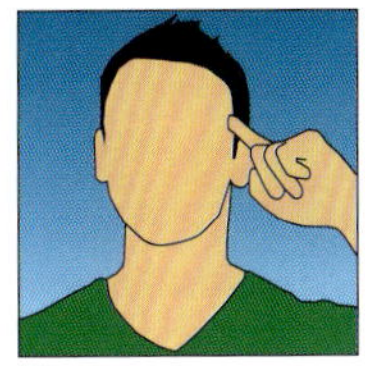

4 Lives wisely
It's more about wisdom than knowledge, being disciplined (1 Tim. 3:2; Tit. 1:8; 2:5; Gal. 5:23).

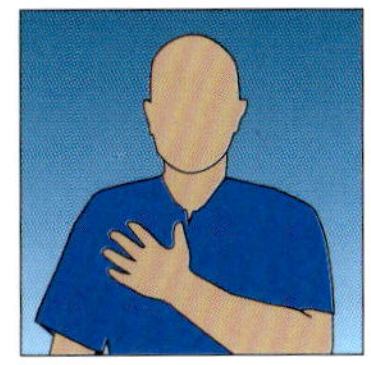

5 Good reputation
Respected, dignified, orderly, and decent. To win respect by one's life (1 Tim. 2:9; 3:2).

6 Guests in his home
Has an open home, a welcoming attitude, is generous and inviting (1 Tim. 3:2; Tit. 1:8; Rom. 12:13).

7 Able to teach
Has sound faith and doctrine, able to teach and refute those who oppose them (1 Tim. 3:2; Tit. 1:9).

8 Not a heavy drinker
Is a role model in his approach to alcohol. Is not a stumbling block to others. (1 Tim. 3:3; Tit. 1:7).

9 Not a violent person
Doesn't hit people, use physical or verbal violence, or threaten people for his cause (1 Tim. 3:3; Tit. 1:7)

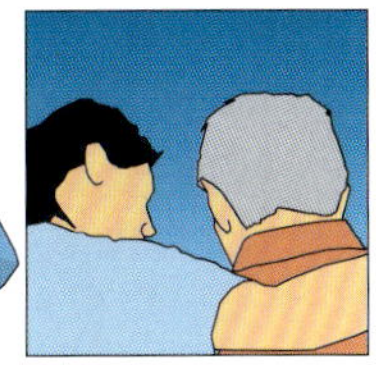

10 Is gentle
Is patient, considerate, and gentle in tone (1 Tim. 3:3; Tit. 3:2; Phil. 4:5; James 3:17; 1 Peter 3:15).

11 Not quarrelsome
Not prone to quarreling and fighting, able to bring order, not division (1 Tim. 3:3; 6:4; 1 Cor. 14:33).

12 Not lover of money
Content, is not controlled by the pursuit of wealth and possessions (1 Tim. 3:3; 6:5; Tit. 1:7; Phil. 4:11).

13 Manages his family
Respected in his own family, has children who are respectful and obedient (1 Tim. 3:4; Tit. 1:6).

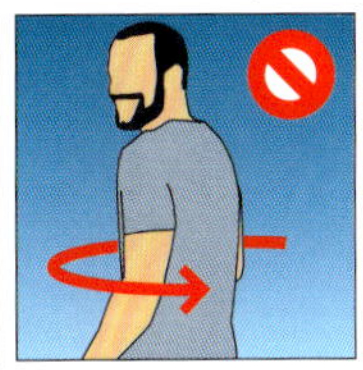

14 Not new believer
Leadership requires spiritual maturity. A young Christian is more likely to fall or go astray (1 Tim. 3:6).

15 Good reputation
Accepted not only by believers, but those outside the church. Wins the esteem of all (1 Tim. 3:7).

16 Not arrogant
Not arrogant, overbearing, or complacent. Does not always insist on being in charge (Tit. 1:7).

17 Not quick-tempered
It's about being able to control one's temper. Isn't contentious or quick to anger and rage (Tit. 1:7).

18 Loves the good
Pursues what is good. A sincere desire for goodness coming from the heart, is morally pure (Tit. 1:8).

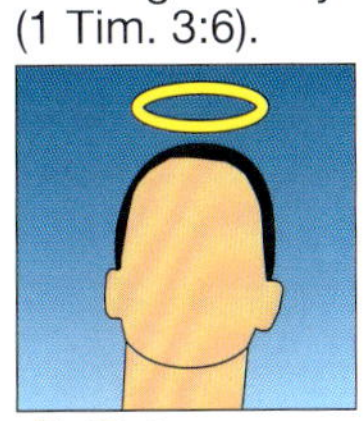

19 Is just
Is an honest person, doesn't lie. Keeps his word, respects the decisions that are made (Tit. 1:8).

20 A devout life
A commitment to holiness. God is the focus of life, set apart and fully surrendered to him (Tit. 1:8).

SECOND TIMOTHY

"You have heard me teach things that have been confirmed by many reliable witnesses. Now teach these truths to other trustworthy people who will be able to pass them on to others" (2 Tim. 2:2).

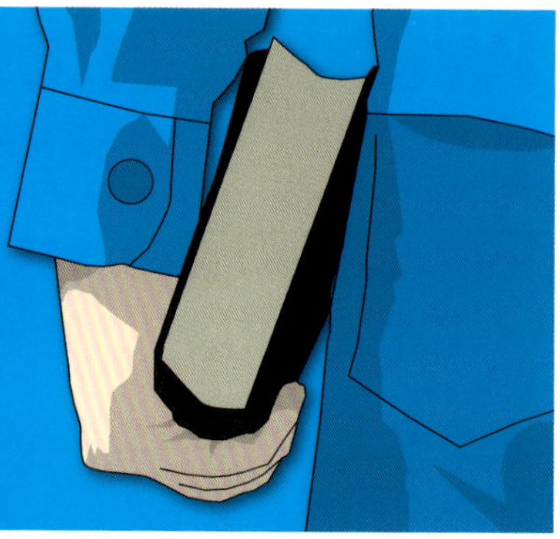

A FEW WORDS ABOUT THE AUTHOR

This is Paul's last surviving letter, written while in prison in Rome (1:1, 16; 2:9). Two early church leaders, Clement of Alexandria and Tertullian, quote from 2 Timothy, demonstrating the letter's early influence in the church. There are those who try to claim that it was written later under a false name. They argue, among other things, that the false doctrines addressed arose at a later date. The arguments are not convincing.

A FEW WORDS ABOUT THE RECIPIENT

This is the last letter we have from Paul to Timothy, his beloved son in the faith, who may have still been in Ephesus, where he was a church leader (1:2–3). It is a spiritual will, in which Paul longs for Timothy's presence, asking him to come as quickly as possible (4:9, 13). But in case Timothy doesn't arrive in time, Paul gives some final admonitions: entrust the message to others and preach the word with all patience (2:2; 4:2).

A FEW WORDS ABOUT DATES

Paul was imprisoned in Rome and martyred under Emperor Nero around AD 66–67 (1:16; 2:9), giving us a last possible date for the letter's composition. It was most likely written shortly before Paul's death, as he gives the impression of someone taking stock of his life (4:6–7). The letter can be seen as Paul's final will for Timothy, his spiritual son. Tradition says that Paul was executed just south of the city of Rome.

THE WHOLE BOOK IN 25 WORDS

Paul's last will to his spiritual son Timothy: do not be ashamed of the gospel, entrust it to trustworthy people, and be focused on Christ.

A SIMPLE STRUCTURE

1. Charge – Guard the gospel deposit
(2 Tim. 1:1–2:26)

2. Challenge – Stand firm amid deception
(2 Tim. 3:1–17)

3. Commitment – Finish well with faith
(2 Tim. 4:1–22)

A FEW WORDS ABOUT KEY THEMES

- **Paul's priorities**—These include sound teaching (4:3), sincere faith (1:5), patient love (3:10), and endurance (3:11).
- **Images of the Christian life**—A child (2:1), a soldier (2:3–4), an athlete (2:5), a farmer (2:6), a worker (2:15), a utensil (2:20–21), and a servant (2:24)
- **Reliability of the Bible**—Scripture is God-breathed, God-given, and useful for transforming lives (3:16–17)—a central text on the Bible's trustworthiness.
- **Exhortations**—The letter is filled with exhortations, with over thirty-five direct exhortations to Timothy, including fan into flames God's gift (1:6), do not be ashamed (1:8), trust (2:2), pursue righteous living (2:22), preach the word (4:2), and keep a clear mind (4:5).
- **Paul's last will**—The letter is Paul's testament in which he summarizes his life and vision. How did he see his life? What did he want to leave behind?

A FEW TIPS ON WHAT TO LOOK FOR

Theme of the book: Serving in the church

- Various images of a true servant of Jesus (7 images)
- All the people Paul mentions (30)
- The reliability of God's Word and the preaching of the Word
- Paul's many exhortations to Timothy (more than 35)
- Faith (at least 7 times)
- Do not be ashamed (4 times)
- What he taught about the person and work of Christ
- The personal tone of the letter

Paul's Words in the Waiting Room of Death

Imprisoned in Rome and knowing the end was near, (2 Tim. 2:9; 4:6–8), Paul wrote his spiritual will to encourage Timothy and remind him of all he had been taught.

Three role models for thinking about the Christian life

1 Suffer like a soldier
Emphasis: Prioritization
Text: 2 Tim. 2:3–4
A soldier does not allow himself to become involved in matters that are not fully connected to his mission.

2 Compete like an athlete
Emphasis: Follow the rules
Text: 2 Tim. 2:5
A sportsman must follow the rules in order to win. The right rules are about our motives before God.

3 Work hard like a farmer
Emphasis: Long term
Text: 2 Tim. 2:6
A farmer needs to plan his work. He must sow in the spring in order to enjoy his harvest in the fall. The work requires patience.

A letter filled with exhortations

In total there are more than thirty-five exhortations in the letter: 1:6, 8a, 8b, 13, 14; 2:1, 2, 3, 7, 8, 14a, 14b, 15, 16, 22a, 22b, 22c, 22d, 22e, 23; 3:5, 14; 4:2a, 2b, 2c, 2d, 2e, 2f; 4:5a, 5b, 5c, 9, 12, 13, 15, 19, 21.

My last will to my spiritual son Timothy

My beloved son Timothy, I have no one else like you. On the eve of my execution, I write to you to remind you of what we have talked about throughout all our years together.

1. HOLD ONTO YOUR GENUINE FAITH (1:5; 3:10; 4:7)
You have a genuine faith that you learned from your family. Fight to preserve it throughout your life.

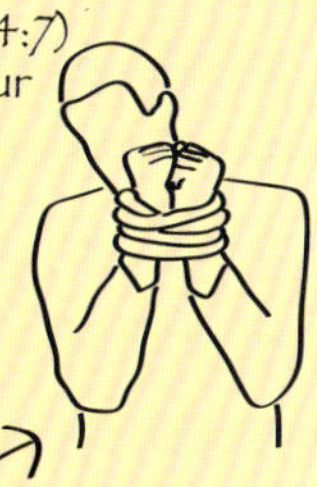

2. CHERISH YOUR SPIRITUAL GIFT (1:6)
You have a spiritual gift from God, received by the laying on of hands, so fan it to flames again.

3. NEVER BE ASHAMED OF THE GOSPEL (1:8)
You should never be ashamed to testify about the gospel of our Lord and Savior (Rom. 1:16).

4. BE PREPARED TO SUFFER FOR THE GOSPEL (1:8; 2:3)
Be ready to endure suffering for the sake of the gospel. God will give you the strength you will need.

5. DRAW STRENGTH FROM GRACE (1:9; 2:1)
God has given you his grace. Draw your strength from that grace he gave you in Christ Jesus.

6. PREACH THE WORD (1:13; 2:24; 4:2)
Preach the word whether or not the time is favorable. In your teaching correct, rebuke, and encourage.

7. TRAIN OTHERS AS I TRAINED YOU (2:2)
You are to pass on what you have received from me to others, who will in turn pass it on to others.

8. KEEP CHRIST AS THE FOCUS (2:8)
Keep Christ at the center of everything. Think of him who has risen from the dead.

9. ARGUMENTS ARE USELESS (2:14, 23)
You should not fight over words. Do not be involved in foolish and ignorant arguments.

10. STAY AWAY FROM UNGODLY PEOPLE (3:2–6)
Stay away from people who are proud, ungrateful boastful, godless, disobedient, and money-loving.

11. TRUST GOD'S WORD AND SOUND DOCTRINE (3:15)
You should trust God's word and not be ashamed of the truth and the way you share it.

12. FOLLOW WHOLESOME TEACHING (4:3–5)
Keep a clear mind and teach the Good News, in contrast to those who reject truth and follow myths.

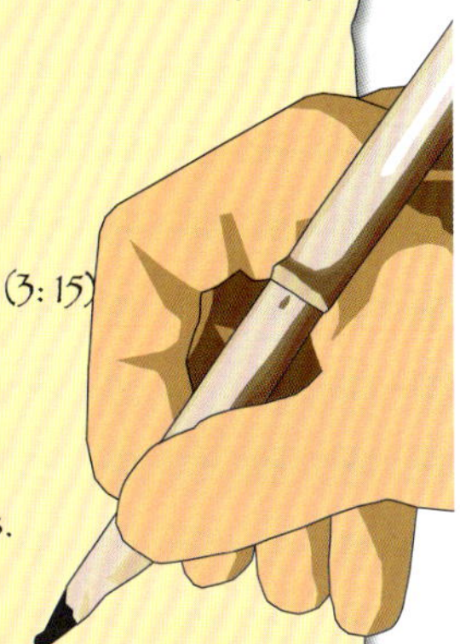

My son, do as I have done. Fight the good fight, finish the race, and remain faithful. Then you will win the crown of righteousness.

Your friend and brother, Paul

The Origin and Purpose of Scripture

One of the most central passages in the Bible regarding the origin and purpose of the Scriptures is 2 Timothy 3:16.

NOTE: Useful for four different things

“ All Scripture is inspired by God

1 Describes scope of Scripture
“All,” “the whole of,” or “every part of.” The context points to “all Scripture.” The preceding verse speaks of the entire Old Testament.

2 Describes the nature and status of Scripture
“What is written down.” A phrase the New Testament reserves for Scripture. The context confirms this is what is meant (see 1 Tim. 5:18).

3 Describes how God gave Scripture to us
“God-breathed,” “inspired.” The Bible is God’s Word because it comes from God himself. God breathed it, humans wrote it down.

4 Describes the source and origin
“God-breathed.” God himself is the source. Scripture is as an expression of God’s will and intentions, reflecting his character.

and is useful to teach us what is true and to make us realize what is wrong in our lives. It corrects us when we are wrong and teaches us to do what is right.

5 It is useful for ...
“Helpful.” It explains what Scripture means in practical terms for those who study it and live by its message.

6 (1) teaching us what is true
“Instruction” Scripture provides the content of our faith—refers to the doctrines that shape our faith.

7 (2) realizing what is wrong
Evidence used to examine a matter. Reveals to us where we are in error and need correction.

8 (3) correcting us when wrong
“To straighten up.” Explains what we should do instead, giving us direction and motivation.

9 (4) teaching us what to do
Instruction on becoming who we should be. The good we already do that can be further developed.

God uses it to prepare and equip his people to do every good work. (2 Tim. 3:16–17)

10 The purpose of this text
“In order to,” “so that.” God uses it to speak of purpose. Scripture is given as a tool for change, for transformation in faith and life.

11 To prepare his people
“Complete”, “skilled,” “capable.” Shows us how Scripture helps us to be prepared and ready to serve God better.

12 To equip his people
“To the end,” “completed.” Scripture gives us everything we need to understand the work God wants us to do.

13 His people
The purpose of Scripture is to help the believer to increasingly reflect the character and attributes of God (Phil. 2:5).

14 To do every good work
“The good,” “intrinsically good,” “right actions.” Context shows that the spiritual life is always expressed through good actions.

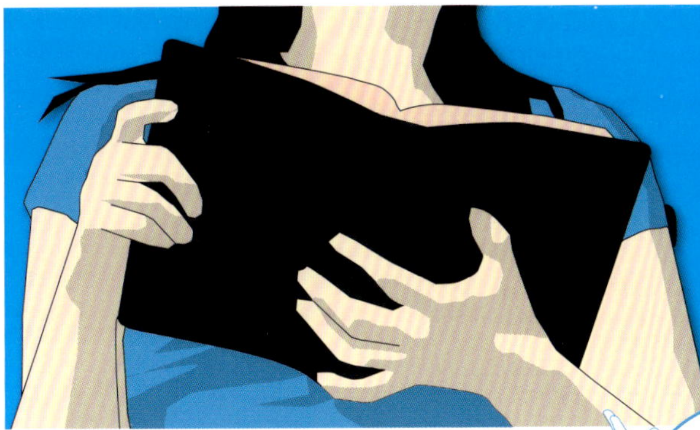

TITUS

"This is a trustworthy saying, and I want you to insist on these teachings so that all who trust in God will devote themselves to doing good" (Titus 3:8).

A FEW WORDS ABOUT THE AUTHOR

The letter was written by Paul, probably from Nicopolis in Greece or possibly from Macedonia (1:1; 3:12). Two early church fathers, Clement of Alexandria and Irenaeus, quote from the letter, showing its early authority in the church. There are those who claim that the letter was written later under a false name. They argue, among other things, that the picture of the church is too developed, but their arguments are not convincing.

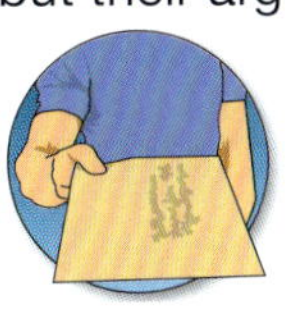

A FEW WORDS ABOUT THE RECIPIENT

The letter was written to Titus (1:4), who was one of Paul's faithful coworkers, a Greek whom he had brought to faith (1:4; Gal. 2:3). After a joint missionary journey to Crete, Paul had left him on the island to organize the new churches. The letter contains instructions and admonitions about church leadership and warnings about false teachers (1:6–9, 10–11; 3:10–11). Paul urges Titus to come to him in Nicopolis (3:12).

A FEW WORDS ABOUT DATES

The letter (see 1:5; 3:12) cannot be harmonized with Paul's travels as described in Acts. This suggests that the letter was written after Paul was released from house arrest in Rome (Acts 28:30). Despite its similarity with 1 Timothy, this letter may have been written later, perhaps as late as AD 65–66 if Paul traveled to Spain (see Rom. 15:24, 28). Otherwise, slightly earlier, closer to the time of 1 Timothy in the mid AD 60s.

THE WHOLE BOOK IN 25 WORDS

Titus is given advice on organizing and leading the churches in Crete. He receives instructions on church leadership and exhorting believers to do good works.

A SIMPLE STRUCTURE

1. Character
– Appoint leaders with integrity
(Titus 1:1–16)

2. Conduct
– Live correctly, whatever your role
(Titus 2:1–15)

3. Compassion
– Do good with humility
(Titus 3:1–15)

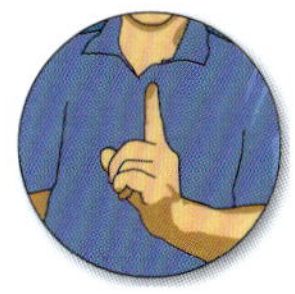

A FEW WORDS ABOUT KEY THEMES

- **Church leadership**—Paul urges Titus to appoint elders and gives him a list of criteria for those who would lead the church (1:5, 6–9).
- **Good deeds**—Our deeds can either deny (1:16) or confirm faith (2:7,14; 3:1, 5, 8, 14).
- **"Wholesome teaching"**—These two words are only used together in the Pastoral Letters (1 Tim. 1:10; 2 Tim. 4:3; Tit. 1:9; 2:1). A criterion for a church leader (1:3, 9; 2:1, 6–8; 3:8, 10). God's Word is revealed and reliable (1:3).
- **Grace is powerful**—Paul highlights how God's grace is active in us. "It teaches us" (2:12 NIV).
- **Deity of Christ**—The letter has one of the clearest passages in the New Testament on the deity of Christ. In Greek, the grammar of "our God and Savior" clearly shows that both words refer to the same person (2:13).

A FEW TIPS ON WHAT TO LOOK FOR

Theme of the book:
A life worthy of the church

- Good deeds (6 times)
- Criteria for church leadership
- Three passages on salvation (1:1–4; 2:11–14; 3:4–7)
- The reliable word of doctrine and references to the Word of God
- The kinds of opposition the church faces, false teachers
- Facts about Paul's travels and travel plans
- Faith (at least 6 times)
- Grace (4 times)

Doing Good Deeds

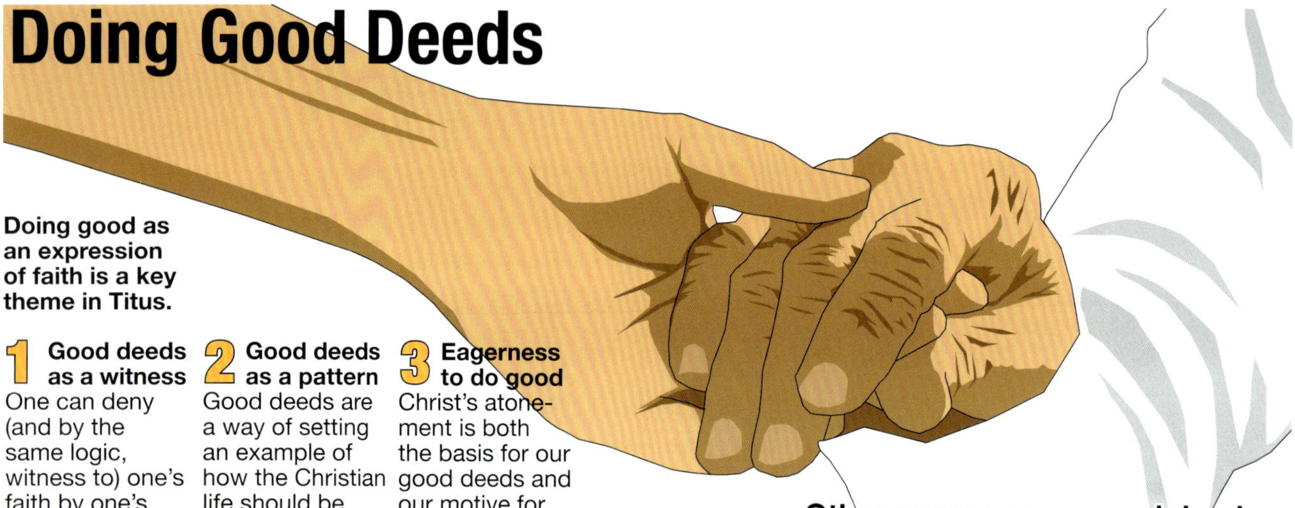

Doing good as an expression of faith is a key theme in Titus.

1 Good deeds as a witness
One can deny (and by the same logic, witness to) one's faith by one's deeds (1:16).

2 Good deeds as a pattern
Good deeds are a way of setting an example of how the Christian life should be lived (2:7).

3 Eagerness to do good
Christ's atonement is both the basis for our good deeds and our motive for doing them (2:14).

4 Ready to do good deeds
All believers are expected to be prepared and ready to do what is good at all times (3:1).

5 Founded on grace
The reason we belong to Christ is not our works but God's mercy (3:5, see Eph. 2:8–9).

6 Devoted to good deeds
Doing good helps everyone, and believers should express their faith through them (3:8).

7 The road to good deeds
Doing good is something that we must learn by meeting the needs of others (3:14).

Other passages on good deeds:

- **Matt. 5:16; 1 Peter 2:12:** Point to the Father
- **Matt. 6:1:** Should be done privately
- **John 10:32:** Jesus did many good works.
- **Acts 9:36; 1 Tim. 6:18:** Be rich in works.
- **Eph. 2:10:** God has prepared good works.
- **Col. 1:10:** Are pleasing to the Lord
- **1 Tim. 2:10; 5:10:** Reflect our inner self
- **1 Tim. 5:25:** Good works will be revealed.
- **Heb. 10:24:** Inspire each other to good works

And holding fast to *wholesome teaching*

The Pastoral Letters, and Titus in particular, highlight "wholesome teaching" as a central theme.

WHERE "WHOLESOME" (*HYGIAINO*) IS USED

Luke 5:31	1 Tim. 6:3	Tit. 1:13
Luke 7:10	2 Tim. 1:13	Tit. 2:1
Luke 15:27	2 Tim. 4:3	Tit. 2:2
1 Tim. 1:10	Tit. 1:9	3 John 1:2

Only in the Pastoral Letters are the Greek words *hygiaino* ("wholesome") and *didaskalia* ("teaching") used together: 1 Tim. 1:10; 2 Tim. 4:3; Tit. 1:9; 2:1. Paul says that leaders should "encourage others with **wholesome teaching**" (Tit. 1:9) and promote lives that reflect it (Tit. 2:1).

WHERE "TEACHING" (*DIDASKALIA*) IS USED

Matt. 15:9*	1 Tim. 1:10	1 Tim. 6:1	Tit. 2:1
Mark 7:7*	1 Tim. 4:1*	1 Tim. 6:3*	Tit. 2:7
Rom. 12:7	1 Tim. 4:6	2 Tim. 3:10	Tit. 2:10
Rom. 15:4	1 Tim. 4:13	2 Tim. 3:16	
Eph. 4:14	1 Tim. 4:16	2 Tim. 4:3	
Col. 2:22*	1 Tim. 5:17	Tit. 1:9	

- The Greek word *hygiaino*, is where we get the word "hygiene."
- **It means:** In the right way, in good condition, a healthy balance, to be sound, to be in good health, correct, someone whose positions are free from error, the true and unadulterated doctrine.
- **Total occurrences:** 12 times, 8 in the Pastoral Letters, 4 of those in Titus

- The Greek word *didaskalia* is also translated as "doctrine."
- **It means:** teaching, instruction, what is taught.
- **Total occurrences:** 21 times, 15 in the Pastoral Letters, 4 of those in Titus.

* Used in a negative sense

The 12 times *hygiaino* is used:

Luke	3
1 Tim.	2
2 Tim.	2
Tit.	4
3 John	1

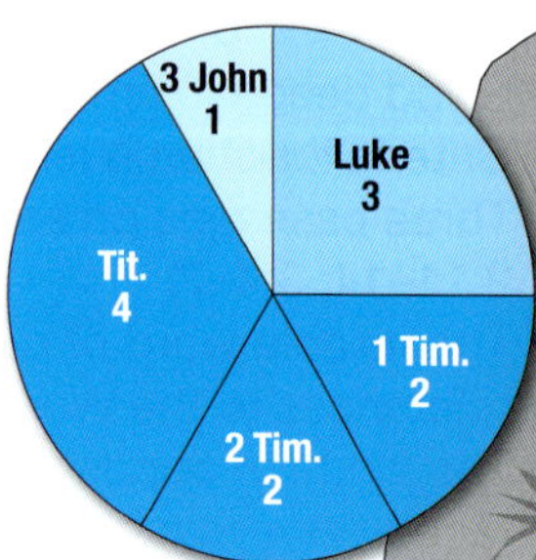

67% 2/3 of all occurrences are in the Pastoral Letters

The 21 times *didaskalia* is used:

Matt.	1
Mark	1
Rom.	2
Eph.	1
Col.	1
1 Tim.	8
2 Tim.	3
Tit.	4

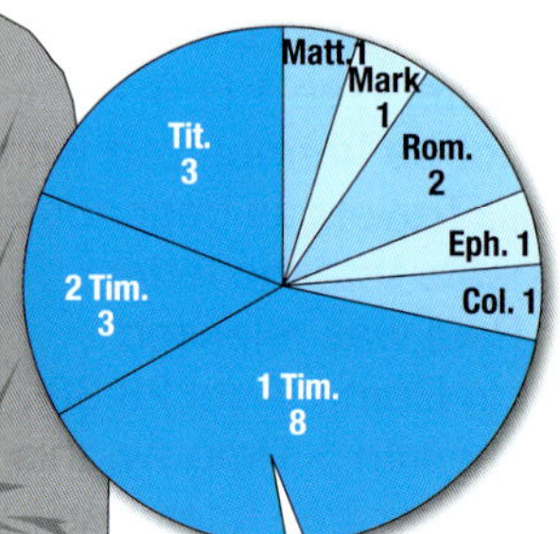

71% more than 2/3 of all occurrences are in the Pastoral Letters

Crete and Other Mediterranean Islands

GORTYN
The Church of St. Titus was built around the sixth century. Perhaps named for Titus as late as 670. Destroyed in an earthquake in 828.

1 Crete and Cauda
Texts: Acts 27:7–21; Tit. 1:5
Paul left Titus on Crete when he moved on (Tit. 1:5). On an earlier trip, he had docked on the island, then sailed south near Cauda (now Gavdos). **Area:** Crete 3,263 sq mi, Cauda 13 sq mi

Titus was probably active in the vicinity of Gortyn, the capital at the time. But clearly there were several churches on the island ("in each town" Titus. 1:5).

The island is:
160 miles long
35 miles wide

HERAKLION
The Church of St. Titus in Heraklion. Probably built around 961. The church was rebuilt in 1925 and today belongs to the Greek Orthodox Church.

TITUS AND CRETE
After Paul's release from Rome, he traveled with Titus to Crete. There, Titus stayed behind as Paul continued on (1:5). Titus was later replaced by Artemas or Tychicus and traveled to meet Paul, either in Nicopolis or Rome (Tit. 3:12; 2 Tim. 4:10).

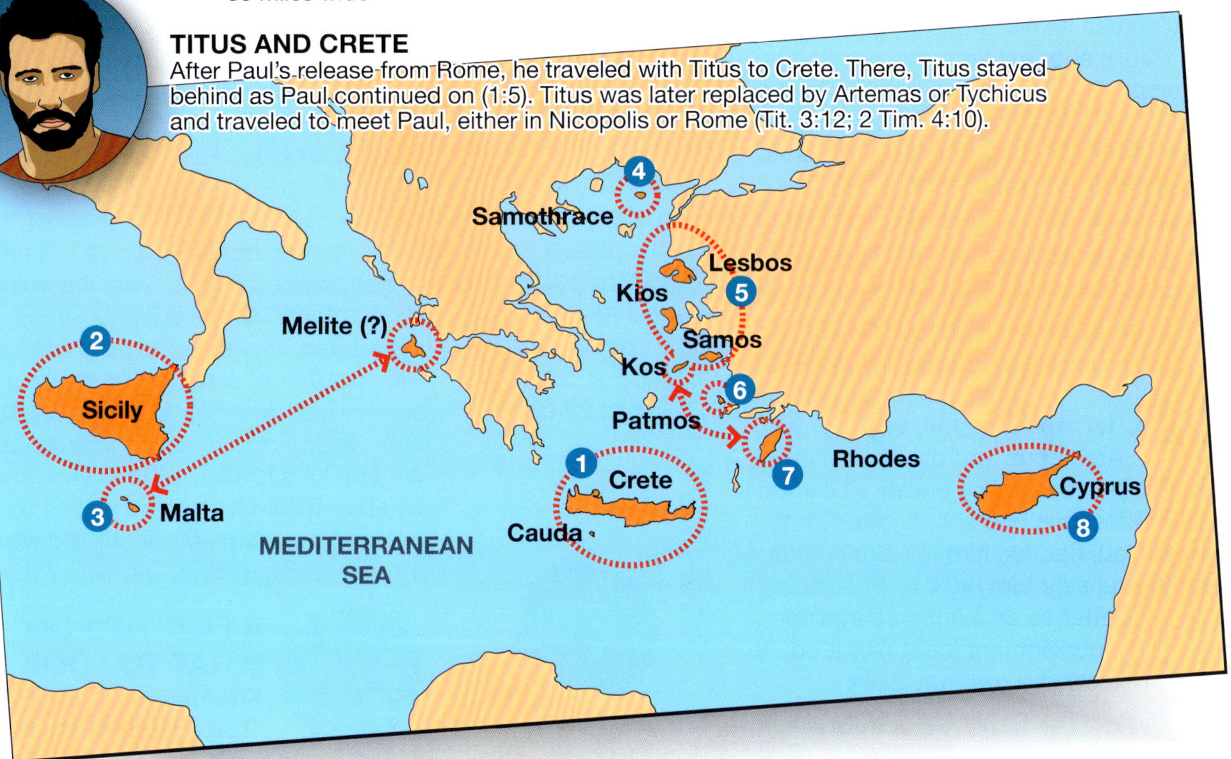

2 Sicily
Paul left Malta and arrived in Syracuse, Sicily. He stayed there for three days before he continued his journey to the mainland and Rome. **Surface area:** 9,927 sq mi (Acts 28:12)

3 Malta
Paul was stranded on Malta after a storm in the Mediterranean. **Surface area:** 122 sq mi (Acts 28:1, 12) One theory has Paul landing on Melite/Cephalonia instead; this is not likely.

4 Samothrace
In Troas, Paul had a vision of a man asking him to come to Macedonia (Acts 16:9). The route from Troas took him to Samothrace and then Neapolis. **Surface area:** 68 sq mi (Acts 16:11)

5 Lesbos, Kios, Samos
Three islands in the Greek archipelago that Paul traveled to or passed by on his way back to Jerusalem. **Surface area:** Lesbos 630 sq mi, Kios 325 sq mi, Samos 184 sq mi (Acts 20:13–15)

6 Patmos
John was exiled to the island when Christians were being persecuted under Emperor Domitian. Patmos is a small island in the Aegean Sea. **Surface area:** 13 sq mi (Rev. 1:9).

7 Kos and Rhodes
On his third journey, Paul spent the night on the island of Kos. **Surface area:** 80 sq mi • The next day, he traveled to Rhodes and then continued on. **Surface area:** 541 sq mi (Acts 21:1)

8 Cyprus
Paul visited the island on his first journey and sailed to the north of the island on his journey to Rome. **Surface area:** 3,572 sq mi (Acts 4:36; 11:19; 13:4; 15:39; 27:4 see 4:36

PHILEMON

"It seems you lost Onesimus for a little while so that you could have him back forever ... He is more than a slave, for he is a beloved brother" (Philem. 1:15–16).

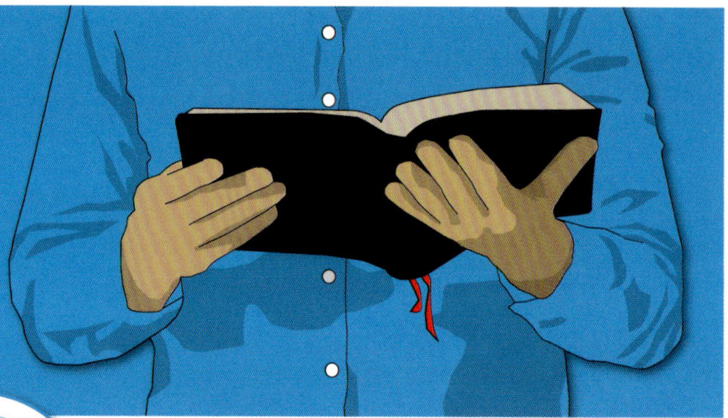

A FEW WORDS ABOUT THE AUTHOR

The letter was written by Paul from Rome while he was a "prisoner of Christ Jesus" (Philem. 1:1, 9, 23; Acts 28:30). Possibly, or perhaps even probably, Timothy served as his scribe (Philem. 1:1). It is Paul's shortest letter and written in a personal style. Paul had never visited Colossae, so his previous meeting with Philemon must have taken place somewhere else, perhaps in the port city of Ephesus (Philem. 1:19).

A FEW WORDS ABOUT THE RECIPIENT

The letter is addressed to Philemon, a Christian who probably lived in Colossae (Philem. 1:1, see Col. 4:9), together with Apphia, Archippus and the church in their house. Sometime earlier, Philemon's slave Onesimus had escaped to Rome where Paul had led him to Christ (Philem. 1:10). Paul sent him back to Philemon with the letter as an insurance against the harsh punishment (death) that could otherwise await a runaway slave.

A FEW WORDS ABOUT DATES

Paul wrote the letter during his first imprisonment in Rome (Philem. 1: 1, 23). A likely date is between AD 60 and 61. The mention of the same people in both Philemon and Colossians (Mark, Aristarchus, Demas, Luke), and that both letters were delivered by Onesimus and Tychicus, indicates a close connection to Colossians (Col. 4:7–9). Though earlier dates for the letter (as early as AD 55) have been proposed, these are unlikely.

THE WHOLE BOOK IN 25 WORDS

The gospel illustrated in real life. Paul is willing to pay the price for Onesimus's sin and save the converted slave from a death sentence.

A SIMPLE STRUCTURE

1. Forgiveness – Gives hope for a new life for the escaped slave
(Philem. 1:1–16)

2. Friendship – Gives hope for a new chance for the returning convert
(Philem. 1:17–25)

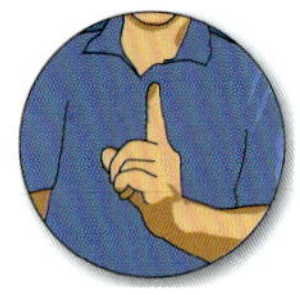

A FEW WORDS ABOUT KEY THEMES

• **To be useful**—Paul points out that previously Onesimus had been not useful but that he would now be useful (Philem. 1:11). The name Onesimus means "useful" (Philem. 1:20).

• **Forgiveness**—The punishment for a runaway slave could be death; Onesimus could have been thrown to the beasts in an amphitheater. Paul appeals to Philemon to forgive Onesimus, as Philemon himself has been forgiven (Philem. 1:19). Paul offers to bear Onesimus's debt as Christ has borne ours. The whole story is an illustration of the gospel.

• **Paul and slavery**—Paul did not call for the abolition of slavery, but showed that slavery can never be a fruit of Christianity, listing slave traders with murderers and liars (1 Tim. 1:10). It is unclear whether Philemon owned slaves only before his conversion or still did when the letter was written.

A FEW TIPS ON WHAT TO LOOK FOR

Theme of the book:
Theme: Christ and forgiveness

- What do you learn about Onesimus's situation?
- What do you learn about Philemon?
- What do you learn about Paul?
- The name Onesimus means "useful" How is this reflected in the letter?
- Can you see how the letter illustrates the gospel? Paul's says "If he ... owes you anything, charge it to me" (Philem. 1:18).
- Note the phrases "send to," "get back," and "receive."

The Story of the Slave Onesimus

By reading between the lines of Paul's letter to Philemon, we can figure out the background of what happened between Onesimus and Philemon.

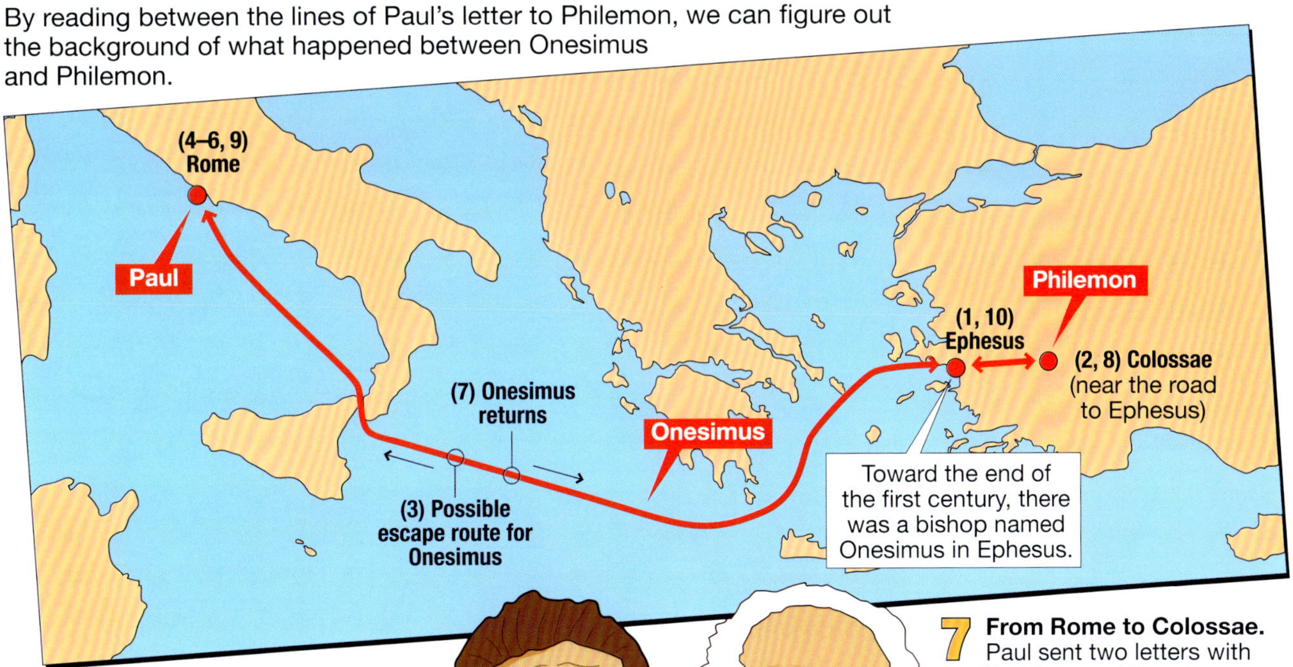

1 **Unknown place.** Paul hadn't been in Colossae (Col. 1:4). He met Philemon and brought him to faith, perhaps in Ephesus (Philem. 1:19; Acts 18:19–21).

2 **Colossae.** Onesimus is a slave of Philemon in Colossae (Philem. 1:11, 16)

3 **From Colossae to Rome.** Onesimus escaped from his master, Philemon, making his way to Rome. His escape may have occurred before Philemon came to faith in Jesus (Philem. 1:15).

4 **Rome.** Onesimus met Paul in his house in Rome and came to faith in Christ (Acts 28:30; Philem. 1:9, 10, 13, 16).

5 **Rome.** Onesimus informed Paul about his background as an escaped slave (Philem. 1:10, 12, 16).

6 **Rome.** Paul wrote the letter to Colossians and the letter to Philemon living in Colossae (Col. 1:1–2; Philem. 1:1, see Col. 4:7–9)

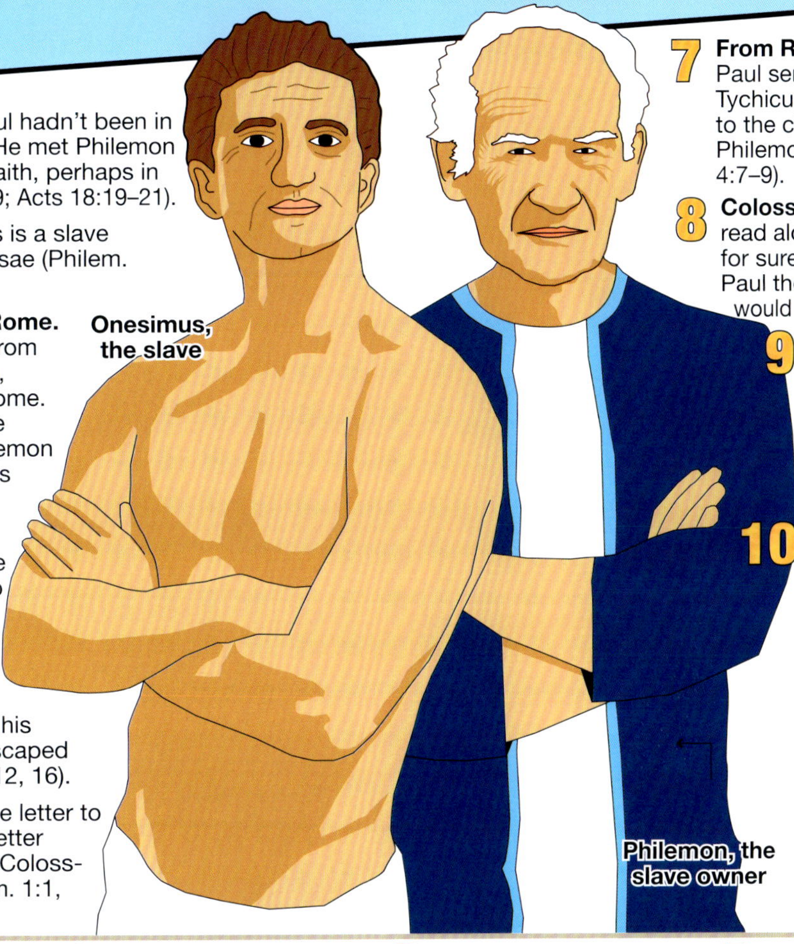

7 **From Rome to Colossae.** Paul sent two letters with Tychicus and Onesimus, one to the church and one to Philemon (Philem. 1:12; Col. 4:7–9).

8 **Colossae.** The letters were read aloud. We don't know for sure what happened, but Paul thought he knew what would happen (Philem. 1:21).

9 **From Rome.** Paul also promised to come to Colossae as soon as he was released, perhaps as an inducement (Philem. 1:22).

10 **Ephesus.** We know that during Emperor Domitian's reign (AD 81–96), there was a bishop named Onesimus in Ephesus. He may have been the runaway slave who was forgiven. Whoever he was, Bishop Onesimus was martyred in Rome for his faith, according to Ignatius of Antioch.

1 The Roman Empire was built on slavery

The Roman Empire was based on slavery. In Italy, 30–40% of the population were slaves, and maybe 10–15% of the entire empire.

2 Slaves had many different tasks

Not all slaves were manual laborers. Many were well educated and some were even able to earn money and buy their freedom.

3 The Bible does not defend slavery, but...

Bible verses about slavery deal with the realities of their time. And Paul lists "slave traders" (1 Tim. 1:10) among murderers.

4 Philemon was a slave owner

We do not know if Philemon kept slaves after he came to faith. Onesimus might have run away before Philemon became a Christian.

Overview of the General Letters

The letters are called:
1. The General Letters—most were written to groups
2. The Catholic Letters—older term for general
3. The non-Pauline Letters—by other authors

The General Letters were originally placed before Paul's letters. They were placed in their current order in later collections of the New Testament.

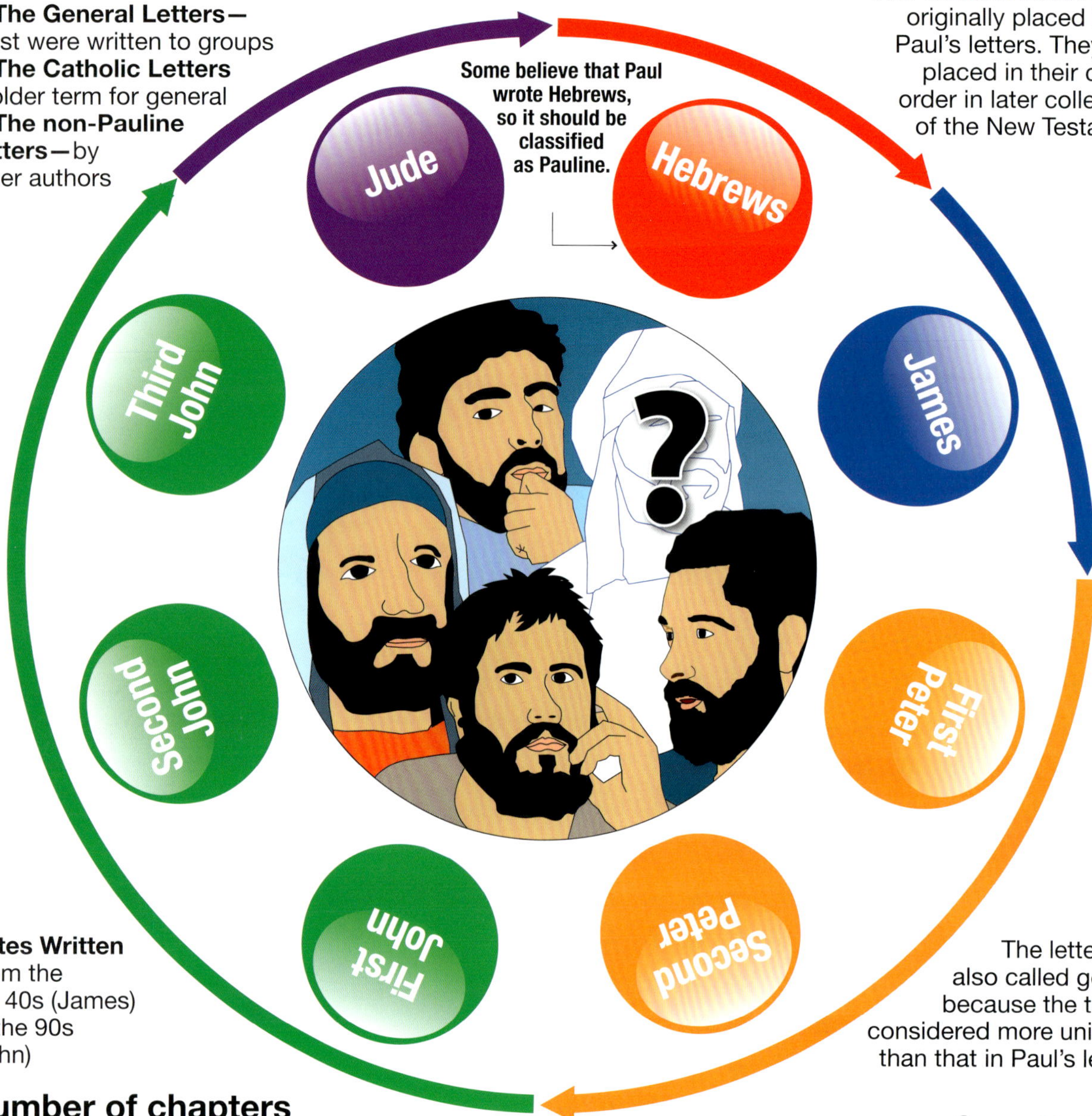

Dates Written
From the AD 40s (James) to the 90s (John)

The letters are also called general because the tone is considered more universal than that in Paul's letters.

Number of chapters in the General Letters

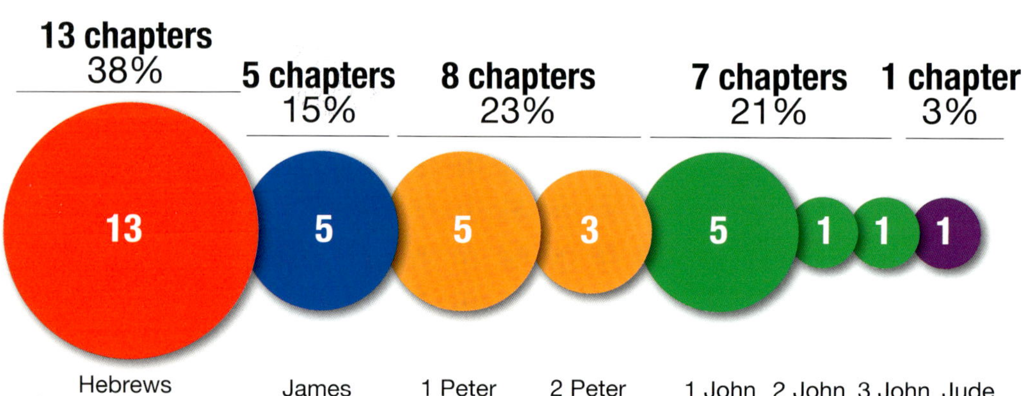

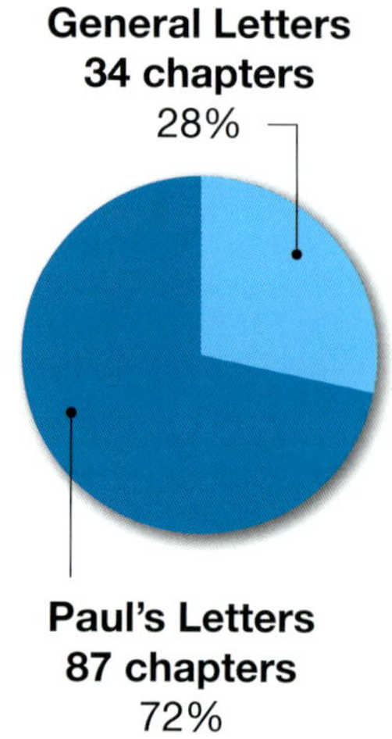

HEBREWS

"For the word of God is alive and powerful. It is sharper than the sharpest two-edged sword, cutting between soul and spirit.... It exposes our innermost thoughts and desires" (Heb. 4:12).

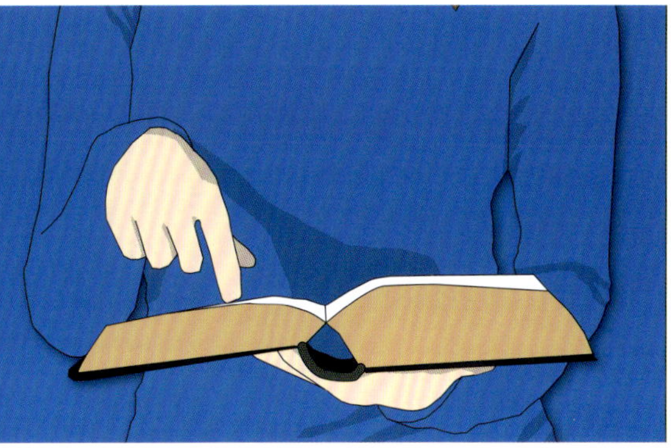

A FEW WORDS ABOUT THE AUTHOR

The author is unknown to us, but was not unknown to the recipients of the letter (Heb, 13:19–24). The author had had the message of Jesus confirmed by others and knew Timothy (2:3; 13:23). His command of Greek was the best among the New Testament writers. This would fit well with Apollos being the author (Acts 18:24), but many others have been suggested as the author, including Paul, Barnabas, and Priscilla and Aquila.

A FEW WORDS ABOUT THE RECIPIENTS

The recipients were Jews who believed in Jesus and were facing severe persecution for their faith, probably under Emperor Nero (12:3). The author's greeting from "the believers from Italy" (13:24) suggests that the recipients might have been in Italy or even in Rome, though this is not known for certain. Other suggestions are Egypt, Asia Minor, or Greece. The believers had probably not seen Christ personally (see 2:3).

A FEW WORDS ABOUT DATES

The dating of the letter is uncertain but it must have been written before the destruction of the temple in AD 70 (8:4; 10:1). The book speaks of severe persecution (10:32–39; 12:4; 13:3) and Timothy's recent release from captivity (13:23). These details fit well with the violent persecution of Christians by Emperor Nero, which began in AD 64. Since Nero died in AD 68, a probable date for the writing of Hebrews is AD 64–68.

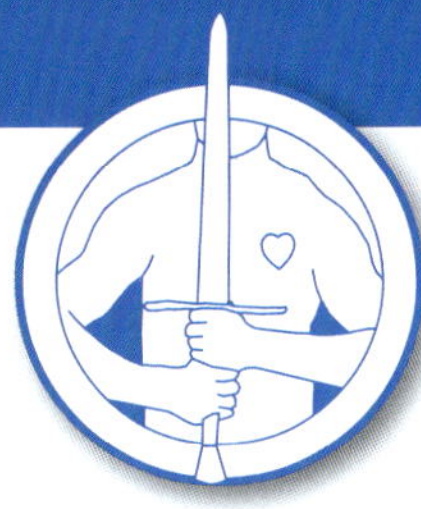

THE WHOLE BOOK IN 25 WORDS

Jesus: greater than angels, Moses, Joshua, and high priests. He brought a better sacrifice for a better covenant that offers a better way of salvation.

A SIMPLE STRUCTURE

1. Supremacy – Christ outshines all others
(Heb. 1:1–4:13)

2. Sanctuary – He opens the holy way
(Heb. 4:14–10:18)

3. Sacrifice – Worship leads to faithful witness
(Heb. 10:19–13:25)

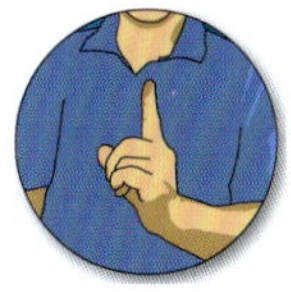

A FEW WORDS ABOUT KEY THEMES

- **Christ is better**—The author compares the Old Covenant with the New, concluding that Jesus is better than the prophets, angels, Moses, Joshua, Aaron, Melchizedek, and many more (1:1–10:18).
- **Can we lose our salvation?**—Are those who are saved secure in their salvation? Some passages in the letter are central to this question (3:7–19; 6:4–6; 10:26–31).
- **Spiritual maturity**—Central to the book is the issue of spiritual growth and stability, for example, see 5:11–6:12.
- **Warnings**—Over the course of the book, the author delivers seven clear warnings (2:1–4; 3:7–12; 4:9–13; 5:11–6:3; 6:4–12; 10:26–31; 12:25–29).
- **The use of the Old Testament**—No other book in the New Testament has as many references to the Old Testament, particularly the faith chapter (11).

A FEW TIPS ON WHAT TO LOOK FOR

Theme of the book: The foundation of salvation

- "Better than ... " (11 times)
- What is learned about Christ and his ministry
- Heaven (15 times), eternal (11 times)
- The many warnings in the letter
- Perfect (15 times)
- Many allusions to and quotations from the Old Testament (at least 90)
- "Let us ... " (4:1, 11, 14, 16; 6:1; 10:22–25; 12:1–2, 28; 13:13, 15)
- Faith, examples of faith
- The expression "once for all"

Who Wrote Hebrews?

Hebrews is the only letter where the identity of the author is completely unknown. But we can draw some plausible conclusions: He was a well-educated theologian, a skilled stylist, an eloquent communicator, a knowledgeable apologist, well-versed in the Old Testament, probably had both a Jewish and a Greek background, likely in Italy or of Italian origin (13:24), does not appear to have been an eyewitness to Jesus (2:3), possibly associated with Paul (13:23).

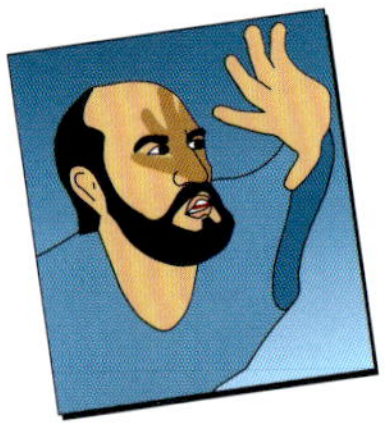

PAUL
Hebrews was placed among the Pauline letters early on. Clement of Alexandria accepted Paul's authorship. But others, Irenaeus and Eusebius, questioned it or moved Hebrews from that section.

LUKE
Some believe that Paul wrote the letter in Hebrew and that it was later translated into Greek by Luke. But the text does not appear to be a translation from a Semitic language. Maybe Luke wrote the letter himself.

BARNABAS
Tertullian says that he quoted from a letter of Barnabas when he cites from Hebrews. Mentioned by Jerome as probable author. He was a Levite, which can explain his deep knowledge of Scripture (Acts 4:36).

CLEMENT OF ROME
Eusebius noted that the letter to Corinth by Clement of Rome (in the late first century) had many references and quotations found in Hebrews. Clement might have edited or written Hebrews himself.

APOLLOS
Martin Luther suggested Apollos as the author. Apollos is described as "an educated man ... very knowledgeable in the Scriptures" (Acts 18:24). But there is no support in early texts.

PRISCILLA (AND AQUILA)
Hebrews13:24 might refer to Italians who had been forced out of Rome, such as Priscilla and Aquila (Acts 18:2). But the masculine pronoun used in "What else shall I say?" (11:32) excludes a female author.

OTHER NAMES
Mary (mother of Jesus), Philip, Silas, Stephen, Timothy, Epaphroditus, other disciples of Paul, and some others have all been suggested. But the arguments are often built on speculative observations.

"The absence both of solid testimony, internal or external, and of any firm traditions means that, as things are, the riddle of the authorship of Hebrews is incapable of solution. (Philip Edgcumbe Hughes)

AN UNKNOWN AUTHOR
We do not know enough to determine the letter's author. As Origen wrote, "Who really wrote the letter, only God knows." However, the author was known to the original recipients (13:19–24).

What we know about the recipients

1 They had come to faith in Jesus
"Dear brothers and sisters who belong to God" (3:1; 2:3). The message was confirmed by those who had heard the Lord themselves, and it continues to be passed down faithfully.

2 They had stalled in their spiritual growth
"You have been believers so long now that you ought to be teaching others. Instead, you need someone to teach you ... the basic things" (5:12a). A reminder of their spiritual immaturity.

3 They needed help to move forward in faith
"You need someone to teach you again the basic things about God's word" (5:12b). They could not get themselves out this situation. They needed help from mature believers.

4 They had faced hardships ...
They faced persecution. "You remained faithful even though it meant terrible suffering ... all you owned was taken from you, you accepted it with joy" (10:32–34).

5 ... so they no longer wanted to listen ...
"You are spiritually dull and don't seem to listen." (5:11). They had reached a situation where they were no longer as willing to take in what was being said, showing signs of resistance.

6 ... and risked falling away from their faith
This had brought them to the point where they were considering giving up, "turning you away from the living God" (3:12). "[Do not] drift away from [the truth]" (2:1).

Jesus is Bigger, Better, Greater

The author of Hebrews addresses Jewish Christians who were tempted to return to their Jewish faith, and thereby escape persecution. So the author emphasizes that Jesus is bigger, better, and greater.

1 ... than the prophets (1:1–3)
• **Previously:** God repeatedly spoke to the fathers through the prophets (1:1). • **But now:** God has spoken to us through his Son (1:2). Jesus not only brings the message, he is the message (Heb. 1:3; John 1:1–4, 14). • **Response:** Listen to what he tells you.

2 ... than the angels (1:4–2:18)
• **Previously:** The angels are God's servants. They are sent to worship the Son (1:6).
• **But now:** Jesus's name is **greater** than the angels', he is the Son of God (1:4–5, 2:5, 8).
• **Response:** Take heed to what we have heard (2:1), receive God's help (2:18).

3 ... than Moses (3:1–19)
• **Previously:** Moses was only a servant who bore witness to what was to come (3:5).
• **But now:** Jesus is worthy of honor, for he is Lord (3:3, 6).
• **Response:** Look to Jesus (3:1), be bold (3:14), do not harden your hearts (3:8), believe (3:19).

4 ... than Joshua (4:1–13)
• **Previously:** Joshua brought them into the land but it was not the final rest God had promised (4:8). • **But now:** Jesus is greater, for he brings us into the promised rest (4:9–10).• **Response:** Do not miss God's promise, try to enter into the rest (4:1–2, 11).

5 ... than the high priest Aaron (4:14–6:20)
• **Previously:** Aaron was a high priest, but also a man among men (5:2–3; 7:11) • **But now:** Jesus is greater for he comes from God and is high priest forever (4:14; 6:20).
• **Response:** Become mature in your understanding of who Christ is (6:1).

6 ... than the high priest Melchizedek (7:1–28)
• **Previously:** Melchizedek was a greater high priest than Aaron because he remains a priest forever (7:3, 9) • **But now:** Jesus is an even better high priest, who lives forever (7:15–16, 22, 24). • **Response:** Come near to God (7:25).

7 ... than the tabernacle (8:1–5; 9:1–11)
• **Previously:** The layout of the tabernacle purposely showed that the way into God's presence was closed (8:5; 9:8). • **But now:** There is a perfect tabernacle where the way into God is opened through Jesus Christ (8:5; 9:11). [Note the change of location of the altar of incense Ex. 26–27] • **Response:** Go in and meet God.

8 ... than the old covenant (8:6–13)
• **Previous:** Since the earlier covenant God had made was not faultless, it is therefore obsolete (8:7, 13). • **But now:** Jesus is the mediator of a new and better covenant (9:15)
• **Response:** Receive forgiveness (8:12).

9 ... than the sacrifices of atonement (9:11–28)
• **Previously:** The sacrifices of goats and bulls could bestow external purification (9:13).
• **But now:** Once for all, Jesus has sacrificed himself, a better sacrificial lamb to win eternal redemption (9:12, 23). He offers a better, inner, cleansing from sin (9:14). • **Response:** Receive forgiveness of sins, serve him (9:15).

10 ... than all the other sacrifices (10:1–18)
• **Previously:** The priests brought inadequate sacrifices, having to do it repeatedly (10:11). • **But now:** Jesus has sacrificed himself once for all with eternal results (10:14).
• **Response:** Receive forgiveness of sin (10:18).

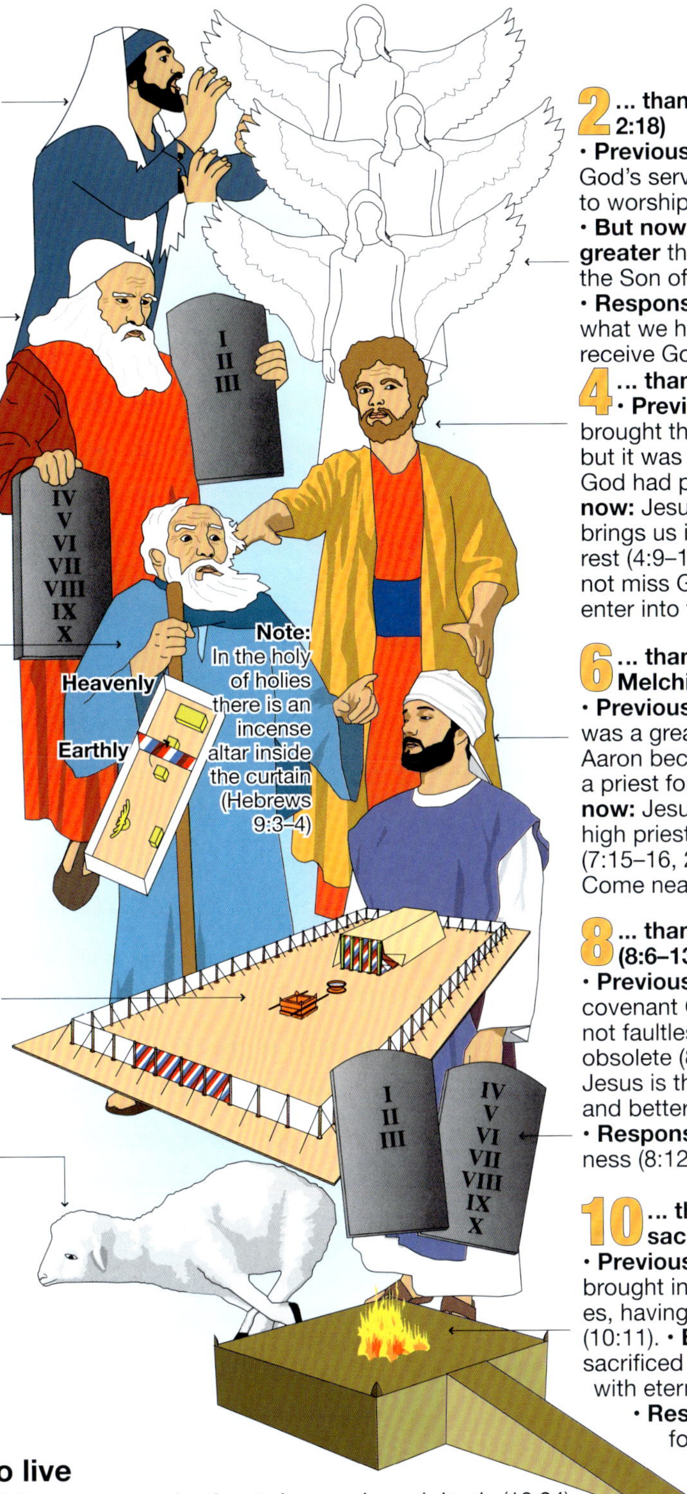

Therefore, we are called to live

- **in a better community (10:19–31)** Encourage each other to love and good deeds (10:24).
- **with a greater boldness (10:32–39)** Hold boldly to the confession despite opposition (10:36).
- **with a greater faith (11:1–40)** Develop an inner certainty about what we do not see (11:1).
- **with a greater persistence (12:1–29)** Keep our eyes on Jesus so we don't lose heart (12:2, 4).
- **with a greater mutual love (13:1–21)** Care for those in need and be hospitable (13:1–3).

Different Stages in the Christian Life

The New Testament speaks of different stages in the Christian life. Five profiles can be identified. Each represents a phase in an individual's spiritual journey. The New Testament gives each believer responsibility for both where they are and where they are going. Where do you belong?

> “Spiritual maturity ... comes from the sustained application of spiritual discipline. (Donald Guthrie)

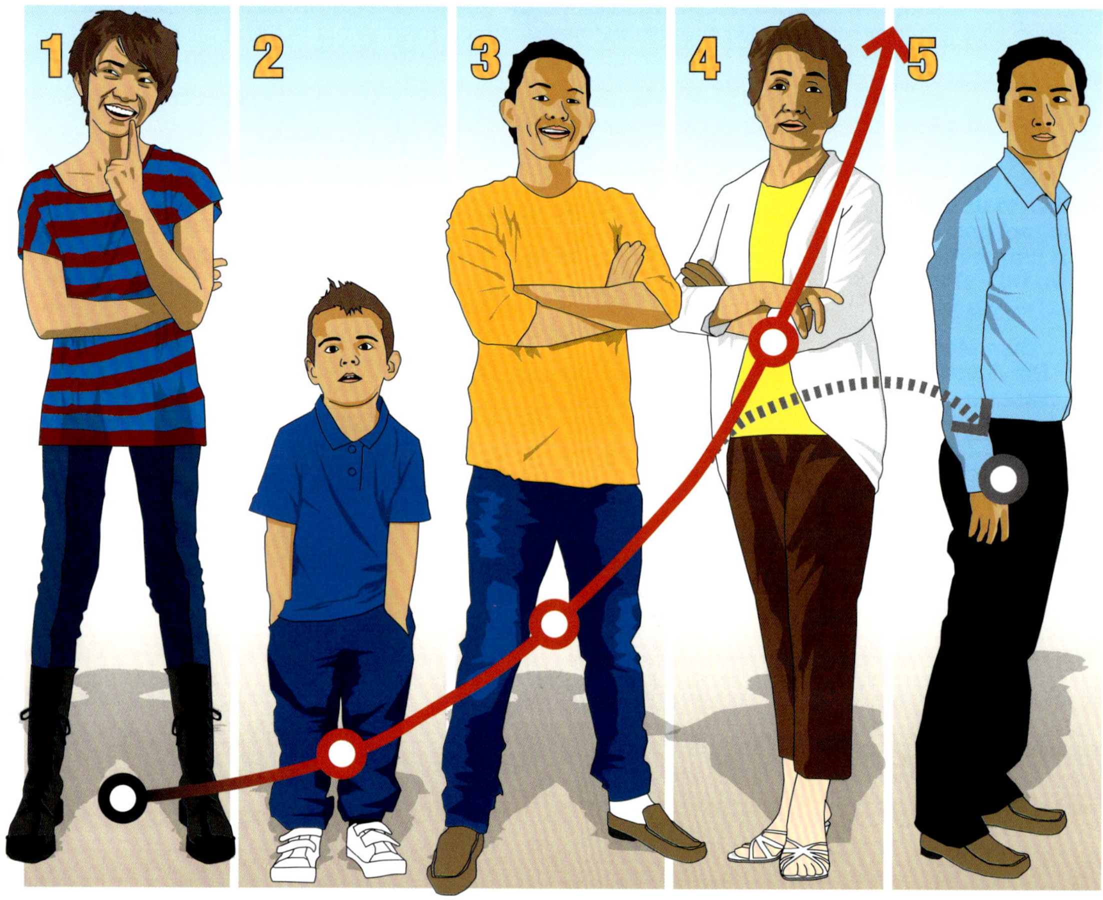

Relationship to faith	**One who has not yet come to faith**	**One who is young in faith**	**One who is growing in faith**	**One who is maturing in faith**	**One who has strayed from faith**
	One who has not yet come to faith. Can be on the way, close to faith or far from it.	**One who has** just come to faith in Jesus and been born again, is spiritually young.	**One who has** started their journey and is on the way to spiritual maturity.	**One who has**, over time, grown and matured in their relationship with Christ.	**One who has** consciously made a wrong choice, leading them away from Christ.
Key phrase	Is still a seeker	Has only just begun	Is on the way	Has come a long way	Has turned down a wrong path
Is called	“Sinner” (Rom. 3:23)	“Baby” (Heb. 5:12–13)	“Young” (1 John 2:14; 1 Tim. 4:12).	“Mature”(Heb. 5:14; Eph. 4:13)	“Turned away” (Heb. 6:6)
Descriptions	Is personally responsible for their sin (Rom. 3:23; James 2:10).	Is still perceived as being worldly (1 Cor. 3:1–3).	Listens to and abides in God's Word (Heb. 5:11; 1 John 2:14).	Has grown through practice over time (Heb. 5:14).	Sins willfully (Heb. 10:26).
	Is being drawn to faith by God (John 6:44).	Is easily carried away by new teachings (Eph. 4:14).	Is increasingly rooted in Christ and faith (Col. 2:6–7).	Is able to distinguish between good and evil (Heb. 5:14).	• **Debate: Can someone who has been saved lose their salvation?** a) **Yes**, if you consciously choose to walk away from Christ. b) **No**, what sin is so great that Jesus did not die for it?
	Needs to be born again (John 3:3).	Needs to be taught the basics of the faith (1 Cor. 3:2).	Is pressing on in their life with Christ (Phil. 3:12–14).	Is standing firm, well grounded in the faith (Col1:22–23, Tit. 1:9).	
	The step to faith is to trust in Jesus's redemption (John 3:16).	Should not be in positions of church leadership (1 Tim. 3:6).	Growing in character and bearing fruit (2 Peter 1:5–8).	Ready and able to teach others (2 Tim. 2:2; Heb 5:12).	

A Gallery of Heroes of the Faith

Hebrews 11, the "Faith Chapter," begins with a definition (11:1). Faith is more than a belief, it is a confidence and can be defined as:

- a conviction of what is hoped for, what will happen one day
- a certainty about things that are unseen—the belief in a spiritual reality.

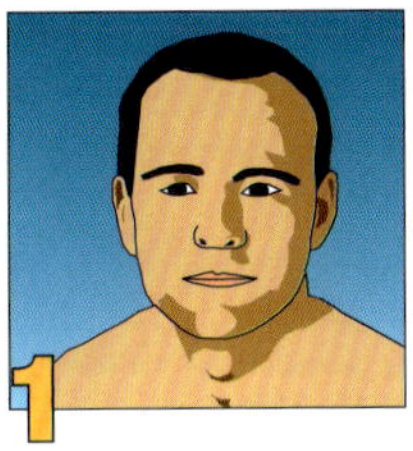

Abel
By faith, Abel offered a sacrifice to God, who accepted it, showing Abel's righteousness (11:4; Gen. 4:4).

Enoch
By faith, Enoch walked with God for 365 years, and one day God took him away (11:5; Gen. 5:23–24).

Noah
By faith, Noah built the ark even though there was no rain when he began to build it (11:7; Gen. 6:8–22).

Abraham (I)
By faith, Abraham left the city of Ur for an unknown land (11:8–10; Gen. 12:1–4, Rom. 4:20–22).

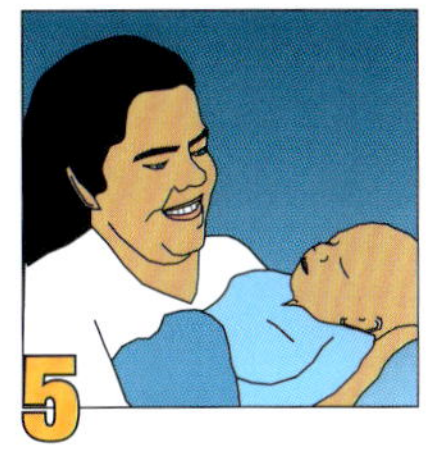

Sarah
By faith, Sarah trusted in God's promises to give her a son (11:11–12; Gen. 17:15–16; 21:1–2).

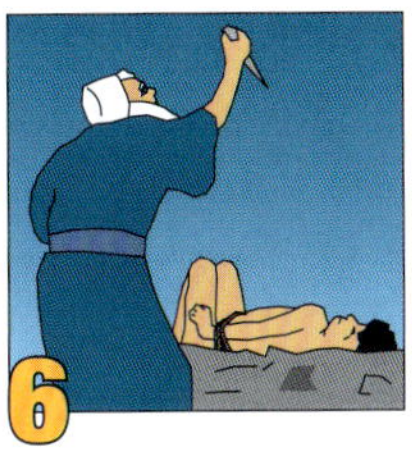

Abraham (II)
By faith, Abraham offered Isaac as a sacrifice, believing that God could raise him (11:17–19; Gen. 22:1–18).

Isaac
By faith, Isaac blessed his two sons, with a good understanding of their futures (11:20; Gen. 27:1–40).

Jacob
By faith, Jacob blessed Ephraim and Manasseh, and worshiped God (11:21; Gen. 47:31; 48:14–16).

Joseph
By faith, Joseph took his brothers' vow, knowing they would return to Canaan (11:22; Gen. 50:24–25).

Moses's parents
By faith, Moses's parents saw he was unusual and kept him hidden for three months (11:23; Ex. 2:2).

Moses (I)
By faith, Moses refused to call himself Pharaoh's grandson when he grew up (11:24–26; Ex. 2:10–12).

Moses (II)
By faith, Moses left Egypt without fear and kept his eyes on the one who is invisible (11:27; Ex. 2:15).

Moses (III)
By faith, Moses celebrated Passover, knowing that the blood would save them (11:28; Ex. 12:10–13).

Moses and the people
By faith, the people walked through the Red Sea on dry ground (11:29; Ex. 14:21–23).

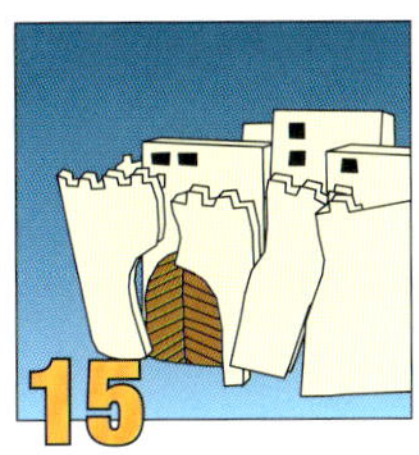

Joshua
By faith, the people marched around Jericho, and the walls of the city collapsed (11:30; Josh. 6:20).

Rahab
By faith, Rahab believed Jericho would fall, and dared to trust the spies (11:31; Josh. 2:1–21).

Gideon
By faith, Gideon defeated the Midianites, even sending some of his soldiers home (11:32; Judg. 6–8).

Barak
By faith, Barak went up against King Jabin and Sisera, the commander of his army (11:32; Judg. 4).

Samson
By faith, Samson received power from God to defeat Israel's enemies (11:32; Judg. 13–16).

Jephthah
By faith, Jephthah trusted God and the Lord gave Israel's oppressors into his hand (11:32; Judg. 11).

David
By faith, David challenged and defeated Goliath, the Philistine giant (11:32; 1 Sam. 16–1 Kings 1).

Samuel
By faith, when he was a boy, Samuel obeyed God's call, serving as Israel's last judge (11:32; 1 Sam. 1–25).

The prophets
By faith, all of the prophets listened to God and faithfully carried his words to the people (11:32).

JAMES

"The tongue is a small part of the body, but it makes great boasts ... But no human being can tame the tongue. It is a restless evil, full of deadly poison" (James 3:5, 8).

A FEW WORDS ABOUT THE AUTHOR

The letter states that it was written by James (1:1). The New Testament mentions four men named James. Both the father of Judas (Luke 6:16) and the son of Alphaeus (Mark 3:18) are extremely unlikely candidates, and John's brother was executed early (Acts 12:2). That leaves Jesus's half-brother as the probable author (Matt. 13:55; 1 Cor. 15:7; Gal. 1:19; 2:9, 12). Early church tradition also supports this.

A FEW WORDS ABOUT THE RECIPIENTS

The letter was written to "the 'twelve tribes'—Jewish believers scattered abroad" (James 1:1). This refers to the Jewish believers who were scattered throughout the Roman Empire. It is obvious in the letter that a Jew was writing to other Jewish believers (see "brothers and sisters" 1:2 and "our ancestor Abraham" 2:21). In response to the testing of their faith, James urged them to see their trials as a challenge to persevere (1:3).

A FEW WORDS ABOUT DATES

The letter does not mention the apostolic council in Jerusalem (AD 49) where Paul and James met and clarified the relation between grace and works (Acts 15:12–13). The fact that the recipients are scattered may refer to Herod Agrippa's persecution in AD 44 (1:1; Acts 12:1–3). This could indicate that the letter had been written early, sometime between AD 44 and 49, and most likely before Galatians.

THE WHOLE BOOK IN 25 WORDS

True faith is expressed in deeds. Therefore, believers must listen to and apply God's Word in practical action. Particularly in how we speak about others.

A SIMPLE STRUCTURE

1. Suffering – Trials shape sincere trust
(James 1:1–2:26)

2. Speech – Words show soul's state
(James 3:1–4:12)

3. Steadfastness – Steady hearts stay hopeful
(James 4:13–5:20)

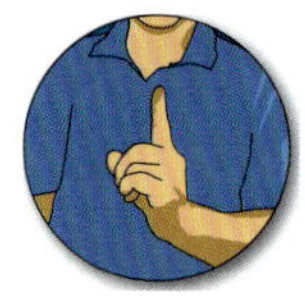

A FEW WORDS ABOUT KEY THEMES

• **Faith and works**—The letter challenges us to reflect on the relationship between faith and works, between grace and performance. How can we harmonize Paul's words on grace with James's words on works?

• **The tongue**—It is a symbol of the mindset behind what we say and do. Controlling the tongue is a challenge, and James points out the consequences of an unruly one (1:26; 3:5–12).

• **Part of the wisdom literature**—The letter is a collection of words of wisdom often seemingly unrelated to each other. Something like Proverbs.

• **Applying Scripture**—The letter emphasizes being doers of the word who apply Scripture, and not just hearers of it (1:22–25).

• **Healing**—Anointing with oil was the medical treatment of the day, not a religious ceremony (5:14–15; Luke 10:34).

A FEW TIPS ON WHAT TO LOOK FOR

Theme of the book:
The works of salvation

- Faith (at least 12 times)
- Doer/doers (5 times)
- Many exhortations, commands
- All illustrations and images (at least 15)
- Speech and the power of the tongue
- Parallels with the Sermon on the Mount (Matt. 5–7)
- Characteristics of a mature Christian (at least 10)
- What we learn about God
- The multiple references to nature (30)

Clothing in Biblical Times

James talks about how we judge people by their clothing. He writes, "Imagine [if] a man comes in with a gold ring on his finger and fine clothes, and at the same time a poor man in dirty clothes" (James 2:2). This is what the typical garments of James's day could have looked like.

1 Tunic: Also *chiton* or long shirt. Made of linen, wool, or cotton. Basic garment, worn closest to the body. May have been the only garment some people owned (Mark 14:52).

2 Abolla: Many men wore an *abolla*, a cloak. It was a square, double-folded piece of woolen cloth, fastened over one shoulder with a metal brooch (2 Tim. 4:13).

3 Himation: Used with or without a tunic. Without a tunic, it is often called an *achiton*. The *himation* is a rectangular piece of fabric wrapped in various ways around the body.

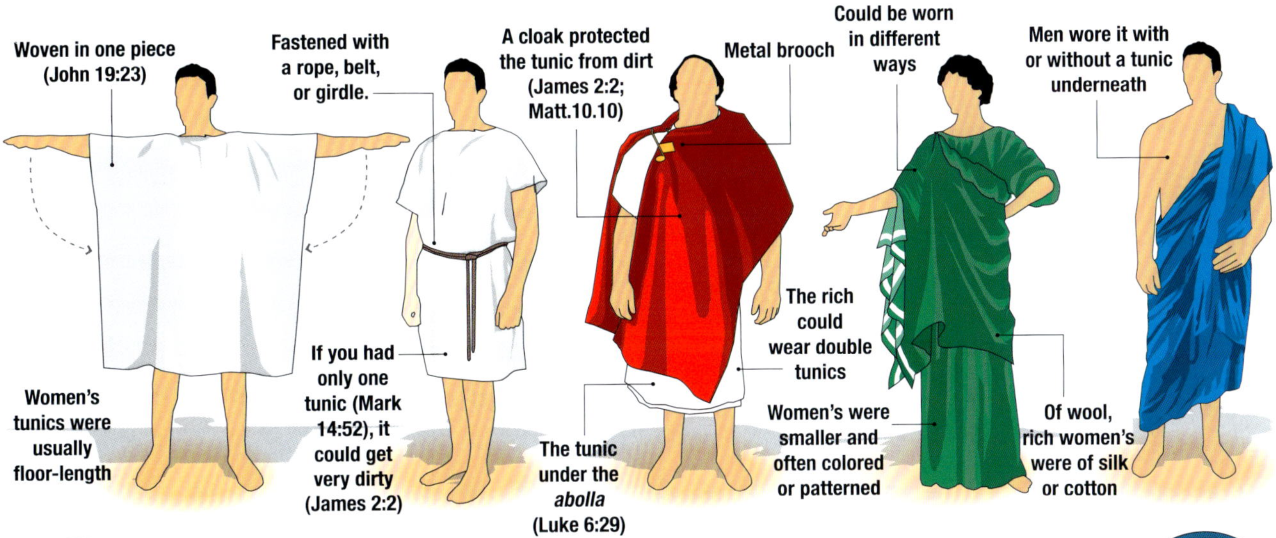

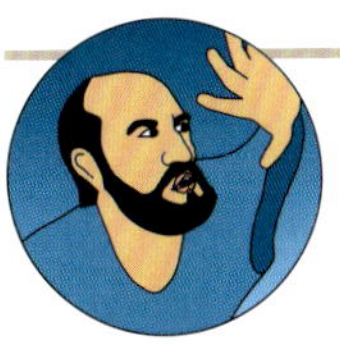

Paul

Do Paul and James say different things?

Because Paul talks about salvation by grace alone without works, while James argues for salvation with works, many think that they contradict each other. But do we really need to see the two authors' positions as being in conflict with each other?

James

	What Paul says about the gospel	What James says about the gospel
Where the issues arises	"By grace you have been saved through faith ... not by works, so that no one may boast" (Eph. 2:8–9 NIV). It is only faith that saves, "faith alone."	"What good is it ... if you say you have faith but don't show it by your actions? Can that kind of faith save anyone?" (James 2:14). It is not only faith that saves, "faith that saves is not alone."
The position summarized	What saves us is faith without works: "So we are made right with God through faith and not by obeying the law" (Rom. 3:28).	Faith is shown by works: "How can you show me your faith if you don't have good deeds? I will show you my faith by my good deeds" (James 2:17–26).
The meaning of "works"	Paul understood **works** as an attempt to earn salvation. But a person is not saved by works.	James understood **works** to be the result of salvation. A saved person does good works.
Where they are in agreement	**Paul agrees with James:** Paul teaches that good works flow naturally from saving faith (Gal. 5:6; Eph. 2:10; Phil. 2:11–12; Tit. 3:8).	**James agrees with Paul:** James teaches that the kingdom is only inherited by faith (James 2:5) and that Abraham was justified by faith (James 2:23).
Misconception	**The misconception Paul wants to correct:** Salvation is a result of our performance (legalism). Paul teaches about how sinners can become righteous before God.	**The misconception James wants to correct:** Works are unnecessary after a person has been saved (lawlessness). James teaches about how believers can show their faith before God.
Were Paul and James in open conflict?	At the apostolic council in Jerusalem (Acts 15), the main question was whether salvation is by grace through faith or by following the Jewish law (Acts 15:1). Peter's conclusion was clear (Acts 15:9, 11). James, who had a leading role in the discussion, never expressed a dissenting view from Peter or Paul on the issue (Acts 15:13–21).	
Perspectives	**Paul's perspective:** Looks at what sinners are expected to do in order to come into a right relationship with God (the sinner is in focus).	**James's perspective:** Looks at what believers are expected to do in order to prove that their faith is genuine (the believer is in focus).

Theology of the Tongue and Face

The Bible uses the human body is as an image, a metaphor, for spiritual truths. The face and its features are often understood to be like a mirror reflecting the inner person.

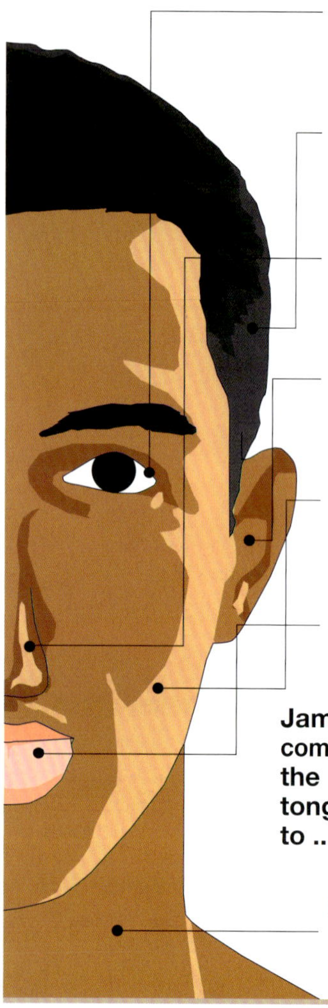

1 **The eye (Matt. 6:22–23):** Seeing is about conviction, beliefs. It reflects the inner person (Ps. 31:9). To have open eyes is to receive insight (Ps. 119:18). To look to the Lord is to turn to God with your inner self (Ps. 34:6). Failing to see is failing to receive or understand (Matt. 13:13).

2 **The hair and beard (Judg. 16:17):** Hair is seen as a symbol of strength and power and spiritual devotion (Num. 6:5). Shaving off one's hair then becomes submission to God (NUm. 6:18; 1 Cor. 11:14). The same applies to beards (Isa. 7:20; Ezra 9:3). Also a sign of being defeated and mourning (Jer. 48:37).

3 **The nose (Gen. 2:7):** We breathe through our nose, therefore the nose represents life itself (Gen. 2:7). To lose the nose is to lose life itself (Ezek. 23:25). A beautiful nose represents a beautiful mind (Song 7:4). Smoke rising from the nostrils refers to anger (Ps. 18:8).

4 **The ear (Matt. 13:15–16):** The ear and hearing are associated with putting what is said into action. To hear the word of God is to apply it (Matt. 7:24). To "listen carefully" to something means to obey what is said (Prov. 4:20; 5:1). "Itching ears" refers to what a person desires or wants (2 Tim. 4:3).

5 **The cheek (Matt. 5:39):** Striking someone on the cheek (face) is a way to humiliate and defeat the person (Job 16:10; Ps. 3:7; Mic. 5:1; John 19:3). Beautiful cheeks represent a beautiful inner character (Song 1:10; 5:13). To turn the other cheek is to submit to someone (Luke 6:29).

6 **The tongue (James 3:2):** Mouth, lips, and tongue refer not only to what is said but also to the attitude behind what is said (Ps. 5:9; 64:3; Matt. 15:18). The mouth (speech) is seen as a mirror of the inner man (Ps. 51:15; Luke 6:45). The tongue is ascribed great power (Prov. 18:21; James 3:3–5).

James compares the tongue to ...

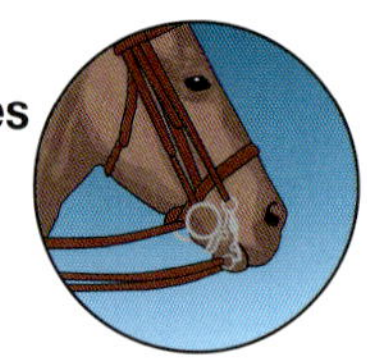

... a bit that guides a horse (3:3)

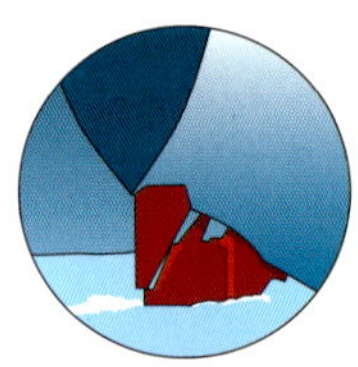

... a rudder that steers a ship (3:4)

... a spark that lights a fire (3:5)

7 **The neck (Prov. 6:21):** Wearing something around the neck reflects a person's character (Prov 3:3, 6:20–21). A stiff or outstretched neck shows pride (Job 15:26; Isa. 3:16; Jer. 27:8). Wearing a yoke around the neck shows submission to an authority (Jer. 27:8, 12; 28:11; Hos. 10:11; Gal. 5:1).

Mirror, mirror on the wall

James likens our relationship with the Bible to looking into a mirror. There are two ways to respond.

When we walk away from the mirror, we forget what we look like (James 1:23–24)

1 **See ourselves, but not care (James 1:23–24)**
God's Word is compared to a mirror in which we see ourselves. The word "look" means to consider, perceive. We don't take what we see with us when we leave the mirror, we aren't letting God's Word change us.

2 **See ourselves and deal with what we see (James 1:25)**
"Looking in" actually means "to bow" which can be understood as an attitude of humility, openness, and obedience. We don't forget, but what we see in the mirror translates into a changed life.

When we pause to look at the image, we see ourselves (James 1:25).

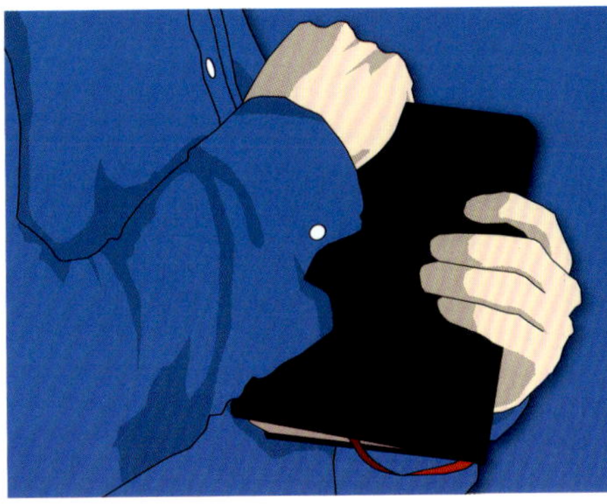

FIRST PETER

"Be very glad—for these trials make you partners with Christ in his suffering, so that you will have the wonderful joy of seeing his glory when it is revealed to all the world" (1 Peter 4:13).

A FEW WORDS ABOUT THE AUTHOR

The author is "Peter, an apostle of Jesus Christ" who claimed to be an eyewitness to the suffering of Christ (1:1; 5:1). The eloquent Greek of the letter may be due to the fact that Silas, a Roman citizen, assisted in its writing (Acts 16:29, 37; 1 Peter 5:12). The early church, including Irenaeus and Polycarp, unanimously affirmed that Peter was the author, also an earlier letter is mentioned in 2 Peter (2 Peter 3:1).

A FEW WORDS ABOUT THE RECIPIENTS

The recipients are called "God's chosen people who are living as foreigners in the provinces of Pontus, Galatia, Cappadocia, Asia, and Bithynia," all areas in Asia Minor (1:1). Peter called them "foreigners" (1:1), implying they were Jews living in scattered communities, and possibly also gentile believers who saw themselves as outsiders in their culture. Though they suffered outwardly, they were rooted in a new spiritual identity.

A FEW WORDS ABOUT DATES

Peter was executed around AD 67, during the reign of Emperor Nero, shortly before Nero took his own life in AD 68. Therefore the letter was probably written in the early or mid AD 60s, perhaps between AD 62 and 65. It was written from Rome, referred to as "Babylon" (5:13), where Peter was active. It may have been written just before or shortly after Rome burned and the Christians were persecuted (July AD 64).

THE WHOLE BOOK IN 25 WORDS

Peter writes about living holy and responsible lives as foreigners, experiencing suffering and hardship. Think about salvation, draw strength from the hope of Jesus's return.

A SIMPLE STRUCTURE

1. Identity
– God's people live set apart
(1 Peter 1:1–2:10)

2. Integrity
– Live honorably among unbelievers
(1 Peter 2:11–4:11)

3. Invincibility
– Hope holds on through hardship
(1 Peter 4:12–5:14)

A FEW WORDS ABOUT KEY THEMES

- **Suffering**—Mentioned about 20 times, talks about our trials (1:6), Christ's suffering (1:11), and how we share in them (2:12, 20–21, 4:12–13; 5:9, 10).
- **The use of the Old Testament**—One of the New Testament books that frequently quotes from and alludes to the Old Testament (1:16, 24–25; 2:3, 4, 6, 7, 9, 10, 22, 24; 3:6, 10–12, 14, 20; 4:8, 18; 5:5, 7).
- **The Christian life**—Grow into salvation (2:2), the goal of faith is the salvation of our souls (1:9), strive for genuine faith (1:7, 13–22).
- **Doctrines about Christ**—His eternal existence, his incarnation (1:20), his substitutionary death (1:19; 2:21–24; 3:18), his resurrection (1:3, 21; 3:18, 21), and his return in the last days (1:7; 4:5).
- **Calling, vocation**—We are called to be holy (1:15), to live in his wonderful light (2:9, 21; 3:9; 5:10).

A FEW TIPS ON WHAT TO LOOK FOR

Theme of the book: Suffering before the return of Christ

- Suffering (at least 20 times, both Christ's and ours)
- Valuable/precious (4 times)
- Hope (5 times)
- Teaching about Jesus's death on the cross (7 references)
- Signs of persecution (under Nero)
- Look for "holy" and "holiness"
- Called (5 times)
- Exhortations (30)
- Similarities with Paul's letters to the Ephesians and Colossians

An Overview of Peter's Life

The striking similarity between Peter and Paul.

1 Both healed a lame man

Peter healed a lame man at the Beautiful Gate (Acts 3:1–10). **Paul** healed a lame man in Lystra (Acts 14:8–10).

2 Both healed people indirectly

Peter when his shadow fell across people (Acts 5:15–16). **Paul** when people touched items he had touched (Acts 19:11–12).

3 Both confronted false teachers

Peter confronted a sorcerer named Simon (Acts 8:9, 18–24). **Paul** confronted the magician Barjesus (Acts 13:6–11).

Peter was called "the rock" (Matt. 16:18). He was Andrew's brother.

> "After Peter came to recognize his own inadequacy, his utter inability ... he became a rock-solid leader. (Charles Swindoll)

4 Both helped others receive the Holy Spirit

Peter helped believers in Samaria to receive the Spirit (Acts 8:14–17). **Paul** did the same in Ephesus (Acts 19:1–6).

5 Both raised someone from the dead

Peter raised Tabitha from the dead (Acts 9:36–41). **Paul** raised Eutychus (Acts 20:9–12).

6 Both received guidance through a vision

Peter had a vision telling him to go to Cornelius (Acts 10:9–20). **Paul** saw Jesus and was warned by him (Acts 22:17–21; 26:12–19).

7 Both were miraculously freed from prison

Peter was freed by an angel (Acts 12:1–11). **Paul** by an earthquake (Acts 16:25–34).

	Work	Calling	Maturity	Confession	Denial	Leadership	Martyrdom
KEY POINTS	• With family in Bethsaida • Worked as a fisherman • Worked with Andrew	• Called for the first time • Given time to grow • Called for the second time	• With family in Bethsaida • Worked as a fisherman • Worked with Andrew	• Confessed Jesus • Tried to stop Jesus • On the Mount of Transfiguration	• Warned by Jesus • Still denied Jesus • Met the risen one	• Received a new mission • Spoke on the day of Pentecost • Leader in the church	• Moved to Rome • Wrote two letters • Died a martyr's death
TOPICS	A fisherman who came to Jesus	A disciple who walked with Jesus	A follower who believed in Jesus	A leader who confessed Jesus	A friend who denied Jesus	An apostle who fought for Jesus	A martyr who gave his life for Jesus
	Peter worked as a fisherman	Peter was called to be a disciple of Jesus	Peter was taught by Jesus	Peter was challenged by Jesus	Peter received forgiveness from Jesus	Peter was filled with and led by the Spirit	Peter was crucified for his faith in Jesus
	Jesus was unknown to Peter	Jesus called Peter to follow him	Jesus lived alongside Peter	Jesus, Messiah, is identified by Peter	Jesus gave his life for Peter	Peter lived his life for Jesus	Peter gave his life for Jesus
PEOPLE	Father was John (John 1:42), had wife, mother-in-law (Luke 4:38)	Andrew, his brother (John 1:40), Philip, Nathaniel	The eleven other disciples: Andrew, James, John, Philip, Bartholomew, Thomas, Matthew, James, Thaddeus, Simon, and Judas Iscariot			James, Paul, John, Stephen, Philip	John Mark (1 Pet. 5:13)
LOCATIONS	Bethsaida	Capernaum, Galilee	Mostly Galilee but also Jerusalem, Judea, and Perea		Jerusalem	Jerusalem, Judea, and Samaria	From Jerusalem to Rome
TEXTS	John 1:40–42 Matt. 4:18–19	John 1:44 Matt. 4:18 Luke 5:1–11	Luke 6:13–14 Matt. 10:1–5 Mark 5:37	Matt. 16:16 Matt. 16:22 Matt. 17:1–2	John 13:38 Matt. 26:69–75 Luke 22:54–62	John 21:17 Acts 2:14 Acts 5:29	1, 2 Peter John 21:18–19, Tertullian
TIME PERIOD	About 30 years About AD 1 to 30	About 1 year AD 30	About 1 year AD 31	About 1 year AD 32	About 1 month April AD 33	About AD 33–62/67	About 1–5 years (?) AD 62/67

To Whom Did Jesus Preach?

Peter writes: "So [Jesus] went and preached to the spirits in prison—those who disobeyed God long ago when God waited patiently while Noah was building his boat" (1 Peter 3:19–20). Who did Jesus preach to? What did he say? And when did this take place?

START HERE: How are we to understand Jesus preaching to the spirits in prison?

WHO: Does "the spirits in prison" refer to humans (1 Peter 3:19)?

YES → **WHAT:** Did Jesus offer them salvation through the ark?

- YES → **WHEN:** Before the cross, in the days of Noah
  - YES → **CONCLUSION:** Jesus preached through Noah **to people in the days of Noah.** They did not believe and are now in hell.
- NO → **WHAT:** Did Jesus offer them salvation after they died?
  - YES → **WHEN:** Between his death and resurrection
    - YES → **CONCLUSION:** Jesus preached the gospel to fallen humans from the days of Noah now in the **realm of the dead**.
  - NO → **WHAT:** Did Jesus proclaim judgment after the cross?
    - YES → **WHEN:** Between his death and resurrection
      - YES → **CONCLUSION:** Jesus preached to fallen people from the days of Noah now in **hell**, confirming their final judgment.
    - NO → **WHAT:** Did Jesus offer deliverance from death/purgatory?
      - YES → **WHEN:** Between his death and resurrection
        - YES → **CONCLUSION:** Jesus preached to people from the days of Noah who then believed but did not enter the ark, who are now in **purgatory**.

NO → **WHO:** Does "the spirits in prison" refer to fallen angels (1 Peter 3:19; Jude 1:6)?

YES → **WHAT:** Did Jesus proclaim judgment after the cross?

- YES → **WHEN:** At the ascension, after the resurrection
  - YES → **CONCLUSION:** Jesus preached to the fallen angels from the days of Noah in **heaven**, confirming their final judgment.
  - NO → **WHEN:** Between his death and resurrection
    - YES → **CONCLUSION:** Jesus preached to the fallen angels from the days of Noah in **hell**, confirming their final judgment.

But why does it say "so he went" (1 Peter 3:19)? If it was through Noah, Jesus went nowhere.

But doesn't Scripture say that everyone must die *once* and then be judged (Heb. 9:27)

But the Greek word for "prison" (1 Peter 3:19) is never used of a place where people go to be punished. It is used of angels (2 Peter 2:4; Rev. 20:7).

But does the Bible even talk about purgatory?

Note that the plural form of "spirits" (1 Peter 3:19) always refers to angels (with one exception, Heb. 12:23).

But "fallen angels" are said to be in heaven (Rev. 12:7; 20:7).

Related Bible Passages: Ps. 16:10; Eph. 4:8–10; 1 Tim. 3:16; 1 Peter 4:4–6

Godly attitude in our relationships

Peter concludes his section on relationships by describing six attitudes that should characterize how Christians treat other people (1 Peter 2:13–3:12).

1 Unity (1 Peter 3:8)
Having the same mind, striving to work together despite differences.

2 Compassion (1 Peter 3:8)
Suffering together, being sensitive to others.

3 Godly love (1 Peter 3:8)
Loving as a family—a sincere, compassionate love that unites all true believers.

4 Mercy (1 Peter 3:8)
Gracious, forgiving, feeling with and for others.

5 Humility (1 Peter 3:8)
Not thinking too highly of yourself. Putting someone else's best interests before your own.

6 Restraint (1 Peter 3:9)
Not repaying evil with evil, not being vindictive, willing to forgive, turning the other cheek.

SECOND PETER

"You already know these things, dear friends. So be on guard; then you will not be carried away by the errors of these wicked people and lose your own secure footing" (2 Peter 3:17).

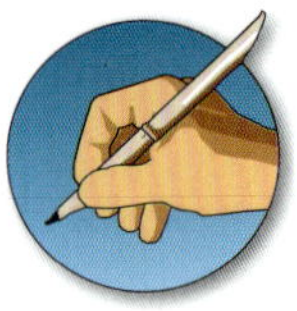

A FEW WORDS ABOUT THE AUTHOR

The authorship of 2 Peter is the most debated in the New Testament. Although Peter is listed as the author (1:1), critics argue that there are reasons to call the letter a pseudepigrapha, a book written later but in the name of a known person. However, the arguments are not convincing. None of the books excluded from the New Testament have anywhere near the amount of evidence and support that exists for the letter of 2 Peter.

A FEW WORDS ABOUT THE RECIPIENTS

It was probably addressed to the same people as his first letter, the churches scattered around Asia Minor. The letter can be seen as a spiritual last will. Peter gave it a personal touch, emphasizing his role as an eyewitness to Christ on the Mount of Transfiguration (1:16–18). He created emotional depth by using expressions from his life as a fisherman, such as "lure," which literally means "to catch with bait" (2:14, 18).

A FEW WORDS ABOUT DATES

Peter was martyred in Rome under Emperor Nero (1:13–15), who took his own life in AD 68. This, Peter's second letter, was probably written in the mid or late AD 60s, perhaps AD 64–67 and after the first letter (3:1). Those who don't believe Peter wrote the book tend to argue that the earliest the letter could have been written was in the early AD 100s. But this argument is less consistent with internal and historical evidence.

THE WHOLE BOOK IN 25 WORDS

As Christians grow in understanding, they stand firm against false teachers, especially those who deny Jesus's return and that the end of time will come.

A SIMPLE STRUCTURE

1. Foundation – God's promises bring certainty
(2 Peter 1:1–15)

2. Falsehood – False teachers are exposed
(2 Peter 1:16–2:22)

3. Future – Christ's return fuels hope
(2 Peter 3:1–18)

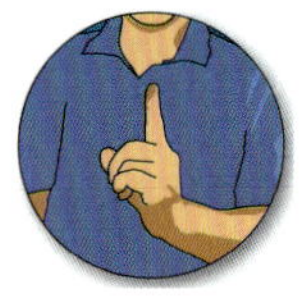

A FEW WORDS ABOUT KEY THEMES

- **Jesus's return**—Scornful people mock believers for Jesus's delay but God keeps his promises (3:3–4, 8–13). At the same time, he shows patience to allow time for repentance (3:9). Therefore, be on your guard against error (3:14–18).
- **Steps to spiritual maturity**—Supplement your faith with moral excellence, knowledge, self-control, patient endurance, godliness, brotherly affection, and love for everyone (1:5–8).
- **Knowledge**—Growing in knowledge of God and Jesus will give us all we need and lead to a fruitful life (1:2–3, 8; 3:18).
- **Reminders**—Wants the recipients to always remember what he has taught them (1:12) and to stimulate wholesome thinking (3:1; also 1:13, 15; 3:2).
- **False teachers**—Peter lists 23 characteristics of false teachers, pointing out their doctrine, character, and methods (2:1–19).

A FEW TIPS ON WHAT TO LOOK FOR

Theme of the book: Apostasy and the return of Christ

- Knowledge (15 times) as opposed to false teaching
- Attitudes toward the day of the Lord and discussion about the return of Jesus.
- Beloved
- Eight steps to spiritual growth (1:5–8)
- Depravity (4 times)
- Remembering/reminding
- Compare 2 Peter with Jude
- Peter's understanding of Paul's writings (2 Peter 3:16)

The Signs of False Teachers

Peter warns against false teachers who were "among you" (2 Peter 2:1). Every church runs the same risk. Here are the signs to look for:

1 They "cleverly teach destructive heresies" (2:1).

2 They "deny the Master who bought them" (2:1).

3 They slander "the way of truth" (2:2).

4 They "make up clever lies to get hold of your money" (2:3).

5 They "follow their own twisted sexual desire" (2:10a).

6 They "despise authority" (2:10b).

7 They "are proud and arrogant" (2:10c).

8 They dare to "scoff at supernatural beings" (2:10d).

9 They "scoff at things they do not understand" (2:12a).

10 They are "like animals" (2:12b).

11 They "indulge in evil pleasures in broad daylight" (2:13a).

12 They are a "disgrace and a stain among you" (2:13b).

13 They "delight in deception" (2:13c).

14 They "commit adultery with their eyes" (2:14a).

15 "Their desire for sin is never satisfied" (2:14b).

16 They "lure unstable people" (2:14c).

17 They "are well trained in greed" (2:14d).

18 They "have wandered off the right road" (2:15).

19 They "are as useless as dried-up springs" (2:17a).

20 They are "as mists blown away by the wind" (2:17b).

21 They "brag ... with empty, foolish boasting" (2:18a).

22 They "appeal to twisted sexual desires" (2:18b).

23 They "are slaves of sin and corruption" (2:19).

Signs of false teachers include:
- their teachings
- their methods
- their character

Peter or ... not Peter

Did Peter write 2 Peter?

The New Testament letter whose authorship is most disputed is 2 Peter. Critics argue that although Peter is the stated author, there are reasons to conclude that the book is a pseudepigrapha, that is, a book written later but put into the mouth of someone who is known—in this case Peter. This is a summary of the arguments for and against the different objections.

Argument	Peter did not write the letter	Peter wrote the letter
Language and style of the letter	The language and style are different from 1 Peter. It also differs in style from anything else we know that Peter said in the New Testament. The letter uses fifty-seven words that are not found in any other New Testament book.	The language and style in the two letters are not as different as some claim. Peter may be deliberately imitating a form of skillful writing found among the recipients. He may also have become more skilled at language and writing in the intervening years.
The use of a scribe	If someone other than Peter wrote the letter, it was not only a scribe but another writer who had a free hand, not only with words and expressions but also with the content.	Peter most likely used a different scribe than for his first letter, which explains the difference in style. It is also possible that Peter wrote the second letter himself, without the help of a scribe.
Heresy	The false doctrine the letter opposes is a form of Gnosticism not found until the AD 100s. This is not consistent with it being written in the AD 60s.	The letter does not explicitly state that it was opposed to Gnosticism. Since we can't identify the heresy, we cannot claim that it is from the 100s.
When Scripture became canon	The letter refers to Paul's letters. However, during Peter's lifetime, there was no complete collection of Paul's letters that could be called Scripture (2 Peter 3:16). The letters were not considered part of Scripture until long after Peter's death.	The apostles considered their own words to have the same authority as Scripture; no collection of letters was needed (2 Cor. 10:11; 2 Thess. 2:15; 3:14; 1 Peter 1:10–12). Attributing authority to Paul's letters during Peter's lifetime is not problematic.
Extra-biblical evidence	The letter is not mentioned by any of the early church fathers until the third century. It is missing from the oldest list of accepted books (late AD 100s). Eusebius expressed uncertainty about the letter and counted it among the disputed letters.	The problem is exaggerated. Several early church fathers show the influence of the letter, for example the Apocalypse of Peter (AD 110–140). No book excluded from Scripture has nearly as much supporting evidence as 2 Peter does.

Some Troublemakers in the New Testament

ANANIAS AND SAPPHIRA
A couple in Jerusalem gave part of the proceeds from a property sale to the church, claiming it was everything. But they secretly kept some. When confronted, they fell down dead (Acts 5:1–11).

SIMON THE SORCERER
Simon of Samaria came to the apostles and offered them money so he could receive the power of the Spirit. But the apostles refused and admonished him: "Your heart is not right with God" (Acts 8:4–24).

ELYMAS (BAR-JESUS)
A Jewish false prophet in Cyprus who practiced sorcery. He opposed Paul and tried to prevent the governor from coming to faith, but Paul, filled with the Spirit, rebuked him (Acts 13:6–12).

DEMETRIUS
Some people in Ephesus listened to Paul and stopped buying silver shrines (idols). Then the silversmith Demetrius started a riot because he and his craftsmen were losing money (Acts 19:21–32).

"A CERTAIN PERSON"
This person's actions had caused Paul grief. Perhaps it was the man "living in sin with his step-mother," who was expelled from the church (1 Cor. 5:1–8), or someone who spoke ill of Paul (2 Cor. 2:5–7).

EUODIA AND SYNTYCHE
Two women who had fallen out with each other. Paul appealed for one of his associates, perhaps Epaphroditus, to help the women "settle their disagreement" (Phil. 4:2–3).

HYMENAEUS
His faith had been shipwrecked and he had caused Paul much harm. He engaged in idle talk and led some astray, claiming that the resurrection of the dead had already occurred (1 Tim. 1:19–20; 2 Tim. 2:16–18).

ALEXANDER
A coppersmith gone astray in the faith, who greatly disappointed Paul and was handed over to Satan to learn not to blaspheme; possibly involved in riots (Acts 19:33; 1 Tim. 1:19–20; 2 Tim. 4:14–15).

PHILETUS
Had engaged in foolish talk, words that spread like cancer. Turned some people's faith upside down, claiming that the resurrection of the dead had already occurred. He had "left the path of truth" (2 Tim. 2:16–18).

DIOTREPHES
A man who spread malicious slander and refused to receive traveling teachers. He also tried to prevent others from being hospitable, driving those people out of the church (3 John 1:9–10).

DEMAS
A disciple of Paul who was with him during his imprisonment in Rome (Col. 4:14; Philem. 1:24). But when Paul was imprisoned a second time, he abandoned him, loving the things of the world (2 Tim. 4:10).

JEZEBEL
The church in Thyatira tolerated a false prophetess referred to as Jezebel—probably a symbolic name. Perhaps named for King Ahab's pagan wife (1 Kings 16:31). She deceived the faithful (Rev. 2:20–23).

PHYGELUS AND HERMOGENES
When Paul was imprisoned in Rome, Christians in the Province of Asia deserted him, including Phygelus and Hermogenes. We know nothing about them, but Paul chose to name these two (2 Tim. 1:15).

FALSE APOSTLES, BROTHERS, TEACHERS, PROPHETS, AND WITNESSES
Apostles: 2 Cor. 11:13, ***Brothers:*** 2 Cor. 11:26, ***Teachers:*** 2 Peter 2:1, ***Prophets:*** Acts 13:6, ***Witnesses:*** Acts 6:13

FIRST JOHN

"If we are living in the light, as God is in the light, then we have fellowship with each other, and the blood of Jesus, his Son, cleanses us from all sin" (1 John 1:7).

A FEW WORDS ABOUT THE AUTHOR

The letter does not mention an author, but it was clearly written by an eyewitness to the life and work of Jesus (1:1). There are significant similarities with the Gospel of John, both in style and theme. Early church fathers such as Irenaeus, Clement of Alexandria, and Papias either quote, allude to, or explicitly speak of John as the author. It is therefore generally accepted that the apostle John wrote the letter.

A FEW WORDS ABOUT THE RECIPIENTS

There is no recipient specified in the letter, but the intended recipients were probably a church in the Roman province of Asia, perhaps near Ephesus. Alternatively, it may have been a circular letter sent to several churches (see Rev. 2:1–3:21). Since John calls them "dear children," it is assumed that there was a personal relationship between him and the recipients (2:18, 28; 3:7, 18; 4:4; 5:21).

A FEW WORDS ABOUT DATES

The dating of the letter is closely linked to the Gospel of John and its dating. The Gospel is often placed between AD 85 and 95. The letter was likely written after John completed his Gospel, before his exile to the island of Patmos in AD 94–95 (Rev. 1:9). Therefore, the letter most likely dates from the late-80s to mid-90s, possibly before or around the same time as 2 and 3 John. It addresses the rising controversy over proto-gnosticism.

THE WHOLE BOOK IN 25 WORDS

As Christians grow in understanding, they stand firm against false teachers, especially those who deny Jesus's return and that time will come to an end.

A SIMPLE STRUCTURE

1. Identity – Believers are God's children
(1 John 1:1–2:14)

2. Integrity – Walking faithfully in the light
(1 John 2:15–4:6)

3. Immortality – Trusting God for eternal life
(1 John 4:7–5:21)

A FEW WORDS ABOUT KEY THEMES

- **Assurance of salvation**—Note how clearly the letter says that we "[may] know [we] have eternal life" (5:11–13).
- **What we learn about Jesus**—The letter is directed against false teachers who question whether Jesus is both true God and true man, God in human form (1:3; 2:22; 4:2–3; 5:15; 2 John 1:7).
- **Sin and forgiveness**—Every Christian sins (1:8, 10), but in Christ we find grace and forgiveness (1:7, 9; 2:1, 2, 12; 3:4–6, 8–9; 4:10; 5:16–18).
- **Contrasts**—John uses many contrasts, such as light and darkness, among others (1:5; 2:7–8, 13–16, 18, 20–21; 3:1–10, 14–16; 4:1–3, 18–19; 5:11–12).
- **A Controversial Verse**—Some medieval manuscripts include extra words about the Father, the Word, and the Spirit (1 John 5:7–8), often called "*Comma Johanneum*." Scholars generally regard it as a later addition.

A FEW TIPS ON WHAT TO LOOK FOR

Theme of the book:
Community in the church

- Know (at least 30 times)
- World (23 times)
- Love (at least 21 times)
- Notice all the contrasts (dark/light, acknowledges/doesn't acknowledge)
- Lie/Lies (7 times)
- Which errors John is trying to correct
- What can be learned about fellowship
- To write down (10 times)
- Parallels with the Gospel of John
- To remain (at least 15 times)

An Overview of John's Life

Seven key events in John's life
These important events shaped John into the man he became.

> "John's perceptive, soaring spirit grasped the inner truths of Christ with eagle-like vision, beyond outward symbols. (Charles Spurgeon)

1 A [possible] cousin of Jesus
His mother Salome may have been the sister of Jesus's mother, Mary (John 19:25), in which case John and Jesus were cousins.

2 Encounter with Jesus at the Sea of Galilee
John was at the Sea of Galilee when Jesus called him to be a disciple, to fish for people (Matt. 4:18–22).

3 With Jesus on the Mount of Transfiguration
Jesus took John up the Mount of Transfiguration, where he saw Jesus with Moses and Elijah (Matt. 17:1–8).

* **The apostle John may have been** a disciple of John the Baptist. Two disciples were there when Jesus met John the Baptist: Andrew (John 1:35–40) and possibly John.

4 Accompanied Jesus in Gethsemane
In Gethsemane, Jesus took three of the disciples, his inner group, deeper into the garden, one of them was John (Mark 14:33).

5 With Jesus and his mother at the cross
Jesus asked John to take care of his mother, Mary. And he asked her to take care of John (John 19:25–27).

6 Saw the empty tomb
John believed in the resurrection when he entered the empty tomb, before he met the risen Lord (John 20:8).

7 Received visions on the island of Patmos
Exiled to Patmos where he was given visions and a glimpse into the future (Rev. 1:9–10; 4:1–2).

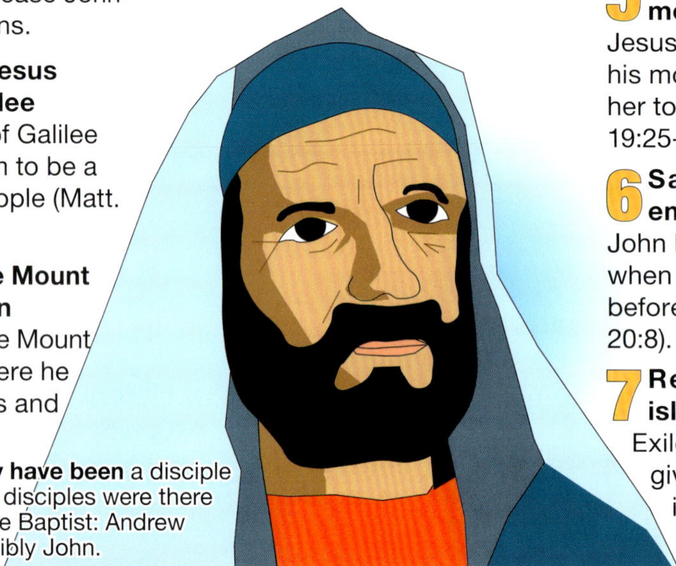

	Employment	Calling	Growing	Trust	Leadership	Education	Vision
KEY POINTS	• Fisherman in Galilee • With John the Baptist* • First encounter with Jesus	• Called to follow Jesus • Left Galilee • Followed Jesus	• Became one of the Twelve • One of the inner circle • On Mount of Transfiguration	• With Jesus at the Last Supper • With Jesus at the cross • Met the risen Jesus	• Participated in miracles • Admonished by the Sanhedrin • Traveled to Samaria	• Moved to Ephesus • Leader in the church • Wrote four texts	• Exiled to Patmos • Had visions from God • Died a natural death
TOPICS	Fisherman (Matt. 4:21)	Disciple (Mark 3:17)	Chosen (Mark 5:37)	Beloved (John 20:2)	Apostle (Gal. 2:9)	Teacher (Acts 4:13)	Prophet (Rev. 1:10)
	Encountered the gospel (Mark 1:19–20)	Followed the gospel (Luke 6:14)	Understood the gospel (Matt. 16:15–17)	Entrusted with the gospel (Matt. 28:18–20)	Shared the gospel (Acts 4:13)	Wrote down the gospel (John 21:24)	Suffered for the gospel (Rev. 1:9)
	Jesus came to John (Matt. 4:21)	Jesus called John (Mark 3:17–19)	Jesus led John (Matt. 10:2)	Jesus entrusted Mary to John (John 19:26–27)	Spirit leads John (Acts 3:1–10)	Spirit spoke through John (1, 2, 3 John)	Jesus revealed himself to John (Revelation)
PEOPLE	Zebedee, James, John the Baptist	The eleven other disciples: Peter, Andrew, James, Philip, Bartholomew, Thomas, Matthew, James, Thaddeus, Simon, Judas Iscariot, as well as Mary, Jesus's mother			James, Paul, Peter, Stephen, Philip, and James the brother of Jesus	The chosen lady and her children, Gaius	The seven churches of Asia Minor
LOCATIONS	Sea of Galilee	Mostly Galilee but also Jerusalem, Judea, and Perea		Jerusalem		Ephesus	Patmos/ Heaven
TEXTS	John 1:35–40; Matt. 4:21–22; Mark 1:19–20	Luke 5:1–11; Mark 5:35–43	Matt. 17:1–13; Mark 10:35–45	John 19:25–27; John 20:2–10; John 21:4–14	Acts 1:13; 3:1, 3, 11; 4:13, 19; 8:14	1, 2 and 3 John	Revelation
TIME PERIOD	Around 20 years AD 10/15–30	1 year AD 30	1 year AD 31	1 year AD 32–33	Around 12 years AD 33–45	Around 45 years AD 45–90	Around 5 years AD 90–96

Do Not Love This World

John highlights the believer's conflict with the world, *kosmos* in Greek. In this context, "world" refers to human culture under the influence of evil. Believers are expected neither to conform to the world nor to love it or anything in it (Rom. 12:2; 1 John 2:15–16).

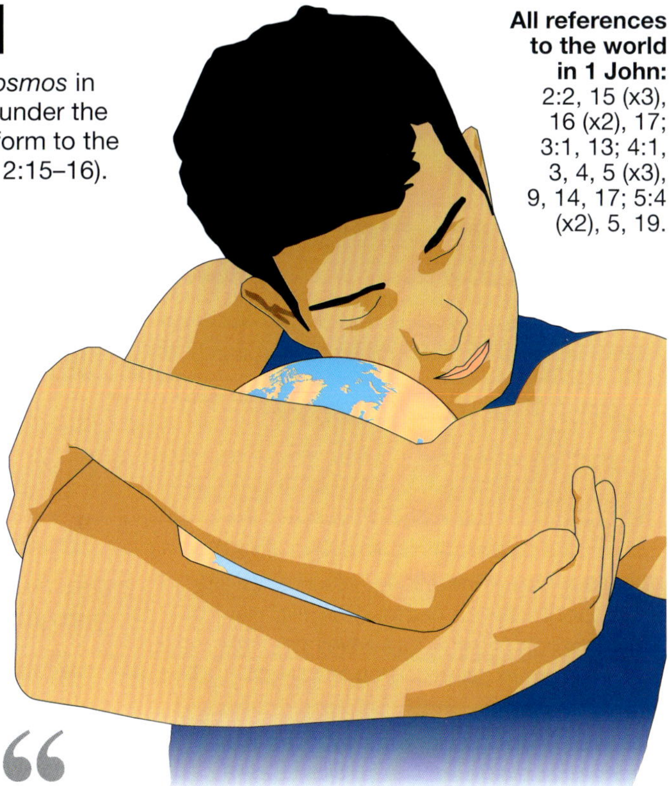

All references to the world in 1 John: 2:2, 15 (x3), 16 (x2), 17; 3:1, 13; 4:1, 3, 4, 5 (x3), 9, 14, 17; 5:4 (x2), 5, 19.

To love the world

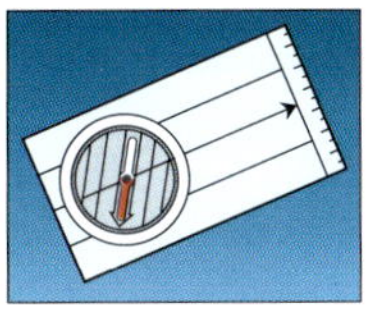

1 About my values
This is about what I think is right or wrong, what the basis for my moral decisions is, and what the motives for my actions are.

2 About my priorities
This is about what I consider important, what I value most, what I give my time, my money, and my thoughts to. What comes first in life my life.

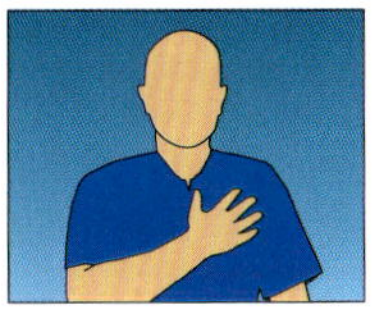

3 About my beliefs
This is about what I stand for, my convictions. It's about what I believe, but also how I arrive at the conclusion that what I believe is true.

To love what is in the world

1 The desires of the flesh
What I want to do. An inner urge to act for my own pleasure—something we struggle to control, the desires that drive us (Luke 9:59–61).

2 The desires of the eyes
What I want to own. An inner longing to have, collect and possess—whether money or property, big or small (Mark 10:20–22).

3 The desires of the ego
Someone I want to be. An inner desire to be seen and noticed—to "be someone," hold a title or position, and seek power (1 Peter 5:3).

> "**Do not love this world nor the things it offers you,** for when you love the world, you do not have the love of the Father in you. For the world offers only a craving for physical pleasure, a craving for everything we see, and pride in our achievements and possessions. These are not from the Father, but are from this world (1 John 2:15–16).

The three great enemies of the Christian

	Scripture	The problem	Our defense	The challenge
 **The world** – the fallen culture	"This **world** [and] the things it offers you … are not from the Father, but are from this **world**" (1 John 2:15–17).	How the world influences us—everything from fashion to moral values.	**The Father** stands against the world (1 John 2:15).	**Flee:** "You, Timothy, are a man of God; so run from all these evil things" (1 Tim. 6:11). "Run from anything that stimulates youthful lusts" (2 Tim. 2:22; see Tit. 2:12).
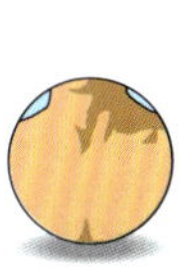 **The flesh** – our sinful nature	"I know that nothing good lives in me, that is, in my **sinful nature**…. Who will free me from this life that is dominated by sin and death?" (Rom. 7:18–24).	The way our sinful nature affects us—the inner desires of fallen humanity.	**The Spirit** stands against the flesh (Gal. 5:16, 23).	**Oppose:** "If through the power of the Spirit you put to death the deeds of your sinful nature, you will live" (Rom. 8:13; 6:12–13).
 **The devil** – the rebellious angel	"Stay alert! Watch out for your great enemy, **the devil**. He prowls around like a roaring lion, looking for someone to devour" (1 Peter 5:8).	The way the evil one's direct attacks affect us—the temptations he uses.	**Christ** stands against Satan (Heb. 2:14–15; 1 John 3:8).	**Stand Firm:** "Stand firm against him, and be strong in your faith. Remember that your family of believers all over the world is going through the same kind of suffering you are" (1 Peter 5:9).

SECOND JOHN

"If anyone comes to your meeting and does not teach the truth about Christ, don't invite that person into your home or give any kind of encouragement" (2 John 1:10).

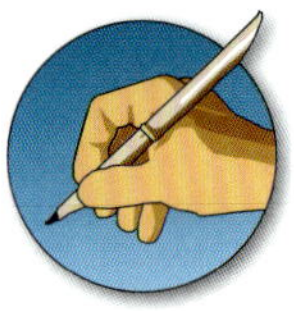

A FEW WORDS ABOUT THE AUTHOR

The letter was written by "the elder" (2 John 1:1). The title probably refers not only to a church elder but also to an older, respected man within the community. Early church fathers identified the author as the apostle John. The letter's strong similarity in style, vocabulary, and content with 1 John suggests that the same arguments made for the authorship of the first letter also apply here, strengthening the case that John was the author.

A FEW WORDS ABOUT THE RECIPIENTS

The letter was written "to the chosen lady and her children" (2 John 1:1, 5). It probably doesn't refer to a specific woman, since that would make the meaning of verse 5 seem ambiguous or uncertain. It is more likely that the "chosen lady" is the personification of a church, and the greeting at the end of the letter from "the children of your sister" is a warm greeting from another closely related church community (2 John 1:13).

A FEW WORDS ABOUT DATES

The dating of the letter is linked to the Gospel of John and its dating. The Gospel is often dated to between AD 80 and 90. The letter was likely written after John completed his Gospel. This means it was probably composed toward the end of the AD 80s or in the first half of the 90s, before John was exiled to the island of Patmos in AD 94–95 (Rev. 1:9), so AD 85–954 Its tone reflects an urgent response to emerging false teaching.

THE WHOLE BOOK IN 25 WORDS

There is a difference between those who live in truth and deceivers. Love one another, but do not tolerate impostors who refuse to confess Christ.

A SIMPLE STRUCTURE

1. Love
– Walk in truth and obedience, faithful love guards against deception
(2 John 1:1–6)

2. Loyalty
– Protect the community's purity, reject false teachers
(2 John 1:7–13)

A FEW WORDS ABOUT KEY THEMES

• **Truth—**The concept is central to John. Mentioned 52 times in his Gospel and 22 times in his three letters. John emphasizes that we should live in the truth (2 John 1:4) and love because of the truth (Jude 1:2, see also 1:1, 3).

• **Love—**We should love one another (1:5), it is a natural consequence of faith (1:2, see also 1:1, 3, 6 [x2]).

• **Fellowship—**John sets a boundary for the church. We are to love one another (1:5), but not all doctrines and teachers are welcome (1:10–11).

• **Foundation of faith**—Living in the truth, as the Father commanded, and accepting the truths about Jesus as expressed in his teachings (1:4, 7, 9).

• **Warning against false teachers—** John warns against teachers who deny Christ's humanity (1:7). He calls them deceivers, the antichrist. They have wandered from Christ's teaching (1:9).

A FEW TIPS ON WHAT TO LOOK FOR

Theme of the book:
False teachers and the church

- Truth (5 times), love (4 times)
- What false teaching is, how we respond to false teachers
- What we learn about Christ
- Command (4 times), teach (3 times)
- The relationship between love, truth, and obedience
- To live (4 times)
- Where John changes tone from praise to warning (1:7)
- The 8 verses that parallel verses found in 1 John (1:1, 2, 3, 4, 5, 6, 7, 9)

How Love, Truth, and Obedience Are Connected

In 2 John, John speaks of three major themes in the letter: love, truth, and obedience to God's commandments. This is how they are connected.

1 Relationship between love and truth

• Truth refers to God's revelation in Scripture (2 John 1:1, 7–9); "whom I love in the truth" (1:1–3) means a love based on common faith.
• **Love** without truth turns emotional; leads away from God (1:5–6).
• **Truth** without love becomes harsh and judgmental (James 2:13) driving people into spiritual pride.
• **Truth and love** in harmony lead to a balanced Christian character, reflecting Christ's nature in both word and deed (2 John 1: 2; Eph. 4:15; 1 John 2:5).

2 Relationship between truth and obedience

• Obedience means "walking" or "living in" (2 John 1:4, 6). Refers to "living according to," putting faith into practice (Eph. 5:2; Phil. 3:17–18; 1 John 1:6–7; 3 John 1:3).
• **Truth** without obedience is an empty confession; life contradicts faith (James 1:22; Tit. 1:16).
• **Obedience** without truth misleads, resulting in practices God never intended (Matt. 15:9).
• **Obedience and truth** in harmony lead to a solid foundation for faith and life (John 14:23).

3 Relationship between obedience and love

• Love means "benevolence toward," "divine love." It is a choice, a commandment we choose to obey (2 John 1:6). The ability to love is a gift from God.
• **Obedience** without love is legalism, it makes demands, and has no grace or forgiveness.
• **Love** without obedience becomes self-affirmation built on emotion.
• **Obedience and love** in harmony lead to care for one another in the spirit of Christ.

The Doctrine of the Incarnation

The letter insists that the Son of God came in human flesh. Yet some considered the body inherently evil, and therefore resisted the idea of God incarnate; their views influenced the community. John says that those who do not confess that "Jesus Christ came in a real body" are deceivers (2 John 1:7).

JOHN'S ARGUMENT:
• **The problem:** Many deny that Christ has come in a real body (2 John 1:7).
• **The warning:** Watch out for them (2 John 1:8); they have no relationship with God (2 John 1:9).
• **The instruction:** Don't invite them or encourage them (2 John 1:10–11).

DEFINITION: The **incarnation** is the doctrine that the eternal Son of God assumed a true and complete human nature, becoming fully human while remaining fully divine, united in one person, and that this union of divine and human natures continues forever, even after his resurrection and ascension.

THE HISTORY OF CHRIST'S INCARNATION
• **From eternity:** Jesus is the eternal Son (John 1:1–3; Col. 1:16–17).
• **Prophecies:** Divine promises point to him as the coming Messiah (Gen. 3:15; 12:3; Isa. 7:13–14; 9:6; Mic. 5:2).
• **Annunciation:** The eternal Son assumes a fully human nature in Mary's womb through the Holy Spirit, marking the actual beginning of the incarnation (Luke 1:26–38; Matt. 1:18–25).
• **Birth:** True human birth—fully human, fully divine (Luke 2:1–20; John 1:14).
• **Life:** Fully God, living with genuine human limitations (Phil. 2:6–8).
• **Death:** A real human death while united to the divine nature, offering himself as our atonement (Rom. 3:25).
• **Resurrection:** He rises bodily, not just spiritually, and his human nature is transformed into a glorified body (Luke 24:39; 1 Cor. 15:35–49).
• **Ascension:** Christ ascends in his glorified human body (Acts 1:9–11).
• **Heavenly reign:** Intercedes for us as a human mediator (1 Tim. 2:5; Heb. 4:14–16; 7:25).
• **Second coming and eternal reign:** Christ returns bodily and visibly, continuing forever as the incarnate Son. His humanity remains for all eternity (Acts 1:11; Rev. 21:1–22:21).

THIRD JOHN

"They have told the church here of your loving friendship. Please continue providing for such teachers in a manner that pleases God" (3 John 1:6).

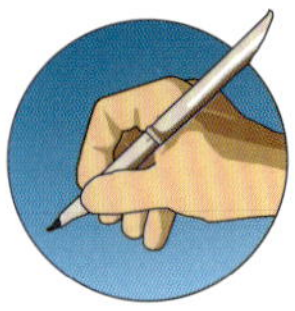

A FEW WORDS ABOUT THE AUTHOR

The letter was written by "the elder" (3 John 1:1), an expression that probably refers to the author's age and authority. Early church fathers point to the apostle John as the author and Origen states that John wrote three letters. The similarity in style and content with 1 John suggests that the arguments for the apostle John's authorship of the first letter also apply to the third letter, which carries a similarly personal and pastoral tone.

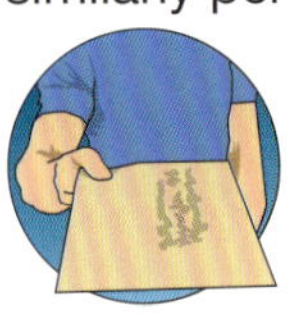

A FEW WORDS ABOUT THE RECIPIENTS

The letter is addressed to "Gaius, my dear friend, whom I love" (3 John 1:1). There are several men named Gaius in the New Testament (Acts 19:29; 20:4; Rom. 16:23; 1 Cor. 1:14). The recipient of the letter is probably not one of them, but a completely different Gaius. We do not know in which city the church to which Gaius belonged was located, but it was most likely close to John's base in Ephesus (1:9, 10, 14).

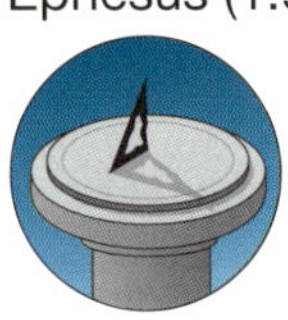

A FEW WORDS ABOUT DATES

The dating of the letter is linked to the dating of the Gospel of John, usually dated to between AD 80 and 90. John probably wrote it after he wrote his gospel. So the letter was most likely written toward the end of the AD 80s or in the first half of the 90s, before John was exiled to the island of Patmos in AD 94–95 (Rev. 1:9). This gives a probable date of AD 85–94, when there was increasing pressure on believers.

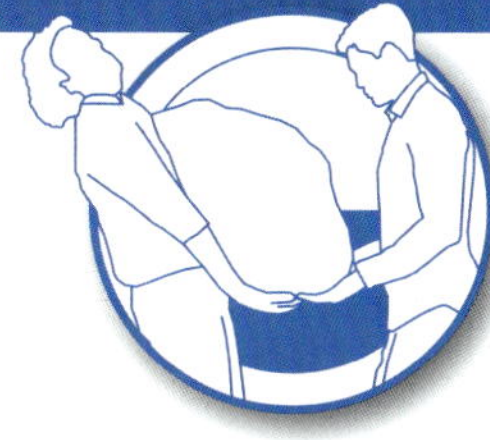

THE WHOLE BOOK IN 25 WORDS

Believers should know and fight for the truth of the gospel. One way is to show hospitality to Christian servants who valiantly work for Christ.

A SIMPLE STRUCTURE

1. Generosity – True faith is shown in love, action, and practical care
(3 John 1:1–8)

2. Greed – Selfish ambition hinders community, truth, and spiritual responsibility
(3 John 1:9–15)

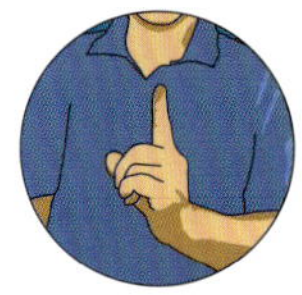

A FEW WORDS ABOUT KEY THEMES

- **Hospitality**—Show it to those who work for the truth. Gives examples of hospitality (3 John 1:6–8) and inhospitality (1:9–10).
- **Pride**—Seeing oneself as most important. Not only did Diotrephes fail to show hospitality, but he also loved his position as a leader (1:9).
- **Faithfulness**—Doing one's duty (1:8), living in truth (1:3), living in love and caring for others (1:6).
- **Truth**—Truth refers not only to purity of doctrine but also to the genuine character of the person. To live in truth (1:3) and to work together for truth (1:8, also 1, 3, 4, 12).
- **Encouragement**—Build up believers through words and deeds (1:5, 8).
- **The book's three named people**—The hospitable Gaius (1:1), the proud and wicked Diotrephes (1:9), and Demetrius with a good testimony (1:12).

A FEW TIPS ON WHAT TO LOOK FOR

Theme of the book: Hospitality in the church

- Similarities with 1 and 2 John
- Compare Gaius, Diotrephes, and Demetrius
- True and truthful
- The words "love" and "beloved"
- The absence of Jesus's name, the use of "for the Lord" (1:7)
- What is learned about Christian character from Gaius (1:4), what it means to "live in truth" (1:3, 4)
- The conflicts reveal deeper spiritual truths

Don't Follow Bad Examples ...

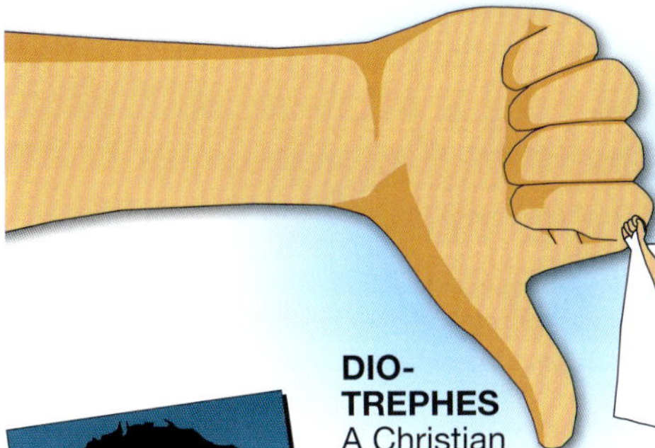

DIO-TREPHES
A Christian who wants to appear as the fore-most among them (3 John 1:9). He spreads malicious slander and actively drives believers out of the church (1:10). Does not listen to reprimands.

1
Wants to be the best
Has a distorted self-image. Cares about position. Wants to be seen as the leader of the church (1:9a).

2
Shows no hospitality
Does not care about showing hospitality. Re-fuses to receive other believers (1:9b–10).

3
Spreads mali-cious slander
Does not hesitate to bad-mouth others. Spreads rumors and mali-cious slander (1:10).

4
Drives believers out of the church
Hinders and drives out mem-bers of the church who dare to disagree with him (1:10).

... but Follow Good Examples (3 John 1:11)

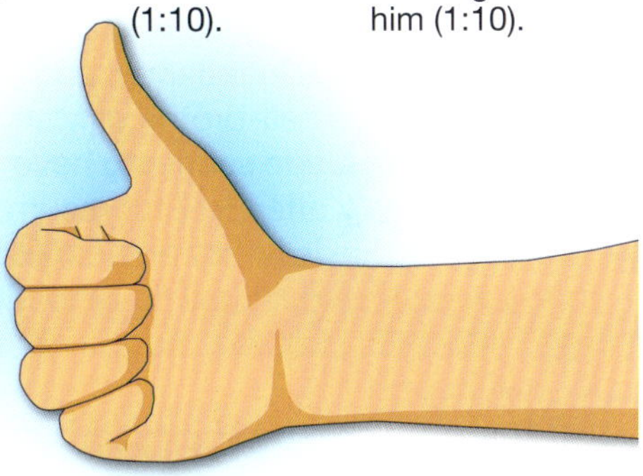

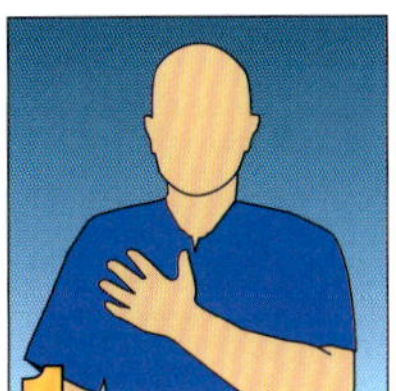

1
Walk in the truth
To walk in truth means to believe in it and follow it. Live your life in accordance with the truth (1:3–4).

2
Be faithful and loving
Show love through generosity and by how you treat others in the church (1:5a, 6).

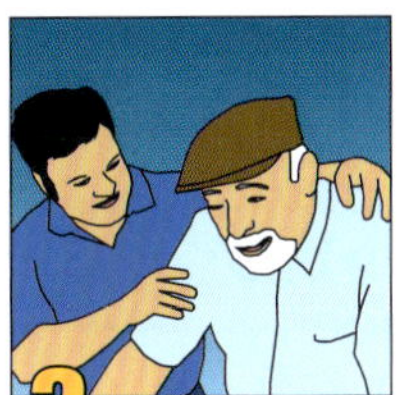

3
Be friendly to strangers
Treat strangers with the same care as family. Show kindness without malice (1:5b, 8).

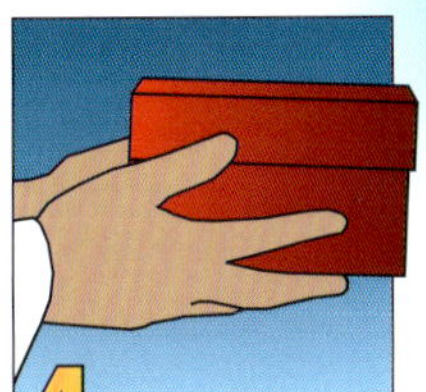

4
Be generous and hospitable
Help others for the sake of the gospel and support those traveling for the Lord (1:6–8).

DEMETRIUS
A role model for others, receiving a good testimony from all. Even John himself testifies to the truth so convincingly that truth itself seems to speak for Demetrius (1:12).

Some people who showed hospitality

The New Testament gives examples of hospitable people. Here are some that we can use as role models:

1
Party at Mary and Martha's
When Jesus visits the sisters, Martha devotes herself to preparing a meal for him (Luke 10:38–42).

2
Matthew's feast
After Jesus calls him to follow, Matthew (Levi) organizes a big party for him (Luke 5:27–29).

3
Zacchaeus's Feast
When Zacchaeus meets Jesus, he gladly welcomes him into his home (Luke 19:1–10).

4
Guest of Aquila and Priscilla
When Paul meets Priscilla and Aquila, they offer hospitality to him and he lives with them (Acts 18:2).

5
Hospitality by leaders
Among other traits, a church leader is expected to enjoy showing hospitality (1 Tim. 3:2).

6
Hospitality by widows
Church widows are also ex-pected to show hospitality, among other things (1 Tim. 5:9–10).

7
Generosity by Gaius
He shows hospitality and equips travelers for their onward journey (3 John 1:6–8).

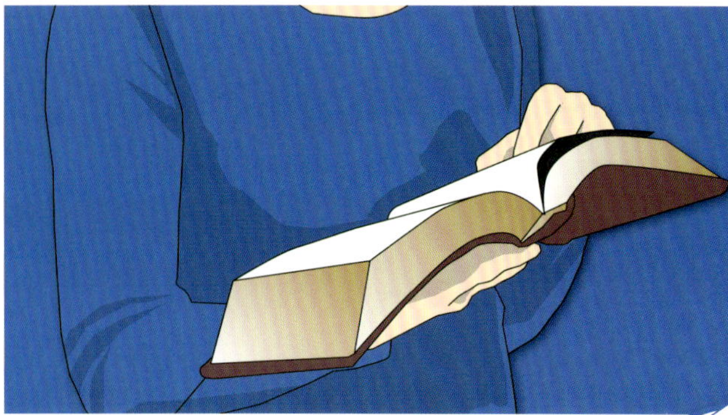

JUDE

"They [false teachers] are like clouds blowing over the land without giving any rain. They are like trees in autumn that are doubly dead" (Jude 1:12).

A FEW WORDS ABOUT THE AUTHOR

The author introduces himself as the brother of James (Jude 1:1), who was the leader of the church in Jerusalem (Acts 15:13; 21:18). Both James and Jude were Jesus's half-brothers (Matt. 13:55; Mark 6:3). Jude seems to have come to faith only after Jesus's resurrection (John 7:5). He is not to be confused with the apostle Jude (Luke 6:16). Jude himself indicates that he is not one of the apostles (Jude 1:17).

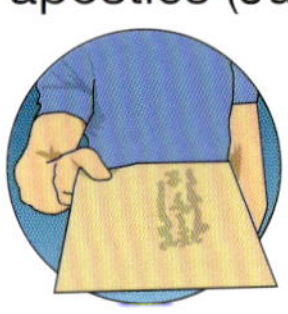

A FEW WORDS ABOUT THE RECIPIENTS

The letter is written to "all who have been called by God the Father, who loves you and keeps you safe in the care of Jesus Christ" (Jude 1:1, also 4, 17). The letter gives no specific information about the recipients, but the author knew them well, "Dear friends" (Jude1:3). Given that Jude quotes Jewish sources (Jude 1:4–5, 7, 11), the letter was probably written to one or more churches from a Jewish background that are unknown to us.

A FEW WORDS ABOUT DATES

Jude quotes 2 Peter 3:3 in his letter (Jude 1:18), or vice versa. This may give us a clue to the dating. It is likely that the two letters were written around the same date. Peter's death is usually dated before Nero's death in AD 68. Perhaps it is sufficient to say that Jude's letter is likely to have been written sometime in the mid- to late AD 60s. Some suggest that it was written later, possibly even in the late AD 80s.

THE WHOLE BOOK IN 25 WORDS

False teachers in the church must be defeated. Jude's history lesson shows the consequences of sin. Don't fall for flattery but fight for the faith.

A SIMPLE STRUCTURE

1. Deception – False teachers corrupt faith, twisting grace and denying Christ
(Jude 1:1–16)

2. Deliverance – Believers are called to persevere, remain faithful, and trust God
(Jude 1:17–25)

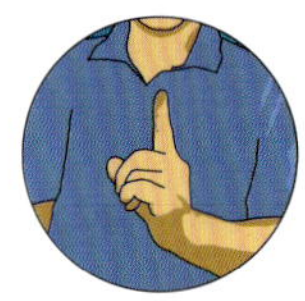

A FEW WORDS ABOUT KEY THEMES

- **Heresy**—Abandoning true doctrine, they say "God's marvelous grace allows us to live immoral lives ... they have denied our only Master and Lord" (Jude 1:4, also 8, 10, 16–19).
- **Rogue teachers**—Their character and activities are described: they are godless (1:4), despise the Lord (1:8), and scoff at what they don't understand (1:10, also 16, 18, 19).
- **References to nature**—Jude uses many images from nature: "unthinking animals" (1:10), "clouds blowing over the land without giving any rain," "trees that bear no fruit" (1:12), "wild waves of the sea churning up foam," and "wandering stars" (1:13).
- **Old Testament Illustrations**—Refers to people and events: the exodus (1:5), fallen angels (1:6), Sodom and Gomorrah (1:7), Cain, Balaam, and Korah (1:11), Enoch (1:14).

A FEW TIPS ON WHAT TO LOOK FOR

Theme of the book: The end times and the return of Jesus

- Godlessness, ungodly people (6 times)
- The Christian life (1:20–24)
- References to the Old Testament (7 times)
- Contrast between the use of "you" and "them"
- How the false teachers are described
- Use of three consecutive words, such as called, loved, preserved (1:1)
- Nature imagery such as clouds, trees, waves, and stars
- The end times and the return of Jesus

The Way Down and the Way Up

Jude draws a contrast between those who are drifting away from Christ and those who are growing closer to him. He points out six steps that lead away from Christ and six steps that lead toward a stronger faith.

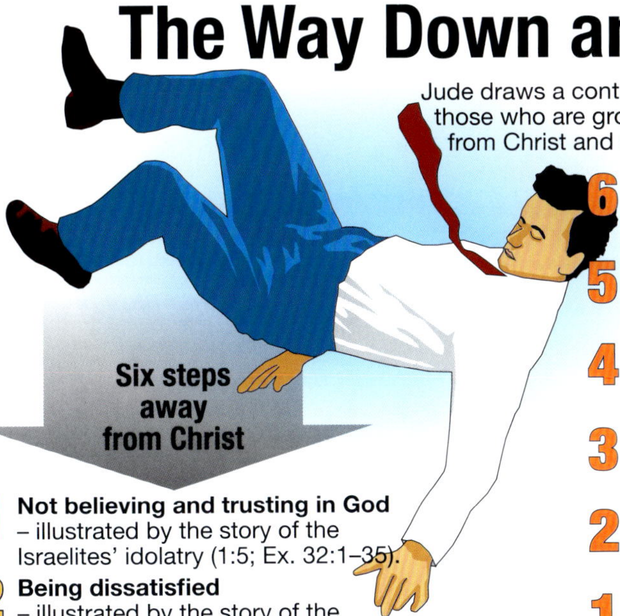

Six steps away from Christ

1 **Not believing and trusting in God**
– illustrated by the story of the Israelites' idolatry (1:5; Ex. 32:1–35).

2 **Being dissatisfied**
– illustrated by the story of the angels' sin (1:6; Gen. 6:1–4; 2 Peter 2:4).

3 **Engaging in sexual immorality**
– illustrated by the story of the immorality of Sodom and Gomorrah (1:7; Gen. 19:23–29).

4 **Being driven by jealousy**
– illustrated by the story of Cain's murder of Abel (1:11; Gen. 4:1–12).

5 **Compromising for money**
– illustrated by the story of Balaam's greed (1:11; Num. 22:1–41; 31:16).

6 **Living with a rebellious attitude**
– illustrated by the story of Korah's rebellion (1:11; Num. 16:1–50).

The use of the Old Testament
Jude references six stories from the Old Testament. He also brings up Enoch, see table below (1:14–15; Gen. 5:19–24).

6 **Trusting Jesus to keep you from stumbling**
– is expressed by trusting in him to bring you into his presence without a single fault (1:24).

5 **Showing mercy to those who doubt**
– is expressed by showing mercy to some and saving others (1:22–23).

4 **Waiting for the mercy of the Lord**
– is expressed through the hope of eternal life through Jesus (1:21).

3 **Living in God's love**
– is expressed by abiding and trusting in him (1:21; 1 John 4:16).

2 **Praying in the Holy Spirit**
– is expressed by praying in the power of the Holy Spirit (1:20).

1 **Letting faith shape your life**
– is expressed by deepening each other's holy faith (1:20).

Six steps to a stronger faith

Does Jude cite extra-biblical sources as authoritative?

Moses and the archangel
Moses died on Mount Nebo (Deut. 34:1–12). After his death, the archangel Michael is said to have fought with the devil over Moses's body (Jude 1:9). There is no mention of this event anywhere in the Old Testament.

Alleged allusion to The Ascension of Moses	Possible source text	Alleged quote from The Book of Enoch 1:9
Also called the Testament of Moses. It is a Jewish apocryphal* pseudepigrapha.** Known only from an incomplete Latin manuscript from the sixth century AD.	What do we know about the source?	Also called the First Book of Enoch, it is a collection of apocryphal* Jewish texts. It is not part of the biblical canon and is considered to be a pseudepigrapha.**
Michael the Archangel disputed with the devil over Moses's body (1:9).	What is it all about?	Enoch prophesies that the Lord will convict the ungodly (1:14–15).
• Jude likely alludes to the Ascension of Moses, even if it comes from Origen; the story is not in any surviving part of that book. • If the story is in The Ascension of Moses, it may point to a common origin. • Just because Jude alludes to it does not mean there is reason to ascribe biblical authority to it.	How should we look at the text?	• Jude seems to quote the Book of Enoch, but the phrases do not match. Jude and the Book of Enoch may have a common origin, come from an oral tradition, or be a direct revelation. • Jude does not attribute the quote to any author. • Jude's focus is on what happened in Enoch's day; not on giving his source biblical authority.

Enoch
Son of Jared and father of Methuselah (Gen. 5:19, 21), he lived 365 years and then "they found him no more, for God had taken him away" (Gen. 5:22, 24). According to Hebrews, Enoch did not die but was taken up to heaven by faith (Heb. 11:5).

** Apocryphal, meaning hidden, reminiscent of Bible books but not recognized as such. ** Pseudepigraphic, means writings published later under a false name.*

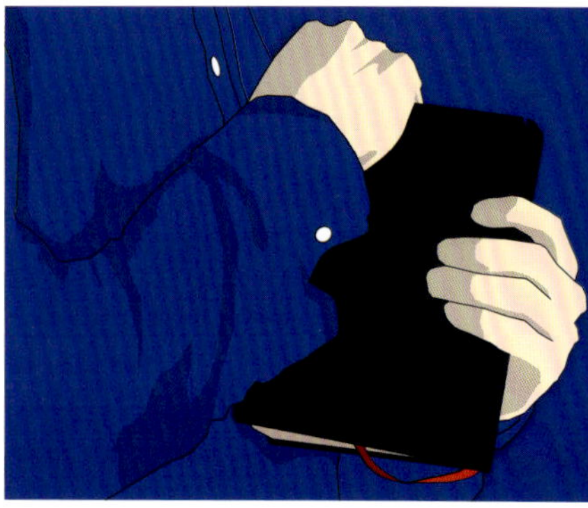

REVELATION

"Look! I stand at the door and knock. If you hear my voice and open the door, I will come in, and we will share a meal together as friends" (Rev. 3:20).

A FEW WORDS ABOUT THE AUTHOR

Four times the book names John as the author (1:1, 4, 9; 22:8). Early church tradition unanimously identifies the apostle John as the author of the book. These witnesses include Justin Martyr, Irenaeus, Clement of Alexandria, and Tertullian. Some of the original recipients may still have been alive when Justin Martyr and Irenaeus wrote their books, both of which stand by apostolic authorship for Revelation.

A FEW WORDS ABOUT RECIPIENTS

The book was written as a letter and sent to seven churches in the region around Ephesus, where John was based (1:4; 2:1–3:21; 22:21). The purpose is to comfort and encourage believers suffering severe persecution under Emperor Domitian. The book depicts the glory of heaven, the final judgment, and God's victory over evil at the end of time. It offers hope through vivid symbols and promises of eternal restoration.

A FEW WORDS ABOUT DATES

The book was probably written sometime between AD 94 and 96. Irenaeus dates the book to the end of the reign of Emperor Domitian (AD 81–96) and is supported by several other church fathers, such as Origen and Victorinus. The struggles in several of the early churches also points to a late date (2:1–3:21). This is reflected in what many consider to be the historical section of the book (1–3), likely contemporary with John.

THE WHOLE BOOK IN 25 WORDS

Jesus, the Lord of history, returns to earth, overcomes all evil and opposition, judges all people justly before eternity breaks in. Amen, come Lord Jesus!

A SIMPLE STRUCTURE

1. Vision
– Christ revealed in sovereign glory
(Rev. 1:1–1:20)

2. Virtue
– Churches called to faithful witness
(Rev. 2:1–3:22)

3. Victory
– God's victory through the Lamb
(Rev. 4:1–22:21)

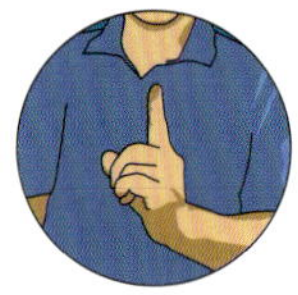

A FEW WORDS ABOUT KEY THEMES

- **Revelation**—The whole book is "a revelation from Christ [He is the source] and of Christ (1:1). It is both from Christ and by Christ.
- **Holiness**—To be set apart, raised above. Describes the character of God (3:7; 4:8; 5:8; 6:10; 8:3–4; 11:2, 18; 13:7, 10; 14:10, 12; 15:4; 16:5, 6; 18:20, 24; 19:8; 20:6, 9; 21:2, 10; 22:11, 19).
- **Worship**—Describes the role of the prayers of the saints in working out God's plan (4:10–11; 5:8, 12; 8:3–5).
- **The last days**—Most interpreters see (20:2–22:21) as about the end of time. Many view most of the book this way. Interpret with caution.
- **Justice**—God's final judgment brings justice, vindicates the faithful, and restores all creation in righteousness.
- **Comparison with Genesis 1–3**—Note how the last chapters (21–22) reverse the first chapters of Genesis (1–3).

A FEW TIPS ON WHAT TO LOOK FOR

Theme of the book:
The triumph of Jesus's return

- All the sevens (7 letters, 7 seals, etc.)
- The seven churches
- Lamb (29 times), angels (70 times)
- The battle between God and Satan, good and evil
- God's attributes, especially righteousness, holiness, and power
- Interaction between heaven and earth
- God's judgments, how many and about whom
- Names of Christ (19)
- Praise and worship

Five Ways of Interpreting Revelation

There is hardly a book in the New Testament whose interpretation is as controversial as that of Revelation. This is an overview of the main views used by biblical interpreters throughout the centuries.

1 PRETERIST VIEW
The book describes historical events before the Christianization of Rome

2 HISTORICIST VIEW
The book provides continuous coverage of the entirety of church history

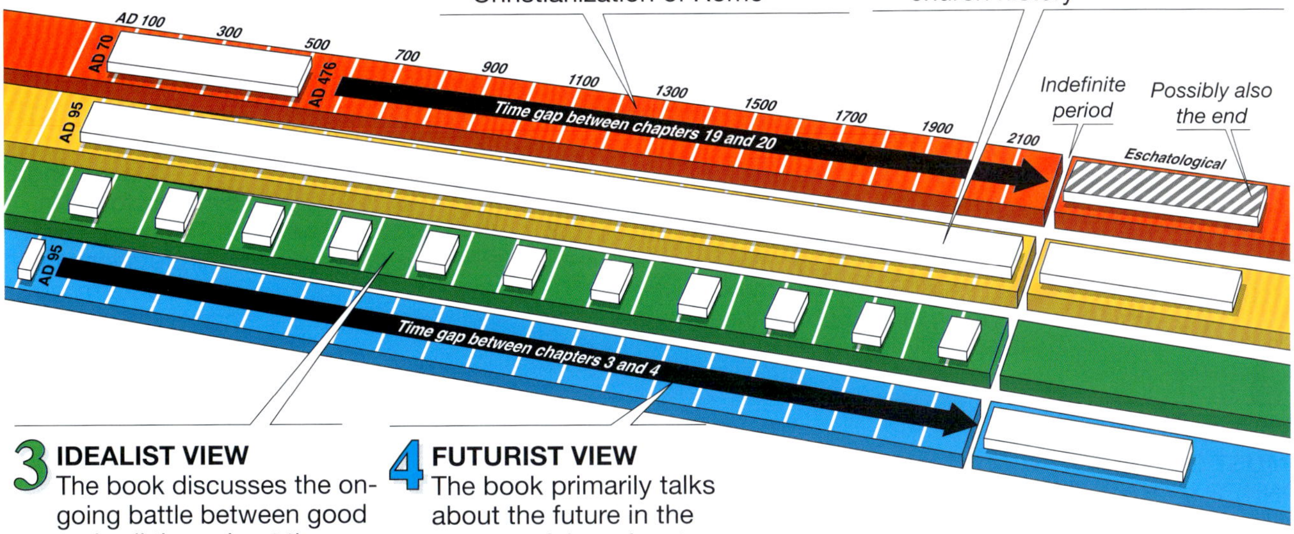

3 IDEALIST VIEW
The book discusses the ongoing battle between good and evil throughout the ages

4 FUTURIST VIEW
The book primarily talks about the future in the context of Jesus's return

1 PRETERIST VIEW

Talks about the first centuries **(past)**, describing the time leading up to the fall of Jerusalem (AD 70), some think even to the fall of the Western Roman Empire (AD 476).
- **Strengths:** Interpretation based on the readers' era, seems consistent with the introduction (1:1, 19).
- **Weaknesses:** Difficult to make the text correspond to historical events. Assumes that the book was written very early, even before AD 70 (unlikely). There is a time gap between Revelation 19 and 20.

2 HISTORICIST VIEW

Talks about the time between the first and second comings of Jesus **(present day)**. The book describes the whole of church history.
- **Strengths:** The book presents a linear narrative from John to the return of Christ. There is no time gap—the book is relevant for all Christians at all times.
- **Weaknesses:** Disagreement on what the different events symbolize. Hard to make the stories correspond to historical events. The interpretation of church history depends on the faith of the reader.

3 IDEALIST VIEW

Talks about all of history **(always)**, sometimes called the allegorical view. Does not believe there is a single literal fulfillment. Describes the ongoing struggle between God and Satan, good and evil.
- **Strengths:** There is no need to harmonize it with historical events. The book becomes applicable to everyone at all times, in both large and small matters.
- **Weaknesses:** The book itself claims to speak of future events (1:1). Can be said to "spiritualize" the text. Stories are seen as imagery (for example, the New Jerusalem is an ideal image of the church).

4 FUTURIST VIEW

Talks about the end times and Jesus's return **(future)**. The book describes the future, the last days.
- **Strengths:** Interprets the text more literally, follows the same divisions as those in the book (1:19). Does not need to be harmonized with historical events. Provides a comprehensive, chronological timeline for the end of the age.
- **Weaknesses:** There is a time gap between chapters 3 and 4. Interpreters often see their generation as the last. Much speculation about the date of Christ's return.

5 ECLECTIC VIEW

"Eclectic" means selective or mixed. It is an approach that, while emphasizing one of the four views, chooses to incorporate elements from several or all of the other interpretive views.
- **Strengths:** The approach takes advantage of the good insights from all the other views while avoiding what can be perceived as extreme and one-sided interpretations.
- **Weaknesses:** Prone to subjective and inconsistent interpretation and arbitrary choices.

How to Interpret Revelation

In order to unlock the insights of Revelation, it is wise to start with some guiding principles. These might help you make both its vivid imagery and its messages more accessible and easier to understand.

1 START FROM A LITERAL UNDERSTANDING

Our starting point is interpreting the book as literally as possible. But that is not always possible. So you need to decide carefully which criteria you will use when deciding not to interpret a passage literally.

2 "APOCALYPTIC" IS A GENRE OF ITS OWN

The book must be understood according to genre, the type of literature it is. Apocalyptic literature has special characteristics. At the same time, you must ask yourself whether everything in the book is apocalyptic.

3 MUST BE READ IN LIGHT OF OLD TESTAMENT

Many of the visions and symbols in the book of Revelation find their roots in the Old Testament. These must be interpreted in harmony with a proper understanding of the images in their original context.

4 MUST ALSO BE READ IN LIGHT OF NEW TESTAMENT

Other New Testament writings also contain material on the same subject, such as Matthew 24–25, Mark 13, and Luke 21. Many other passages must also be taken into consideration as the book is interpreted.

5 THE BOOK INTERPRETS MANY IMAGES

It is important to understand that the book itself interprets many of the images and symbols found in it. The book's own interpretations provide a pattern we can apply to other passages.

6 INTERPRETATION MUST SHOW AN INNER LOGIC

The interpretation of the text must display an internal logic. For example, seven heads must represent seven things of the same kind, ten horns must represent ten things of the same nature.

7 HOW DOES THE CHURCH RELATE TO ISRAEL?

The question of the relationship between Israel and the church also enters into the interpretation. When the book speaks of Israel (7:4; 21:12), is it referring to Jews or to Christians?

> "What people believe about the End Times impacts how they operate in their daily lives (Darrell Bock)

UNDERSTANDING THE LETTERS IN REVELATION

Here are four ways to understand the seven letters in Revelation 2–3.

1 Seven churches in John's time
Many believe that there are seven letters because there were seven real churches that John wrote to. This is most likely.

2 Seven types of churches
Others see the seven churches as representative of seven different types of churches existing throughout history.

3 Seven ages in church history
Still others see them as symbols of seven ages in church history, from the early church to the time of Jesus's return to earth.

4 Seven churches in the end times
There are others who believe that these are seven types of churches that exist at the time of Jesus's return to earth.

The Seven Churches in Revelation

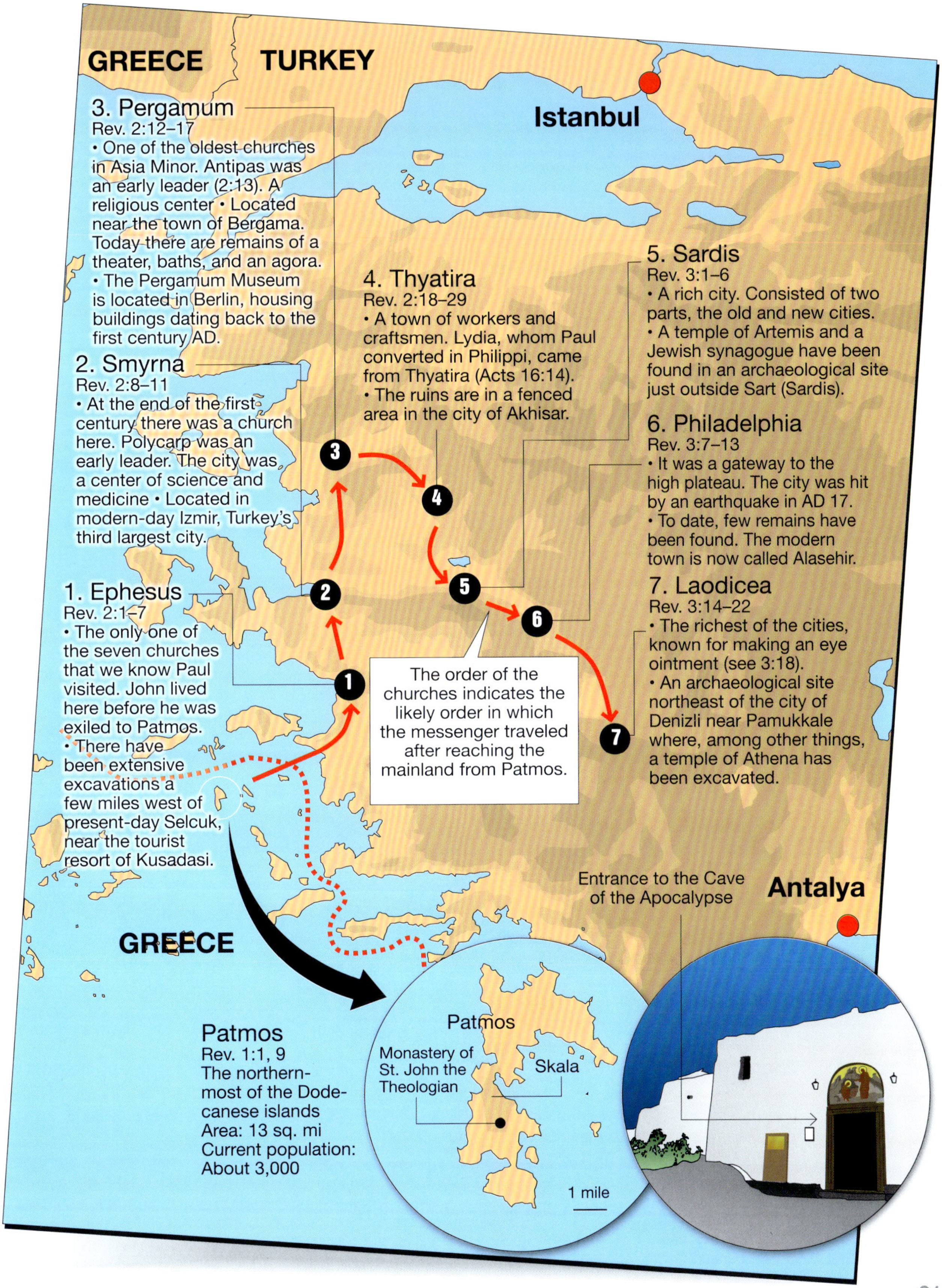

Letters to the Seven Churches

	JESUS	PRAISE	REPRIMAND	EXHORTATION	PROMISE
1. EPHESUS—the church that lost its first love (Rev. 2:1–7) PATMOS AD 95 POST OFFICE 18 To the church in Ephesus	Jesus, holding the seven stars, walks among the golden lampstands (2:1).	You do not tolerate evil people, you have suffered patiently (2:2–3).	You have abandoned your first love (2:4).	Repent and do the works you first did (2:5–6).	Then you will eat of the tree of life, which is in the paradise of God (2:7).
2. SMYRNA—the church undergoing persecution (Rev. 2:8–11) PATMOS AD 95 POST OFFICE 18 To the church in Smyrna	He is the First and the Last; he was dead and has come to life again (2:8).	You have suffered and you are poor, but you are rich (2:9).	**No reprimand**	Don't be afraid. Be faithful, even to death (2:10).	You will receive the crown of life and not be harmed by the second death (2:10–11).
3. PERGAMUM—the church in need of repentance (Rev. 2:12–17) PATMOS AD 95 POST OFFICE 18 To the church in Pergamum	He has the sharp, double-edged sword (2:12).	You remain loyal to me and have not denied me (2:13).	Some of you follow the teachings of Balaam or the Nicolaitans (2:14–15).	Turn from your sin (2:16).	You will receive hidden manna and a white stone with a new name (2:17).
4. THYATIRA—the church of the false prophetess (Rev. 2:18–29) PATMOS AD 95 POST OFFICE 18 To the church in Thyatira	He has eyes like flames of fire and feet like polished bronze (2:18).	I know your deeds, love, faith, service, and patient endurance (2:19).	You tolerate Jezebel with her immorality and idolatry (2:20–23).	Hold on to what you have (2:24–25).	You will receive the morning star and authority over nations (2:26–29).
5. SARDIS—the church that has fallen asleep (Rev. 3:1–6) PATMOS AD 95 POST OFFICE 18 To the church in Sardis	He has the sevenfold Spirit of God and the seven stars (3:1).	You have a few who have not soiled their clothes (3:4).	You are dead, your deeds do not measure up (3:1–2).	Wake up and strengthen what remains. Hold firmly to what you had, repent (3:2–3).	You will be dressed in white, with your name in the Book of Life (3:5–6).
6. PHILADELPHIA—the church that showed patience (Rev. 3:7–13) PATMOS AD 95 POST OFFICE 18 To the church in Philadelphia	The holy and true one, who has the key of David (3:7).	You obeyed my word and did not deny my name (3:8–10).	**No reprimand**	Hold on to what you have (3:11).	You will become pillars in God's temple, have his name written on you (3:12–13).
7. LAODICEA—the church that has become lukewarm (Rev. 3:14–22) PATMOS AD 95 POST OFFICE 18 To the church in Laodicea	He is the Amen, the true witness, the beginning of God's new creation (3:14).	**No praise**	You are lukewarm, neither hot nor cold; you are miserable and blind (3:15–17).	Buy gold, white clothes, and ointment. Open the door to me (3:18–20).	Then you will sit with Christ on his throne (3:21).

Imagery in the Book of Revelation

The book of Revelation is filled with many seemingly strange images. Trying to interpret their meanings is something of a key to the book. Some of them have their origins in the Old Testament (for example, the four horsemen in Zechariah chapters 1 and 6).

The Four Riders
When the first four seals of the scroll are broken by the Lamb, four horsemen are sent out over the earth. Four living beings stand around the throne and when they speak with voices of thunder, the four horsemen are sent out (Rev. 4:6; 6:1–8).

The Red Dragon
Another sign appeared in the heavens: a great red dragon throwing the stars of heaven to earth (Rev. 12:3–4).

The Beast of the Earth
Another beast that exercised the authority of the first beast (Rev. 13:11–12)

The Son of Man
In a vision, John sees Jesus standing among seven gold lampstands. He is "like the Son of Man" (Rev. 1:13–16).

The Pregnant Woman
A great sign appeared in heaven. A woman with special characteristics (Rev. 12:1–2).

Beast of the Sea
Out of the sea comes another beast. The dragon gives the beast his own power and great authority (Rev. 13:1–3).

Artwork: Anders Parsmo

What (Almost) Everyone Agrees On

While it is easy to focus on the different ways of interpreting Revelation, there are plenty of reasons to note the many similarities in interpretation. Here are key points the vast majority of interpreters agree on.

God has the future in his control. The texts about Jesus's return show that God, in his power, wisely controls the course of history (Rev. 5:13).

Jesus will come back as promised. At his ascension, Jesus's return to earth, both bodily and visibly, was promised (Rev. 19:11–13; Acts 1:11).

We do not know when it will happen. The time is not for us to know. Jesus will come when he comes. It is hidden with God (Matt. 24:36).

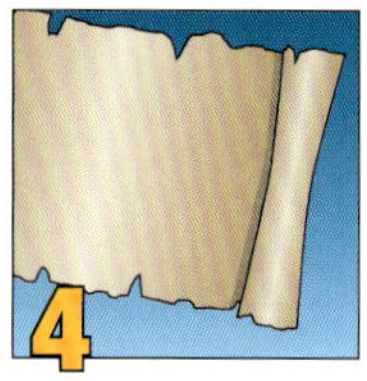

Revelation is written to believers living in John's day. Revelation is written to people in churches that John knew, not primarily to us today (Rev. 1:11).

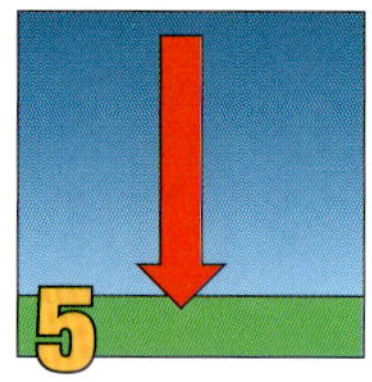

What happens in heaven affects what happens on earth. The heavenly world is interconnected with the earthly world (Rev. 6:1–17).

The prayers of believers have a role in fulfilling God's plan for history. Prayers reach heaven and influence the development of history (Rev. 5:8; 8:3).

Angels are actively involved in what happens on earth. There is a spiritual world where the struggle between good and evil takes place (Rev. 7:1; 12:7).

Believers are not exempt from suffering. Scripture teaches that God strengthens our faith in and through suffering (Rev. 2:9–10).

Christ will triumph over his enemies. His triumph is certain because it is securely and eternally based on God's omnipotence (Rev. 20:10).

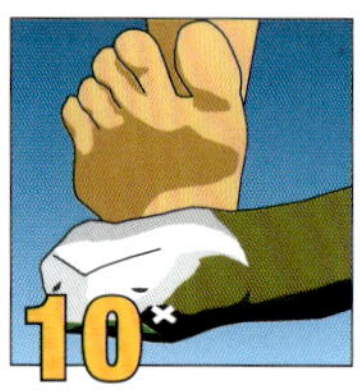

Satan will be defeated once and for all. The evil one will be utterly defeated, suffering eternal punishment under God's justice (Rev. 20:10).

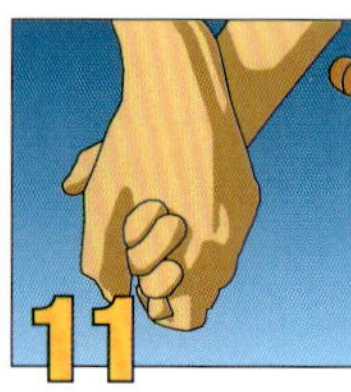

Believers will have eternal communion with God. For the believer, there is a joyful new beginning in God's eternal presence (Rev. 22:4–5).

Everyone will recognize God's works as righteous. His righteous nature is revealed, resulting in praise and worship from all (Rev. 15:3–4).

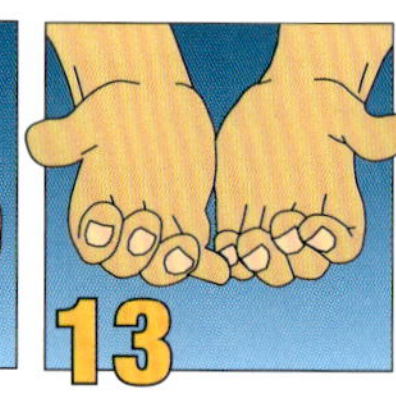

Believers' confidence in the future is based on God's character. God's power and wisdom guarantee what is to come (Rev. 7:9–17).

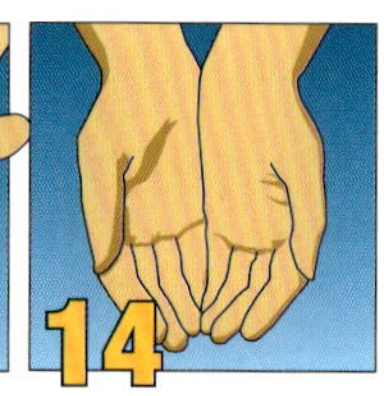

Be humble when considering others' interpretations. Interpretation is not always easy and it is wise not to be overconfident.

Some Images that Revelation Itself Interprets

- **The seven lampstands** (1:12) are the seven churches (1:20; 2:1–3:22).
- **The seven stars** (1:16) are the angels of the seven churches (1:20).
- **The seven torches at the throne** (4:5) are the sevenfold Spirit of God (4:5).
- **The seven eyes** (5:6) are the sevenfold Spirit of God upon the earth (5:6).
- **The golden bowls filled with incense** (5:8) are the saints' prayers (5:8).
- **The vast crowd before the throne that no one could count** (7:9) are those who died in the tribulation and washed their robes in the blood of the Lamb, making them white (7:13–14).
- **The ten horns of the beast** (17:3) are ten kings who (then?) had not yet received their kingdoms (17:12).
- **The seven heads of the beast** (17:3) are seven hills and seven kings (17:9–10).
- **The woman** (17:3) is the great city (Babylon) (17:18).
- **The waters** (17:15) are multitudes from every nation and language (17:15).

One might wonder what the explanations in Revelation mean. But at least it points in a certain direction.

The New Testament—Book by Book

The 27 books take us through the history of the New Testament. The books are grouped into three sections: the historical books, the teaching letters, and the apocalypse. Here are keywords for all the books in order.

HISTORICAL BOOKS
5 books

MATTHEW
Jesus is presented as the king

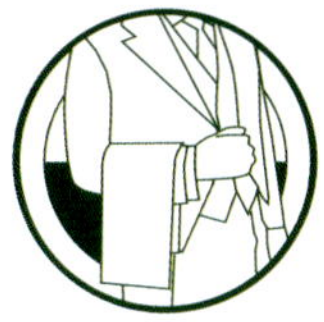

MARK
Jesus is presented as the servant

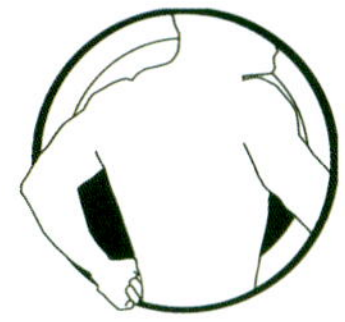

LUKE
Jesus is presented as the true man

JOHN
Jesus is presented as the Son of God

ACTS
From Jerusalem to Rome (Fire of the Spirit)

PAUL'S LETTERS
13 letters

ROMANS
The way of salvation (Colosseum in Rome)

FIRST CORINTHIANS
Problems in the church (Faith, hope, love)

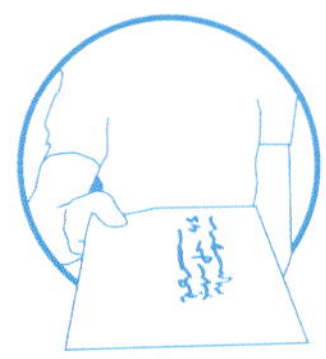

SECOND CORINTHIANS
You are letters of Christ

GALATIANS
Freedom of salvation (Fruit of the Spirit)

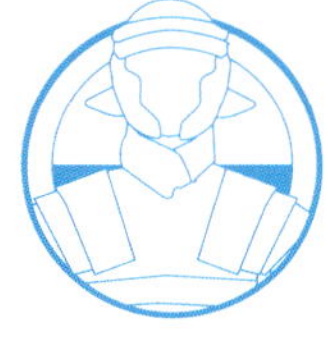

EPHESIANS
Christ and the church (Armor of God)

PHILIPPIANS
Christ and joy (Rejoice in the Lord!)

COLOSSIANS
Christ and the cosmos (He canceled our debt)

FIRST THESSALONIANS
The comfort of Jesus's return (Like a thief in the night)

SECOND THESSALONIANS
Waiting for the return of Jesus (Do not be intimidated)

FIRST TIMOTHY
Leadership in the church (Train yourself in godliness)

SECOND TIMOTHY
Serving in the church (Entrusting to others)

TITUS
A life worthy of the church (A word to trust)

PHILEMON
Christ and forgiveness (The slave who became free)

GENERAL LETTERS
8 letters

HEBREWS
The basis of salvation (faith) (God's word, a double-edged sword)

JAMES
Works of salvation (Control your tongue)

FIRST PETER
Suffering for Christ's return (Sharing Christ's sufferings)

SECOND PETER
Apostasy and the return of Christ (Watch out)

FIRST JOHN
Community in the church (Walking in the Light)

SECOND JOHN
False teachers and the church (Do not accept false teachers)

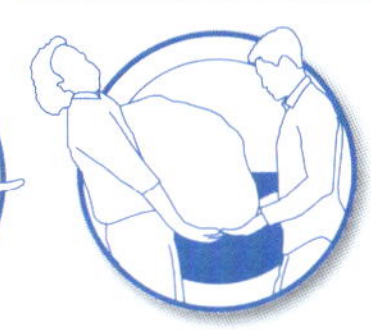

THIRD JOHN
Hospitality in the church (Equip for further travel)

JUDE
The end times and the return of Jesus (As clouds without rain)

REVELATION
1 book

REVELATION
The triumph of Jesus's return (Standing at the door and knocking)

DIFFERENT TYPES OF TEXTS

- **NARRATIVES** – Tell what has happened. Gives historical information about the life of Jesus and Paul's travels, among others. Historical documents rather than theological treatises.
- **TEACHING LETTERS** – Address problems, point to theological and practical solutions, encourage, give doctrinal reasons why we should act in a certain way.
- **APOCALYPTIC TEXT** – Through dramatic scenes, the text gives a picture of the future. The texts often dramatic, spectacular. And the images require careful interpretation.

Three Aspects of Spiritual Maturity

The pursuit of spiritual maturity is a central theme of the New Testament. Paul writes: "We pray that you will become mature" (2 Cor. 13:9). Maturing spiritually is a long process involving convictions, motives, and actions.

CONVICTION

1 What I believe in

Conviction is about what I think and believe. God's Word is the source of our knowledge of God and of ourselves. "The Bible is the divine means of developing spiritual maturity. There is no other way." (Howard Hendricks)

2 A stable faith

- **Doctrinal beliefs**
Growing in understanding and soundness of doctrine (2 Tim. 3:14; Tit. 1:9)
- **A biblical worldview**
Balance in understanding the connection between the spiritual and the material (Rom. 12:2; 1 John 2:15–16)
- **Ethical beliefs**
Understanding what is right and wrong—and why—as well as grace and forgiveness (Matt. 18:22; 1 Tim. 3:2; 2 Peter 1:5)
- **A biblical view of humanity**
Respect for human dignity and integrity (Gen. 1:27; Matt. 25:40)

3 Goal: Stable convictions

An inner conviction that creates stability in the Christian life, which gives birth to a security that gives peace and rest to the soul. "Then we will no longer be immature like children. We won't be tossed and blown about by every wind of new teaching" (Eph 4:14, see Tit. 1:9).

MOTIVE

1 What drives me

Motive is about what drives me. It's what makes me put what I believe into practice and apply it in everyday life. "Work willingly at whatever you do, as though you were working for the Lord rather than for people" (Col. 3:23).

2 A change of mindset

- **The mind of Christ**
Developing a mindset that is Christ like. It is about an inner change (Phil. 2:5–8, Mark 7:21–23)
- **Grace as a driving force**
Understanding grace as a driving force to a changed mindset (Tit. 2:11–12)
- **Internal struggle**
At the same time, recognizing the reality of an inner struggle (Rom. 7:15–20)
- **Fruit of the Spirit**
Revealing itself, bearing fruit, through my character (Gal. 5:22–23)

3 Goal: Pure motives

Pure motives are about what drives me. My will and desire to let faith express itself in my life. True spirituality grows from the inside out. "Let God transform you into a new person by changing the way you think" (Rom. 12:2; 1 John 2:15–16).

ACTION

1 What I do

Action is about how I put into practice both what I believe and what I am driven by: "Don't just listen to God's word. You must do what it says. Otherwise, you are only fooling yourselves" (James 1:22).

2 A transformed life

- **Putting faith into action**
Putting my faith into practice in my everyday life (Ezra 7:10)
- **Observing and taking initiative**
Being aware of what is happening around me and actively taking the initiative (James 2:18; 1 John 3:18)
- **Controlling my speech**
Consciously controlling what I say, honoring God, not hurting others (James 3:5–11)
- **Having a servant attitude**
Doing what is best for others and the Lord, making a difference, reflecting his love, through small but significant acts (Col. 3:23)

3 Goal: Changed character

Putting my convictions, driven by inner motives, into practice in daily life. The goal is that the servant of God is prepared and equipped for every good work (2 Tim. 3:17). "You must be holy in everything you do, just as God ... is holy" (1 Pet. 1:15).

> There is no saint without a past, no sinner without a future. (Augustine)

> The path of spiritual growth is a path of lifelong learning. (Scott Peck)

> The proof of spiritual maturity is not how pure you are but awareness of your impurity. That very awareness opens the door to grace. (Philip Yancey)

How to Grow a Christian Character

Applying the words of the Bible is the path to spiritual maturity. Scripture is given to us because "God uses it to prepare and equip his people to do every good work" (2 Tim. 3:17). Here are some steps on the road to developing Christian character.

1 Sow a thought ...

It starts with a thought from the study of God's Word. What does the passage say? How can I understand what it means for me? I ask: How can it change me? "They **listened eagerly** to Paul's message. They searched the Scriptures ... to see if Paul and Silas were teaching the truth" (Acts 17:11).

2 ... reap an action, sow an action ...

The path toward spiritual maturity continues with a decision to put into practice what I see and understand. I take what I learned from the Bible and express it in daily life in concrete actions. "Don't just listen to God's word. You must **do what it says.** Otherwise, you are only fooling yourselves" (James 1:22).

3 ... reap a habit, sow a habit ...

The constant repetition of an action creates a habit in my daily life. I do this because I have learned how to express my inner beliefs through my actions. The habit becomes foundational for my ongoing spiritual growth and maturity. "[Jesus] went **as usual** to the synagogue on the Sabbath" (Luke 4:16, see 2:22, 41).

4 ... harvest a character.

A good habit that becomes permanent will, over time, be a natural part of my personality. I act not only because I decided to, but because the pattern has become part of my character. "Then we will **no longer be immature like children**. We won't be tossed and blown about by every wind of new teaching" (Eph. 4:14).

Words to help you apply the Word of God

Describe the application you are working on by beginning a sentence with "I will" followed by one of the following expressions:

- accept...
- analyze...
- answer...
- appreciate...
- ask for...
- ask myself...
- avoid...
- be willing to...
- build...
- buy...
- call...
- cancel...
- cease...
- choose...
- claim...
- confess...
- confide...
- consider...
- collect...
- count...
- create...
- decide...
- develop...
- devote time to...
- eliminate...
- encourage...
- entrust...
- evaluate...
- exemplify...
- find...
- follow...
- give...
- give away...
- give notice...
- give up...
- go to...
- help...
- implement...
- invite...
- keep...
- listen to...
- look at...
- look for...
- look up...
- love...
- make a list...
- make time for...
- meet...
- memorize...
- opt out of...
- organize...
- participate in...
- plan...
- praise...
- pray for...
- pray with...
- prefer...
- protect myself against...
- question...
- read...
- realize...
- recognize...
- reconsider...
- record...
- rejoice over...
- repair...
- replace...
- sacrifice...
- save...
- say...
- search for...
- sell...
- send...
- share...
- show...
- sing...
- spend time with...
- stop...
- strive to...
- stay away from...
- study...
- switch off...
- take away...
- take control of...
- talk to...
- teach...
- tell...
- testify to...
- thank...
- think about...
- throw away...
- track down...
- try to...
- visit...
- wake up...
- watch...
- wait...
- write down...
- write to...
- work with...

> "More heresy is preached in application than in Bible exegesis ... You're saying what God doesn't say ... I cannot make that passage mean something today that it did not mean in principle in the ancient world. (Haddon Robinson)

Comparing the Beginning and the End

The end of the New Testament mirrors the beginning of the Old Testament: What is broken will be repaired. But that is not all. The Bible does not describe a return to the Garden of Eden—it anticipates something more.

The serpent and man (Gen. 1; 3:1–24)

I am the Alpha and the Omega,* the First and the Last, the Beginning and the End (Rev. 22:13).

The lion and the lamb (Isa. 65:25; Rev. 5:5–6)

Genesis 1–3	Revelation 20–22
"In the beginning God created the heavens and the earth" (1:1).	"I saw a new heaven and a new earth" (21:1).
"God called ... the darkness night" (1:5b).	"There is no night there" (21:25).
"God made two great lights" (the sun and moon) (1:16).	"The city has no need of sun or moon" (as light) (21:23).
"If you eat [the tree's] fruit, you are sure to die" (2:17).	"There shall be no more death" (21:4).
Satan emerges as the seducer of humanity (3:1).	Satan is cast out forever (20:10).
We see a garden, into which sin enters (3:6–7) .	There is a city where "nothing evil will be allowed to enter" (21:27).
God's walk with humanity is interrupted (3:8–10).	God's walk with humanity is restored (21:3).
The snake triumphs—at first (3:13).	The Lamb triumphs—in the end (20:10; 22:3).
"In pain you will give birth" (3:16).	"There will be no more ... sorrow or crying or pain" (21:4).
"The ground is cursed because of you" (3:17).	"No longer will there be a curse" (22:3).
Humanity falls from a high position in the first man, Adam (3:19).	Humanity is reinstated to a high position, reigning in the new man, Christ (22:5).
The first paradise closes (3:23).	The new paradise opens (22:5).
Access to the tree of life is lost by Adam (3:24).	Access to the tree of life is regained in Christ (22:14).
They are driven away from the face of God (3:24).	"They shall see his face" (22:4).
Old Testament	**New Testament**

** Alpha and Omega are the first and last letters of the Greek alphabet, the equivalents of A and Z in ours.*